Movies and Mental Illness

Dedication

For Lester R. Bryant, MD, ScD,
who continues to be a great mentor, model, scholar, and friend.
DW

For my newborn, Ryland Zander,
who inspired the revamping of Chapter 2, and elicits the goodness in me each day.
RMN

About the Authors

Danny Wedding, PhD, MPH, is associate dean for management and international programs at the California School of Professional Psychology, Alliant International University. He is the editor of *PsycCRITIQUES: Contemporary Psychology – APA Review of Books*, the senior editor for Hogrefe's book series on *Advances in Psychotherapy: Evidence-Based Practice*, and the coauthor of *Positive Psychology at the Movies: Using Films to Build Virtues and Character Strengths*. Wedding lectures widely on international psychology and the portrayal of mental illness in contemporary cinema.

Ryan M. Niemiec, PsyD, is education director of the VIA Institute on Character, a global nonprofit organization that advances the science and practice of character strengths. He is a licensed psychologist, adjunct professor at Xavier University, and an international speaker. He is author of *Mindfulness and Character Strengths: A Practical Guide to Flourishing* and coauthor of *Positive Psychology at the Movies: Using Films to Build Character Strengths and Well-Being,* and a number of articles and book chapters on films. He is film editor of *PsycCRITIQUES* and received a specialization in film studies from Michigan State University. His website is www.ryanniemiec.com

Movies and Mental Illness

Using Films to Understand Psychopathology

4th edition

Danny Wedding
California School of Professional Psychology
Alliant International University
San Francisco, CA

Ryan M. Niemiec
VIA Institute on Character
Cincinnati, OH

Library of Congress Cataloguing-in-Publication Data
is available via the Library of Congress Marc Database
under the LC Control Number 2014937622

National Library of Canada Cataloguing in Publication

Wedding, Danny, author
    Movies and mental illness : using films to understand psychopathology / Danny Wedding, California School of Professional Psychology, Alliant International University, San Francisco, CA, Ryan M. Niemiec, VIA Institute on Character, Cincinnati, OH. -- 4th edition.

Includes bibliographical references and index.
Issued in print and electronic formats.
ISBN 978-0-88937-461-4 (pbk.).--ISBN 978-1-61676-461-6 (pdf).--
ISBN 978-1-61334-461-3 (epub)

    1. Psychology, Pathological--Study and teaching--Audio-visual aids.
2. Mental illness in motion pictures. I. Niemiec, Ryan M., author II. Title.

RC459.W43 2014   616.89   C2014-902339-1
                                                 C2014-902340-5

© 2014 by Hogrefe Publishing
http://www.hogrefe.com

PUBLISHING OFFICES

USA: Hogrefe Publishing, 38 Chauncy Street, Suite 1002, Boston, MA 02111
            Phone (866) 823-4726, Fax (617) 354-6875; E-mail customerservice@hogrefe-publishing.com
EUROPE: Hogrefe Publishing, Merkelstr. 3, 37085 Göttingen, Germany
            Phone +49 551 99950-0, Fax +49 551 99950-425; E-mail publishing@hogrefe.com

SALES & DISTRIBUTION

USA: Hogrefe Publishing, Customer Services Department,
            30 Amberwood Parkway, Ashland, OH 44805
            Phone (800) 228-3749, Fax (419) 281-6883; E-mail customerservice@hogrefe.com
UK: Hogrefe Publishing, c/o Marston Book Services Ltd, 160 Eastern Ave., Milton Park, Abingdon,
            OX14 4SB, UK
            Phone +44 1235 465577, Fax +44 1235 465556; Email direct.orders@marston.co.uk
EUROPE: Hogrefe Publishing, Merkelstr. 3, 37085 Göttingen, Germany
            Phone +49 551 99950-0, Fax +49 551 99950-425; E-mail publishing@hogrefe.com

OTHER OFFICES

CANADA: Hogrefe Publishing, 660 Eglinton Ave. East, Suite 119 - 514, Toronto, Ontario M4G 2K2
SWITZERLAND: Hogrefe Publishing, Länggass-Strasse 76, CH-3000 Bern 9

Hogrefe Publishing
Incorporated and registered in the Commonwealth of Massachusetts, USA, and in Göttingen, Lower Saxony, Germany

Printed and bound in the USA

ISBNs 978-0-88937-461-4 (print), 978-1-61676-461-6 (pdf), 978-1-61334-461-3 (epub)
http://dx.doi.org/10.1027/00461-000

Foreword to the Fourth Edition

I have been a fan of the *Movies and Mental Illness* from the first edition, so I am delighted to write this Foreword with Ruth Richards. Prior to becoming a psychologist, I worked for over 20 years in Hollywood as a television writer and producer. I saw firsthand how powerful TV and of course, movies, can be in impacting viewers.

I was lucky enough to work as a writer on *The Mary Tyler Moore* show, which was seen by many women as a breakthrough depiction of a woman who "could make it on … [her] own." I also worked on *Room 222*, an Emmy-winning show, where some episodes I wrote were used in schools of education for teaching. An episode of *Silver Spoons* I wrote about a child who was being physically abused by his father triggered thousands of calls to a hotline by abused children.

Based on my experience both professionally and personally, I suggested the concept of *audience flow* could apply to watching television and movies. *Audience flow* is defined as watching "in an active and mentally engaged state that may allow insights and new perspectives to develop. … A 'conversation' develops between the viewer and the work that is so engaging that all sense of time is lost. This cognitive engagement means that being part of an au-

dience can be enjoyable, educational, active and creative" (Pritzker, 2007).

An example of the emotional power of film to influence the viewer was described to me by a Saybrook University Creativity Studies doctoral student. He said that he was watching a scene in the movie *Good Will Hunting* in which Will Hunting (Matt Damon) is talking to his psychologist (Robin Williams) about Will's foster father coming up the stairs to beat him. His psychologist repeatedly tells him: "It's not your fault, it's not your fault, it's not your fault …" until Will finally breaks down and cries. The student who told me this story found himself crying as he connected the scene to his mother coming up the stairs to beat him with a belt, and he realized for the first time it really was not his fault.

What is interesting about the hundreds of films in *Movies and Mental Illness* is the pervasive fascination with psychopathology. It is a testament to how deeply mental illness touches almost everybody's life in one form or another. Screenwriters and psychologists have a great deal in common in trying to understand the dynamics of mental illness, which is a positive development because understanding can lead to compassion.

Steven R. Pritzker, PhD
Professor and Director, Creativity Studies Specialization
Saybrook University
President, Division of Aesthetics, Creativity, & the Arts
American Psychological Association
Co-Editor-in-Chief, *Encyclopedia of Creativity*

Steve and I teach together at Saybrook University and started one of the first graduate programs in psychology with a specialization in creativity, offering certificates and MA and PhD degrees. We do not offer these just for fun (although it often is fun), but because we truly believe that the process of creating can change lives. It can bring us more fully into the present moment, aware, open, flexible, and adaptive – more in tune with life, its richness, beauty, and potential, and with our many life options. Creative *process*, all else being equal, tends to be healthy and good for us. As Steve notes, being

in "flow" with the movies, as an active and aware observer, can also fit our criteria for creativity, including *originality* and *usefulness*. Creativity can be good for us – and for society as well.

I am a psychiatrist as well as educational psychologist and professor, and have studied issues of creativity and mental health for quite a few years – in schools, clinics, and in our spiritual lives. I am cheered by how much people can learn about psychopathology at the movies – and how the best movies can even change how culture views certain disorders and treatments. Take, for instance, *Silver*

Linings Playbook, with Jennifer Lawrence winning Best Actress for 2013 for both the Oscars (7 other nominations) and Golden Globes (3 other nominations). The film received 5 out of 5 stars in *Movies and Mental Health.* Most people would never curl up on Saturday night with a diagnostic and treatment manual, yet they might well say, "let's go to the movies – what was that new Oscar winner …?"

Every person and every experience is different, yet in *Silver Linings,* I was immediately struck by the authenticity of the characters. A well-done film can give a real three-dimensional flavor of the lived experience of a psychiatric disorder, along with the distinguishing central features. Meanwhile it can show real people, their lives, and their individual patterns and challenges – along with hopes and ways of coping. This one touched a great many of those bases – as do selected others receiving high ratings in *Movies and Mental Illness.*

In *Silver Linings,* Bradley Cooper played a young man with bipolar disorder, type I (manic-depressive illness), and Ms. Lawrence's character suffered from her own challenges. We see disruption of lives, why medications can make a huge difference (and what happens without them), the magic of a good therapist (meds don't do everything!), major influences of (and effects on) family and friends, and on the larger community, and even the value of – and behavioral benefits, resilient coping, and triumph possible from – creative work. Talk about overcoming adversity; how marvelous when this young and creative couple … well you need to see it for yourself.

As Steve suggests, we can learn not only by living our own challenges, but by living them through the lives of others, by entering the magic of film and imagination, and enlarging our experience, consciously as well as vicariously. Our "empathetic" *mirror neurons* jump right in to know that mood swing, that awkwardness or desperate fear of loss; suddenly the pain becomes our own.

Film can meanwhile impart vital information – and perhaps even save lives. For instance, it turns out that enhanced everyday creativity (originality of everyday life) can be found associated with certain forms of psychopathology – yet the message is relatively more about *health* than illness – as I, with Dennis Kinney and other colleagues at McLean Hospital and Harvard Medical School, among others, have shown (see Kinney & Richards, 2011). The results of these studies do support a higher rate of everyday creativity, on the average, among per-

sons falling on the *bipolar spectrum* than among control participants.

Yet this is in connection with *higher* function (not with greater illness). The chance of creativity is enhanced with milder compared with the more severe bipolar spectrum disorders (e.g., the milder cyclothymic disorder compared with full manic-depressive syndrome, again on average), or for a particular person during better functioning states, compared with very ill states (e.g., mild hypomania versus mania). We see this last difference in *Silver Linings.*

It is important that treatment may not only reduce terrible suffering, but also potentially free a hindered potential, toward a richer life and more productive contributions to society. Yet how many people at risk for bipolar disorder think it is a matter of "the sicker, the better" with regard to creativity – a serious misunderstanding. Some even refuse treatment. This can be dangerous. Please note these findings potentially generalize to millions of people.

Before leaving this example, let us be careful to note that there *are many routes to creativity,* and not just ones linked to personal or familial psychiatric disorder. It is human to be creative.

Meanwhile what an important chance the movies have to lower the stigma of mental disorders, in general, to raise self-esteem, and to share accurate information, including information about treatment, and renew hope in life. *Movies and Mental Illness* helps us find just those films of the greatest value.

I was privileged to speak on the topic of the arts and self-expression in mental health at the Carter Presidential Center in Atlanta, for the Mental Health Program chaired by Former First Lady Rosalynn Carter. This Carter Center program has related objectives for improving how mental illness is understood, viewed by, and treated in society, goals that resonate with the objectives of *Movies and Mental Illness.*

Finally, while we moviegoers can learn bitter truths about mental illness, and see how people learn to cope with their painful symptoms, do we not also want to see how people triumph and overcome, how they build on their strengths, passions, and positive qualities? Do we not wonder how suffering individuals try to find meaning in life, perhaps a greater good, or even transcendence? Unfortunately, individuals' strengths sometimes get overlooked by well-meaning mental health professionals who are more focused on what has "gone wrong" than what could "go right." It seems enough to some clinicians to reverse the depression, psychosis, loss and heartbreak, substance abuse, stress, or crippling anxiety. Yet who needs the hope more than the struggling patient?

As can be seen in the companion book *Positive Psychology at the Movies 2* by the same authors, themes of resilience, resurrection, and renewal are often found in the movies. We in the audience can again live the drama, this time ascending to a higher human promise. We can imagine, experience, and sometimes soar. For the person in pain, and for friends and family – which is to say, for pretty much all of us – here is the chance not only to regain one's life vicariously, but also to discover what one is living for.

Ruth Richards, MD, PhD
Professor, Saybrook University
Lecturer, Dept. of Psychiatry, Harvard Medical School
Member-At-Large, Division of Aesthetics, Creativity, and the Arts
American Psychological Association
Editor, *Everyday Creativity and New Views of Human Nature*

Foreword to the Third Edition

You know a book is valuable when it enters multiple editions in tumultuous economic times. Such is certainly the case for *Movies and Mental Illness,* now entering its third edition as a classic resource and an authoritative guide.

Movies play a powerful and pervasive role in our culture and, increasingly, in our classrooms. Psychologist Ken Gergen (*The Saturated Self,* 1991, pp. 56–57) opined that movies have become one of the most influential rhetorical devices in the world: "Films can catapult us rapidly and effectively into states of fear, anger, sadness, romance, lust, and aesthetic ecstasy – often within the same two-hour period. It is undoubtedly true that for many people film relationships provide the most emotionally wrenching experiences of the average week."

If a picture is worth a thousand words, then a movie is worth tens of thousands of words in even the most engaging of textbooks. My students – all students – clamor for immediate, personal, and riveting examples of mental disorders and their treatment.

Movies can easily be integrated into education to illustrate psychopathology, but can also be used for clinical purposes. The use of films for treatment can be traced back to the 1930s, but more professionals are recommending or prescribing specific films. Whether it's called cinematherapy, movie treatment, or reel therapy, the goal is to enhance health and happiness.

Many of the movies featured in these pages portray healing stories. The best of them typically increase awareness about a disorder or treatment; *As Good as It Gets* springs to mind for its accurate and humorous depiction of obsessive-compulsive disorder. The best movies also show flawed, yet effective role models struggling realistically with problems and ultimately triumphing; a case in point is the inspiring film *The Soloist* about living well with psychosis. Such films stir the soul as they generate hope and offer a fresh perspective on ourselves and our relationships.

Like the very movies it recommends, *Movies and Mental Illness* is a powerful medium for teaching students, engaging patients, and educating the public. Wedding, Boyd, and Niemiec have produced an invaluable guide for all those committed to understanding the human experience.

John C. Norcross, PhD
University of Scranton
Editor, *Journal of Clinical Psychology*
2009 President of the Society of Clinical
Psychology

Foreword to the Second Edition

John Milton, in *Paradise Lost*, tells us that we must "strike the visual nerve, for we have much to see." So, too, in this present work, do Wedding, Boyd, and Niemiec admonish us that there is much to learn by seeing with the mind's eye what these well-chosen films, by turns sad and silly, offer us in illuminating the psychopathologies set forth in the *Diagnostic and Statistical Manual* of the American Psychiatric Association.

Ranging from such classics as the depiction of alcoholism in *The Lost Weekend*, to relatively obscure films perhaps known only to the aficionado of foreign films, Wedding, Boyd, and Niemiec have achieved a work which may itself become a classic in this genre, particularly with respect to its intended purpose of teaching how the various psychopathologies might play themselves out in an approximation of real-life, real-world situations of which these films are a simulacrum.

Wedding, Boyd, and Niemiec provide a brief synopsis of each film in relation to the major category of psychopathology being covered in a chapter, and they relate the manifest and latent content of the film to the various diagnostic symptoms within a category, such as childhood disorders, and further provide an illustrative case study to assist in the process of generalizing from the film to actual diagnostic work.

As a didactic tool, the work by Wedding, Boyd, and Niemiec should have a salutary effect in engaging the attention of the student, as well as in engaging the affective response of the student through a vicarious identification with the film characters portrayed, and hopefully, enhancing the learning process of what otherwise tends to be a rather tedious pedagogical process for most students.

The authors provide a lively expository style, and the use of epigraphs for each chapter is a particularly happy device for setting a tone for each chapter and for capturing a pithy bit of dialogue that may cause the reader to engage in some cognitive restructuring, as when one of the characters says, "I recall every fall, every hook, every jab" in the chapter on the dementias, a quote which instantly evokes an image of the prizefighter with organic brain damage. Other such examples abound and contribute significantly to the teaching potential of the work.

On balance, this is a work that is likely to become a classic of its type and a particularly useful teaching tool for the diagnosis and understanding of the various psychopathologies for students of the helping professions. I commend it to the reader, be the reader a student or professor.

Allan Barclay, PhD
St. Louis, Missouri

Table of Contents

Preface

The whole of life is just like watching a film. Only it's as though you always get in ten minutes after the big picture has started, and no-one will tell you the plot, so you have to work it out all yourself from the clues.
Terry Pratchett, *Moving Pictures*

We wrote *Movies and Mental Illness* because of our conviction that films are a powerful medium for teaching students (in psychology, social work, medicine, nursing, and counseling), engaging patients, and educating the public about the fascinating world of psychopathology. In addition, we wrote the book because we genuinely love watching and talking about movies. While this book's title is *Movies and Mental Illness*, we also discuss serious problems that do not reflect mental illness per se, including neurodevelopmental disorders, physical or sexual abuse, and violence.

We have made numerous changes in this edition. A new edition was necessary because dozens of excellent films have been released in the past 5 years that need to be included in any book that purports to be both contemporary and comprehensive. We have added over a hundred recent films to Appendix H that illustrate psychopathology. Although it is impossible to list every film depicting every disorder, we feel we have seen and critiqued the majority of important films that illustrate psychopathology. The reader will find a significant number of these new films discussed in the relevant chapters.

The release of the fifth edition of the *Diagnostic and Statistical Manual of Mental Disorders (DSM-5)* required that we rework our Table of Contents to line it up with the new nosology that was developed by the American Psychiatric Association. In our clinical examples, we include the appropriate codes from the *International Classification of Diseases* (ICD-11) after each diagnosis. We hope students will debate the merits of the various diagnoses we assign, discussing differential diagnosis and alternate possibilities.

We have updated the sample course syllabus, and we have selected numerous new headliner films to teach students the look and feel of the various disorders they are likely to encounter in clinical practice. For example, we believe watching Michael Haneke's *Amour* captures the pathos of Alzheimer's disease with raw emotion and a vivid power that can never be had by simply reading about neuropathol-

ogy and neurofibrillary tangles. One way to approach *Movies and Mental Illness* is to simply start with Appendix H and a highlighter, identifying interesting films, and then seeing what we have to say about them in the book.

We have also updated our list of our favorite films in each category ("Authors' Picks"). We did not always agree about which films were most important for readers to see, but we negotiated and debated each list and eventually selected around 10 films for each chapter that balanced artistic merit and clinical relevance. This addition is in response to the frequent request for our recommendations for movies that can be used to help train mental health professionals and students from various health professionals.

We have continued the practice of recommending a single book and a single article in the "Future Exploration" section at the end of each chapter. We envision that these additional readings will be used in honors courses or perhaps as supplemental readings to compensate for a missed class, exam, or assignment. All students will benefit from taking time to read the recommended books and the key articles we identify.

Finally, we have continued to expand the sections on international films in each chapter. Often these films are more powerful and accurate than anything filmmakers in the United States have produced. We hope this will entice readers to watch more foreign language films; we have found this an especially interesting and rewarding way to learn about other cultures.

In discussing psychopathology, we occasionally reveal endings or surprise twists to films, and we realize this may spoil these films for some readers. We apologize in advance if this occurs.

The book was originally designed to supplement core texts in abnormal psychology; if the book is being used in this way, the relevant core chapters in the primary text should be read before reviewing the corresponding chapter in *Movies and Mental Illness*. (However, it is almost always helpful to review the "Questions to Consider" section that introduces each chapter on psychopathology before seeing the recommended film.) We will occasionally present detailed and specific information about mental illness, but these facts are almost incidental to the discussion of the films themselves, and we have tried to avoid redundancy with the many fine textbooks that already explain psychopathology in considerable detail. We assume the reader will look up unfamiliar terms or discuss them in class, and we have not always defined each new term.

Each chapter is introduced with a fabricated case history and Mini-Mental State Examination. We have developed composite presentations linked as closely as possible to the character being portrayed in the film being discussed. In every case, the diagnoses we present reflect hypotheses, not facts; the case studies are designed to generate ideas, enliven discussion, and stimulate learning. Our diagnoses and character descriptions are always derived from our own judgment and clinical experience, and our fabricated evaluations are anchored in the events portrayed on screen, even when films are based on actual figures (e.g., the characters of John Nash in *A Beautiful Mind*, Ray Charles in *Ray*, and Teena Brandon in *Boys Don't Cry*).

We are clinical psychologists and educators, and we have both learned that the judicious use of films dramatically increases students' and clients' understanding of abnormal behavior. For example, when lecturing about alcoholism, we might supplement our lectures with a "demonstration" of delirium tremens using *The Lost Weekend* or illustrate withdrawal and tolerance using Denzel Washington's character in *Flight*. Before a lecture on bipolar disorder, we will ask our students to watch *Michael Clayton* or *Silver Linings Playbook*. All four films provide a rich intensity that simply cannot be captured by a classroom lecture or the printed page. Likewise, when working with a client going through a divorce who becomes incensed over the behavior of his or her spouse, we might recommend watching *Kramer vs. Kramer* or *The Squid and the Whale*. A counselor working with parents attempting to understand and cope with their adolescent child's suicidality might consider reviewing *Boy Interrupted*. We have found that the discussion of relevant films offers a wonderful way to open clinically relevant areas that have not previously been explored.

We discuss a variety of films throughout the book; however, we usually use one or two films as primary illustrations of each disorder. These head-

liner films are movies we have watched repeatedly. In many cases, they are popular movies that students are likely to have already seen (e.g., *A Beautiful Mind*); in other cases, they are simply films that we believe every student learning to be a mental health professional should see (e.g., *Temple Grandin*).

Usually the connection between the films being discussed and the chapter is immediate and direct, but we occasionally include obscure films when a small section relates in a meaningful way to the points made in the chapter. There are also some classic films such as *Psycho*, *A Clockwork Orange*, and *One Flew Over the Cuckoo's Nest* that have tremendous pedagogical value, and we take great pleasure in introducing a new generation of students to these movies. In addition, films such as *Pelle the Conqueror* or *Antonio's Line* are occasionally included, even when there is no direct connection to psychopathology, because the films are provocative and moving and are good illustrations of various psychological phenomena. For detailed examples of these and other films depicting character strengths, resilience, and various positive psychological phenomena, we recommend our book, *Positive Psychology at the Movies: Using Films to Build Character Strengths and Well-Being*, which discusses 1,500 films.

Films can be integrated into courses in abnormal psychology and psychopathology in a variety of ways. The particular approach selected will vary from course to course, depending on the needs of the instructor and the interests of students.

First, students can be asked to take responsibility for seeing many of these films on their own. Because we have selected popular films as the exemplars for each clinical chapter, students can easily attain them from any number of commercial sources. Costs are minimized if students choose to see the films in small groups. This promotes the intellectual camaraderie, discussion, and debate that characterize effective learning. We recommend that whenever possible students see the films before coming to class to discuss the corresponding topic.

Second, we have used films in classes that meet twice weekly. The first class meeting is devoted to seeing the film; the second is spent discussing the content of the related textbook chapter and determining whether or not the film accurately represents the disorder being discussed. It is ideal when such courses can be team taught by a mental health professional and a literature/drama professor. Danny

Wedding used this approach in the abnormal psychology course he taught at Yonsei University in Seoul, Korea, where he spent a year as the Fulbright-Yonsei Distinguished Scholar.

Finally, most professors choose to use class time to show selected vignettes from pedagogically powerful films, and they encourage students to view the entire film and other related films on their own time. The goal with this approach is to augment lectures with relevant in-class discussion while minimizing the total amount of class time spent watching films. Using a film vignette that vividly depicts a psychiatric disorder circumvents the ethical issues (confidentiality, securing releases and permission, etc.) associated with using real cases and clients as illustrations in the classroom. We have found it useful for our students to present selected film clips along with diagnostic criteria from the *DSM-5*, arguing the merits and limitations of potential diagnoses for particular film characters.

When films are used in the classroom, it may be necessary for the educational institution (or the professor teaching the class) to pay a fee for public usage. Most colleges and universities have audio-visual departments well equipped to handle such administrative details.

Many readers will disagree about the ratings we have assigned films included in Appendix H. However, it is important to remember that our ratings are based *primarily* on the utility of the film as a teaching tool and only secondarily on the film's artistic merit.

We are including our e-mail addresses below so we can get feedback about the book. We hope those readers who share our enthusiasm about movies as a teaching tool will recommend additional films that we can include in the next edition of *Movies and Mental Illness*.

Danny Wedding, PhD, MPH
danny.wedding@gmail.com

Ryan M. Niemiec, PsyD
rmjn@sbcglobal.net

Acknowledgments

We are constantly writing about and discussing movies, and there are numerous friends and colleagues to acknowledge. Many of our ideas and the selections of films to be included in each new edition of *Movies and Mental Illness* grew out of discussions with these individuals, especially those who are mental health professionals interested in the fascinating ways in which psychopathology is portrayed in film.

Rob Dimbleby at Hogrefe Publishing is an extraordinary publisher, a true visionary, and a valued friend. We appreciate his enthusiasm for publishing an expanded and enhanced edition of this book.

We are also grateful to Mary Ann Boyd, our colleague and friend, who served as coauthor on the first three editions of *Movies and Mental Illness*.

Christoph Zepeda and Chris Pearce are two colleagues who help with each week's release of a new issue of *PsycCRITIQUES*; both helped immeasurably with this new edition.

Many people gave us specific feedback or suggestions relating to the psychopathology or movie portions of the book. We believe these have helped us make solid improvements throughout this particular edition. Thanks go to our colleagues in two divisions of the American Psychological Association: The Society for Media Psychology and Technology, and the Society for the Psychology of Aesthetics, Creativity, and the Arts. The members of these two divisions made multiple recommendations for films we include in this new edition.

Danny Wedding benefited from hundreds of discussions about films with his two sons, Joshua Wedding and Jeremiah Wedding (whose decision to major in film studies was no doubt influenced by his father's habit of watching two or three movies each week). Kayley Harrington, Kristine Harrington, and Thomas Harrington also made numerous useful suggestions, along with their respective partners, Aaron Bach, Steve Rutkowski, and Krystle Bartholomew.

Danny Wedding's work on this edition was delayed by his October 2013 marriage to Karen Harrington; however, she has proven herself to be a stalwart partner who shares his passion for both language and films (if not his passions for films dealing with depression, pathology, and suicide). Karen's mother, Dorothea (Dody) Schwaiger, also helped with this edition – in part by walking away from several films partway through, helping Danny know when films were too confusing, provocative, or disturbing for the typical viewer (e.g., *Cloud Atlas* and *We Need to Talk About Kevin*).

Danny Wedding is the editor of *PsycCRITIQUES: Contemporary Psychology – APA Review of Books*, and Ryan Niemiec is the associate editor for films for this American Psychological Association publication. When Wedding became editor, he reinstated the practice of reviewing psychologically relevant films in the journal, a practice first introduced by the journal's founding editor, E. G. Boring. Reading weekly film reviews written by psychologists has both sharpened and deepened our appreciation for the psychological relevance of films. Although the journal itself requires a subscription, interested readers can read and comment on selected film reviews at no cost by visiting the website (http://psyccritiquesblog.apa.org).

This book has opened up some incredible speaking opportunities for Danny Wedding. For example, Drs. Moira Nakousi, Daniel Soto, John Norcross, and Roberto Opazo Castro arranged for him to present talks on *Movies and Mental Illness* in Santiago, Chile; Dr. Catherine Sun invited Danny to keynote a conference in counseling psychology in Hong Kong, presenting a talk on films and mental illness; Dr. Saths Cooper invited him to present on the topic at the 2012 International Congress of Psychology in Cape Town, South Africa; Professor Paul Crawford arranged for Danny to present at an International Health Humanities conference sponsored by the University of Nottingham; and Danny was able to present on the topic of bipolar disorders and cinema at the 12th International Review of Bipolar Disorders in May, 2012, in Nice, France. The Nice talk coincided with the by-invitation-only Cannes Film Festival (*Festival de Cannes*), and Danny was able to use a flyer for *Movies and Mental Illness* to establish his credentials as a serious scholar and a journalist with a genuine interest in films.

Special thanks goes to Ryan Niemiec's wife, Rachelle Plummer, who continues to support his compulsive need to watch movies; this often entails light-up pens in movie theaters, tolerating the ubiquitous laptop he keeps by his side while watching movies at home, and frequent interruptions from new alerts on recent movies on his iPhone. His young sons, Rhys and Ryland, have slept through many hours of films in their father's arms as he studied the characters on the screen.

Finally, we want to thank two world class scholars: Dr. Antonio Díez Herranz, who translated *Movies and Mental Illness* into Spanish, and Professor Seung-hwa Beack, from Myong-Ji University, who translated our book into Korean. We were also gratified to receive copies of recent transla-

tions in Japanese, German (*Psyche Im Kino*) and Polish (*Kino I Choroby Psychiczne*).

We appreciate the feedback from our colleagues, friends, family, and the many readers who have taken the time to share suggestions, opinions, and support for our work. We hope you will contribute to our blog (http://moviesandmentalillness.blogspot. com) and let us know when you come across a great film that should be discussed in the next edition.

Chapter 1

Films and Psychopathology

For better or worse, movies and television contribute significantly to shaping the public's perception of the mentally ill and those who treat them.

Steven E. Hyler

For contemporary audiences, attending movies is an experience that provides catharsis and unites the audience with their culture in much the same way that the tragedies of Sophocles and Aeschylus performed these functions for 5th-century BC Greek audiences.

Glen Gabbard and Krin Gabbard

Introduction

In all of human perceptual experience, nothing conveys information or evokes emotion quite as clearly as our visual sense. Filmmakers capture the richness of this visual sense, combine it with auditory stimuli, and create the ultimate waking dream experience: the movie. The viewer enters a trance, a state of absorption, concentration, and attention, engrossed by the story and the plight of the characters. When someone is watching a movie, an immediate bond is set up between the viewer and the film, and all of the technical apparatus involved with the projection of the film becomes invisible as the images from the film pass into the viewer's consciousness. The viewer experiences a sort of dissociative state in which ordinary existence is temporarily suspended, serving as a *psychological clutch* (Butler & Palesh, 2004) in which the individual escapes from the stressors, conflicts, and worries of the day. This trance state is further enhanced in movie theaters where the viewer is fully enveloped in sight and sound, and in some instances experiences the sense of touch through vibration effects. No other art form pervades the consciousness of the individual to the same extent and with such power as cinema. Many consider movies to be the most influential form of mass communication (Cape, 2003).

Hollywood took the original invention of the cinematic camera and invented a new art form in which the viewer becomes enveloped in the work of art. The camera carries the viewer into each scene, and the viewer perceives events from the inside as if surrounded by the characters in the film. The actors do not have to describe their feelings, as in a play, because the viewer directly experiences what they see and feel.

To produce an emotional response to a film, the director carefully develops both plot and character through precise camera work. Editing creates a visual and acoustic **gestalt**, to which the viewer responds. The more effective the technique, the more involved the viewer. In effect, the director *constructs* the film's (and the viewer's) reality. The selection of locations, sets, actors, costumes, and lighting contributes to the film's organization and shot-by-shot **mise-en-scene** (the physical arrangement of the visual image).

The Pervasive Influence of Films

Film has become such an integral part of our culture that it seems to be the mirror in which we see ourselves reflected every day. Indeed, the social impact of film extends around the globe. The widespread popularity of online movies, DVDs by mail (e.g., through Netflix), nominally priced Redbox rentals at the street corner, the use of unlimited rentals for a monthly fee, and in-home, cable features like On-Demand make hundreds of thousands of movies available and accessible to virtually anyone in the world (and certainly anyone who has Internet access). No longer are individuals limited solely to the film selection and discretion of the corner video store. People now have wide access to films beyond Hollywood, including access to films from independent filmmakers, even those from developing countries. Moreover, with the affordability of digital video, neophyte and/or low-budget filmmakers can now tell their stories within the constraints of a much more reasonable budget without sacrificing quality (Taylor & Hsu, 2003); this increases the range of topics and themes that can be covered. Recent award-winning films such as *Gravity* (2013), *Rust and Bone* (2012), and *Life of Pi* (2012) were all shot using digital video.

We believe films have a greater influence than any other art form. This influence is felt across age, gender, nationality, and culture – and even across time. Films have become a pervasive and omnipresent part of our society, and yet people often have little conscious awareness of the profound influence the medium exerts.

Films are especially important in influencing the public perception of mental illness because many people are relatively uninformed about the problems of people with mental disorders, and the media tend to be especially effective in shaping opinion in those situations in which strong opinions are not already held. Although some films present sympathetic portrayals of people with mental illness and those professionals who work in the field of mental health (e.g., *The Three Faces of Eve*, *David and Lisa*, *Ordinary People*, and *A Beautiful Mind*), many more do not. Individuals with mental illness are often portrayed as aggressive, dangerous, and unpredictable; psychiatrists, psychologists, nurses, and other health professionals who work with these patients are often portrayed as "arrogant and ineffectual," "cold-hearted and authoritarian," "passive and apathetic," or "shrewd and manipulative" (Niemiec & Wedding, 2006; Wedding & Niemiec, 2003). Psychiatrists in particular have been negatively portrayed in the cinema (Gabbard & Gabbard, 1992).

Films such as *Psycho* (1960) perpetuate the continuing confusion about the relationship between schizophrenia and dissociative identity disorder (formerly multiple personality disorder); *Friday the 13th* (1980) and *Nightmare on Elm Street* (1984) both perpetuate the misconception that people who leave psychiatric hospitals are violent and dangerous; movies such as *The Exorcist* (1973) suggest to the public that mental illness is the equivalent of possession by the devil; and movies such as *One Flew Over the Cuckoo's Nest* (1975) make the case that psychiatric hospitals are simply prisons in which there is little or no regard for patient rights or welfare. These films in part account for the continuing stigma of mental illness.

Stigma is one of the reasons that so few people with mental problems actually receive help (Corrigan, Roe, & Tsang, 2011). The National Institute of Mental Health (NIMH) estimates that only 20% of those with mental disorders actually reach out for help with their problems, despite the fact that many current treatments for these disorders are inexpensive and effective. In addition, there is still a strong tendency to see patients with mental disorders as the cause of their own disorders – for example, the National Alliance for the Mentally Ill (NAMI) has polling data that indicate that about one in three US citizens still conceptualizes mental illness in terms of evil and punishment for misbehavior.

Psychiatrist Peter Byrne has pointed out that films rarely portray mental illness or mental health practitioners accurately, but he also makes the compelling point that the job of a director is to create a film that will generate revenue for producers and investors, and it is not necessarily their job to educate the public. In a recent article, he described five rules of movie psychiatry (Byrne, 2009):

1. Follow the money: film-making is a commercial enterprise and producers may include inaccurate representations in their films to 'give the public what they want';

2. Film begets film: every new film draws on previous films within the genre;
3. Skewed distribution hides more films than censorship ever did;
4. There are no mental health films, just mental illness ones;
5. If it bleeds it leads: violence, injury and death often ensure prominence of a story in both news and film. (Byrne, 2009, pp. 287–288).

Byrne's points are well-taken, although we would challenge Number 4 because we have written a book titled *Positive Psychology at the Movies* (Niemiec & Wedding, 2014) in which we document nearly 1,500 movies that display character strengths and other healthy aspects of human psychology, including positive mental health. This edition of *Movies and Mental Illness* also describes many films that offer positive depictions of mental health.

Cinematic Elements

A film director must consider countless technical elements in the making of a film, often orchestrating hundreds of people, many of whom monitor and pass down orders to hundreds or thousands of other collaborators. There are three general phases involved in making a film.

The time spent prior to filming in the **preproduction phase** is often seen as the most important. Many directors *storyboard* (draw out) every shot and choreograph every movement for each scene to be filmed. Countless meetings with each technical supervisor (e.g., cinematographer, costume designer, set designer, electrician) are held to facilitate preparation, coordination, and integration. The director will also scout out locations, work with casting appropriate actors and actresses for the various roles, and may rework the screenplay.

In the **production phase**, the director attempts to film his or her vision, working closely with the actors and actresses to encourage, stimulate, guide, or alter their work, while carefully monitoring camera angles, lighting, sound, and other technical areas.

In the **postproduction phase**, editing and laying out the musical score and background sounds are major areas of focus. The director integrates each of these elements while working to honor the original purpose, message, and underlying themes of the film.

Some of the most important cinematic elements are summarized with film examples in Table 1. Of course, these three phases exclude countless other tasks involving financing, budgeting, marketing, and other business, administrative, consulting, and legal aspects. A mental health consultant may be used with certain films and may play an important role in any phase, particularly involving fine tuning the screenplay and helping the director and actors understand psychological and related phenomena; we believe mental health consultants should be sought out for *every* film portraying a psychological condition or a therapeutic encounter. Unfortunately, such consultants are sorely underutilized in cinema. However, the directors of films such as *A*

Beautiful Mind, *Antwone Fisher*, and *Analyze This* did use psychologists and/or psychiatrists as consultants.

Directors attempt to artfully integrate the technical elements of sound, camera, and lighting fluidly with the plot, themes, pacing, and tone of the film, while eliciting quality acting performances. Danis Tanovic, director of a film that won the Academy Award for Best Foreign Film, *No Man's Land* (2001), about the Bosnian-Serbian war, speaks to many of these elements as he describes the shock and disharmony of the war that he attempted to depict in his film:

"This shock is something I have reproduced through my film. On one side, a long summer day – perfect nature, strong colors – and on the other, human beings and their black madness. And this long, hot summer day re-

Table 1. Film elements with movie examples

Film element	Explanation	Classic example	Recent example
Themes	Overall meaning, messages, motifs	*It's a Wonderful Life* (1946)	*12 Years a Slave* (2013)
Cinematography	Visual appeal, framing, camera work, lighting	*Lawrence of Arabia* (1962)	*Gravity* (2013)
Pacing	Movement, fluidity	*M*A*S*H* (1970)	*Life of Pi* (2012)
Sound	Music, score, sound effects	*Ben-Hur* (1959)	*Django Unchained* (2012)
Mood	Tone, atmosphere	*M* (1931)	*Beasts of the Southern Wild* (2012)
Art	Set design, costumes	*Star Wars* (1977)	*The Great Gatsby* (2013)
Dialogue	Conversation, modes of communication	*Annie Hall* (1977)	*Blue Jasmine* (2013)
Acting	Character portrayal, depth and quality, casting	*The Philadelphia Story* (1940)	*Dallas Buyers Club* (2013)
Editing	Continuity, transitions	*Citizen Kane* (1941)	*Captain Phillips* (2013)
Screenplay	Storyline, plot; original or adapted to the screen	*One Flew Over the Cuckoo's Nest* (1975)	*Silver Linings Playbook* (2012)
Direction	All elements together, quality of film overall	*A Clockwork Orange* (1971)	*Cloud Atlas* (2012)

flects the atmosphere of the film itself. Movements are heavy, thoughts are hard to grasp, time is slow and tension is hiding – hiding but present. When it finally explodes, it is like fireworks – sudden, loud, and quick. Panoramic shots of landscape become unexpectedly mixed with nervous details of action. It all lasts for a moment or two, and then tension hides again, waiting for the next opportunity to surprise. Time slows down again."

Danis Tanovic, quoted in the DVD insert for
No Man's Land

Changes in color and sound have a significant impact on the viewer's experience of a film. Butler and Palesh (2004) offer the example of Steven Spielberg's manipulation of these cinematic elements in *Saving Private Ryan* (1998). In addition to screams turned slowly into sobs or mumbles, colors are subdued to an almost black-and-white appearance so that when the color red is introduced in the battle scenes amid the muted background, the depiction of the reality of war becomes even more vivid for the viewer.

For the most skilled directors, virtually everything that the camera "sees" and records is meaningful. The sense of subjective experience produced by a sequence of **point-of-view** shots facilitates the viewer's identification with the film's characters, their perceptions, and their circumstances. Extreme **close-up shots** and a variety of **panning techniques** facilitate the importance of an emotional expression or inner conflict, or develop pacing for the film. High-angle and low-angle shots give emphasis to character control, power, strength, weakness, and a variety of other dynamics. For example, in *American Beauty* (1999), high-angle shots are used at the beginning of the film focused on Lester Burnham (Kevin Spacey) to indicate a passiveness and submission to authority prior to his transformation to a strong-willed, commanding character.

Each viewer possesses unique perceptual preferences, prior knowledge about the film's content, and preconceptions about the images the film contains that mediate his or her perceptions and experience. Rarely, if ever, do any two viewers have an identical experience when viewing the same film. Each viewer subjectively selects, attends to, and translates the visual and acoustic images projected in a theater into his or her own version of the story. Often viewers are affected by, or identify with, the

film's characters so strongly that it appears clear that the defense mechanism of **projection** is present. This process is facilitated when the viewer can anticipate the storyline, the plot, or the outcome. The avid moviegoer quickly realizes familiar themes, similar settings, and "formulas" for plots and endings across a variety of films.

The Close-Up

When we see an isolated face on the screen, our consciousness of space is suspended, and we become vividly aware of all the nuances of emotion that can be expressed by a grimace or a glance. We form beliefs about a character's emotions, moods, intentions, and thoughts as we look directly into his or her face. Indeed, many of the most profound emotional experiences (such as grief) are expressed much more powerfully through the human face than through words. Consider the dynamic film, *Amélie* (2001), in which director Jean-Pierre Jeunet purposefully chooses characters (as he does for all of his films) who have very expressive faces. There are numerous close-ups on several of the characters' faces throughout the film. He explains that he wants to have characters who are interesting for the viewer to look at. In turn, this enhances viewer interest and character development.

Director Woody Allen uses close-up shots smoothly and effectively, and they are a hallmark of many of his films. Some of the close-up images of Cate Blanchett playing the role of Jasmine in *Blue Jasmine* (2013) are unforgettable, and they linger with the viewer long after he or she leaves the theater (see Figure 24 on page 250).

This ability to share and comprehend subjective experiences through empathic interpretation of the language of the face is clearly evident in early **silent films**, and these films still have the power to evoke strong emotions. In fact, many early directors of silent films, confronted with the development of "talkies," feared that the addition of sound would place a barrier between the spectator and the film and restore the external and internal distance and dualism present in other works of art. The principles of observing emotional nuances can be extended from the human face to the background and surroundings in which the character moves, and a character's subjective vision can be reproduced by a film as objective reality. For example, film can show the frightened, paranoid individual, but also the distorted, menacing houses and trees which the protagonist views. This technique was used in the expressionist film *The Cabinet of Dr. Caligari* (1920).

What we see in a facial expression is immediately apparent to the spectator without the distraction of words, and a good actor can convey multiple emotions simultaneously. It has been shown repeatedly that real people playing themselves are less convincing than actors. This is true with instructional films, advertisements, and docudramas, as well as feature films. In *Ordinary People* (1980), director Robert Redford attempted to cast an actual psychiatrist in the role of the therapist, but the effect was unconvincing. Redford finally decided to cast actor Judd Hirsch in the role, and the film ended up winning an Academy Award for Best Picture, and Hirsch received a nomination for Best Actor. A notable exception was *One Flew Over the Cuckoo's Nest* (1975), a film in which a bona fide psychiatrist actually played the role of the psychiatrist, and filming occurred on the grounds of an actual psychiatric facility.

Identification

As a film is being projected onto a theater screen, we project ourselves into the action and identify with its protagonists. At one time it was thought that to maintain the attention of viewers, a film had to have a central character and theme. At times this central figure has been an antihero. However, directors such as Robert Altman and Quentin Tarantino have experimented with techniques in which they rapidly shift among short vignettes that may be only loosely linked with a storyline or central character. Altman's *Short Cuts* (1994) and Tarantino's *Pulp Fiction* (1994) are two examples of this approach. *Crash* (2005), directed by Paul Haggis, was so masterful at interweaving stories to enhance meaning and viewer engagement that it won an Academy Award for Best Picture, among many other awards. The most recent example of this approach is *Cloud Atlas* (2012), a film in which multiple actors play multiple roles in vignettes that are loosely but meaningfully connected. The film addresses the obscure links between past, present, and

future events. Critics were divided over whether directors Tom Tykwer, Andy Wachowski, and Lana Wachowski were entirely successful; however, we found the film engaging and provocative.

Suture

Viewers integrate separate, disjointed photographic images into coherent scenes and weave different scenes into the whole film experience without conscious effort or appreciation of the complicated psychological processes involved. **Suture**, to use a medical metaphor, occurs when cutting or editing is necessary, and the resulting cinematic gaps are "sewn" shut by viewers.

According to suture theory, instead of asking, "Who is watching this?" and "How could this be happening?" viewers tacitly accept what is seen on the screen as natural and "real," even when the camera's gaze shifts abruptly from one scene, location, or character to another. Suture works because cinematic coding makes each shot appear to be the object of the gaze of whoever appears in the shot that follows. The most commonly cited example of suturing is the **shot/reverse shot**, in which each of two characters is alternately viewed over the other's shoulder.

The Representation of Psychological Phenomena in Film

Film is particularly well suited to depicting psychological states of mind and altered mental states. The combination of images, dialogue, sound effects, and music in a movie mimics and parallels the thoughts and feelings that occur in our stream of consciousness. Lights, colors, and sounds emanate from the screen in such a way that we readily find ourselves believing that we are actually experiencing what is happening on the screen.

In *Secrets of a Soul* (1926), German director Georg Wilhelm Pabst dramatized psychoanalytic theory with the help of two of Freud's assistants, Karl Abraham and Hanns Sachs, and depicted dream sequences with multilayered superimposition (achieved through rewinding and multiple exposures). Freud himself did not want his name connected with the project and had misgivings about the film's ability to convey the nuances of psychoanalytic process. In a letter to Abraham, Freud wrote, "My chief objection is still that I do not believe satisfactory plastic representation of our abstractions is at all possible" (Freud, cited in Greenberg, 1993, p. 19). Freud remained skeptical about the cinema all his life. This perspective is in direct contrast to that of the late, renowned filmmaker Stanley Kubrick, who noted, "If it can be written, or thought, it can be filmed."

Film is frequently used to objectively portray subjective states such as dreams. Perhaps the best example of this is Hitchcock's collaboration with Salvador Dali on the dream sequence in *Spellbound* (1945). Hitchcock wanted to "turn out the first picture on psychoanalysis." He was determined to break the traditional way of handling dream sequences through a blurred and hazy screen. Hitchcock wanted dreams with great visual sharpness and clarity, and images sharper than those in the film itself. He chose Salvador Dali as a collaborator because of the architectural precision of the artist's work. Hitchcock originally wanted to shoot *Spellbound* in the open air and in natural light, but he wound up shooting the film in the studio to cut costs. *Spellbound* depicts the cathartic recovery of repressed memories, and an emotional experience intense enough to eliminate the hero's amnesia. This is a psychological process that has been depicted in film since its early days.

Films can also be used to interweave fantasy and reality, and a director may intentionally set up situations in which the viewer cannot tell if the film portrays reality or the unconscious fantasies of a character. Examples of this technique include Ingmar Bergman's *Persona* (1966), Federico Fellini's *Juliet of the Spirits* (1965), Luis Buñuel's *Belle de Jour* (1966), Robert Altman's *Images* (1972), and Derek Cianfrance's *Beasts of the Southern Wild* (2012). Director David Lynch has made this approach his trademark with such films as *Mulholland Drive* (2001), *Lost Highway* (1997), *Blue Velvet* (1986), and *Eraserhead* (1977).

Processes such as thinking, recalling, imagining, and feeling are not visible, but the language of the **montage** and camera techniques such as **slow fades** can suggest these invisible processes. Also, the film can be edited in such a way that the viewer is forced to think about psychological phenomena.

The inclusion of images with symbolic meaning, such as a hearse passing by or the well-known chess game with Death in *The Seventh Seal* (1957), can evoke certain moods or prepare the viewer for events that are about to occur. Symbolic sounds, such as a baby crying, can have a similar effect.

Another symbol often used in film is the mirror. When a character is filmed looking in the mirror, it often represents self-reflection, insight, a new identity emerging or changing, or even a narcissistic preoccupation with oneself. *Monster's Ball* (2001) uses mirrors and other reflective objects to symbolize self-distortion and negative self-perception in the two lead characters who are numb to their own lives. Mirrored images depict Marlon Brando's broken and distorted character in *Last Tango in Paris* (1972), self-deprecation in *American Splendor* (2003), self-criticism in *Soldier's Girl* (2003), deterioration in *Ben X* (2007), *Black Swan* (2010), and *Focus* (2001), self-reflection and distortion in *Chloe* (2010), and externalization of blame in a dramatic, comical scene in *25th Hour* (2002).

"Beyond all physical and palpable reality another dimension defined only in painting, a mirror which deforms life ... an instant reflected ... a magical reality where all is possible."

Goya in Bordeaux (1999)

Films offer numerous examples of unconscious motivation and **defense mechanisms**, involuntary patterns of thinking, feeling, or acting that arise in response to the subjective experience of anxiety. **Acting out** in reaction to stress or inner conflict is present in *The Hammer* (2010), *Intimacy* (2000), *You Can Count On Me* (2000), and *Lantana* (2001), and in Michael Douglas' response to the stress in his life in *Falling Down* (1993). **Altruism** can be seen in *Patch Adams* (1998), and the character of the doctor who devotes himself to the indigent people of India in *Streets of Joy* (1994). **Denial** is dramatically illustrated in Katharine Hepburn's and Ellen Burstyn's gripping roles as drug addicts in *Long Day's Journey into Night* (1962) and *Requiem for a Dream* (2000), respectively, as well as the Oscar-winning film *The White Ribbon* (2009), and most of the townspeople in both *The Village* (2004) and *Dogville* (2003). **Intellectualization** is present in *Lorenzo's Oil* (1992), and **suppression** is apparent in *A Dangerous Method* (2011), *Rabbit Hole* (2010), *The United States of Leland* (2003), *Caramel* (2007), and *Kill Bill: Vol. 2* (2004), and is commonplace in *Gone with the Wind* (1939).

"I'll think about it tomorrow. Tara! Home. I'll go home, and I'll think of some way to get him back! After all, tomorrow is another day!"

Gone with the Wind (1939)

The Depiction of Psychological Disorders in Films

This book organizes the categories of mental disorders in the fifth edition of the *Diagnostic and Statistical Manual of Mental Disorders (DSM-5)* with appropriate film examples. Table 2 presents an overview of well-recognized and accepted disorders and some of the best representations of them in cinema. Watching any of these films will provide the viewer with insights into the presentation of the particular disorder portrayed.

Psychopathology in Different Film Genres

The depiction of mental illness in films most commonly appears in three popular genres: the drama, the horror film, and the suspense film. Often the most effective portrayals of mental illness are those that infuse surreal and expressionistic images into a montage that is realistic and plausible, powerfully conveying the "interior" of a character's psyche.

The popular genre of **drama** is perhaps the most fertile ground for psychopathology to be portrayed in movies in a very realistic, engaging way. Every chapter in this book has numerous examples of dramatic films depicting psychological disorders. The range is vast, and it extends from the slow-moving drama of *The Human Stain* (2003) and the disjointed, complex drama of *21 Grams* (2003), to the affectively engaging dramas of *12 Years a Slave* (2013) and *Captain Phillips* (2013).

An early film that served as a prototype for **horror** films, Wiene's *The Cabinet of Dr. Caligari* (1920), is highly expressionistic, and it established a precedent for setting macabre murders in mental institutions. Like dozens of films that followed, it linked insanity and the personal lives of psychiatrists and implied that mental health professionals are all "a little odd." Evidence of the enduring effects of these themes is found in the successful and highly acclaimed film *The Silence of the Lambs* (1991), in which Anthony Hopkins plays a mentally deranged and cannibalistic psychiatrist. The various *Saw* (2004; 2005; 2006; 2007; 2008; 2009) movies and *House of 1000 Corpses* (2003) portray psychopathic villains who are clearly out of touch with reality, as does the dreadful trilogy of films that tell the story of *The Human Centipede* (2009; 2011; 2014).

The seminal films of Alfred Hitchcock provide the best examples of the **suspense** genre. They are unique in the way they engage the viewer and pander to his or her anxieties in subtle, unrelenting, and convincing ways. The majority of Hitchcock's films, noted for their stylized realism, invariably evoke a sensation of vicariously pulling the viewer "in" to the plight of the characters as a not-so-innocent bystander, through a carefully edited montage of a variety of objective and subjective camera shots. Hitchcock's filmography reflects not only a fascination with pronounced and extreme psychopathology (e.g., *Psycho, 1960*), but more importantly, an appreciation of more subtle psychological phenomena such as acting out, reaction formation, idealization, repression, and undoing. These defense mechanisms are depicted in Hitchcock's films *Shadow of a Doubt* (1943), *Spellbound* (1945), and *Marnie* (1964). Hitchcock's style is immensely popular and has been imitated frequently by other directors such as Brian De Palma and Roman Polanski.

More recent examples of suspense films include Robert Redford's *All Is Lost* (2013), Sean Durkin's *Martha Marcy May Marlene* (2011), and Ben Affleck's *Argo* (2012). *Argo* won the Academy Award for Best Picture.

Mental illness is also depicted, although less often, in the genre of **documentary** films. Frederick Wiseman's *Titicut Follies* (1967) and *Capturing the Friedmans* (2003) illustrate clear cases of psychopathology. It is interesting to contrast the former movie with the horror film *Bedlam* (1945) or "docu-

Table 2. *DSM-5* categories and movies that portray them

Category	Classic film examples	More recent film examples
Neurodevelopmental disorders: Intellectual disability	*Sling Blade* (1996); *My Left Foot* (1989)	*Me, Too* (2009); *Monica and David* (2009); *Rory O'Shea Was Here* (2004)
Neurodevelopmental disorders: Autism spectrum	*David and Lisa* (1962); *Rain Man* (1988)	*Adam* (2009); *The Horse Boy* (2009); *The Black Balloon* (2008)
Neurocognitive disorders	*On Golden Pond* (1981)	*Away From Her* (2006); *Amour* (2012)
Substance-related and addictive disorders	*The Lost Weekend* (1945)	*Half Nelson* (2006); *Walk the Line* (2005); *The Fighter* (2010); *Bob and the Monster* (2013); *Owning Mahowny* (2002); *Smashed* (2012)
Schizophrenia spectrum and other psychotic disorders	*Clean, Shaven* (1994)	*Take Shelter* (2011); *Shutter Island* (2010); *A Beautiful Mind* (2001)
Depressive disorders	*Ordinary People* (1980)	*A Single Man* (2009); *Melancholia* (2011)
Bipolar disorders	*Mr. Jones* (1993)	*Silver Linings Playbook* (2012); *Crooked Beauty: Navigating the Space Between Beauty and Madness* (2010); *Michael Clayton* (2007)
Anxiety disorders	*Vertigo* (1958)	*The Perks of Being a Wallflower* (2012)
Obsessive-compulsive disorders	*As Good As It Gets* (1997)	*Phoebe in Wonderland* (2008); *Matchstick Men* (2003)
Trauma- and stressor-related disorders	*The Deer Hunter* (1978)	*The Hurt Locker* (2008); *The Dry Land* (2010)
Somatic symptom disorders	*Persona* (1966)	*Therese* (2004); *Hollywood Ending* (2002)
Dissociative disorders	*Psycho* (1960)	*Peacock* (2010); *Unknown White Male* (2005)
Paraphilic disorders	*Lolita* (1962)	*The Woodsman* (2004); *Secretary* (2002);
Gender dysphoria	*Boys Don't Cry* (1999)	*Transamerica* (2005); *Normal* (2003)
Feeding and eating disorders	*The Best Little Girl in the World* (1982)	*Primo Amore* (2004); *Center Stage* (2000); *Black Swan* (2010)
Sleep-wake disorders	*My Own Private Idaho* (1991)	*Inception* (2010); *The Machinist* (2004); *Insomnia* (2002)
Disruptive, impulse-control, and conduct disorders	*Marnie* (1964)	*2 Days in Paris* (2007); *Klepto* (2003)
Adjustment disorders	*The Wrong Man* (1957)	*The Upside of Anger* (2005); *Best in Show* (2000)
Sexual dysfunctions	*Bliss* (1997)	*The Sessions* (2012)
Personality disorders	*Compulsion* (1959); *Fatal Attraction* (1987)	*Side Effects* (2013); *Jobs* (2013); *Blue Jasmine* (2013); *We Need to Talk About Kevin* (2011); *The Iceman* (2012)

Note. DSM-5 = Diagnostic and Statistical Manual of Mental Disorders, 5th edition.

dramatic" films such as *The Snake Pit* (1948), *Pressure Point* (1962), and *One Flew Over the Cuckoo's Nest* (1975), all dealing with mental institutions and the treatment of people with mental illness. At least two heralded films, *The Three Faces of Eve* (1957) and *Sybil* (1976), provide viewers with full-scale case histories and the struggles between patient and psychiatrist.

The **comedy** genre has its share of films portraying psychopathology. *Drop Dead Fred* (1991), *What About Bob?* (1991), *High Anxiety* (1977), and *Scotland, PA* (2001) portray psychological aberrations with quirky humor that is used to defuse the sense of anxiety that is produced by the behavior of the lead characters in each of the films. Director Woody Allen has made a career out of portraying anxiety, neuroticism, and somatization in various films such as *Hannah and Her Sisters* (1988) and *Hollywood Ending* (2002), but more recently has turned to subtle, dark, and complex psychopathology as seen in the portrayal of personality disorders in *Match Point* (2005), *Vicky Cristina Barcelona* (2008), and *Blue Jasmine* (2013).

Misconceptions and Stereotypic Themes in Films

Otto Wahl, an authority on media psychology, summarizes the media's portrayal of mental illness in his book *Media Madness: Public Images of Mental Illness* (1995): "Overall, the mass media do a poor job of depicting mental illness, with misinformation frequently communicated, unfavorable stereotypes of people with mental illness predominating, and psychiatric terms used in inaccurate and offensive ways" (pp. 12–13). This is largely due to **media framing**, a concept that refers to the way a form of media presents and organizes information that leads to interpretations by the public. In the case of mental illness in films, media framing is overwhelmingly negative and usually inaccurate (Goffman, 1986; Sieff, 2003). The media frames for mental illness are typically narrow and distorted, frequently presenting those with mental illness as violent, dangerous, simplistic, disillusioned, and/or innocent. This is troubling for at least two reasons: (1) Mental health literacy levels for the general public are low (Orchowski, Spickard, & McNamara, 2006); (2) Research has shown that people's primary source of information about mental illness are the mass media (Wahl, 1995).

Steven Hyler (Hyler, Gabbard, & Schneider, 1991) has provided a compelling analysis of the portrayal of mental illness in films. Hyler and his colleagues describe six common stereotypes that perpetuate stigma. The first of these is that of the mental patient as **rebellious free spirit**. Examples of this portrayal can be found in films such as *Frances* (1982), *Nuts* (1987), *The Dream Team* (1989), *The Couch Trip* (1989), *An Angel At My Table* (1990), *Shine* (1996), *K-Pax* (2001), *Asylum* (2005), and perhaps most clearly in *One Flew Over the Cuckoo's Nest* (1975). The stereotype of the **homicidal maniac** is present in many of the slasher/horror films described earlier. However, the authors point out that this stereotype can also be traced back as far as D. W. Griffith's 1909 film *The Maniac Cook*, in which a psychotic employee attempts to kill an infant by cooking the child in an oven.

The patient as **seductress** is seen in films such as *The Caretakers* (1963) and *Dressed to Kill* (1980), and most clearly in the 1964 film *Lilith*, which stars Warren Beatty as a hospital therapist who is seduced by a psychiatric patient played by Jean Seberg. The stereotype of the **enlightened member of society** is linked to the work of writers such as R. D. Laing and Thomas Szasz and is illustrated in films such as *King of Hearts* (1966) and *A Fine Madness* (1966). The **narcissistic parasite** stereotype presents people with mental disorders as self-centered, attention-seeking, and demanding. It is reflected in films such as *What About Bob?* (1991), *Annie Hall* (1977), *High Anxiety* (1977), and *Lovesick* (1983). Finally, the stereotype of **zoo specimen** is perpetuated by films that degrade people with mental illness by treating them as objects of derision or a source of amusement or entertainment for those who are "normal." Films that exemplify this stereotype include *Bedlam* (1948) and *Marat/Sade* (1966). A variation on this theme occurs in Brian De Palma's *Dressed to Kill* (1980), in which a psychotic and homicidal psychiatrist murders a nurse in a surrealistic amphitheater-like setting, with dozens of other patients sitting in the gallery and watching in silent approval.

Hyler (1988) describes three dominant themes in film that contribute to stereotypes about the etiology manifestation of mental disorders. The first is the **presumption of traumatic etiology**. This theme reinforces the belief that a single traumatic event is the cause of mental illness. Examples include the amnesia experienced by Gregory Peck that was eventually shown to be related to his role in the childhood death of his brother (revealed by Hitchcock in a dramatic and unforgettable flashback scene) in *Spellbound* (1945), and the dissociative identity disorder that resulted when a child was required to kiss the corpse of her dead grandmother in *The Three Faces of Eve* (1957). Other examples of this theme are found in films such as *Suddenly, Last Summer* (1959), *Home of the Brave* (1949), *Nuts* (1987), and Robin Williams' character in *The Fisher King* (1991).

Hyler's second theme is that of the **schizophrenogenic parent**. This is a widely held misconception that holds parents (most often, the mother) accountable for serious mental illness in their children. NAMI has worked hard to dispel this unfounded but pervasive belief, but it is deeply rooted in popular culture and commonplace in films. Examples include *Agnes of God* (1985), *Face to Face* (1976), *Sybil* (1980), *Carrie* (1976), *Frances* (1982), *Fear Strikes Out* (1957), and *Shine* (1995).

"Insanity runs in my family. It practically gallops."

Mortimer Brewster (Cary Grant) in
Arsenic and Old Lace (1944)

The third misconception discussed by Hyler is that **harmless eccentricity is frequently labeled as mental illness and inappropriately treated**. We see this theme most vividly presented in the film *One Flew Over the Cuckoo's Nest* (1975). Jack Nicholson's character, Randle P. McMurphy, is charismatic, flamboyant, and colorful. The only diagnosis that seems at all appropriate is that of antisocial personality disorder, although it is not even clear that this is justified. However, once in the system he cannot get out, and he is eventually treated with electroconvulsive therapy and lobotomy, presumably as a way of punishing his misbehavior in the name of treatment. The same theme is found in two films released in 1966, *King of Hearts* and *A Fine Madness*, and in the film *Chattahoochee* (1990). A related theme, that treatment in mental health facilities is actually a form of social control, is reflected in the work of Thomas Szasz (e.g., in books such as *The Myth of Mental Illness* and *Psychiatric Slavery*). It is also reflected in films depicting excesses in treatment, such as the aversion therapies portrayed in *A Clockwork Orange* (1971). For

a full list of misconceptions perpetrated in movies accompanied by film examples see Appendix D. Appendix E looks specifically at the mental health profession and delineates a list of both "balanced" and "unbalanced" portrayals of psychotherapists.

Another myth, although one not specifically addressed by Hyler, is the belief that **love will always conquer mental illness**. This myth is promulgated by films like *Shine* (1996) and *Benny & Joon* (1993). Although the benefits and buffering effects of love are important for anyone coping with mental illness or addiction, the reality is that some people with these disorders do not improve no matter how much they are loved. The pernicious corollary to this myth is that if people who are mentally ill *do not* improve, it must be because they simply were not loved enough.

Psychopathology and its representation in films will be discussed in some detail in the chapters that follow. In general, we will follow the nosology of the American Psychiatric Association's *DSM-5*, while also including diagnostic codes from the *International Classification of Diseases*, whenever appropriate. Appendix H includes a filmography broken down by diagnostic category. Readers who take time to review even a few of the films included in Appendix H will find that the experience will supplement and enhance their understanding of psychopathology.

Mental Illness, Mental Health, and the Human Condition

Mental illness is one of the most fascinating phenomena a filmmaker can depict on screen. There is, of course, much more to the human condition than psychopathology and what is going wrong with individuals. The positive aspects of human beings – happiness, achievement, talents, character strengths, interests, etc. – should not be viewed as mutually exclusive from mental struggles and disorders. Indeed, both can co-occur, and certainly one (i.e., positive psychology) can frequently benefit the other (i.e., mental disorders). In fact, while mental disorders are associated with lower levels of happiness, most people with mental disorders are happy (Bergsma, ten Have, Veenhoven, & Graaf, 2011). High levels of distress do not preclude happy moods, and happiness does predict recovery from mental disorders (Bergsma et al., 2011).

In another book, *Positive Psychology at the Movies 2: Using Films to Build Character Strengths and Well-Being* (Niemiec & Wedding, 2014), we focus on what is right with people, and review nearly 1,500 cinematic portrayals of triumph, virtue, and positive influence. We use the VIA Classification system from the work *Character Strengths and Virtues* (Peterson & Seligman, 2004) of 24 universal character strengths, and discuss important cinematic examples of each (e.g., creativity, curiosity, kindness, fairness, etc.). Indeed, there is an overlap with the discussion here, as individuals with mental illness have character strengths and virtues (like all people) and often use their strengths to overcome mental adversity. Character strengths, in general, buffer people from vulnerabilities that can lead to depression and anxiety, such as the need for approval and perfectionism (Huta & Hawley, 2010). The specific character strengths of hope, kindness, social intelligence, self-regulation, and perspective buffer against the negative effects of stress and trauma (Park & Peterson, 2009). Such films are often more true to the human condition, as they are less likely to offer one-dimensional portrayals or shock-value sensationalism, and more likely to reveal the complexity and intrigue of what it means

to be human. Films like *A Beautiful Mind* (2001) offer a compelling portrayal of schizophrenia, but this film also illustrates the character strengths of love, bravery, and perseverance. See Table 3 for examples of films that speak clearly to both dimensions of the human condition.

The entertainment industry presents **PRISM Awards** to recognize the most accurate depictions of social issues in movies and television (Appendix F). Recent PRISM Award winners include *Silver Linings Playbook*, *Flight*, *Warrior*, and *Take Shelter*. The mental health community comes also together each year to present the **Voice Awards**; these awards recognize films that promote awareness of mental health issues and the power of recovery. The recipients are writers and producers of entertainment programming (film and television) who have given voice to individuals with mental health problems by building in dignified, respectful, and accurate portrayals in their scripts and productions. While each of the feature film winners can be found in this book, we give particular attention to *Canvas* (2006), *Reign Over Me* (2007), and *The Aviator* (2004). The Voice Awards are sponsored by the Center for Mental Health Services (CMHS), a division of the Substance Abuse and Mental Health Services Administration (SAMHSA); a complete list of the Voice Awards for movies is presented in Appendix G.

Table 3. Films portraying psychopathology as well as character strengths and virtues

Film	Psychopathology	Virtue	Character strength(s)
Elling (2001)	Anxiety disorder	Courage	Bravery and perseverance
Away from Her (2006)	Dementia	Humanity	Love
Mishima: A Life in Four Chapters (1985)	Suicide	Temperance	Self-regulation
Canvas (2006)	Schizophrenia	Wisdom and transcendence	Creativity and Hope
The Soloist (2009)	Schizophrenia	Wisdom	Creativity
Insomnia (2002)	Sleep disorder	Courage	Bravery and perseverance
American Beauty (1999)	Mood disorder	Transcendence	Appreciation of beauty
It's a Wonderful Life (1946)	Adjustment disorder	Transcendence	Gratitude and hope
A Clockwork Orange (1971)	Personality disorder	Wisdom and transcendence	Curiosity and appreciation of excellence

⚙ Critical Thinking Questions

➤ Do directors and producers have an obligation to present mental illness accurately, or are their sole objectives to entertain and to make films that maximize box office returns for investors?

➤ What cinematic element do you believe is most crucial to the portrayal of psychopathology in movies (e.g., musical score, lighting, etc.)?

➤ Consider a film character who has had an impact on your understanding of a psychological disorder. How did the cinematic elements of the film accentuate or contribute to your understanding?

➤ Do you believe that a purist approach to filmmaking (e.g., the Dogme 95 films that avoid special effects, sound external to the film, etc.) does more justice to psychological phenomena than an approach that emphasizes special effects?

➤ Describe some examples of how a film's music has enhanced the portrayal of depression, schizophrenia, and anxiety disorders. In what way was the music different for each? Was this dependent on the genre?

➤ Do most films that portray a dynamic, complex character with mental illness also portray the character's strengths and virtues? For those that don't, can this still be an accurate, full depiction of the individual?

➤ How much time do you spend watching movies or engaging in other activities in which you automatically enter a state of trance-like absorption and concentration? What is the function of this state of mind for you in terms of your everyday life?

➤ Can you think of additional myths that are promulgated by films? What are they?

If you have time to read just one book on stigma, make it:

Corrigan, P.W., Roe, D., Tsang, H.W.H. (2011). *Challenging the Stigma of Mental Illness: Lessons for Therapists and Advocates.* Chichester, UK: Wiley. doi: 10.1002/9780470977507

If you only have time for one article, read:

Bryne, P. (2000). Stigma of mental illness and ways of diminishing it. *Advances in Psychiatric Treatment, 6,* 65–72. doi: 10.1192/apt.6.1.65

If you have time to become an activist working for social change, listen to In Our Own Voice (online) and join

NAMI Stigmabusters (http://www.nami.org)

Wedding and Niemiec's Top 10 Psychopathology Films

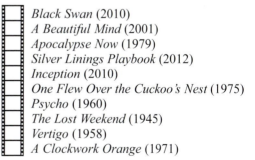

Black Swan (2010)
A Beautiful Mind (2001)
Apocalypse Now (1979)
Silver Linings Playbook (2012)
Inception (2010)
One Flew Over the Cuckoo's Nest (1975)
Psycho (1960)
The Lost Weekend (1945)
Vertigo (1958)
A Clockwork Orange (1971)

Chapter 2

Neurodevelopmental Disorders

My name is Temple Grandin.
I'm not like other people.
I think in pictures and I connect them.

Temple Grandin

Questions to Consider While Watching *Temple Grandin* (2010)

➤ Does Temple Grandin present as a typical person with autism spectrum disorder? If not, how is she different?

➤ Using *DSM-IV*, Temple Grandin would have been diagnosed as someone with Asperger's disorder. Why did the committee that developed the *DSM-5* do away with this diagnosis?

➤ How could a psychologist or social worker help Temple Grandin improve her social interactions?

➤ Why has the incidence of autism spectrum disorder been increasing in recent years?

➤ Are most people with autism spectrum disorder able to live and work independently?

➤ What are the heritability estimates for autism spectrum disorder?

➤ Is autism spectrum disorder diagnosed more frequently in boys or girls?

➤ Do you believe autism spectrum disorder can be caused by inflammatory damage, autoimmune disease, environmental factors, nutritional deficiencies or vaccinations? Cite research to support your view.

➤ Is autism spectrum disorder found across cultures? Is the incidence highest in the United States?

Patient Evaluation[1]

Name: Temple Gradin

Patient's stated reason for coming

"I'm different from other people. I don't like stimulation, and I feel uncomfortable in social situations. I just don't understand people. I hate noise and confusion. People keep giving each other looks, and I don't know what they mean. I'm just not like everybody else."

History of present illness

Ms. Temple Grandin is a 21-year-old college student who is studying animal husbandry at Arizona State University. She becomes anxious when around other people or in situations that deviate from her normal routine. Although clearly intelligent, she has always struck others as odd and eccentric; these differences were first noted around the age of 2 and they have been present ever since that time. She engaged in stereotypical and repetitive behaviors as a child and reverts to these behaviors when under stress or when she hears loud noises. Ms. Grandin maintains strict routines and engages in elaborate ritualistic behaviors (e.g., sharpening each pencil on her desk before beginning to study each evening); these habits have persisted since childhood.

Past psychiatric illness, treatment, and outcomes

Ms. Grandin has no history of psychiatric illness or hospitalization. However, language onset was delayed for approximately 3 years. In addition, as a child she would line up objects and become very disturbed if these items were moved or changed in any way. She also engages in rhythmic rocking (or sometimes spinning) when she is stressed. Several sessions with a psychologist at the university counseling center were apparently unproductive, and Ms. Grandin has decided not to continue treatment at the center.

Medical history

Her tonsils were removed at age 8, but there is no other history of hospitalization. Ms. Grandin did not begin to speak until age 4. She was diagnosed as a child and labeled an "infantile schizophrenic." She displayed little interest in playing with toys or interacting with other children. Her mother reports, "She was a perfectly normal baby." Her mother has been supportive and encouraging, refusing to institutionalize her daughter. Ms. Grandin reports that her mother taught her from a very young age that she was "different – but not less!"

---

[1] This fictitious interview has been developed for pedagogical purposes. It is based solely on the character of Temple Grandin as portrayed by Claire Danes in the movie *Temple Grandin*.

Psychosocial history

Ms. Grandin currently lives on campus in a dormitory where she is sometimes ridiculed and tormented by other students. She has a female roommate who is blind. These two students appear to have developed an effective and rewarding mutual support system. Ms. Grandin frequently sees an aunt who lives nearby, but she has few friends. She does have a loving mother who visits Temple at the university at least once each semester. Ms. Grandin has improvised what she describes as a "squeeze machine," and she utilizes this apparatus whenever she feels tense or overwhelmed by life and its demands.

Drug and alcohol history

Ms. Grandin denies any history of drug or alcohol use. She reports that she finds the odor and taste of both tobacco and alcohol repugnant.

Behavioral observations

Ms. Grandin was cooperative and polite during my interview. She was alert, and she cooperated fully with my evaluation. She avoided direct eye contact, but she did laugh appropriately several times during the evaluation. Her responses were sometimes tangential to the questions being asked, and she responded to all queries with very concrete responses.

Mental status examinations

Ms. Grandin was alert and oriented to time, place, situation, and person. She denied hallucinations and delusions. She was able to complete serial sevens very quickly (counting backwards all the way to zero, despite my attempts to stop her), and she had no difficulty with memory recall and copying a complex drawing. She had no problems with short-term memory questions. She denied suicidal and homicidal ideation. Her thinking is concrete, but otherwise her judgment appears above average. She achieved a perfect score of 30 on the Folstein Mini-Mental State Examination.

Functional assessment

Ms. Grandin is succeeding as a college student. She reports grades of A or B in all her classes so far. She is genuinely excited about science and the study of animal husbandry, and she is passionate about ensuring humane treatment for animals. She has little interest in French or some of the other elective courses she is required to take. She does not date, and claims she is not interested in romantic relationships or becoming married in the future. She occasionally watches television and she goes to see movies about once each month.

Strengths

Ms. Grandin is a pleasant individual with a good sense of humor. She is cooperative and friendly. Despite her limited social skills, she is clearly a very intelligent woman. She attends classes on a regular basis and does well in her university courses. On the VIA Survey, a measure of character strengths, Ms. Grandin's signature strengths were love of learning, perseverance, self-regulation, prudence, creativity, and appreciation of beauty/excellence.

Diagnosis

Autism spectrum disorder without accompanying language or intellectual impairment (F84). Rule out social anxiety disorder.

Treatment plan

(1) Social skills training. (2) Supportive counseling to discuss use of her character strengths to manage stress or anxiety relating to her social difficulties. (3) Consider including her mother in sessions as adjunctive support.

Prognosis

Excellent. This patient may continue to struggle in social situations despite treatment, but her keen intelligence and good education will help her compensate for the interpersonal difficulties she encounters because of her autism spectrum disorder.

Autism and *Temple Grandin*

Temple Grandin (2010) is a remarkable movie about a remarkable woman, portrayed in the film by Claire Danes. When Temple first goes to her aunt's home in Arizona, she initially has to put a sign on her door so she will know which room is hers. She experiences tremendous stress when the sign is removed, and she copes by running outdoors and putting herself in a "squeeze machine," a device her uncle uses when inoculating cattle. She develops a similar device in her college dormitory room, and later at an autism conference attempts to explain how the device was soothing: "Being held by another person is scary, but rolling or being held by surfaces reproduces the calming effect that ordinary children get from a hug." However, she continues to experience the challenges associated with being a person with autism spectrum disorder (e.g., she is threatened by an automatic sliding glass door in a supermarket). Later in the film, "going through doors" becomes a metaphor for overcoming the challenges Temple faces in her day-to-day life; Betty Goscowitz (the friendly wife of the owner of a slaughterhouse with "a grandson who's artistic") symbolizes how others in the life of a person with an autism spectrum disorder can be helpful. Temple Grandin (the actual person on whom the film is based) provides a useful commentary that is available on the DVD for this film. She reports that antidepressants she began taking in 1980 have been helpful in eliminating most of her panic attacks and helping her deal with her anxiety in those situations that she finds overly stimulating. Imaging studies of Grandin's brain and neuropsychological tests reveal exceptional nonverbal intelligence and spatial ability, enhanced brain volume, a left lateral ventricle much larger than the one on the right, and an abnormally large amygdala. She obtained a perfect score on Ravens Progressive Matrices, a widely used measure of nonverbal intelligence. Figure 1 shows Grandin upset by the discovery that she had received an "F" grade for one of her papers.

Figure 1. *Temple Grandin* (2010, HBO Films, Ruby Films). Produced by Scott Ferguson. Directed by Mick Jackson.

Movies and Persons With Disabilities

Similar to films portraying people with psychological disorders, films depicting individuals with disabilities can perpetuate misconceptions and stereotypes. These films are often shocking, inaccurate, implausible, and/or overly sentimental. From one vantage point, the person with a disability might be the subject of cheap jokes and bullying; from another angle, the portrayal can be patronizing or melodramatic. Such stereotyping can be made worse by casting actors without a disability who are expected to "fake it," or by having writers base their stories on stereotypes when they have no personal experience interacting with people with disabilities. Such contrived portrayals miss the uniqueness of the individual and lead to the misconception that all people with a particular disability are the same (e.g., the belief that all people with autism behave in a certain way).

Disabilities often are used as a plot device, and the character of the person with the disability is not developed fully in the story. For example, *The Other Sister* (1999) is a romantic comedy depicting the intellectual and developmental struggles of Carla Tate (Juliette Lewis) as she works hard to become an independent adult. But, many film critics found the film offensive and argued that intellectual disability was being used as a gimmick for the plot. The comedy *The Ringer* (2005) received similar criticism. In this Farrelly brothers' film, Steve Barker (Johnny Knoxville) is desperate for money and decides to enter the Special Olympics to beat the reigning champ in the racing event. Special Olympics International supported the film, and consequently there are over 150 Special Olympics athletes in the film, with a handful having important supporting roles. Some stereotyping is present, including the use of the outdated and offensive word "retard" and the depiction of a person of average intelligence faking an intellectual disability with a false voice, unlikely behavior, mussed hair, and a contrived laugh. On the other hand, the film normalizes intellectual disability by showing that people with an intellectual disability experience normal emotions and activities – we see them struggling to compete, laughing, and supporting others; in addition, several of the characters with intellectual disability use sarcasm and wit to provide clever comic relief.

Films have also frequently perpetuated the misconception that individuals with a disability are more likely to be violent. Films like *Sling Blade* (1996) and *The Village* (2004) clearly convey this message. In fact, the opposite is true: Research has documented that individuals with an intellectual disability, for example, are less likely to be aggressive than the "typical" individual. A similar misconception is that people with disabilities necessarily display outrageous behavior or exceptional talents. This can go in the negative behavior direction (e.g., smearing feces) or the positive behavior direction (e.g., savant/genius level talents). The film *The Black Balloon* (2008) is an example of the former while *Rain Man* (1988) is an example of the latter. Of course, both ends of the continuum are possible, but they are clearly not the norm, as some films suggest. Stereotypes of women with disabilities have been categorized into four types by Norden (1994): the "sweet innocent" in *Stella Maris* (1918), the "obsessive avenger" in *Freaks* (1932), the "civilian superstar" in *Interrupted Melody* (1955), and the "bitter" in *What Ever Happened to Baby Jane?* (1962). Norden also discusses realistic depictions of women with disabilities in *The Other Side of the Mountain* (1975), *Gaby: A True Story* (1987), *Passion Fish* (1992), and *The Theory of Flight* (1998).

For information on the Reel Abilities Film Festival, the largest disabilities festival, which is held in several US cities, go to http://reelabilities.org **or** http://cincinnati.reelabilities.org. For free short films starring (and in some cases, created by) individuals with different disabilities, go to http://sproutflix.org.

The Optimal Portrayal of Persons With Disabilities in Film

No doubt it is challenging for filmmakers to offer a portrayal of persons with disabilities that is accurate, substantive, and entertaining. Filmmakers are improving, however, and better films are being made. This may reflect enhanced societal awareness about the lives of people with disabilities. As one examines films on a deeper level, the philosophical question emerges: Does art (film) imitate life/society or vice versa?

There is probably no "perfect" portrayal of a person with an intellectual disability, an autism spectrum disorder, or a similar condition. However, there are a number of factors that are important for filmmakers to consider as they ponder potential film projects; viewers, too, can take such factors into consideration when making choices about the films they will watch.

We believe an optimal portrayal of persons with disabilities will contain all – or at least most – of the following elements:

- **Humanizing**: The film offers unique insight into who the human being is – the person "beyond" the disability. This means that the film takes a person-first approach.
- **Dynamic**: Viewers will witness – and be able to identify – many important aspects of the individual's life from the film – positive traits, deficits, positive relationship/environmental factors, and negative relationships/environmental factors.
- **Balanced**: The filmmaker strikes a balance between overemphasizing the disability/disorder/deficits and oversentimentality/glorification of it.
- **Meaningful**: The best films offer a compelling and substantive story about the characters they portray. In many cases, these are stories and characters that are inspiring and that depict the person with a disability transcending his or her disability/disorder.

Ultimately, film is a type of entertainment and this remains the main reason people view movies. However, even very entertaining films can still educate the viewer.

Neurodevelopmental Disorders

The *DSM-5* categorizes neurodevelopmental disorders into seven broad categories: intellectual disabilities, communication disorders, autism spectrum disorders, attention-deficit/hyperactivity disorder, specific learning disorder, motor disorders, and other developmental disorders. Neurodevelopmen-

tal disorders are characterized by onset early in development (typically before a child enters grade school) and impairment in functioning in important life activities such as self-sufficiency, socializing with others, learning, and working. These disorders often co-occur and overlap. This chapter focuses on those conditions most frequently portrayed in films: intellectual disabilities, autism spectrum disorders, attention-deficit/hyperactivity disorders, and to a lesser degree, communication disorders and motor disorders.

Intellectual Disability

The term intellectual *disability* has replaced the pejorative term *mental retardation*. Rosa's law, a unanimously supported, bipartisan bill signed into US federal law in 2010, removes the terms *mental retardation* and *mentally retarded* from federal health, education, and labor policy. It replaces these words with *individual with an intellectual disability* and *intellectual disability*. The *DSM-5* and *ICD-11* have also made these changes. The American Association on Intellectual and Developmental Disabilities considers intellectual disability from a dimensional perspective and notes that disability is a state of functioning that exists within the fit between a person's capacities and the context in which he or she functions, as opposed to the previous term *mental retardation*, which viewed disability as a defect within the person (Wehmeyer et al., 2008). These scientists explain how this change in terms improves the accuracy in describing individuals as well as the social impact:

> The changing understanding of disability reflected in the term intellectual disability, however, has marked impact on how society responds to people who manifest intellectual disability. The adoption of the term intellectual disability implies an understanding of disability consistent with an ecological and multidimensional perspective and requires that society respond with interventions that focus on individual strengths and that emphasize the role of supports to improve human functioning. (p. 317)

In short, use of the term *intellectual disability* emphasizes a "person-first" approach.

According to the *DSM-5*, intellectual disability is prevalent in about 1% of the population. The range of intellectual disability extends from mild to profound, and has historically been defined in terms of scores on tests of intellectual ability. However, *DSM-5* rejects the arbitrary use of IQ scores in favor of clinical assessment of adaptive functioning, using historical categorical labels (mild, moderate, severe, and profound). Deficits in adaptive functioning include not meeting the expected standards for a child of his or her age or cultural group in communication, not using community resources, lacking self-direction, limited academic skills, or experiencing problems with leisure, health, or safety. There are numerous causes of intellectual disability – these include drug or alcohol abuse in the mother, chromosomal or genetic disorders, or lack of oxygen during a difficult delivery.

Today a child who is diagnosed with an intellectual disability is usually kept at home and integrated into the school system when he or she reaches school age. Schools, the design of buildings, and community support organizations are becoming more and more **inclusive** for individuals with intellectual (and other) disabilities, integrating them into society-as-usual. New approaches in early intervention when the child is in his or her first few years of life have a significant impact and can help the child improve intellectually and adaptively and reach the goal of functioning as independently as possible with minimal support. With appropriate training, the majority of adults with intellectual disability live productive, independent lives.

Down syndrome is the most common genetic cause of intellectual disability, and most but not all individuals with Down syndrome have a below-average IQ. This is a disorder caused by the individual having three chromosomes 21; the incidence is approximately 1 per 1,000 live births. These children have distinctive physical characteristics that often include hypotonia, midface depression, and short ear length. People with Down syndrome have frequently been victims of stereotyping and prejudice. In the early 1960s, about 10% of all residents who were institutionalized had Down syndrome. They were institutionalized because it was thought that anyone with Down syndrome needed to live apart from the rest of society. This has been shown to be a very inaccurate stereotype. Families of children with Down syndrome have become pioneers in the understanding of developmental disabilities, and institutionalization has become increasingly uncommon.

Me, Too

We hesitate to include this film in this section because the primary character, while having Down syndrome, may not have an intellectual disability. (However, there are other characters in the film who clearly have an intellectual disability and are well portrayed in the film.) The protagonist of *Me, Too* (2009) is played by actor Pablo Pineda, an award-winning Spanish actor who has Down syndrome. Pineda portrays Daniel, a young man who has just earned a bachelor's degree (similar to Pineda himself, who earned a bachelor's degree in educational psychology, the first person in Europe with Down syndrome to accomplish this) and is working in his first job for regional social services. Daniel does his work well and has good adaptive functioning. There are some elements that suggest adaptive limitations, such as the fact that he continues to live with his mother and at times he has difficulty tying his shoes, although he sometimes pretends to struggle with the latter in a strategic way to get a love interest to help him, allowing him to be in closer proximity to her. There are other instances in which Daniel uses his social intelligence, humor, and Down syndrome to his advantage, such as when he purposefully displays inappropriate behavior in an elevator with two strangers and his work colleague with the intention of embarrassing his colleague. When the colleague claims that Daniel is "faking it," the strangers are shocked that she would say such a thing about a person with a "handicap," and she and Daniel then roar with laughter at the humor and subtlety of the situation. Daniel is often reflective and observant and displays clear social intelligence in his interpretation of a woman's inner experience when he asks her: "Is that why you have such a sad expression on your lips?"

The drama in the film centers on Daniel falling in love with a work colleague (someone who does *not* have an intellectual disability). As he pursues her, they develop a friendship and engage in a number of activities such as dancing, traveling, swimming, and having fun at the beach. She likes Daniel and acknowledges that she loves him; however, the Down syndrome acts as a barrier to an intimate relationship, which is what he wants. She is forthright about her feelings, and says they cannot be a couple, but they can be close friends. Daniel is disappointed, but he understands the situation. He maintains resilient in response to social barriers and others' perceptions of him.

Daniel is aware of his Down syndrome and describes the physical characteristics associated with the syndrome to others. When asked about the severity level of his intellectual disability and whether or not he has a more minor form, Daniel replies with humor: "No, not at all. I'm Down syndrome from head to toe." When asked why he seems to be doing so well, he explains the reason is his mother talked to him a lot when he was young about various topics such as history and politics, frequently asked him questions, and made sure he went to school. Daniel spends his time learning another language, working out, swimming, socializing with family, listening to hypnosis recordings to help him stop smoking, and continuing to learn.

The actor Pineda is an active advocate for the Down syndrome community. When interviewed about his role in the film and his experience of living with Down syndrome, he replied that he views the condition as just "another personal characteristic."

We highlight *Me, Too* as an exemplary film for filmmakers interested in depicting intellectual disability, and as a stellar example for educators and professionals teaching and exploring the topic and working with individuals with intellectual disabilities.

Monica and David

The marriage between the title characters, both of whom have Down syndrome, is the subject of the documentary *Monica and David* (2009). The film portrays the daily life of this couple, including their desires, hopes, and family interactions. Monica and David initiated their wedding following years of a loving relationship they spent living apart. After a successful wedding and California honeymoon, they move in together along with Monica's mother and stepfather. Both characters have their own limitations – including cognitive impairment, obsessive-compulsive behavior, and adaptive limitations. Each makes an effort to improve: Monica learns to cook and David learns to regularly test his blood sugar and self-administer his insulin. There are scenes of tension – such as when the whole family moves into a bigger home – and scenes demonstrating deep caring, such as when David offers insight, support, and a "loving

playfulness" for his wife after she explains she has written an honest and emotional letter sharing her anger with her biological father who abandoned her.

Monica's mother shares the rewards of being so close to her daughter and son-in-law and explains that she enjoys spending time with them. She also shares the difficult balance she must maintain between protecting David and Monica from exploitation while at the same time not wanting to control and restrict them too much. She wonders and worries about how they will get by when she and her husband are no longer around – who will help support or care for them? How will they be treated by society? This film, directed by Alexandra Codina, won Best Documentary Feature at the Tribeca Film Festival and was nominated for an Emmy for outstanding informational programming.

Forrest Gump

The now classic film *Forrest Gump* (1994) portrays 40 years in the life of a man who has a marginal IQ of 75 but whose innocence, innovation, and common sense make him wise. Forrest's condition would be classified as **borderline intellectual functioning**, and he would probably be tested for a learning disability.

This superb film begins with Forrest, played by Tom Hanks, telling his life story. When Forrest is a child, his mother (Sally Fields) believes in him and is determined that he should have a full, complete life. Forrest has a weak spine and needs to wear leg braces. He is forced to run from other children to protect himself, so that even with the leg braces he becomes an outstanding runner. Eventually, a local football coach spots Forrest and signs him to play college football. He begins a brilliant career that eventually leads him to the army and service in Vietnam. He wins a medal and becomes a table tennis star. After being discharged from the army, Forrest goes into the shrimp business and becomes a millionaire. Forrest has a life-long friend, Jenny Curran (Robin Wright Penn), who often came to his aid as a child. As an adult, he is able to help her as she and her son cope with disability and death resulting from AIDS.

Even with a limited intelligence and modest academic ability, Forrest is able to feel good about himself and who he is – a simple man who leaves his mark on the world. The development of his self-esteem has its roots in his childhood and his mother's confidence in him. The friendship with Jenny encourages him. Because of the support of these two women, it never occurs to Forrest that he might not succeed.

Drill Sergeant: "Gump! What's your sole purpose in this army?"

Forrest Gump: "To do whatever you tell me, drill sergeant!"

Drill Sergeant: "God damn it, Gump! You're a goddamn genius! This is the most outstanding answer I have ever heard. You must have a goddamn I. Q. of 160. You are goddamn gifted, Private Gump."

Forrest Gump (1994)

Shorty and *Radio*

Two films that portray adult males with intellectual disabilities who are accepted and integrated into the community of a football team are the documentary *Shorty* and the feature film *Radio*.

Shorty (2003) tells the story of Walter Simms (nicknamed "Shorty"), a man with Down syndrome, who for 28 years has been an important member of the Hampden-Sydney College community – the football team, the college campus, and the larger community. The film follows Shorty in his daily work and his interactions with coaches, players, students, and others at the college. He is frequently referred to as part of the family. Shorty's passion for the football program is so strong that his one birthday wish is that Hampden-Sydney College defeats their archrival, Randolph-Macon, in the 107-year rivalry known as "The Game." Despite his cognitive limitations, Shorty exhibits tremendous zest and energy and is loving and humorous with everyone in his life. Whenever Shorty is around, people seem happier. The film also depicts Shorty's induction into the Hampden-Sydney College Athletic Hall-of-Fame and his acceptance speech.

When the real-life Shorty was initially approached about the potential for making of this film, he was hesitant and humble, saying he did not think he had enough personality for a film to be made about him. The community and filmmakers disagreed, finding

him to be charming, friendly, passionate, humorous, caring, honest, brave, and hopeful. The film was made by actor Danny Aiello's production company, Revolution Earth; when interviewed about the film, Aiello explained that he wanted to make a film about the regular life of a person with Down syndrome and to educate the public about this disorder.

Inspired by a true story, *Radio* (2003) is the story of Coach Harold Jones (Ed Harris) who takes in a young man, Radio (Cuba Gooding, Jr.), and makes him an assistant coach for the football team. Though he is never given a diagnosis in the film (other than the label "slow"), Radio has an intellectual disability. At the beginning of the film, Radio barely speaks a word, mostly uttering sounds, is hunched over in posture, and walks around with a shopping cart for several miles to get groceries. He lives alone with his mother and is almost completely isolated. He is never given a chance at life. Early in the film, Radio is cruelly ridiculed and mistreated by several football players. One particular player continues his cruel taunting of Radio, but he accepts the criticism without complaining. Given an opportunity to help out the football team, Radio agrees and begins to talk much more, interacts with others, and helps out the team in significant ways; in fact, he becomes a symbol of inspiration for the players, and his life changes. Coach Jones goes out of his way to help give Radio opportunities; he defends Radio in front of the community, and integrates him into the school system. When the coach is asked why he is helping Radio, he responds: "It's the right thing to do." The story speaks to the courage and sacrifices of two men who influence one another and in turn grow in courage and dedication. Coach Jones admits part of his dedication and care for Radio arises from childhood shame for not taking action to protect a boy with a disability who was being tortured.

Dominick: "Gene tell me about when we were born."

Eugene: "You were born first. And 12 minutes later I was born. You are the big brother. Our mother died when we were born. Our father worked in the steel mill."

Dominick: "And you and me was always together. Our father had to go away. I fell down and hurt my head and that is why I can't remember."

Dominick and Eugene (1988)

Dominick and Eugene

Dominick and Eugene (1988), directed by Robert M. Young, is a movie about twin brothers Dominick (Tom Hulce) and Eugene Luciao (Ray Liotta), who live together in a low-income Pittsburgh neighborhood. Dominick ("Nicky") experienced brain trauma as a child and is developmentally disabled. He also has a learning disability and memory problems. The story begins as the twins approach their 26th birthday. Nicky is interested in the Hulk; Eugene ("Gino") is completing medical school and has been accepted into a California residency program. Gino, who feels responsible for his brother and who is afraid to tell him about his plans to move, is frequently angry with Nicky. The movie depicts the change in the brotherly relationship as each matures and responds to his respective need to live separately. It also highlights the strength of people with intellectual disabilities.

Other Films Portraying Intellectual Disability

The film *I Am Sam* (2001) depicts an adult, Sam (Sean Penn), with intellectual disability and some autistic behaviors who lives independently. He thinks very concretely and has difficulty with any task requiring abstract thought. His reading and math ability are limited. Sam lives in an apartment with his 7-year-old daughter, Lucy, whom he has cared for since birth. Sam has assumed responsibility for raising Lucy with the help of a neighbor. He has not had contact with any family members. He has several friends who also have developmental disabilities who provide support to Sam and his daughter. The father and daughter have approximately the same intellectual abilities, and they enjoy playing in the park, singing songs, and reading together. When Lucy surpasses her father's intellectual capacity, she is embarrassed by his limited cognitive abilities. She struggles to cope with classmates and friends making fun of Sam, and frequently tells her friends that she is adopted. At a birthday party planned by her father, Lucy becomes distraught over her father's child-like behavior. Child Protective Services eventually takes Lucy away from her father.

> "You don't know what it is when you try, and you try, and you try and you never get there!"
>
> Sam expressing the challenges of his life in *I Am Sam* (2001)

Ira Wohl's film *Best Boy* (1979) is a documentary that examines the life of Wohl's cousin, Philly, a man with an intellectual disability who has spent his entire life living with, and being protected by, his parents. The film beautifully documents the concerns of Philly's parents about who will take care of him after their death, a common theme in films depicting parents of children with intellectual disabilities. Philly's father dies while the film is being made, and his mother reluctantly allows Philly to become involved in an adult day services program. In addition, the film does a beautiful job portraying the emotional richness of Philly's life and the strong bonds that have been formed between this man and his family. Ira Wohl produced a moving sequel to *Best Boy* titled *Best Man: 'Best Boy' and All of Us Twenty Years Later* (1997). This film brings the viewer up to date on the life of Philly, who now lives in a group home in Queens. He has a full and meaningful life, and he is shown preparing for a significant, albeit delayed, rite of passage – his bar mitzvah.

The challenges and concerns of parents who have young children (or adult children) with Down syndrome is a common theme in films about intellectual disabilities. Examples can be found in *Praying with Lior* (2008, UK), *The Memory Keeper's Daughter* (2008), *Girlfriend* (2010), *Me, Too* (2009), and particularly in *Monica and David* (2009). *Any Day Now* (2012) is a sensitive film describing the attempt of a gay couple to provide a loving home for a boy with Down syndrome and the challenges they confront as they deal with bigotry and stereotypes. This powerful film is based on a true story.

Some films depict a character with a disability who significantly influences other characters, as in the comedy *There's Something About Mary* (1998). The protagonist's brother Warren (W. Earl Brown) has intellectual disability and autistic tendencies. He exhibits **echolalia**, perseverates in his play, displays finger-flicking behavior, and wears earmuffs to block out disturbing sounds. He clearly likes the lead character, Ted (Ben Stiller), but when Ted touches him near his ears, Warren's sensitivity leads to a violent reaction – he picks Ted up and spins him around before throwing him down on the coffee table. It is an upsetting incident, but the whole family realizes that it happened due to a triggering event and was not due to malevolence on Warren's part. Mary (Cameron Diaz) lives near Warren and remains an active part of his life. She volunteers and spends time with Warren and other people with disabilities. Mary is not simply a "do good" person; she is also a good sister. The antagonists in the film attempt to fake being "good," but eventually their manipulations fall short. In addition, although Warren has a significant disability, he does do comical and outrageous things. Since this film is a comedy, and all of the other nondisabled characters do things that are comical, it does not appear that the director has singled out Warren. His behaviors clearly influence the lives of the other characters.

Characters with intellectual disabilities can also be found in Philip Seymour Hoffman's socially awkward character, Jack, in *Jack Goes Boating* (2010), and in the films *Caramel* (2007, Lebanon) and *The Secret Life of Bees* (2008).

Films sometimes show persons with disabilities, particularly intellectual disability, being exploited by others. In *Amélie* (2001), one character is ridiculed and mistreated by his boss in front of others. Though he is depicted with an intellectual disability, his character is more developed as he takes charge of a fruit stand, demonstrates competence in this new role, enjoys painting with a friend, and experiences a deep appreciation of life. In one of the many disturbing scenes in *Gummo* (1997), a girl with an intellectual disability is sold to young boys for sex.

A number of older films have poignantly illustrated the difficulties – and sometimes the beauty – in the lives of people who have an intellectual disability such as *Charly* (1968), *A Day in the Death of Joe Egg* (1972), and *Of Mice and Men* (1939; 1992). There are also reprehensible films, such as *Tropic Thunder* (2008), that deliberately use offensive language to get laughs at the expense of people with intellectual disabilities. Timothy Shriver (2008) in the *Washington Post* described the film this way: "By all accounts, it is an unchecked assault on the humanity of people with intellectual disabilities – an affront to dignity, hope and respect."

Short Films

A number of **short films** have been made about people with an intellectual disability, some of which can be accessed online, such as the whimsical *3:15 to Brunswick* (2012, Australia), the charming *Be My Brother* (2009, Australia), the honest *Between Sasquatch and Superman* (2010), and a film with several intersecting stories, *Beyond Borders* (2009, Belgium). The film *Waiting for Ronald* (2003) is discussed in Chapter 5; *Jacob's Turn* (2010) depicts a 4-year-old boy's early experiences on a T-ball team with "typical" kids; and *Hannah* (2010) is a striking film with no dialogue and no characters other than the dancer/athlete Hannah Dempsey, a young woman with Down syndrome displaying significant strength, endurance, and suave finesse as she conquers snowy mountain landscapes, ocean waves, and chilling temperatures while downhill skiing, spinning, swimming, and sprinting.

The Ups of Downs (2002) is a short documentary depicting the unique interests, talents, and personality of Danny, a young man with Down syndrome, who leads a very active and productive life. Danny performs and dances in a theatrical group, and he is the lead singer of a hardcore band with which he performs live shows sporting his red, spiked hair. He has a girlfriend whom he regularly has sex with; dabbles in photography; is a prolific painter; and he drinks beer when socializing with friends. "It's very, very important to let me speak," says Danny, referring to his desire for people to be patient with his slow and sometimes unclear speech. In the film, the filmmaker asks Danny, "Do you know that not everyone allows Down syndrome people to be born?" Danny responds, "I feel ashamed," in regard to such individuals.

> "I am a free person and I need my own life ... because having my own life is very, very important."
>
> Danny in *The Ups of Downs* (2002)

Danny is not the only person with Down syndrome featured in short films and music videos. In addition, there is Cam Lasley, a talented rapper with videos such as *Against These Walls*. There is also the popular Australian rock band, Rudely Interrupted, in

which five of the six members have a major disability, including intellectual disabilities (e.g., two members have Down syndrome), other developmental
disabilities, autism spectrum disorders, blindness,
and deafness. The documentary *Rudely Interrupted*
(2009) follows this inspiring band on a world tour
that includes the first performance by any band in
front of the United Nations. The one person without a disability is Rohan Brooks, the band manager
and one of the guitarists. The film portrays the
strengths of each individual in the band as well as
the challenges brought forth by each of their disabilities. It is clear that the band comes together as
a unit to offer strong musical performances as well
as support one another when one of the band members is struggling.

Autism Spectrum Disorder

Autism spectrum disorder is usually diagnosed
before the age of 3. This condition occurs four times
more frequently in males than in females and according to data released in 2014 by the Centers for
Disease Control and Prevention, autism occurs in 1
in 68 children in the United States (a 30% rise over
the course of 2 years). Approximately 75% of persons with autism spectrum disorder also have an intellectual disability, and about half do not communicate verbally. Autism spectrum disorder is a
complex problem and requires special treatment and
family support.

Problems in social interaction and communication and restricted, repetitive patterns of behavior
are the primary symptoms of autism spectrum disorder. Many children with autism spectrum disorder are not able to maintain eye-to-eye gaze, respond with facial expressions, or use normal body
posture and gestures. As children with autism grow
older, they do not typically develop peer relationships that are appropriate to their developmental
level. They often do not express pleasure in other
people's happiness or participate in interpersonal
give and take. The behaviors of these children can
be very frustrating to parents because of a lack of
emotional warmth that is clear and visible. There is
often a delay and sometimes a complete lack of development of spoken language. If there is speech,
there is impairment in the ability to initiate or sustain a conversation with others. Their use of lan-

guage is often repetitive or idiosyncratic. As children, they may not be able to engage in make-believe
play or social imitative play appropriate to their developmental level.

Other symptoms of autism spectrum disorder are
repetitive and stereotyped patterns of behavior, interests, and activities. For example, children may
rock for hours, twist their fingers, rub their hands
on their legs, spin, or repeat complex body movements. People with autism spectrum disorder compulsively adhere to specific, often nonfunctional,
routines or rituals. The children are frequently preoccupied with objects rather than people. A child
with autism may be fascinated with a motor, a piece
of equipment, or a model automobile. The child
may spend hours taking the object apart and putting
it together again.

Most adults with autism spectrum disorder continue to be inattentive to social convention, lack social skills, have few or no friends, and often do not
marry. They may also be troubled by chronic anxiety. Their repetitive behavior and movements usually persist.

In addition to treatment with medication, behavior modification, and individualized educational approaches, the family plays a critical role. Most families need support in helping their child with autism,
and implementing treatment programs within the
home to help the child generalize from an academic
setting to the home is often useful. Parents learn
how to teach their children appropriate social and
communication skills, as well as behavior modification techniques. Family therapy is sometimes recommended to help the family cope with the stress
and problems associated with raising a child with
autism spectrum disorder.

The prognosis for children with autism spectrum
disorder is mixed. If a child begins to acquire language, is socially responsive, and shows improvement in cognitive skills by the age of 5–7, the child
will have a better prognosis than those children who
do not.

Because the manifestations of autism vary tremendously across patients, depending on the severity of the condition, the child's age, and his or her
developmental level, the *DSM-5* now classifies autism as a *spectrum disorder*. The diagnosis of autism spectrum disorder includes children and adults
who would have previously been diagnosed as people with high functioning autism or Asperger's dis-

order. Temple Grandin is clearly an example of someone with an autism spectrum disorder who is functioning at a very high level (e.g., she has a PhD, she lectures around the world, and she has published numerous books). People with this condition are frequently labeled as odd and eccentric. However, language skills are generally intact, and cognitive development is not delayed.

"Kids get a lot of labels – dyslexic, ADHD, autism – and people get hung up on the label. Well, these labels are not precise diagnoses … [People] get so hung up on the deficit, they forget about developing the strengths."

Temple Grandin in an interview with *Great Falls Tribune* reporter Briana Wipf, January 7, 2014

Adam (2009) is a film about a high functioning, 29-year-old man with autism spectrum disorder who falls in love with his neighbor Beth. Adam has a fixated interest in astronomy, and this reaches the savant level, because he knows more about this subject than almost anyone. When he first invites Beth to come to his room, it is literally an invitation to watch the planets move as they are projected on his bedroom wall. Because of Adam's limited social skills, he is intimidated by an upcoming job interview, and Beth coaches him, teaching him how to maintain eye contact with the interviewer and demonstrate enthusiasm about the potential new job. Adam is aware of many of his social limitations, his excessive focus on logic and facts, and his tendency to take everything literally. He has difficulty with the analogies people use, and he does not understand social nuances or jokes or how to respond to the emotions of others. When he gets stressed or nervous, he talks rapidly and provides many more details than the situation or interaction calls for. The film demonstrates some of the challenges inherent in loving someone with this condition. It is a rare and accurate depiction of what *DSM-IV* termed Asperger's disorder.

The movie *Mozart and the Whale* (2005) is based on the real life story of Jerry and Mary Newport, two high functioning people with autism spectrum disorder. Jerry Newport is a savant who has the abil-

ity to calculate numbers and dates and who reportedly was unaware that he had a form of autism until he saw *Rain Man*. He subsequently organized support groups around the country. Mary has prodigious artistic talents. The title for the movie is based on a Halloween party where Jerry was dressed as a whale expressing his adoration of *Free Willy*. Mary arrived in the guise of Nannerl Mozart, the brilliant musician whose life was overshadowed by her famous brother. The ups and downs of their relationship and their struggles to live a quality life are documented in their publications, presentations, and various television programs. The movie deals with the development of a meaningful relationship between Donald and Isabelle in spite of their opposing personalities and the symptoms associated with their disorders. For example, when Donald nervously brings Isabelle to the cluttered apartment he shares with an array of uncaged birds, she announces in her typically forthright manner, "This is about sex" – an approach too direct for Donald. Isabelle is extremely labile and emotionally insecure, creating legitimate doubt as to whether she, more than Donald, can ever handle a permanent relationship. The film received mixed reviews, but has the advantage of having been written by individuals who actually have the disorder.

In *Breaking and Entering* (2006), Will (Jude Law) and his live-in girlfriend, Liv (Robin Wright Penn), raise a young adolescent girl, Beatrice (Poppy Jones), who has an autism spectrum disorder. Beatrice displays behaviors typical of autism spectrum disorder, including limited social skills, repetitive behaviors (endlessly watching herself on video), and being upset by changes in her environment or routine. She also demonstrates sensory issues related to music. When stressed, she closes her eyes and repeats words. She thinks concretely and has an unusual collection of batteries. Her behavior places strain on Will and Liv's relationship. Liv becomes closer to Beatrice, while Will avoids the situation by working and distancing himself from the two of them.

American Splendor (2003) is about Harvey Pekar (Paul Giamatti), a comic book writer whose friend and coworker is a man (Toby Radloff) with what was formerly called Asperger's. Toby is socially awkward, has a monotone voice, and restricted patterns of interest and behavior. Toby is a self-proclaimed "world-class nerd" who wears a button reading "Genuine Nerd" and proudly recounts once driving over 200 miles to see the movie *Revenge of the Nerds*. Overall, the portrayal is realistic and challenges the viewer's stereotypes about Asperger's.

The Horse Boy (2009) is a documentary of two parents (a journalist/author and a professor/scientist), Rupert Isaacson and Kristin Neff, who travel to remote areas throughout Mongolia searching for shamans and reindeer herders to bring healing to their young son, Rowan, who has an autism spectrum disorder. Rowan is incontinent and has horrible tantrums, after which he is inconsolable. He spends hours lining up objects. The film educates the viewer about autism and emphasizes its genetic links; however, it also notes the interaction of genetics with environmental factors. The film clearly depicts the persevering love the parents have for Rowan, as well as their bravery and open-mindedness in pursuing novel treatments and alternative forms of healing. While on this long journey and through various interactions with shamans, Rowan experiences some changes – for example, he becomes more social – and after the trip his incontinence disappears, he develops new social skills, and he begins to regularly ride horses. Rupert is clear to say that he is not arguing that he found a "cure" for autism spectrum disorder; however, his son did experience healing. Rupert documents his son's changes – and notes that he does not know specifically what accounted for the changes (it could have been the vastly different environment and culture or the shamanistic rituals or some other change in Rowan's life) – as well as the positive impact the trip had for their family. The film includes interviews with Simon Baron-Cohen, Steve Edelson, and Temple Grandin, all of whom comment on the nature and treatment of autism.

Equine therapy is discussed quite positively in this film. However, this form of therapy for autism spectrum disorder remains controversial, as Oswald (2011) noted in his review of *The Horse Boy* for *PsycCRITIQUES*:

> There has been little systematic investigation of the effects of animal-assisted therapy for children with autism. While some positive effects have been reported (Martin & Farnum, 2002; Solomon, 2010), the studies are methodologically weak. A meta-analysis of 49 studies of animal-assisted therapy included only four studies involving children with autism with effect sizes ranging from 0.10 to 1.42 (Nimer & Lundahl, 2007). The most commonly reported animal-assisted therapies for children with autism involve dogs, dolphins, or horses. (np)

"Why does autism have to be a limitation? Why can't it be a gateway to healing?"

Rupert Isaacson sees his son benefit from a unique connection with a horse in *The Horse Boy* (2009)

Rain Man

While many people in the autism community have grown tired of the synonymous connection between the word *autism* and the film *Rain Man* (1988), the film continues to be the quintessential media example of raising awareness about the condition. Part of the weariness is perpetration of the misconception that all people with an autism spectrum disorder have **savant** abilities.

Rain Man won Academy Awards for Best Actor, Best Director, Best Picture, and Best Original Screenplay. The film stars Dustin Hoffman as Raymond Babbitt and Tom Cruise as Raymond's younger brother, Charlie. The drama opens with Charlie, a cynical hustler in his mid-20s, unemotionally learning of his father's death. Charlie and his father had been estranged for many years. Charlie's father only left a 1949 Buick to his youngest son, but he left $3 million in a trust fund for a secret beneficiary.

Charlie traces the beneficiary and discovers that he has an older brother, Raymond, who has an autistic spectrum disorder and lives in the sanatorium Walbrook. Raymond's world is bound by the rituals of watching television programs and eating certain foods on certain days. The books and baseball memorabilia in his room must be in order, or Raymond becomes agitated and begins reciting the Abbot and Costello routine, "Who's on First?" When the sanatorium administrator refuses to give Charlie half of the inheritance, Charlie removes his brother from Walbrook.

Charlie wants to return to the coast, but Raymond refuses to fly. The story unfolds as Charlie and Raymond cross the country in their father's Buick. Their adventures include viewing an accident, after which Raymond refuses to travel on interstate highways, and a day in a motel because Raymond refuses to go out in the rain. Raymond has many idiosyncrasies, such as having maple syrup on the table before the pancakes are served, insisting upon snacks of apple juice and cheese balls, imitating any noise he hears, and being preoccupied with television. One of Raymond's most significant symptoms is his tendency to constantly repeat the same word or phrase.

Raymond has savant abilities, which occur in only about 10% of people with autism spectrum disorders (and in less than 1% of those without autism). When this occurs, the individual usually scores low on standardized IQ tests but has one or two outstanding talents, such as calculating dates, drawing, or musical performance. Raymond is able to memorize several pages of a telephone book after just one reading, and he quickly memorizes baseball player statistics. When a box of toothpicks falls open, Raymond almost instantly knows how many toothpicks are on the floor. Upon discovery of Raymond's unusual memory and mathematical skills, Charlie decides to capitalize on these to recoup his business losses through gambling in Las Vegas. When Raymond inadvertently makes a date with a prostitute, Charlie teaches his brother how to dance. When the woman fails to show up, Raymond dances with Charlie's girlfriend, Susanna (Valeria Golino), who gives Raymond his first kiss.

Charlie develops an appreciation for the complexity of the illness when Raymond becomes upset after being frightened by the noise of a smoke detector. The movie ends when Charlie, who has developed a sensitivity and love for his brother, turns down a $250,000 settlement and lets his brother voluntarily admit himself back into Walbrook.

Overall, this is a technically correct portrayal of a character with an autism spectrum disorder – Raymond has all the correct mannerisms, tics, and tendencies of any number of real-life people with autism. The story surrounding the characters is also realistic – many families were separated by institutionalization as people with disabilities were simply erased from family memory. (For example, Charlie never knew he had an older brother.)

Rain Man does reinforce the misconception that "it's an institution or nothing" for people with significant disabilities. However, the assumption that someone like Raymond would be happiest in a large institution is foolish. Although the familiarity and smooth routines often occurring in an institutional setting enhance Raymond's comfort and adaptation, people like Raymond can also live fully, success-

fully, and happily in their own homes, with individualized supports as needed and with housemates of their own choosing.

Additional Questions for Discussion (*Rain Man*)

➤ Is the scene in which Raymond calculates complex square roots but cannot make change for a dollar realistic?
➤ Why is Raymond unable to appreciate the humor in Abbott and Costello's "Who's on First?" routine?
➤ Would Raymond realistically be "a voluntary admission free to leave at any time," as Dr. Bruner maintains?
➤ Identify examples of repetitive behavior in the film. Are these behaviors more likely to occur when Raymond is stressed?
➤ Why is Raymond's favorite word "definitely"?
➤ Raymond smiles at one point and appears to appreciate the ironic humor involved in asking for maple syrup when it is already on the table. Is the appreciation of subtle humor like this characteristic for someone with autism?
➤ How would you rate the quality of care provided for Raymond at Walbrook?
➤ Raymond's knowledge of trivia serves him well when watching the quiz show Jeopardy. What sorts of games or activities would Raymond find the most difficult?
➤ What do you know about the real life of Kim Peek, a man with autism spectrum disorder who inspired the film?

In *Silent Fall* (1994), a retired child psychiatrist (Richard Dreyfuss) works with Tim Warden (Ben Faulkner), a young boy with autism spectrum disorder who was a witness to his parents' murder. Tim rocks, enjoys spinning and movement, twirls and fidgets with his fingers while watching them in front of his face, and has limited communication through grunting and moaning noises. He displays a distant look in his eyes with flat affect, and adheres to rigid rules such as never eating anything that is round in shape. He communicates through cards, nonverbal signals, drawings, and figures. He displays **echolalia**, repeating others' speech at certain times while impersonating them. He bangs his head against the wall when he gets upset or stressed.

August Rush (2007) is a film about an orphan (Freddie Highmore) in search of his musician parents. It turns out that Freddie, who is mute and has behaviors characteristic of a person with autism spectrum disorder (though he may not meet the full diagnostic criteria for the disorder), has inherited his parents' musical ability; in fact, he is a savant who teaches himself to play a guitar almost immediately after picking one up. He eventually winds up training at the Juilliard School where he astonishes the faculty with his precocious musical ability. Somewhat predictably, he becomes reunited with his parents by the end of the film.

Leonardo DiCaprio plays the protagonist's autistic younger brother in *What's Eating Gilbert Grape?* (1993). This character is not a savant, and he certainly is no saint; however, he is realistically portrayed as a needy, younger sibling growing up in a family that loves him.

In the classic *To Kill a Mockingbird* (1962), a young Robert Duvall makes his film debut as Boo Radley, a neighbor with autism spectrum disorder who kills a man to protect two young children. His diagnosis is never mentioned, and it probably would not have been recognized as autism at the time the film was made.

Molly (1999) is a disappointing film about a woman with autism spectrum disorder. Molly (played by Elisabeth Shue) undergoes experimental surgery that temporarily brings her back to normal functioning; her brain eventually rejects the cells used in the operation and she returns to her presurgery levels of functioning. Molly's brother, Buck, initially avoids and fears his sister and agrees to try anything to make her better, but this enthusiasm is followed by disappointment in the surgery's failure. The film ends with a stereotypic "change-of-heart" ending when Buck arranges for Molly to live with him.

The Boy Who Could Fly (1986) tells the story of a young girl, Millie Michaelson (Lucy Deakins), who moves to a new house and neighborhood after the death of her father who had committed suicide following a diagnosis of cancer. She copes with her grief by becoming involved with the boy who lives next door, a boy with autism spectrum disorder who spends much of each day on his roof, preparing to fly. His parents were killed in a plane crash, and the boy developed his fixation of the idea of flying immediately after their death.

Attention-Deficit/Hyperactivity Disorder

Children and adolescents are frequently diagnosed with attention-deficit/hyperactivity disorder (ADHD). Diagnosis of ADHD using the *DSM-5* requires evidence of "a persistent pattern of inattention and/or hyperactivity-impulsivity which interferes with functioning or development" (p. 59). Six or more symptoms of **inattention** must be present and/or six or more symptoms of **hyperactivity and impulsivity**. Common symptoms of inattention are failure to attend to details, difficulty sustaining attention, failure to listen, difficulty following through with tasks such as homework, difficulty organizing tasks, avoidance of any task that requires sustained mental effort, losing things, easy distraction, and forgetfulness. Symptoms of hyperactivity and impulsivity include fidgeting, leaving one's seat at inappropriate times, running or climbing in inappropriate situations, the lack of ability to engage in quiet leisure activities, always being "on the go," talking excessively, blurting out answers to questions, difficulty in waiting for one's turn, or frequent interruption. At least some of these symptoms have to had been present before the age of 12 years. Clinicians must specify if the disorder predominately involves inattention or hyperactivity/impulsivity or both conditions, and they specify severity level (mild, moderate, or severe).

Dory, the blue fish in *Finding Nemo* (2003), is a character who displays many of the symptoms of ADHD. While Dory describes herself as having a neurological condition of short-term memory loss, the behavior she exhibits parallels the inattentive qualities of ADHD. Dory is forgetful and often loses track of her current task or activity, and she is easily distracted such as when she becomes preoccupied with a baby jellyfish, a distraction that leads her and Nemo into danger. She impulsively approaches various fish in the sea and often displays hyperactive behavior as she swims, almost as if "driven by a motor," another classic quality of ADHD.

In another children's film, *Winnie the Pooh* (2011), many of the characters may have a psychological disorder – Tigger has ADHD symptoms (also evident in *The Tigger Movie* [2000]), Piglet is anxious, Eeyore is depressed, Owl has obsessive-compulsive disorder (OCD), and Pooh has a binge eating behavior. While we may not agree with each of these being a full-blown disorder (remember that a formal diagnosis requires that the symptoms must cause serious distress or impairment or affect the individual's everyday functioning), it is clear that some symptoms are present in each character.

Many adult characters display symptoms of ADHD. John Cusak portrays an air traffic controller who notes he was diagnosed with ADHD, in the film *Pushing Tin* (1999). He attempts to use his ADHD to focus his attention on his work; however, at times it leads to recklessness. Clark Griswold (Chevy Chase), in the National Lampoon films *Vacation* (1983) and *Christmas Vacation* (1989), portrays many of the symptoms of ADHD such as distractibility, impulsivity, and especially inattention. The Mr. Bean character (played by Rowan Atkinson) from the TV series of the same name and the film *Mr. Bean's Holiday* (2007) is another comedic character who exhibits the inattentive and impulsive characteristics of ADHD.

"It used to be kind of a hassle to put on underwear in the morning, Now its kinda easy ... ya know."

Justin Cobb in *Thumbsucker* (2005)

Thumbsucker and ADHD

In the award-winning coming-of-age film *Thumbsucker* (2005), 17-year-old Justin Cobb (Lou Pucci) comforts himself by sucking his thumb, but is also highly distressed by his infantile habit and his inability to stop the obsessive behavior. As an awkward, self-conscious teenager, his psychological stress leads to failure on a debate team, poor performance in school, and a break-up with his girlfriend. Justin's dentist, Perry Lyman (Keanu Reeves), confronts Justin about his thumb sucking and uses hypnosis to make the thumb distasteful. Justin's frustration increases when he is unable to find an adequate substitute for his thumb sucking. A well-meaning, but ill-informed school counselor diagnoses Justin as having ADHD and strongly recommends a stimulant (Ritalin) as treatment. After starting the stimulant, Justin's behavior improves, and he begins to excel on the debate team. The transition from a shy and socially inept teenager to debate team star is dramatic.

Errors in diagnosing ADHD are common. To be diagnosed with ADHD, the patient must be carefully evaluated. If ADHD is present, treatment should include counseling in addition to medication. This film demonstrates the negative outcomes associated with a misdiagnosis and inappropriate medication. It is unlikely that Justin had ADHD, and it is certainly unlikely that he would have had legal access to the amount of Ritalin he eventually wound up taking.

? Questions to Consider While Watching *Thumbsucker* (2010)

➤ How does Justin's obsession with his thumb influence his psychosocial development?
➤ There are many self-gratifying habits; why does thumb sucking attract so much attention?
➤ Is hypnosis, as depicted in the film, a useful treatment for thumb sucking and other childhood habits? Is it helpful to use hypnosis with children?
➤ How often do children with ADHD abuse stimulants?
➤ What percentage of children and adolescents are incorrectly diagnosed as having ADHD? What percentage is not diagnosed with ADHD when they should be?
➤ Describe the relationship between the two brothers. Is it a typical sibling relationship?
➤ How can a clinician optimally differentiate between normal adolescent development and psychiatric disorders?

Communication Disorders

Communication disorders involve deficits in language, speech, and communication. A Best Picture Academy Award winning film, *The King's Speech* (2010) illustrates stuttering disorder (also called childhood-onset fluency disorder). In the film, Colin Firth portrays King George VI of the United Kingdom (Bertie) who suffers from stuttering and is helped by Lionel Logue (Geoffrey Rush), a speech therapist (see Figure 2). Prior to consulting with Lionel, Bertie attempts many unsuccessful treatments (e.g., trying to speak with marbles in his mouth). Lionel's approach, however, is warm, insightful, and challenging, and certainly an approach that promotes self-acceptance, which is one of the more current approaches to stuttering, in addition to a nonavoidance approach in which the person with stuttering is encouraged to embrace communication (Ghiselli & Davis, 2010; Jackson, 2006). With Lionel, King George is able to forge a meaningful "therapeutic" relationship, and he engages Bertie in a variety of innovative techniques (e.g., reading aloud while listening to music with headphones so he cannot hear himself speak). Figure 2 depicts Lionel coaching Bertie using one of his idiosyncratic methods. In their *PsycCRITIQUES* review of the film, Ghiselli and Davis (2010) observe that these techniques have been used by actors and actresses who stutter, such as Marilyn Monroe, which led to her whispery, sexy voice; they go on to say:

> These techniques do not cure stuttering, but instead mask stuttering. Additionally, people who utilize these techniques may become dependent on them to avoid or conceal their stuttering. This experience is oftentimes referred to as "covert stuttering." Although the outside world may view covert stuttering as the stutterer transcending his or her speech impediment, it can also come at an emotional and psychological cost because the person who stutters (PWS) may not be expressing themselves in the way and with the words that they desire. (np)

The film was written by a person who struggles with stuttering, David Seidler, and was directed by Tom Hooper. Due to the popularity, acclaim, and critical success of the film, *The King's Speech* is likely to promote public awareness about stuttering, just as *Rain Man* promoted public awareness about autism spectrum disorder. While both films have flaws, *The King's Speech* helps to educate the public about the realities and struggles of stuttering. Ghiselli and Davis (2010) also observe:

> Although stuttering is often regarded as a speech disorder that must be overcome and avoided, one must also remember that it is still a component of a person's identity that, like any other facet of the self, should not only be acknowledged, but also appreciated. Despite the incongruences between *The King's Speech* and what we now know about the origins of stuttering and its treatment, it is clear from a sociological point of view that the film has provided a positive role model for the stuttering community, as well as a solid base from which to educate others about stuttering. (np)

Two other films that depict a character with stuttering disorder are *The Straight Story* (1999) and *Liam* (2000).

Figure 2. *The King's Speech* (2010, Weinstein Company, UK Film Council, et al.). Produced by Iain Canning, Emile Sherman, and Gareth Unwin. Directed by Tom Hooper.

Another major diagnosis that falls under the communications disorder category is language disorder, which is characterized by persistent difficulties in the acquisition and use of language due to deficits in comprehension or production. *The Wild Child* (1970, France) depicts a young boy who was found living on his own in a French forest in 1798. This feral child was unable to speak, read, write, or walk. He would easily have met the criteria for a language disorder, but he also exhibited signs of an intellectual disability and autism spectrum disorder. Based on a true story, the film was directed by the famous filmmaker Francois Truffaut, who stars in the film as Dr. Jean Itard, the child's teacher.

Motor Disorders

Motor disorders include tic disorder, developmental coordination disorder, and stereotypic movement disorder; however, tic disorders are the most recognizable motor disorder in films. A tic is a sudden, rapid, recurrent, nonrhythmic event that can occur in movement or in vocalization. Tourette's disorder is the dominant type of tic disorder and occurs when both motor and vocal tics are present for more than a year, even though the frequency may increase and decrease over time. The documentary *I Have Tourette's But Tourette's Doesn't Have Me* (2005) depicts a number of children speaking about their experiences with the condition. The children express themselves directly with humor, charm, and insight, and describe their experiences in the home, school, and social environments. *The Tic Code* displays a mentoring relationship between two individuals with Tourette's disorder – a child prodigy and an adult musician. Tourette's disorder is also evident in characters in the films *Maze* (2000), *Niagara, Niagara* (1997), *Front of the Class* (2008), and *Phoebe in Wonderland* (2008). In the latter film, a young girl diagnosed with both Tourette's and OCD displays vocal tics as she barks out inappropriate phrases to her neighbor. Unfortunately, the depiction of Tourette's disorder, especially vocal tics (e.g., cursing), is routinely used for cheap comic relief as in *Deuce Bigalow: Male Gigolo* (1999).

Cerebral palsy is not a *DSM-5* diagnosis, but individuals with this physical disability are frequently portrayed in films, and so we discuss it in this section. Cerebral palsy is a central motor dysfunction that affects muscle tone, movement, and posture. Cerebral palsy is accurately and diversely portrayed in a number of films, such as *Dance Me to My Song* (1998, Australia), *Music Within* (2007), *Oasis* (2002, South Korea), *Storytelling* (2001), and *My Left Foot* (1989, Ireland). This last film is the story of Christy Brown, a successful artist and author with cerebral palsy who grows up in a poor working class family in Ireland. Brown was never idle and – using only his left foot to paint and write – was able to cope with painful feelings, confront social struggles, transcend isolation, and express himself through his art.

Rory O'Shea Was Here (2005) depicts the friendship, dependence, struggles, and joys of two young men, Rory and Michael: Rory has muscular dystrophy and Michael has cerebral palsy. This drama displays genuine interaction and care between the friends as well as their arguments and disagreements. A resounding core theme of the film is the ability of these two men to use the physical strengths of one another to cooperate in solving problems and be more successful as a team than they could ever be as separate individuals. *Magnifico* (2003, Philippines) displays a family under increasing duress. With limited finances, the grandmother becomes ill and needs costly medical care, the eldest son loses a precious academic scholarship in Manila, and the daughter has cerebral palsy. She displays significant muscle rigidity and shaking and is unable to speak other than with occasional grunting sounds. The family takes care of her basic needs but does not go out of their way to discover her interests, passions, and strengths. The other son, Magnifico, is a young, kind, and perseverant boy who is eager to improve his family's situation. He applies his creativity and love to help each member of the family – for example, he discovers what his sister is interested in (e.g., attending a carnival) and puts her on his back and takes her to experience the various carnival rides. Magnifico's impact on his sister, family, and ultimately the larger community is significant.

> "Independent living helps me to grow and mature as a person. It helps me to fulfill the potential I have within myself. It's not always realized by institutional living. It opens the way for me to make a real contribution to live a fuller life"
>
> Michael in *Rory O'Shea Was Here* (2005)

International Films: Neurodevelopmental Disorders

Many films do not present a character who "happens to have" a disability where the disability is treated as just another aspect of the character's life. An exception are films by French director Jean Pierre-Jeunet, whose *Amélie* (2001, France) and *The City of Lost Children* (1995, France) depict such characters and suggest that their meaningful contributions far outweigh the significance of their intellectual disability.

Pauline and Paulette (2001, Belgium) is an award-winning Belgian comedy-drama directed and cowritten by Lieven Debrauwer. Pauline (Dora vander Groen) is a 66-year-old woman with an intellectual disability who has been cared for by her sister Martha. When Martha dies, her younger sisters Paulette (Ann Petersen) and Cecile (Rosemarie Bergmans) become responsible for Pauline. Both sisters are very busy in their own lives. According to Martha's will, her wealthy estate will only be divided into three equal parts if one of the sisters looks after Pauline. If they decide to place her in an institution, Pauline will be the only heir. This film depicts a family's dilemma and difficulties when faced with making decisions about loved ones. It also highlights the reality of intellectual disability and underscores the degree of love and commitment required by family members taking care of another family member who has an intellectual disability. In contrast to the film *I Am Sam* (2001), this movie focuses more on character development (e.g., kindness, curiosity, creativity, playfulness, and love).

Adam Elliot, director of the popular Australian clay animation films, *Harvey Krumpet* (2003, Australia) and *Mary and Max* (2009, Australia), references and depicts neurodevelopmental disorders in his films, usually in a comical and inoffensive manner. In the former Academy Award winning film, Harvey is diagnosed with Tourette's disorder and incorrectly diagnosed with an intellectual disability. Despite suicidal intentions, a brain tumor, testicular cancer, being struck by lightning, and growing senility, Harvey remains optimistic. *Mary and Max* uses the voices of Toni Collette and Philip Seymour Hoffman in the roles of Mary and Max, respectively, to portray a long-distance, pen pal friendship. Max is labeled with Asperger's syndrome, which is correctly described as "a neurobiological, pervasive developmental disability;" however, Max prefers to simply refer to himself as an "aspie." He explains that he finds people confusing and has never had a friend, and he describes his mind as literal and logical. He has trouble understanding the emotions of others, cannot interpret people's faces, is hypersensitive to sound, likes solving problems, and has trouble expressing his own emotions. Mary goes to college to study "disorders of the mind" and later writes a book about Asperger's, which offends Max and temporarily stifles their friendship.

"Is the decline in her abilities inherent in her condition? Will she ever be without medication? Will we take that trip again? Can the damage of institutionalization ever be repaired?"

Filmmaker Sandrine Bonnaire wondering about her sister in *Her Name Is Sabine* (2007)

The negative impact of institutionalization is clearly outlined in the documentary, *Her Name Is Sabine* (2007, France). This is an honest and vivid portrait of Sabine Bonnaire, a woman with autism spectrum disorder who is the sister of the famous French actress Sandrine Bonnaire, who wrote and directed the film. The film depicts the present-day life of Sabine interspersed with family history and home movies. Prior to hospitalization, Sabine lived at home with her mother and sisters, and she flourished. She engaged in various creative arts, music and crafts and studied topics like geography. After her sisters moved out of the home, she traveled to visit them independently; however, she increasingly began to exhibit problematic behaviors. Her aggressive and destructive behavior became so significant that her family decided to place her in a psychiatric hospital when she was 28 years old, and she stayed there for 5 years. Sabine languished and suffered in the hospital. During family visits, it was clear she was heavily medicated; she exhibited slowed speech, and she was perseverative and lethargic. Physically, she shifted from slim and attractive to obese and unkempt, walking hunched over with her mouth gaping open; socially, she shifted to communicating in screams and cursing, and she drooled, picked her nose, looked dazed, and frequently spat. In addition, she became untrusting and self-injurious; she banged her head, became aggressive, was often mute and was troubled by intrusive thoughts. She began to claim that she would marry a fireman and raise children. The changes were dramatic. After leaving the hospital, some of these behaviors improved; however, many of the physical and psychological characteristics persisted, and her social functioning remained limited at the time of the filming. One expert who worked with Sabine offered a psychoanalytic interpretation of autism spectrum disorder:

> It's the impossibility at a certain point to live with others. It's withdrawal, the inability to express anxiety in a way other than within a boundary. Always hitting against a boundary and looking for bodily limits … a psychological structuring like you no longer exist. An annihilation of the self … it's one heck of an adaptation to me.

The Dead Mother (1993, Spain) portrays Leire, a mute, young girl with characteristics of intellectual disability and autism spectrum disorder, who is the only witness to a burglar who breaks into her house and kills her mother. Twenty years later, Leire is in an institution and by chance the criminal sees her and, fearing she might turn him in, kidnaps her and holds her for ransom. Leire displays flat affect and muscle rigidity. She is easily distracted by details (e.g., a crack on a wall, bubbles in a bathtub, and her own hands), has poor eye contact, and reacts to loud noises. While living in the institution, Leire displays a traumatic response to blood and shakes and cries when a boy falls and cuts himself. She is not toilet trained and is obsessed with chocolate, which makes her vulnerable to manipulation and exploitation. She rarely, if ever, laughs and is limited in her social responses. She displays some adaptive difficulties, such as difficulty in dressing, and she is unable to bathe herself. Leire is an innocent character whose behavior stands in marked contrast to the pathological criminals around her.

The Black Balloon (2008, Australia) depicts the challenges, joys, stressors, and coping patterns of a family raising a child, Charlie, who was diagnosed with an intellectual disability, autism, and ADHD. Charlie giggles constantly, makes strange noises, taps repeatedly, rocks, and engages in various repetitive behaviors. The film displays several dramatic incidents such as Charlie running out of the house and down several blocks of his neighborhood in his

underwear; wiping his feces all over the floor, his clothes, and body; placing his brother's girlfriend's tampon in his mouth; making a scene in a busy grocery store by rolling around on the floor; smashing a window when punished; and masturbating at the table during a birthday celebration. Clearly, the impact on the entire family is significant, and each family member copes in his or her own way, communicating with Charlie and connecting with the family unit. The film will help viewers understand and appreciate some of the potential challenges associated with raising a child with autism spectrum disorder. The film accurately depicts the conflicting emotions of love and anger and the explicit and implicit tensions that exist in family interactions. The film's director, Elissa Down, grew up with two brothers who were coping with autism spectrum disorder, and it is likely that this experience contributed to the film's integrity, honesty and veracity. In another Australian film, *Somersault* (2004), a young female protagonist encounters a boy with autism spectrum disorder. He is passive and taciturn with blunted affect and is shown studying emotions on cards with his mother.

"All's I know is he's my own, and you're weak as piss if you don't look after your own."

Charlie's father's response when asked whether he ever wished Charlie was "normal" in *The Black Balloon*

Ben X (2007, Belgium) is a Flemish film about a young man, Ben, who is taciturn, quirky, and awkward in his interactions. He is quick to take things personally. He displays a wide range of symptoms, presenting an interesting differential diagnosis challenge for health profession students seeing this film. Ben sees a range of doctors who give him different diagnoses and descriptors for his symptoms, ranging from "emotionally dysfunctional," "a bit stressed," "a light form of psychosis," and "sensitive," to "Asperger's syndrome." The film does portray **equine therapy**, an emerging treatment that is sometimes used successfully with autism spectrum disorders. Ben's struggles with emotions and social interaction, and his sensitivity to sound and touch, support a diagnosis of autism spectrum disorder. In addition, he is quick to identify small details but has trouble seeing the bigger picture. In many situations, he has no idea how to interact or make a connection; for example, after a girl has traveled across town to meet him, he sits next to her but is unable to muster a single word and eventually just runs off. He is often judged, teased, and called names by other students. The film depicts two brutal bullying scenes that are humiliating, abusive, and torturous. He is so affected by this social abuse and disconnection that he becomes preoccupied with suicide; he begins to plan his own suicide, which he eventually attempts by jumping off a boat.

> It's hard to explain. It's hard to explain myself. But I never tell lies. Everything I say is true, even when I don't say a thing.
>
> Ben in *Ben X* (2007, Belgium)

Despite the emotional turmoil some of these scenes will cause in some viewers, the film has a surprising and uniquely redemptive ending that makes the painful earlier scenes all the more rewarding. The film leaves the viewer with the message that one sometimes has to go to great lengths to effect substantive social change.

Critical Thinking Questions

➤ Howard Gardner describes seven kinds of intelligence (verbal, visual, physical, musical, mathematical and logical, introspective, and interpersonal) in his book *Frames of Mind* (1983). How does this model help you understand individuals such as Raymond Babbitt, Sam Dawson, and Forrest Gump?

➤ Why are people with disabilities stigmatized in today's society?

➤ Are movies about people with disabilities improving in their portrayal? Cite film examples that support your answer.

➤ If you are working with the parent of a child with autism or an intellectual disability who was driven to search for a miracle cure or pursue an untested treatment, what is the best way to respond? In what situations might you champion this search? In what situations might you discourage it?

➤ Some films, such as *Temple Grandin* (2010), *Mozart and the Whale* (2005), and *I Am Sam* (2001), have actors without disabilities playing lead characters who have a disability in the film. How much does this enhance or detract from the overall film?

➤ Explain how films that portray autism spectrum disorder such as *Molly* (1999) and *Rain Man* (1988) do a disservice to people with these conditions.

➤ Is there anything a person with a disability cannot do that a person without a disability can? How about the reverse?

➤ How are persons with disabilities stigmatized in today's society? In your town or city?

➤ If a child without a disability was substituted for the murdered child with autism spectrum disorder in *The United States of Leland* (2003), would this change the story and the film's meaning?

➤ How have the parents of children with autism spectrum disorder been stigmatized in the past? Are there comparable examples of inappropriate stigmas today for the parents of children with other conditions?

➤ Do people with intellectual disability experience sexual feelings like everyone else? If so, how can health professionals support natural sexual expression while at the same time avoiding exploitation and abuse?

➤ Which labels are more useful: Specific terms such as "autism" or "Asperger's" or more generic labels such as "autism spectrum disorder"?

➤ Why does it matter what labels are used to refer to people with disabilities?

Authors' Picks

If you only have time to read just one book relevant to this chapter, make it

 Grandin T. (2012). *Different ... not less: Inspiring stories of achievement and successful employment.* Arlington, TX: Future Horizons.

If you only have time for one article, read

Shogren, K.A., Wehmeyer, M.L., Buchanan, C.L., & Lopez, S.J. (2006). The application of positive psychology and self-determination to research in intellectual disability: A content analysis of 30 years of literature. *Research & Practice for Persons with Severe Disabilities, 31*(4), 338–345.

Wedding and Niemiec's Top Neurodevelopmental Disorders Films

Intellectual Disabilities

Me, Too (2009)
Shorty (2003)
Monica and David (2009)
Forrest Gump (1994)
Pauline and Paulette (2001)

Communication Disorders

The King's Speech (2010)

Autism Spectrum Disorder

Temple Grandin (2010)
Rain Man (1988)
The Black Balloon (2008)
Adam (2009)

Attention-Deficit/Hyperactivity Disorder

Finding Nemo (2003)

Motor Disorders

I Have Tourette's But Tourette's Doesn't Have Me (2005)

Chapter 3

Schizophrenia Spectrum and Other Psychotic Disorders

My name is John Nash!
I'm being held against my will!
Someone call the Department of Defense!

John Nash (Russell Crowe) in *A Beautiful Mind* (2001)

➤ How is schizophrenia typically portrayed in films?

➤ Are auditory hallucinations more or less common than visual hallucinations in people with schizophrenia?

➤ Describe the course and progression of John Nash's illness as depicted in the film.

➤ Can mental health providers make accurate predictions about the likelihood of violence in people with mental illness?

➤ Is there any relationship between John Nash's mathematical genius and the course of his illness?

➤ What elements of anxiety and depression are present in John Nash, and at what points in the film are they heightened?

➤ Can a patient with schizophrenia usually comprehend the fact that he or she is delusional when confronted with absolute and contradicting truths?

➤ John Nash is depicted as having aged quite a bit in the film when compared with his wife and other characters. How does the lifestyle of someone with an untreated mental illness contribute to aging?

➤ How were Nash's delusions of paranoia and conspiracy affected by the realities of his job working for the government?

➤ How common are self-mutilation, other forms of self-harm, and suicidality in people with schizophrenia?

➤ What clues does director Ron Howard give in the first half of the film to indicate John Nash is in the early stages of schizophrenia?

➤ How do the cinematic elements, such as lighting and musical score, enhance the depiction of John Nash's schizophrenia?

Patient Evaluation[2]

Name: John Nash

Patient's stated reason for coming

"They say I've been diagnosed with schizophrenia. I take medicine for this condition. I don't see why I should be here today to talk about my problems. I can find the solution myself. I only came because I promised my wife I would."

History of the present illness

Prof. John Nash is a 38-year-old, White man who presents to this outpatient clinic with a complex history of visual and auditory hallucinations, intense periods of agitation, confusion, paranoia, and delusional thinking. He experiences frequent visual hallucinations that are delusional and usually dangerous, although, on occasion, benign and supportive. The former most commonly take the form of a demanding Department of Defense agent who gives orders. The latter hallucinations are described as a young man and little girl, whom Prof. Nash states are an old college roommate and the roommate's niece, respectively. He reported significant delusions of reference and claims he decodes messages from newspapers and magazines as a part of his top-secret work for the Pentagon. Nash eventually became convinced that his psychiatrist, whom he assaulted at one point, was a Russian spy and that his hallucinated friend had betrayed him. Prof. Nash believes a radium die containing access codes has been implanted in his arm. There is a history of self-mutilation of his left arm in an apparent attempt to remove this device.

Past psychiatric illness, treatment, and outcomes

Prof. Nash's symptoms began during his doctoral studies at Princeton University. He first received inpatient psychiatric treatment at the age of 33. He reports a history of two previous hospitalizations and a past diagnosis of "schizophrenia." His most recent hospitalization began 10 months ago when he was hospitalized for a total duration of 4 months. Records

---

[2] This fictitious evaluation is written as if John Nash were interviewed shortly after his release from one of his psychiatric hospitalizations.

of these hospitalizations will be requested. In both instances, he received insulin-shock therapy five times per week for 10 weeks.

Medical history
Prof. Nash suffers from impotence as a result of the medication he is taking. There is also a long scar on his left arm; this apparently resulted from a previous attempt to cut out an imaginary communications device he believed was implanted in his arm. There is no other significant medical history.

Psychosocial history
Prof. Nash quotes his first-grade teacher who once said he was "born with two helpings of brain and only a half a helping of heart." He added, "my wife is helping me with the latter." He has been married for 8 years. He reports that this is a happy marriage and describes his wife as the most beautiful, accepting person he has ever met. They have one child together, a two-and-a-half-year-old son. Professor Nash earned a PhD in mathematics from Princeton University. He has a history of various academic awards, including the distinguished Carnegie fellowship.

Drug and alcohol history
Prof. Nash denied any significant history of alcohol or drug abuse. He stated he has an occasional beer, and there is a history of occasional binge drinking during graduate school.

Behavioral observations
Prof. Nash presented as disheveled and unshaven, with clothes that did not match. He entered and left the office with his head down and a shuffling gait. He occasionally talked to himself in the form of "asides." His eye contact was poor, particularly when answering questions. Mood and affect were dysphoric. Speech was coherent but at times tangential. There was a marked tremor present, possibly a symptom of tardive dyskinesia. Prof. Nash has some insight into the nature of his condition but refuses to accept its seriousness. He seemed to be preoccupied with objects in the office, such as the reflection of the light shining on a water glass.

Mental status examination
Professor Nash scored 30/30 on the Folstein Mini-Mental State Examination. He was fully oriented at the time of the interview. He was particularly strong with the serial sevens as he swiftly counted backwards from 100 down to 23 accurately, despite the interviewer telling him he could "stop" several times.

Functional assessment
Prof. Nash graduated with his PhD 10 years ago. He worked as a professor at MIT for 6 years, teaching classes and conducting research. He is currently unemployed. He is a well-known and highly respected scholar in his field. Socially, he is quite withdrawn, has limited social skills, and his current social support consists of two work colleagues and his wife. He states that he does not like to socialize but that he enjoys teaching "eager, young minds."

Strengths
This patient is clearly gifted in the areas of science and mathematics. He has conducted seminal work in his field. His love for his wife is strong and apparent. He enjoys stargazing, going on walks, and spending time with his wife. His results on the VIA Survey, a measure of strengths of character, reveal his highest character strengths are creativity, curiosity, judgment (critical thinking), love of learning, and perseverance.

Diagnosis
Schizophrenia, multiple episodes, currently in acute episode, severe (F20.9). There is clear evidence of both visual and auditory hallucinations and paranoid delusions. There is no evidence of medical conditions or a history of substance abuse that could account for these symptoms. He experiences mild depression as a result of the challenges of rehabilitation, though these do not appear to warrant a separate diagnosis.

Dimensions of psychosis symptom severity
Hallucinations (4)
Delusions (4)
Disorganized speech (1)

Abnormal psychomotor behavior (0)
Negative symptoms (2)
Impaired cognition (0)
Depression (3)
Mania (1)

Treatment plan
Relapse is highly likely if this patient does not follow up with treatment recommendations, particularly his medication regimen. He could be dangerous if he responds to his delusions. He requires outpatient treatment focused on relapse prevention and regular psychiatric visits to provide medication review and monitoring until his condition further stabilizes. He would likely benefit from a psychiatric rehabilitation approach that emphasizes social skills training, peer support, and facilitated occupational integration into the community.

Prognosis
Good, pending adherence to medication regimen and psychiatric rehabilitation.

Schizophrenia and *A Beautiful Mind*: Realities, Misconceptions, and Recovery

A Beautiful Mind (2001) is based on the biography of the same name by Sylvia Nasar, written about the life of John Forbes Nash Jr., who won the Nobel Prize for Economics in 1994. John and Alicia Nash have noted in interviews that they are satisfied with the final film product. Dr. Nash was often on the set of *A Beautiful Mind* and consulted with Russell Crowe and Ron Howard in the production process. Although the film is true to the "spirit" and major events of John Nash's life, it does leave out some of the less flattering details such as his divorce and remarriage to Alicia and an arrest history.

One of the many artistic achievements of the film is that the viewer is given a glimpse of the perspective/experience of schizophrenia. Ron Howard accomplishes this by depicting life from the perspective of John Nash's character and the unfolding of his genius while temporarily omitting the fact that Nash is hallucinating characters including secret military agents and a roommate. When the film is halfway over, the viewer learns that much of what has been witnessed from Nash's perspective is unreal. This underscores the fact that oftentimes individuals are completely unaware that they are experiencing hallucinations or delusions, and that others are actually not experiencing the present moment in the same way. *Shutter Island* (2010) takes a similar perspective with the protagonist, played by Leonardo DiCaprio; however, the effect is not as successful.

A Beautiful Mind depicts the horrors, traumas, and suffering of schizophrenia, and it illustrates that people with schizophrenia can find a sense of normalcy in life, certainly outside of mental institutions, sometimes functioning as well as anyone in society. The film has educated millions of viewers about the realities and challenges of schizophrenia. However, it has flaws and may mislead viewers in some significant ways. For example, auditory hallucinations are more common and occur far more frequently than visual hallucinations, yet visual hallucinations are portrayed as one of John Nash's most salient symptoms, and the public is left to believe that this is a standard presentation for those with schizophrenia. Director

> "Often what I feel is obligation ... or guilt over wanting to leave, rage against John, against God. But then I look at him and I force myself to see the man that I married and he becomes that man. He's transformed into someone that I love and I'm transformed into someone that loves him. It's not all the time but it's enough."
>
> Alicia Nash in response to a question about how she is coping with her husband's illness in *A Beautiful Mind* (2001)

Ron Howard was using the visual medium of film, and therefore he chose to emphasize visual phenomena. The film may also mislead viewers because it shows John Nash overcoming his illness by putting himself on a "diet of the mind" (i.e., he learned to simply ignore his hallucinations and delusions); this may have worked for Prof. Nash, but it is highly unlikely to work for the average person coping with this illness. Finally, the film depicts Nash receiving insulin shock therapy (Figure 3), although many viewers mistakenly assume he is receiving electroconvulsive therapy (ECT).

The film digs deep into the challenges associated with treatment and rehabilitation of a person coping with a severe mental illness. Few films have done as good a job depicting the impact of a schizophrenia spectrum disorder upon healthy family members. The latter part of the film depicts John Nash's wife, Alicia, playing an important role in helping him "live with the realities of schizophrenia." She helps him remember to take his medications. She works longer hours, takes a large role in

child rearing, and manages household chores, all in support of her husband's recovery.

Relapse is common in people with schizophrenia due to numerous challenges, such as depression associated with recovery, the reality of remembering to take medications several times per day, and the multiple unpleasant side effects of the medication. This film is an accurate depiction of the difficulty of compliance with medication regimens, and it shows the impact of psychotropic medications on John Nash's ability to work, his difficulties in taking care of his son, and his inability to sexually satisfy his wife.

"He's been injected with a serum. I can see him because of the chemicals enlisted in my bloodstream when my implant dissolved. I couldn't tell you, it was for your own protection."

John Nash during a relapse after not taking his medication in *A Beautiful Mind* (2001)

Figure 3. *A Beautiful Mind* (2001, Universal Pictures, Dreamworks SKG, et al.). Produced by Brian Grazer and Ron Howard. Directed by Ron Howard.

It is a challenge for the person with schizophrenia to adapt and become integrated into the community. The depiction of John Nash's struggle to adapt is another strength of the film. Stress triggers his delusions, and he longs to give up and become further isolated, but he also has moments of grace and connection with others.

The film illustrates the fears of the public about schizophrenia, and specifically examines the impact of the illness on Nash's friends. His best friend goes to Nash's house and is visibly nervous, hesitant in his speech, and laughs uncomfortably. Another friend watches Nash closely when Nash enters the office. Other reactions are more negative: Some students at the university make fun of Nash and mimic his awkward gait and posture, while others stare in disbelief at his odd behavior.

A Beautiful Mind can be compared to the film, *Proof* (2005), starring Anthony Hopkins as a world-class mathematician with schizophrenia working at an elite university. *Proof* also depicts the impact of schizophrenia on family members (in *Proof*, the father–daughter relationship is emphasized). Frederick Frese, a psychologist and professor of psychology who has a schizophrenia spectrum disorder, reviewed this film for *PsycCRITIQUES* and made the observation that *Proof* "does an excellent job of capturing what is happening in the mind as it experiences the expanded horizon of meaningfulness that occurs in schizophrenia" (Frese, 2006).

Psychotic Disorders

The *DSM-5* now classifies schizophrenia as a spectrum disorder, in much the same way that autism was redefined as a spectrum disorder. This practice recognizes that psychotic symptoms vary in severity along a continuum. *The key features of psychotic disorders are delusions, hallucinations, disorganized thinking, abnormal behavior, and negative symptoms.* Delusions are fixed beliefs that resist change, despite evidence contrary to the delusion. Delusions are often paranoid, grandiose, erotomanic (e.g., romantic fixation on a celebrity or public figure), or somatic. People with delusions may or may not meet the diagnostic criteria for schizophrenic spectrum disorder. Delusions often take the form of a belief that someone else has control of one's thoughts and/or behavior.

Hallucinations are perceptual experiences that distort reality or which exist in the absence of a realistic stimulus. They are most often auditory in nature; the presence of olfactory or gustatory hallucinations should almost always trigger a referral for evaluation by a neurologist. People with psychotic disorders also frequently present with disorganized thinking that most often takes the form of distortions in speech such as loose associations, tangential thinking, or "word salad."

Movement may also be distorted in psychotic disorders. This sometimes takes the form of **catatonia**; catatonia may result in either marked diminution of activity, or exaggerated motor activity. It is sometimes difficult to distinguish catatonic excitement from the mania that accompanies bipolar disorder. **Waxy flexibility**, the tendency of a patient to maintain a position or posture once the position has been established, is one of the defining features of catatonic stupor.

Delusions, hallucinations, and movement disorders are all considered positive symptoms. In contrast, the negative symptoms associated with psychotic disorders are less salient and dramatic; however, they can be just as limiting for the individual with a disease like schizophrenia. The most common negative symptoms associated with psychotic disorders are diminished emotional expression and a lack of motivated, purposeful activity. Patients with negative symptoms appear vacant and hollow; they may avoid eye contact and often sit for long hours without engaging in meaningful activity. They may wander aimlessly, say little, and appear to have no interest in other people or other activities.

Note that the diagnosis of schizotypal personality disorder is considered part of the schizophrenia spectrum, but the DSM-5 emphasizes discussion of this disorder in the chapter on personality disorders. We take the same approach – readers will find film examples of schizotypal personality in Chapter 13.

The Diagnosis of Schizophrenia

Schizophrenia usually first occurs during late adolescence or early adulthood, although it sometimes – but rarely – begins in childhood or middle/late adulthood. Even though the frequency of the illness is approximately equal in men and women, symptoms in males often occur earlier than in females. Peak onset occurs in the early to mid 20s for males and mid to late 20s for females. In general, the outcome of the illness is worse with earlier onset.

For a person to be diagnosed with schizophrenia, certain symptoms must be present. According to the *DSM-5*, there must be continuous signs of the disturbance for at least 6 months and, during 1 month (the active phase), two or more of the following must be present: delusions, hallucinations, disorganized speech, grossly disorganized or catatonic behavior, or negative symptoms. In addition, at least one of the symptoms must be the presence of delusions, hallucinations, or disorganized speech (i.e., the presence of catatonic behavior and negative symptoms alone would not be sufficient to justify the diagnosis). The individual's ability to function in work, social relations, and self-care decreases during the active phase and rarely returns to the individual's premorbid level of functioning.

"The nightmare of schizophrenia is not knowing what's true. Imagine if you had suddenly learned that the people, the places, the moments most important to you were not gone, not dead, but worse ... they've never been. What kind of hell would that be?"

Psychiatrist Dr. Rosen educating Alicia Nash about her husband's schizophrenia in *A Beautiful Mind* (2001)

Patients with schizophrenia spectrum disorder frequently have systematized delusions or frequent hallucinations related to a single theme (e.g., hearing denigrating voices). These individuals are often extremely anxious, angry, or argumentative, and may become violent. However, there is *not* the strong relationship between violence and schizophrenia that many people expect (and which most movies suggest is common). When violence does occur, it most often occurs in young males with a history of violent behavior who are nonadherent to their medication regimens, or with those individuals whose illness is complicated by substance abuse.

Elaine Walker and her colleagues examined early childhood home movies from families in which one of the children subsequently developed schizophrenia. Trained observers rated facial affect in the children who became schizophrenic and their nonschizophrenic siblings. For females, there were consistently fewer expressions of joy in the preschizophrenic children than in their same-sex siblings who did not develop the disorder. This difference was present at every age, but only for females. However, both preschizophrenic males and preschizophrenic females displayed greater negative affect than their nonschizophrenic same-sex siblings (Walker, Grimes, Davis, & Smith, 1993). A subsequent study demonstrated a higher rate of neuromotor abnormalities and poorer motor skills in the preschizophrenic subjects in the first 2 years of life, with deficits noted predominately on the left side of the body (Walker, Savoie, & Davis, 1994).

Among people diagnosed with schizophrenia spectrum disorder, paranoid patients are the most likely to commit acts of violence. This is a common subtype portrayed in films; it is popularized in films such as *A Beautiful Mind* (2001), *Donnie Darko* (2001), and *Gothika* (2003). The documentary *People Say I'm Crazy* (2004) is a remarkably honest and real portrayal of the daily life of a courageous man coping with paranoia and schizophrenia spectrum disorder.

Incoherent speech and disorganized behavior are common with schizophrenia spectrum disorders. These patients rapidly shift from one idea to another; often these ideas are unrelated. They may also express inappropriate emotion, such as laughing on a sad occasion. They usually have very strange mannerisms and are extremely socially impaired. Robin Williams' character in *The Fisher King* (1991) and Geoffrey Rush's portrayal of David Helfgott in *Shine* (1996) both illustrate these symptoms. Ralph Fiennes' title character in *Spider* (2002) is another excellent example of this type of schizophrenia spectrum disorder.

Some patients with schizophrenia spectrum disorders display catatonia. For example, catatonic persons may appear to be in a stupor, completely unaware of their environment. They may maintain one posture for a long time, crawl into a fetal position, hold an arm in a bizarre position, or sit stiffly in a chair; it may be difficult to move the individual because of the muscle rigidity. At times these individuals become very excited or agitated, but then slip into the previous mannerisms. At times they are mute. The film *Awakenings* (1990) is a dramatic portrayal of catatonia (although this particular film depicted a neurological rather than psychiatric condition). Many films depicting psychiatric institutions have one or two characters (often in the background) who display catatonia, as in *K-Pax* (2001) and *House of Fools* (2004).

Some patients with schizophrenia spectrum disorders will not hallucinate or have delusions, but they will display social withdrawal or eccentric behavior. Eugene Levy's character, Mitch, in *A Mighty Wind* (2003) illustrates this phenomenon. Mitch sits alone and stares for hours in a drab motel room; displays psychomotor retardation; exhibits blank, distant, and quizzical facial expressions; and has inappropriate social skills, yet he does not appear to be in the active phase of a schizophrenia spectrum disorder. These are residual effects. The viewer learns Mitch had previously been hospitalized for severe depression, anger outbursts, and eccentric behavior, though an actual diagnosis is never given.

Dr. Mittag-Leffler: "I'm afraid what you're describing is schizophrenia."

Harold Crick: "No, no. It's not schizophrenia. It's just a voice in my head. I mean, the voice isn't telling me to do anything. It's telling me what I've already done ... accurately, and with a better vocabulary."

Dr. Mittag-Leffler: "Mr. Crick, you have a voice speaking to you."

Harold Crick: "No, not TO me. ABOUT me. I'm somehow involved in some sort of story. Like I'm a character in my own life. But the problem is that the voice comes and goes ..."

Dr. Mittag-Leffler: "Mr. Crick, I hate to sound like a broken record, but that's schizophrenia."

A physician argues with Will Ferrell's character about his diagnosis in
Stranger Than Fiction (2006)

Stranger than Fiction (2006) stars Will Ferrell as Harold Crick, an IRS agent who leads a fairly insipid life until he begins to hear someone narrating his life and telling him he is going to die soon. Harold recognizes the voice; it was the voice of an esteemed author he had heard on television. He

begins to look for the author to convince her that she cannot end the story by having the protagonist die.

The Content of Movies About Schizophrenia Spectrum Disorders

Patricia Owen (2012) identified 41 English language movies released between 1990 and 2010 in which a major character was coping with the challenges associated with schizophrenia. The majority of these characters were White and male, and they most commonly had positive symptoms. Delusions were the most common symptom, followed by auditory and visual hallucinations. Violence was commonplace: Nearly a third of these characters were homicidal, and approximately one in four committed suicide. In addition, one in four of the films suggested an early traumatic event was responsible for the schizophrenia spectrum disorder that was being portrayed. Owen concluded, "The finding that misinformation and negative portrayals of schizophrenia in contemporary movies are common underscores the importance of determining how viewers interpret media messages and how these interpretations inform attitudes and beliefs both of the general public and of people with schizophrenia" (p. 655).

Family Dynamics and Schizophrenia Spectrum Disorder

In the 1960s and 1970s, a popular theory implicated dysfunctional family communication patterns in the etiology of schizophrenia. Communication within the family of a person with schizophrenia was believed to be indirect, unclear, incongruent, and growth impeding. Communication within theses families was thought to be distorted and based on "double messages." The child received two opposing messages from the parent and, thus, was in a **double bind**. For example, a parent might say, "Come here and give me a hug," and when the child responded, the parent would tense up and push the child away. The child then would feel that pleasing the parent was an impossible no-win situation and would develop schizophrenia in response to this psychological bind. The

schizophrenogenic family was characterized as being severely fused. Members of these families never adequately separated or developed into individuals, and thus the family had no boundaries. This view of distorted family communication has been largely discounted as a cause of schizophrenia.

Despite the fact that no one seriously believes that parents "cause" their children's schizophrenia spectrum disorder, this misconception persists in both popular culture and contemporary cinema. Peter Winter's mother in *Clean, Shaven* (1993) is portrayed as cold, aloof, and withdrawn; there is a clear implication that she is at least in part responsible for her son's illness. Likewise, the movie *Shine* (1996), Scott Hick's fascinating film about the life of child prodigy and pianist David Helfgott, clearly implicates David's father as the root of his son's subsequent mental illness. The father is alternately loving and hateful, telling his son, "No one can love you like me!" while at the same time actively working to limit his son's future and potential. A similar theme can be found in the 1962 film *David and Lisa*, in which David's mother – a woman focused on appearances – makes some efforts to support David but ends up appearing insensitive to her son's abilities and problems. The father is depicted as passive, distant, and unavailable to David in his younger years. Both parents are ineffective in dealing with David's problems, and the film suggests there is a link between the dysfunctional parental communication and David's mental illness.

Misconception: People With Mental Illness Are Frequently Violent

One of the most profound yet common stereotypes in contemporary cinema is the connection filmmakers draw between mental illness and violence. This misconception is strongest in films that portray schizophrenia spectrum disorder. It is often not directly stated in the film; however, the plotline and ensuing messages are usually clear to the viewer: They see a character being treated for a psychological problem, or they see a character begin to deteriorate with mental illness, and the next thing the viewer sees is that person perpetrating a violent act. This is unfortunate because the general public is not educated on the relationship between violence and

mental illness, and many individuals, influenced by media reports, are likely to exaggerate their own personal risk when interacting with someone who has a mental illness. The reality is that *people with mental illness are far more likely to be the victim of a violent act than to be the perpetrator of violence*; moreover, research also shows that mental illness is neither a necessary nor a sufficient cause for violence (Stuart, 2003). The data are mixed as to whether people with mental illness are more or less likely to react with violence than the general public. Yet filmmakers use this stereotype as it provides a clear understanding of what is often unspeakable and perplexing; it is a way to clear up ambiguity and to make sense of the human psyche.

"I was Mr. Nobody till I killed the biggest somebody on earth ... I was nothing and [then] I was a big shot." "There was no emotion in my blood, there was no anger, there was nothing. It was dead silence in my brain, dead cold quiet. He looked at me, he looked past me. Then I heard my head, [it] said do it, do it, do it, over again."

Mark Chapman explaining his murder of John Lennon in *The Killing of John Lennon* (2006)

Films portraying the assassination of public figures are a clear example of filmmakers leveraging this idea. Two in particular – *The Killing of John Lennon* (2006) and *The Assassination of Richard Nixon* (2004) – portray men who obsess over a public figure and subsequently murder or attempt to murder as a result of a strong delusional process. Both men are scruffy, irritable, quirky, socially awkward, and withdrawn. Each has a deep insecurity and inferiority and anger toward some aspect of the social system (e.g., consumerism, politics), and each uses violence to deal with these frustrations. Each is a fascinating, accurate portrayal of the internal dialogue and reasoning that fosters a grandiose delusional state. In *The Killing of John Lennon*, Mark Chapman is very grandiose and paranoid, displaying mood changes and delusional explanations for his behavior. He shows no remorse or regret and believes he later received a message from God to plead guilty. In the end, both films leave the viewer with a strong sense that there is a connection between schizophrenia/delusions and violence/murder.

"That little guy can't do it anymore. He just can't do it anymore ... because there's a cancer in the system. The whole system has a cancer and I'm being punished because I resist. But somebody has to resist, just somebody has to resist."

"I know what it's like to not be respected, to be lied to, and to be treated like a great big nothing."

Samuel J. Bicke's (Sean Penn) delusions that led to his assassination attempt on Richard Nixon in *The Assassination of Richard Nixon* (2004)

Another film that makes people fear those with mental illness is *Keane* (2004), a movie in which a man frantically searches for his daughter whom he has lost at a Port Authority bus terminal in New York City. Damian Lewis as the protagonist, a man with a schizophrenia spectrum disorder, does a marvelous job portraying how he struggles to hold reality together even while he continues to deteriorate. Nevertheless, the aspects of the film that most viewers will remember are the scenes of intense and bizarre behavior. In one particular scene, William Keane chases and attacks a stranger in a parking garage.

William H. Macy's portrayal of a man losing touch with reality in *Edmond* (2005), written for the screen and the stage by David Mamet, is equally chilling. Edmond breaks up with his wife and slowly deteriorates as he starts to wander the streets of New York City looking for sex. As he begins to self-destruct, his loneliness, isolation, instability, and lack of responsibility and empathy become clear. The viewer will easily remember standout scenes of Edmond impulsively screaming at a woman who does not listen to him on the subway and his murder of a waitress after having sex with her. He later rationalizes his killing as the result of too much coffee, and he claims that there are just too many people in the world.

There are literally hundreds of suspense and horror movies about "psychotic killers" who are on a rampage, usually attacking women. While entertaining for some, these films typically have nothing to do with any particular mental disorder, and they perpetuate the stigma associated with mental illness. The term *psychotic* is used to induce fear and suggest unpredictability. Pictures such as *The Caretak-*

ers (1963), *The Silent Partner* (1979), *Alone in the Dark* (1982), *Angel in Red* (1991), and *Cape Fear* (1991) have contributed to shaping the stigma experienced by people with mental illness.

Two horror/thriller films that portray characters deteriorating with mental illness who consequently become violent are *May* (2002) and *Love Object* (2003). *May* is a macabre, well-acted character study of a veterinary technician whose best friend is her doll. As she continues to fail at intimate and social relationships, she becomes psychotic and begins to kill to get ideal body parts that she combines to form a whole. In *Love Object*, a young man believes his lifelike sex doll is real and comes to believe he is being controlled and attacked by the doll; these delusions deepen and extend to violence in the outside world.

"If you can't find a friend, make one."

An example of psychotic thinking in *May* (2002)

Even the portrayal of schizophrenia in the widely popular *A Beautiful Mind* (2001), albeit helpful in educating the public in a number of ways, also highlights scenes in which John Nash becomes violent or dangerous to his wife and to their newborn baby, particularly when he is in a paranoid state. Other classic examples of this stereotype include Annie Wilkes, the delusional character played by Academy Award winner Kathy Bates, who tortures a writer she is obsessed with in *Misery* (1990), the isolated female protagonist in Roman Polanski's *Repulsion* (1965, UK), and Robert De Niro's classic role as a delusional killer, Travis Bickle, in *Taxi Driver* (1976).

Schizophrenia Spectrum Disorders in Contemporary Films

Schizophrenia

Can films educate students and the general public about the realities of schizophrenia spectrum disorders? In one study, a video was constructed with segments from popular movies depicting inaccurate and accurate portrayals of schizophrenia (Owen, 2007). The researchers randomly assigned college students to either a video presentation or a traditional lecture on schizophrenia, and later tested the students' knowledge of schizophrenia. The results showed knowledge improvement following both the movie clips and the lecture; however, the movie clips had a greater corrective effect for female students.

There have been a number of intriguing films portraying schizophrenia in the fairly recent past. We discuss several of them below.

Canvas

This 2006 film from first-time director/writer Joseph Greco is an outstanding portrayal of the paranoid symptoms that are often associated with schizophrenia spectrum disorders. It is based on some of Greco's experiences growing up with a parent coping with the symptoms of schizophrenia. Indeed, some individuals in the mental health community believe Marcia Gay Harden's portrayal of schizophrenia is the most accurate in film history. Harden plays Mary Marino who desires to be close to her husband and son, but who finds that her illness is a significant obstacle to achieving this goal. She regularly has auditory hallucinations and tries to drown out the sound, first with running water and later by literally pouring water on her forehead. She displays inappropriate affect (e.g., laughing at the dinner table during conversation about a serious matter), embarrasses her son by running after the bus saying that she was concerned about his safety, and she seems to be socially unaware of the discomfort her symptoms cause others with whom she interacts. In a memorable scene, Mary runs around in the rain, fear-struck and paranoid as she wakes up the neighbors searching for a wiretap. The film references the Baker Act (also called the Florida Mental Health Act), a law that can be invoked by judges, police, physicians, or mental health professionals. The Baker Act allows for involuntary examination of individuals who have mental illness and who are believed to be likely to harm themselves or others or who neglect their own basic needs. Mary is routinely picked up by the police when her paranoid behavior puts her safety at risk.

Important themes in the film include the loss of a family member (to institutionalization), the struggles associated with coping with mental illness, and the challenge of finding hope at the most trying of times. The realities of severe mental illness are not minimized – Mary is often in and out of the hospital, she frequently stops taking her medication, and her illness has a profound impact on her family. Her husband obsesses about building a boat, and her son begins to avoid school. Nevertheless, each of the three taps into an outlet of creativity to cope with the situation – each has a different "canvas," whether it be painting, knitting, or construction/building.

"When you paint, they go away."
"Who?"
"The voices."

Mary Marino interacting with another
patient in Canvas (2006)

The film is a wonderful portrayal of the impact of mental illness on the family; it is also tender, hopeful, and positive, with an ending that is neither contrived nor forced.

The Soloist

The Soloist (2009) is an outstanding film starring Jamie Foxx as Nathaniel Ayers, a homeless man and brilliant musician who has schizophrenia. Robert Downey Jr. plays the Los Angeles Times columnist Steve Lopez, the reporter who stumbles upon Ayers playing a broken violin on the street next to a statue of Beethoven. Intrigued by Ayers, Lopez writes a series of stories about him, and their relationship develops into a lasting friendship. The Soloist does an excellent job at portraying the symptoms of schizophrenia and the resulting impact on daily functioning and social interaction. Director Joe Wright emphasizes auditory hallucinations through a haunting series of various voices that increase in intensity, tone, and frequency; unlike in the film A Beautiful Mind – and more true to the reality of schizophrenia – visual hallucinations are de-emphasized. Ayers exhibits a significant level of paranoia but shows a modest degree of symptom awareness when he observes that he might "make a spectacle" of himself. Lopez encourages Ayers to take medication; however, Ayers refuses. A counselor advises Lopez that Ayers cannot be forced to take medication unless he is a danger to himself or others. The film flashes back to scenes in Ayers' childhood when he isolated himself in a dark basement repeatedly practicing his music and to his early symptomatic days at the Juilliard School before his illness forced him to drop out of that prestigious academy.

"Life has a mind of its own."

Nathaniel Ayers in *The Soloist*

Unfortunately, the film falls into the prevalent trap of perpetrating the misconception that all people with schizophrenia eventually become violent and dangerous. Of course, a person with a mental illness can be violent, like anyone else. The problem is that filmmakers notoriously make disorders such as schizophrenia spectrum disorders synonymous with violent, dangerous, and often lethal behavior. The everyday moviegoer and consumers of mental health films looking for education about a disorder that they or a family member have been diagnosed with are then misled, simply because filmmakers want to enhance the drama of the film. Unfortunately, it is the dramatic and violent scenes that viewers will remember.

Bug

The William Friedkin film *Bug* (2006), based on a play, is an excellent, moody, mysterious, and raw depiction of mental illness. Most of the film takes place in one room, which heightens emotions, gives the viewer a claustrophobic feel and forces him or her to focus on the characters. An emotionally wounded and exhausted woman, Agnes (Ashley Judd), lives in a small motel room and uses cocaine with her occasional lesbian lover. Her only child vanished several years ago at age 9 and she has been struggling with an abusive husband, Jerry (Harry Connick Jr.), who was recently released from prison. Agnes befriends a strange man, Peter, who claims he is able "to sense things." Peter is a highly intuitive person with keen social intelligence; he quickly and correctly realizes that Agnes is someone who has suffered a lot in her life. He also senses that she has a "bad" husband, and he quickly picks up on times when she has lied to him. But he also believes

her motel room is infested with microscopic bugs. Soon the room is filled with bug traps, sprays, fumigation devices, and even a microscope. He takes his own blood samples and points out the bugs that appear to be multiplying. He later painfully explains that he had been kicked out of the military because of his paranoid beliefs. Peter's next step in eliminating the "bugs" is to cover the entire rooms in tin foil, from top to bottom including all the furniture and household items. He claims that the tin foil scrambles the "signals" of the bugs, making it impossible for them to communicate. He shares extensive details about his persecutory delusions, describing special experiments, prototypes, biochips, and military testing conducted on a global scale.

Peter's psychiatrist arrives at the motel explaining that Peter has been hospitalized for 4 years at an Army hospital where he was diagnosed as a "delusional paranoid with schizophrenic tendencies." After resisting the psychiatrist's advice, Peter brutally and repeatedly stabs him. In a scene reminiscent of another film portraying schizophrenia (*Clean, Shaven*), Peter graphically yanks out his teeth believing there is a transmitter in his gums. Agnes, a vulnerable, traumatized, and lonely woman desperate for a connection, begins to share Peter's psychotic beliefs (i.e., shared psychotic disorder or folie à deux). The tension accelerates, and the mental status of both characters continues to deteriorate, culminating in a decision to set themselves on fire to destroy the bugs. This film is an excellent portrayal of schizophrenia, and it provides salient examples of tactile and visual hallucinations and paranoia; however, it also perpetuates the myth that people with mental illness are almost always violent.

Take Shelter and *Revolution #9*

These are two excellent films that illustrate late-onset psychosis. Each film demonstrates the symptoms of schizophrenia that are largely left untreated, causing significant decline in the protagonists' functioning and social well-being.

Take Shelter (2011) is a Gus van Sant film that features Curtis, a small-town construction worker. Curtis begins to experience symptoms of night terrors that seem to specifically target him and his daughter. He experiences hallucinations and delusions; he subsequently conducts research on mental illness and concludes that he has symptoms of schizophrenia. He believes terrible storms are coming and observes signs of storms that no one else can see; he sees figures in the storm, sees flocks of birds that are not there, and hears storms that are not present. His coworkers notice and remark on his strange behavior. His symptoms result in a decision to taking time off from work to build a tornado shelter. He sees a counselor who tells him she can listen to him but cannot prescribe medication. Curtis receives mild antianxiety medication from his family doctor, yet avoids communicating about his symptoms with his wife. The film reviews some of the family history of Curtis and points out that his mother left him in a parking lot at age 10 and he was found a few days later eating trash out of a dumpster. His mother was diagnosed with paranoid schizophrenia and taken to a state hospital, and Curtis was raised by his father (who had recently died, exacerbating the stress Curtis was experiencing). Interestingly, the age of onset of symptoms for both mother and son was the mid-30s. As the film concludes, the whole family is able to see a big storm looming, as if to symbolically challenge the viewer's assumptions about Curtis and his presumed illness. While the film is excellent and one of the better portrayals of schizophrenia, there is one episode of violence, which contributes to the misconception that all people with mental illness are violent.

Revolution #9 (2001) is a dramatic and unsentimental illustration of paranoid schizophrenia and the complexities and failings of the US health care system. James Jackson is a freelance writer/reviewer who was recently engaged. As he goes about his work and social life, he begins to realize something is wrong, but he believes his problems are external (i.e., other people are causing his problems). His exhibits diminished eye contact, angry facial expressions, and agitation. He thinks that his fiancée's brother's son is sending him messages, that his fiancée is involved, and that his coworkers are rearranging his desk behind his back. James's writing becomes muddled and confused. His confusion and paranoia escalate as he firmly believes that others are manipulating him. After a month of gradual deterioration, he becomes convinced that a perfume commercial for Revolution 9 contains hidden messages and was made especially for him. He says to his fiancée: "look at that … they're good aren't they … it's a code, it hits you underneath." He watches the commercial repeatedly – completely consumed

and paranoid. He later stalks the director of the commercial, calling him, creating anonymous, threatening pictures, and he then tricks the director into participating in an interview that ends in violence. A common thread of his social interactions is his belief that he is the subject of a grand conspiracy that involves his fiancée, coworkers, hospital staff, a judge, and others he meets. He is admitted to a hospital and placed on medication for 2 weeks. He is later released and becomes suicidal.

Revolution #9 is particularly effective in depicting the impact of mental illness on the protagonist's fiancée. She expresses concern, agitation, and helplessness, and while she perseveres in trying to get him help, he gives her almost no reason to sustain hope. She persuades him to visit a psychiatrist, but he walks out, defensive and angry. She repeatedly compromises and ends up giving up her job because of her efforts to help her fiancé.

Director Tim McCann confuses the viewer with humor, and close-up shots are used to enhance the feeling of claustrophobia. McCann also skillfully manages sounds – for example, he stifles sounds, cuts out words, and uses rapid nondiegetic sound. This effect contributes to the cinematic depiction of the progression of schizophrenia. The film offers a sympathetic portrayal of mental health professionals and shows them as competent and knowledgeable about the condition they are treating. The film also provides a rare glimpse of how the mental health community (along with insurance companies) tries to take care of mentally ill people within the cost–benefit constraints of modern health care. The film also depicts manipulation and exploitation by insurance companies determined to avoid paying for necessary care.

Spider

The viewer realizes this is a deeply psychological movie as he or she sees the opening credits. Inkblots, similar to those used with the classic psychological assessment tool, the **Rorschach Inkblot Test** are integrated into the opening. The viewer is thus invited to "interpret" and challenge what he or she is seeing from the very start to the ambiguous ending.

Director David Cronenberg sets the tone of this 2002 film in the first scene, which depicts "the flow of humanity" – an arriving train, the hustle of activity, and a multitude of people heading toward their own destinations – contrasted with the lead character, Spider (Ralph Fiennes), slowly stepping off the train, disoriented and isolated from everyone else. This dark and dreary film maps out the psychological terrain of a man with schizophrenia. Spider has minimal dialogue, so the viewer learns about his inner world through his facial expressions, body language, and utter isolation.

The adult character Spider, played by Ralph Fiennes, has been discharged from an institution and attempts to integrate into a group home. He has many symptoms of schizophrenia, including delusions, mumbling and disorganized speech, incoherent and grossly disorganized behavior, an unclean and disheveled appearance, and negative symptoms including severely flattened affect and shuffling gait.

Ingeniously, Cronenberg places the present-day Spider character in all of the memory scenes as Spider tries to reassemble his past. The adult Spider is shown observing his parents and himself as a boy interacting with the world. Some of these memories are false and some are accurate, but neither the viewer nor Spider himself knows the truth. To make matters more complicated, Spider fuses identities of his memories as well as his past and present, which results in further confusion and distortion.

This is also a good depiction of **childhood schizophrenia** as we see the young boy distort reality, express the paranoid belief that his father and his father's mistress killed his mother, and the boy's complete isolation from social contact.

"You're by yourself too much. You need some mates. When I was your age I had mates. Every young lad needs ... some mates."

Bill Cleg (Gabriel Byrne) speaking to his delusional son, Spider in *Spider* (2002)

Throughout the film, several metaphors are used to portray Spider's struggle to recognize reality and the disintegration of that reality into psychosis. In one scene, Spider is carefully putting together a very complex puzzle of hundreds of pieces, and in a later scene after putting together some painful memory fragments, he angrily destroys the puzzle, throwing the pieces to the floor in the day room. Broken mirrors, pieces of glass, and twine, used to create what appears to be a spider's web, symbolize his mental state.

Additional Questions for Discussion (*Spider*)

➤ What makes this character's portrayal of schizophrenia so provocative and realistic?

➤ Are some of the behaviors portrayed by Spider (e.g., collecting little objects from the street, lying in a fetal position in the bathtub) common characteristics of schizophrenia?

➤ What does this film have to say about the etiology of schizophrenia?

➤ In interviews, director David Cronenberg has spoken to the potential for multiple endings for this film. Reflect on different options and cite which fits best with this portrayal of schizophrenia.

➤ Cronenberg states that he wants the viewer to "become Spider." Why? Does this happen for you?

➤ This film obviously deals with a person with schizophrenia. Why isn't the word or any other diagnosis ever mentioned in the movie?

K-Pax

In this 2001 film, Kevin Spacey plays Prot, a man claiming to be from the planet K-Pax who has traveled to Earth by light beams. At the outset, we see Prot appear in a busy train station among sparkles of light. Soon he is falsely accused of a crime and admitted to a psychiatric institution. The psychiatrist, Dr. Powell (Jeff Bridges), takes an interest in working with Prot when he learns Prot is unresponsive to conventional psychiatric medications. As their relationship progresses, Dr. Powell learns much about the identity of Prot and the differences between K-Pax and Earth. Prot offers extensive (and savant-like) explanations of his planet's rotational patterns, discusses the ways in which men and women procreate on his planet, and gives descriptions of the differences between the planets. Many of Prot's delusions are bizarre, which keeps him from being given a diagnosis of delusional disorder. The viewer essentially has two options at this point: Prot is either a man with schizophrenia or a spiritual guide from another planet. We can view the film accepting the former as true to help us understand the predicament in which a delusional patient finds himself. He is completely trapped by his delusions and does not have a way out; the painful challenge of this is that the patient is not aware he is delusional.

Viewers who choose the latter option are choosing a fascinating, inspirational take on the film, while at the same time buying into the misconception that the person with mental illness is an "enlightened member of society" (Hyler, Gabbard, & Schneider, 1991). It is worth noting, however, that some cultures do indeed believe that a person with schizophrenia is an enlightened member of society; therapists and educators should appreciate and acknowledge such cultural beliefs and spend time exploring these beliefs with their patients.

The situation in *K-Pax* gets more complex. As Dr. Powell questions Prot about where he comes from and where he has visited on this planet, another diagnostic explanation emerges. We learn through flashbacks and hypnotic regression that Prot is Robert Porter, a man who found the bodies of his murdered and raped wife and child, and then experienced the trauma of encountering the killer in his home and breaking the murderer's neck. Prot then washes his bloody hands with a water hose (hence his water phobia) and attempts suicide in a nearby river. The viewer is left to assume Prot was found and taken to the psychiatric hospital. Consequently, additional diagnostic considerations emerge, such as posttraumatic stress disorder (PTSD) and dissociative fugue. His sudden travel, assumption of a new identity, and inability to recall his past (other than under hypnosis) make a strong case for the diagnosis of dissociative fugue.

In the end, Prot becomes catatonic – unresponsive and rigid as he is pushed around in a wheelchair – providing further evidence to support a diagnosis of schizophrenia.

Additional Questions for Discussion (*K-Pax*)

➤ What diagnoses do you believe are appropriate for Prot's character? Explain.
➤ How does Prot fit the other patients on the ward into his delusional framework?
➤ What would be appropriate criteria for releasing Prot from the hospital?
➤ Compare the portrayal of mental illness depicted in this film and in *A Beautiful Mind* (2001).
➤ Discuss the differences of the role of the psychiatrist and treatment in this film and in *A Beautiful Mind*. How does the time period each film is set in play a role?

Black Swan

Darren Aronofsky's *Black Swan* (2010) is a provocative and unforgettable film starring Natalie Portman who won an Academy Award for Best Actress in a Leading Role for her portrayal of Nina Sayers, the Swan Queen. Sayers is a ballerina who gradually decompensates as she competes for, wins, and then prepares for the lead role in the ballet *Swan Lake*, which ends in a dramatic finale (see Figure 4). She is under tremendous pressure to succeed in the highly competitive world of ballet, and the stress of competition is complicated by a dysfunctional relationship with her mother (played by Barbara Hershey, in a role depicting a woman who gave up her career in ballet after her daughter was born) and sexual harassment by her director. She also experiences the drug ecstasy for the first time and likely has a lesbian encounter with Lily, her doppelgänger and the dancer who plays the role of the Black Swan. While Nina's character presents a diagnostic quandary because she exhibits symptoms associated with several disorders, she clearly exhibits anorexic and bulimic behavior, and she has a history of scratching herself to the point where she bleeds (i.e., excoriation). It is also clear that she is delusional and

---

Nina: "I came to ask for the part."

Thomas Leroy: "The truth is when I look at you all I see is the white swan. Yes you're beautiful, fearful, and fragile. Ideal casting. But the black swan? It's a hard fucking job to dance both."

Nina: "I can dance the black swan, too."

Thomas Leroy: "Really? In four years every time you dance I see you obsessed getting each and every move perfectly right but I never see you lose yourself. Ever! All that discipline for what?"

Nina: [whispers] "I just want to be perfect."

Thomas Leroy: "What?"

Nina: "I want to be perfect."

Thomas Leroy: [scoffs] "Perfection is not just about control. It's also about letting go. Surprise yourself so you can surprise the audience. Transcendence! Very few have it in them."

Nina: "I think I do have it in me."

Dialogue between Thomas Leroy and Nina in *Black Swan* (2010)

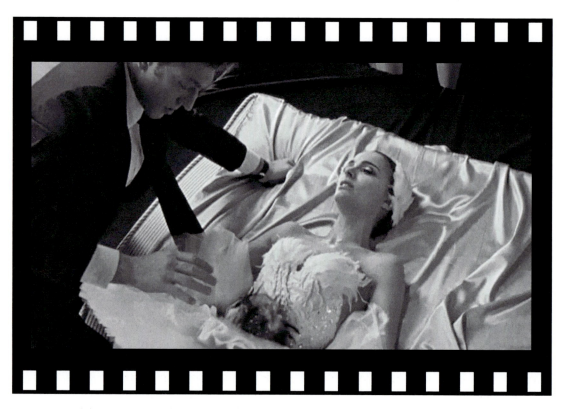

Figure 4. *Black Swan* (2010, Fox Searchlight Pictures, Cross Creek Pictures, et al.) Produced byScot Franklin, Mike Medavoy, Arnold Messer, and Brian Oliver. Directed by Darren Aronofsky.

psychotic; however, the film is unrealistic insofar as someone experiencing a psychosis as profound and as complicated as that experienced by Portman's character would never be able to perform at the high level required by the lead role in *Swan Lake*. Nadine Kaslow, 2014 president of the American Psychological Association and the staff psychologist for the Atlanta Ballet, called the film "intense and disturbing and fascinating and mysterious." The dramatic climax of this psychologically complex film is seen in Figure 4.

Delusional Disorders

Contrary to popular belief, a delusional disorder is not synonymous with schizophrenia, it is not a subtype of schizophrenia, and hallucinations are not a predominant feature. Delusional disorder is, however, one of the less severe conditions on the schizophrenia spectrum. The delusions experienced by someone with a delusional disorder are not bizarre; instead, they involve situations of everyday life, such as being poisoned, followed, or loved, when in fact this is not happening. The delusions can be erotomanic, grandiose, jealous, persecutory, somatic, or a combination of these types. A person with delusional disorder can usually function fairly well in his or her daily life.

Lars and the Real Girl (2007) is an exceptional portrayal of delusional disorder. Ryan Gosling portrays Lars, a taciturn, aloof young man who lives in a detached residence near his brother's family. Lars does everything he can to avoid social contact, intimacy, and conversation. One day he purchases a life-like doll on the Internet, names it Bianca, and comes to believe Bianca is his actual girlfriend. He takes Bianca to parties, to church, and to family dinners, and he treats her with respect, telling her his innermost secrets and feelings. Interestingly, the small community decides to join Lars' delusion, talking to, spending time with, and even fighting over who will be able to interact with her. It is this community support that fosters Lars' connections with real people until he feels safe enough to let the delusion go.

A less powerful example of one or more characters who might meet criteria for delusional disorder (although more information is needed) is found in the film *Confessions of a Superhero* (2007). This independent film offers a glimpse into the lives of the "characters" who walk along the Hollywood Walk of Fame posing for pictures for tips, such as Superman, Batman, Wonder Woman, and Hulk, Some individuals are aggressive and get arrested, such as Batman, portrayed by a man who has a secret past and may have worked for the mafia; the film shows Batman describing his problems with anger control, and some of his sessions with a psychiatrist are depicted. The man portraying Superman is shown to be obsessed with his character; he persistently believes he has a mother who was an actress who sent him to various psychiatric facilities; other characters are shown challenging this belief system.

In *The Truman Show* (1998), no psychotic disorders are portrayed. However, this Peter Weir movie is a useful teaching tool in understanding delusional disorders. It flips the essence of a delusion. The film is about the unreal life of Truman Burbank. Everything around him has been created for him (or, better stated, created for the public viewing his reality show) – all of the people in the city, all of the buildings, the street lamps, the water, even the sun! It is all an extensive production set for a television show, yet Truman accepts his town of Seahaven as his reality; it is all he has known from birth to young adulthood. His name is appropriate as he is the only "true man" because everyone else, including his wife, best friend, mother, and father, are set actors. Eventually, Truman senses that he is trapped in a "world within a world" and tries to escape this contrived reality.

"We accept the reality with which the world is presented to us."

Christof (Ed Harris) in *The Truman Show* (1998)

Imagine that there was no television show and that Seahaven was like any other town; in this scenario, would Truman's behavior be seen as delusional? All of his behaviors *would* probably be seen as paranoid: His questioning and threatening of his wife with a knife, his suspicious looking around the store, his pausing in the middle of the street and stopping traffic. Most of the world around him would be in-

corporated into his delusional framework. He would include various environmental elements in his delusions: The camera equipment that suddenly falls from the sky, the rain water that just rains down on him and then follows him when he steps out of it, the observation of inconsistency in his wife's behavior. Further paranoid behaviors are exhibited when he follows his wife, and he questions whom he can trust. Truman explains that he believes his whole life is "building to something" and that he needs to escape to Fiji for a while. We would probably interpret this as delusional thinking.

Instead, what really happens is Truman does what a person with delusional disorder does not typically do. He challenges his own perception of reality, and this is ultimately what sets him free.

💬 Additional Questions for Discussion (*The Truman Show*)

➤ How can this movie help the therapist or client understand the popular treatment approach of cognitive-behavioral therapy?

➤ In some ways, this film is a psychological study. What are the moral and ethical drawbacks and possibilities in creating a research case study in a controlled environment as seen in this film? Will this be done in the future? Would it better society in some way?

➤ In Truman's world, the society revolves around him. Is this belief common for a person who has symptoms of paranoia, delusions, or schizophrenia?

➤ As Truman is leaving his world, Christof encourages him not to leave saying, "I know you better than you (know yourself)." If Truman were to believe this, would this suggest psychosis? Do most people with a psychotic disorder believe some variation of this?

Other Films Portraying Psychotic Disorders

People with schizophrenia spectrum disorders often get stereotyped as being the "crazy person on the street," which generalizes to the misconception that all eccentric behavior is "crazy." Films depict such instances with minor characters that may or may not have much impact on the plot, but nevertheless this misconception helps shape the stigma associated with mental illness. In *Cinema Paradiso* (1988), one man who appears to have schizophrenia makes a serious claim to a public square at a certain time each evening. Each day, he runs around a small area of the street he believes he owns exclaiming, "The square is mine. It's twelve o'clock, the square is mine!" refusing to allow anyone to step in this area. Later in the film (many years later), he continues the behavior, claiming "It's my square. It's mine. The square is mine." Though these are not critical scenes in the film, the eccentricity and subsequent label do not go unnoticed by the viewer.

At times, the psychosis depicted in films is a brief break with reality (i.e., a **brief psychotic disorder**), often with an obvious trigger. Consider the Bernardo Bertolucci film *The Dreamers* (2003), in which a young man triangulates with a pair of enmeshed fraternal twins (male and female). At one point, when the young man and the female twin are about to have sex, she begins to hear her twin brother in the next room with another woman. She breaks with reality screaming to the young man, "Who are you? What are you doing in my room? Get out!" while pounding on her brother's wall. The next morning, after a restful sleep, she is coherent and once again oriented to reality. If her symptoms lasted longer than 1 day, she would be likely to receive a diagnosis of brief psychotic disorder. The experience of the female twin in *The Dreamers* is similar to the experience of a character in *Jesus of Montreal* (1989, Canada/France) who has a psychotic break in the subway, in which he suddenly begins to blurt random, abstract sentences to strangers and then passes out; in such cases, one would immediately wonder if there were an underlying medical cause for the syncopal episode.

Shared psychotic disorder (also called folie à deux [French for "a madness shared by two"]), a condition emphasized in *DSM-IV* but not included in *DSM-5*, occurs when an individual develops a delusion in the context of a close relationship with someone who already has a delusion. Shared psychotic disorder is seldom depicted in films; however, the film *Birth* (2004) is a notable exception. This independent film features Nicole Kidman as Anna, who encounters Sean, a young boy with the delusion that he is the incarnation of Anna's deceased husband. Anna is skeptical at first, but as she begins to spend time with Sean she begins to believe him,

sharing his delusion. Of course, no other characters believe this could be anything but a delusion, and the boy is later confronted by Anna's husband's mistress, who claims the husband would have sought out others first. This breaks the delusional framework – and the boy, who "only feels love" for Anna – disappointedly tells Anna he is not the husband. Her folie à deux no longer possible, Anna moves on with her life. Another example is the independent film *Apart* (2011), in which a teenager coming out of a coma gets sucked into the delusional belief system of his girlfriend. *Who's Afraid of Virginia Woolf?* (1966) also portrays a husband and wife who appear to have characteristics of a shared psychotic disorder involving a son who never existed.

John Cassavetes' *A Woman Under the Influence* (1974) presents some challenging differential diagnosis questions. With Mabel Longhetti (Gena Rowlands), there is some evidence for **schizoaffective disorder,** as she is clearly not in touch with reality and has various mood problems; however, it is unclear whether she experiences her psychosis for 2 weeks without any mood symptoms. In addition, she meets a hallmark borderline personality criterion – an intense fear of abandonment – and she self-mutilates. She is referred to as chronically nervous by others including her own child, and a diagnosis of anxiety disorder would have to be considered as well. More information would be needed to be able to ensure a proper differential diagnosis.

Psychotic disorder due to a general medical condition can arguably be seen in *Synecdoche, New York* (2008). Philip Seymour Hoffman portrays Caden Cotard; the name "Cotard" is a direct reference to **Cotard's syndrome**, a nihilistic or negation delusion. This is a rare neuropsychiatric disorder in which the individual holds a delusional belief that he or she is dead or does not exist. The character Cotard struggles with a number of existential, relationship, and life problems, bordering on the somatic and delusional, with accompanying mood disturbances. The actual diagnosis is not certain, largely due to the surrealistic filmmaking and complexly layered plot of filmmaker Charlie Kaufman.

There are a number of **classic genre films** that portray schizophrenia spectrum disorders, and Martin Scorsese and Francis Ford Coppola have each directed numerous films over the decades that depict these disorders. Coppola's film *Apocalypse Now* (1979), which is a commentary on the conflicts in the human heart – rational versus irrational and good versus evil – stars Marlon Brando as the infamous Colonel Kurtz, an officer who drops out of the Vietnam War, takes the law into his own hands, and makes his home in the jungle. Kurtz is described throughout the film as "mad"; this label does not provide much information, but the viewer witnesses moments of insight and brilliance as well as psychosis in this character. Kurtz had witnessed terrible atrocities during the war, and he believed that such horrors could not be explained in words, noting: "Horror and moral terror are your friends. If they are not, they are enemies to be feared. They are truly enemies." His dying words are some of the most famous in movie history: "The horror, the horror."

"It's better to be king for a night than a schmuck for a lifetime."

Robert DeNiro as Rupert Pupkin in
The King of Comedy (1982)

Martin Scorsese directed *The King of Comedy* (1982), a dark comedy about a famous talk show host, Jerry Langford (Jerry Lewis), who is hounded by his fans. The film focuses on two fans in particular: the unknown stand-up comic, Rupert Pupkin (Robert De Niro), and his friend (Sandra Bernhard). Pupkin is an obsessive, out-of-touch man who lives predominantly in a fantasy world filled with imaginary successes. His delusions become even more pronounced when he has a one-time, "forced" conversation in a cab with Jerry and convinces himself that this is evidence of a substantive and meaningful friendship. His delusions deepen, and he becomes motivated to do anything necessary to support and maintain his delusional beliefs (e.g., kidnapping Jerry).

Terry Gilliam's 1991 film *The Fisher King*, stars Robin Williams as Parry, an obsessed yet benign street person. Parry believes himself to be a knight whose mission is to save the Holy Grail. Throughout the film, Parry has several hallucinations, including seeing friendly "little people" who communicate with him regularly and give him guidance. The Red Knight is a frightening hallucination that appears at times of extreme stress or when he is reminded of his personal tragedy.

In *Sophie's Choice* (1982), Sophie (Meryl Streep), Nathan, (Kevin Kline), and Stingo (Peter MacNi-

col) become inseparable friends, with Sophie and Nathan maintaining a turbulent romantic/sexual relationship and Stingo eventually falling deeply in love with Sophie. Sophie and Stingo struggle to understand Nathan's eccentric, erratic behavior, which at different times involves intense love, suspiciousness, anger, hostility, and paranoia. Initially, Nathan merely appears to be an unstable, "moody" person who claims to be a Harvard graduate and an overworked research biologist. As the story unfolds, the viewer learns that Nathan has been diagnosed with schizophrenia and he is only marginally coping with life. His symptoms are exacerbated by the use of amphetamines and cocaine, and his psychotic thinking leads to vicious accusations and unpredictable behavior. His bizarre behavior becomes more pronounced as his interpersonal stress increases and his denial is challenged. It is unclear how much Nathan's drug use influences his symptoms; if it were determined that his symptoms developed during or within a month of his substance intoxication or withdrawal, he would qualify for a **substance/medication-induced psychotic disorder** diagnosis.

One of the most vivid cinematic portrayals of psychiatric decompensation occurs in *The Caine Mutiny* (1954). Humphrey Bogart plays Lieutenant Commander Philip Francis Queeg, the obsessive-compulsive captain of a World War II destroyer. The ship's crew silently watches the deterioration that occurs as Queeg is put under increasing pressure, and eventually a junior officer, Lieutenant Barney Greenwald (José Ferrer), takes command. Greenwald is later court-martialed, and the film's most dramatic moment comes when Queeg cracks under the stress of the courtroom examination while playing with steel ball bearings, as he does when he is anxious.

"Ah, but the strawberries! That's, that's where I had them. They laughed at me and made jokes, but I proved beyond the shadow of a doubt, and with, with geometric logic, that, that a duplicate key to the wardroom icebox did exist."

Captain Queeg in *The Caine Mutiny* (1954)

Other films that illustrate psychotic disorders – some with more success than others – include *404* (2011), *Angels of the Universe* (2000), Lars von Trier's unforgettable film *Antichrist* (2009), *Deranged* (2012),

Lilith (2011), *Pi* (1998), *Secret Window* (2004), *Some Voices* (2000), *The Experiment* (2010), *The Jacket* (2005), *The Number 23* (2007), and *Gigantic* (2008).

International Films: Schizophrenia and Other Psychotic Disorders

Oil on Water (2009, South Africa) explicitly deals with the ways in which schizophrenia spectrum disorder affects a loving relationship; the protagonist – an artist – begins to decompensate about halfway through film. We first become aware of his illness when we see Japanese masks on the wall begin to speak. The voices escalate and become increasingly **ego dystonic**. The protagonist experiences loss of libido, experiences both hallucinations and delusions, and becomes suicidal. The film ends with some somber statistics: "Over 51 million people in the world suffer from schizophrenia. More than 50% will attempt suicide at least once. Between 10 and 15% will succeed."

Two films from South Korea are particularly noteworthy for their portrayal of mental illness: *Save the Green Planet* (2003) and *I'm a Cyborg, But That's OK* (2006). In the former, a young man pursues individuals he perceives are aliens that come from Andromeda, and he must stop them from destroying the planet. He and his girlfriend capture these individuals and torture them; by doing so, he believes he is taking away their powers by going after their "sensitive zones" (eyes, feet, and genitals) and by limiting their telepathy (which aliens do through their hair). He is genuinely convinced that he is heroic and saving the human race. He experiences a number of **ideas of influence** as seen in his correspondence with the aliens. In *I'm a Cyborg, But That's OK*, a young woman, Young-goon, is admitted to a psychiatric institution. She embodies a delusion that she is a cyborg and frequently communicates with clocks and vending machines. She refuses to eat, believing she will break down if she eats. She wears her dead grandmother's dentures in order to communicate and feels she has to kill the staff so she imagines shooting the doctors, nurses, and hospital staff with guns that are her fingers. In the memorable opening scene, while working on an assembly line, Young-goon matter-of-factly follows what her auditory hallucinations ("a broadcast") say

to her – she cuts her arm, put wires in it, and then plugs the wires into the wall. The film also touches on the origins of Young-goon's psychosis: Her grandmother, also treated for schizophrenia, thought she was a mother-mouse caring for a number of baby mice and ate a diet of only radishes.

The depiction in *I'm a Cyborg, But That's OK* is a good illustration of the power of psychotic beliefs and the futility of a helping professional in challenging such beliefs when the professional is contending with the client's psychosis, culture-bound issues (the secrecy and shame of such beliefs thus leading to a lack of disclosure, as evidenced in this film), mutism, and the client's own lack of awareness of her own beliefs and their impact. Suprisingly, most of the psychological jargon and diagnoses are accurate in the film. As is the case for most films portraying psychiatric hospital wards, the portrayal of the psychiatric patients suggests that people with mental illness are wild and crazy, with some rolling around on the floor. It raises the question, should the emphasis of such films be to educate the viewer or help the viewer to better empathize? This film emphasizes the dramatic, the interesting, and the eccentric, revealing the character's innermost, highly distorted delusional beliefs; this helps the viewer empathize with the character but the film sacrifices an opportunity to educate the viewer about the realities of mental illness and its treatment.

He Loves Me, He Loves Me Not (2002, France) might be the most effective and clear-cut use of the cinema to depict a delusional disorder. It is the directorial debut of French director Laetitia Colombani. First, viewers are completely taken in as they see reality from Angelique's (*Amélie's* Audrey Tautou) perception of her blossoming love relationship with a man named Loic. Midway through, the film rewinds, flashes back to the beginning, and then gives us the vantage point of Loic, who is a married doctor who barely knows Angelique exists. It is only as the second half of the film unfolds that the viewer can then backtrack in his or her mind to remember how Angelique perceived the relationship, and compare that with what Loic sees and experiences. It is the latter that becomes reality. Thus, the viewer eventually realizes everything in the first half of the film is Angelique's delusion. The viewer learns she obsessively calls Loic, leaving 23 messages. Her obsessions with drawings, following him around, and writing notes, all reinforce and maintain her delusional framework.

The delusional person can readily function in society, as shown with Angelique successfully taking care of her house, working a regular job, wearing appropriate attire, and communicating with others around her. Without knowing her thinking, we would not know she is delusional, particularly with her very sweet, often smiling, and innocent presentation. The film also depicts the risk in breaking the framework of a person's delusional mindset. It is here we see the stereotype of the violent psychiatric patient, as Angelique takes on the frame of mind "if I can't have him, no one will" and attempts to murder two innocent people.

Many films are ambiguous in their portrayal of delusional disorder, and they leave the viewer confused about whether the disorder is real or whether the character is simply idiosyncratic or eccentric. However, *He Loves Me, He Loves Me Not* is not at all ambiguous. The film maintains an honest and clear narrative about the disorder and stays with its purpose in showing drastically different truths, where one side is actually much "more real" than the other. Angelique's diagnosis of delusional disorder is discussed in the end when she is taken to a psychiatric hospital. The filmmakers knew what they specifically wanted to achieve with this deeply psychological film, and they accomplished it.

The film *11'09"01 – September 11* (2002, UK/France/Egypt/Japan/Mexico/US/Iran) is what followed when producer Alain Brigand proposed to 11 renowned directors to each "create a film lasting eleven minutes, nine seconds and one frame – September 11 – around the events of September 11 and their consequences." He asked them to look toward their own cultures, memories, stories, and language in constructing their short film segments. The filmmakers include directors from Bosnia-Herzegovina, India, the United States, Japan, Egypt, Mexico, Iran, the United Kingdom, France, West Africa, and Israel. In one segment, Japanese director Shohei Imamura depicts a man who heads off to war as a soldier and returns home as a snake (in human form). He maintains and embodies this severe, bizarre delusion, slithering around, hissing like a snake, biting the woman who feeds him, and eating a live rat. He is eventually kept in a cage and then forced out of the home. Before slithering into a body of water, he is asked, "Does being a man disgust you that much?" In a terrifying and poignant way, this simple question (and the psychosis) speaks to the horror of war.

House of Fools (2002) is a Russian/Chechnyan film based on a true story. Set in 1996, during the first Chechen war, the film depicts a psychiatric hospital located on the border of a war-torn area. The hospital staff flees due to conflict in Chechnya, leaving the patients to fend for themselves. Soldiers find refuge in the hospital and interact with the patients. As with most films depicting psychiatric institutions, there is a hodge-podge of psychopathology depicted. One patient, Jana, has hallucinations (or are they daydreams?) of herself in a video that portrays the famous singer Bryan Adams, who appears in the film as himself, often singing the lyrics "have you ever really loved a woman?" Jana has a **delusional disorder, erotomanic type**, as she believes Bryan Adams is her fiancé and that he is in love with her. Her room is covered in Bryan Adams posters. In a later scene, she naïvely believes the mock marriage proposal made to her by a soldier seeking refuge. Soon she finds herself in a bind, struggling to choose between the deceptive solider and the delusion of Bryan Adams. In one scene, Jana is gripping broken glass so hard that her hand becomes cut and bloodied. She uses a fantasy of Bryan Adams to cope with the pain. Jana denies her illness, telling people she was once sick but is not anymore. Furthermore, she believes she is a teacher for her fellow patients, teaching them yoga and how to play the accordion. Jana tries to help other patients when they make mistakes or need guidance. Cinematically, the viewer sees her reality of bright colors and light where the staff and patients are dancing to her music. This cinematic technique – weaving from patient perception to reality – is used frequently in the film. Other patients include a person with delusions, a psychotic fire starter, a psychotic transvestite, a psychotic midget, and a person who is catatonic.

Something Like Happiness (2005, Czech Republic) portrays the complex dynamics among three adults who are friends from childhood: Tonik, Monika, and Dasha. A single mother of two, Dasha deteriorates into psychosis, neglects her children and is only concerned about having a male companion. She is admitted to a psychiatric ward and becomes determined to become pregnant. In an upsetting scene, Dasha, upon being released from the ward, goes to her friend's home where her children have been properly cared for and interrupts the children's special party, grabbing them, forcing them into her car, and refusing to let them get their belongings.

Werner Herzog's *Aguirre, the Wrath of God* (1972, West Germany/Peru/Mexico) shows the Spanish conquistadors' search for the mythic treasure of El Dorado deep in the Amazon reaches of Peru. Aguirre is a defiant, competitive, power monger who leads a mutiny. During long, fruitless journeys in the jungle, he loses touch with reality and develops a **delusional disorder, grandiose type**. His appearance becomes boggy eyed, shaky, hypervigilant, and preoccupied. Aguirre's grandiosity continues to increase as he speaks of getting larger ships for bigger conquests. He shows a blatant disregard for his men's needs and leads them to suffering and destruction. At one point he exclaims, "I, the wrath of God, will marry my own daughter" and speaks of ruling with her.

"If I, Aguirre, want the birds to drop dead from the trees then the birds will drop dead from the trees. I am the wrath of God. The earth I walk upon sees me and quakes. But whoever follows me and the river will win untold riches."

Aguirre's delusions of grandeur in
Aguirre, the Wrath of God (1972)

As previously noted, filmmakers often link violence and psychosis. *Rampo Noir* (2005, Japan) is a collection of four short, surreal horror films – *Mars's Canal*, *Mirror Hell*, *Caterpillar*, and *Crawling Bugs* – that are adaptations and tributes to the Japanese poet Rampo. Each gives a different perspective on violence and a disturbing environment or situation relating to hell. Since each has a strong surreal component, each provides a different perspective on mental illness, violence, and psychosis. *Mars's Canal* uses no sound, with the exception of static, and creates intentional defects in the visual image. The viewer sees surrealist images of a naked man along a landscape, violence with a naked woman, and darkness slowly creeping over a character's face (e.g., to show the slow deterioration that is often associated with mental illness). This segment ends with a quote from Rampo: "Reality is seen in dreams. What you dream at night is real." Another character portraying a link between psychosis and violence is the thief in *The Cook, the Thief, His Wife & Her Lover* (1989).

An Angel at My Table (1990), Jane Campion's film biography of New Zealand writer Janet Frame,

is a compelling story of misdiagnosis and malpractice. Frame, an awkward, anxious, and socially inept adolescent, is misdiagnosed as having schizophrenia after an apparent panic attack and winds up receiving shock treatment and being hospitalized for 8 years. She narrowly avoids receiving a frontal lobotomy, a popular treatment at the time.

Crimson Gold (2003, Iran) illustrates themes of classism, highlighting the distance and tension between the wealthy and the poor in modern-day Iran. Hussein is a taciturn pizza delivery man who delivers pizza to both rich and poor; however, when he is treated poorly and rejected – both when wearing a suit and tie and when dressed more casually – by a jewelry store manager, he explodes. It is interesting to note that the lead actor (in real life) has been diagnosed with schizophrenia; this is never mentioned or explicitly portrayed in the film, but it potentially helps account for the uncanny accuracy of the character's flat affect and distant behavior.

The disturbing film *Dogtooth* (2010, Greece) portrays a seemingly psychotic family. The husband and wife appear to share their psychosis (i.e., they have a "shared psychotic disorder"), and their odd beliefs have a dramatic impact on their three children. The various characters all exhibit absurd, shocking, psychopathic, incestuous, and odd behavior. The film begins with the children listening to an audiotape of someone teaching a foreign language, but the words are being taught incorrectly. The parents teach the incorrect meaning of words throughout the film (e.g., "pussy" is a "bright light" and "zombie" is "a small yellow flower"). The children then begin a "game" of endurance in which each puts his or her finger under hot water, and the last to pull away is the winner. The father then blindfolds a security guard and drives her to the family home to then engage in paid sex with his son (later in the film when the woman is killed, the father has his son fondle the son's two sisters to decide which one the son wants as a sexual partner). The father returns home from work in clothes he has deliberately tattered and colored with red food coloring and tells the family that a dangerous (domestic) cat in the neighborhood is attacking and killing people; the family then get on their knees and bark like dogs. One of the children, caught between reality and delusion, believes that to escape from the house she must extract a tooth (referred to as "the dogtooth"), and she smashes herself repeatedly in the face with a heavy barbell to extract the tooth. The film clearly depicts psychopathology as well as its impact on children and their development. Viewers who can handle the consistently dis-turbing behavior may learn something from this film; however, it is not recommended for classroom teaching.

Critical Thinking Questions

➤ Compare and contrast how *Canvas* (2006), *Spider* (2002), and *Lars and the Real Girl* (2007) treat the impact of illness on families.

➤ Consider a quote from John Nash in *A Beautiful Mind* (2001): "She never gets old. Marcee can't be real. She never gets old." How common is this kind of insight for a person with a schizophrenia spectrum disorder?

➤ In *A Beautiful Mind*, John Nash explains that he won't talk back to his visual hallucinations so as to not feed them and keep them alive. How effective is this approach for most people with schizophrenia?

➤ Do familial environment and parental role contribute to development of mental illness in a child? How?

➤ Do films such as *Clean, Shaven* (1993), *Shine* (1996), and *David and Lisa* (1962) do a disservice to parents by blaming them for what is essentially a biological disorder over which they have no control?

➤ Films such as *Shine*, *David and Lisa*, and *Benny & Joon* (1993) all suggest that love can at least partially offset the deleterious effects of a disease such as schizophrenia. Is there any evidence suggesting this is true?

➤ In one memorable scene in the film *Clean, Shaven*, Peter Winter is in the library, hitting his head against the stacks. If you had been present, would you have ignored the behavior or tried to intervene and help in some way?

➤ John Nash in *A Beautiful Mind* is a genius, Prot in *K-Pax* has many savant-like qualities, and Peter Winter in *Clean, Shaven* graduated "in the top 5 percent of his high school class." Is there any relationship between schizophrenia, psychosis, and intelligence? Are extremely bright people more or less likely to develop such a disorder?

➤ What other films can you think of that present good and bad portrayals of schizophrenia or delusional disorder?

Authors' Picks

If you have time to read just one book relevant to this chapter, make it:

 Chase, R. (2013). *Schizophrenia: A brother finds answers in biological science*. Baltimore, MD: Johns Hopkins University Press.

If you only have time for one article, read:

 Owen, P. R. (2012). Portrayals of schizophrenia by entertainment media: A content analysis contemporary movies. *Psychiatric Services, 63*(7), 655–659.

Wedding and Niemiec's Top 10 Schizophrenia Spectrum and Other Psychotic Disorders Films

☐ *A Beautiful Mind* (2001)
☐ *Clean, Shaven* (1993)
☐ *The Soloist* (2009)
☐ *Shine* (1996)
☐ *Take Shelter* (2011)
☐ *Spider* (2002)
☐ *Revolution #9* (2001)
☐ *Canvas* (2006)
☐ *Lars and the Real Girl* (2007)
☐ *He Loves Me, He Loves Me Not* (2002, France)

Chapter 4

Bipolar and Depressive Disorders

We reach a point where, in order to go on, we have to wipe the slate clean. We start to see ourselves as a box that we're trapped inside and no matter how we try and escape, self-help, therapy, drugs, we just sink further and further down. The only way to truly break out of the box is to get rid of it all together … Starting over isn't crazy. Crazy is being miserable and walking around half asleep, numb, day after day after day. Crazy is pretending to be happy. Pretending that the way things are is the way they have to be for the rest of your bleeding life. All the potential, hope, all that joy, feeling, all that passion that life has sucked out of you. Reach out, grab a hold of it and snatch it back from that bloodsucking rabble.

Walter Black in *The Beaver* (2011)

➤ How does this film demonstrate the genetics and heritability of depressive disorders?

➤ We see Walter Black attempting suicide several times – and failing. Were these merely half-hearted attempts? Are suicidal people usually ambivalent about their decision to commit suicide?

➤ Walter Black becomes quite drunk before he attempts to hang himself. How common is it for depression to be complicated by alcoholism or substance abuse?

➤ Would electroshock therapy have been helpful in this case?

➤ Does this patient meet *DSM-5* criteria for a delusional disorder?

➤ If you were treating Walter Black, would you encourage him to give up his puppet and deal with his depression in a more straightforward and traditional way?

➤ Is there any significance in the screenwriter's decision to name the film's protagonist Walter Black?

Patient Evaluation

Name: Walter Black

Patient's stated reason for coming
"My wife insisted I come, Mate, although the Beaver and I have been making quite a good go of it on our own, and I'm not at all sure I need to see a doctor."

History of the present illness
Walter Black has been profoundly depressed for the past year. He reports weight loss of approximately 20 pounds, marked insomnia with frequent early morning risings, extreme fatigue, significant anhedonia, psychomotor retardation, difficulty with concentration, and loss of libido. He made two suicide attempts in a hotel room after his wife asked for a divorce, insisting he move out of the family home; both attempts were unsuccessful, in part because he was significantly intoxicated at the time he attempted to kill himself. There is no history of mania; however, approximately 2 months ago this patient stopped talking in his own voice and adopted an alter ego, a beaver hand puppet, and Mr. Black now refuses to communicate except when speaking through the puppet. In spite of this bizarre behavior – or perhaps because of it – Mr. Black's symptoms have significantly abated, and he has returned to work. However, his family and coworkers remain concerned about behavior that is eccentric at best and, at worst, psychotic.

Past psychiatric illness, treatment, and outcome
There is no significant history of psychopathology. Mr. Black had a normal childhood, and he had never received psychological or psychiatric services before the current period of depression. However, his father committed suicide when Black was a teenager, and his oldest son has seen a psychologist off and on for the past 3 years for depression and self-harm (head banging during periods of stress).

Medical history
Unremarkable.

Psychosocial history
Mr. Black was born in Australia to successful parents. He was the sixth of 11 children. He reports a happy childhood that he shared with his brother and parents until the time of his father's suicide. He is a well-educated individual who earned an undergraduate degree from St. Leo's Catholic College in New South Wales. This patient is now a CEO of a large but struggling toy company; it appears that the company's recent fiscal difficulties are directly related to Black's passivity, low energy levels, and lack of interest in the business. Interestingly, Mr. Black had previously acquired an American accent, and his Australian accent was hardly noticeable; however, it is present in the persona of his doppelgänger, the Beaver.

Drug and alcohol history

Mr. Black denies significant drug or alcohol use or abuse prior to the onset of his depression. He would drink beer on the weekends and occasionally when returning from work. However, he began to drink heavily, primarily vodka, after the onset of depressive symptoms approximately 1 year ago.

Behavioral observations

This patient arrived on time for the evaluation. He was unshaven and unkempt. He maintains that he only scheduled the appointment to placate his wife who accompanied him for the appointment. Mr. Black was cooperative; however, he refused to answer questions in his own voice. Instead, he communicated only through the talking Beaver puppet he brought with him to the examination. The Beaver would frequently laugh and joke during the evaluation.

Mental status examination

Mr. Black was oriented to person, place, time, and situation. The Folstein Mini-Mental State Examination was administered, and he scored 30 out of 30. This patient is exceptionally intelligent, and appeared to be amused by the simple questions he was asked as part of the mental status examination.

Functional assessment

Mr. Black has a clear history of a major depressive disorder; however, he has made considerable gains over the past 2 months, and these gains appear to be directly related to the adoption of a hand puppet as a separate and distinct identity, one which navigates the environment with considerable skill and far more success than that seen in Mr. Black's recent behavior when he was suffering from depression.

Strengths

Mr. Black is a highly intelligent individual with multiple strengths. He is handsome, educated, articulate, and socially skilled. He possesses a wry sense of humor and appeared to be at ease throughout the evaluation. Of course, his decision to communicate solely through a hand puppet significantly interferes with his ability to appear to be a normal human being. His results on the VIA Survey, a measure of strengths of character, reveal his highest character strengths are perseverance, love, hope, humility, and creativity.

Diagnosis

Major depressive disorder with mood-incongruent psychotic features, severe, in partial remission (F33.3). Rule out bipolar disorder, delusional disorder, and alcohol use disorder.

Treatment plan

(1) Weekly psychotherapy aimed at insight regarding the role and purpose of the hand puppet. (2) Neurological consultation. (3) Referral for marital therapy.

Prognosis

Guarded.

The Beaver (2011)

Jodi Foster directed *The Beaver*, and she costars with Mel Gibson, playing a generally supportive wife who has reached her wits end with her profoundly depressed husband (Gibson, playing the role of Walter Black). She kicks him out of the house, and he goes to a hotel where he becomes quite drunk and makes two suicide attempts; one attempt involves hanging himself from a shower curtain rod, and the other involves an attempt to jump from the balcony of his hotel. Both attempts fail, in part because of his profound intoxication. Walter has been able to maintain a positive relationship with his youngest son, but his older adolescent son is quite estranged and hostile toward his father. Walter stops going to therapy and adopts a radical treatment plan for his depression: He stops speaking for himself and only communicates with others through a hand puppet (the Beaver ; see

Figure 5. *The Beaver* (2011, Summit Entertainment, Participant Media, et al.) Produced by Steve Golin, Keith Redmon, and Ann Ruark. Directed by Jodie Foster.

Figure 5). The puppet has a different accent, a keen sense of humor, and it is decidedly upbeat and optimistic. The puppet berates Black for his depression and his low energy; with encouragement from this **alter ego,** presumably representing that part of Black that wanted to get well, the protagonist proceeds to put his life back together. However, in a dramatic and surprising ending to the film, Black literally severs his relationship with the Beaver by cutting off his arm with a buzz saw, finally realizing that he has always had the internal resources necessary for him to overcome his illness.

Depressive and Bipolar Disorders

Periods of depression are normal in most persons' lives. For example, failing an examination or the ending of a relationship often precipitates a predictable period of sadness. In addition, the feelings of high energy that accompany major events such as a graduation or marriage are also common in every-

day life. However, some illnesses involve affective states that resemble these normal periods of depression or elation, but in fact they are very different. The individual experiencing a mood disorder is consumed by negative emotions and is unable to alleviate them through normal coping mechanisms. These illnesses are characterized by emotions that are so intense they begin to dominate a person's life. Mood disorders include many different cognitive, emotional, and behavioral manifestations, but the overriding symptoms of all mood disorders are *emotional* in nature. The *DSM-5* categorizes types of mood disorders in separate chapters, specifically as **bipolar and related disorders** (bipolar I, bipolar II, or cyclothymic) or as **depressive disorders** (disruptive mood dysregulation disorder, major depressive disorder, persistent depressive disorder [dysthymia], and premenstrual dysphoric disorder). As with almost all *DSM-5* diagnoses, there are also diagnoses provided in both categories for substance/medication-induced, due to another medical condition, and other specified and unspecified disorders. Sadness, irritability, and somatic/cognitive changes that impact functioning are common features of both bipolar and depressive disorders; however, these categories of disorders differ from one another by duration, timing, and etiology.

Depressive Disorders

Depressive disorders, one of the most common types of mental disorders, occur in approximately one in 10 adults in the United States. Most surveys show that depression is two to three times more prevalent in women. There is a relationship between depressive disorders and social class, and depressive symptoms are more common in individuals with fewer economic advantages.

A **major depressive disorder** is associated with depressed mood and a loss of interest or pleasure in daily activities. Sleep, eating habits, appetite, concentration, motivation, self-esteem, and energy level are the areas most often affected. An episode can range from mild (few symptoms) to severe, and in some instances major depressive episodes can be accompanied by delusions and hallucinations. Some people experience a **masked depression** in which they unconsciously mask their depression and experience physical aches and pains rather than traditional depressive symptoms. These physical manifestations of depression are often misdiagnosed as physical illnesses. Others experience an **agitated depression** where frustration and anger seem to dominate and cover up depressive symptoms. If chronically depressed moods, low self-esteem, and feelings of pessimism, despair, or hopelessness are present for 2 years without suicidal thoughts or limitations in functioning, the diagnosis of **persistent depressive disorder** is made. (This condition is still widely diagnosed as **dysthymia**.) While the diagnosis of major depressive disorder requires symptoms that last for at least a 2-week period, the diagnosis of persistent depressive disorder requires a history of depressed mood that has lasted for at least 2 years.

Excellent portrayals of depression can be found in *Mind the Gap* (2004) and *Shopgirl* (2005). The first film interweaves several vignettes of characters honestly and earnestly struggling to change their lives. In one vignette, an African American man is clearly depressed, with considerable evidence of suppressed anger. He sits around watching television all day in his lonely apartment. He is riddled with guilt for having cheated on his wife and abandoned his son. He purchases a shotgun at a store and writes a suicide note telling his son that the son is not to blame. However, before pulling the trigger, he consults a priest who gives him some wise advice on the distinction between saying "I'm sorry" and asking "Will you forgive me?"; the man then travels to speak face-to-face with both his ex-wife and his son to ask for their forgiveness in two powerful scenes. *Shopgirl*, based on actor/screenwriter Steve Martin's novella, is another film that offers a realistic, nonstereotyped portrayal of depression. In this film, a young, isolated, depressed woman, Mirabelle, falls in love with an older man; the film uses muted colors and positions Mirabelle's work station in a way that highlights her isolation from the other workers.

In *American Splendor* (2003), comic strip writer Harvey Pekar (Paul Giamatti) displays the symptoms and behaviors associated with persistent depressive disorder. His dysthymia is expressed through agitation and negativity, and he kicks and breaks objects and sees life through a very pessimistic filter, frequently describing himself as "a nobody." He has a chronically furrowed brow that emphasizes his agitated affect and frustrated view of the world.

Harvey has few social skills; he is socially distant, unfriendly, and awkward, and acts inappropriately and has poor eye contact. Despite success with his comic books, he remains cynical and pessimistic; this theme is emphasized when he repeatedly appears on the David Letterman Show and comes across as a defensive misanthrope. Harvey denies having any sense of spirituality. He is lonely and makes a quick decision to marry after one meeting with a woman who travels from out of state to visit him; to the viewer, it seems obvious that these are two lonely people covering up their pain. Nevertheless, Harvey seems to have found a good match in his wife (Hope Davis) who also has a dysthymic quality; she is easily agitated, highly somatic, pessimistic, and suffers from hypersomnia.

Various coping strategies are exhibited in the film. When diagnosed with cancer, Harvey explores creative expression of the disease through comics. Responding in a less healthy way, Harvey exhibits characteristics of **hoarding disorder**: His home is dirty and cluttered; there are stacks of comic books everywhere; and he regularly goes to thrift stores and garage sales to acquire more "stuff."

In the emotionally intense *Monster's Ball* (2001), Hank (Billy Bob Thornton) and Leticia (Academy

Award winner Halle Berry) are two lost, self-hating people who become even more lonely and raw after each loses an only child – Hank's son commits suicide in front of him, and Leticia's son is hit by a car. Both parents had been physically and verbally abusive to their sons as they attempted to work through their inner turmoil and struggles. The film emphasizes how both characters are trying to escape from their internal hell; in some ways, the prison in which Hank works is a metaphor for their inner pain, loneliness, isolation, and futility. Hank quits his job at the prison, where he works with death row inmates, realizing the emotional toll his job has taken on his personal life. A relationship between the racist Hank and the beautiful Black woman Leticia begins following an act of kindness by Hank when he aids a screaming Leticia he finds on the side of the road; he explains that he just felt like "doing the right thing" and that he is trying to get "outside of his insides." After becoming drunk, Hank and Leticia engage in raw, uninhibited sex "just to feel." Both are emotionally numb and overwhelmed by their personal pain; scenes of the two lovers interacting are juxtaposed with flashes of human hands reaching into a "cage" to release a bird desperately flapping its wings. Through their connection, which becomes more intimate and genuine over time, both characters find meaningful, expressive outlets for their depression for the first time.

The Cooler (2003) is about Bernie (William H. Macy), an "unlucky" man, who works for a traditional, antisocial casino boss (Alec Baldwin). Bernie's job is walking around successful casino patrons to bring them bad luck. Bernie is "the cooler" because he turns winners into losers; his appearance at a table is enough to make a winning gambler quickly go bankrupt. He claims he can do this easily; "I just be myself." He is stuck in the past and trapped by it, unable to move on, since he is forced to use his "bad luck" to pay off his extensive gambling debt or be killed by the casino boss. When we look deeper beyond the plot, the viewers see that Bernie's personality is very self-critical, self-defeating, and negativistic. His "unlucky" quality is a self-fulfilling prophecy. He is isolated, lives alone, and is too passive to take action to change his life.

This film presents a classic **depressive triad**: The protagonist is hapless (unlucky), hopeless, and helpless. A cognitive therapy approach emphasizing the impact of one's thoughts, beliefs, and attitudes as affecting mood states is highlighted. Upon falling

in love, Bernie's luck changes, he becomes assertive, and his presence at casino tables enhances the success of others. The power of attitude is an overriding theme in the film, and we see Bernie's negative attitudes keeping him from love and luck, while positive attitudes bring him good luck and success.

In many ways, the story is clichéd – the fight for love to the death, escape from a tyrannical boss, and tremendous luck in the end save the heroes from their seemingly inevitable demise.

In *Scent of a Woman* (1992), Lieutenant Colonel Frank Slade exhibits many of the classic symptoms of a major depressive disorder and clearly would qualify for the diagnosis. He has both a depressed mood and a loss of interest and pleasure in everyday activities (**anhedonia**). Slade's angry comment "I have no life, I'm in the dark" clearly suggests his depression is related to his blindness, and the sentence captures the lack of meaning and purpose in his life. His daily activities, sitting alone and drinking himself into oblivion when he is not tormenting his 4-year-old niece, are clear indications of his loss of interest in life. It is a useful pedagogical exercise to list the numerous risk factors for suicide present in the character of Frank Slade.

Some people who are depressed are not pleasant, and can be quite difficult to be around. They are often agitated and easily angered. This serves to hide their underlying need for help. Colonel Slade is irritable, intimidating, and verbally abusive to anyone who approaches him. Expression of this type of anger and abuse has a distancing effect on

---

Additional Questions for Discussion
(*Scent of a Woman*)

➤ Will the use of alcohol alleviate depression?
➤ The Colonel decides to shoot himself while in uniform. Would his previous military experience increase the likelihood that Slade would actually kill himself?
➤ Does the likelihood of suicide increase because Slade is blind?
➤ Who should determine if a decision about suicide reflects an accurate appraisal of life and its likely rewards? Who is qualified to determine if a decision to commit suicide is the consequence of a disease such as depression?
➤ Should people who are believed to be at risk for suicide be involuntarily hospitalized?

others, who naturally withdraw from unpleasant situations. Charles Simms, a college student hired to accompany the Colonel on a trip, does not want to stay with Slade after meeting him, and Simms dreads the weekend he is forced to spend with the Colonel.

Another interesting film depicting depression is the 1971 Academy Award winning film *The Hospital* starring George C. Scott as Herbert Bock, a middle-aged, depressed, suicidal physician who is trying to cope with the mayhem of a crowded and disorganized institution, where negligence and confusion result in a series of deaths. Bock's personal life is as chaotic as the hospital he runs. He is recently divorced, alienated from his children, and suffering from both personal and sexual impotence. He had been believed to be a medical genius in his early career; however, at the point we are introduced to him in the film, he is washed up and discouraged. At one point in the film, Bock is seen sitting in his office, preparing to inject a fatal dose of potassium. He exclaims: "I've lost my reason for being ... my purpose!" and later when he is upset and drinking: "People are sicker than ever. We cure nothing. We heal nothing."

Bock demonstrates the classical symptoms of a major depressive disorder. His depressed mood is expressed through his explosive angry episodes and chronic irritability. He is anhedonic and expresses little interest in his patients, his profession, or any of the activities of daily living through which most of us find meaning and purpose. Bock cannot sleep, he feels worthless, and he is plagued by recurrent thoughts of suicide. Dr. Bock's behavior is remarkably similar to that of Lt. Colonel Slade – it is similar because both men are clinically depressed.

Marlon Brando plays a depressed man trying to come to grips with the meaning of his wife's suicide in Bernado Bertolucci's powerful film *Last Tango in Paris* (1972). The character of the coach's wife in Peter Bogdanovich's *The Last Picture Show* (1971) is clearly depressed, and her affect and behavior offer good teaching examples of depressed affect for students learning how to give a mental status examination. The despair that overcomes a man when he is abandoned by his wife is presented in the Australian film *My First Wife* (1984). Finally, Joanne Woodward gives a memorable performance as a depressed housewife in *Summer Wishes, Winter Dreams* (1973).

We highly recommend *Prozac Nation* (2001) as a film that illustrates the devastation caused by depression in a gifted but deeply troubled Harvard freshman (Lizzie) played by Christina Ricci. The film presents a compelling portrayal of Lizzie's slow descent into depression, and Lizzie provides an insightful description of her illness: "Hemingway has this classic moment in *The Sun Also Rises* when someone asks Mike Campbell how he went bankrupt. All he can say is, 'gradually, then suddenly.' That's how depression hits. You wake up one morning afraid that you're going to live." Lizzie knows she needs medication, but she also knows that it is not sufficient to solve her myriad personal problems. At one point she states, "I call this the crack-house where I come to score. Dr. Sterling is my dealer. Seems like everyone's doctor is dealing this stuff now. Sometimes it feels like we're all living in a Prozac nation."

"If only my life could be more like the movies. I want an angel to swoop down to me like he does to Jimmy Stewart in *It's a Wonderful Life* and talk me out of suicide. I've always waited for that one moment of truth to set me free and change my life forever. But he won't come. It doesn't happen that way."

Lizzie in *Prozac Nation* (2001)

The Visitor (2007), directed by Tom McCarthy, is a sensitive portrayal of the human suffering associated with social isolation and with the restrictive immigration policies in the United States. The film stars Richard Jenkins as a depressed and ineffectual college professor who has never recovered from the death of his wife. Jenkins' character, Prof. Walter Vale, makes a half-hearted attempt to learn to play the piano, but lacks the energy, passion, and talent necessary to succeed at this task. Watching Vale interact with his colleagues and students reminds the viewer of Hamlet's lament, "O God, O God, how weary, stale, flat, and unprofitable seem to me all the uses of this world!" Vale's life has become weary, stale, flat, and unprofitable, and he finds meaning, purpose and some degree of contentment only when he stops contemplating his own unhappiness and becomes invested in helping a pair of undocumented workers he finds living in his infrequently used New York City apartment. Walter's transition from a staid, discouraged, and unhappy college professor to someone genuinely interested in life and in others is symbolized by the transition from his desultory attempt to learn to play classical music on the piano to his enthusiasm for the *djembe* (an African drum that he passionately plays in the subway in the film's final moments). The film illustrates both persistent depressive disorder and burnout, and it is a convincing demonstration of the therapeutic truism that one helps oneself most by learning to reach out and help others.

To address the overdiagnosis of bipolar disorder in children, **disruptive mood dysregulation disorder** was added as a new depressive disorder category for *DSM-IV*. This label is applied to individuals who display severe temper outbursts behaviorally and/or verbally that are inconsistent with their developmental level and accompanied by persistent irritable or angry mood. It is recommended that this diagnosis be restricted to ages 7–18, those ages in which validity for the condition have been established. This condition is a tricky one to diagnose in films; to make the diagnosis one must have enough information to differentiate the condition from conduct disorder, oppositional defiant disorder, bipolar disorders, and impulse control disorders.

Hyler (1988) has pointed out that many of the characters who appear depressed in films would meet the *DSM-IV* criteria for **adjustment disorder with depressed mood** rather than major depression. The examples Hyler cites include Jimmy Stewart's character in Frank Capra's *It's a Wonderful Life* (1946) and Henry Fonda's character in *The Wrong Man* (1956). In the latter film, Fonda becomes depressed after he is unjustly accused of murder.

Bereavement-related depression is a controversial condition due to the difficulty inherent in defining what a normal bereavement period should be. The *DSM-5* lists it both as a disorder needing further study and as a condition that can be diagnosed in the trauma- and stressor-related disorders category (the actual label is **persistent complex bereavement disorder** and is coded as an "other specified trauma- and stressor-related disorder). We discuss this further in Chapter 6.

Bipolar and Related Disorders

Bipolar disorder occurs less frequently than depressive disorders but affects approximately 0.6% of the US population. Prevalence rates for bipolar disorder tend to be somewhat lower in other countries, but it is unclear if this reflects true differences in incidence or simply differences in diagnostic patterns and training for psychiatrists and other mental health professionals.

Unlike depression, bipolar disorders occur approximately equally often among men and women. Like most mental disorders, the prevalence is greater in lower socioeconomic groups, in part because these illnesses interfere with a person's ability to work, and in part because the cost of the illnesses quickly depletes the economic resources of all but the very wealthy. Even wealthy clients can quickly become impoverished, however, because of the poor judgment and spending sprees often associated with manic episodes.

A **manic episode** is a distinct period of an abnormally and persistently elevated, expansive, or irritable mood, lasting at least 1 week, during which the mood disturbance causes marked impairment of work or functioning. The manic episode may range from mild to severe and may be accompanied by psychotic features. During manic episodes, people develop exaggerated sense of self-esteem, decreased need for sleep, and increased energy levels. These individuals often display a flights of ideas (jumping rapidly from one thought to another) and speak very speak rapidly.

A **hypomanic episode** results in a period of sustained elevated mood, lasting at least 4 days. This change is obvious to others and alters a person's level of functioning. However, by definition, a hypomanic episode is *not* severe enough to impair work or social functioning.

People with bipolar illnesses are often very likable. Their basic personality is usually outgoing, and they often work in people-intensive occupations such as sales. During a manic episode, they feel good about themselves, and their moods are contagious. They are often very generous and may buy strangers expensive gifts. Judgment is typically very poor during a manic episode, and these individuals may gamble away their life savings or spend money they cannot afford to lose on an expensive vacation. They often have multiple sexual partners during their manic episodes. They also seem to have endless physical energy, appear to function perfectly well without sleep, usually eat very little, and may lose 30 or 40 pounds within a few weeks. The potential for physical exhaustion during a manic episode is very real, and the long-term consequences of a manic episode can be devastating for families. For example, it may take years to pay back a debt or forgive infidelities.

Bipolar I illnesses are diagnosed when a person has *both* manic and depressive episodes and cycles from one to another. The depressive episode may last 3–6 months before the person swings to a manic phase. The diagnosis of **bipolar II** disorder is reserved for those who have primarily depressive episodes, with occasional hypomania. These patients do not have full-blown manic episodes. **Cyclothymic disorders** are found in individuals who never experience a major depressive or manic episode but who have had hypomanic and depressive symptoms that persisted for at least 2 years.

Silver Linings Playbook

Silver Linings Playbook (2012) is one of the most recent films to depict bipolar I disorder. It was nominated for numerous Academy Awards, and Jennifer Lawrence won the Academy Award and a Golden Globe Award for Best Performance by an Actress in a Leading Role for her portrayal of Tiffany, a distraught widow who deals with her grief

---

Tiffany: "What meds are you on?"
Pat: "None. I used to be on Lithium and Seroquel and Abilify, but they make me foggy, and they also make me bloated."
Tiffany: "Yeah. I was on Xanax and Effexor. I wasn't as sharp."
Pat: "You ever take Klonopin?" Tiffany: "Klonopin, yeah ..."
Pat: "What day is it? How about Trazodone?"
Tiffany: "Trazodone?"
Pat: "It flattens you out. I mean you are done. It takes the life right out of your eyes."

Pat and Tiffany compare notes
of their reactions to several
psychiatric medications in
Silver Linings Playbook (2012)

Figure 6. *Silver Linings Playbook* (2012, Weinstein Company). Produced by Bruce Cohen, Donna Gigliotti, and Gordon). Directed by David O. Russell.

by indiscriminate sex with strangers and with all of her male coworkers. Bradley Cooper plays Pat, an unemployed high school teacher who has just been released from a psychiatric hospital where he spent 8 months after discovering his wife in the shower with another man, subsequently beating the man almost to death. Pat hopes to become reunited with his wife, but she has a restraining order in place and clearly no longer wants him in her life. There is clear sexual chemistry between Pat and Tiffany, and this leaves other family members feeling uncomfortable and tense in their presence (Figure 6).

Pat is clearly still manic after his release from the hospital. In one scene he becomes visibly disturbed by what he perceives to be an unsatisfactory ending of Ernest Hemingway's *A Farewell to Arms*. He throws the book through the window, shattering the pane, and then bursts into his parents' bedroom at 4:00 a.m. to share his disappointment with the way the book ends. This is a realistic portrayal of the way someone with bipolar I disorder might act. Unfortunately, the film only shows Pat behaving normally or in a manic phase, and the profound depression that accompanies bipolar I is never shown in the film. However, the film does illustrate the importance of peer and family support for someone coping with this disorder, and the film ends with an optimistic message about the possibility of recovery.

Mr. Jones

Alan Greisman and Debra Greenfield's 1993 film *Mr. Jones* is about a musician, Mr. Jones, played by Richard Gere, and his psychiatrist, Dr. Libbie Bowen, played by Lena Olin. *Mr. Jones* is a clear-cut illustration of bipolar I disorder. The film portrays Jones as elated, seductive, and euphoric. He is a charismatic man with tremendous personal charm. He persuades a contractor to hire him, proceeds to the roof, and prepares to fly after rhythmically pounding a few nails into the roof. Before climbing to the front of the roof, he insists that Howard, his newfound friend, accept a $100 bill. After realizing that Jones really believes that he can fly, Howard persuades him to move away from the beam where he is teetering. An ambulance arrives and takes Jones to a local psychiatric emergency unit, where he is released after a few hours. At the hospital, he

is misdiagnosed and given inappropriate medications.

Mr. Jones: "I'd like to close my account, please."

Susan: "You just opened this account last week."

Mr. Jones: "Yeah, I'm a fickle kind of guy."

Susan: "Oh, my goodness."

Susan: "Okay, you have $12,752 in your account. Do you want that in hundreds?"

Mr. Jones: "I'll leave that up to your impeccable judgment."

Richard Gere's character displaying the poor judgment characteristic of bipolar I disorder in *Mr. Jones* (1993)

Next, Jones goes to a bank and withdraws over $12,000; he seduces the teller in the process, and then goes on a spending spree. He purchases a baby grand piano, checks into an expensive hotel, and then attends a concert. He is arrested and returned to the hospital after he disrupts the symphony by attempting to take over for the conductor as the orchestra is playing Beethoven's "Ode to Joy" – Jones is convinced that Beethoven would have wanted the piece played at a much faster tempo. Jones is once again hospitalized in a state of manic exhaustion, but this time he is accurately diagnosed and treated by psychiatrist Elizabeth (Libbie) Bowen.

Jones knows he has a bipolar disorder. He was first diagnosed in late adolescence and had several hospitalizations. However, he refuses to take his medication because it makes his hands shake. It is during the "highs" or the manic phases that he feels best about himself. The rest of the time Jones is lonely and depressed. His lows are life threatening and result in several suicide attempts. The viewer is able to gain some insight into the impact of a mental illness on the promising career of a classical musician. In addition, the film illustrates the ways in which interpersonal relationships are affected by a condition such as bipolar disorder. Jones's one important prior relationship ended when a woman he loved could no longer deal with his mood swings.

Unfortunately, the rest of the movie involves the romantic relationship that develops between Dr. Bowen and Jones. Even though Dr. Bowen resigns from the hospital, underscoring the unethical nature of this doctor–patient relationship, the true impact of the psychiatrist's behavior is never addressed in the movie.

| 💬 | **Additional Questions for Discussion (*Mr. Jones*)** |

➤ Why does Dr. Elizabeth Bowen question the resident's admitting diagnosis of paranoid schizophrenia?

➤ At what point is the doctor-patient relationship first compromised? Are there early warning signs that should have alerted the psychiatrist to her countertransference to this patient?

➤ Does Jones's history of a previous suicide attempt increase the likelihood of another attempt?

➤ Is an affair between a doctor and a patient more serious than one between an orderly and a patient?

➤ Would it have mattered if the patient had been discharged? Why?

➤ Is it ethical for a psychiatrist to visit a university to get historical information that may be relevant to a patient she is treating? Should school officials release the information?

➤ Should patients with illnesses such as bipolar disorder be required by the courts to take medication, even if they dislike the effects of the medication and find it dampens their creativity?

Other Films Depicting Bipolar Disorder

Some films describe characters with bipolar disorder but do not show them as symptomatic. In *The Last Days of Disco* (1998), for example, one character is stereotyped as "looney" and "crazy"; however, he is also depicted as compliant with lithium, and shown to be stable, kind, and balanced. *Garden State* (2004) also depicts a patient diagnosed with bipolar disorder. However, this patient becomes noncompliant with his medication and finds that his life improves dramatically when he is not taking lithium, and there is no apparent exacerbation of his bipolar symptoms. While **drug holidays** might be recommended by physicians on occasion, films of this sort mislead the public and suggest that these important decisions can be made without medical consultation. Matt Da-

mon's character in *The Informant* (2009), a Steven Soderbergh film, is diagnosed with bipolar disorder, and he receives hospitalization and medication; his symptoms at least partially explain his illegal behavior and the web of lies that spiral out of control.

One of the best films depicting a bipolar illness is *Call Me Anna*, a 1990 made-for-TV movie starring Patty Duke, who plays herself in this adaptation of her best-selling autobiography. The film traces her career and her battle with a bipolar disorder and vividly portrays her mood swings and the accompanying personality changes she experienced. In real life, Patty Duke has become a vocal advocate for persons with mental illness.

Gena Rowlands plays a woman who appears to have a bipolar I disorder in the John Cassavetes film *A Woman Under the Influence* (1974). She is quite convincing during a manic episode, and there is a memorable scene in which a neighbor stops by to drop off his children and then decides that it is not safe to leave them with Rowlands. He does not know exactly what is wrong, but it is clear to him that *something* is not right. Unlike *Mr. Jones*, the actual diagnosis is never specified in *A Woman Under the Influence*, despite the fact that Rowlands character spends 6 months in a psychiatric hospital.

Another example of an apparent bipolar disorder is found in the Harrison Ford character in *Mosquito Coast* (1986), although that character's eccentric habits and obsessional style are probably adequate to support multiple diagnoses. In addition, the biographical film *Mommie Dearest* (1981) suggests that Joan Crawford had a bipolar disorder.

Examples of the type of rapid speech, quick thinking, and impulsive behavior associated with a hypomanic episode can be seen in the college president character played by Groucho Marx in *Horse Feathers* (1932) and in *Good Morning, Vietnam* (1987), a film in which Robin Williams plays an Air Force disc jockey with a rapid and clever repartee that endears him to his military audience.

Blue Sky (1994) stars Jessica Lange and Tommy Lee Jones. Lange, who won an Academy Award for her role in this film, plays the role of Carly Marshall, a woman whose bipolar disorder (diagnosed with the then appropriate term *manic-depressive disorder*) gets her family in considerable trouble. She sunbathes topless and acts out sexually, and the film illustrates the profound effects of a disease like bipolar disorder on families.

> "You take water, for example. Sometimes it's water, sometimes it's ice. Sometimes it's steam, sometimes vapor. It's always the same old H$_2$O. It only changes its properties. Your mother's like that. She's like water."
>
> Henry Marshall (Tommy Lee Jones) tries to explain their mother's erratic behavior to his children in *Blue Sky* (1994)

Two other films that have presented fairly accurate portrayals of bipolar I disorder are *Running with Scissors* (2006) and *Michael Clayton* (2007). In the first film, Annette Bening plays the role of a bipolar mother who turns over her son's life to her psychiatrist; in the second film, Tom Wilkinson portrays a senior attorney in a large law firm who becomes manic. Wilkinson's character displays inappropriate behavior (e.g., stripping in court), pressured speech, and grandiose thinking. His illness is controlled by medication, but he becomes quite ill when he stops taking his lithium, and the film illustrates the critical importance of adherence to medication regimens for anyone with this disorder.

In the poetic, experimental film *Crooked Beauty: Navigating the Space Between Beauty and Madness* (2010), director Ken Paul Rosenthal weaves photographic images and the mercurial weather patterns of the San Francisco Bay area with voice-over storytelling and artwork by activist–artist Jacks Ashley McNamara, a woman who suffers from a severe mental illness. This short film is stunning as a positive psychology film, one that depicts psychological struggle and turmoil while simultaneously depicting resilience, creativity, humanity, and ultimately triumph (Niemiec & Wedding, 2014). In their *PsycCRITIQUES* review, Larry Leitner and Hideaki Imai (2011) cite studies that document that people with schizophrenia often can achieve better outcomes in treatment programs without medication. The pervasiveness of psychiatry and the medical model can sometimes lead to the alternative: "the client can be condemned to a lifetime of medication, many of which will shorten the client's lifespan by as much as 20 years." The film elicits important questions for psychologists about mental illness and its treatment. Here are some of those questions relevant to *Crooked Beauty*:

- What are the limitations of psychiatric treatment?
- Should people with severe mental illnesses be encouraged to try to live their lives without medication, or should medication always be the first treatment implemented?
- Many psychologists, such as Dean Simonton, have studied the relationship between creativity and mental illness. In the film, Jacks discusses this connection as it relates to her life and the importance of healing. How important is creativity in helping people with bipolar disorder cope with their condition? Can creativity be increased if the person with bipolar disorder is low in creativity?
- Which character strengths are most important for a person suffering from a mental illness like bipolar disorder? What will help them become more resilient and triumph over their suffering?
- Is it the character strengths of hope, wisdom, spirituality, perseverance, zest, kindness, humor, or self-regulation that make the critical difference, or is it some intricate combination of these strengths and others?

Theories of Mood Disorders

There are three main theoretical explanations associated with mood disorders: **Genetic theories**, which are useful in understanding familial tendencies; **Biological theories**, which explain the physiological changes and the rationale for pharmacotherapy and electroconvulsive therapy; and **psychological theories**, which support the use of psychotherapy and other psychological approaches to treatment. The environment and external events are an extremely important factors in the manifestation of mood disorders, e.g., loss of a job or a recent divorce.

Genetic Theories

Twin and adoption studies have documented that there is a genetic vulnerability to mood disorders. Bipolar disorder, in particular, has been shown to have a very high heritability estimate of 93% in identical twins (Kieseppa, Partonen, Haukka, Kaprio, & Lonnqvist, 2004).

When researchers compared the incidence of mood disorders in identical twins (who share the same genetic code) with that of fraternal twins (who have different genetic material), the concordance rate was 67% for the identical twins and 15% for fraternal twins. The high concordance for identical twins has also been found in twins who were raised in different environments. It is clear that there is a significant genetic component in mood disorders.

Biological Theories

The biological approach to mood disorders focuses on the activity of the neurotransmitters in the limbic system. The neurotransmitters involved include **dopamine**, **serotonin**, **acetylcholine**, and **norepinephrine**. In depression, it is believed that there are fewer available neurotransmitters in the synaptic junction; in contrast, in mania there is an excess.

The limbic system also regulates the pituitary hormone, a key element in the highly complex endocrine system. Changes in the endocrine system also influence mood. There have been many studies documenting the changes in the functioning of the pituitary gland and thyroid that occur with mood disorders. Some depressed persons have been found to secrete an excessive amount of cortisol, a hormone produced by the pituitary gland. Additionally, persistently low thyroid hormone levels have been noted in some cases of depression, and an elevated thyroid hormone level is present in some rapid cycling bipolar disorders.

Psychological Theories

Psychological theories have always played an important role in the understanding and treatment of mood disorders. While the depressive and bipolar disorders clearly have a biological basis, the psychodynamic conceptualization of these disorders provides a different way of understanding the behavioral and emotional problems associated with these conditions. Many of the psychological features of depression are readily apparent in films.

The early psychoanalysts (e.g., Sigmund Freud, Karl Abraham) noticed that people with depression

experienced **ambivalence** toward significant persons in their lives. That is, they often acted as if they loved and hated the same person. In *Scent of a Woman* (1992), Lt. Col. Slade is both affectionate and antagonistic toward his niece, brother, and other family members. He also becomes antagonistic and aggressive when Charlie Simms tries to help him.

Introjection, the unconscious "taking in" of qualities and values of another person or a group with whom emotional ties exist, was also identified as a characteristic feature of depression. In *Scent of a Woman*, Slade introjected the values of the military and continued to treat everyone as if they were subordinates who reported to him. Interestingly, Slade had been discharged from the military because of his overbearing behavior. Colonel Slade's difficulties in the Army were likely related to a long-standing history of untreated depression.

Regression, another characteristic of depression, refers to a return to an earlier pattern of behavior. During a depressive episode, childhood behavioral patterns may appear, and a person may act less mature. In *Scent of a Woman*, Slade's ongoing battle with a 4-year-old is not acceptable adult behavior for a retired colonel.

Denial, ignoring the existence of reality, is characteristic of persons experiencing a manic episode. These patients often stop taking their medication because they believe that there is nothing wrong with them. They reject any advice from family members and may become belligerent at any suggestion that they are ill. Jones had been hospitalized multiple times after he discontinued his medication in *Mr. Jones*, and he is smart enough to know it will happen again. However, each time, he convinces himself that this time will be different. This is a classic example of denial.

Cognitive behavior theorists have contributed significantly to the understanding of the experience of depression. Aaron Beck has described a **cognitive triad** that is common in these patients. The triad consists of (1) perceiving oneself as defective and inadequate, (2) perceiving the world as demanding and punishing, and (3) expecting failure, defeat, and hardship. These "automatic thoughts" are readily apparent in *American Splendor* (2003), *The Cooler* (2003), *Scent of a Woman* (1992), and *The Hospital* (1971), and in Julianne Moore's character in *The Hours* (2002).

Mood Disorders and Creativity

There is compelling evidence that mood disorders may be related to the creative process, and numerous artists, poets, and composers have been diagnosed as depressed or bipolar, or have biographies that suggest that these disorders were present. Dean Simonton, who has studied creativity and creative genius for over 35 years, notes that artists and those in professions involving skills that are subjective, intuitive, and emotive are more likely to have mental illness than those who are scientists or in professions using skills that are rational, logical, and formal (Ludwig, 1998; Simonton, 2009). Simonton adds that some creators are able to control their bizarre thoughts and use them productively. Similarly, Kay Redfield Jamison, a psychologist with bipolar disorder, notes that the periods of creativity in many individuals with this disorder typically happen during healthy periods in which the person draws upon the experiences that occurred in their manic, hypomanic, or depressed phase (Jamison, 1993). Two recent short documentaries discuss this link between psychopathology and art – *Between Madness and Art* (2007), which tells the story of Dr. Hans Prinzhorn, a man who collected hundreds of artistic creations by patients with mental illness, from various institutions, and *Hidden Gifts: The Story of Angus MacPhee* (2005), a film about a mute man with schizophrenia who made incredibly creative objects and clothes out of twigs and sticks.

Several actors and actresses have struggled with bipolar disorder, including Richard Dreyfuss, Patty Duke, Carrie Fisher, Linda Hamilton, Jean-Claude Van Damme, and Vivien Leigh. Examples of poets believed to have experienced mood disorders include William Blake, Ralph Waldo Emerson, Edgar Allan Poe, Lord Byron, Alfred Lord Tennyson, John Berryman, Sylvia Plath, Theodore Roethke, and Anne Sexton; examples of painters and composers with mood disorders include Vincent van Gogh, Georgia O'Keefe, and Robert Shuman (Jamison, 1993). Sylvia Plath's difficulties with depression are detailed in *Sylvia* (2003), the film adaptation of her semiautobiographical novel *The Bell Jar* (1979), in which Gwyneth Paltrow plays the title role. Novelist Virginia Woolf's mood disorder is portrayed in the highly recommended movie *The Hours* (2002). The troubled life of Beethoven is portrayed in the 1995 film *Immortal Beloved*. Vincent van Gogh's life, work, and mental illness (which may have been bipolar disorder) have been documented in the films *Vincent* (1987), *Vincent & Theo* (1990), and *Van Gogh* (1991). However, none of these match the artistic achievement established by the 1956 film *Lust for Life*, in which Kirk Douglas plays van Gogh and Anthony Quinn plays the supporting role of Paul Gauguin. The final days of influential Nirvana lead singer/guitarist, Kurt Cobain, are portrayed in Gus van Sant's *Last Days* (2005) and *Kurt Cobain: About a Son* (2006); Cobain had been diagnosed with bipolar disorder and committed suicide in 1994. Wedding (2000) provides examples of the cognitive distortions found in the poems of Anne Sexton; these particular distortions are common in depressed and suicidal people.

Shakespeare was fascinated by people who took their own lives, and his plays and their film adaptations provide a useful and fascinating way to approach the study of suicide. Major Shakespearean plays in which suicide is a prominent theme include *Romeo and Juliet*, *Julius Caesar*, *Hamlet*, *Anthony and Cleopatra*, *Macbeth*, *Othello*, and *King Lear*. There have been multiple film adaptations of each of these plays.

Creativity does not always have to come in the form of great art and writing – it can also present

Additional Questions About Creativity

➤ Are people with certain mental illnesses more creative than people without such disorders?

➤ How do you make sense of such a significant split between dramatic creativity and the complete chaos and disorder that often mark such individuals' lives? What are your own views on van Gogh? What behaviors support a diagnosis of bipolar disorder? What evidence suggests a seizure disorder may have been present? Are there any other competing hypotheses?

➤ If you had the power to cure someone like van Gogh, but you knew that the treatment would destroy his creativity, would you proceed?

➤ What other artists and writers have experienced mood disorders?

➤ Can you name other artists, writers, and poets who have committed suicide?

simply as creative thinking. This is known as **divergent thinking** – coming up with many ways to solve problems. In *Sherlock Holmes* (2009) and *Sherlock Holmes: A Game of Shadows* (2011), the character of Holmes may have a bipolar disorder as evidenced by episodes of depression and his intense, elevated mood periods. However, Holmes' character happens to be exemplary in divergent thinking.

Suicide

Suicide and Depression

Suicide is the eighth most frequent cause of death throughout the world, but suicide rates vary widely between different countries. Generally, the suicide rate is low in the less prosperous countries and highest in the more affluent ones, such as Germany, Switzerland, and Sweden. However, the suicide rate is also high in all Eastern European nations. The suicide rates in the United States and Canada are in the middle range. Among adolescents, suicide is the third most frequent cause of death. While men are more likely to commit suicide, women attempt suicide more frequently than men. Men are more successful in their attempts because they are more likely to choose a more lethal means (e.g., guns).

Mortality rates for suicide are generally higher in urban areas, and prevalence rates for suicide have been shown to be positively correlated with the size of cities. Although suicide has a low incidence in closely knit rural communities, the problem is more common among older persons, in areas where agriculture is in decline, and among workers who are immigrating into cities. The incidence of suicide increases with age, with older persons at greatest risk for killing themselves (NIMH, 2003).

People with bipolar disorder are at least 15 times more likely to commit suicide than those in the general population and may account for one quarter of all completed suicides, according to *DSM-5*.

One of the best predictors of who will attempt suicide is a history of a psychiatric disorder. Those who are at the highest risk for suicide are those who have no hope. People who express hopelessness are more likely to commit suicide than those who have some hope for the future. The association between suicidality and hopelessness is stronger and more stable than the association of suicidality with the presence of depression and substance use disorders (Kuo, Gallo, & Eaton, 2004). The lead characters in two films discussed earlier, *Scent of a Woman* (1992) and *The Hospital* (1971), each have a strong sense of hopelessness.

Risk Factors and Antecedents

There are many risk factors associated with suicide. The demographic risk factors include being adolescent or elderly, male, white, separated, divorced or widowed, isolated, and unemployed. Other risk factors include depression, alcoholism, bipolar disorders, and neurological disorders.

Unfortunately, even though risk factors and the antecedents of suicide have been well established, accurately predicting who will commit suicide is extraordinarily difficult. Most clinicians include a suicide assessment in their initial interaction with any client who has an emotional problem or a mental illness. An assessment for suicide focuses on three issues: intent, plan, and lethality.

Intent, or thinking about suicide, is a specific indicator of an impending suicide and probably the single most important predictor. Those people most intent on suicide have worse insomnia, are more pessimistic, and are less able to concentrate than those with less intent. In the film *Night, Mother* (1986), the entire story focuses on Jesse's plan to kill herself. Those individuals most intent on killing themselves are more often males, older, single or separated, and living alone. However, experts also know that intent is episodic, and that even if there is no intent today, there may be tomorrow. In *Dead Poets Society* (1989), there is no mention of Neil's intent, and the viewer is led to believe that he does not intend to kill himself; however, he eventually returns home, feels helpless, and convinces himself there is no way out of an untenable situation. If someone had recognized his intent or if he had reached out for help (e.g., by calling a suicide hotline), Neil might have been able to identify creative alternatives to suicide.

Most experts believe that even though a person is intent on suicide, there is almost always an underlying wish to be rescued. Thus, a person who is very intent on killing himself or herself may consciously or unconsciously send out signals of distress, evidence of helplessness, or pleas for help. Some of the verbal cues may be "I am going away" or "You won't be seeing much of me from now on." There may also be unusual behaviors such as putting one's affairs in order, giving away prized possessions, engaging in atypical acts, or becoming socially isolated. These behaviors are all present in *Scent of a Woman* (1992). Lt. Colonel Slade puts his financial affairs in order, visits his family, says good-bye, and has his "last fling" before he attempts to kill himself.

People who have a **plan** for committing suicide are more likely to actually kill themselves than those who have vague thoughts about not wanting to live. Clinicians are trained to determine whether their patients have a plan to kill themselves and how specific these plans are. An individual who does not have a plan is considered to be at lower risk than someone who knows how he or she can commit suicide, and who has access to the planned method. In *The Hospital* (1971), Dr. Herbert Bock plans to kill himself by injecting a lethal dose of potassium. He demonstrates both plan and intent, and, because of his easy access to potassium, he is clearly at high risk.

The **lethality** of the method is also an indicator of the risk of suicide. The more lethal the chosen means, the more likely it is that the person will commit suicide, especially if there is easy access to the method selected (e.g., guns in the home). The most lethal suicide methods are using guns, jumping off buildings and bridges, and hanging. Slashing one's wrists and ingesting 15 or fewer aspirin are common methods of attempting suicide, but they are seldom lethal. Other methods that carry a moderate to high risk of lethality are drowning, carbon monoxide suffocation, and deep cuts to the throat. In both *Scent of a Woman* (1992) and *Dead Poets Society* (1989), the lethality was high because guns were the means selected for the suicidal act.

Colin Firth portrays a gay man living alone in *A Single Man* (2009). Firth's character has recently lost his lover in an automobile accident. He is suffering, dysphoric, isolated, and suicidal. He displays a number of signs suggesting he is preparing to kill himself: He announces that "this day" will be different. He packs a gun and then gives unique, out-of-character compliments to his housekeeper and assistant, picking out details which he appreciates, both of which seem to surprise the women and brighten their day. He shares his fears and notes the challenge of being fully honest.

Boy Interrupted

Boy Interrupted (2009) is an important and powerful documentary about a young man who committed suicide in his early teens in 2005. It was filmed by his parents who are filmmakers. Evan Scott Perry was diagnosed with bipolar disorder after inpatient hospitalization due to a suicide attempt during which he stood on top of a tall building until a teacher talked him down. After inpatient treatment, Evan went to a center that focused on milieu therapy, which helped Evan tap into his "boy-ness," offering a shift from his current behavior in which he acted like an immature adult. Evan was highly moody and as a young child, and he seemed to act like two different people. He was preoccupied with death and suicide. He displayed aggression, periods of depression, intense emotions, explosiveness, and he had difficulty managing his feelings. His poor impulse control and personal belief in his negative thoughts seemed to worsen. During his tantrums, he would destroy most items in his room. There was a family history of suicide by an uncle. Evan left a poignant suicide note marked with teenage angst, similar to the notes left by thousands of other teens. As one psychiatrist notes in the film, bipolar disorder is "psychiatry's cancer" – it kills people. In addition to being an emotional film, *Boy Interrupted* is thought-provoking and educational and represents a creative way to cope with an incomprehensible tragedy (i.e., make a film about the tragedy). The film is also important in depicting the impact of suicide on parents, a sibling, friends, and the family unit as a whole. It shows that suicide is not without significant consequences and significant lasting impact on others (e.g., a grandmother of another suicide victim shares in the film that as a family member, "one never recovers"). The film emphasizes how the fantasy of family and friends simply saying wonderful things at the funeral of a suicide victim is both naïve and transient, while the pain and suffering of the living is ongoing and salient.

Seven Pounds

Will Smith initially worked with Italian director Gabriele Muccino to produce the movie *The Pursuit of Happyness* (2006), a moving portrayal of a man and his son who triumph over economic difficulties and homelessness. The actor and the director teamed up again to produce *Seven Pounds* (2008), a provocative and controversial movie in which the protagonist, Ben Thomas, attempts to atone for a single tragic mistake in an otherwise charmed life by committing suicide and giving away his home, his wealth, and various body parts (including his eyes and his heart) to seven decent and deserving individuals. In some obscure way, this allows Thomas to "undo" his responsibility for the death of his fiancée and the six other individuals killed in an accident that he clearly caused when attempting to read a Blackberry message at the same time he was driving a vintage Corvette far too fast. Thomas becomes romantically (but not sexually) involved with Emily Posa (Rosario Dawson), a woman who will die unless a suitable donor can be found and she receives a heart transplant. Thomas works with a childhood friend to ensure that his heart goes to Emily, his eyes go to Ezra Turner (a blind, vegan telemarketer played by Woody Harrelson), and other needy individuals receive other body parts. The movie is overtly sentimental, and there is not clear evidence of psychopathology in Will Smith's character; however, we do believe the film raises interesting questions about the movie industry's tendency to glamorize suicide, and it suggests that suicide can sometimes be an altruistic act. The movie illustrates that mental health professionals are hard pressed to identify suicidal thinking in any patient who denies it, and we believe the film can provide a springboard for lively class discussions about depression, suicide, and the societal responsibilities of directors and producers.

House of Sand and Fog

House of Sand and Fog (2003) offers a compelling illustration of the ways in which depression can present. The movie stars Jennifer Connelly as Kathy, a depressed, recovering alcoholic; Ben Kingsley as Behrani, a former high-ranking Iranian colonel working hard at two menial jobs to create success for his family; and Ron Eldard as Lester, a married police officer who protects Kathy and wants to start a new life with her. Director Vadim Perelman succinctly describes the dynamics of each character's psyche as follows: "Behrani wants up, Kathy wants in, and Lester wants out. Those are their motivations." Kathy's house is seized due to

tax payment delinquency, and Behrani wins the house in an auction, thus beginning a complex web of morality, conflict, individual needs, and pursuit of one's dreams.

> "The woman has come here and tried to take her own life. We must help her. She's a bird, a broken one. Your grandfather used to say the bird which flies into your house is an angel. You must look upon its presence like a blessing."
>
> Behrani giving advice regarding Kathy's first suicide attempt in
> *House of Sand and Fog* (2003)

Kathy lives alone in a house she and her brother inherited from their father. In one of the opening scenes, Kathy is sleeping when she is awakened by her advice-giving mother on the phone; after discussing the need for her to attend support group meetings, Kathy ends the conversation with a single tear streaming down her cheek and hangs up the phone. She then rises from her shaking waterbed (an early symbol of her instability) and begins to walk around her dirty house that includes a dripping faucet and a large stack of unopened mail blocking her front door. The opening scenes set up a depiction of an unsteady woman with a history of alcoholism who lives a sedentary, isolated, and unmotivated life. These scenes set the stage for Kathy's battles with alcoholism and depression.

Kathy's symptoms include agitation, numbed and blunted affect, and social isolation. Early on, she alludes to her struggle with depression and remarks, "I'm trying not to harp on the negative." Kathy also has financial problems, and because she is unable to afford a motel for 2 days, she begins to live and sleep in her car, turning the engine on for heat. She finds some comfort and escape from her loneliness through an affair with a married man. As stress increases, she begins to smoke cigarettes again. There is a clear link between alcohol and depression, yet this begins with denial. Kathy says, "See, when I think of my sobriety I don't think about wine, alcohol was never a problem." She then begins to drink wine with a subtle smile. This is a break in her 2 years of sobriety, and it rapidly results in physical and emotional deterioration. This is a serious and severe relapse for

Kathy, clearly triggered by the stress and chaos in her life.

Kathy's overt "cry for help" comes when she calls her brother, pleading with him to visit and support her: "I just feel lost, Frankie, I just feel lost." Her brother, a typical busy American, claims there are new things needing attention at his job and quickly gets off the phone. Kathy's despair continues to escalate. With tearfulness and bloodshot eyes from crying, Kathy purchases several miniature bottles of whiskey and some gasoline. She drinks the whiskey while driving and crying. Her depression and helplessness then lead to two suicide attempts. While despairing over the house she has lost, she tries to kill herself with a gun, pulling the trigger several times; however, the gun is not loaded. She is found, taken in and cared for by her rival Behrani and his family, and she attempts suicide a second time, swallowing several bottles of unnamed prescription medicine. She is saved again, this time because she is found early and forced to throw up most of the medicine.

Metaphors for depression abound in this film. The emergence of the moon and the setting or rising of the sun represent character transitions and shifts into different moods and mental states. As the title suggests, sand and fog are important elements in the film; one possible interpretation is that both represent the symptoms of depression. Sand is a naturally unsteady element representing the sinking nature of suicide. As Kathy sinks deeper into depression, fog is seen in many scenes, becomes thicker and more concealing until in one scene it completely surrounds the house. There are several camera shots of moving fog in which the fog quickly covers trees, mountains, water, and homes. This is similar to the rapid clouding associated with the negative thoughts, helplessness, and self-destructive behaviors one finds in depression. The film opens with life being cut down (trees) and concludes with a shot of a tree surrounded and protected by a fence.

The viewer is particularly challenged with this film, as he or she can empathize with both characters and can see the needs of both sides. As tension rises and conflict continues, this challenge becomes more complex, even to the point where a state of helplessness is induced in the viewer which mirrors the helplessness portrayed on screen.

Additional Questions for Discussion (*House of Sand and Fog*)

➤ Based solely on the film, does Kathy meet the criteria for a diagnosis of mood disorder?
➤ At what point would hospitalization be recommended for Kathy?
➤ What are the negative automatic thoughts likely to occur in Kathy?
➤ What is the relationship between alcohol and depression in this film? How commonly does alcohol and drug abuse co-occur with mood disorders?
➤ How much more likely is a depressed drinker to commit suicide than a depressed nondrinker?
➤ Describe the ways characters react to Kathy's suicide attempts. Are these reactions typical?
➤ What suicide signs are evident for Kathy? Compare and contrast the suicide risk factors for Kathy and Behrani?
➤ What is suggested by the film's title? Does it relate to depression or addiction?
➤ Some reviewers have described Kathy as a weak person. Do you agree?
➤ What are Kathy's healthy and unhealthy coping strategies?

The Hours

The Hours (2002) is a film of enormous psychological, emotional, and cinematic proportions. The film was nominated for Academy Awards as Best Picture, Best Director, and Best Adapted Screenplay. The all-star cast includes Nicole Kidman, Meryl Streep, Julianne Moore, Ed Harris, Claire Danes, Jeff Daniels, Toni Collette, John C. Reilly, and Miranda Richardson. Music was brilliantly composed by the renowned Philip Glass, and the script was adapted by David Hare. Ironically, one of the least known figures in this film is perhaps the most important – the director. This was director Stephen Daldry's second feature film, though his extensive work and awards in the London theater show he was more than equal to the challenge of directing a movie.

> "If I were thinking clearly, Leonard, I would tell you that I wrestle alone in the dark, in the deep dark and that only I can know, only I can understand my own condition."
>
> Virginia Woolf (Nicole Kidman) talking to her husband in *The Hours* (2002)

The film depicts three stories about three women who are closely connected although they live in different periods. Each struggles with both serious depressive symptoms and suicide issues.

Kidman plays the now celebrated novelist Virginia Woolf, struggling to write her soon-to-be-famous novel *Mrs. Dalloway* in the early 1900s while suffering with what would be identified today as bipolar disorder. The film dramatically begins and ends with the suicide of Virginia Woolf, who drowns herself in a quickly flowing river with heavy rocks in her pockets to weigh her down. Woolf's depression is emphasized in the film, though some mania symptoms are depicted, including her agitation, decreased need for sleep, poor judgment, and indecisiveness, such as when she decides to leave her house against doctor's orders with the intention to move to and live in London. She has a history of "fits," problems with mood, she hears voices, and she has made two suicide attempts. Although her life has been set up to protect her, the inner turmoil she experiences is simply too painful for her to continue to live. She smokes marijuana to calm herself, focus her thoughts, and numb the pain.

The character of Laura (Julianne Moore) is living in a quaint neighborhood home in the 1950s. She reads *Mrs. Dalloway* with interest and passion, finding comfort and inspiration in the lead character. Laura's character is an enigma, but she is clearly depressed and overwhelmed by life and its demands. She is socially awkward and skittish, at times unsure of how to respond socially and at other times standing near the door (after the doorbell rings) but not answering it. She is overwhelmed by easy tasks (e.g., baking a cake) and she is extremely critical of herself when she makes mistakes. Laura, like Woolf, feels alone and craves connections though does not seem to know how to make them. She kisses her visiting neighbor, Kitty (Toni Collette), on the lips,

clearly trying to connect with another person in a meaningful way. She spends a lot of time alone and experiences frequent crying spells. At one point, she decides to commit suicide, leaves her son with a babysitter and checks into a hotel – a suicidal dream seems to be the catalyst that changes her mind. Ultimately, life is too much for her to cope with and rather than committing suicide, she travels to Canada to restart her life, abandoning her husband and children.

> "There are times when you don't belong and you think you're going to kill yourself. Once I went to a hotel. Later that night I made a plan. The plan was I would leave my family when my second child was born. That's what I did. I got up one morning, made breakfast, went to the bus stop, got on a bus, left a note ... What does it mean to regret when you have no choice? It's what you can bear. There it is. No one's going to forgive me. It was death. I chose life."
>
> Laura (Julianne Moore) explaining herself in *The Hours* (2002)

The third interweaved story is set in New York City in 2001 and involves Clarissa (Meryl Streep), a woman trying to impress others and cover up her pain by throwing a party (just as in *Mrs. Dalloway*) for Richard (Ed Harris), her former lover, a prize-winning poet dying of AIDS. Clarissa is a strong woman who is socially confident and appears sure of herself. Her vulnerability is slowly disclosed through her struggles to help Richard, through her distant relationship with her partner of several years, and in her emotions that rush to the surface when she confronts a former lover (Jeff Daniels).

> "I still have to face the hours, don't I? ... I mean the hours after the party and the hours after that."
>
> Richard (Ed Harris) alluding to his suicidal thoughts when speaking to Clarissa in *The Hours* (2002)

Clarissa covers her inner pain through self-sacrifice, trying to help Richard cope with his hallucinations, noncompliance with medication, depression, and cynicism. Ultimately, Richard commits suicide by allowing himself to fall from a high apartment window in front of Clarissa.

💬 Additional Questions for Discussion (*The Hours*)

➤ Compare and contrast Virginia Woolf's decision to commit suicide and Laura's decision to live but abandon her family. Is one decision healthier? More just?

➤ Is suicide the right decision for a person such as Woolf who feels trapped in life and consumed by intense inner turmoil, or is suicide a selfish attempt to escape one's pain?

➤ How might a therapist approach a predicament and character such as Woolf's?

➤ What is the prognosis for Clarissa at the film's conclusion?

➤ What depression elements are paralleled in each woman across the generations?

➤ Can someone painfully dying of AIDS (e.g., Richard) still have a life worth living? What can be said to a patient who would answer no to this question?

Other Films Dealing with Depression and Suicide

A number of recent films portray protagonists who end their life, suggesting there is no trend to decrease the frequency of the portrayal of suicide in films; consider *Revolutionary Road* (2008), *The Reader* (2008), *Boy A* (2007), and the sacrificial suicide in *Gran Torino* (2008). An interesting educational exercise is to assign students to select two films portraying suicidality and write a paper comparing/contrasting method, etiology, risk factors, level of suffering, diagnoses, familial/social impact, and so forth.

Hopelessness and suicidal intent are well depicted in the film *Night, Mother* (1986), starring Sissy Spacek as Jesse and Anne Bancroft as the mother, Thelma. This film is a thought-provoking and gripping film adaptation of a Pulitzer Prize-winning stage play about suicide. The entire film takes place in the mother's home, where Jesse has lived since her divorce. As the play begins it is 6:05 p.m.,

and Jesse has just informed her mother that she plans to kill herself that night. The two women examine their lives as Thelma tries to protect her daughter from her decision. Ultimately, Jesse explains that she has no hope and ends her life at 7:45 p.m.

Suicidal intent, hopelessness, cynicism, and serious depression are also depicted in the fascinating film, *Sunset Limited* (2011), which has a cast of two. This dialogue film between White (Tommy Lee Jones) and Black (Samuel L. Jackson) initially centers on Black trying to understand why White has just attempted suicide in a train station. White is a professor who displays sadness, anhedonia, fatigue, poor self-care, low appetite, insomnia, social isolation, severe work and relationship dissatisfaction, anomie, and a lack of meaning and purpose in life. He says he does not believe in anything any longer, that everything he previously believed in was "flimsy," and that he yearns for blackness, for silence, for nothingness, for death, for the end. He reports that both medication and group therapy for depression were unsuccessful. Black, at times, is encouraging, insightful, and challenging, occasionally using religious arguments to impact the atheist White. The film offers a compelling depiction of depression and shows the resistant power of the mind, the power of negative thoughts and beliefs on behavior, and the suffering that results.

Suicide makes for high drama, and it is a common theme in films. Some examples include the unforgettable Russian roulette death of the soldier who remained in Vietnam in *The Deer Hunter* (1978); the suicide by drowning of a young man who feels he cannot please his critical father in *The Field* (1990); the murder/suicide by a Marine recruit in *Full Metal Jacket* (1987); the lead character in the Roman Polanski film *The Tenant* (1976), who becomes suicidal after renting the apartment of a woman who in fact had recently committed suicide; the female protagonist (played by Greta Garbo) committing suicide by stepping in front of an oncoming train in *Anna Karenina* (1935); and the suicide staged to look like a hunting accident in *Mountains of the Moon* (1990). Japanese novelist Yukio Mishima, one of the most fascinating characters in contemporary literature, committed *seppuku* (ritualistic suicide), and his life and death are portrayed in the film *Mishima: A Life in Four Chapters* (1985). Peter Finch, playing Howard Beale, the mad prophet of the evening news, announces to the world that he will commit suicide on the air in 2 weeks and sees his ratings soar in the film *Network* (1976). In the independent film, *Eye of God* (1997), a young boy views his mother's suicide. He is left in acute stress, confusion, and terror, unable to speak and catatonic. Shortly after, he kills himself at the age of 14.

Often a failed suicide attempt is a means by which a director can heighten tension or set the stage for future character development. After Olivia (Patricia Clarkson) attempts suicide in *The Station Agent* (2003), her relationship with two other lonely characters deepens and the three become close and mutually supportive friends. When Pu Yi, the last emperor of China, attempts to commit suicide by slashing his wrists in a railroad station restroom in Bernardo Bertolucci's *The Last Emperor* (1987), we get some insight into his character and a better sense of the despair he is experiencing. Alex Forrest (Glenn Close) attempts suicide by slashing her wrists in *Fatal Attraction* (1987), and the attempt is necessary to establish the extent to which she is willing to go to manipulate and control her lover. After Emmett Foley (Gary Oldman) shoots himself in the chest in the opening scenes of *Chattahoochee* (1989), we learn that he is afraid to die and not genuinely psychotic.

Suicide is sometimes romanticized in film, such as in the hauntingly beautiful *Elvira Madigan* (1967), in which two lovers decide on a double suicide. In *The Hairdresser's Husband* (1992), the female protagonist jumps to her death by drowning in order not to lose the happiness she has found with her new husband.

Finally, suicide is often treated as a humorous topic. Examples include Burt Reynolds' character in *The End* (1978), the multiple suicide attempts of Harold in the black comedy *Harold and Maude* (1972), the Italian judge who tries to get his sister to commit suicide in *Leap into the Void* (1979), the elaborate last supper for the impotent and suicidal camp dentist in *M*A*S*H* (1970), and the inadvertent death by hanging in *The Ruling Class* (1972).

The Virgin Suicides (1999) was Sofia Coppola's directorial debut. The story involves a repressed family with five daughters who commit suicide in response to their mother's overbearing control and repression. Unfortunately, this film supports the public misconception that suicide is caused by overcontrolling parents, when in fact it is the opposite that is more likely.

Dead Poets Society

Dead Poets Society (1989) stars Robin Williams as John Keating, an unconventional English teacher at a strict boys' preparatory school. This film was nominated for several Academy Awards. Set in 1959, this drama contrasts institutional values and individual creativity. By fostering "critical thinking" in his classroom, Keating broadens students' educational experience and their ability to think independently. The students also discover that when Keating was a student at the school, he started a secret society, the Dead Poets Society, dedicated to intellectual creativity. These students reactivate the society.

One important conflict in the film is between Neil, a student who wants to be an actor, and his father, a domineering businessman who wants his son to be a doctor. Neil's father will not allow him to try out for a campus production of *A Midsummer Night's Dream*. Neil disregards his father's demands, goes to the audition, and is selected for the lead role. Keating encourages Neil to explore the relationship with his father and to enlist his father's support. Neil's father is enraged when he views his son's successful performance. Neil is immediately brought home, and in an act of desperation, believing that his father will never "allow" him to become an actor, Neil shoots himself with his father's gun. Keating becomes the scapegoat for Neil's suicide, and the school's administration uses the suicide as an excuse to fire the unconventional teacher. The film ends with the other students protesting against Keating's dismissal.

Additional Questions for Discussion (*Dead Poets Society*)

➤ Would Neil qualify for a psychiatric diagnosis under *DSM-5*? If so, which one?

➤ How common is it for someone to commit suicide as a way of punishing someone else?

➤ Does the presence of a handgun in a house increase the likelihood of suicide?

➤ Would a daughter have been as likely to shoot herself?

➤ What else could John Keating have done to reduce the conflict between Neil and his father?

Wristcutters: A Love Story (2006) opens with Zia, the lead character, slashing his wrists. He then finds himself in a kind of purgatory, populated by other people who have committed suicide. He considers killing himself again, but suspects he will only wind up in a still worse setting. The film will teach you very little about depression and suicide, and it insults the viewer's intelligence by making use of a cheap "it was all just a dream" plot device that explains everything away.

Harold and Maude (1971) is a cult classic that opens with Harold, a troubled teenager, pretending to hang himself. He routinely fakes suicide attempts, primarily to annoy his intrusive mother, and he amuses himself by attending funerals of people he has never met. At one of these funerals he meets Maude, a 79-year-old woman who also enjoys attending funerals. These two unlikely companions become fast friends, and Harold professes his love for Maude shortly before she dies.

There is a memorable suicide by hanging in *The Shawshank Redemption* (1994), and few viewers are able to forget the Russian roulette games that prisoners of war are forced to play in *The Deer Hunter* (1978).

Prevention of Suicide

Since there are no clear predictors of suicide, there are no foolproof prevention strategies. Treatment of an acutely suicidal individual involves protecting him or her and connecting with that part in each person that wants to be rescued. Usually, a person who is suicidal is hospitalized and not allowed to be alone. Even in those instances, if a person wants to commit suicide, a hospital environment cannot prevent it, and many suicides have been completed in a protected environment. In the film *Crossover* (1983), a psychiatric nurse is plagued by self-doubt after one of the patients he works with commits suicide.

An important part in any suicidal person's care plan should include support from others and open communication. This is exhibited in the dark comedy, *It's Kind of a Funny Story* (2010), in which a 16-year-old admits himself to a psychiatric hospital for suicidality related to stress from his academic and social life. He reports depression and cessation of the medication Zoloft on his own accord. He shares a number of vulnerabilities – fear of rejection, perfectionism, and people-pleasing behavior (these are con-

trasted with more dramatic vulnerabilities such as history of abuse, trauma, and drug abuse – conditions that characterize other patients in the hospital). Catastrophizing, magnification, and helplessness are further cognitive and emotional vulnerabilities of the protagonist. The film depicts the importance of open communication, the ability to both give and receive support, learning positive reframing, acts of kindness, role playing, self-expression through art, optimistic thinking, directly confronting one's difficulties, and establishing new connections as distinct, healthy coping approaches to manage depression and stress.

Ordinary People

Ordinary People (1980), an Academy Award winning film based on Judith Guest's novel by the same name, depicts the aftermath of a suicide attempt. Conrad Jarret, played by Timothy Hutton, is a sensitive teenager who has attempted suicide following a boating accident that killed his brother, Buck. Conrad could not overcome his feelings of guilt, attempted suicide, and subsequently was hospitalized for 4 months. The film begins following Conrad's return home and traces his struggle for personal redemption and his futile attempts to communicate with his parents. His father, Calvin, played by Donald Sutherland, is a successful tax attorney who tries to respond to Conrad's needs. His mother, Beth, played by Mary Tyler Moore, is well intentioned but ultimately unable to meet the needs of her son. Beth is the nucleus of a family in a crisis.

Upon his return from the hospital, Conrad is inattentive in class and distant with classmates. He is also ill at ease with his parents. His father encourages Conrad to contact a psychiatrist, and eventually he begins therapy with Dr. Tyrone Berger, played by Judd Hirsch. In therapy, Conrad explores his relationship with his parents. When Dr. Berger suggests that the entire family meet together, Beth refuses. Throughout the movie, Beth's feelings toward her living son become obvious. Calvin begins to question his relationship with Beth and unsuccessfully attempts to reengage his wife in their relationship. Beth eventually leaves her husband and son, who come to terms with Beth's limitations and begin to rebuild their lives around their love for each other.

Other characters play an important role in the movie. Conrad's swimming coach quizzes him about his hospitalization, asks him whether he received shock treatment, and is demanding during training sessions. Conrad finally decides to quit the swimming team.

Another important character is Karen, a girl Conrad met at the hospital. While hospitalized, Conrad and Karen had a completely "open and honest" relationship. When Conrad contacts her at home, she is distant but appears to be in control. She is involved in school activities and maintains she no longer thinks about the problems that resulted in her suicide attempt. She also decides not to see a therapist. Karen's newfound confidence is startling to Conrad, who begins to question his own fragile condition. When he tries to get in touch with her later, however, Conrad learns that she has committed suicide.

Karen's death forces Conrad to relive the boating accident that took Buck's life. At last, he is able to explain his guilt – he lived and Buck did not. Conrad realizes that he was angry with Buck because he did not hang on to the boat. With the help of Dr. Berger, he experiences the intense pain of his loss and resolves his guilt.

If a suicide attempt is survived, the meaning of the attempt should be examined. Even though the viewer is not told whether Conrad has symptoms of depression, it is safe to assume that they were present prior to the suicide attempt. Conrad's suicide attempt was both an attempt to kill himself and a cry for help. His family fails to appreciate or respond to his distress over his brother's death. His mother is unable to relate to anyone, and his father is withdrawn from family interaction. Through a suicide attempt, Conrad got his family and friends to acknowledge his desperate situation.

Every suicide threat should be taken seriously. While attempting suicide is often an impulsive act, it is also an act of communication. If Conrad had possessed the necessary communication skills, he could have discussed his feelings and explored their meaning.

Additional Questions for Discussion (Ordinary People)

➤ How would you describe Conrad's family in Ordinary People?
➤ If you were a therapist working with this family, how would you proceed?
➤ Do any of the characters in the film meet DSM-5 criteria for depression?

International Films: Depressive Disorders, Bipolar Disorders, and Suicide

Melancholia (2011, Denmark), an intriguing, at times surreal and beautiful, and at times tragic and disturbing film, depicts Kirsten Dunst as a woman with severe depression. On occasion this reaches levels in which she struggles to function and take care of herself, and in one instance, she is unable to lift her leg to get into the bath and instead doubles-over on the floor. She also displays crying spells, inappropriate affect, and exhaustion. Her erratic and impulsive behavior is evidence of the need for differential diagnoses including bipolar and an impulse control disorder. Freud's comments on melancholia are applicable to the film: "a profoundly painful dejection, cessation of interest in the outside world, loss of the capacity to love, inhibition of all activity, and a lowering of the self-regarding feelings to a degree that finds utterance in self-reproaches and self-revilings and culminates in a delusional expectation of punishment." *Melancholia* was written and directed by the controversial Lars von Trier who is known to suffer from serious depression, which has, at times, significantly disrupted his filmmaking.

Respiro (2002) is a highly recommended Italian film about a woman whose behavior would meet criteria for the diagnosis of bipolar disorder. Her behavior is erratic, unpredictable, and frequently inappropriate (e.g., she invites her sons to go swimming with her in the nude). The people in her small Mediterranean fishing village insist that she be sent to Milan for psychiatric hospitalization after she releases a pack of mad, caged dogs that have to be shot from the rooftops. She avoids psychiatric hospitalization when her oldest son helps her find refuge in a cave, and her husband and the villagers eventually come to miss her eccentric but life-affirming behavior.

The slow-moving but powerful Iranian film *Taste of Cherry* (1997) won the Palme d'Or at the Cannes Film Festival. The movie illustrates the grim determination of a man who has decided to take his own life, but who cannot find anyone to help him. He has dug a hole in the ground and plans to lie in the hole and die after taking a handful of pills; however, it is important to him that he find someone to fill up the hole after he has died. One person he attempts to persuade to take on this task asks a poignant question that leads to the suicidal man questioning his decision: "Do you want to give up the taste of cherries?"

In the graphic, disturbing film, *Suicide Room* (2011, Poland), Dominik is a wealthy normal adolescent with many friends. After kissing a classmate while drunk at a party, a stream of bullying is set off, mostly through electronic media. Life spirals out of control for Dominik. Eventually, he connects with a girl in the "suicide room," an online chat room. The room graphically depicts suicides and self-injurious behavior (cutting); one girl in the room explains she has not left her house for 3 years and that she only wishes for pain, abuse, and suffering, and that she has a strong desire to die, all of which give her a sense of freedom. This influences Dominik to stay away from school. He stays locked in his room for 10 days where he engages in self-mutilation. His parents are disengaged, workaholic parents who do attempt to help him but are limited in their parenting skills. While the film depicts atrocious events in the chat room, there are positives shown as well such as connection and shared pain. The film includes scenes of animation to depict Dominik's interactions as an avatar attempting to cope. Symptoms of depression, anxiety, insomnia, and negative thinking are illustrated. A psychiatrist makes a house call and speaks with Dominik behind the locked door to his room. Finally, his parents get into the room and take away his Internet connection; Dominik is devastated and experiences emotional withdrawal when he can no longer connect with his new chat room friends.

Turtles Can Fly (2004, Iran/France/Iraq), filmed on the Iraq-Turkey border, depicts an adolescent with severe posttraumatic stress disorder (PTSD) who is depressed, homicidal, and suicidal, clearly in reaction to the horrors and atrocities of war; the film does not hold back in depicting what happens to children in war-torn countries.

The Japanese film *Maborosi* (1995) shows how a young woman is affected after the seemingly senseless and random suicide of her husband, who chooses, without any apparent reason, to deliberately walk into the path of an oncoming train.

Suicide Club (2002) is a Japanese film that explores the phenomenon of suicide and raises more questions than it answers. It assesses possible links between suicide and crime, music, violence, group contagion, internal compulsions, consumerism, evil, and various external factors. After 54 young girls mysteriously and collectively commit suicide by jumping in front of an oncoming subway train, mass hysteria and confusion develop, and several individuals and groups around the country take their lives. One scene depicts a group of students joking about creating a suicide club, and they gather at the edge of a building's roof, chanting to encourage each other to "jump." One by one, they watch each other plummet to their death. The film illustrates the phenomenon of suicide **contagion** (de Leo & Heller, 2008; Hacker et al., 2008), a serious problem that is compounded by media such as the Internet (Mehlum, 2000).

Rain (2001) is a New Zealand film about a young girl coming of age as she interacts with family and neighbors on a beach. The film is included in this chapter because of the girl's depressed mother, an alcoholic who acts out sexually and only seems to be happy when she is drinking. The drinking clearly helps her escape from her depression.

The Scottish film *Wilbur Wants to Kill Himself* (2002) is educational only insofar as it allows the viewer to witness the various stereotypes and misconceptions possible in a movie. Wilbur is a depressed and angry man who curses children, rejects women, and cheats with his brother's wife even though his brother is the person who repeatedly keeps Wilbur from killing himself. The brother is depicted in the role of protector, frequently checking up on Wilbur, supporting him, and removing sharp objects from his home. Wilbur's persistent suicide attempts include pills, gas from the oven, hanging, drowning, cutting his wrists in the bathtub, and standing at the edge of the roof of a building. Wilbur's determination to commit suicide ends once his love for his brother's wife becomes mutual. This perpetuates the misconception that love conquers mental illness. Equally disturbing is the film's blatant stereotypes of two psychologists leading a group; one smokes cigarettes during sessions and comments that the patients would be better off without group therapy; the other violates boundaries with a patient, licking his ear, going out on a date, engaging in sexual activity in a hospital closet, and violating confidentiality.

Another film about a character repeatedly attempting suicide, and failing, can be found in *The Face* (1999, South Korea). The protagonist is a diagnostic quandary – she lives a completely isolated life, rarely leaves her house, and has no friends, and her only social contact is her younger sister who berates her and abuses her. She is socially inept and spends her life sewing, until her mother dies suddenly, after which she strangles her younger sister to death. This character seems to lose touch with reality, suggesting a link between dissociation and suicide attempts. The film ends with the protagonist escaping from life by swimming away on an inflatable tube in the ocean; this is simultaneously a suicide attempt (similar to the protagonist in Kate Chopin's *The Awakening*) and the realization of her ultimate dream (to learn to swim). The viewer may also be reminded of another attempted suicide by drowning in *The Piano* (1993).

A classic film, *Diary of a Country Priest* (1951, Italy), directed by Robert Bresson, chronicles the life of a young priest who has somatic depression. This is apparent from the opening shot which depicts him tired, wiping his forehead, and behind the bars of a gate as if locked in his own prison. He is isolated and displays sadness, low appetite, and a variety of somatic symptoms such as light-headedness, sweating, and an upset stomach. He is quick to self-criticize, usually because he believes he has not prayed enough (which might be considered **scrupulosity**). He eventually receives a diagnosis of stomach cancer and continues to deteriorate.

Critical Thinking Questions

➤ Are dysthymic disorders, major depressive episodes, and major depressive disorders qualitatively different phenomena, or are they simply different quantitative expressions of a single disorder?

➤ If you genuinely believe a friend is suicidal, what are your ethical and moral obligations? Do your responsibilities to that person change if you are a therapist rather than a friend?

➤ Is there a suicide hotline in your community? Do you know how to access it?

➤ How do you distinguish between idle, passing thoughts of suicide and a cry for help?

➤ The suicide rate for both men and women is much higher in Asian countries and in Sweden, Denmark, and Austria than in the United States. What cultural factors could account for these differences?

➤ Kathy in *House of Sand and Fog* (2003) does not receive treatment for her depression. What percentage of depressed individuals go untreated? About how long does it take a depressed individual to seek treatment following the onset of their disorder?

➤ At one point in *Mr. Jones* (1993), a physician compares bipolar disorder to diabetes. In what way is the comparison apt? In what way is it misleading?

➤ Patty Duke is a well-known personality who has "come out of the closet" and openly shared the story of her mood disorder (see *Call Me Anna*; 1990). Can you think of other celebrities who have been candid about their own struggles with mental illness? Did any of them have bipolar disorder?

➤ How might you distinguish between someone experiencing a manic episode, someone experiencing the elation and energy associated with amphetamine abuse, and someone with a high level of enthusiasm/vitality?

➤ Dr. Bowen in *Mr. Jones* (1993) states, "You're not a sick person; you're a person with a sickness!" What is the significance of this semantic distinction?

➤ Do filmmakers have a responsibility to avoid glamorizing suicide to prevent contagion, or is a director's sole responsibility to make the best possible film without worrying about things like social influence?

If you have time to read only one book relevant to this chapter, make it:

 Jamison, K. R. (2000). *Night falls fast: Understanding suicide*. New York: Vintage Books.

If you only have time for one article, read:

 Picture this: Depression and suicide prevention. Entertainment Industries Council, for the Substance Abuse and Mental Health Services Administration. Enter the title into a Web search engine to download a PDF copy, or go to http://www.eiconline.org/resources/publications/z_picturethis/Disorder.pdf

If you have time to watch a video relevant to this chapter, watch:

 Jamison, K. R. (2011). *Assessment and psychological treatment of bipolar disorder* [DVD]. Mill Valley, CA: Psychotherapy.net. Available from http://www.psychotherapy.net/video/jamison-bipolar-disorder

Wedding and Niemiec's Top 10 Mood Disorders and Suicide Films

Bipolar Disorder

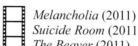 *Mr. Jones* (1993)
Michael Clayton (2007)
Silver Linings Playbook (2012)

Depression

 Melancholia (2011)
Suicide Room (2011)
The Beaver (2011)
Scent of a Woman (1992)

Suicide

House of Sand and Fog (2003)
The Hours (2002)
Boy Interrupted (2009)

Chapter 5

Anxiety and Obsessive-Compulsive Disorders

Sometimes I truly fear that I ... am losing my mind.
And if I did it ... it would be like flying blind ...

Howard Hughes in *The Aviator* (2004)

➤ Howard Hughes experiences symptoms of several anxiety disorders. How often do other anxiety disorders co-occur with obsessive-compulsive disorder (OCD)?

➤ How are Howard Hughes' obsessions related to his compulsions? Are there any compulsions that appear to be illogical and unrelated to his obsessions?

➤ What other psychiatric disorders are clearly present throughout the film, but are not addressed?

➤ What is the treatment of choice for OCD? What comorbid symptoms compromise this treatment?

➤ Is it possible to separate Howard Hughes' personality from his disorder?

➤ Would Howard Hughes have been as successful in aviation and entertainment industries without having OCD?

➤ Can people with OCD experience hallucinations? Is the episode of a germ-free environment realistic for someone with OCD?

➤ When would have been the optimal time to begin treatment for Howard Hughes? What treatment would have produced the best results?

➤ Hughes had not made a will at the time of his death, and his fortune was divided between 22 cousins. Do you think Hughes would have been competent to write a will during the last years of his life? Why or why not?

➤ Why did the American Psychiatric Association decide to "break out" OCD as a separate category distinct from anxiety disorders in the *DSM-5*?

➤ Why is posttraumatic stress disorder (PTSD) now included in a new, separate category for trauma- and stressor-related disorders in the *DSM-5*?

Patient Evaluation[3]

Name: Howard Hughes

Patient's stated reason for coming
"There is no safe place; there is no safe place."

History of the present illness
Mr. Howard Hughes, a 42-year-old White male, was brought to the clinic by his accountant who reports that the patient has been living in one room of his mansion which he has turned into a "germ-free environment." All entrances to his room are covered with masking tape, he uses tissue to pick up items, and he refuses to use dishes or glassware. He has numerous obsessions and compulsions that have been present for several years, but are becoming increasingly debilitating. The most troubling obsession is his fear of germs, which has developed into a severe phobia. He burns his complete wardrobe when he is exposed to anyone who is sick. He also requires his friends and employees to follow very strict hygiene practices. Recently, he has begun to experience severe panic attacks caused by extreme fear of dirt, messiness, or any perceived disorder in his life. He once reported "seeing things" that others cannot see. He has panic attacks daily and is very afraid that he will have an attack in public.

Past psychiatric illness, treatment, and outcomes
There is no reported history of mental health treatment, but symptoms have been present for years. He adamantly denies having a mental illness, but is aware that some of his behavior might make him appear mentally disturbed.

Medical history
Mr. Hughes has a long history of minor physical illnesses beginning in childhood. Driven by fear of developing life-threatening diseases, his mother frequently sought treatment for young Howard for colds and somatic complaints. At age 13, Mr. Hughes developed a medically unexplained paralysis that confined him to a wheelchair for 2 months. His parents be

---

[3] This fictitious interview is based on the character portrayed in the film *The Aviator*. It is not intended in any way to represent an interview with the late Howard Hughes.

lieved that he had contracted polio, but the diagnosis was never confirmed. He has chronic pain from a series of plane accidents that resulted in serious facial, leg, and internal injuries. He currently takes pain medication from multiple prescribers.

Psychosocial history

Mr. Hughes, an only child, enjoyed a close relationship with his parents, Howard Sr. and Allene Hughes. His mother died unexpectedly when he was 16. Two years later, his father died of a heart attack. During childhood, his mother is reported to have been overly protective of her only child and was preoccupied with his physical and emotional condition. Mr. Hughes noted he learned early in life that he could attract attention or avoid unpleasant situations by complaining of an illness. His father was rather flamboyant and well known for his gregarious lifestyle. Devastated and lonely following his wife's death, Mr. Hughes Sr. removed his son from a private school and brought him back home. Until his father's death, he lived in California, where he engaged in a glamorous Hollywood lifestyle, often meeting with celebrities from the film industry. His paternal uncle was a noted film producer. Even though Howard never earned a high school diploma, his influential father managed to have him admitted to Rice University. He later quit college (after his father's death) and became the sole beneficiary of a very successful family-owned business.

Mr. Hughes married at age 19 and divorced 5 years later. There were no children. He continues to oversee the family business and is a well-known movie producer. He is also a celebrated aviator who started a successful airline. He never remarried, but has had multiple short-term, romantic relationships including several with teenage girls. His accountant is his closest friend.

Drug and alcohol history

Mr. Hughes uses legally prescribed narcotics for pain control. He uses alcohol on a daily basis, often in combination with narcotics. There is strong evidence suggesting addiction.

Behavioral observations

Mr. Hughes is a disheveled, tall, emaciated, white male appearing older than his stated age. He arrived with his accountant. He entered the room hesitantly and refused to shake hands. He brushed off his chair before sitting down and answered most questions with anger and impatience. He avoided eye contact. During the interview, he frequently covered his mouth with a tissue making his words unintelligible. His shoulder-length hair was uncombed, and his fingernails were dirty and unusually long. His clothes were dirty and wrinkled. He was agitated and restless throughout the interview and answered most questions with a one-word response, usually a mere yes or no.

Mental status examination

Mr. Hughes was alert and oriented to person and place, but did not know the day or date. He denied suicidal or homicidal thoughts, but stated he would like to go to sleep and not wake up. He admitted to occasionally seeing things (bugs, germs, images) that others do not see. While these events are disturbing to him, he explained them as his mind playing tricks on him. He also admitted that these events usually occur following use of alcohol and codeine substances. He completed serial sevens to 65 until he became distracted by an outside noise. When asked the meaning of "why does a rolling stone gather no moss?" he sat in silence and then said "that's me." When anxious, he repeated phrases over and over.

Functional assessment

Within a very short period of time, Mr. Hughes has become a successful filmmaker, aviator, airplane designer, and airline executive. He is independently wealthy, living on profits from his manufacturing company. He has not worked for the last 6 months, following a break-up with a girlfriend and a collapse of a business venture. His food is prepared by a personal chef who follows very specific directions including disinfecting all cooking utensils. Even though he is very concerned about transmission of disease, he bathes infrequently and does not attend to personal hygiene. He lives like a hermit, rarely seeking outside contact.

Strengths

Mr. Hughes is clearly a creative, ingenuous, and innovative man. He has had periods of successful functioning in which he established new businesses and engaged in friendships and romantic relationships. He recognizes that his psychosis may be related to substance use. He easily discusses his childhood experiences. He is motivated to manage his panic attacks. Mr. Hughes' results on the VIA Survey, a measure of strengths of character, reveal his highest character strengths are creativity, love of learning, judgment (critical thinking), perseverance, leadership, and hope.

Diagnosis

Obsessive-compulsive disorder (OCD) with absent insight/delusional beliefs; tic related (F42); agoraphobia (F40.00). Rule out bipolar disorder; alcohol use disorder; addiction to codeine.

Treatment plan

(1) Consider an intensive outpatient/inpatient anxiety management program that employs the evidence-based treatment of in vivo exposure and response prevention; (2) Psychiatric consultation to initiate pharmacotherapy for managing OCD symptoms; (3) Weekly cognitive behavior therapy to identify and manage obsessions, compulsions, and panic attacks; (4) As anxiety management improves, target residual substance abuse problems via psychotherapy, support groups, and other adjunctive sources; (5) Psychoeducation for lifestyle changes, nutrition, and general self-care/hygiene.

Prognosis

Fair, if Mr. Hughes adheres to the treatment plan. However, he is likely to resist, and it will be challenging to engage him fully in treatment.

The Aviator and OCD

The Aviator (2004), an award-winning film directed by Martin Scorsese and starring Leonardo Di-Caprio, illustrates many factors that may contribute to the development of obsessive-compulsive disor-der (OCD) – overprotective parents, fear of germs, impulsivity, need for immediate gratification, and the untimely death of both parents. Based upon the real life of the tycoon Howard Hughes Jr. (1905–1976) from age 24 to 42, the film depicts his psy-chosocial and physical deterioration. The underly-ing effect of his addiction to codeine is not as clearly

Figure 7. *The Aviator* (2004, Warner Bros. Pictures, Miramax). Produced by, Sandy Climan, Charles Evans Jr., Grahma King, and Michael Mann al. Directed by Martin Scorsese.

portrayed, but the use of alcohol can be clearly seen. Like symptoms of many people with OCD, the obsessions and compulsions develop over time. The film also shows how stress can exacerbate one's symptoms. Leonardo DiCaprio prepared for his marvelous portrayal of Hughes by spending time interacting with patients with OCD. Figure 7 captures Hughes' physical and mental state at the end of his life, a time when he was clearly debilitated and disabled by his illness.

"I want ten chocolate chip cookies. Medium chips. None too close to the outside."

Howard Hughes (Leonardo DiCaprio) in
The Aviator (2004), displaying OCD
behavior

Anxiety Disorders

Anxiety, a normal reaction to a situation or stressor, is a motivator for performance and can be a healthy warning signal of danger or something that needs attention. The *DSM-5* distinguishes anxiety from fear noting that "*Fear* is the emotional response to real or perceived imminent threat, whereas *anxiety* is anticipation of future threat" (American Psychiatric Association, 2013, p. 189). Existential writers and mental health specialists agree that anxiety is an expected part of the human condition.

There are a variety of theoretical explanations for anxiety. Richard Lazarus, a well-known psychologist, described anxiety as a negative emotion that occurs when facing an uncertain, existential threat (Lazarus, 1999). Psychoanalysts view anxiety as a warning signal that danger is present and that overwhelming emotions are imminent, giving rise to unmanageable helplessness. Cognitive behaviorists associate persistent anxiety with a negative self-view, along with a strong sense of desperation and vulnerability.

When anxiety significantly interferes with school, work, or social interactions, an underlying psychiatric disorder may be present. The *DSM-IV-TR* included OCD, panic disorders, phobias, and PTSD as subcategories under the broad rubric of anxiety disorders. In contrast, the *DSM-5* privileges OCD and trauma- and stressor-related disorders as major categories separate and apart from anxiety disorders. The commonality of all anxiety disorders is an abnormal or exaggerated anxiety response that negatively affects physical health, psychological well-being, and cognitive and social functioning. Stress exacerbates the symptoms. Untreated, anxiety disorders can result in physical deterioration, despair, extreme fear, broken relationships, and unemployment. Suicide may be the ultimate outcome.

The subcategories of anxiety disorder included in the *DSM-5* are separation anxiety disorder, selective mutism, specific phobias, social anxiety disorder, panic disorder, agoraphobia, and generalized anxiety disorder. As with other disorders, there are specific diagnoses to cover anxiety that results from substance- or medication-induced disorders or medical conditions, and there is the option of coding the disorder as specified or unspecified.

The subcategories of OCD include OCD, body dysmorphic disorder, hoarding disorder, trichotillomania (hair-pulling disorder), excoriation (skin-picking) disorder, and OCD that relates to substances or medications or due to another medical condition.

Obsessive-Compulsive Disorder

People with **obsessive-compulsive disorder** (OCD) are distressed by recurring thoughts and/or irrational behaviors that can be so time consuming that they interfere with work and social relationships. In severe cases of OCD, these thoughts and behaviors dominate virtually every minute of every day.

Obsessions are intrusive, inappropriate, recurrent and persistent thoughts, impulses, or images that cause marked anxiety or distress. Obsessions are of greater magnitude than the everyday worry that is part of almost all our lives. Those with OCD repeatedly try to suppress these thoughts, but the very act of suppression serves to increase their intensity. These recurrent thoughts are disagreeable and alien to the sense of self (i.e., ego-dystonic). Common obsessional themes include harming others (especially children or helpless individuals), contamination with germs or feces, exposure to toxins or infectious diseases such as AIDS, blasphemous thoughts, and sexual misbehavior. Obsessions can also coexist with other disorders such as post-traumatic stress disorders.

Figure 8. *Matchstick Men* (2003, Warner Bros.). Produced by Sean Bailey, Ted Griffin, Jack Rapke, Ridley Scott, and Steve Starkey. Directed by Ridley Scott.

Compulsions are repetitive behaviors or mental acts that are carried out to reduce the discomfort associated with the obsessions. Sometimes there is a logical connection between the compulsion and the obsession (e.g., repeated hand washing *may* help prevent contamination from germs). However, in other cases there is no logical connection between the two (e.g., the patient who feels a compulsive need to sing the first few lines of a popular commercial before pulling away from every stoplight knows there is no meaningful connection between the behavior and the likelihood of an accident).

Matchstick Men (2003) does an outstanding job of highlighting the psychological consequences of OCD. Roy Waller, played by Nicholas Cage, is a successful con man who is able to use his attention to detail to execute complicated bait-and-switch schemes. When his life is disrupted by the appearance of his estranged teenage daughter (whom he has never seen), he is no longer able to maintain control over his illness or his life. His symptoms

erupt, and he deteriorates. The viewer is able to not only observe the numerous odd, incapacitating behaviors of a patient with OCD, but also his therapy sessions in which he vividly explains internal conflicts typical of OCD. Figure 8 illustrates Roy Waller's obsessive need to take a placebo medication that he is convinced is necessary to control his symptoms.

In another popular film, *As Good As It Gets* (1997), Melvin Udall, a misogynist and a homophobe played by Jack Nicholson, has a pronounced obsession with cleanliness. He eats at the same restaurant every day, sits at the same table, insists on the same waitress (Helen Hunt), and always orders the same meal. Melvin always brings his own paper-wrapped plastic utensils to this restaurant, so he does not have to "risk" contamination from dirty silverware. Whenever anything disrupts this well-established routine, Melvin becomes anxious and belligerent. He wipes off door handles before opening doors, and he carefully avoids stepping on cracks as he walks to his therapist's office. Melvin's obsessions are his repetitive thoughts about germs and disease; his compulsions are the ritualistic behaviors he engages in as a consequence of his thoughts. Patients with OCD frequently have multiple obsessions, and the film *As Good As It Gets* provides a realistic presentation of the disorder (with the possible exception that a patient with an obsession about cleanliness as severe as that present in Nicholson's character would be unlikely to be willing to touch a small dog). Some clinicians argue that Melvin also would meet the *DSM-5* criteria for a dual-diagnosis of OCD and obsessive-compulsive personality disorder (OCPD) due to his pervasive rigidity, interpersonal control, and inflexibility.

It is rare to find a film that depicts OCD patients who are compulsive hand-washers. Two exceptions can be found in a short film and a feature-length film, *Waiting for Ronald* and *Phoebe in Wonderland*. *Waiting for Ronald* (2003) is a short film about a man, Ronald, leaving a supervised residence to take a bus to live in the community with his friend, Edgar. Both men have developmental disabilities. Edgar has OCD and he is a compulsive hand-washer. He is very precise in the way he places his hat, fixes the folds in the hat, and places objects in his bag. He arrives early at the bus stop, and since Ronald misses the first bus, Edgar has to wait longer than he had anticipated. Edgar has a strong need to use the restroom, which he finally does, knowing he might miss Ronald's arrival. Edgar begins to wash his hands and continues, even though he has heard the bus arrive. He wants to stop washing but cannot; his anguish is palpable. He winces and struggles, moaning in mental pain. He washes his hands harder, crying, trying to push himself away from the sink. The viewer can clearly see the pain and suffering the hand washing causes him. Edgar coaches himself over and over (using the words and name of his therapist): "You can do it. Joe says you can do it … just breathe." Eventually, he slowly pulls his hands away from the sink one hand at a time.

Phoebe in Wonderland (2008) is a feature film that portrays a child with OCD. Phoebe displays repetitive hand washing, to the point that her hands bleed. The impact of her disorder is clear when her obsessive-compulsive behavior causes her to run late for an audition and to be late for a family dinner. She uses elaborate rituals; for example, she employs a particular jumping pattern while clapping a certain number of times to win a particular role; as is common in individuals with OCD, she gets frustrated when she is interrupted, and she explains that she cannot avoid engaging in her behavior. Phoebe quickly generates rituals when she becomes afraid, such as jumping up and down repeatedly to the extent that she has cuts and burn marks on knees. Other OCD behaviors include her repeating what is said to her as well as spitting in the face of other children who provoke her. She is also diagnosed with Tourette's disorder.

"All the answers are in a bottle. I've seen that solution! I've seen it all around me and that is a life of side effects and dull minds. Your profession just doesn't like kids to be kids.

Felicity Huffman, as Phoebe's mother,
challenging the psychiatrist in
Phoebe in Wonderland (2008)

The comedy *What About Bob?* (1991) stars Bill Murray as a patient with multiple problems, including overwhelming anxiety when he cannot be close to his therapist, played by Richard Dreyfuss. The character of Bob would likely be diagnosed with both OCD and dependent personality disorder.

Body dysmorphic disorder, formerly noted as a "somatoform disorder" in *DSM-IV*, refers to a preoccupation with a perceived physical imperfection that is not observable or which appears slight to others. Individuals with this problem may spend hours each day looking into a mirror and brooding about the perceived defect or flaw.

In 1987, Steve Martin played the role of a modern-day Cyrano de Bergerac in the film *Roxanne*. However, in this film, his nose is truly of grotesque proportions, and he would not qualify for the diagnosis of body dysmorphic disorder (which requires an *imagined* defect in appearance). In the French film version of *Cyrano de Bergerac* (1990), Depardieu's nose is elongated but not grotesque, and one suspects that his concerns are at least as much psychological as real.

The artistically eccentric Peter Greenaway directed the film *The Belly of an Architect* (1987) in which the viewer is introduced to Stourley Kracklite

"The most important words in the English language are not 'I love you' but 'It's benign.'"

Woody Allen's character obsesses over his health in *Deconstructing Harry* (1997)

(Brian Dennehy) who is a prominent American architect putting on an exhibition in Rome. Kracklite is too preoccupied with himself to care much about his wife's flirtations with a younger man. In particular, Kracklite becomes obsessed with his stomach. This begins to occupy all of his attention. His doctor states it is nothing more than gas and egotism. Kracklite examines other options – dyspepsia, fatigue, overexcitement, lack of exercise, too much coffee, too much constipation – but his stomach obsession continues. He makes photocopies of a statue of Augustus, obsesses over the statue's stomach region, and compares it with his own. In a memorable scene, Kracklite's obsession with his stomach extends to his covering his entire room including the floor with photographs of bellies. The film presents interesting differential diagnosis challenges involving somatoform disorders, OCD, and delusional disorder. Support for a diagnosis of hypochondriasis can be found in his unshakable belief that his body is being consumed by a tumor. There are other psychological elements contributing to his disorder: fear of being embarrassed, fear of death, isolation, psychological stress, and narcissistic grandiosity and self-preoccupation.

Compulsive hoarding was not an official *DSM-IV-TR* diagnosis; however, hoarding disorder is now recognized as a bona fide condition in the *DSM-5*. Hoarding disorder is commonly associated with OCD; the term refers to the collecting and saving of excessive quantities of possessions (e.g., newspapers, pets, sticks) that are of little use or value in large quantities; in severe cases, safety and health can be at risk. Hoarding is portrayed briefly in Juliette Binoche's character in *Bee Season* (2005) and in the character of Harvey Pekar, the comic strip artist portrayed in *American Splendor* (2003). In *Winter Passing* (2005), Ed Harris portrays an alcoholic who is a disheveled mess, perhaps partly as a reaction to his wife's recent suicide. He lives in a home filled with trash. He is a compulsive hoarder, and the numerous stacks of books in his home serve as a symbolic boundary outlining the entire house, including the stairs and each room, making it challenging to maneuver. It is estimated that the prevalence of hoarding disorder in the United States and Europe is 2–6%, with a somewhat greater prevalence among males and in older adults.

Animal hoarding is a special case of hoarding disorder; people diagnosed as animal hoarders typically fail to provide adequate sanitation or nutrition for the animals in their homes, and the animals sometimes die because of overcrowding or starvation. *Cat Ladies* (2009) is a documentary film that depicts four women whose lives revolve around the animals they own.

Trichotillomania (hair-pulling disorder) refers to pulling out one's hair to such an extent that it results in noticeable hair loss. There is an increase in tension prior to pulling the hair, and pleasure or relief upon pulling the hair out. Trichotillomania is rarely depicted or even referred to in movies, and it is one of the least represented psychological disorders in film. An exception is the brief portrayal of the disorder in *Dirty, Filthy Love* (2004, UK), a film about a man with OCD. In attempting to manage his condition through treatment, self-help, and support groups, the protagonist meets a woman who has been diagnosed with OCD but displays behaviors of trichotillomania. The viewer observes her pulling out a couple of hairs. She later gets in a fight, and her wig is pulled off exposing the bald patches fairly typical for those suffering from this condition. In the recent comedy, *The Internship* (2013), one individual on the Google "team," with the protagonists played by Vince Vaughn and Owen Wilson, is a young man with trichotillomania who pulls out his hair when he becomes stressed. By end of the various team challenge tasks, his eyebrows need to be painted on.

Excoriation disorder (skin picking) is portrayed briefly in several films. Nina, the ballet dancer who portrays both the "white" and "black" swans in *Black Swan* (2010), exhibits criteria for a number of *DSM-5* disorders, including skin picking and scratching. The excoriation is connected with her competitiveness and her difficulty managing stress, and this condition coincides with other OCD phenomena such as perfectionism, rigidity, anxiety, and ritualistic behavior. The film *Personal Velocity* (2002) depicts an adolescent boy who pricks the skin on his fingers, arms, and other areas of his body. Many of the areas are infected. The boy appears to have been severely abused and is running away by hitchhiking; he presents as severely withdrawn.

Panic Attacks

Panic Attacks

Intense, irrational fears and very distressing physical reactions are the primary symptoms of **panic attacks**. Some persons fear losing control, while many others fear dying. Panic attacks peak within minutes, and the *DSM-5* diagnosis requires four or more of the following symptoms: palpitations, sweating, trembling, shortness of breath, choking, chest pain, nausea, dizziness, chills or heat sensations, numbness or tingling, derealization, fear of going crazy, or fear of dying. Panic attacks are most commonly found in the various anxiety disorders; however, they can be associated with any number of other disorders (e.g., depression, PTSD, substance use disorders), and when this occurs panic attacks are coded as a *DSM-5* specifier (e.g., major depressive disorder with panic attacks). Note that a panic attack itself is NOT a mental disorder.

Even though these fears are recognized as illogical, they *feel* very real. Events associated with loss of control such as being in an enclosed space or being raped or abused can also be antecedents to the attacks. Patients usually vividly recall their first panic attack.

In *Dirty, Filthy Love* (2004), Mark's anxiety often leads to panic attacks. In *Matchstick Men* (2003), Roy has several panic attacks throughout the film. In *Something's Gotta Give* (2003), Jack Nicholson's character, Harry Sanborn, experiences panic attacks on two separate occasions. This film makes the point that panic can often present with symptoms very similar to those accompanying a heart attack; the cause of Harry's panic appears to be relational stress with the main female character, Erica Barry, played by Diane Keaton. In the film *The Departed* (2006), Billy Costigan (Leonardo DiCaprio), experiences panic attacks that contribute to the suspense of the movie; his medication (lorazepam) is discussed as an anxiety treatment. Panic attacks are also depicted in the Australian clay ani-

mation, *Mary and Max* (2009) about two overseas pen pals, in which one character, Max, experiences panic attacks when he receives a letter from Mary as it triggers deep emotions and memories.

In *Broken English* (2007), Parker Posey portrays an event planner who sits around much of the day bored at her computer. When she begins to date and moves toward a relationship commitment, she begins to experience panic attacks in public. She immediately escapes from the situation back to the comfort of her home. She later faces her anxiety directly, symbolized in her traveling to another country where the man whom she had been trying to avoid lives; she initially travels with a supportive friend, but when the friend leaves, she is forced to confront her anxiety on her own.

Panic Disorder, Agoraphobia, Specific Phobias, Social Anxiety Disorder, and Selective Mutism

Panic Disorder

A **panic disorder** is diagnosed when panic attacks become regular, but are still unpredictable, events AND the individual has at least 1 month of concern or worry that they will have additional panic attacks or feel that they are "going crazy," losing control, or having a heart attack. It is the latter criteria that are most challenging when attempting to diagnose cinematic movie characters, as films often do not reveal the internal dialogue of the characters.

Panic attacks seem to come out of nowhere. The fact that they seemingly occur anywhere and at any time is one of the reasons that a panic disorder is such a debilitating condition. Some people will have daily panic episodes, while others may be able to go for weeks or months without experiencing panic. Misdiagnosis often leads to delays in treating panic disorder, which in turn exacerbates the anxiety disorder. In the true story *Nobody's Child* (1986), patient rights' advocate Marie Balter (Marlo Thomas) is misdiagnosed as having schizophrenia and spends more than 15 years in a state psychiatric institution. In reality, she suffers from depression and panic disorder. Following her release she earns a baccalaureate and master's degree and returns to the state hospital as an administrator.

Robert De Niro plays a mob boss with panic disorder who meets with a psychiatrist, played by Billy Crystal, in both *Analyze This* (1999) and *Analyze That* (2002). Paul Vitti (De Niro) believes he is suffering a heart attack, but Dr. Ben Sobel (Crystal) explains the important difference between a panic attack and a heart attack and eventually helps Vitti get in touch with the deep pain and suffering that trigger his attacks. Although Vitti resolves some important issues in his life, this therapeutic approach risks misleading the viewer into believing this is the typical treatment for panic disorder; in fact, empirically validated treatments such as medications, cognitive behavior therapy, and exposure therapy are much less dramatic, and require much more work on the part of the patient. Another hit man who suffers from panic disorder is Pierce Brosnan's character in *The Matador* (2005).

In *Panic Room* (2002), Meg (Jody Foster) and her young daughter, Sarah, move into an extravagant mansion on the Upper West side of Manhattan, and while spending their first night in their new home, three thieves, expecting an empty house, break in hoping to steal millions of dollars. Meg and Sarah find refuge in the steel-plated, impervious "panic room" which holds both the money and their safety. The viewer sees Meg experiencing symptoms of a panic disorder as she experiences difficulty breathing. Her face expresses fear when she is enclosed in the panic room for the first time in a nonthreatening situation, and her daughter asks, "Mom you're not gonna wig out, are you?" When confronted with a dangerous situation, Meg shows resilience, and her panic is justified. It is interesting to note that the stress of the situation triggers Sarah's anxiety and causes a hypoglycemic response so severe her face changes color.

In *Lady in a Cage* (1964), Olivia de Havilland stars as Mrs. Hilyard, an upper class woman who is trapped inside her home elevator when the electricity in her house goes out. In making a call for help, she attracts thieves who rob her and try to hurt her. The film melodramatically and metaphorically illustrates claustrophobia and panic attacks. Panic attacks are also frequently depicted in a realistic way but with only a minor role in the overall story, as in *Das Experiment* (2001), *My First Mister* (2001), *Monster's Ball* (2001), and *Hannah and Her Sisters* (1986).

Agoraphobia

Agoraphobia is diagnosed when there is marked fear or anxiety in two or more of five fairly specific situations: (1) Using public transportation; (2) Being in open spaces; (3) Being in enclosed spaces; (4) Standing in line or being in a crowd; and (5) Being outside of the home alone. Although the word *agoraphobia* comes from the Greek word for fear of the marketplace, the idea that people with agoraphobia only fear "open places" is incorrect; the person may associate any number of situations or places with fear and anxiety. In the film *Matchstick Men* (2003), it is unclear if Roy has fear of panic or fear of situations and places. If it is the latter, then it is more likely he is experiencing *situational* panic due to his fear of contamination (relating to his OCD), and this is what causes him to avoid public places – nevertheless, these symptoms would not be sufficient to justify a diagnosis of agoraphobia.

Drew Barrymore and Jessica Lange portray the infamous mother and daughter, Edie and Edith Beales, in *Grey Gardens* (2009). Edith Beales (Jessica Lange) was a first cousin to Jacqueline Kennedy Onassis, and in the film displays dependent personality and extreme symptoms of what is likely agoraphobia. The extreme avoidance and pathology of the characters results in a deteriorating mansion that is nothing but a cesspool of filth, cat urine, and dilapidation. Agoraphobia would be diagnosed if a fear of panic attacks is also present; the viewer does learn that she just wants to be home as it is the only place she feels she can be herself, and her behavior of never leaving her house and refusing to sell it are further evidence. In real life, President John F. Kennedy actually paid for the home to be revamped.

Columbus Circle (2012) is set up as a murder mystery and depicts a woman with agoraphobia who has not left her apartment in many years. She rarely interacts with others and has a manager shop for her. She is reticent to speak with the detective investigating the mystery and displays rigid behavior and is meticulous about keeping her apartment a particular way. She is afraid to leave her apartment, but when she witnesses domestic abuse outside her door, she finally breaks "the plane" of her doorway to help the victim. This new "friend" later helps her step fully out of the doorway and to then take small steps down the hall. She experiences physiological and psychological anxiety symptoms – including a strong desire to avoid being outside the home – with this exposure to her fear.

Sean Connery's character William Forrester in *Finding Forrester* (2000) could probably be diagnosed with agoraphobia (he also has characteristics of avoidant personality disorder, a clinical problem with features that overlap with anxiety disorders). Forrester does not leave his apartment (in part out of a fear he will have a panic attack in public), is socially awkward, and experiences panic when he is required to go into a public place. He does what many people with agoraphobia do – he has his groceries delivered so he does not have to leave his apartment. The film captures the subjective experience associated with Forrester's panic attacks when the camera shows his "spinning" feeling, and sound is blurred. In the throes of his anxiety, Forrester wanders off and gets lost. At the end of the film, the viewer sees the potential for successful treatment of agoraphobia when Forrester is shown riding his bike on busy and crowded streets.

One of the most interesting cinematic portrayals of agoraphobia is found in Robert Taicher's movie *Inside Out* (1986). In this film, Elliott Gould plays Jimmy Morgan, a New York businessman with marked agoraphobia who has not left his house for 10 years. He has food delivered to him, arranges for call girls to come to his apartment for anonymous sex, places bets over the phone, and almost never ventures out of his house until forced to by circumstances beyond his control. Sigourney Weaver plays the role of Helen Hudson, an agoraphobic psychologist, in the murder mystery *Copycat* (1995).

Specific Phobias

Fears are labeled as **phobias** only when specific conditions are met. Marked anxiety must be present in the presence of a specific phobic stimulus and must routinely occur with exposure to the stimulus. In addition, the phobic individual must generally be aware that the magnitude of the fear response is excessive. Most people with specific phobias will avoid the stimulus situations that leave them fearful, to avoid the extreme distress they experience in these situations. Successful treatment of phobias involves exposing the person to the phobic object in a safe and controlled environment. Over time and with continual exposure, the person becomes comfortable with the object. However, the fear never truly leaves, and at times of extreme stress, the original fear and anxiety around the object can reappear.

Tom Hanks' character Dr. Robert Langdon in *The Da Vinci Code* (2006) is afraid to go into small, enclosed spaces such as an elevator or the back of a locked truck. He experiences shortness of breath and becomes hyperfocused (intense mental concentration focusing on a narrow subject). Claustrophobia is also depicted in producer M. Night Shyamalan's *Devil* (2010) in which five people are trapped in an elevator in a Philadelphia skyscraper, along with the devil. A guard in the film displays this specific phobia, and the film deliberately provokes anxiety in the viewer since it is filmed in such a small space. Mel Brooks' character in *High Anxiety* (1977) suffers from severe acrophobia which generalizes to a fear of planes, escalators, elevators, higher numbered floors in hotels, and any high places where he can look down. He experiences dizziness, nausea, and vertigo in these situations.

Specific fears are sometimes justified. Spiders can bite us; people do fall from high spaces; and even small cats can scratch us. Specific phobia occurs when there are excessive or unreasonable fear of an object or situation, and the anxiety-provoking stimulus is avoided. Various subtypes of this disorder include animals (e.g., dogs and insects), natural environment (e.g., storms and water), blood-injection injury (e.g., medical procedures), situations (e.g., bridges, elevators), or other miscellaneous stimuli (e.g., situations that might lead to choking). Specific phobias will occasionally remit spontaneously in the absence of treatment, but this is relatively rare. A fear of flying is depicted in Rachel McAdams's character in the Wes Craven thriller *Red Eye* (2005).

Many specific phobias are triggered by a specific traumatic event (at least traumatic to the individual experiencing the event). This was clearly the situation in *Vertigo* (1958), a classic Alfred Hitchcock film that stars Jimmy Stewart as John Ferguson, a San Francisco police detective, who is paralyzed by his fear of heights. The phobia has a traumatic etiology: While chasing a criminal across a rooftop, John almost falls to his death. A fellow officer, trying to aid John, is killed when he plunges to the street below. John, overcome with guilt, develops **acrophobia**, a debilitating fear of heights. The term *vertigo* refers to either marked dizziness or a confused, disoriented state of mind. Both meanings apply in this complex and the engrossing film. At one point in the film, John designs his own behavior modification program, stating, "I have a theory that I can work up to heights a little bit at a time." He puts a stepladder near the window, stands on the first step, waits, gets down, stands on the second step, waits, goes to the third step, becomes frightened and dizzy, and then falls to the floor.

In *Batman Begins* (2005), 8-year-old Bruce Wayne (Christian Bale) develops a bat phobia after falling into a cave and encountering a swarm of bats. After Bruce urges his parents to leave an opera featuring actors dressed as bat-like creatures, his parents are murdered in front of him. He blames himself for his parents' murder by reasoning that they would not have left the theater if he had not been afraid of bats. In response to these traumatic events, he gradually exposes himself to the feared stimulus and eventually transforms himself into a superhero with a bat-like appearance. By becoming "batman," he further reduces his anxiety and conquers his fear.

Arachnophobia (1990) is a film that builds on the widespread fear of spiders; one of the lead characters is Dr. Ross Jennings, played by Jeff Daniels, who has an intense and debilitating fear of spiders. Claustrophobia also is evident in Dakota Fanning's character in *War of the Worlds* (2005). Her father repeatedly teaches her to use coping skills involving an integration of safety reminders, closing her eyes, positioning her arms in a self-soothing way, imagination, and self-talk.

Social Anxiety Disorder

Intense and persistent fears of criticism and rejection characterize social anxiety disorders, which are also known as social phobias. People with social anxiety disorders experience anxiety in response to the possibility of, or the thought of, negative evaluation or scrutiny, and consequently they avoid situations in which they are likely to be observed by others. The disorder can take many different forms and occurs in situations that require public speaking, public performance, test taking, or social skills.

Some male patients with social phobias are unable to urinate in public places (also called **paruresis**), as shown briefly in *Roger Dodger* (2002); other patients are unable to eat in public for fear they will make a mistake and be ridiculed. The disorder is related to common phenomena such as performance anxiety, stage fright, and shyness. The specifier "performance only" is used if the debilitating fear is restricted to public speaking or performing in public.

The onset of social phobias typically occurs in childhood or adolescence, and the clinical course, if left untreated, is usually chronic, unremitting, and associated with significant impairment. Few people with social anxiety seek professional help. The symptoms of social phobia include tachycardia, trembling, sweating, blushing, dizziness, and hyperventilation and occur in anticipation of or during a social interaction. Even more distressing is the sensation of impending doom that frequently occurs. Finally, patients feel an overwhelming need to escape from the social situation that is causing their distress. In the *The 40 Year Old Virgin* (2005), Andy Stitzer (Steve Carell) avoids dating and sexual relationships due to anxiety. The film's premise is that Andy is a virgin due to intense fear of criticism or rejection.

Woody Allen's character in *Play It Again, Sam* (1972) is an exaggerated portrayal of someone with social anxiety (related to dating) and other neuroses. His portrayal personifies the worst-case-scenario thinking that individuals may engage prior to and even during a date. His character bumbles about and knocks things over, all in chaotic, comical movements. Any person nervous about an upcoming date can watch this portrayal and think, "At least I won't be that bad!" It is important to remember that shyness, performance anxiety, stage fright, and anticipatory anxiety are *normal* anxiety experiences in stressful and/or social situations.

Anticipatory anxiety about social situations often sets up a self-fulfilling prophecy. The phobic individual worries excessively about the performance demands of an upcoming event, loses sleep worrying about the situation, becomes tremendously anxious just before the event, and in fact performs poorly in the actual situation because of the high levels of anxiety. This poor performance then confirms people's beliefs about their inability to perform adequately in these situations, and their fear is exacerbated, causing them to perform even more poorly in similar situations in the future.

Social phobias are portrayed or implied in numerous films. In *Coyote Ugly* (2000), a young woman, Violet, moves to New York City to try to make it as a songwriter. Her social anxiety disorder keeps her from reaching her full potential, so she takes a job as a "coyote" bartender at a wild nightclub. At this bar she begins to perform in front of large groups, deliberately "exposing" herself to those situations that she fears; moreover, her boyfriend helps to desensitize her by having her sing in the dark. It is this exposure that helps her manage and work through her anxiety symptoms. In the film's climax, she begins to get stage fright while performing and attempts to leave the stage; however, when the lights are turned off she is able to perform and she continues performing when the lights come back on. Violet believes the etiology of her social phobia is genetic; her mother also went to New York City to be a singer but left because of her own social phobia, and Violet believes she is carrying a "gene" for her inability to sing in front of others and her other avoidance symptoms. After she is able to perform, Violet learns it was her father who encouraged her mother to move home, and her mother never had a social phobia.

The painfully shy woman is a common film motif found in *Amélie* (2001), *Lonely Hearts* (1981), *Rocky* (1976), *The Fisher King* (1991), and *I've Heard the Mermaids Singing* (1987). Shy and socially unskilled men are portrayed in *Bubble* (2005), *The Shape of Things* (2003), *Dummy* (2002), *Marty* (1955), *Untamed Heart* (1993), *Awakenings* (1990), *Goodbye, Mr. Chips* (1939), *Howard's End* (1992), *The Remains of the Day* (1993), and all of the Charlie Chaplin films in which he played the Little Tramp. The ways in which two shy adolescents come to grips with their emerging sexuality and a racist society are portrayed in a wonderful Australian film, *Flirting* (1990).

Generalized Anxiety Disorder

Some people are characterologically anxious; they walk around with a sense of apprehension and experience physiological arousal in a variety of different situations. They display what is sometimes called **free-floating anxiety**. Their condition can be quite debilitating. These individuals frequently re-

ceive a diagnosis of **generalized anxiety disorder**; the diagnosis requires that worry and anxiety be present more days than not.

The *DSM-5* diagnosis of generalized anxiety disorder requires the presence of excessive anxiety or worry that occurs more days than not for at least 6 months. In addition, at least three of the following six symptoms must be present: restlessness, fatigue, difficulty concentrating, irritability, muscle tension, or sleep disturbance.

Anxiety symptoms associated with generalized anxiety disorder include the same physiological, cognitive, and behavioral symptoms associated with other anxiety disorders, but the symptoms are chronic. The individual with this disorder may have multiple somatic complaints such as tachycardia, a dry mouth, and gastrointestinal distress. He or she will worry constantly about the multiple things that can go wrong in life and may be irritable and short-tempered because of anxiety. The lifetime morbid risk for generalized anxiety disorder is about 9%, but relatively few of these patients actively seek out treatment. Onset of symptoms typically occurs in childhood or adolescence, and females are about twice as likely as males to experience the disorder.

In *Greenberg* (2010), Ben Stiller portrays Roger Greenberg, a selfish man who is consistently neurotic. His generalized anxiety disorder leads him to be anxious in a variety of everyday situations, and it dampens his life ambitions (e.g., his goal in life is to do nothing). He uses alcohol to cope with his anxiety. He is hospitalized for "mental problems," and has a history of a suicide attempt. He experiences intense anxiety. While his primary diagnosis appears to be generalized anxiety disorder, a mental health professional treating Roger would need to differentiate generalized anxiety disorder from his symptoms of depression and social phobia as well as interrelated personality factors such as OCPD.

Nicholas Cage plays two twin brothers, Charlie and Donald, in *Adaptation* (2002). Both brothers are screenwriters, but one is much more neurotic than the other. No makeup or artistic tricks are used to differentiate the two twins; instead, Cage's talent alone is sufficient to portray both the worried and neurotic Charlie and the easy-going Donald. This provides a nice contrast for people studying anxiety. Charlie anxiously struggles with writer's block and is plagued with self-doubt and preoccupation with himself, both hallmark symptoms of generalized anxiety disorder. In another scene, Charlie is too anxious to approach an attractive woman played by Meryl Streep. The viewer learns about Charlie's anxiety, worry, and rumination not only through cinematic close-ups displaying his anxiety symptoms (e.g., sweating), but also through the voice-over indicating his thought processes. A major theme of this film speaks to how people try to "adapt" to circumstance, problems, and, in this case, anxiety.

Kissing Jessica Stein (2002) explores sexuality and relationships through the character of a New York journalist, Jessica Stein, who is tired of the dating scene and its limited offerings. She places an ad for "women seeking women" and meets a woman who turns out to be a great match. As their relationship develops, Jessica must battle her own neuroses about a lesbian relationship as well as her feelings for an ex-boyfriend who is still in love with her. Jessica experiences generalized anxiety as a worrier and classic neurotic. She is uptight and rigid, and very anxious about anything new or different. She does not have the self-confidence necessary to defend herself when she is criticized in public. She rarely stands up for herself and is unable to be honest to family or friends about her female lover. Jessica describes her experiences with panic attacks and mentions various other anxiety symptoms. She stumbles over her words and tries to control situations in which she be-

comes nervous. After reading a book about lesbians she realizes she is afraid of both sexuality and sensuality. Her anxiety is particularly noticeable at the dinner table prior to a family member's wedding; she is preoccupied with what people think of her and is unable to be honest, covering up the truth with repeated lies. This film emphasizes honesty, individuality, and the potential for change.

Most Woody Allen comedies will include at least one character with an anxiety disorder, and many depict characters with generalized anxiety disorder (usually played by Woody Allen himself). Indeed, neurotic, insecure, and self-absorbed characters and the existential anxiety produced by the need to cope with a complex and impersonal world form the basis for much of Allen's humor. *Annie Hall* (1977) and *Manhattan* (1979) are the Woody Allen films that best illustrate generalized anxiety disorder.

Mel Brooks' classic film *High Anxiety* (1977) makes fun of numerous movies with Hitchcock-like psychological motifs. Mel Brooks plays Dr. Richard H. Thorndyke, an anxiety-ridden psychiatrist, who takes over a prestigious mental institution, "The Psycho-Neurotic Institute for the Very Very Nervous." Thorndyke must battle an unethical and murderous staff to save his patients and himself. Meanwhile he struggles with his own generalized anxiety and phobias.

"I check my answering machine nine times every day and I can't sleep at night because I feel that there is so much to do and fix and change in the world, and I wonder every day if I am making a difference and if I will ever express the greatness within me, or if I will remain forever paralyzed by muddled madness inside my head. I've wept on every birthday ... and I feel that life is terribly unfair and sometimes beautiful and wonderful and extraordinary but also numbing and horrifying and insurmountable and I hate myself a lot of the time. The rest of the time I adore myself and I adore my life in this city and in this world we live in. This huge and wondrous, bewildering, brilliant, horrible world."

Jessica Stein describing the ways her anxiety disorder has limited her life in *Kissing Jessica Stein* (2002)

Selective Mutism

Selective mutism involves the failure to speak in specific social situations in which one is expected to speak, and this interferes with educational, social, or occupational functioning. This condition is seldom depicted in movies. In *Disco Pigs* (2001), the character of Runt, one of two dizygotic twins, has a period of mutism when sent to a psychiatric institution. Other diagnoses would need to be ruled out to determine if selective mutism is the primary diagnosis for Runt. When mutism is portrayed in films, it is customary to portray mutism as the result of trauma. In *My House in Umbria* (2003, UK/ Italy), it is clear that the mutism of a little girl is due to a traumatic reaction to a train crash. Similarly, in *Henry Poole Is Here* (2008), a young girl becomes mute for a year after being abandoned by her father. In these instances, acute stress disorder and PTSD would need to be ruled out as possible diagnoses.

International Films: Anxiety and Obsessive-Compulsive Disorders

An excellent portrayal of OCD is seen in *Dirty, Filthy Love* (2004, UK). This short but powerful film begins with a successful architect, Mark Furness (Michael Sheen), taking a leave of absence from work due to his OCD. His wife leaves him because she can no longer deal with his odd behaviors. During periods of stress, his OCD symptoms are exacerbated and his tics (from Tourette's disorder) worsen. This film depicts a warm and sensitive person who is trying to cope with the challenges and consequences of mental illness. Many typical compulsions are displayed, such as climbing the stairs by walking up four stairs and down two, flicking lights on and off, and touching walls going up and down the stairs. Throughout the film, rituals dominate every aspect of Mark's life. Seeing Mark find acceptance in a "support group" allows the viewer to glimpse the variety of behaviors associated with OCD and the spectrum of behavioral interventions used in treating anxiety disorders. As Mark becomes increasingly ill, the destructive nature of mental illness is portrayed.

In the comedy, *Nothing* (2003, Canada), two roommates, Dave and Andrew, struggle with the stress and demands of everyday life. Andrew has one or more anxiety disorders, most likely panic disorder and agoraphobia. He refuses to leave the house and has avoided going outside since his teen years. He has arranged to work as a travel agent so he can stay at home. He reacts to situations with anxiety and distress, always thinks the worst in any situation, catastrophizes, jumps to conclusions, and is exceedingly fearful. Dave and Andrew discover that they are able to make something disappear by hating it. The problem is if they go too far with this ability, they are unable to make things reappear again.

Andrew: "Oh my God, we are going to die."
Dave: "For once I don't think you're overreacting."
Andrew: "For as long as I can remember I've been afraid of going outside and now it's not there. But I'm not going to be around to enjoy it not being there."

Two best friends in *Nothing* (2003, Canada)

The Norwegian film *Elling* (2001) presents an honest and fair portrayal of what it is like to cope with the debilitating effects of mental illness. A small, feeble man named Elling is taken to a psychiatric hospital after his mother, who was his caregiver for 40 years, dies. It is there Elling meets another eccentric, Kjell, who has sexual obsessions about women and problems with anger management. The two men are discharged together and placed in supportive housing under the guidance of a social worker. The film is about their return to the reality of everyday living. Each man must prove he can live on his own.

Elling states he has two enemies: dizziness and anxiety; "they follow me everywhere." He refuses to leave his house and believes he is unable to answer the phone (even when it is only the social worker checking in). He has learned to be completely dependent on his mother and the hospital staff, so it is a great achievement when he is able to walk to the end of the block to go to a store. Further challenges are met when Elling begins to talk on the phone, eat at a restaurant, and go on vacation. Elling takes another big risk in battling his anxiety by going to a public poetry reading; arriving several hours early, he befriends an isolated, famous poet. Elling is rigid in his behavior, worries constantly, and is terrified of losing his only friend Kjell to Kjell's new girlfriend. Elling expresses this fear in jealous passive aggressiveness whenever he feels he has been left out or abandoned. His friendship with Kjell develops and deepens as they sacrifice for one another and stick together through the difficult times. "Hard work pays off" is a theme applied to the psychological challenges Elling and Kjell face. Rather than avoiding their fears, they face them and in turn, find freedom – freedom from dependency, from the hospital, and from isolation.

The interaction between the social worker, Frank, and Elling is noteworthy and inspirational. Frank sets firm boundaries and gives clear directives to Elling, taking a "tough love" approach that emphasizes that Elling must take chances to challenge himself, or he will lose his new residence. Frank is accepting and understanding of Elling's eccentric ideas, and tolerant at the film's end when he walks into the home and finds Elling lying on the couch, drunk, and having thrown up on himself. Elling awakens and believes he is sure to lose his house and his freedom; instead, the opposite happens because this all-too-human behavior confirms in Frank's mind Elling's readiness to live on his own in the outside world.

The protagonist in *She's One of Us* (2003, France) clearly struggles with social anxiety. She is socially awkward, frequently displays inappropri- ate affect, and misperceives social situations. In in- teractions, she pauses, looks away, hesitates and shakes; heavy breathing can be heard off-camera to simulate her anxiety. She is eager to please and to seek reassurance.

⚙ Critical Thinking Questions

➤ If anxiety is a natural human condition, at what point does it become a problem? At what point does concern become a disorder? Cite examples from your personal, family, or social life to support your views.
➤ Which anxiety disorder do you believe is most powerfully captured by the cinema? Why?
➤ How does anxiety play a role in OCD, and how does this differ in panic disorder?
➤ Compare and contrast the symptoms of Howard Hughes in *The Aviator* (2004), Mark Furness in *Dirty, Filthy Love* (2004), and Roy Waller in *Matchstick Men* (2003).
➤ Some existential therapists such as Irvin Yalom and Rollo May have argued that anxiety is an essential part of the human condition, and that it needs to be confronted rather than avoided (e.g., they discourage the use of benzodi- azepines after the experience of intense trauma). Do you agree?
➤ Are there some occupations in which it might be adaptive to have OCD?
➤ Compare the dysfunction associated with the specific phobia of John Ferguson (*Vertigo*, 1958) with that experi- enced by Dr. Robert Langdon (*The Da Vinci Code*, 2006).

Authors' Picks

If you have time to read just one book relevant to this chapter, make it:

Grills-Taquechel, A.E., & Ollendick, T.H. (2013). *Advances in psychotherapy. Phobic and anxiety disorders in children and adolescents.* Cambridge, MA: Hogrefe.

If you only have time for one article, read:

Rapee, R.M. (1997). Potential role of childrear- ing practices in the development of anxiety and depression. *Clinical Psychology Review, 17*(1), 47–67. doi: 10.1016/S0272-7358(96)00040-2

Wedding and Niemiec's Top 10 Anxiety Disorders Films

Obsessive-Compulsive Disorders

The Aviator (2004)
Matchstick Men (2003)
Dirty, Filthy Love (2004)
As Good As It Gets (1997)
Phoebe in Wonderland (2008)

Anxiety Disorders

Vertigo (1958)
Adaptation (2002)
Elling (2001)
Batman Begins (2005)
Play It Again, Sam (1972)

Chapter 6

Trauma- and Stressor-Related Disorders

I've been on edge ... mood swings ... that sort of thing.

An inarticulate soldier describing his PTSD symptoms in *The Dry Land* (2010)

➤ James exhibits abnormal reactions to seemingly normal events (e.g., a dog waking him by licking his face). Would this be common in cases of posttraumatic stress disorder (PTSD)?

➤ Many of James's most serious problems occur when he has been drinking. How often is substance abuse comorbid with PTSD?

➤ How does the military environment contribute to alcoholism and substance abuse?

➤ James does not remember the explosion that resulted in his injuries and discharge. How common is memory loss following a traumatic brain injury?

➤ Why is James so very reluctant to discuss the symptoms he is experiencing with those people who love him most?

➤ James keeps a loaded gun in his closet. How would you deal with this if you were his therapist?

➤ James believes only his Army buddies can fully understand what he experienced in Iraq and what his life is like after returning. Why?

➤ Why would work in a slaughterhouse probably not be a good job for a returning combat veteran?

➤ What is the significance of the film's title?

➤ How would you personally be affected by the experience of killing people in a combat situation?

➤ Are the injuries sustained in Iraq and Afghanistan any different from those experienced by soldiers in Vietnam, Korea, and during World War II? If so, how are they different?

Patient Evaluation

Name: James Wilson

Patient's stated reason for coming

"I can't sleep; when I do sleep I have nightmares. I don't remember what I did, but I still feel guilty. I can't concentrate. My wife left me because I've been drinking too much and she was afraid I'd hurt her. I probably deserve it. I'm always on edge, and everything seems to get to me. Nothing makes sense any more, and I just can't seem to get my life back."

History of the present illness

Mr. Wilson has experienced multiple personal and interpersonal problems since returning to Texas after receiving a medical discharge from the Army 2 months ago. He experienced a serious traumatic event in Iraq, although he denies any memory of the event. He now has serious problems with insomnia, and on three occasions he has hit his wife while sleeping, apparently in response to nightmares. He denies any history of domestic violence apart from these events; however, he does sometimes become "rough" when having sex with his wife. He has been drinking heavily and has trouble with commonplace social interactions. He becomes especially angry when his friends press him for details about his combat experience in Iraq; these conversations have degenerated into fistfights on several occasions. James has felt detached and estranged.

Past psychiatric illness, treatment, and outcomes

Mr. Wilson denies any history of previous psychiatric or psychological illness or treatment. He had an uneventful childhood, and he joined the Army as soon as he graduated from high school. Shortly after returning from Iraq, James saw a VA general medical officer for anxiety; he was prescribed Xanax 0.5 mg to be taken three times each day. A follow-up visit was not scheduled, and it is likely that there has been a significant interaction between Xanax use and this patient's heavy use of alcohol. Mr. Wilson appears to be adherent to his medication schedule. He is not taking any other medications at this time.

Medical history

The patient reports being knocked unconscious once when playing football in the 10th grade; however, he soon came to and did not receive any subsequent evaluation. He had asthma as a child, but apparently his condition was not serious enough to keep him out of the Army.

Psychosocial history

Mr. Wilson is an Army veteran who was honorably discharged with the rank of Sergeant approximately 2 months ago after returning from a tour of duty in Iraq. James lives in a rural community in West Texas where he shares a mobile home with his dog and his wife, a Latina woman he met in high school and married before joining the Army. This is a first marriage, and there are no children.

Drug and alcohol history

Mr. Wilson denies any use of recreational drugs. He drank alcohol "occasionally" in high school, but denies any history of drinking to excess. He and his buddies managed to secure and drink beer in Iraq despite military regulations prohibiting the use of alcohol in a Muslim country. However, James has been drinking heavily with his friends since returning from Iraq, and he routinely drives his truck after drinking, even though he knows he is drunk and his driving is impaired. He also finds that his suicidal ideation is most intense when he has been drinking heavily.

Behavioral observations

Mr. Wilson arrived on time for his examination. He is a pleasant and polite young man who was appropriately dressed. James repeatedly referred to me as "Sir," despite the fact that I am not a military psychologist. He fidgeted in his chair throughout my evaluation, and he appeared somewhat uncomfortable.

Mental status examination

James was alert and oriented to person and place, but did not know the day or date. He denied homicidal thoughts, but acknowledged frequent fantasies about shooting himself with the .45 Winchester Magnum he keeps in his bedroom closet. He completed serial sevens to 65 until he became distracted with an outside noise. James experienced some difficulty with abstraction; when asked the meaning of "why does a rolling stone gather no moss?" he sat in silence, and then said "I guess that's me."

Functional assessment

Mr. Wilson is a somewhat quiet individual with limited social skills. He is experiencing considerable difficulty making the transition from military to civilian life, and there is a great deal of tension in his marriage. He reports he hates his job in a slaughterhouse, and he has only been able to maintain his job there because the slaughterhouse is owned by his wife's father.

Strengths

James is affable and friendly, albeit somewhat shy. He cooperated with the evaluation completely and was quick to respond to almost all questions. He appears to have at least average intelligence. Although he has few remaining friends in his hometown, he still maintains close ties with his military buddies. His results on the VIA Survey, a measure of strengths of character, reveal his highest character strengths are bravery, honesty, humility, fairness, and teamwork.

Diagnosis

Posttraumatic stress disorder (F94.2). Rule out major depressive disorder; alcohol use disorder.

Treatment plan

(1) Psychiatric assessment to evaluate the need for continued use of Xanax and possible treatment with antidepressant medications; (2) Implement a care plan to prevent suicide to include the patient leaving his gun with a friend or relative; (3) Monitor closely for continuing suicidal ideation; (4) Meet with the patient's wife on the next visit to explore the potential for reconciliation; (5) Progressive muscle relaxation training; (6) Weekly psychotherapy sessions focusing on client's guilt about Iraq and follow-up on a care plan to prevent suicide; (7) Continuing evaluation of the possibility of alcohol use disorder and/or major depression.

Prognosis

Guarded. This patient is estranged from his wife and has limited social support. His prognosis is especially poor if he continues to drink heavily, and an auto accident seems almost inevitable if he continues to drive while intoxicated.

The Dry Land and Posttraumatic Stress Disorder

The Dry Land (2010) offers students a compelling and realistic introduction to the symptoms of post-traumatic stress disorder (PTSD). The film revolves around the experiences of James, an Iraq war veteran, who returns to a small West Texas town, and the friends, family, and life he led there, only to discover that you cannot go home again. He has changed as a result of his combat experiences: He is irritable, labile, and anxious, and he seriously considers suicide with a gun he keeps in his trailer closet. He drinks heavily when he is out with his friends, and his suicidal ideation is most apparent when he is intoxicated. Relatively simple events like seeing someone shooting a rabbit, something that would have seemed perfectly normal at one time, now trouble him deeply and led to a fistfight with the shooter. His marriage is on the rocks, and his wife, fearing for her own safety, leaves him to stay with her parents. James is only comfortable with his former combat buddies, and he traveled several days to visit one of these friends who had been hospitalized because of his Iraq injuries (Figure 9).

Trauma- and Stressor-Related Disorders

The **DSM-5** now includes a separate chapter for those disorders that originate as a result of exposure to a traumatic or stressful event. The diagnoses included in this chapter are reactive attachment disorder, disinhibited social engagement disorder, PTSD, acute stress disorder, and adjustment disorders. The chapter makes it clear that there is wide individual variability in the ways in which people respond to stress: Some people will react with anhedonia and dysphoria; others with anger or aggression; still others with dissociative symptoms. Reactive attachment disorder and disinhibited social engagement disorder are both disorders of childhood that result from social neglect. The former is

Figure 9. *The Dry Land* (2010, Maya Entertainment). Produced by Heather Rae. Directed by Ryan Piers Williams.

expressed as an internalizing disorder (e.g., depression, withdrawal), while the latter is expressed as an externalizing disorder (e.g., disinhibition). PTSD, acute stress disorder, and adjustment disorders are described below.

Posttraumatic Stress Disorder

PTSDs occur after exposure to traumatic events. The individual with a PTSD must have personally witnessed or experienced some event that involved actual or threatened death or serious injury and must have responded with fear, helplessness, or horror. The traumatic event is then reexperienced by the individual in the form of nightmares, recurrent recollections, and flashbacks or as physiological distress. The PTSD victim works hard to avoid these recurrent experiences. In addition, the individual usually experiences sleep disturbance, irritability, difficulty concentrating, hypervigilance, or an exaggerated startle response.

Military combat is a common cause of PTSD, but the disorder can also occur in response to earthquakes, fires or floods, mugging, rape, the witnessing of violence, or any of a variety of other traumatic situations. Often, seemingly innocuous stimuli will cause an individual to relive the anxiety-producing experience; for example, hearing a car backfire may trigger a terrifying war memory of combat for a war veteran.

What we now call posttraumatic stress disorder was referred to as battle fatigue or combat neurosis in previous wars. *Patton* (1970) depicts George C. Scott in the title role slapping a soldier with PTSD whom he accuses of being a "dirty coward." The horrors of war are also vividly depicted in older, classic films like *All Quiet on the Western Front* (1930) and *Paths of Glory* (1957).

In war films such as the award-winning *Saving Private Ryan* (1998), even though PTSD is not portrayed per se, it would be easy to understand how one could develop PTSD as the viewer observes the ubiquitous trauma the soldiers experience. *Gran Torino* (2008) depicts the adjustment problems of Clint Eastwood playing the role of Walt Kowalski, a decorated but racist and embittered Korean war veteran. The award-winning film, *In the Valley of Elah* (2007) is based on the July 13, 2003, murder of Richard Davis, a 23-year-old army soldier who had just returned to Fort Benning, Georgia, when he was declared AWOL. The young veteran's charred remains were discovered in the woods 4 months later. Hank Deerfield (Tommy Lee Jones), father of the murdered soldier and a retired army investigator, uncovers the events surrounding his son's murder.

Patton: "What's the matter with you?"

Soldier:"I ... I guess I ... I can't take it, sir."

Patton: "What did you say?"

Soldier: "It's my nerves, sir. I ... I ... I just can't stand the shelling anymore."

Patton: "Your nerves? Well, hell, you're just a God-damned coward."

[Soldier starts sniveling]

Patton: "Shut up! I won't have a yellow bastard sitting here crying in front of these brave men who have been wounded in battle! ... . You're going back to the front, my friend. You may get shot, and you may get killed, but you're going up to the fighting. Either that, or I'm going to stand you up in front of a firing squad. I ought to shoot you myself, you god-damned ... bastard! Get him out of here!"

General George S. Patton slapping and denigrating a soldier coping with PTSD, which would have then likely been called "combat exhaustion."

"Every man I kill, the farther away from home I feel."

Capt. John H. Miller (Tom Hanks) in
Saving Private Ryan (1998)

Waltz with Bashir (2009) is an acclaimed, animated documentary inspired by actual events. Ari Folman, an Israeli veteran of the first Lebanon war, is unable to remember much of what happened when he was engaged in war. His memory is mostly full of gaps as he tries to figure out what happened on the day of a massacre in which he has one distinct memory. He asks questions and confronts his past to deal with his trauma. As students consider the PTSD criteria Ari meets, they might need to extrapolate from particular statements and scenes to fill in gaps where there is a lack of clarity. In an interview about the film, the director shared the experience of finding that the making of the film was therapeutic and healing for him because it helped him directly confront the trauma and reality of war.

Many victims of combat or natural disasters experience what is sometimes referred to as **survivor guilt**. Some might feel guilty when they realize that their lives were spared while those of more "worthy" individuals (e.g., children, young parents) were taken. Consider Tom Cruise's character Ron Kovic, who would meet the criteria for PTSD, in *Born on the Fourth of July* (1989). Kovic's guilt about the death of his buddy "Wilson" is an example of survivor guilt. A brother meets the criteria for PTSD and experiences considerable survivor guilt after his brother dies during a storm in *Ordinary People* (1980).

In the fictitious film *Reign Over Me* (2007), Adam Sandler plays the role of a dentist coping with PTSD and survivor guilt after the death of his wife and three daughters who were passengers on one of the planes involved in the 9/11 destruction of the World Trade Center. Refusing to acknowledge his past or the tragedy, the character Charlie Fineman enters extreme isolation, regressing to a child-like existence in which he spends his time playing video games, listening to loud music, riding around on a scooter, watching movies, and pounding on his drums. He gets considerable emotional support as a results of the efforts of an old friend, another dentist played by Don Cheadle. However, the film is somewhat clumsy in dealing with this delicate subject, and teaches the viewer very little about the sequelae associated with something as traumatic as loss of one's entire family.

Suicide and suicide attempts are common in patients with PTSD. In addition, it is essential to assess for comorbidity (especially substance abuse) in cases of PTSD. Nearly all PTSD patients who are suicidal will be found to have a concomitant psychiatric condition.

The movie *Fearless* (1993) provides an interesting picture of an unusual reaction to trauma. Max Klein (Jeff Bridges) is one of a small group of survivors of a devastating plane crash. He assists a number of other passengers and is celebrated as a hero and a saint. He becomes convinced he is invulnerable and grows increasingly impatient with the banal concerns of his wife and child. After a near-death experience precipitated by an allergic reaction to strawberries, he returns to normal and reestablishes a loving relationship with his wife and son. The movie includes a very interesting segment in which a psy-

chiatrist (who is employed by the airlines because he has written a best-selling book about PTSD) leads a discussion group for survivors of the crash.

Kevin Spacey's portrayal of Prot, a man who claims to be from another planet, presents a diagnostic enigma in *K-Pax* (2001). One way to view the film (another way is discussed in Chapter 3) is to assume that this character has PTSD. The viewer learns through flashbacks that Prot is Robert Porter, a man who experiences trauma when he returns home to find his wife and daughter murdered and the killer still in the house. Prot/Porter reexperiences the trauma under hypnosis and displays significant physiological arousal (e.g., a racing heart rate, elevated blood pressure) when his psychiatrist (Jeff Bridges) forces him to recall the traumatic incident. Porter engaged in extensive avoidance following the trauma – denial, estrangement from his home town, inability to recall information, and a restricted range of affect.

In *The Fisher King* (1991), Robin Williams plays a former college professor who becomes homeless and psychotic after witnessing his wife being gunned down in a restaurant. However, the active, well-formed, and specific hallucinations Williams experiences (e.g., a red knight riding a horse in Central Park with flames shooting out of his head) would be very unlikely to occur as a result of a traumatic experience. The character Jeff Bridges plays in the same film, a disc jockey who withdraws from life and abuses alcohol and drugs after a traumatic event, presents a far more realistic portrayal of PTSD. Although *The Fisher King* is imprecise and confusing in the way it links trauma to psychosis, PTSD is not uncommon among people who are homeless.

The stressors experienced by homeless people are illustrated in the films *Ironweed* (1987) and *The Saint of Fort Washington* (1993). *Ironweed* (1987) is a compelling film in which Jack Nicholson plays an alcoholic whose drinking is apparently related to his guilt about dropping and killing his infant son. Many of the symptoms of PTSD have become obliterated by Nicholson's alcoholism, which has become the dominant theme in his life. *Ironweed* illustrates the way in which alcohol abuse can develop as a secondary problem in response to trauma and can then become the primary psychological problem as abuse progresses to addiction.

Dozens of movies have been made about the Vietnam War, and many of these (as well as other

Figure 10. *The Hurt Locker* (2008, Warner Bros., Summit Entertainment, et al.). Produced by Katheryn Bigelow, Mark Boal, Nicholas Chartier, and Greg Shapiro. Directed by Kathryn Bigelow.

war movies) illustrate either acute stress disorders or, more commonly in those that follow the hero home after the war, PTSD. Some of the most powerful of these films are *Coming Home* (1978); *The Deer Hunter* (1978); *Apocalypse Now* (1979); *The Killing Fields* (1984); *Rambo: First Blood* (1982) and the numerous *Rambo* sequels; Oliver Stone's trilogy *Platoon* (1986), *Born on the Fourth of July* (1989), and *Heaven and Earth* (1993); *Full Metal Jacket* (1987); *Good Morning, Vietnam* (1987); *Hamburger Hill* (1987); *We Were Soldiers* (2002); and *The Hurt Locker* (2008), in which a soldier assigned to a bomb disposal unit finds readjustment to civilian life almost impossible. *The Hurt Locker* is especially effective in dramatizing the stress associated with making quick life or death decisions in combat situations (Figure 10). The film *Heaven and Earth* (1993) addresses multiple traumas, including those associated with rape, torture, war, and suicide.

In the original version of *The Manchurian Candidate* (1962), Frank Sinatra plays a brain-washed trauma victim who has recurring nightmares. He wakes up screaming with extensive sweating and a recollection of traumatic dreams that seem real. In a recent remake of *The Manchurian Candidate* (2004), director Jonathan Demme updates the film by including contemporary politics and more recent wartime experiences. Denzel Washington plays a major who returns from the Gulf War with PTSD, paranoia, nightmares, and memories he cannot understand. He displays flat affect when he describes events surrounding the war, and he experiences intrusive memories. He becomes obsessed with trying to uncover the truth about what happened to him and his men. He hallucinates blood oozing from the forehead of a woman and has a flashback to a time when he was seeing a hypnotist; this symbolizes a real memory coming back and triggers a panic attack. He slowly begins to put together the sinister pieces of a political plot that involved extensive trauma and torture as well as physical and psychological abuse and brainwashing. PTSD symptoms are also displayed by Nicole Kidman's character in *The Human Stain* (2003) as well as by characters in *Open Hearts* (2002), *The Princess and the Warrior* (2000), and *The Pawnbroker* (1965). The last of these films portrays a defeated concentration camp survivor who has become numb and indifferent in response to wartime experiences that included seeing his wife raped and his children killed.

The film *Mystic River* (2003) portrays multiple characters who experience PTSD, most notably the character of David Boyle (Tim Robbins), who was sexually abused as a young boy, and Jimmy Markum (Sean Penn), whose daughter is murdered. In *Shutter Island* (2010), Leonardo DiCaprio plays the role of Teddy Daniels, a federal marshall who was initially traumatized by his experiences liberating a Nazi concentration camp in World War II, and later by seeing his wife burn to death in a fire. *The Brave One* (2007) deals with the trauma that results when a woman is molested in Central Park and sees her boyfriend being killed.

EMDR: A Documentary Film (2011) presents a series of case histories of people who have benefited from eye movement desensitization and reprocessing (EMDR), a popular but still controversial treatment for PTSDs. Another documentary, *The Invisible War* (2012), documents an epidemic of rape in the military and the ways in which victims are affected by rape (often experiencing PTSD symptoms every bit as serious as those experienced by combat veterans).

Acute Stress Disorder

Acute stress disorder results from exposure to threatened death, serious injury or sexual trauma; it requires at least nine of 14 symptoms be present (e.g., recurrent intrusive memories or dreams, dissociative symptoms, avoidance, sleep disturbance). Acute stress disorder is in many ways similar to PTSD. However, acute stress disorder occurs between 3 days and 1 month following a traumatic event and may resolve quickly or develop into PTSD. In contrast, the symptoms of PTSD by definition have to last more than a month, and the onset of symptoms may occur months or even years after exposure to trauma.

According to the *DSM-5*, acute stress disorder occurs in less than 20% of cases in which the traumatic event did not involve interpersonal assault; however, much higher rates are reported following interpersonal traumatic events such as rape or witnessing public bombings like those that occurred in 2013 during the Boston Marathon. The risk for acute stress disorder is greater for woman, and there

is wide variability across cultures in how people respond to acute stress situations.

Brothers (2009) is a compelling film that offers a rare cinematic depiction of the symptoms of acute stress disorder as they develop into PTSD. The film contrasts the lives of two brothers, Captain Sam Cahill (Toby Maguire) and Tommy Cahill (Jake Gyllenhaal). Sam is happily married to Grace Cahill (Natalie Portman), and Sam can be described as a man of strong character, very involved with his family, responsible, and a hardworking leader. Tommy, on the other hand, is volatile, angry, lacks self-control, has family problems, drinks too much, and cannot sustain a long-term relationship. Their father makes the distinction that Sam is perseverant (there is "no quit in him") while Tommy is a "quitter" who easily gives up. A surprising yet realistic role-reversal takes place. Sam goes to war and is captured and tortured for months in Afghanistan and then forced to do the unthinkable – to beat another soldier to death with a lead pipe, Sam escapes and returns home, hardened, unemotional, and profoundly affected by the traumatic experiences. Tommy, on the other hand, steps up to help his brother's family (his sister-in-law Grace and his two girls). Tommy takes on responsibilities such as remodeling the kitchen, providing genuine care for his nieces, and participating in family gatherings; these acts pave the way for him to then express kindness to a woman he had previously robbed. Meanwhile Sam's acute stress disorder worsens as he is unable to share any of his internal experience with his family, and the intensity of his mental suffering worsens significantly. He projects his pain onto his wife, brother, and daughters. Sam becomes easily irritated and difficult to be around; his daughters pick up on this behavior and even share that they would rather have "Uncle Tommy" around than their dad. Sam's full-blown PTSD becomes so serious that the only thing Sam can imagine doing to cope is to leave his family and return to combat or commit suicide. Then, a turning point emerges when Tommy repeatedly and lovingly reminds him: "You're my brother. You're my family." This breaks through Sam's hardened shell, and he agrees to inpatient treatment. During a hospital visit by his wife, Sam finally shares his horrible secret: "I have seen the end of war. The question is: Can I live again?"

Brothers is directed by Jim Sheridan who tends to make films that deal with redemption within the complexities of family life (e.g., *In America* [2002]). He explains that this film, although ostensibly about war trauma, also is about how a family can put "Humpty Dumpty" back together again. Indeed, PTSD victims often seem to be "shattered."

Martha Marcy May Marlene (2011), directed by Sean Durkin, depicts a young woman, Martha, who has escaped from a cult after being indoctrinated for 2 years. The film shows both the present day coping (acute stress disorder) and flashbacks depicting the cult's abusive practices – drugging, manipulation, subtle inconsistencies, distortion of the word *family,* and use of women to recruit new members into a self-sustaining farming commune. After Martha escapes from the cult through the woods, she calls her estranged sister and finds solace at her sister's remote retreat home. Martha begins to experience memory flashes, paranoia, and blunted affect. She becomes isolated, refuses to share details of her past experiences, and manifests inappropriate behavior. At a party, her paranoia peaks and she loses control. Clearly, she is haunted by her traumatic past, frequently thinking people she meets are cult members trying to recapture her. This film offers a good portrayal of acute stress disorder that is likely to turn into PTSD about a month posttrauma. The related short film, *Mary Last Seen* (2010), also by Durkin, depicts manipulative tactics to indoctrinate a girl into a cult.

In the small, but powerful movie *Grace Is Gone* (2008), Stanley Philips (John Cusack) is unable to accept and process his wife's death in Iraq. Instead, he drives his daughters from the upper Midwest to a Disneyland-like park for a brief vacation. Marisa Tomei's character in the film *In the Bedroom* (2001) experiences a traumatic event when her boyfriend is murdered by her estranged husband. In a subsequent scene, she is shown as depressed and expressionless. Acute stress disorder is also present in Roman Polanski's *Death and the Maiden* (1994) and the TV movie *My House in Umbria* (2003, UK/Italy)

Adjustment Disorders

An adjustment disorder is diagnosed when a person develops significant emotional or behavioral symptoms in response to a particular psychosocial stressor, and the response exceeds what would typically be expected in such a situation. Social, academic, or occupational functioning may be affected. Adjustment disorders are usually associated with depression, anxiety, disturbance of conduct, or some mix-

ture of each.

The adjustment disorder displayed by Terry Ann Wolfmeyer (Joan Allen) in *The Upside of Anger* (2005) includes a mixture of disturbance of conduct and emotions. We see this in her reaction when she learns her husband has been having an affair, and she becomes convinced that he has gone off to Sweden to be with a younger woman. Terry becomes incredibly bitter, irritable, lonely, and explosive. She begins to drink alcohol regularly and becomes increasingly angry and cynical, particularly when interacting with her daughters.

It is not difficult to find other films portraying adjustment disorders – numerous movies exhibit characters facing a stressor, conflict, or challenge, and frequently this affects an area of their functioning in a significant way. Many films depicting relationship stress or those addressing problems with work include characters with adjustment disorder symptoms, such as the anxiety displayed by Harry Sanborn (Jack Nicholson) in *Something's Gotta Give* (2003) and the disturbance of conduct exhibited by Tommy Rowland (Matt Dillon) in *Beautiful Girls* (1996). The protagonist in *Meet Bill* (2007), played by Aaron Eckhart, is a man languishing in several areas of his life. He struggles to cope with his wife's infidelity, and this leads to numerous changes in his life; while at first it disturbs his functioning, he eventually finds ways to make meaning out of the stress he is experiencing. A similar theme (adjusting to infidelity) can be found in *Tennis, Anyone ...?* (2005).

Films that integrate several vignettes or stories are almost certain to have at least one character with an adjustment disorder. Some good examples include *Lantana* (2001), *The Last Kiss* (2006), and *13 Conversations About One Thing* (2001).

Persistent Complex Bereavement Disorder

Persistent complex bereavement disorder, a controversial diagnosis, is noted as a "condition for further study" in *DSM-5*, and at the same time, it can be diagnosed under the coding for other specified trauma- and stressor-related disorder. This means that grief symptoms following the death of a loved one cause clinically significant distress or impairment in social, occupational, or other important areas of functioning. *DSM-5* suggests that this "disorder" occurs if the symptoms last longer than

12 months after the death of a loved one for adults and longer than 6 months after the death for children. The individual may have a reactive distress to the death (e.g., difficulty with positive reminiscing, accepting, and believing the death) and social/identity disruption (e.g., a desire to die to be with the deceased, feeling life is meaningless). One of the controversies with the *DSM-5* involved the decision to remove the *DSM-IV* "bereavement exclusion," which stated that major depressive disorder could not be diagnosed in anyone who had experienced a recent loss of a loved one; this change ostensibly helps clinicians avoid overlooking cases of major depressive disorder that could be helped by aggressive treatment. However, many mental health providers feel that grief and bereavement are existential challenges all of us will face at some point, and they believe it is inappropriate to pathologize those emotions that are quite naturally associated with loss. These clinicians emphasize that the experience of bereavement symptoms and suffering is normal, especially following the loss of someone close to oneself. Indeed, to *not* experience these symptoms after the loss of someone you deeply love would be pathological.

Two poignant films about bereavement of parents following the loss of a child are the independent film *Morning* (2010) and the popular film *Rabbit Hole* (2010), the latter starring Nichole Kidman and Aaron Eckhart. Each film shows unproductive and unhealthy coping and a significant impact of loss on marital relationships. Grief counselors and support groups are depicted in both films. *Morning* offers a somewhat melodramatic illustration of coping; for example, the husband regresses to childlike behavior as he makes a mess of the house, hits the tops of indoor flowers with his golf club, and runs around the house as if playing "cowboys and Indians," while the wife dissociates while putting on makeup at a department story and runs to the bathroom to vomit. Whenever she is reminded of her son, she screams – wherever she is. Although we would caution against giving ANY of these characters this diagnosis, we include these films because of their compelling portrayal of bereavement. In addition they would not meet *DSM-5* criteria, because the films do not depict the characters' lives post-12 months from the death of each child. A third movie depicting bereaved parents following the loss of a child is Lars von Trier's *Antichrist* (2009), a film that takes the disturbing content (i.e., the recent, untimely death of a child) and devastated parents to a new level, in which the parents deal with their grief by beginning to torture one another. Each of the characters in these films should be monitored over the months and years for not only complicated bereavement but also depression and conditions relating to stress/trauma.

In *Mother Ghost* (2002), a man begins to have significant conflicts with his wife, ignores his son, numbs his pain by getting drunk, and is unable to sleep. At the same time, his deceased mother's jewelry begins to appear. The reactions to deaths in both *Truly, Madly, Deeply* (1991) and *In the Bedroom* (2001) seem to go beyond "healthy" bereavement and consequently would warrant a diagnosis, though by the end of each film, the viewer gets the sense that the characters have found healing and have learned to cope with their losses. Sandy Edwards (Toni Collette) in *Japanese Story* (2003) and a young girl in *Ponette* (1996) both experience protracted bereavement.

In each of the following three films the bereaved character copes by immediately going on a journey in reaction to his or her pain: Jack Nicholson as Warren loses his wife of many years in *About Schmidt* (2002), a young woman loses her beloved father in *Searching for Paradise* (2002), and another young woman loses her boyfriend to suicide in *Movern Callor* (2002).

International Films: Trauma- and Stressor-Related Disorders

Enduring Love (2004, UK) is a film about a freak hot air balloon accident in which several men attempt to save a young boy by grabbing onto a hot air balloon that is out of control. As the balloon rises higher and higher, each man saves himself by letting go soon enough, except for one who eventually dies. This traumatic incident leads the protagonist to develop symptoms of acute stress disorder and to vacillate from avoidance to rumination and from detachment to agitation in his relationships. His emotional distress is palpable as he displays inappropriate affect and struggles with guilt and anger.

In the Australian film *Walking on Water* (2002), an assisted-suicide plan for a man dying of AIDS goes awry, and a friend forcefully suffocates the dying man. The friend is plagued by intrusive images and memories of the suffocation; he tries hard to avoid his memories, acts out in self-destructive ways, and displays considerable irritability and interpersonal conflict. He appears to be suffering from acute stress disorder.

 Critical Thinking Questions

➤ How might the cinematic characters who have returned from the Iraq war with PTSD differ from those who returned from Vietnam with PTSD?

➤ At what point does normal, healthy bereavement become unhealthy and abnormal? Is it possible to put symptom labels and a timeline on bereavement?

➤ Are EMDR and hypnosis effective treatments for PTSD? What is your evidence?

➤ Can adjustment disorders be more severe than other major psychiatric disorders? At what point should they be treated with medication?

➤ Can adjustment disorders last for years, or is this contrary to the definition?

Authors' Picks

If you have time to read just one book relevant to this chapter, make it:

Vasterling, J. J., Bryant, R. A., & Keane, T. M. Eds. (2012). *PTSD and mild traumatic brain injury.* New York: Guilford Press.

If you only have time for one article, read:

Kearns, M. C., Ressler, K. J., Zatzick, D., & Rothbaum, B. O. (2012). Early interventions for PTSD: A review. *Depression and Anxiety, 29,* 833–842. doi: 10.1002/da.21997

Wedding and Niemiec's Top 10 Trauma- and Stress-Related Disorders Films

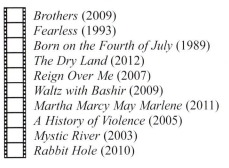

- *Brothers* (2009)
- *Fearless* (1993)
- *Born on the Fourth of July* (1989)
- *The Dry Land* (2012)
- *Reign Over Me* (2007)
- *Waltz with Bashir* (2009)
- *Martha Marcy May Marlene* (2011)
- *A History of Violence* (2005)
- *Mystic River* (2003)
- *Rabbit Hole* (2010)

Chapter 7

Dissociative Disorders

Matricide is probably the most unbearable crime of all ... so he had to erase the crime, at least in his own mind.

A police psychiatrist attempts to explain Norman Bates' behavior in *Psycho* (1960)

➤ Alfred Hitchcock's *Psycho* (1960) is regarded as one of the greatest films ever made. Is it an accurate presentation of mental illness?

➤ Do films like *Psycho* do a disservice to people with mental disorders by perpetuating the myth of the homicidal psychopath?

➤ Bates's voyeurism seems almost innocuous compared with his other behaviors. How often are paraphilic disorders (such as voyeurism) linked with violence?

➤ Bates has trouble saying the word *bathroom* when he shows the hotel room to Marion (Janet Leigh). Is it common for people who commit sexual crimes to be uncomfortable with mature discussions of sexuality or elimination?

➤ How often in a lifetime of clinical experience would a therapist treat a patient with a dissociative disorder? How often would a Norman Bates come along?

➤ Marion has stolen $40,000. How does Hitchcock manage to make her a sympathetic character with whom we can all identify?

➤ How does a patient with a dissociative disorder suppress the evidence presented by everyday experience (e.g., the nonresponsiveness of the dead Mrs. Bates)?

➤ How does Hitchcock's storyline fit with the psychological zeitgeist of the 1960s?

➤ Would you feel comfortable working with a patient like Norman Bates? Would you insist that security officers be present during your evaluation?

Patient Evaluation

Name: Norman Bates

Patient's stated reason for coming
"I had to come. They made me. Of course, I'm eager to get any help you can offer. I truly do suspect you can be helpful."

History of the present illness
Norman Bates is a 27-year-old White man who has been referred for psychological evaluation by the Madison County Court. Mr. Bates is awaiting sentencing on four counts of murder. The alleged murder of his mother and stepfather occurred more than a decade ago; the two recent killings are reported to have occurred within the past 30 days.

Past psychiatric illness, treatment, and outcomes
Mr. Bates has a long history of eccentric and odd behavior, including isolation, withdrawal, reclusiveness, and secrecy. Local authorities have noted these behaviors; however, there has never been any evidence of danger to self or others, and Mr. Bates has never received treatment in the mental health system.

Medical history
There is a history of the usual childhood diseases, such as mumps and chicken pox. Aside from these childhood experiences, Mr. Bates has never seen a physician. He has never been hospitalized.

Psychosocial history
Mr. Norman Bates reports that he started to walk and talk at about the normal times. He has a long history of self-imposed isolation. He is reported to have been lonely and withdrawn in school, and he cannot identify anyone he regarded as a friend when he was growing up. He obtained passing grades, although he dropped out of school at the age of 16 to help run a family motel. When the expressway bypassed the motel, business dwindled to almost nothing. His mother and stepfather died approximately 10 years ago; since that time, Mr. Bates has managed the motel and the

family home on his own. He manages the books for the motel, and he performs routine maintenance on both the motel and the family home. He has no brothers or sisters, and there are no living relatives. He reports devoting almost all of his leisure time to his hobby of taxidermy. Mr. Bates has never been married or involved in a significant romantic relationship. He does not date, and he has no regular or routine social activities.

Drug and alcohol history
Mr. Bates denies any history of drug or alcohol use. He believes drunkenness is a sin, and he prefers not to be tempted by social drinking. He does not smoke.

Behavioral observations
Mr. Bates arrived on time for the evaluation, accompanied by a deputy sheriff. He was appropriately groomed and dressed. He was polite to the point of being obsequious. He cooperated fully with all tasks, except for those instances in which his identity would be questioned or challenged. At these points, the patient became resentful and stopped cooperating with the evaluation.

Mental status examination
Mr. Bates was alert and oriented to place and time. He was disoriented to person, however, and steadfastly maintained that he was actually his mother. He became agitated and threatened to leave the room when the obvious was pointed out (e.g., he had male features, she had been buried some years ago, etc.). After the evaluator stopped challenging his assertion that he was in fact his mother, he cooperated with the evaluation and was able to answer all other questions on the Mini-Mental State Examination, obtaining an overall score of 29.

Functional assessment
The patient appears to be of average intellectual ability. He has not completed high school, and he has no significant occupational abilities other than minimal bookkeeping skills. However, he appears to have been able to manage on his own for the past 10 years. He has no living family, and there are no friends to provide social support. (Mr. Bates appears comfortable in his isolation and does not appear to be distressed by the solitary nature of his existence.) Mr. Bates's social skills are limited, and he tends to be quite awkward and uncomfortable in social situations. However, his entrenched and well-defended delusional disorder appears to be his most limiting feature, and he is unlikely to function successfully in either occupational or social settings as long as he continues to maintain he is his mother.

Strengths
Mr. Bates has normal intellectual ability, and he possesses the skills necessary to manage on his own. He is usually friendly, and he has many years of experience as a hotel manager. On the VIA Survey, a measure of character strengths, Mr. Bates scored high on prudence, self-regulation, humility, and honesty.

Diagnosis
Dissociative identity disorder (F44.81).

Treatment plan
Mr. Bates was referred by the court for a forensic evaluation, and therefore no systematic treatment plan has been developed. Given his legal problems, it is likely that Mr. Bates will be imprisoned for life, and it is unlikely he will be offered the benefits of active psychological treatment in the correctional system. Even if treatment is available, it will require years of daily work before Mr. Bates begins to understand himself or his problems.

Prognosis
Mr. Bates lacks insight into the nature of his problems or their causes. He resists efforts to change his belief system. He has maintained these fallacious beliefs for the past decade, and they are likely to prove intractable. If he is acquitted by reason of insanity, he will be remanded to the state hospital for intensive treatment. However, even then his prognosis is poor.

Psycho and Psychopathology

In the latter half of the 1900s, films began depicting the psychological complexities of the human personality. *Psycho*, Alfred Hitchcock's 1960 film, describes a young man who assumed the personality of his mother after he murdered her and her lover. This film is regarded by many as Hitchcock's finest film. It is a superb movie; unfortunately, it also contributes to the negative stereotype of persons with mental illnesses.

The film begins in a hotel room in Phoenix, with Marion Crane, played by Janet Leigh, who is scantily dressed. She is discussing her future with her lover, Sam Loomis, played by John Gavin. Marion wants to get married, but Sam is unable to make a commitment because of previous financial commitments to his ex-wife. After the afternoon rendezvous, she returns to work, where she steals $40,000. The next morning she heads toward Sam's hometown with the money.

During a rainstorm, she seeks shelter at the Bates Motel, only 15 miles from Sam's home. Nor-

man Bates, played by Anthony Perkins, invites her to dinner at his home behind the motel. Marion hears Norman's mother yelling at him for wanting to bring a girl to dinner. Norman fixes sandwiches for Marion and apologizes for his mother's behavior. They talk in a room adjacent to the office, and Norman shows off his taxidermy collection. Norman later watches her undress through a peephole separating her room from the office. That night Marion is brutally murdered by someone who appears to be Norman's mother. The murder scene occurs in a shower, and this scene (with its dramatic, nondiegetic music) is one of the most famous scenes in film history.

Norman cleans up the blood from the shower and puts Marion's body in the trunk of her new car (and unknowingly hides the stolen $40,000 there as well). He then drives the car to an isolated area, where he is able to sink the car and its contents into a swamp.

Instead of telling the police about the stolen money, Marion's boss hires a private detective, Milton Arbogast, to track Marion and recover the money. He traces her to the Bates Motel after fol-

Figure 11. *Psycho* (1960, Paramount Pictures/Universal Pictures). Produced by Alfred Hitchcock. Directed by Alfred Hitchcock.

lowing Marion's sister, Lila, to Sam's. Neither Lila nor Sam know anything about the stolen money. Mr. Arbogast is killed when he visits the Bates home to investigate his hunch that Norman Bates is somehow involved in the disappearance of Marion.

"I'll just sit here and be quiet, just in case they do suspect me. They're probably watching me. Well, let them. Let them see what kind of a person I am. I'm not even going to swat that fly. I hope they are watching. They'll see. They'll see and they'll know and they'll say, 'Why, she wouldn't even harm a fly.'"

Norman Bates sits in his (her) cell, smiling and thinking to himself (herself) about the future in *Psycho* (1960)

Lila and Sam then contact the local sheriff, who is willing to investigate Marion's disappearance if an official missing persons report is made. He also informs Sam and Lila that Norman's mother has been dead for 10 years and that she killed herself after poisoning her lover.

Lila and Sam return to the motel to solve the case. In a very suspenseful ending, they find that Norman Bates had exhumed his mother's grave, mummified her corpse, and kept her body with him in the house for the past 10 years. Bates had always been a disturbed child, and, after he killed his mother and her lover, he coped with his guilt by assuming her identity. By the end of the movie, Norman has totally assumed the alter ego of his mother, as can be seen when he attempts to kill Lila dressed in his mother's clothes (see Figure 11).

Gus Van Sant remade *Psycho* in 1998, this time in color. Van Sant's version is faithful to the original script and pays homage to Hitchcock, but the remake lacks the power and fascination of the original.

Dissociation and Films

Alteration in consciousness can occur under many different conditions. With alcohol intoxication, there is a clouding of consciousness, with attenuated awareness of sensory stimuli and diminished attention to the environment and self. Some drugs produce a dream-like state in which the individual is conscious but inattentive. Heightened states of attention, concentration, and absorption brought about through hypnosis, meditation, or relaxation are further examples of alterations in consciousness.

Dissociation involves an unwelcome shift in consciousness that is accompanied by the sense that one's core identity has changed. In dissociation, events and information that would ordinarily be connected or integrated are divided from one another. Dissociation is often viewed as a normal defense mechanism that can be used in frightening, stressful, or painful situations to cope with stress. It allows an individual to detach from overwhelming fear, pain, and helplessness generated by trauma.

Dissociation can be viewed on a continuum from minor dissociative experiences of everyday life (i.e., daydreaming) to major forms of psychopathology, such as multiple personality disorder (Allen & Smith, 1993; Bernstein & Putnam, 1986). Most people have minor dissociative experiences, such as driving a car over a familiar route and suddenly realizing that they do not remember what happened during all or part of the trip. In some cultures, dissociative states, such as trances, are common and accepted cultural activities or a routine part of religious experience. The development of extreme dissociative behavior patterns has been linked to trauma. For example, in *Sybil* (1976), the lead character's development of 16 different personalities was found to be the result of repeated physical and psychological abuse she experienced at the hands of a deranged and delusional mother.

Numerous films depict characters experiencing a traumatic event and many depict the lead character dissociating from the traumatic experience in order to cope. However, it is unlikely that any of the characters in the following five examples would be given a dissociative disorder diagnosis, as there is not enough evidence in the film to meet all of the diagnostic criteria. In *Lilya 4-Ever* (2002), a young girl is prostituted against her will in a foreign country, and she is neglected and abused; she dissociates during sexual intercourse with a paying customer. In *The Princess and the Warrior* (2001), a man is trapped in a bathroom stall while his wife is killed; his various traumatic reactions include "freezing," dissociating from reality, feeling tense and shaky, and experiencing flashbacks. In *Natural Born Kill-*

ers (1994), Woody Harrelson and Juliette Lewis play characters who are both victims and perpetrators of various violent and traumatic events; in the film, dissociative numbing, dissociative perceptual distortion, dissociative time distortion, and dissociative derealization are depicted. *Swimming Pool* (2002) portrays a young woman exhibiting dissociative amnesia in her inability to remember killing a man. One particular dissociative episode occurs when she thinks she is seeing her mother; she screams when she is told her mother is not there, and then she faints. In the independent film *Searching for Paradise* (2002), a woman, in the middle of sex with a "fantasy-come-true" man, suddenly stops and states she feels betrayed by her partner; this seems to be a dissociative experience in which she is confusing her father who had left her and this "fantasy" man who has become real.

Another dissociative experience often present in traumatic situations is **derealization** or **depersonalization**. In derealization, a person feels detached from familiar people or places that seem unreal and unrecognizable. The size or shape of objects may be perceived as altered or strange, and people may seem mechanical. During the 1989 San Francisco Bay Area earthquake, 40% of the 101 persons interviewed afterward reported feeling as though their surroundings were unreal (Cardea & Spiegel, 1993). David Lynch's films seem to induce a derealization state for both his characters and his viewers, his characters' identities are often confused, and locations seem unreal. The films *Lost Highway* (1997) and *Mulholland Drive* (2001) are particularly good examples of this kind of derealization. Depersonalization is related and occurs when someone feels that he or she is "outside their body" observing themselves behave and think as though they were watching a third party interacting with the world. In *DSM-5*, derealization/depersonalization are linked into a single syndrome.

Dissociative Disorders in Films

There is controversy in the mental health community about the categorization of dissociative experiences as psychiatric disorders. Dissociation, by itself, does not necessarily lead to impairment and is not clear evidence of psychopathology. However, if dissociative states lead to distress and im-

pairment in psychological, interpersonal, social, or vocational functioning, then they should be evaluated as psychiatric problems. Because dissociative symptoms such as amnesia and depersonalization can be present in other psychiatric disorders such as PTSD and schizophrenia, no other psychiatric disorders can be present if a person's symptoms are diagnosed as a dissociative disorder. In addition, the disorder cannot be caused by a traumatic brain injury; this is the reason films such as *Memento* (2000) are discussed in Chapter 12 "Neurocognitive Disorders." There are three primary dissociative disorders: dissociative identity disorder, dissociative amnesia, and depersonalization/derealization disorder.

Dissociative Identity Disorder

Dissociative identity disorder (DID), formerly called multiple personality disorder, is an extremely rare condition characterized by disturbances in memory and identity along with a marked discontinuity in one's sense of self. The essential feature is the presence of two or more distinct identities, or alters (personality states), that assume control over behavior. Amnesia is present in one or more of the personalities. Usually, the more passive the personality, the greater the amnesia. DID is usually believed to be a posttraumatic condition that emerges after overwhelming traumatic childhood experiences.

The symptoms of DID are associated with many other psychiatric states such as anxiety symptoms (phobia, panic attacks, and obsessive-compulsive behaviors), mood symptoms (manic and depressive), other dissociative symptoms (amnesias, fugues, and depersonalization), somatic symptoms (conversion), sexual dysfunctions, suicide attempts, self-mutilations, substance abuse, eating disorders, sleep disturbance, symptoms of schizophrenia, symptoms of PTSD, and borderline personality disorder. Since many symptoms of PTSD occur in DID, some argue that these two are variants of the same disorder (Piper & Merskey, 2004).

The *DSM-5* cites a study suggesting a 12-month prevalence for DID of 1.5%, with males slightly more likely to develop the condition than females. However, many mental health professionals challenge the very existence of DID, and they would be very dubious about a prevalence as high as that suggested by the *DSM-5* (Lilienfeld & Berg, 2012; Nathan, 2011). Debbie Nathan's book *Sybil Exposed: The Extraordinary Story Behind the Famous Multiple Personality Case*, suggests that the Sybil story is "scant[ly] more than an elaborate fabrication, an intricate web of lies spun by an ambitious psychiatrist and eager journalist" (Lilienfeld & Berg, 2012, n.p.). In their review of this book, Scott Lilienfeld and Joanna Berg (2012) note that

> Prior to the publication of *Sybil*, DID was presumed to be an exceedingly rare condition, even a psychiatric curiosity. As of 1970, there were fewer than 80 documented cases of DID in the world literature … . Yet not long after Sybil's story appeared in print and on the small screen, the number of DID cases skyrocketed. By 1986, there were approximately 6,000 reported cases of DID; by 1998, this number had mushroomed to 40,000. Today, some DID experts place the prevalence of DID at several million individuals in the United States alone; psychiatrist Colin Ross (1991) contends that DID is at least as common as schizophrenia.

> Sybil's influence did not end there. As Spanos (1994) observed, prior to the publication of *Sybil*, few if any individuals with DID reported a history of child abuse. Following *Sybil*, severe abuse became a virtually ubiquitous fixture of DID's clinical portrait, so much so that some experts regarded it as a *sine qua non* for the condition's emergence. Furthermore, before *Sybil*, most individuals with DID reported only one alter (the so-called split personality); following *Sybil*, most reported multiple alters (Lilienfeld et al., 1999). … From its inception, the DID epidemic (Boor, 1982) was dogged by a vexing question. Are the alters in DID discovered, as DID advocates insist, or are they created? (Lilienfeld & Berg, 2012)

There is no evidence of spontaneous remission or integration of personality alters without mental health treatment. Therapy is long-term and requires the establishment of a strong therapeutic relationship with the individual. Hypnosis may be used at varying stages of treatment. Through the support of the relationship, the original traumas are accessed and examined, and the psychological pain is soothed and viewed from an adult perspective. At this point in therapy, internal conflict can be addressed and resolved.

Peacock

Cillian Murphy offers an extraordinary performance as both the male and female personalities of the same character in *Peacock* (2010), a film that clearly focuses on depicting DID. The film offers an in-depth character analysis, accurate depiction of a dissociative disorder, and realistic psychopathology origins. Unfortunately, this otherwise great portrayal of DID is marred by the significant violence of the protagonist, hence perpetrating the misconception that all people with mental illness are violent. This stereotype is rampant in the majority of films attempting to portray DID.

The protagonist in *Peacock* is John, a passive, taciturn, and socially awkward man. He is a compliant and hard worker who isolates himself at work and at home. The viewer learns that after John's mother died over a year ago, a new personality called Emma emerged; Emma is sweet and quiet, but thoughtful. Emma writes love notes to John and prepares his food. Following a random incident of a train going off the track and ending up in his front yard, John and his house are thrust into the public eye, as townspeople and political figures attempt to learn more and even take advantage of the situation. As a result, John becomes more controlling, irritable, and impulsive, and he begins to unravel. Interestingly, Emma develops in a positive way: She becomes more altruistic and caring while maintaining insight. Both personalities know of the other's existence but are not necessarily aware of everything the other says and does.

DID is associated with trauma, abuse, neglect, and other overwhelming experiences. In *Peacock*, significant abuse is indeed alluded to, but it is not depicted in the film. The viewer learns that John's mother forced John to have sex with a call girl named Maggie (Ellen Page) who became pregnant. His mother then gave Maggie monthly child support.

The interior of the home is eerie and dark, and the identity switch from John to Emma occurs in John's mother's room where he puts on extensive makeup and dresses up in dainty clothes. In one scene, Maggie comments that she thought Emma was the mother due to the similar appearance. As the film progresses, the Emma alter appears to have taken substantial control of John and becomes protective, generous, and supportive of Maggie and her son. She encourages them to safely leave the town of Peacock, Nebraska. At one point Emma takes a photo of the son playing, which appears to replace the painful childhood memories. In an attempt to outsmart Emma, John kills a vagabond and burns the body and a motel room in order to fake his own death.

Cillian Murphy engaged in extensive analysis of DID to play the roles of John and Emma. He reported that he studied the origins, pathogenesis, and diagnosis of DID to fully capture the complexities and subtleties of this interesting condition.

Fight Club, Identity, and Secret Window

None of these three popular, contemporary film examples of DID is especially helpful in portraying important and accurate psychopathology information of this disorder, and they are not as educational as *The Three Faces of Eve* (1957) and *Sybil* (1976) (to be discussed in the section "Sybil"). In their defense, these films do not pretend to educate viewers about DID; instead, the condition is used as an important plot device to enhance excitement, in-

trigue, fascination, and entertainment. Each of the three films is unique in its cinematic approach and has something to offer the viewer interested in dissociative disorders, and therefore each is worth seeing.

David Fincher's fast-paced, visceral *Fight Club* (1999) begins with the narrator, Jack (brilliantly played by Edward Norton), struggling with insomnia and perhaps depression. Jack begins to deteriorate as he is entrenched in an unsatisfying consumerist lifestyle, feels apathetic at work, and becomes addicted to attending different support group meetings each day just for emotional release. The culmination of his deterioration happens early on in the film when he meets Tyler Durden (Brad Pitt), although he (and the viewer) do not realize Tyler is Jack's alter ego for much of the film. Tyler is everything Jack is not: flamboyant, exciting, seductive, unconventional, and self-empowering. The dramatically different personalty types are illustrated in

Figure 12. *Fight Club* (1999, 20th Century Fox). Produced by Art Linson, Ross Grayson Bell, and Ceán Chaffin. Directed by David Fincher.

Figure 12. The two (really just Jack) fight one another (he fights himself) and begin a "fight club" that attracts other disenfranchised men wanting a release. It is interesting to note that there are many clues to Jack's DID given in the film, including one-frame cinematic flashes of Tyler Durden until the full alter develops, illustrating Jack's full dissociation. Some mental health professionals argue that the identities of DID typically are not aware of one another; this is the case in *Fight Club*.

Identity (2003) takes a different approach to DID. The viewer sees two stories: One story depicts 10 characters stranded at an isolated motel trying to hide from and elude a mysterious serial killer on the loose in the area; the other story portrays a convicted serial killer, Malcolm Rivers, on the night of his final hearing before having the death penalty carried out. The viewer later learns these two stories are integrated in that Malcolm has DID and that the 10 characters represent Malcolm's alters whom he is trying to kill off to achieve integration.

Secret Window (2004) manipulates the viewer, and it is not until the conclusion of the film that the protagonist's DID is revealed. Johnny Depp plays Mort, a man who experiences the trauma of seeing his wife cheating on him in a motel room. Mort confines and isolates himself in the woods to write his next novel and subsequently begins to deteriorate (this is a direct parallel with Jack Nicholson's famous and more dramatic character in *The Shining* [1980]). Coinciding with his deterioration (which takes the form of angst about his deteriorating marriage, anger toward his wife's boyfriend, an inability to quit smoking, alcohol abuse, and writer's block), are Mort's provocative encounters with Shooter (John Turturro) who wants amends, claiming Mort has stolen his story. These interactions become more dangerous and threatening, and Shooter kills various people and Mort's dog. Toward the end, a frustrated Mort throws an ashtray against the wall – the wall and house begin to crack, and he hallucinates the crack spreading around the house; this scene is a metaphor for his own fragility and continuing decompensation. We then see Mort talking to himself and begin to hear his inner voice, which then shows up visually and multiplies. Mort had been so afraid of the Shooter part of his personality that he developed it as an alter and suppressed it from his conscious awareness.

The Three Faces of Eve

In *The Three Faces of Eve* (1957), narrator Alistair Cooke prepares the viewer for a true story about a woman with multiple personality disorder (i.e., DID). This black-and-white film takes place in 1951 in a small Georgia town. Joanne Woodward introduces the viewer to Eve White, a quiet, passive, modest homemaker who begins having severe headaches, followed by "spells." She cannot remember what she does during these spells. Mrs. White is married to a rigid, dull, unimaginative man named Ralph, who is frustrated with the changes in his wife's behavior. Their unhappy marriage is even more stressed by these unexplained events.

During these spells, Eve Black, the second personality, "comes out." Eve Black is a seductive, sexually promiscuous single woman, who buys flashy and provocative clothes, smokes, drinks, and frequents nightclubs. Eve White, who is unaware of Eve Black's existence, is afraid she is going crazy because of her unexplained periods of amnesia and hearing voices. Eve Black, on the other hand, knows of Eve White, dislikes her husband and their child, Bonnie, and delights in having Eve White feel the hangover following Eve Black's night of carousing. Eve White and her husband seek psychiatric treatment from Dr. Curtis Luther, played by Lee J. Cobb, for her headaches and spells.

It is well over a year before Dr. Luther is able to identify the existence of Eve Black. Following an incident in which Eve Black attempts to strangle Bonnie, Eve White is admitted to the hospital. She vows not to be reunited with her daughter until she is well. While Eve is in the hospital, Dr. Luther is able to establish a therapeutic relationship with both personalities and attempts to integrate them into one. The diagnosis of multiple personality disorder is explained to Eve White and her spouse, who both attempt to understand the problem. Ralph is never able to understand the disorder and eventually divorces Eve.

As Eve White struggles to work during the day, Eve Black parties at night. They both continue to be treated by Dr. Luther. Eventually, a third personality, Jane, emerges who is aware of both Eve White and Eve Black, even though neither is aware of her. Following a visit with her daughter, Bonnie, at her parents' home, Jane begins to have memories of playing under the porch as a child. Gradually, through the use of hypnosis, Dr. Luther is able to help Eve recall the trauma that precipitated her personalities splitting (being forced to kiss her dead grandmother's corpse). After reliving the memory, only Jane remains.

Sybil

The film *Sybil* (1976), based upon a true story, stars Sally Field as Sybil and Joanne Woodward as Dr. Cornelia Wilbur. It is interesting to note that Woodward, who received an Academy Award in 1957 for her lead role in *The Three Faces of Eve,* returned almost 2 decades later to play the psychiatrist treating Sybil. The viewer is introduced to Sybil, a distressed young woman who is working as a preschool teacher while attending art school. As Sybil is talking with the children, the creaking sound of a swing stirs traumatic childhood memories. Sybil unsuccessfully attempts to attend to her assigned task of organizing the children into a game of follow-the-leader. In the next scene, Sybil is standing in the middle of a fountain, obviously confused. Her supervisor is scolding her for leading the children the wrong way. Sybil returns to her apartment, where she curls into a fetal position, trying to escape her tormenting memories. In desperation, she breaks her apartment window, which seems to give her some psychological relief. Because of her cut wrist, she ends up in an emergency room. Due to her confusion, she is referred to a psychiatrist, Dr. Wilbur, who evaluates her and begins treatment that lasts for 11 years.

This episode represents one of many in which Sybil is initially overwhelmed with flashbacks of traumatic childhood events that lead to periods of irrational behavior followed by a climactic event, such as breaking a window and injuring herself. The viewer gradually realizes that as Sybil recalls traumatic memories, one of her 16 other personalities, or "alters," gains control and triggers the irrational behavior. Each of the other alters represents a part of Sybil and serves a particular purpose. For example, Vanessa is musical and enjoys playing the music Sybil once played. Vicki is very much in charge of life and is fearless. Peggy is a child who feels the terror and anger of childhood trauma. Marsha represents her despair and is often suicidal.

Through interaction with the different personalities and the use of hypnosis, Dr. Wilbur gradually pieces together Sybil's traumatic past. The goal of

therapy is to integrate the personalities by helping the alters remember the past, experience the emotions associated with the traumatic events, and develop an adult perspective on the trauma. Patiently, Dr. Wilbur develops a warm, therapeutic relationship with all of the alters who are able to share their experiences. Dr. Wilbur, in turn, is able to help Sybil remember parts of her life that were previously shut off. Gradually, as the repeated abuse of her childhood is relived, Sybil is able to remember her childhood experiences and integrate them into her whole personality.

Frankie & Alice

Frankie & Alice (2010) stars Halle Berry as Francine (Frankie) Murdoch, a woman with DID. Frankie works in a strip club, and she has multiple problems in her life that ultimately bring her to a psychiatric hospital where she meets Dr. Joseph Oswald (Dr. Oz) who diagnoses three distinct personalities: Frankie, a right-handed 32-year-old Black woman; Alice, a left-handed Southern White woman of indeterminate age; and "Genius," a very bright but very frightened young child. Interestingly, the personality of Alice is quite racist. Dr. Oz uses hypnosis to treat and eventually integrate the three distinct personalities. The movie is based on a true story. Although we appreciate and admire Halle Berry, the film is ultimately disappointing and teaches little about DID.

Frankie Murdoch: "Multiple personality, huh? But, who are they?"

Oz: "Well, they're you. Your aspects of you. Your subconscious."

Frankie Murdoch: "Okay, but why?"

Oz: "That's what we'll have to find out."

Frankie Murdoch: "So, what you're saying is, I got all these different … people living inside of me, right? But, I don't know who they are."

Oz: "Well, we all have different personalities and different selves. "Do I contradict myself? Very well, then I contradict myself. I am large, I contain multitudes." It's Whitman."

Dr. Oz describes dissociative identity disorder in *Frankie & Alice* (2010)

Other Dissociative Identity Disorder Films

The film *Primal Fear* (1996) should be seen to provide a certain degree of skeptical balance, as it portrays a man (Edward Norton) who feigns DID in an attempt to evade murder charges. This film reminds clinicians of the potential for malingering in suspected cases of multiple personality disorder.

In *X-Men: The Last Stand* (2006), superheroine mutant Jean Grey is portrayed as someone with a dissociative personality disorder. She quickly becomes a danger to herself and others and, as is painfully common in most films depicting "split personalities," the alter becomes dangerous, murderous, out-of-control, and perpetrates the misconception that people with mental illness are violent. Actress Famke Janssen, who researched DID to make her character more realistic, plays the part. The movie is an allegory in which society's need to control and limit the mutant's powers parallels society's inevitable attempts to make "them" more like "us."

DIDs are also illustrated in *Raising Cain* (1992) and *Voices Within: The Lives of Truddi Chase* (1990), a made-for-TV movie based on the bestselling book *When Rabbit Howls*. The movie *Birdy* (1984) stars Matthew Modine and Nicholas Cage playing the roles of Birdy and Al, two Vietnam veterans who have been traumatized by the war. Birdy has always been obsessed with birds, and he is passionate in his attempts to fly; after Vietnam, he is hospitalized because of his mutism and his belief that he is in fact a bird. With help from Al, Birdy recovers, begins to speak, and the two men escape from the military hospital where they have been confined. It is not at all clear whether Birdy's condition is best conceptualized as a DID or a delusional disorder; however, it is apparent that Birdy has become amnestic for much of what happened to him while in Vietnam.

In *Me, Myself & Irene* (2000), Jim Carrey plays Charlie, a state-trooper and a cuckold with a double identity as Hank. Charlie is insecure, hesitant, and bumbling; Hank is confidant, self-assured, and quite a ladies man. Despite occasional funny moments, the movie ultimately disappoints and gets laughs at the expense of people with mental illness. For example, when someone incapacitates Hank with a Taser and shouts to his friends "Let's kick the shit out of this bastard," Irene (Renée Zellweger) comes to Hank's rescue, shouting, "Wait, he's a schizo!" Most audiences laugh at both lines.

Dissociative Amnesia

Dissociative amnesias are characterized by an inability to recall important personal information, usually of a traumatic or stressful nature (e.g., the death of a child). Affected individuals can usually remember events up to the time of the trauma but have memory loss for events that occur after the event. Even though significant personal information is lost with dissociative amnesias, cognitive abilities and the ability to remember new information remain intact. This memory impairment is reversible. In the classic disorder, the person is quickly brought to a mental health provider because of the overt, dramatic change in memory. Persons with amnesia may have intense emotional reactions to stimuli without knowing the reasons for the reaction or the significance of it.

Even though filmmakers do not typically focus on the psychological etiology of amnesia, they have often used amnesia as a central theme. One example is the 1940 Academy Award–winning satire, *The Great Dictator*, starring Charles Chaplin, Paulette Goddard, and Jack Oakie. Chaplin plays a dual role as a Jewish barber and Adenoid Hynkel, dictator of Tomania. This spoof of Adolf Hitler begins when Chaplin plays a Jewish barber in a "Tomanian" ghetto who is recovering from amnesia and wakes up to find himself living under the thumb of Hynkel (also played by Chaplin). He escapes to Austria with a Jewish laundress, played by Paulette Goddard, who is in love with him. In Austria, he is mistaken for Hynkel, who had recently assumed control of the country. Chaplin then assumes the role of the dictator.

Amnesia is also portrayed in the excellent film *Sullivan's Travels* (1941) starring Joel McCrea and Veronica Lake and directed by Preston Sturges. The main character becomes amnestic when he is hit over the head and ends up being sentenced to 6 years on a chain gang. An example of traumatic amnesia triggered by a murder can be found in the film *Dead Again* (1991).

Amnesia allows a spoiled, self-centered, rich woman to experience life at the other end of the social ladder in the comedy *Overboard* (1987), directed by Garry Marshall. Dissociative amnesia is also illustrated in the classic films *Spellbound* (1945) and *Suddenly, Last Summer* (1959).

It would appear that the Jim Carrey and Kate Winslet characters in *Eternal Sunshine of the Spot-*

less Mind (2004) have some form of dissociative amnesia, as they are unable to remember certain events and people, particularly those related to a former significant other. However, because the memories are intentionally eliminated with the help of a specialist who erases traumatic memories with sophisticated technology, the diagnosis would not apply.

Hollywood movies have reaped some financial gain with action films using amnesia as a plot device, such as the successful *The Bourne Identity* (2002), and the unsuccessful *Paycheck* (2003). In the former, Jason Bourne, a CIA assassin, loses his memory after a failed spy mission, and he is left to try to uncover who he was, before he is killed.

The Forgotten (2004) stars Julianne Moore as Telly Paretta, a mother grieving over the loss of her 9-year-old son, who was killed in an airplane accident. The plot thickens when Telly's husband and her therapist tell her that she never had a son, and that she created all the memories she has of her son as a response to a miscarriage. The movie is spoiled by a silly ending that negates the value of what could otherwise have been a meaningful psychological exploration.

In *50 First Dates* (2004), Adam Sandler plays the role of Henry Roth, a happy veterinarian living in Hawaii. Henry falls in love with Lucy (Drew Barrymore), a woman who suffers from anterograde amnesia as a result of a motor vehicle accident. Henry arranges to meet Lucy each day, and eventually marries her.

Mirage

In the film *Mirage* (1965), David Stillwell, played by Gregory Peck, develops amnesia after witnessing the accidental death of his boss and mentor, Calvin Clark. Stillwell, a scientist, has just discovered a method for neutralizing the effects of nuclear fallout. Believing that his mentor was working for world peace, Stillwell shares the information with him. When Stillwell realizes that his formula would end up being used to produce nuclear weapons, he sets the formula on fire in front of an open window. In an attempt to save the piece of paper, Calvin lunges toward Stillwell and falls to his death from the 27th floor. Stillwell observes the fall, is horrified, and then calmly picks up his empty briefcase and leaves the office. He has developed amnesia. The lights in the office building go out.

The audience has none of this information until the end of the film. The film actually opens during a blackout in an office building in New York City. David Stillwell appears to be a very calm, rational individual who leads a woman, Sheila, played by Diane Baker, down the darkened stairs. He does not recognize Sheila, but she recognizes him. Upon returning to his apartment, he is greeted by a man who attempts to kill him. Stillwell overpowers the intruder and leaves him unconscious in the service quarters. Gradually, Stillwell begins to realize that he has lost his memory, but he becomes convinced that he has been in an amnestic state for 2 years instead of 2 days. He seeks help from a psychiatrist, who questions his amnesia and throws him out of the office.

In this Hitchcock-style thriller, Stillwell's belief that he had been an accountant in New York is reinforced by his enemy, the Major, who hires thugs to follow Stillwell and get the formula. Stillwell next employs Detective Ted Caselle, played by Walter Matthau, to discover his identity and figure out who is trying to kill him. Caselle attempts to fit the pieces together but is killed in the process. A romance is rekindled between Sheila and Stillwell, who had previously been lovers.

Following the detective's death, Stillwell desperately contacts the same psychiatrist, who is again skeptical of Stillwell's amnesia. By now, Stillwell's memory is beginning to return, and he realizes that his memory loss has been present for only 2 days. The psychiatrist asks some questions that provoke the retrieval of more memories. Gradually, the amnesia for his mentor's death lifts, and he is able to face the horror of the event.

Dissociative **fugue**, emphasized as a separate, distinct diagnosis in *DSM-IV*, is now only a specifier under dissociative amnesia in *DSM-5* (e.g., dissociate amnesia with dissociative fugue [F44.1]). Fugue states are characterized by sudden, unexpected travel away from home or one's customary place of work, an inability to recall one's past, and confusion about personal identity or the assumption of a partial or completely new identity (e.g., a person whose business is failing may show up in a new city with a new identity and no memory of previous problems). With the onset of fugue, a person begins a new autobiographical memory that replaces the original one. These individuals appear normal and will not reveal any evidence of dissociative symptoms unless asked. When the fugue resolves, the original memories are recovered, but the fugue memories are lost. The individual then has a permanent void in personality history. Even though the prevalence of dissociative fugue has been reported to be only 0.2% of the general population, it may be more common in times of war, natural disaster, and dislocation (Fullerton, Ursano, & Wang, 2004).

Some patients with dissociative fugue disorders will travel short distances over brief periods; others may travel far and remain in a fugue state for months or years. The acclaimed and thought-provoking Wim Wenders film, *Paris, Texas* (1984) introduces the character of Travis Clay Henderson, an individual suffering from dissociative fugue. He has been lost for 4 years and is found wandering in the desert. Eventually, he (partially) puts the pieces of his shattered life back together.

Renée Zellweger's character in *Nurse Betty* (2000) witnesses her husband's murder and shortly thereafter becomes convinced she is the former fiancée of her soap opera idol, and she travels across the country to find him. This character provides a fascinating springboard for a discussion of the differentiation between delusional disorder and other potential diagnoses. Jim Carrey's lead role in *The Majestic* (2001) would be another example of dissociative fugue had the experience not been caused by a head injury from an automobile accident; Carrey's character has amnesia, has traveled away from home, and readily takes on the identity of a missing-in-action soldier in a small town.

Amnesia and identity are central themes in *Identity Unknown* (1945), starring Richard Arlen and Cheryl Walker. In this film, a soldier develops amnesia during World War II and works to recover his identity.

Unknown White Male

Perhaps the best film to date to examine the life of someone experiencing a fugue state is *Unknown White Male* (2005). This documentary, directed by Rupert Murray, is based on the real-life experience of Doug Bruce, a man who seemingly without reason developed a profound retrograde amnesia for everything that happened to him before July 3, 2003. Bruce is disoriented when he discovers himself on a subway bound for Coney Island with no recollection of any of the previous 37 years of his life. He is taken to a Coney Island hospital where he is examined for neurological injuries and then taken to a psychiatric ward where he is given a wristband that reads "Unknown White Male."

"There are aspects of his experience I do envy. Everything is new to him. To eat chocolate mousse for the first time and to have the language to describe it ... that is an experience we won't have. To wipe the slate clean is desirable in a way. The first film he saw at the cinema was a restored print of *Taxi Driver*. Someone gave him a list of 50 films he had to see, and he's become a real movie buff [because] he's never seen a bad one."

Unknown White Male (2005)
director Rupert Murray

The film underscores the fascinating complexity of what we unthinkingly call memory. Bruce cannot remember his own name, but he remembers how to *sign* his name (although the signature is illegible). He goes to the beach and remembers how to swim – but he does not *know* that he remembers until he is actually in the water. He is unable to recall the names of his parents, but he can still speak French. He does not remember that he once liked the Rolling Stones, but he enjoys their music when it is played for him. Signing his name, swimming, typing, playing a musical instrument, and riding a bike are all examples of **procedural memory**.

How much of our past lives, the thousands of moments we experience, help to make us who we are? If you took all of these remembrances, these memories, away, what would be left? How much is our personality, our identity, determined by the experiences we have? And how much is already there, pure "us"?

Prologue commentary for
Unknown White Male (2005)

Unlike many individuals who experience fugue states, Bruce is frustrated and deeply troubled by his loss of memory. He has a girlfriend's phone number in his pocket, and she agrees to take him from the hospital and help him reestablish his past life. The cause of Bruce's memory loss was never determined. The film underscores the intimate and profound link between memory and one's sense of self, and illustrates what it is like for someone to genuinely experience what Buddhists call *beginner's mind*.

K-Pax

Kevin Spacey as both Robert Porter and Prot in *K-Pax* (2001) is a diagnostic quandary. In addition to hypothetical diagnoses of schizophrenia and PTSD, a valid and highly arguable case can be made for dissociative amnesia with a dissociative fugue specifier.

From this vantage point, a man named Robert Porter experiences a highly traumatic event. Upon returning from work one day, he finds his wife and child murdered with the perpetrator still in his house; Porter quickly kills the man, cleans up, and jumps in a nearby river. He then travels from his home in New Mexico to New York City under a completely new identity as Prot, a highly spiritual person with a great knowledge of planetary rotations. Porter interacts with other people comfortably with this new identity and claims no knowledge of any other past history. Under clinical hypnosis (age regression), the amnesia is lifted, and he painfully faces his past trauma.

Depersonalization/Derealization Disorder

Depersonalization/derealization disorder is diagnosed when there is evidence of persistent or recurrent feelings of detachment from one's mental processes or body. In depersonalization, there is an alteration in the perception of self and often a sense that one is living out a dream. The person feels like an outsider looking in but continues to be connected with reality during the experience. Transient experiences of depersonalization are common in adolescents and decline with age in normal individuals (Putnam, 1985). During a traumatic event such as rape, depersonalization is sometimes experienced by women who report they were floating above their own bodies during the assault (Classen, Koopman, & Spiegel, 1993). Closely related to depersonalization experiences are **out-of-body experiences** in which the individual has the distinct feeling that he or she is leaving his or her body. Often these individuals are able to describe scenes as if viewed from above and report a sense of being isolated and detached from their bodies. In de-

realization, the external environment seems unreal, and there is a sense of detachment from one's surroundings; individuals experiencing derealization often feel like they are caught in a dream or that they exist in an unnatural environment. These patients frequently have a distorted sense of time, and time may seem to move very rapidly or very slowly.

Since depersonalization and derealization occur as a symptom in a variety of disorders, some authorities have questioned whether these two phenomena constitute a distinct disorder. The cause of depersonalization/derealization is unknown. Some authorities speculate that the phenomenon is related to a neurobiological disturbance produced by temporal lobe dysfunction. Others claim that depersonalization is an adaptation to overwhelming trauma. Still other authorities argue that depersonalization is a defense against painful and conflictual stimuli, or that it is a split between the observing and participating selves that allows the person to become detached from self (Steinberg, 1991).

Transient depersonalization/derealization is very common in the general population, and about half of adults will have this experience at some point. However, it is far less common for people to meet the full criteria for this diagnosis. *DSM-5* estimates the lifetime prevalence is approximately 2%, with the disorder occurring equally often among men and women.

Numb (2007) is one of the few films in which a leading character is explicitly diagnosed with depersonalization disorder (a term likely to be very unfamiliar to most viewers). The movie stars Matthew Perry as Hudson, a screenwriter who apparently developed his profound sense of detachment as a result of taking 12 hits from a bong in 12 minutes (it is important to note that if depersonalization symptoms occur exclusively as a direct effect of a substance, then the diagnosis of depersonalization disorder would not be given). He feels chronically detached, much as though he were watching himself in a film. He has no interest in himself, others, or anything that is happening around him. He spends his days and most of his nights watching the golf channel or very long-running movies (e.g., *Star Wars*). His neurological exam is normal, but he tells the doctor "stab me with a fork and I wouldn't feel it." He is treated with clonazepam but finds the medication dramatically diminishes his libido (a genuine potential side effect of the drug). He engages in extensive "doctor shopping," seeing one therapist after another. One psychiatrist is only interested in pharmacological management of Matthew's problems ("Fuck talking … take drugs!"). However, Matthew is able to overcome his malady only when he becomes genuinely interested in a new woman in his life, Sara (Lynn Collins). The film perpetuates the misconception that love is sufficient to conquer mental illness. While it is questionable whether Hudson actually has either depression or depersonalization (since depersonalization is being used as a convenient plot device), it makes for interesting discussions on differential diagnosis.

"I just wanted to let you know that if you lost all your limbs, we'd still be together forever. I mean I really hope that doesn't happen because I think your limbs are pretty great. And when I said your name, it would always sound safe. I'm not sure about the perfume and the cologne thing but I could try … And if you like this shirt, I wouldn't take it off for a month. And I would be more than willing to paint your grandmother's toenails so your grandfather doesn't have to do it anymore. You don't have to save me, Sara. But I am going to love you for the rest of my life, so things would be a lot better for me if you were around."

Matthew admits his love for Sara in
Numb (2007)

The Butterfly Effect

It might be a stretch to place the film *The Butterfly Effect* (2004) under this diagnostic category; however, while it does not seem to fit any category neatly, it can inform us about depersonalization. Evan, a 20-year-old college student, experiences frequent blackouts during highly emotional or stressful times. When he reflects on his amnestic blackouts and reads his copious journal entries about a given memory, he is transported to the actual past memory. He is then able to change the memory with various ensuing consequences on his and others' lives in the present.

Each of the memories he engages can be seen as his detachment from his body; he enters the memory, relives it, and changes it while maintaining reality testing to his world and the new world (due to

the changed memory) around him. This process causes him significant personal and social distress as he realizes each of these "detachment" episodes has a profound effect on his own life and on the lives of the people he loves.

Other Examples of Dissociative Disorders in Films

Dissociative disorders are among the most fascinating forms of mental illness, and it is not surprising that relative to their prevalence, they are portrayed fairly often in films. In addition to the clinical examples cited, film history is replete with examples of quasidissociative conditions in which one character exchanges personalities (or sometimes even bodies) with another. The classic example is Bergman's *Persona* (1966, Sweden), in which two characters gradually exchange personalities. A similar theme is found in the Robert Altman film, *3 Women* (1977), in which two of the women appear to exchange personalities.

In the mock-documentary/comedy, *Zelig* (1983), Woody Allen plays a human chameleon whose personality changes to match whatever situation he is in – if he is around black musicians, he talks and acts like black musicians; if he is around politicians, he becomes a politician. Ronald Coleman finds himself merging his own personality with that of Othello in *A Double Life* (1947). The comedy *Prelude to a Kiss* (1992) is about an old man and a young bride who mysteriously exchange bodies after kissing on the bride's wedding day. The film raises interesting questions about what it is that one person loves in another: Is it a physical body or a set of personality characteristics, such as wit, charm, and grace? The means through which the transformation is effected are never specified in *Prelude to a Kiss*. In contrast, it is very clear in *Black Friday,* a 1940 horror film in which Boris Karloff transplants the brain of a criminal into the body of a college professor.

The theme of contrasting personalities in the same person is seen in those films in which someone presumed to be dead returns to his or her old social roles, usually as a vastly improved human being. We see this in *Sommersby* (1993) and *The Return of Martin Guerre* (1982). The dramatic force of both films is heightened by the sexual excitement both women feel as they go to bed with a man who may or may not be the husband who left them years earlier.

Dissociation is also used in a plethora of films that contrast the forces of good and evil inherent in all of us. Oftentimes, the evil is inherent in a twin. For example, the personalities of good and evil twins are juxtaposed in *The Dark Mirror* (1946) and in Brian De Palma's *Sisters* (1973). The latter film adds an interesting twist by making the two women Siamese twins who were separated as children.

Films have often presented the duality of the human personality, usually depicting a struggle between good and evil. In 1920, *Dr. Jekyll and Mr. Hyde* was first introduced as a silent film, starring John Barrymore and Martha Robinson. The 1931 remake, directed by Rouben Mamoulian, was the first sound version of this Robert Louis Stevenson classic. In this film, Dr. Harry Jekyll (played by Fredric March, who won an Academy Award for his performance) represents all that is good and kind. He is a well-respected physician who devotes endless hours to hospital charity work. His innate curiosity, as well as his own socially unacceptable feelings, have led him to speculate about good and evil within human beings. He believes that the evil of humans can be captured and isolated. As the film opens, he is engaged to Muriel, played by Miriam Hopkins, with whom he is deeply in love. According to the custom of the time, Muriel's father has set a marriage date that is far in the future, but too far to suit Harry. The audience gets a glimpse of Dr. Jekyll's underlying impulsiveness, his impatience, and the sexuality that he is trying hard to repress.

When Muriel's father takes her away for an extended trip, Dr. Jekyll tests his theory about inherent evils. He mixes and swallows a potion that he believes can isolate the evils of human beings. He then becomes the evil Mr. Hyde, who seduces, abuses, and finally kills a woman who is his social inferior. Eventually, he can no longer control the "coming out" of the alter personality (Mr. Hyde), and he confides his mistake to his future father-in-law. After attacking his fiancée, Dr. Jekyll is caught and killed.

Dr. Jekyll and Mr. Hyde was remade in 1941, this time starring Spencer Tracy and Ingrid Bergman. It was filmed again in 1968, with Jack Palance, and given the full title *The Strange Case of Dr. Jekyll and Mr. Hyde*. One of the best adaptations of the Dr. Jekyll and Mr. Hyde story is in the more recent *Mary Reilly* (1996), starring John Malkovich and Julia Roberts. A somewhat different twist on the same theme is found in *Steppenwolf* (1974), an adaptation of the Hermann Hesse novel, illustrating the problem of a single individual grappling with these two competing aspects of self.

Additional film examples of depersonalization disorder are found in the fascinating movie *Tarnation* (2003), as well as *Dead of Night* (1945), *Altered States* (1980), and Martin Scorsese's *The Last Temptation of Christ* (1988).

International Films: Dissociative Disorders

Persona (1966, Sweden), the complex Ingmar Bergman film regarded by critics as one of the greatest films ever made, deals with a famous actress, Elisabeth Vogler (Liv Ullmann), who suddenly, and seemingly without reason, stops talking. Her doctor can find nothing wrong with her and is at a loss to explain her patient's symptom. However, she prescribes rest and constant attention, and Elisabeth spends the summer at a house on the coast in the care of a full-time nurse, Alma (Bibi Andersson). Although Elisabeth almost never speaks, we know that she retains the capacity for speech. At one point, when Alma appears to be about to throw boiling water on Elisabeth, the actress shouts, "Don't."

Although the conversion disorder portrayed in the film is fascinating, the more interesting element is the merging of the personalities of the two women. There are a number of interesting dream sequences, and one scene presents a face on the screen that is a composite of Elisabeth and Alma (one half of each woman's face is shown). In selecting the title for the film, Bergman was likely thinking both about the masks worn by Greek actors in classical theater and of Carl Jung who used the term to refer to those parts of our personality that we show to the outer world. Perhaps Elisabeth quit speaking because she had resolved to stop acting and wear no more masks. The ending of the film is somewhat unclear, but it appears that Elisabeth returns to acting, Alma returns to nursing, and the personalities of the two women do not remain merged.

Interpersonalities (2008, Canada) is a short thriller/mystery that unfolds like a puzzle for the viewer. A young boy is depicted talking with a psychiatrist, then the viewer sees different characters suddenly pop into and out of the scene; these are the other personalities or alters. Those alters that are present at any given time are able to communicate with one another. The film portrays the killing off of one alter, and the reluctance of an alter not wanting to kill another. In one scene, an alter suggests shifting the approach to "focus on the strengths," but the psychiatrist replies that is too dangerous and that one alter must eliminate the other.

Critical Thinking Questions (Dissociative Disorders)

➤ Why do movies so frequently link DID with violent behavior?
➤ How can an understanding of the phenomenon of hypnosis help us understand dissociative disorders?
➤ Movies such as *Primal Fear* (1996) suggest it is relatively easy to fool lawyers and therapists into believing you have a DID. How would you assess the likelihood of malingering if you were a clinician evaluating a patient with an alleged dissociative disorder?
➤ Many reputable psychologists believe DID does not exist. What evidence do you find for and against this claim? Consider having a class debate about the existence or nonexistence of DID.
➤ Are there instances where dissociation occurs, but not amnesia?
➤ Compare and contrast dissociative experiences that are culturally acceptable with those that are considered abnormal.
➤ What are some other causes of dissociative disorders aside from trauma?
➤ Name a few of the inaccuracies and misconceptions perpetrated in the DID depiction in the film *Identity* (2003).
➤ Compare and contrast Edward Norton's character in the modern-day film *Fight Club* (1999) with Joanne Woodward's character in the classic, *The Three Faces of Eve* (1957).

Authors' Picks

If you have time to read just one book relevant to this chapter, make it:

Nathan, D. (2011). *Sybil exposed: The extraordinary story behind the famous multiple personality case.* New York: Free Press.

If you only have time to read a review of the book *Sybil Exposed: The Extraordinary Story Behind the Famous Multiple Personality Case*, by Debbie Nathan, read:

Lilienfeld, S. O., & Berg, J. M. (2012). A psychological urban legend with disastrous consequences. *PsycCRITIQUES, 57* (20). doi: 10. 1037/a0028043

Wedding and Niemiec's Top 10 Dissociative Disorders Films

☐ *Dr. Jekyll and Mr. Hyde* (1920)
☐ *Psycho* (1960)
☐ *Unknown White Male* (2005)
☐ *Paris, Texas* (1984)
☐ *Sybil* (1976)
☐ *The Three Faces of Eve* (1957)
☐ *Peacock* (2010)
☐ *Primal Fear* (1996)
☐ *Birdy* (1984)
☐ *Numb* (2007)

Chapter 8

Sleep-Wake, Eating, and Somatic Symptom Disorders

Let me sleep ... just let me sleep.

Will Dormer suffering from sleep deprivation in *Insomnia* (2002)

➤ How long can a person go without sleep?

➤ Is insomnia more often a primary condition, or is it usually secondary to other psychological disorders?

➤ What are the most common psychological disorders of which insomnia is a symptom?

➤ How common is the degree of insomnia Will Dormer experiences?

➤ How does stress contribute to Dormer's insomnia?

➤ What are the physical and psychological causes of insomnia depicted in the film?

➤ What is the impact of Dormer's insomnia on his mental status and interpersonal relationships?

➤ How is the condition of insomnia expressed through the film's landscape and cinematography?

➤ What coping strategies does Dormer use in attempting to get to sleep? What are some strategies he does not try?

➤ What is the psychological role of guilt in the film? Who is really guilty? What is guilt's role in Dormer's mental status?

➤ Is Dormer a "good" cop or a "bad" cop? Is his character redeemed in the end?

➤ Is it appropriate for nonmedical therapists to prescribe over-the-counter medications like melatonin and kava-kava?

➤ Should psychologists be permitted to prescribe sleep medications like Ambien for patients with insomnia?

Patient Evaluation

Name: Will Dormer

Patient's stated reason for coming
"I can't sleep. It's too bright in this place. I haven't slept for days. You got any tricks up your sleeve?"

History of the present illness
Detective Will Dormer is a 52-year-old White male who has self-referred himself to this clinic because of serious problems with insomnia. Detective Dormer arrived from out of town 5 days ago for a murder investigation he is leading. He has not slept in 5 and a half days. Prior to this episode of insomnia, he reports some problems sleeping for about a month or two, sleeping an average of 5 hours per night. He frequently awakens during the night, unable to get back to sleep; overall, his sleep is not restful. As the current insomnia symptoms have worsened, he has experienced concentration problems, forgetfulness, and several visual and auditory hallucinations. He states he has experienced all of these symptoms in the past but only as a consequence of insomnia. Work performance has been seriously affected, and he believes if he continues without sleep he risks losing his job. He is not interested in social relationships – the insomnia only contributes to this lack of interest.
Three days ago, Detective Dormer's partner was murdered while on duty. Detective Dormer feels significant guilt and responsibility, and he believes he should have saved his partner or somehow prevented the murder.

Past psychiatric illness, treatment, and outcomes
Detective Dormer has no previous psychiatric history. He reports he has battled insomnia throughout his adult life, with the longest span of no sleep prior to the present episode of insomnia having been 3 days.

Medical history
Detective Dormer reports he may have sleep apnea, but he has never been formally tested for sleep problems. He reports previously being diagnosed as hypertensive, but this is currently untreated. He has no history of psychiatric treatment, severe medical illness, or diseases. He has been injured twice on the job. On one occasion he was shot in the arm, and on another occasion he was cut on the neck with a knife; the resulting scar was visible during the interview.

Psychosocial history

Detective Dormer has worked as a criminal investigator for the police department for 30 years. He states, "I've always worked in the city so I've seen everything. I've caught a lot of scum." He was married for 10 years but divorced 15 years ago. He maintains occasional, friendly communication with his former wife. He has not remarried. He has no children. He has few meaningful friendships. From time to time, he isolates himself from others; however, this behavior does not appear to be related to depression.

Drug and alcohol history

Detective Dormer denied a history of drug abuse. He drinks alcohol frequently after work. He reports having two drinks each evening to relieve the tension and stress he experiences on his job. He drinks to the point of intoxication about twice per month. He denies significant problems due to his alcohol use.

Behavioral observations

Detective Dormer was appropriately dressed. His overall appearance was unkempt. He appeared exhausted with bags under his eyes, slightly open mouth, and poor eye contact. He intermixed periods of blank stares and periods of frequent blinking as if he was trying to keep his eyes open. At times, his speech was slurred; this appeared to be due to fatigue. Detective Dormer's mood and affect were agitated. He also reported some apathy about the case on which he is currently working.

Mental status examination

Detective Dormer scored a 28/30 on the Mini-Mental State Examination. His concentration was appropriate for serial sevens and other tasks. He did not recall all three objects at first but then suddenly exclaimed, "It's all in the details," and he remembered two of the three. He chose not to copy the drawing, stating, "I'm too exhausted to put forth that kind of effort."

Functional assessment

Despite the extreme fatigue and sleeplessness Detective Dormer has recently experienced, he continues to function at work. He reports his concentration and attention have worsened. He continues to drive a vehicle despite his fatigue and difficulty with concentration.

Strengths

Detective Dormer is a very adaptable, strong-willed man. He is an experienced and hard-working police officer. His results on the VIA Survey, an assessment of character strengths, reveals his highest strengths of character are judgment/critical thinking, curiosity, perseverance, fairness, and bravery.

Diagnosis

Insomnia disorder, episodic (G47.00). Detective Dormer reported experiencing symptoms of insomnia over the last 1 to 2 months, and these symptoms have worsened over the past week.

Treatment plan

(1) Detective Dormer was cautioned about driving anywhere before he gets some sleep, and in fact he was encouraged to take a taxi home. We called a cab from the office. (2) Discussed the principles of stimulus control, with instructions to begin sleep hygiene practices this evening. (3). Suggested Detective Dormer keep a sleep diary. (4) Referred Detective Dormer to a local psychiatrist for sleep medication and further assessment. (5) Recommended making an appointment for polysomnography in a university-based sleep lab when he returns home, to rule out other sleep-related conditions such as sleep apnea.

Prognosis

Good.

Insomnia Disorder as Portrayed in *Insomnia*

Sleep disorders are rarely portrayed in films, particularly not to the extent they are highlighted in this film. *Insomnia* (2002), a remake of a well-done, 1997 Norwegian film of the same name, is deeply psychological with multiple layers of complexity. One of these layers is the deteriorating mental status of Al Pacino's character, Los Angeles police officer Detective Will Dormer. Director Christopher Nolan accurately depicts this deterioration, documenting both the realities and dangers of the sleep disorder, primary insomnia. This film provides a powerful illustration of the ways this disorder can devastate someone's life.

Dormer flies to Alaska to lead a murder investigation. He arrives in Alaska, already tired, at a time of year when the sun never sets ("white nights") so it never gets dark outside. (His travel to Alaska from California takes him across just one time zone, so he would not meet the criteria for circadian rhythm sleep-wake disorder). Throughout the investigation, Dormer lies in bed with his eyes open, struggling to get some sleep. Under internal pressure to sleep, Dormer employs various strategies, such as blocking all light coming into the room, drinking water, hiding the alarm clock, chewing gum, and turning the phone off. As his insomnia worsens, he sees flashes and trickles of light that become associated with flashes of memory. His vision becomes blurry; he nods off during conversation, often has an unkempt appearance, and frequently stares blankly into space. The longer Dormer goes without sleep, the more severe the consequences; his agitation develops into anger outbursts, he nearly runs a woman over with his car, and he begins to hallucinate. Ultimately, Dormer goes 6 nights without sleep; his exhaustion and irritability are clearly depicted in Figure 13.

Dormer's insomnia symptoms are clearly exacerbated by the psychological pressure he is experiencing. Two major stressors include the pressures of the murder case, and his guilt about killing his

Figure 13. *Insomnia* (2002, Alcon Entertainment, Section Eight). Produced by Broderick Johnson, Paul Junger Witt, Andrew A. Kosove, and Edward L. McDonnell. Directed by Christopher Nolan.

partner and lying about it to protect himself in the upcoming Internal Affairs investigation. His current guilt triggers memories of other events in his life about which he feels guilty.

Insomnia is a powerful metaphor in the film. Director Christopher Nolan has discussed the challenges involved in making a film about insomnia that will not tire viewers; to avoid this problem, Nolan utilized various images in the film to symbolize the experience of insomnia. At the film's onset, the viewer is shown miles and miles of Alaskan glaciers – representing something of a dreamscape, followed by endless green trees covered by moving fog. Other examples of sleep-related imagery include empty streets with blinking traffic lights, flashes of light, tunnels and escape hatches, and things as mundane as trance-inducing windshield wipers. These all symbolize haziness, drifting, mental confusion, and disorientation.

"A good cop can't sleep because a piece of the puzzle's missing, and a bad cop can't sleep because his conscience won't let him."

Ellie Burr to Will Dormer in *Insomnia* (2002)

Sleep-Wake Disorders

The *DSM-5* lists 10 categories of sleep-wake disorders: Insomnia disorder, hypersomnolence disorder, narcolepsy, breathing-related sleep disorder, circadian rhythm sleep-wake disorder, non–rapid eye movement (NREM) sleep arousal disorder, nightmare disorder, rapid eye movement (REM) sleep behavior disorder, restless legs syndrome, and substance/medication-induced sleep disorder. The common denominator for each of these disorders is patient dissatisfaction with their sleeping habits and daytime fatigue or impairment. Due to the complexity and extent of sleep disorders, we will focus on insomnia in this chapter, the most common sleep complaint found in clinical settings.

Sleep researchers recognize five **sleep stages**: Stages 1 through 4 and rapid eye movement (REM) sleep. Each of the first 4 stages of sleep gets progressively deeper, and each has distinct differences on an electroencephalogram (EEG). Stage 1 is a

transition stage from wakefulness (light sleep), Stage 2 occupies about 50% of the time spent asleep, and Stages 3 and 4 (slow-wave sleep) are the deepest levels of sleep. REM sleep is where most dreams are reported; it occurs cyclically throughout the night, and alternates about every hour and a half with NREM sleep (the first four stages). Individuals with insomnia will typically have increases in Stage 1 sleep and decreases in Stages 3 and 4. In narcoleptic individuals, the onset of REM sleep is more rapid after sleep onset, and there is an increase in REMs.

Sleep laboratories are used to conduct sleep studies to ascertain accurate diagnoses. **Polysomnography** (PSG) is the most common sleep test and takes into account both electroencephalographic (EEG) and electrocardiographic (ECG) readings, as well as respiration, leg movements, and other physiological activities during sleep. The PSG helps to diagnose different forms of **sleep apnea** (most often the cause of breathing-related sleep disorder). The **Multiple Sleep Latency Test** (MSLT) is used by sleep labs to diagnose narcolepsy. Referrals to sleep labs are usually done through physician prescription, which can often be encouraged by mental health professionals.

Film depictions of sleep disorders are rare. When depicted, they are usually either very brief or flawed. The film *Insomnia* is an exception.

Insomnia Disorder

Insomnia disorder can present in three ways: Some patients will experience tremendous difficulty falling asleep; others will find it difficult or impossible to sleep through the night; still others will be plagued by early morning awakenings and be unable to fall back asleep. The sleep disturbance must cause distress or impairment to qualify for the diagnosis, and it must be present at least three nights per week for at least 3 months. About a third of the adult population report experiencing the symptoms of insomnia, and 6%–10% will meet the criteria for insomnia disorder. Insomnia disorder is about 44% more common in women than in men, and it is frequently comorbid with other conditions (most often major depressive disorder).

The effects of insomnia are graphically portrayed in *The Machinist* (2004). Christian Bale lost 60 pounds to play the role of the gaunt Trevor

Reznik in this film. Trevor is a depressed and lonely man who has been unable to sleep for a significant period of time. He uses stimulants such as caffeine and nicotine, not uncommon among individuals who struggle with insomnia. Trevor is accused of using drugs, although this is never depicted or indicated. The insomnia clearly affects his daily functioning – he causes an accident, becomes paranoid that his coworkers are plotting against him, and at one point he throws himself in front of a moving car. He displays symptoms of both an amnestic disorder and a psychotic disorder (e.g., hallucinations, paranoia); however, his inability to sleep would need to be treated as the immediate clinical concern. Cinematically, the film's images become less distinct to the viewer as a result of the director's use of muted colors, distorted views through mirrors, and showing Trevor behind and beyond things in his environment.

> "I haven't slept in a year."
>
> Trevor Reznik in *The Machinist* (2004)

In addition to the film *Insomnia*, Christopher Nolan created the remarkable film *Inception* (2010), an incredibly complex story that portrays characters in a dream within a dream within a dream (within a dream). It stars Leonardo DiCaprio, a thief who is able to infiltrate the dreams of high-powered individuals and steal secret information. He suffers from insomnia, and this is an important theme in the film.

Insomnia is one of the many symptoms experienced by Travis Bickle (Robert Di Niro) in *Taxi Driver* (1976). Because of his chronic insomnia, Bickle applies for and secures a job as a taxi driver; as his insomnia worsens, his psychiatric symptoms become all the more apparent.

The symptoms of insomnia are experienced by the two characters in *Lost in Translation* (2003), played by Bill Murray and Scarlett Johansson. Both characters are Americans who have traveled to Japan and experience apathy and loneliness in this unfamiliar setting. Both deal with their insomnia symptoms by going to the hotel bar and watching late-night television. Eventually they meet and build a friendship. One important scene depicts them lying awake in bed together at night; director Sofia Coppola seems to be showing they are facing their symptoms (symbolized by being awake in

bed) in a nonsexual, healthy way through communication.

Edward Norton's character in *Fight Club* (1999) suffers from serious insomnia. The insomnia may be a symptom caused by **circadian rhythm sleep-wake disorder** due to his work, which requires frequent travel. He states he feels as though he is never awake or asleep and that he loses weight because he cannot sleep. He exhibits blank stares, and his body language suggests that he is exhausted. It may be that jet lag exacerbates a preexisting problem with primary insomnia. His experience of sleeplessness triggers a break with reality leading to the development of dissociative identity disorder (DID). It is important to note that individuals with prolonged severe insomnia may experience dissociative symptoms or psychotic states, but there is no evidence it will cause DID.

> "With insomnia, nothing's real. Everything's far away. Everything's a copy of a copy of a copy."
>
> The narrator in *Fight Club* (1999)

In the movie *Return to Oz* (1985), based on the books *The Marvelous Land of Oz* and *Ozma of Oz* by L. Frank Baum, Fairuza Balk portrays Dorothy who is shown suffering from sleep problems. Aunt Em (Piper Laurie) decides to send Dorothy to a facility for treatment of insomnia where her tendency to repeatedly relate things to Oz is treated as a psychiatric symptom. The psychiatrist explains that electroconvulsive therapy (ECT) will be used to treat her insomnia and her "bad waking dreams" of Oz and its characters. Of course, there is virtually nothing accurate in the depiction here of insomnia treatment; however, the film provides an example of how filmmakers can create their own treatments to better fit their plotlines.

Hypersomnolence Disorder

Hypersomnolence disorder is diagnosed when a patient presents with a history of excessive sleepiness evidenced in prolonged, nonrestorative sleep or daytime sleep episodes that occur at least three times each week for at least 3 months, which causes significant distress or impairment. Like insomnia, hypersomnia can be a symptom of other disorders (e.g., major depressive disorder) or a separate entity itself. Although there are widespread individual differences in the amount of sleep people require, sleeping less than 7 hours each night suggests inadequate nocturnal sleep, while sleeping more than 9–10 hours suggests hypersomnolence.

In *American Splendor* (2003), Harvey Pekar's girlfriend moves in with him and sleeps all day. She seems to have an agitated depression that manifests itself in irritability and in sleeping on the couch well into the middle of the day. This may reflect hypersomnia; the long periods she spends in bed may also be a symptom of depression.

Narcolepsy

Narcolepsy is a devastating sleep disorder in which the individual experiences uncontrollable and unwanted daily "sleep attacks." People with narcolepsy can fall asleep while talking, eating, or walking. The disorder is frequently accompanied by **cataplexy** (sudden loss of muscle tone without loss of consciousness). Narcolepsy most often occurs in obese individuals. A rare but accurate portrayal of narcolepsy occurs in the character of Mike Waters (River Phoenix) in *My Own Private Idaho* (1991).

The portrayal of narcolepsy in movies is often brief, unkind, and superficial, with the sole purpose of ridiculing the person with narcolepsy. This type of humor is highly predictable as it almost always involves a character falling asleep at an inopportune, unexpected, or embarrassing moment. Though the portrayals are not entirely inaccurate (since sleep attacks in narcolepsy are of rapid onset and can be triggered by intense emotion), they are grossly exaggerated and almost uniformly unflattering. Minor characters in *Moulin Rouge* (2001), *Deuce Bigalow: Male Gigolo* (1999), *Rat Race* (2001), and *Bandits* (2001) have narcolepsy. In *Rat Race*, Enrico Pollini (Rowan Atkinson, best known as Mr. Bean) falls asleep at a critical moment when he is about to win a race, and in *Bandits*, a bank manager falls asleep during a robbery due to the stress of the experience.

Nightmare Disorder

Nightmare disorder is a parasomnia in which an individual repeatedly awakens from sleep recalling a frightening dream. When waking, the individual quickly becomes alert and oriented. Themes of the nightmare usually involve threats to survival, security, or self-esteem. Four different specifiers are included in *DSM-5*: (a) during sleep onset; (b) with associated conditions (non-sleep disorder, associated other medical condition, or associated other sleep disorder); (c) acute, subacute, or persistent; and (d) severity (mild, moderate, or severe). About 6% of adults have nightmares that occur at least once a month.

Countless movies depict characters experiencing nightmares, yet only a handful of those characters would qualify for the diagnosis of nightmare disorder. Many filmmakers enjoy manipulating the plot in such a way that the viewer is never sure whether a film is a dream (or nightmare) or reality. This plot device is used in Cameron Crowe's *Vanilla Sky* (2001). Sometimes the character awakens from a nightmare the viewer may or may not have known was happening; other films leave the viewer confused as to what has actually been experienced or just occurred. David Lynch is famous for the use of this approach; the strategy can be seen in his films *Blue Velvet* (1986), *Lost Highway* (1997), and *Mulholland Drive* (2001). The last of these films is very confusing, and its second half is usually assumed to reflect a character's dream/nightmare. In *Wristcutters: A Love Story* (2006), the two lead characters wake up in adjacent beds in a hospital room following suicide attempts, and it is assumed that everything the two had experienced together was only a linked nightmare.

Nightmares also are dramatically portrayed in two classic films: They are shown as a part of alcohol withdrawal in *The Lost Weekend* (1945), and the detective Scottie Ferguson (James Stewart) has vivid nightmares after the apparent bell tower suicide of Madeleine (Kim Novak) in Alfred Hitchcock's *Vertigo* (1958). The final scene in *Deliverance* (1972) shows the character of Ed (Jon Voight) wakening from a nightmare in which he had seen his friend Drew's hand rising out of a lake. Michael Shannon plays the role of Curtis in *Take Shelter* (2011), a film that opens with Curtis having a dramatic nightmare about a coming storm during which his own dog attacks him. A few of the other films in which nightmares are portrayed include *David and Lisa* (1962), *Mysterious Skin* (2004), *The Pact of Silence* (2003), and Wim Wenders' *Land of Plenty* (2004, US/Germany).

Non–Rapid Eye Movement Sleep Arousal Disorders

NREM sleep arousal disorders usually occur during the first third of a major sleep episode, and they are accompanied by either sleepwalking or sleep terrors. **Sleepwalking** (somnambulism) involves repeated episodes of rising from bed and walking around during sleep. During these episodes, the person has a blank stare, is unresponsive to others, and can only be awakened with great difficulty. The person does not remember the episode, and there is no impairment in mental activity or behavior upon awakening. **Sleep terrors** are diagnosed when someone experiences recurrent episodes of abrupt awakening from sleep, often with a panicky scream. The person experiencing sleep terror disorder shows signs of significant distress (e.g., rapid breathing, sweating) and is generally disoriented and unresponsive to attempts to comfort him or her. The individual does not recall the dream itself or the experience of screaming.

Some films illustrate sleep terrors when a character screams in his or her sleep only to wake up unaware of what they were dreaming. This is depicted by an amnestic woman in *Dead Again* (1991), in an adolescent girl screaming during sleep while on an inpatient unit in *Manic* (2003), in a woman on a psychiatric unit of a woman's prison in *Gothika* (2003), and in a young boy who has been cloned partially with cells taken from a murderous child in *Godsend* (2004).

In *Secondhand Lions* (2003), Hub (Robert Duvall) sleepwalks each night and goes to stand near a pond; sometimes he acts out an imaginary battle. Garth (Michael Caine) warns others not to awaken the sleepwalker, particularly because Hub will fight in his sleep if he is disturbed. The film suggests that Hub is searching for a love who has died. A young adolescent, played by Haley Joel Osment, enjoys watching Hub but is anxious about his safety.

In *Donnie Darko* (2001), the lead character, Donnie (Jake Gyllenhaal), hallucinates and is discovered by his psychiatrist to be a sleepwalker, often following his hallucinations outside when sleeping or napping.

Waking Life (2001) blends animation and drama in a surrealist film with the feel of a lucid dream. The movie addresses existential themes and questions our own wakefulness during the day, utilizing the metaphor of humans as "sleepwalking" through the days often unaware of what is going on around them. The film explores dream states, reality, and the insights that can be reached with each. Many important questions and issues are raised for the viewer to reflect upon, with themes of "creating one's own life," reality versus illusion, lucid dreaming, free will versus determinism, mindfulness versus automatic pilot, destiny, and the experience of suffering in life. Similar themes are explored in the 2004 film *Sleepwalking*.

"The trick is to combine your waking rational abilities with the infinite possibilities of your dreams. Because, if you can do that, you can do anything."

Guy Forsyth in *Waking Life* (2001)

Feeding and Eating Disorders

There are two major categories of eating disorder: anorexia and bulimia. New diagnoses for *DSM-5* include binge-eating disorder and avoidant/restrictive food intake disorder. Other problems with feeding and eating usually diagnosed in infancy or early childhood are **rumination disorder** and pica. For a graphic depiction of **pica**, see the film *The Princess and the Warrior* (2000), which portrays an adolescent psychiatric patient chewing and swallowing glass.

Anorexia Nervosa

In anorexia, the individual refuses to maintain an appropriate body weight for his or her age and height and has an intense fear of gaining weight or becoming fat even though he or she is underweight. The anorectic patient also has a distorted perception of his or her weight and shape. Many symptoms are similar to those associated with starvation, such as amenorrhea, abdominal pain, and lethargy. Depression and obsessive-compulsive features associated with food are quite common co-occurring disorders. Anorexia presents serious health risks and may lead to death by starvation, suicide, or electrolyte imbalance (more than 10% of anorectics are likely to die, making anorexia one of the most lethal psychological disorders). The *DSM-5* includes three specifiers for anorexia nervosa: (a) restricting or binge-eating/purging type; (b) in partial or in full remission; and (c) severity (mild, moderate, severe, or extreme. The disorder is *far* more common among young females than among young males, with a female to male ratio of at least 10:1.

Thin (2006) is an HBO documentary that provides an inside look at the lives of women with eating disorders and their residential treatment from intake to discharge. Four women, aged 15–30 and living in South Florida, suffer from anorexia or bulimia. The film depicts the young women in their counseling sessions, weighing in, during group activities, and socializing. Anxieties about weighing in, avoidance of food, medication misuse, and other issues common to those with eating disorders are portrayed. The film illustrates important themes related to the intense challenges of recovery, the significant cost of treatment, noncompliance, the sabotage of a fellow patient's treatment, and the high relapse rate.

Big budget films rarely portray anorexia; however, the disorder is often portrayed accurately in television movies (which sometimes can be rented at video stores). A compelling examination of anorexia and its treatment is found in the film *The Best Little Girl in the World* (1981). Jennifer Jason Leigh dropped her weight down to 90 pounds for the role of Casey Powell in this movie. Other films depicting anorexia include *For the Love of Nancy* (1994), which stars Tracey Gold; *Dying to Be Perfect* (1996); *Dying to Dance* (2001); and *Hunger Point* (2003). Anorexia nervosa is common among professional dancers, especially ballerinas, and it is clearly present in the film *Black Swan* (2010).

Bulimia Nervosa

Bulimia is characterized by **binges**, which are self-indulgent and unrestrained eating episodes. In addition, some behavior is used to prevent weight gain, such as **purging** (self-induced vomiting), misuse of laxatives, diuretics, enemas, or medications, fasting, and/or excessive exercise. Bulimics are preoccupied with their body weight or shape. Depression, anxiety, substance abuse, and borderline personality are the most common co-occurring diagnoses.

In *Center Stage* (2000), one of the dancers, Maureen, suffers from bulimia. She has a very controlling mother who is trying to relive her life through her daughter. The mother talks about little other than dance opportunities for Maureen. Maureen has been restricted as a child, and she was not allowed to play tennis or similar games with other children. To please a new boyfriend, she eats junk food and later purges to stay fit for the dance competitions. Elements of denial are evident when she is on a boat with her boyfriend who hears her purging; Maureen claims she is simply experiencing motion sickness. Her boyfriend later confronts her about "hurting her body." An element of insight emerges when Maureen sees another dancer fall and hurt herself, thus becoming unable to dance in the competition; she finds herself wishing she had been the one who was injured, because then the intense pressure both externally (her mother) and internally (herself) would have been gone.

In *Life Is Sweet* (1990), a rebellious adolescent girl, Nicola, is bulimic, binging and purging on chocolate bars hidden in her bedroom. She attempts to include the chocolate in her sex life by rubbing it over her body. It is clear that she lives in a dysfunctional family obsessed with food, cooking, and the restaurant business. In *Girl, Interrupted* (1999), one of the characters hospitalized with Susanna Kaysen (Winona Ryder) has a serious eating disorder and self-mutilates; her rich, codependent father supports his daughter's eating disorder by bringing her baked chicken that she hides and hordes under her hospital bed. The film hints at an incestuous relationship between her and her father, and a pivotal moment occurs in the film when she commits suicide by hanging herself in her shower. *Requiem for a Dream* (2000) includes one character who is obsessed with food but needs to lose weight to appear on a television game show; her obsession with weight loss leads her to become addicted to diet pills.

In *Elephant* (2003), numerous characters are shown going through a typical day before a school tragedy occurs. Three adolescent girls, Brittany, Jordan, and Kelly, focus on the caloric contents of their lunch food. After eating, they walk into the bathroom together and, each using separate stalls, collectively purge. They do it quickly and without a word about the behavior – acting nonchalantly in the middle of their continuing conversation. They are depicted as attractive with slender bodies, and the three girls obviously want to maintain their appearance. Purging together provides social support for their aberrant behavior. *I Want Someone to Eat Cheese With* (2007) portrays an overweight man struggling with food; he frequently binges on snacks while sitting alone on the front of his car in an empty parking garage, he routinely breaks his diet, and he attends Overeaters Anonymous support group meetings.

Bulimia nervosa is much more common among young people than among older adults. Although 90% of people with bulimia are females, the prevalence seems to be rising in males. The film *Seabiscuit* (2003) displays a male horse-racing jockey (Tobey Maguire) who forces himself to throw up to maintain his low weight so he can ride faster. Ben Stiller's narcissistic, male-model character in *Zoolander* (2001) refers to purging after meals to lose weight, to look better, and keep his job.

Maggie: "What are you doing?"
Carol: "Donkey kicks. I've eaten every thing in the place, and I'm trying to work it off before morning. I used to be bulimic. A year ago, I'd be in the bathroom throwing it all up. I'm much healthier now!"

Carol explains her vigorous exercise routine in Kenneth Branagh's film *Peter's Friends* (1992)

Bulimic themes are also evident in *Heathers* (1989), *Peter's Friends* (1992), the Korean film *301, 302* (1995), *Angus* (1995), *When Friendship Kills* (1996), and *Drop Dead Gorgeous* (1999).

Binge-Eating Disorder

Binge-eating disorder (BED) was listed in an appendix to *DSM-IV*; however, in *DSM-5*, it is identified as a bona fide, albeit controversial, disorder. BED involves eating an excessive quantity of food in a discrete period with the sense that one's eating is out of control and cannot be stopped. Three of five criteria must be present: (a) rapid eating; (b) discomfort from eating; (c) eating large amounts of food even when not hungry; (d) eating alone because of embarrassment about one's eating habits; (e) feeling depressed, disgusted, or guilty after bing eating. In addition, binging has to occur, on average, at least once a week for 3 months. In *Monster's Ball* (2001), the son of Halle Berry's character routinely binges

on food he keeps hidden in his room. Binge-eating symptoms, along with symptoms of depression, can be found in the minimalist film *Visioneers* (2008), starring Zach Galifianakis.

Body Image and Eating Disorders

Body image is one of the most significant problems with regard to both anorexia nervosa and bulimia nervosa. Many films, however, display characters struggling with their body image, though not all of them suffer from formal eating disorders. Often the use of a mirror or reflective surface shows characters viewing and assessing themselves, to convey a character's dissatisfaction with his or her body. Many times the image in the reflection is shown as distorted, blurred, formless, or unclear to emphasize self-hate, self-deprecation, or self-distortion.

Soldier's Girl (2003) and *I've Heard the Mermaids Singing* (1987) depict characters with problems with body image who stand in harsh self-judgment in front of a mirror. Toward the end of the acclaimed docudrama *What the Bleep Do We Know?!* (2004), the lead character (Marlee Matlin) stares in the mirror at her body, wearing only underwear, examining it with distaste, distortion, and rage. *What's Eating Gilbert Grape?* (1993) has a key character, Gilbert's mother, who weighs over 500 pounds and is too large to leave the house or even get off the sofa where she lives out her dreary existence. Gilbert (Johnny Depp) gives other children a "leg up" when they come to peer in the window at this morbidly obese woman.

Somatic Symptom Disorders

Somatic symptoms and related disorders is the subject of a new chapter in the *DSM-5*. This rubric encompasses a number of disorders that all involve significant distress or impairment as a result of preoccupation with somatic symptoms. Individuals with somatic symptom disorders commonly present in primary care settings rather than mental health settings. The diagnoses included in this section of the *DSM-5* include somatic symptom disorder, illness anxiety disorder, conversion disorder, and factitious disorder.

Somatic symptom disorder replaces the confusing term *somatoform disorder* in *DSM-IV* although somatic symptom disorder is far less complex in that only one symptom that causes distress is needed for the diagnosis, as opposed to the previous condition in which multiple somatic complaints affecting multiple organ systems were needed for the diagnosis. Individuals with somatic symptom disorder have excessive thoughts, feelings, or behaviors associated with their somatic symptoms, and these are typically disproportionate, often requiring extensive time and energy . The previous *DSM-IV* condition, pain disorder, is now subsumed as a specifier (i.e., *with predominant pain*) under this condition.

Safe

The Todd Haynes film *Safe* (1995) focuses almost exclusively on a woman with a somatic symptom disorder. Carol White (Julianne Moore) slowly begins to deteriorate with unexplained symptoms related to a chemical sensitivity. Doctors tell her stress is the cause of her problem, and advise her to learn to relax. However, it is difficult to see what is stressful in her life – she has a loving husband, beautiful home, good social life, and servants to do the cooking and cleaning. Her bodily system becomes overloaded and overwhelmed by fumes, toxins, fragrances, and other "pollutants" – these come from traffic, her shampoo, her husband's cologne, and a new sofa. It is as if she is being attacked by plastics, ozone, chemicals, high-energy wires, pollution, additives, preservatives, and hamburger fumes. Carol continues to get physically sicker and sicker, leaving her physicians baffled. At one point, she is hospitalized due to extensive bleeding.

Carol makes the decision to travel to another part of the country to a specialized clinic that offers group therapy, seminars, and social activities for people suffering from similar anomalous problems. During a casual group session, the therapist asks probing questions of the patients (and metaphorically to society and the viewer): "Why did you get sick?" and "What's behind your sickness?" One character speaks of abuse experienced as a child, how she made herself sick to remember, and how she had not forgiven the perpetrator and took it out on herself. Other characters believed their illness was due to self-blame or anger, and in one man's case, a drug addiction. Upon hearing other characters speak of coming to terms

with their inner self-hatred, Moore's character admits to also having a deep sense of self-hatred. However, despite all of her treatment, she seems to just get worse. The treatment emphasizes simplistic themes of a need to love oneself more, that we all make ourselves sick, and the role of the mind. These factors can play an important role in the etiology and outcome of illness, and we know that thoughts and feelings affect the immune system; however, the approach in the film comes across as trite and misleading. Ultimately, the film is a dark comedy and a satirical social commentary. Todd Haynes cleverly uses the cinematic element of a subtle background hum to suggest to the viewer that we can never fully escape the impact of the environment.

Illness Anxiety Disorder

Patients with **illness anxiety disorder** are preoccupied with their health problems, despite the fact that their somatic symptoms are either nonexistent or minimal. These are anxious patients who repeatedly check their body for evidence of illness (or, more rarely, who avoid physicians or hospitals because of their anxiety about being diagnosed with a serious illness).

Patients who now receive either of the above diagnoses would have formerly been labeled as having hypochondriasis; however, *DSM-5* avoids this term because it has become "loaded" and clearly stigmatizes individuals who are given this diagnosis. It is estimated that about 25% of patients formerly called hypochondriacs would be appropriately labeled as having illness anxiety disorder; the remaining 75% are more appropriately diagnosed with somatic symptom disorder – a far less stigmatizing label.

Patients with either somatic symptom disorder or illness anxiety disorder are often poor historians, and their complaints may vary from session to session. This problem is complicated by the fact that these patients easily become dissatisfied with their health care provider and may constantly be changing providers, sharing different parts of their story with each new provider. In addition, since most visits result in a prescription of some sort, these patients are often taking multiple medications, some of which produce side effects that result in general somatic distress. This pattern sets up a vicious cycle and makes diagnosis of the patient with a somatization disorder a challenging dilemma. Diagnosis is further complicated by the fact that some genuine medical conditions, such as multiple sclerosis, hyperparathyroidism, and systemic lupus erythematosus, can have vague symptoms that affect multiple organ systems.

The person with an illness anxiety disorder is preoccupied with thoughts of disease, infirmity, and death. This individual worries that simple, benign body sensations or symptoms may be indicative of a serious disease. In the extreme, such a person might interpret routine stomach pain as cancer of the bowel, headaches as a consequence of a brain tumor, and/or misplaced keys or glasses as an undeniable early indication of Alzheimer's. The preoccupations persist despite physical exams, lab tests, X-rays, and other examinations suggesting there is no illness present.

Some patients who have been labeled as hypochondriacs in the past are later found to have bona fide medical disorders. This is especially common with disorders that have vague symptoms and a slow progression (e.g., multiple sclerosis). In addition, patients who are initially believed to have hypochondriasis are sometimes later found to have somatic concerns related to anxiety, depression, or another psychiatric disorder.

In *2 Days in Paris* (2007), a relationship-oriented film directed by Julie Delpy, the male protagonist, Jack, has illness anxiety disorder. He is preoccupied with developing an illness, and he tries to control his environment in any way possible and avoids anything that might elicit symptoms. The viewer can clearly see how his somatic condition affects his relationships.

In *Dogville* (2003), one character is a doctor with illness anxiety disorder who misinterprets lumps and various other physical complaints; he is someone who needs the reassurance of others to tell him he is not dying. In *Something's Gotta Give* (2005), Jack Nicholson plays a 63-year-old man obsessed with dating younger women and develops illness anxiety symptoms after suffering his first heart attack; all subsequent episodes turn out to be panic attacks.

Bandits

In *Bandits* (2001), Billy Bob Thornton plays Terry Collins, a bank robber with illness anxiety disorder. Terry is convinced he has various illnesses despite his physician assuring him there is nothing wrong.

While in prison, he ruminates about how helpful garlic is and becomes upset when it is banned from the prison cafeteria; in a subsequent scene, he incessantly screams in the prison yard about ringing in his ears. In his leisure time, he reads a medical dictionary and while driving listens to *Merck Manual* cassette tapes alphabetically defining diseases.

After escaping from prison and robbing a bank with his cohort in crime, Joe Blake (Bruce Willis), Terry's arm becomes numb, he complains of seeing spots, and makes weird noises with his throat. When challenged by his partner, he explains, "I have sanitation issues, Joe."

When stressed, Terry experiences a sneezing attack and a tic in his left eye. He then begins to talk rapidly and speak in medical jargon. He also becomes preoccupied about one pupil being larger than the other. Each of his senses is affected in some way throughout the film. In addition, Terry suffers from food allergies, lactose intolerance, and various obscure phobias such as a fear of getting smaller, a fear of antique furniture, a fear of historic figures, and a fear of black-and-white movies. He experiences numbness in his arm, lips, and legs that leads him to collapse and flail about on the floor in one scene.

Hannah and Her Sisters

Hannah and Her Sisters (1986) is one of Woody Allen's funniest and most gratifying films. Allen plays Mickey, a neurotic television executive, who is a classic example of someone with an illness anxiety disorder. He is on his way to get a blood test when the film opens, and we soon realize that he is preoccupied with doctors, hospitals, and his own fragile mortality. He works in a high-stress job, and early on in the film he remarks, "Has anybody got a Tagamet? My ulcer is starting to kill me." (Director Woody Allen has a remarkable sense for the prevailing concerns and habits of the American public.

"This time I think I really have something ... It's not like that adenoidal thing, where I didn't realize I had them out."

Mickey Sachs (Woody Allen) discussing his hearing loss with his physician in *Hannah and Her Sisters* (1986)

A decade earlier, he had amused his viewers with a similar line about Valium.)

Mickey has experienced some hearing loss and is convinced that he has a brain tumor. He suspects that his doctors have known this all along but "they don't tell you [these things] because sometimes the weaker ones will panic." He awakens in the middle of the night, terrified, crying out, "There's a tumor

---

? Questions to Consider While Watching *Bandits* and *Hannah and Her Sisters*

➤ How can nonmedical therapists rule out organic pathology?
➤ Does *every* client with a psychological problem have to be worked up medically to ensure that there is no medical disease present?
➤ How common is it for a patient who has headaches actually to have a brain tumor?
➤ Should patients be able to insist on expensive tests (such as computerized axial tomography [CAT] and magnetic resonance imaging [MRI] scans), or is this
➤ decision ultimately up to the physician? Should it matter if a patient has insurance?
➤ Is the percentage of clients who visit psychologists for what are eventually determined to be medical problems about equivalent to the percentage of patients who visit physicians for treatment of what are ultimately determined to be psychological problems?
➤ Do the symptoms of anxiety illness disorder worsen under stress?
➤ Is the reassurance typically offered to hypochondriacal patients possible in a world of managed care? Will these changes in policy exacerbate or ameliorate the patients' concerns and symptoms?
➤ What is the optimal approach for a physician or medical professional to take in working with a person with suspected illness anxiety disorder?

Figure 14. *Hanna and Her Sisters* (1986, Orion Pictures Corporation). Produced by Robert Greenhut. Directed by Woody Allen.

in my head the size of a basketball." He engages in an "organ recital" with each new physician (Figure 14), and with each new doctor and each new test, he grows more apprehensive. When his computed tomography scan turns out to be completely negative, he is at first elated and then plunges into despair as he realizes that this is just a temporary reprieve and eventually he must die.

Conversion Disorder

A **conversion disorder** exists when (1) patients experience significant distress or impairment from motor or sensory symptoms that appear to be neurological but for which no adequate neurological explanation can be determined, and (2) it appears that psychological factors have played a significant role in the etiology or maintenance of the disorder. In addition, the clinician must rule out malingering, before the diagnosis is made.

The very name *conversion disorder* is linked to a psychological theory that maintains that unconscious psychological distress can be "converted" into physical manifestations. Interestingly, symptoms are far more likely to occur on the left side of the body (presumably because most people are right-handed).

Conversion disorders are fascinating, in part because the underlying dynamics seem so transparent to an external observer. The soldier who cannot fire a rifle because his arm is paralyzed has found a convenient way of avoiding battle; the woman who becomes functionally blind after witnessing a car wreck in which her son was killed can never see anything this awful happen again. In actual practice, few cases of conversion disorder are this tidy.

Woody Allen's character, Val Wawman, in *Hollywood Ending* (2002) develops a clear example of hysterical blindness, a previously frequent but currently rare conversion disorder. Just prior to the first day of directing a new film (in which there is the added stress of his ex-wife being the coproducer with her new fiancé), he loses his sight. This would suggest a neurological condition, but an extensive medical examination fails to produce medical or physiological reasons for Wawman's blindness. He goes to see a psychologist who explains this is psychological in origin and supports this comment with individualized interpretations – Val's fears of failure, internal conflicts, and poor relationship with his son. Val also exhibits numerous hypochondria-

cal symptoms including his extreme fear of getting an illness and preoccupation with illness. He previously thought he had experienced many outlandish diseases (e.g., diseases that only trees can get, the plague, etc.), all due to his misinterpretation of bodily symptoms. Another case of hysterical blindness is portrayed in the 1939 film *The Secret of Dr. Kildare*. In this film, Dr. Kildare performs a sham operation to restore his patient's sight, raising interesting ethical questions that probably would not have been debated in the 1930s.

The film *Sorry, Wrong Number* (1948) stars Barbara Stanwyck as a bedridden heiress who is partially paralyzed, although her doctors cannot determine any neurological reason for her inability to walk. One evening, she happens to overhear two men planning a murder; later she realizes that she is the intended victim. Much of the suspense of the film revolves around the realization that she must get out of bed in order to save herself.

Thérèse: The Story of Saint Thérèse of Lisieux (2004), tells the story of Saint Thérèse who became a Carmelite nun at age 15 and died from tuberculosis when she was 24. Thérèse's mother died when Thérèse was only 4 years old, and she experienced marked periods of depression. She also appears to have multiple psychosomatic complaints including stomach pains when she thinks about minor sins, and pounding headaches. One evening she faints at the dinner table. She experiences restless sleep, and at one point she is delirious for 2 weeks. During the period of delirium, she does not eat, loses weight, cries out, and hallucinates. She coughs repeatedly and spits up blood when her father's health deteriorates. Her influence on the Catholic Church has been tremendous; her memoir, *Story of a Soul*, has been translated into over 60 languages and has sold over 100 million copies.

Agnes of God

The complex film *Agnes of God* (1985), stars Meg Tilly as a young nun (Sister Agnes), Anne Bancroft as the mother superior of the convent, and Jane Fonda as the psychiatrist sent to investigate the apparent murder of a newborn baby who was found wrapped in bloody sheets and stuffed in a wastebasket at the convent. The film juxtaposes reason and faith and quickly convinces the viewer that, although Sister Agnes is surely one of "God's innocents," she is just as surely the mother and the murderer of the child.

Fonda, playing the psychiatrist, uses hypnosis in treating Sister Agnes, and it turns out that her mother sexually molested her when she was a child. It also turns out that the mother was the sister of the mother superior. At the end of the film, the court finds Sister Agnes not guilty by reason of insanity, and she returns to the convent, where she will continue to receive psychiatric care.

Sister Agnes's confusion seems very real, and the label of insanity seems justified. It appears that a dissociative amnesia may have been present, and the viewer becomes convinced that Sister Agnes had repressed the memories of her rape and was genuinely amnestic for the incident in which she strangled the child with his umbilical cord. Agnes begins to experience stigmata, once in a convent room and once in a chapel while praying. **Stigmata** is the name given to bleeding in the hands and feet, presumably from the sites that nails were driven into when Christ was crucified. It is a relatively rare but well-documented phenomenon that is found in people with deep religious convictions. In the case of *Agnes of God*, the blood of Christ, the blood of the murdered infant, and the blood of Agnes all seem to comingle. The somatic element of the stigmata in this film is much more complex, powerful, and integrated into the story and personal life of Agnes than the stigmata depicted in the suspense film titled *Stigmata* (1999).

Factitious Disorder

Patients with somatic symptom disorder or illness anxiety disorder will often experience some amount of **secondary gain** as a result of their medical problems, such as extra care and attention from others, worker's compensation benefits, reduced expectations from family, or avoidance of difficult activities. It is important to be cognizant of normal secondary gain factors while separating a given somatoform disorder from both malingering and factitious disorder. In **malingering**, a person deliberately "fakes" his or her symptoms to achieve a clearly understood goal (e.g., one character in *Memento* (2000)). A death row inmate may feign symptoms of mental illness – for example, believing that the state cannot execute someone who is not mentally competent. Likewise, a small child may complain of stomach pain, remembering that the last time this occurred he or she was allowed to stay home from school and eat ice cream.

In contrast to malingering, **factitious disorders**, a completely separate diagnostic category, involve feigning illness with the specific intent of assuming the sick role. Some patients with factitious disorders will present with predominantly psychological symptoms, while others will have predominantly physical symptoms. While the patient who is malingering reports symptoms for personal gain (e.g., insurance payment or disability benefits), the patient with a factitious disorder develops and reports his or her symptoms without any clear expectation of payment or benefit from the illness.

Factitious disorder imposed on another (previously called factitious disorder by proxy or Munchausen syndrome by proxy) occurs when symptoms are intentionally produced in another person, the classic example being the mother who makes her child sick so the child will assume a "sick role" and the mother can assume the role of a long-suffering and loving mother with a sick child. We see an example of factitious disorder imposed on another in Kevin Bacon's film *Loverboy* (2004), which stars Bacon's wife, Kyra Sedgwick, playing an enmeshed and overly protective mother (Emily), and the couple's real-life daughter, Sosie Bacon, who plays the role of Emily seen as a 10-year-old child in a series of flashbacks.

The term **psychosomatic** is often used as a derogatory term for people suffering with the disorders mentioned in this chapter. The term usually refers to physical disorders in which emotional processes play a role indicating a mutual influence of physical and psychological factors; the generality of this concept can be applied to not only somatoform disorders but most medical and psychological conditions as well.

International Films: Sleep-Wake, Eating, and Somatic Symptom Disorders

Sleep Disorders

Control (2003, Hungary) is a comedy/drama filmed in a Budapest subway dealing with fictitious characters reflecting universal themes of good versus evil and feeling trapped in life. There are various odd characters in the film, one of whom is a worker with narcolepsy who falls asleep on the job when he gets angry or stressed. When conflicts arise between coworkers, he immediately falls asleep and experiences an utter sense of confusion upon awakening.

Nightmares in an adult that are related to childhood sexual abuse are portrayed in *Don't Tell* (2005, Italy/UK/France/Spain) and *The Celebration* (1998, Denmark/Sweden), and they play an especially important role in the former film. The seventh 1-hour film in renowned Polish director Krzysztof Kieslowski's 10-film series *The Decalogue* (1989, Poland) offers a good portrayal of sleep terrors. A child in the film has recurrent night terrors in which she screams in her sleep each night, is difficult to awaken, and is unable to recall her troubling dreams after she awakes. In the film, she is described as suffering from nightmares.

Eating Disorders

In the dark psychodrama *Primo Amore* (2004, Italy), a goldsmith, Vittorio, becomes obsessed with molding the perfect female body (paralleling his work of transforming metals into pure forms). He finds an already slender art school model, Sonia, and rigorously controls her diet to get her to lose more weight. Sonia, desperate to please him, is willing to submit to his delusional plans. His role can be seen as the extreme of a "controlling parent." Self-disgust, exhaustion from starvation, secrecy, and sneaking food are characteristic features found in the characters with eating disorders portrayed in this film. Vittorio's behavior is clearly abusive. While not a pure depiction of an eating disorder nor an accurate portrayal of all of the dy-

namics that surround eating disorders, the film is nevertheless useful as a thematic illustration of this serious clinical problem.

Somatic Symptom Disorders

Gerard Depardieu stars in a French film, *The Pact of Silence* (2003, France), in which he plays a Jesuit priest who is also a physician trying to make sense out of a nun's "spells" during which she falls to the floor, experiences tremendous pain, and speaks incoherently. The psychosomatic episodes coincide with occasions when her twin sister, who is incarcerated, is in danger (e.g., when her prison cell is set afire by other inmates).

Georgette in *Amélie* (2001, France) would probably meet all the criteria for somatic symptom disorder if she were to appear at a doctor's office. While operating a cigarette counter, she complains of various symptoms from sciatica to the discomfort of smoke getting in her eyes. One interesting quote used in the film describes Georgette precisely: "A woman without love wilts like a flower without the sun." When Georgette's mind is not occupied with love, she is preoccupied with enough symptoms to meet the criteria for somatization disorder, but when she has a love interest, she feels perfectly healthy and happy.

The Spanish film *Unconscious* (2004, Spain) is set in Barcelona in 1913 and satirizes psychoanalysis and psychoanalysts; for example, in one scene, a psychiatrist tries to hypnotize a patient using a swinging pocket watch, only to become hypnotized himself, eventually revealing his deepest secret (he is a transvestite). The film shows multiple examples of hypochondriasis and conversion disorder, and a character playing Sigmund Freud makes a brief appearance to promote his new book, *Totem and Taboo*.

Critical Thinking Questions (Somatic Symptom Disorders)

➤ Why are somatic symptom disorders often portrayed for comedic purposes?

➤ The majority of Woody Allen's earlier films contain a character with one of the somatic symptom disorders, and often this character was portrayed by Mr. Allen himself. Why do you suppose this is a consistent theme? Is the work of filmmakers a reflection of themselves in some ways? Are their films a way of working through their own anxieties and challenges?

➤ Are the criteria for somatic symptom disorder too lenient? What are the effects of having too many individuals qualify for a *DSM* diagnosis?

➤ How do somatic symptom disorders affect the national health care budget?

➤ How are people with illness anxiety disorders affected by the adoption of managed care practices?

➤ What percentage of major medical illnesses is missed when these conditions are being mislabeled as psychosomatic?

➤ What particular mind–body treatment strategies are most useful with these disorders?

➤ What personality characteristics are most closely associated with somatic symptom disorders?

➤ Why is pain one of the most common and least understood problems facing the medical profession?

➤ How does the film *Safe* (1995) both add to and detract from the understanding of somatic symptom disorders?

➤ What roles can psychologists and other mental health professionals who work in medical settings play in managing the various somatic symptom disorders?

➤ How have mental health professionals in primary care settings made an impact on health care in general in the last decade?

Authors' Picks

If you have time to read just one book relevant to this chapter, make it:

Arnold, C. (2013). *Decoding anorexia: How breakthroughs in science offer hope for eating disorders*. New York: Routledge/Taylor & Francis.

If you only have time for one article, read:

Vitiello, M. V., McCurry, S. M., & Rybarczyk, B. D. (2013). The future of cognitive behavioral therapy for insomnia: What important research remains to be done? *Journal of Clinical Psychology, 69*(10), 1013–1021.

Wedding and Niemiec's Top Sleep-Wake, Eating, and Somatic Symptom Films

Sleep Disorders

- *The Machinist* (2004)
- *Insomnia* (2002)
- *Waking Life* (2001)
- *Inception* (2010)

Eating Disorders

- *Primo Amore* (2004)
- *Girl, Interrupted* (1999)

Somatic Symptom Disorders

- *Sorry, Wrong Number* (1948)
- *Agnes of God* (1985)
- *Hannah and Her Sisters* (1986)
- *Safe* (1995)

Chapter 9

Gender Dysphoria and Sexual Dysfunctions

I'm not like everybody else. I'm a hermaphrodite.

Teena Brandon's self-diagnosis in *Boys Don't Cry* (1999)

➤ How do films promote gender roles and sexual stereotypes?

➤ Which actors do you identify as especially masculine or feminine? Why?

➤ How would you react if you discovered that the person you were flirting with was actually impersonating someone of a different gender?

➤ Why are John and Tom so angry when they discover that Teena is actually female?

➤ Can you imagine yourself falling in love with someone who is a transsexual?

➤ How should parents decide about how to raise a child if the child is born with ambiguous genitalia?

➤ Freud is reported to have once written: "Anatomy is destiny." What did he mean by this? Do you agree?

➤ Are gender dysphoria problems like those illustrated in *Boys Don't Cry* common?

➤ Does gender dysphoria occur more often in (anatomical) males or females?

➤ Is it accurate to describe Teena Brandon as a lesbian?

➤ What are the behavioral characteristics that we use to identify whether or not a given individual is male or female?

➤ Is it more respectful to use masculine or feminine pronouns when referring to someone who is anatomically male but psychologically female?

➤ Is there any evidence that sex reassignment surgery contributes to the happiness of transsexuals? If so, should insurance companies be required by law to pay for this surgery if it is desired?

➤ What is the sexual orientation of a man who has a happy, well-adjusted relationship with a postsurgery male-to-female transsexual?

➤ Is it likely that someone like Teena Brandon would have been more comfortable and safer living in a large, metropolitan environment like San Francisco or Boston?

Patient Evaluation[4]

Name: Teena Brandon

Patient's stated reason for coming
"There's something wrong with me. I've got a gender identity disorder."

History of the present illness
Teena Brandon is a 21-year-old woman who presents with self-diagnosed gender dysphoria. She reports feeling "like a boy" since early childhood. Her identity as a psychological male has been strong and persistent. Even as a very young child, Teena expressed little interest in playing with girls' toys. She remembers envying boys both their status and their games. Although she has never seen a psychiatrist or psychologist, Teena has read widely about gender identity disorders and gender dysphoria, and she is quite knowledgeable about her current condition. She has told a woman she was dating that she is a hermaphrodite; however, she realizes this is incorrect, and reports she only uses the term because it makes it easier for others to understand her concerns about gender and self-identity. Teena has been – and remains – preoccupied with her wish to be identified as a male and to live as a man.

Past psychiatric illness, treatment, and outcomes
There is no significant history of psychiatric illness. Teena has never been hospitalized or treated by a psychologist or psychiatrist. She has frequently contemplated suicide but has never made a suicide attempt or gesture. She saw a guidance counselor in high school when she believed she was depressed, but she did not share her concerns about gender at that time.

---

[4] This fictitious interview is based on the character portrayed in the film *Boys Don't Cry*. It is not intended in any way to represent an interview with the real Teena Brandon.

Medical history

The medical history is not significant. According to the patient, she has been examined by several physicians, including gynecologists, all of whom assured her that her genitalia were anatomically and functionally "normal." Menses are regular, although this patient goes to great lengths to hide the fact that she is menstruating. Breast development is normal; Teena binds her breasts so they will not show underneath her clothes.

Psychosocial history

Teena Brandon was put up for adoption shortly after she was born, and she has never met her biological parents. She lived with a variety of foster parents; after turning 18, she moved to a trailer park in Lincoln, Nebraska, where she lived with her older brother until approximately 6 months ago when she moved to Falls City. Teena was socially isolated and ostracized in school, and she reports that other children always regarded her as "peculiar." At the age of 13, Teena began to refer to herself as "Brandon Teena," and this is the name she uses whenever possible. She met normal developmental milestones, but has never had any interest in dating boys. She has been attracted to females since puberty, and typically fantasizes about women. Teena does not identify herself as a lesbian, but all of her sexual experiences to date have been with women. Teena does not allow the woman she dates to touch or view her genitals. There is a history of petty theft and forging checks.

Drug and alcohol history

Teena has been using and abusing both alcohol and drugs since her early teens. The list of abused substances includes marijuana, LSD, and (most frequently) methamphetamine. She has avoided legal difficulties, but acknowledges "blackouts" that have occurred on many occasions. Alcohol use occurs almost daily; recreational drugs are typically used at weekends, in part because Teena cannot afford more frequent use. Teena cannot remember the last time she went 24 hours without drinking beer; however, there is no evidence of withdrawal or other signs of alcoholism.

Behavioral observations

Teena is a slender and attractive young woman who came in for the evaluation dressed in blue jeans and a flannel shirt. Her hair was closely cropped. She asked that she be called Brandon, although she acknowledges that her legal name is Teena Brandon. She was diffident and quiet, but answered all questions that were asked. She was polite and cooperative. She appeared mildly anxious.

Mental status examination

Teena identified the day of the month as the 23rd rather than the 24th. There were no other errors on the Mini-Mental State Examination, and this patient earned an overall score of 29/30.

Functional assessment

Teena is intelligent and friendly. She possesses considerable insight into her gender identity concerns, and she has read widely about these issues. Although she has only attained a high school education, it is likely that she could compete successfully in a college setting. Her excellent interpersonal skills and her self-effacing sense of humor will serve her well in a variety of occupational roles.

Strengths

Teena displays good social skills, self-awareness, and insight. On the VIA Survey, a measure of character strengths, her highest strengths were social intelligence, love, fairness, honesty, and humor.

Diagnosis

Gender dysphoria (F64.1); alcohol abuse; rule out alcohol use disorder.

Treatment plan

Continue to see Teena on a weekly basis to establish rapport and explore her feelings regarding gender. Consult with a specialist in gender dysphoria to see if Teena might be a candidate for sex reassignment surgery.

Prognosis

Guarded. Teena's intelligence and interpersonal skills make her a good candidate for psychotherapy. She is adamant that she is a male, and no ambivalence is present; however, I continue to be concerned about both the deception involved in her attempts to "pass" as a male, and her misuse of alcohol and drugs.

Boys Don't Cry and Gender Dysphoria

Hilary Swank is unforgettable as Teena Brandon in Kimberly Peirce's 1999 film *Boys Don't Cry*, and she won a Best Actress Academy Award for her role in this film. The film is based on a true story that had earlier been portrayed in a 1998 documentary titled *The Brandon Teena Story*.

Boys Don't Cry vividly portrays Brandon's attempts to pass as a male by using a rolled up sock as an ersatz penis (see Figure 15), as well as her dismay when she is menstruating. She develops a loving, sensual, and happy relationship with Lana, portrayed by Chloë Sevigny. The film accurately presents Brandon's story, and it precisely captures the hatred and homophobia displayed by John Lotter and Marvin Nissen, two men who initially befriended Bran-

don and later raped and killed her after learning that they had been deceived about her gender identity. The interrogation by a prurient, insensitive, and bumbling sheriff is chilling and sadly accurate. The film does not glamorize Brandon, and it accurately presents the confusion, dismay, pathos, and despair that frequently accompany those situations in which one's anatomical gender does not match one's deepest perception of self. The film is required viewing for anyone interested in understanding more about gender dysphoria.

Gender Dysphoria

Sex and **sexual** refer to the biological indicators of male and female whereas **gender** refers to the individual's lived role as a boy or girl, man or woman. **Gender dysphoria** thus refers to the indi-

Figure 15. *Boys Don't Cry* (1999, Fox Searchlight Pictures). Produced by John Hart, Eva Kolodner, Jeffrey Sharp, and Christine Vachon. Directed by Kimberly Peirce.

vidual's cognitive/emotional discontent with his or her assigned gender as male or female. The *DSM-5* refers to gender dysphoria rather than using the label "gender identity disorder"; the new terminology underscores the point that the problem to be treated is not identity per se, but rather the discomfort and unhappiness that results from the lack of correspondence between anatomy and identity. The term **transsexual** refers to an individual who is in process or has undergone a social transition from male to female or female to male. **Transgender** refers to the larger spectrum of individuals who identify with a gender different from their birth gender. Individuals who experience gender dysphoria are uncomfortable with their anatomic sex and often believe they are trapped in the wrong body. There is often a strong desire to replace their genitals with the genitalia of the opposite sex; these urges can be intense enough to lead to self-castration in males. Separate but linked diagnoses are available for children and for adolescents and adults, and specifiers are given when there is a concomitant disorder of sex development (e.g., congenital adrenal hyperplasia). There is also a "posttransition" specifier for those individuals who have undergone or who are preparing to undergo at least one relevant medical procedure (e.g., penectomy, mastectomy). People with marked gender dysphoria often suffer from concomitant depression, and suicide attempts are common. Before diagnosing someone with gender dysphoria, clinicians have to rule out simple nonconformity to gender roles, transvestic disorder (discussed in Chapter 14), body dysmorphic disorder, and psychosis.

Other films focusing on gender dysphoria include *Normal* (2003), *Beautiful Boxer* (2005), and *Soldier's Girl* (2003). These three films, together with *Boys Don't Cry*, show the pain that a person with gender identity disorder faces and the struggles associated with sharing information about sexual identify with loved ones and society. In *Normal*, Roy (Tom Wilkinson) believes he was born in the wrong body, and he wants a sex change operation. His wife of 25 years (Jessica Lange) expresses a variety of reactions – denial, shock, anger, rejection, depression, and finally acceptance – as they ultimately work to keep their marriage intact. Roy desires to be accepted by his congregation, coworkers, boss, children, and society, but each presents a

> "God meant for me to be somebody else."
>
> Roy in *Normal* (2003)

different struggle. *Soldier's Girl* is based on the tragic true story of Barry Winchell, a young man who enters the military and falls in love with a transsexual (a man who dressed as a woman in preparation for gender modification surgery). Likewise, *Beautiful Boxer* (2005) tells the true story of Parinaya Charoemphol, a Thai transgender kickboxer who took up the sport to earn money for gender reassignment surgery.

Transamerica (2005) is a touching film that stars Felicity Huffman as Bree, a presurgical male-to-female transsexual who is saving money and seeing a therapist in preparation for her upcoming operation. She receives a phone call from her son, Toby, a son she did not know she had (he was the byproduct of a casual college affair). Her therapist makes reuniting with her son a prerequisite for surgery, and this leads to a long road trip from New York to Phoenix, where Bree reunites with her dysfunctional family.

> "Don't you find it odd that plastic surgery can cure a mental disorder?"
>
> A fascinating comment explored in *Transamerica* (2005)

Interest in the phenomenon of transsexualism burgeoned in the United States and Europe 6 decades ago after the 1951 gender modification surgery of Christine Jorgensen. (*The Christine Jorgensen Story*, a low-budget and somewhat insipid film, was released in 1970.) The mid-1980s witnessed a revival of interest, after widespread publicity and a television movie *(Second Serve)* about the sex reassignment of male surgeon Richard Raskins into a female tennis star, Renee Richards. Other films that have explored transsexualism include *Myra Breckinridge* (1970) (starring film critic Rex Reed), *Dog Day Afternoon* (1975), *The World According to Garp* (1982), and *Come Back to the 5*

Figure 16. *The Crying Game* (1992, Palace Pictures, Channel Four Films, et al.). Produced by Stephen Woolley. Directed by Neil Jordan.

Fergus: "Do they know?"

Dil:"Know what, honey?"

Fergus: "Know what I didn't know? And don't call me that."

Dil: "Can't help it! A girl has her feelings."

Fergus: "Thing is, Dil, you're not a girl."

Dil: "Details, baby, details."

Fergus: "So they do know?"

Dil: "Alright, they do."

Fergus: "Don't. I should've known, shouldn't I?"

Dil: "Probably."

Fergus: "Kind of wish I didn't."

Dil: "You can always pretend."

Fergus: "That's true. Your soldier knew, didn't he?"

Dil: "Absolutely."

A candid discussion of gender and sexual ethics in *The Crying Game* (1993)

& *Dime, Jimmie Dean, Jimmie Dean* (1982). *The Crying Game* (1993) is a rich and nuanced film that explores a complex transsexual relationship; in one especially vivid scene, the protagonist throws up after discovering his transsexual lover is anatomically male (Figure 16).

The surgical treatment of transsexuals remains controversial, although tens of thousands of patients have undergone the procedure. Transsexualism occurs more often in biological males than in biological females, and many more males apply for sex reassignment surgery. Transsexuals can be heterosexual, homosexual, or asexual, both prior to and after their surgery. Many professionals who have worked with these patients have been struck by the fact that sexual behavior per se is often a secondary concern; the core issue is one of gender discontent, not sexual behavior.

There are a number of documentary films on gender dysphoria and gender identity, and a quick search on Netflix will reveal several of these.

The Range of Normal Sexual Behavior

Few areas of human behavior are as complex, varied, and interesting as sexual behavior. Both social scientists and the public are fascinated by the multitude of possibilities inherent in our sexuality. It is important to appreciate that the range of normal sexual behavior is exceptionally broad, and many behaviors that seem unusual or disturbing to some people do not qualify for a *DSM-5* label. As a rule, remember that complex or elaborate sexual fantasies are commonplace and do not suggest that any type of psychological disturbance is present. A psychological problem exists when a person acts on his or her fantasies with unwilling partners or behaves in ways that distress other people.

Filmmakers have been quick to exploit our fascination with sexual behavior, and contemporary cinema is replete with examples of sexual psychopathology. A serious student can learn a great deal about abnormal psychology from selective viewing.

Sexual Dysfunctions

The human **sexual response cycle** includes the following four phases:

1. *Desire*: fantasies related to sex;
2. *Excitement*: arousal, sense of pleasure with physiological changes;
3. *Orgasm*: peaking of sexual pleasure with release of sexual tension;
4. *Resolution*: sense of muscular relaxation and general well-being.

There can be a sexual disorder at any level. For example, **erectile disorder** (impotence) is an excitement/arousal disorder while a male's **premature ejaculation** is an orgasm disorder. Another significant sexual dysfunction problem for women is **genito-pelvic pain/penetration disorder**; this diagnosis brings together disorders formerly labeled as **dyspareunia,** which is recurrent genital pain during sexual intercourse, and **vaginismus,** which is a recurrent involuntary spasm of the outer muscle area of the vagina that interferes with sexual intercourse. Approximately 15% of women in the United States report experiencing recurrent pain during intercourse.

Other *DSM-5* diagnoses include delayed ejaculation, female orgasmic disorder, female sexual interest/arousal disorder, male hypoactive sexual desire disorder, and substance/medication-induced sexual dysfunction. Sexual dysfunctions can be lifelong, acquired, generalized or situational; these subtypes have important clinical implications and are indicated by a specifier included with the diagnosis.

Erectile disorder is diagnosed when at least one three symptoms are present on almost all occasions of sexual activity: Marked difficulty in *obtaining* an erection, marked difficulty *maintaining* an erection, and marked *decrease* in erectile rigidity during the sex act. These problems must have existed for at least 6 months and result in clinically significant distress for an individual to be diagnosed using *DSM-5* criteria.

Erectile disorder is much more common in older males: According to the *DSM-5*, only about 2% of men younger than 40–50 years have frequent problems with erections, but about half of all men 60 or older experience problems achieving or maintaining an erection.

The treatment of erectile dysfunction took a quantum leap forward in 1996 when Pfizer patented **sildenafil citrate** (Viagra) in the United States. Since that time, the US Food and Drug Administration (FDA) has approved four additional oral drugs to treat erectile dysfunction: Cialis, Levitra, Staxyn, and Stendra.

There is a vivid portrayal of **premature ejaculation** in *The Squid and the Whale* (2005). Erectile dysfunction followed by premature ejaculation is depicted in *Boy A* (2007). The films *Sex, Lies and Videotape* (1989), *Boxing Helena* (1993), *Noise* (2007), *The Hospital* (1971), *Italian for Beginners* (2001), and *Monster's Ball* (2001) each include at least one scene in which a man becomes impotent and has to face the consequences. Warren Beatty plays an impotent Clyde Barker in *Bonnie and Clyde* (1967), assuring Bonnie: "Ain't nothing wrong with me. ... I don't like boys." Peter O'Toole is impotent as a result of age and prostate cancer in *Venus* (2006). *Intimacy* (2000) depicts the frustration associated with premature ejaculation. John Voight play

Joe Buck in *Midnight Cowboy* (1969), a wanna-be stud who is impotent the first time he is paid to perform, and William Hurt plays an impotent drug dealer in *The Big Chill* (1983). The sexually addicted protagonist in *Shame* (2011) also experiences erectile dysfunction when attempting to make love to someone who is not a prostitute.

"Impotence is beautiful. Power to the impotent!"

Part of a soliloquy by a distraught physician/ chief of staff played by George C. Scott in *The Hospital* (1971)

Antiwar films often portray characters that are impotent as a result of war. These include Ron Kovic (Tom Cruise) in Oliver Stone's *Born on the Fourth of July* (1989) and an earlier film, *Coming Home* (1978), in which John Voight plays a paraplegic Vietnam veteran who is impotent but still able to satisfy his partner (Jane Fonda) with fellatio in ways her Marine husband never could.

In Billy Wilder's *Some Like it Hot* (1959), Tony Curtis, playing Joe, pretends to be impotent in order to seduce Marilyn Monroe, playing the role of Sugar. Richard Burton plays an impotent college professor, George, in Mike Nichols adaptation of Edward Albee's play *Who's Afraid of Virginia Woolf?* (1966).

The Oh in Ohio (2006) depicts a high school teacher who is frustrated by his wife's inability to achieve an orgasm and sexual satisfaction during their 10 years of marriage. He eventually has an affair with one of his students. His wife feels abandoned and becomes open to sexual exploration for the first time in her life, eventually having a satisfying sexual experience (an affair) with a character played by Danny DeVito, a swimming pool salesman. During a workshop on orgasm, one woman describes her vagina as a "velvet volcano." *Amy's Orgasm* (2001) is a film in which a confident, self-assured woman who writes self-help books about how women can manage just fine without men falls in love with a "shock jock" radio announcer and finds sexual fulfillment.

Kinsey (2004) is an important film about a college professor, Alfred Kinsey (Liam Neeson), who helped reshape the way people viewed sexuality in the middle of the last century. Kinsey published

Sugar: "Have you ever tried American girls?"
Joe:"Why?" (She takes a drumstick from him – and kisses him.)
Sugar: "Was it anything?"
Joe: "Thanks just the same." (He retrieves the drumstick and chews on it.)
Sugar: "You should see a doctor – a good doctor."
Joe: "I have. I spent six months in Vienna with Professor Freud, *flat on my back*." (He lies on the sofa.) "Then, there were the Mayo Brothers, injections, hypnosis, mineral baths. If I wasn't such a coward, I'll kill myself."
Sugar: "Don't say that!" (She rushes over to him.) "There must be some girl some place that could ..."
Joe: "If I ever found the girl that could, I'd marry her just like that."
Sugar: "Would you do me a favor?"
Joe: "Certainly, what is it?"
Sugar: "I may not be Dr. Freud or a Mayo brother, or one of those French upstairs girls, but could I take another crack at it?"
Joe: "All right, if you insist." (They kiss deeply accompanied by a phallic image – his foot rises at the end of the sofa behind her.)
Sugar: "Anything this time?"
Joe: "I'm afraid not. Terribly sorry."
Sugar: "Would you like some more champagne? Maybe if we had some music? How do you dim these lights?"

Tony Curtis feigning impotence in order to seduce Marilyn Monroe in *Some Like it Hot* (1959)

---

two landmark books based on interviews with tens of thousands of people across the country: *Sexual Behavior in the Human Male* (1948) and *Sexual Behavior in the Human Female* (1953). Many people criticized Kinsey's methodology and research, but his impact on society is undeniable. Kinsey contributed to normalizing homosexuality, premarital sex, and the use of multiple sexual positions; he also debunked numerous misconceptions (e.g., the belief that masturbation is harmful). The film portrays Kinsey training his team in conducting interviews that are objective and unbiased, reminding them that "maintaining a nonjudgmental attitude is harder than you think." A particularly striking scene occurs during Kinsey's straightforward teaching approach in his course on human sexuality where he displays slides of human genitalia. The film also depicts many of the shortcomings of this famous researcher, including his ritualistic compulsiveness (suggesting an obsessive-compulsive personality), barbiturate abuse, lack of personal sexual boundaries, and his superficiality in his interpersonal relations.

The Sessions (2012) stars John Hawkes as Mark, a man in an iron lung who has never experienced a mature sexual relationship. He discusses the situation with his priest, Father Brendan, played by William H. Macy, and decides to seek out the services of a sexual surrogate (played by Helen Hunt). The film, based on a true story involving a University of California student in Berkeley, delightfully explores nascent sexuality and makes the point that genuine and enduring love relationships can exist between people who are very different.

"I have a feeling that God is going to give you a free pass on this one. Go for it."

Father Brendan encourages Mark to explore his sexuality in *The Sessions* (2012)

(A)sexual (2011) is a documentary depicting people who do not experience sexual feelings (e.g., people who are not attracted to either men or women). **Asexuality** is not a disorder or diagnosis because if you ask many of these individuals, they will report that their lack of sexual desire is simply not a problem. Many of the female characters in *(A)sexual* would meet the main criteria for the *DSM-5* condition, female sexual interest/arousal disorder: absent or minimal interest in sex, absent/minimal erotic thoughts/fantasies, reduced or no sexual initiation, etc. However, the majority of these females in the film are entirely comfortable with their asexuality and thus would not meet the key requirement that the symptoms causing significant distress. As a result, no diagnosis would be given. Asexual individuals do not seem to have a problem with sexual arousal. Some scientists have begun to study asexuality, a topic mostly neglected over the

decades. One survey of the general population found that 1% of people report they are not attracted to men *or* women; this number suggests there are 3 million asexual people in the United States. Research reported in the film notes that these individuals do not have any higher rates of depression, anger, trauma, or any mental illness than the normal population.

International Films: Sexual Dysfunctions and Gender Dysphoria

Breakfast on Pluto (2005, Ireland/UK), Neal Jordan's adaptation of a novel by Patrick McCabe, is an Irish film that presents the life of "Kitten," an orphan and a transvestite who enjoyed dressing up in women's clothes from a very early age. This film is less a gender identity study than the story of societal abuse, ostracism, tragedy, and diagnostic misadventure. It is about an individual who happens to cross-dress and have gender issues and overcomes enormous stressful and tragic experiences, including but not limited to serious life threats, prostitution, homelessness, job loss, and a fire that destroys his home. Kitten perseveres through all of this.

She Male Snails, originally released with its Swedish title *Pojktanten* (2011, Swedish), is a documentary about the life of a transgender artist named Eli Leven. The film's director, Ester Martin Bergsmark, identifies as transgender. *Tomboy* (2011, France) is a touching French film about a 10-year-old girl, Laure, who moves to a new neighborhood with her sister and mother. When Laure sets out to meet the other kids in her neighborhood, she meets Lisa who assumes Laure is a boy because of her pageboy haircut. Laure almost effortlessly slides into her new, masculine identity, and she introduces herself to Lisa as "Mikael."

Wild Tigers I Have Known (2006, United Kingdom), directed by Cam Archer, is a sensitive film that tells the story of Logan, a 13-year-old boy coming to terms with his sexuality. Logan keeps a wig and a tube of lipstick hidden in his dresser drawer, and it is never clear if he is gay or transsexual. He becomes romantically involved with another boy,

Rodeo, as a result of a series of late-night phone calls in which Logan pretends to be a girl. Although this is a film worth seeing, we recommend you watch *Tomboy* first.

Rayan: "We hear you're a girl. We're gonna check that."

Lisa: "Stop it! What do you think you're doing?"

Rayan: "We're gonna check if she's really a girl."

Lisa: "Leave him alone."

Rayan: "You're right. It's YOU who'll check."

Lisa: "No, I won't."

Rayan: "If she's a girl, then you kissed her. It's disgusting. Right?"

Lisa: "Yes, it's disgusting."

Rayan: "Then, you're gonna do it."

[Lisa pulls down Laure's pants]

Children trying to make sense of the mystery of gender in *Tomboy* (2011, France)

Y Tu Mamá También (2001, Mexico) includes a memorable scene depicting premature ejaculation when a Mexican teenager has sex with an older traveling companion. One of the boys in the film *That's the Way I Like It* (1998, Singapore) has gone through his life trying to please his parents. For example, he goes to medical school and works hard in school to get stellar grades. One day he announces that he has been hiding the fact that he is a woman. He then shares that he will be undergoing sex reassignment surgery (involving genital surgery and hormone treatment). His father's reaction is negative. Later in the film, despite being disowned by his father, he shows up dressed fully as a woman. His father remains rigid in his disgust and exclaims that he will kill his son if he sees him again. Although this film is a comedy/musical, it depicts the significant impact of such interactions and decisions on the family. The young man then, distraught by the shame he believes he has brought upon his family, attempts suicide. However, he lives and his brother provides the financial support he needs for the operation.

Critical Thinking Questions

➤ Homosexuality was deleted from the *DSM* of the American Psychiatric Association in 1973. What brought about this decision? What have been its effects?

➤ Did the previous *DSM-IV-TR* diagnosis of gender identity disorder perpetuate social stereotypes and discrimination toward members of the trans community?

➤ Why is it that women's clothes (e.g., dresses and slips) are distinctly feminine, while men's clothes (e.g., pants and belts) are far less likely to be regarded as exclusively male?

➤ Is it ethical for therapists to work with gay and lesbian individuals to modify their sexual orientation? If so, under what conditions would it be appropriate?

➤ What do these terms mean: *androphilia, gynephilia,* and *polyamory*?

➤ What is the PLISSIT model for the treatment of sexual dysfunction?

➤ How did the introduction of drugs to treat erectile dysfunction (Viagra, Cialis, Levitra) change the social and sexual landscape in the United States with its rapidly aging population?

➤ How do films and other media shape our expectations about what is sexually normal?

If you have time to read just one book relevant to this chapter, make it:

 Dworkin, S.H., & Pope, M. (Eds.). (2012). *Casebook for counseling lesbian, gay, bisexual, and transgendered persons and their families*. Alexandria, VA: American Counseling Association.

If you only have time for one article, read:

 Green, R. (2010). Robert Stoller's sex and gender: 40 years on. *Archives of Sexual Behavior, 39*(6), 1457–1465. doi: 10.1007/s10508-010-9665-5

Wedding and Niemiec's Top 10 Gender Dysphoria and Sexual Dysfunctions Films

Gender Dysphoria

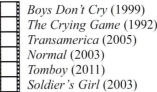

Boys Don't Cry (1999)
The Crying Game (1992)
Transamerica (2005)
Normal (2003)
Tomboy (2011)
Soldier's Girl (2003)
That's the Way I Like It (1998)

Sexual Dysfunction

Love and Other Drugs (2010)
The Oh in Ohio (2006)
Kinsey (2004)

Chapter 10

Disruptive, Impulse-Control, and Conduct Disorders

Eva: Why would you have something like that?
Kevin: I collect them.
Eva: Isn't that a weird thing to collect?
Kevin: I don't like stamps.
Eva: Well, what's the point?
Kevin: There is no point. That's the point.

Kevin tries to explain to his mother why he collects computer viruses
in *We Need To Talk About Kevin* (2012)

➤ Do evil children like Kevin really exist? Have you ever known one?
➤ How common is it for children to bond more closely with one parent than the other?
➤ Do children who "turn out bad" as teenagers show warning signs early in childhood?
➤ Would a high school counselor have been able to identify Kevin as someone likely to commit mass murder?
➤ Should all adolescents who commit murder be tried and punished as adults?
➤ Are there ever times when the death penalty is appropriate for an adolescent?
➤ When is a child's brain fully developed?
➤ Why did Kevin choose to kill his father and sister but spare his mother?
➤ Kevin was raised in what appears to be a happy and loving home. Are his problems strictly genetic?
➤ Why are the neighbors so hostile to Kevin's mother, a woman who has done nothing wrong?
➤ How could Kevin's father be so oblivious to what was really happening with his only son?
➤ Kevin's mother visits him in prison after the mass murder and attempts to maintain a relationship with her son. Is this realistic? How would you have reacted in such a situation?

Patient Evaluation

Name: Kevin Khatchadourian

Patient's stated reason for coming
"Fuck this. They made me come in for counseling. I don't need this shit. ... I don't need you. ... I don't need nothin'. Everything's all fucked up! Nothin' you can say or do will make a bit of difference."

History of the present Illness
Kevin is a 17-year-old high school student referred by the school principal after a series of verbal altercations with teachers and other students. He is described as a loner who has few friends. He makes poor grades in almost all classes but is seemingly indifferent to his poor performance. He excels in art, and he is reported to be quite skilled as an archer, although he did not try out for the school archery team.

Past psychiatric illness, treatment, and outcome
There is no history of past psychiatric illness, although Kevin has always been recognized by his parents and teachers as different from other children and somewhat odd.

Medical history
Kevin was slow to speak and he did not talk in complete sentences until the age of 3. Toilet training was also delayed; Kevin would frequently wet or soil himself until starting preschool at age 5; his mother believes this was deliberate. He was apparently an obstinate child who frequently disobeyed parental instructions.

Psychosocial history
Kevin lives at home with his parents and his 8-year-old sister. He is estranged from his mother, but has a reasonably positive relationship with his father and sister. He has few friends, and he does not date. He spends much of his time alone in his room watching violent pornography and masturbating; occasionally he masturbates openly in front of other family members and seems to take delight in shocking and upsetting his mother and sister. There is a history of angry arguments with other children and with teachers, and he has been suspended from school on two different occasions for fighting. Kevin denies any history of bed-wetting, fire-setting, or stealing. He was an obstinate child who frequently disobeyed parental instructions. He does acknowledge a history of animal cruelty – "Yeah, I've killed a kitten or two along the way." He becomes annoyed easily and often loses his temper. He frequently argues with his teachers and other authority figures, even over trivial issues. He was expelled for 2 weeks last year after clipping the hair of the girl sitting in front of him in class. He was also expelled for 3 days earlier for vandalizing the locker of a fellow student. Kevin denies

any responsibility for his interpersonal problems or his academic difficulties, blaming everything that happens to him on others. Kevin denies any suicidal intent or plan to hurt himself or others.

Drug and alcohol history
Kevin denies use of illicit drugs. He is not allowed to drink alcohol, but reports surreptitious drinking in his bedroom, usually on weekends.

Behavioral observations
Kevin was casually dressed and fairly unkempt. His hair was uncombed. He is thin, almost to the point of emaciation. He appeared sullen, resentful, and indifferent; he slouched in his chair and clearly resented being required to see a school counselor. His language is profane, and he adopted a superior, supercilious attitude during the interview.

Mental status examination
Kevin was oriented to time, place, situation, and person. He appears to have above-average intelligence despite his poor grades. There is no evidence of psychosis or delusions.

Functional assessment
Kevin is withdrawn, reclusive, and hostile. He has limited social skills. He presents as someone full of anger. He clearly did not feel any need for assistance or advice, and came to the interview only because he would be expelled if he didn't show at least minimal cooperation.

Strengths
Kevin's skills in archery suggest good hand–eye coordination. He is an attractive young man. He is able to think abstractly, and he appears to be of above-average intelligence. I requested that Kevin complete the VIA Survey, a measure of character strengths; however, he remarked, "This is stupid," and refused to complete the questionnaire. In reviewing the VIA Classification list of 24 character strengths, my clinical judgment is that he might be high in bravery, curiosity, creativity, and perseverance. Further testing is needed to confirm these impressions.

Diagnosis
Oppositional defiant disorder, severe (91.3). Rule out intermittent explosive disorder, conduct disorder, and antisocial personality disorder.

Family consultation
I will meet with his parents soon to learn more about his home life and developmental history.

Treatment plan
Individual counseling: I plan to see Kevin on a weekly basis if he is willing to be seen. I hope to establish rapport, serve as a role model, and monitor his angry outbursts and the frequency of his altercations with teachers and other students. At present, Kevin denies any intention to harm others; should this change, I will notify local authorities immediately.

Prognosis
Guarded.

We Need To Talk About Kevin

We Need to Talk About Kevin (2012) is a powerful and compelling drama directed by Lynne Ramsey that stars Tilda Swinton and John C. Reilly as Kevin's parents. The film is a horror story for any parent who sees the film, and every parent watching finds himself or herself wondering how he or she would have responded to the challenges presented by a child like Kevin. The film has frequent flashbacks that depict Kevin at various developmental stages, all of them difficult for his parents but especially for Eve, Kevin's mother. It is clear that Kevin does not bond with his mother (or she with him); in contrast, he appears friendly and loving around his sister and father, presumably to underscore how very alienated he is from his mother. Figure 17 shows Kevin's mother, Eve (Tilda Swinton) feeling shocked and overwhelmed by the challenges associated with raising a child like Kevin.

Figure 17. *We Need to Talk about Kevin* (2011, BBC Films, Oscilloscope Laboratories, et al.). Produced by Jennifer Fox, Luc Roeg, and Bob Salerno. Directed by Lynne Ramsay.

Kevin is a skilled archer, and he eventually sets up a premeditated mass murder at his school where he locks the gym doors and kills dozens of children before the police take him into custody. When his mother returns to the family home, she discovers that her husband and daughter have also been killed. Kevin presumably spared his mother's life because having her witness the full horror of the atrocity he committed was more hateful than anything he could have done, including murdering her.

Child Mental Health

In the majority of cases, the diagnoses discussed in this chapter originate in childhood. Psychiatric problems of children are not as easily diagnosed as those of adults, and the symptoms of mental illness in children are sometimes difficult to distinguish from those changes associated with normal growth and development. For example, it is normal for a 4-year-old to have an imaginary friend, but for an adolescent, an invisible friend that only he sees would be considered a psychotic hallucination.

Children who receive mental health treatment usually fall into one of the following categories:

1. Children whose behavior is a response to family disruptions, crisis, or dysfunction;
2. Children whose behavior does not conform to social norms and is troublesome to others (e.g., disruptive behaviors and conduct disorders);
3. Children who experience repeated and excessive depression, anxiety, or states of personal distress;
4. Children whose cognitive or neuromotor development is not proceeding normally (e.g., developmental disabilities).

Oppositional Defiant Disorder and Conduct Disorder

The diagnosis of **oppositional defiant disorder** is typically given to children and adolescents who have a pattern of negativistic, hostile, and defiant behavior, such as losing their temper, being argumentative, and being easily annoyed and resentful. The *DSM-5* requires the presence of four out of eight symptoms, and the aberrant behavior pattern must have existed for at least 6 months. People, most often children, who receive an ODD diagnosis lose their temper easily and often. They are quickly annoyed and are often angry and resentful. They refuse to comply with instructions or demands from authority figures. They annoy other people, and their peers typically dislike them. They blame other people for their mistakes and have a history of spiteful or vindictive behavior. These individuals have little insight into their own behavior and the reactions of other people. The *DSM-5* suggests the prevalence of the disorder is about 3.3%, with males outnumbering females by about 40% until adolescence, when the number of males and females with the disorder becomes approximately equal.

A diagnosis of **conduct disorder** is given to children and adolescents who violate the basic rights of others or societal norms by engaging in aggression towards people or animals, destruction of property, theft, deceit, and/or truancy. The *DSM-5* diagnosis requires the presence of three out of 15 criteria occurring in the past 12 months, with at least one criterion present in the past 6 months. (Note that five children could each receive this diagnosis without a single overlapping symptom among the five.) The criteria used in making this diagnosis include bullying, frequent fighting, use of a weapon, cruelty to people or animals, stealing, rape, fire setting, destruction of others' property, lying, stealing, truancy, and running away.

It should be clear that there is an overlap in these diagnoses (and with intermittent explosive disorder, discussed in the section "Intermittent Explosive Disorder"), and differential diagnosis is often challenging. In many countries, these diagnostic labels are not used. However, these behavioral problems are universal, as are the movies that depict them.

Oppositional defiant disorder in late teens is beautifully illustrated in the film *Don't Come Knocking* (2005), in which a young man displays outrage and defiance after his biological father, a washed-up actor, returns to town wanting to see him. In *Manic* (2003), the viewer gets an inside look at the adolescent unit of a psychiatric hospital. This well-acted independent film presents interesting questions about differential diagnosis, demonstrates friction between various adolescents with clashing behavioral prob-

lems (e.g., bipolar disorder, impulse-control disorder, conduct disorder, and depression), and offers a good portrayal of group psychotherapy.

My Flesh and Blood (2004) is a documentary about a woman who takes care of special needs children; one child, whose life is explored in detail, has a severe conduct disorder in addition to cystic fibrosis. His anger outbursts and sexual acting out are at times tempered by a needy softness and emotional vulnerability. His behavioral problems are directly related to the loss of his mother as a caretaker (she continues to visit him), the stress of his environment (one caretaker serves 11 special needs children), and the stress of his illness.

Holes (2002), an excellent Disney feature film, depicts various oppositional and rule-breaking youth who are sent to a working camp because of their disruptive and behavioral problems. One adolescent steals cars and has a tic disorder. *Beautiful Boy* (2012) is a film in many ways similar to *We Need To Talk About Kevin*; it deals with the way a couple is affected after learning that their son who was away at college shot and killed 17 people and then killed himself.

Life as a House and *My First Mister*

Two important films portray highly troubled, isolated, suicidal, and oppositional adolescents – *Life as a House* (2001) with the character of Sam (Hayden Christensen) and *My First Mister* (2001) with Jennifer (Leelee Sobieski) as the protagonist. Each film presents a highly troubled and alienated young person who is transformed through meaningful relationships. The major difference between the lead characters is their gender, and watching both films will help you appreciate the differences in psychosexual development between boys and girls.

In *Life as a House*, we are introduced to Sam, a character with a rebellious, gothic appearance as evidenced by his colored hair, lip ring, eye makeup, and tough exterior. In an early scene, he huffs paint while choking himself (autoerotic asphyxiation) in his closet. He resorts to this practice whenever he needs to escape from people and reality: He locks his door, plays loud music (e.g., Marilyn Manson), uses drugs (pills, pot, and huffing), and masturbates. With his extreme negativism and oppositional personality, it is easy to see how he believes that no one understands him and why he must come up with complicated ways to isolate himself. At one point in the film, he reveals he has been using drugs since the age of 12. He earns money to buy drugs through prostitution, finding this preferable to working hard to earn less money. Sam can articulate that he wants to become something he is not and does not know how; this leaves him to feel like "nothing." Beneath his rough exterior is a wounded and isolated adolescent longing for a meaningful connection. He finds the needed friendship and love when he establishes a relationship with his dying father; at that point, Sam's behaviors, attitude, and appearance are transformed.

"I like how it feels not to feel."

Sam (Hayden Christensen) in
Life as a House (2001)

My First Mister portrays a similarly troubled youth, 17-year-old Jennifer, who is also gothic in appearance. She wears mostly black and has multiple facial piercings. She is very isolated with no real

Additional Questions for Discussion (*Life as a House* and *My First Mister*)

➤ Contrast the lead characters and the parental figures in each film.

➤ How likely is it for a teen to undergo rapid, positive transformation as depicted in these films? What type of transformation is most common (i.e., physical, attitudinal, social, or emotional)?

➤ Is there a connection between music preferences (e.g., rap, grunge, heavy metal) and adolescent behavior?

➤ Do body piercings provide any evidence of psychopathology, or are they simply a manifestation of healthy adolescent rebellion?

➤ Both characters live in good homes and had opportunities to thrive in those environments. How do you account for the oppositional behavior we see at each film's onset?

➤ Both characters engage in some severe self-destructive behavior (e.g., prostitution, self-cutting). How common is such self-destructive behavior in adolescents? In children?

➤ If a troubled adolescent were to watch one of these films, how likely is it he or she would be inspired to change his or her behavior?

friends and no genuine interest in her needy mother or distant stepfather. She comments that she has never had a boyfriend or, for that matter, any friends. The closest Jennifer can get to people is when she views them through her binoculars. She fantasizes about living with the Partridge family. She has a blunted, sad affect and is highly negativistic and critical about life. She is preoccupied with death, and she writes melancholy poetry about dying, hopelessness, and "not existing." She likes to lie on gravesites, and exclaims, "I'm gonna go to hell anyway." More serious problems include self-injurious behaviors (cutting her arm) and visual hallucinations of her deceased grandmother. She finds meaning and purpose in a random, healthy relationship that blossoms with a man who she works with in a men's clothing store.

Both films include characters in search of their identity. These two teens work through oppositional and conduct problems to find themselves.

Thirteen

This film depicts a nightmarish reality for some parents; for others, it may serve as a wake-up call. *Thirteen* (2003), directed by Catherine Hardwicke, depicts a rapid transformation from childhood to adolescence and the pervasive influence of peer pressure during the teen years.

Tracy Freeland (Evan Rachel Wood), a 13-year-old seventh grader, is eager to be accepted by the "in group" in her school. She earns acceptance from this group when she rejects her current, less popular friends, and spontaneously steals money from a woman on the street. She takes her soon-to-be best friend Evie Zamora (Nikki Reed) on a shopping spree, buying clothing and shoes. A friendship soon develops, and an emotional roller coaster ride begins, characterized by rebellion, acting out, parental opposition, and misconduct. Tracy gets her tongue and belly button pierced, exhibits self-injurious behavior, abuses substances, tells numerous lies, and lets her grades plummet. She also becomes sexually pro-

---

"I'll die for you but I won't leave you alone right now."

Melanie Freeland (Holly Hunter) to her
daughter who has been used and betrayed
in *Thirteen* (2003)

---

miscuous. An opening scene (a flash-forward) depicts Tracy and Evie getting high and amusing themselves by punching one another in the face.

As these oppositional behaviors escalate, Tracy becomes more and more isolated from her mother (Holly Hunter). Tracy becomes angry with her mother and resists any attempts to set parental limits on her behavior. The mother works hard to establish appropriate boundaries, yet frequently falls short because of her own struggles and limitations as a recovering drug addict. The mother and daughter eventually come to know each other better as a result of their frequent fights. Evie's mother, on the other hand, is a self-absorbed abuse victim who allows and even encourages the girls to drink and smoke. The plot culminates in a bitter betrayal by Evie, demonstrating that peer relationships can end as abruptly as they begin.

Additional Questions for Discussion (Thirteen)

➤ Would one of these two teens benefit more than the other in a juvenile detention program?

➤ How common is it for seventh graders to use drugs and alcohol, become promiscuous, have their bodies pierced, or practice self-injurious behaviors?

➤ What does current research say about the social influences of peers? At what age does peer influence peak?

➤ Does Tracy become involved with an African American athlete primarily to upset her mother?

➤ Is peer influence more important than parental influence?

➤ How should parents respond when adolescents refuse to accept parental boundaries?

Elephant

The award-winning (Cannes Film Festival) 2003 independent film *Elephant,* directed by Gus Van Sant, is a realistic and artful portrayal of an American high school and the routine life of students just prior to a massive school shooting, reminding the viewer of Columbine, Sandy Hook, and subsequent tragedies. The film is eerie and foreboding in that it is much more about nonverbal behavior than about dialogue; this heightens the importance of the cinematic craft, a craft Van Sant has mastered, particularly in his unique camera work and use of **nondiegetic sound**

(i.e., sounds whose source cannot be seen in the film). The viewer is taken along as the camera slowly follows several major characters as they go through their daily routines (e.g., walking down long hallways, greeting fellow students), and going in and out of buildings (into danger or safety zones, unbeknownst to them), often with nondiegetic music in the background. It is interesting to note the title outside the building reads simply "high school," letting this particular school represent every high school.

Two characters, Eric (Eric Deulen) and Alex (Alex Frost), are depicted playing a video shooting game and looking up information about guns on the Internet. They order guns without difficulty and receive them in the mail in a large package. Later, these two teens plot their shooting spree with a map of the school, planning to "pick off" as many classmates as possible in the school's high-traffic areas.

Although the film is realistic, the viewer is left with more questions than answers about causes, prevention, psychopathology, and etiology. At the same time, this is part of the director's craft, and he deliberately lets each member of the audience draw his or her own conclusions.

Additional Questions for Discussion (Elephant)

➤ Why did the director, Gus Van Sant, choose this title?

➤ The film provides considerable latitude for viewers to explain the behaviors of Eric and Alex. Which explanations seem most compelling?

➤ Did Eric and Alex have a history of violent, delinquent, or deviant behavior?

➤ What is the purpose of the film? How does the director's style enhance this purpose?

➤ What warnings signs are presented in the behaviors of these two characters? Could this shooting have been prevented? How?

➤ Would stricter gun control laws have reduced the likelihood of the mass murder of children and teachers that occurred at Sandy Hook Elementary School in 2012?

Kids and Gummo

These two movies are discussed together because both are extraordinarily disturbing films. Harmony Korine, who wrote the script for *Kids* (1995), was both writer and director for *Gummo* (1997). Both films provide a frightening perspective on the lives of adolescents, the former in an urban setting and the latter in a small town/rural setting.

Kids, directed by Larry Clark, is a fast-paced film that allows the viewer to experience the thoughts, words, and behaviors of young adolescents as they interact with each other. One unforgettable scene depicts 15 or so skateboarding teens who brutalize a man who made the mistake of criticizing one of the skateboarders. The plot revolves around the character of Telly (Leo Fitzpatrick), a scrawny but confident adolescent who takes tremendous pride in his ability to seduce virgins. Unbeknownst to him, Telly is HIV positive, and he is rapidly spreading the virus to his vulnerable partners, most of whom have never had sex before. Telly is extremely narcissistic, and the viewer assumes he would not change his behavior even if he knew of his diagnosis. One of Telly's victims, a teenage girl, finds out she has been infected by Telly, and much of the film involves her frantic attempts to get him to stop spreading the disease. In this film, HIV is a metaphor for the spread of violence among inner-city youth.

Gummo is a realistic but disturbing film that portrays lower-class, antisocial children and adolescents. The film includes numerous disturbing scenes of animal torture, drug abuse, and bizarre behavior such as that exhibited by one man who has a fight with an inanimate object. The film's two main characters, Solomon (Jacob Reynolds) and Tummler (Nick Sutton), bicycle around shooting stray cats and collecting them in garbage bags to sell them to a storeowner so they can get high on glue or have sex with a girl with an intellectual disability. At times, these two characters are violent just for the sake of violence; they repeatedly whip a hanging dead cat and later take turns shooting a dead cat in the pouring rain. They break into the home of their competitor (another cat killer), masked with guns and a golf club, and unhook the life support of an infirm elderly woman. Each adolescent is reared by a single parent with limited parenting skills; Solomon's mother threatens to kill him with a toy gun for not smiling, and later washes him in filthy bathwater while serving him spaghetti and milk.

There are many other quirky and disturbed characters in the film, including a boy who dresses like a bunny, urinates on traffic from overpasses, drowns a cat, and fakes his own death, and a developmen-

tally disabled girl who laughs while she shaves her eyebrows and compulsively treats her doll as if it were a real infant. The director, Harmony Korine, has a cameo appearance in the film as a drunken adolescent who randomly pours beer on his head while describing his history of sexual abuse and trying to seduce a gay, African American midget. Korine's character recollects throwing marbles on his mother's belly when he was a young child – if he hit her navel, he would get five dollars but whenever he missed, he was hit with a rolling pin.

These characters lack insight into their behavior, and they are not able to appreciate the consequences of their acts. Most lack empathy and have little regard for ethical or moral standards; it is reasonable to assume that many will become adults who qualify for a diagnosis of antisocial personality disorder.

Many viewers stay to the end of the credits of *Gummo* to confirm that the animal abuse scenes are simulated, that prosthetic animals are used, and that the characters and situations are fictitious; despite the assurance of the credits, viewers know that for some children, the scenes portrayed are all too real.

> **Additional Questions for Discussion (*Kids* and *Gummo*)**
>
> ➤ Is there any artistic merit in films as shocking as these?
> ➤ Compare and contrast potential diagnoses for the main characters in the two films.
> ➤ What role does the lack of authority figures play in the lives of these teens?
> ➤ What redeeming scenes are included in each film? How do you react to these?
> ➤ What would be appropriate treatment for the characters in these films? Should these children be treated in the juvenile justice system or the mental health system?

Dysfunctional Families in Contemporary Films

There are a myriad of dysfunctional families captured in films. We have included a handful of examples here. These films show the impact of familial problems on the children and provide a view of children with both healthy and unhealthy coping.

A child's behavior may appear to be symptomatic of a psychiatric disorder but, in reality, be a response to parental marital discord or family dysfunction. Complex family relationships provide filmmakers opportunities to dramatically portray multiple plots and subplots with relatively few characters. In Noah Baumbach's highly acclaimed film *The Squid and the Whale* (2005), two brothers, 16-year-old Walt (Jesse Eisenberg) and 10-year-old Frank (Owen Kline), are the center of their divorcing parents' feuds. The father, Bernard (Jeff Daniels), is an impossible character – jealous, self-absorbed, condescending, and narcissistic. He is a self-proclaimed novelist who feels victimized by being relegated to a college teaching position. The mother Joan (Laura Linney) is emerging as a legitimate writer whose success only fuels her husband's animosity toward her. When the parents separate, Walt, who idolizes and imitates his father, chooses to live with Bernard. Frank, the more emotional of the two brothers, stays with his mother, Joan. Both boys develop abnormal behaviors. Frank drinks alcohol, masturbates, and smears his ejaculate on books and a locker at school. Walt plagiarizes a Pink Floyd song as his own, breaks up with his girlfriend, and refuses to see his mother because she had an affair while still married. Walt is referred to a therapist who helps him increase his self-awareness. In isolation, any of these abnormal behaviors could have been evaluated as symptoms of a mental disorder. Instead, these behaviors are all reactions to the chaotic family crisis.

Another interesting but disturbing film, one that explores a child's attempt to make sense out of chaotic and dysfunctional family interactions, is *Running with Scissors* (2006). This award-winning film is based on the real-life memoirs of Augusten Burroughs who was handed off to his mother's psychiatrist after his parents' divorce. Burroughs is the son of poet and writer Margaret Robison and the late John G. Robison, head of the philosophy department at the University of Massachusetts at Amherst. The Augusten Burroughs' character, played by Joseph Cross, is a young gay child who is consumed with adoration for his mother Deirdre (Annette Bening), who is attempting to launch her career as a poet. Augusten spends his childhood skipping school and practicing to become a performer. Augusten's father Norman (played by Alec Baldwin) teaches philosophy and abuses alcohol. The mother and father spend most of their time arguing. When the parents separate, Augusten, aged 12, is given to Deirdre's psychiatrist, Dr. Finch (Brian Cox), an eccentric physician. As Deirdre sinks into her mental illness, Augusten avoids school, keeps a diary, becomes sexually involved with one of Finch's patients, and develops a friendship with Finch's younger daughter. During this time, he perfects his cosmetology skills. In real life, Burroughs dropped out of school after the sixth grade and obtained his high school diploma (GED) at age 17. He became a successful advertising executive, then left the field and became a successful writer.

"I want rules ... and boundaries ... because ... what I've learned is that ... without them ... all life is ... is a series of surprises ..."

Augusten Burroughs in
Running with Scissors (2006)

The Academy Award-winning satiric comedy *Little Miss Sunshine* (2006) portrays a family in crisis. Olive Hoover (Abigail Breslin) has fantasized about winning a beauty pageant for her entire young life. Although she does not fit the stereotypic contestant profile, Olive does manage to become a finalist in the Little Miss Sunshine pageant. Her family takes off in an old Volkswagen bus to attend the pageant. The family characters are unforgettable – her father (Greg Kinnear) is an unsuccessful motivational speaker/author, her brother Dwayne (Paul Dana) is a lost soul who has not spoken for months but has dreams of being an air force pilot, and her uncle Steve (Frank Ginsberg), who has just been released from a psychiatric facility after a suicide attempt, requires close observation. One of the best performances is that of Olive's grandfather (Alan Arkin), who supports Olive's confidence and sense of self-worth. Olive, probably the healthiest member of the family, does not have a mental illness or emotional problem, but she is an example of a child much wiser than her years who helps an unhealthy family grow psychologically.

Intermittent Explosive Disorder

Intermittent explosive disorder is a diagnosis that requires to recurrent behavioral outbursts characterized by verbal aggression or misbehavior such as destroying property or harming animals or other people. This behavior is grossly out of proportion to the provocation, and the outbursts are not premeditated and appear to be out of the individual's control. These outbursts are typically relative short, but highly disruptive in family interactions or in the classroom. The diagnosis is more prevalent among young individuals (under age 35) than those older than 50, but can be applied to anyone with anger management problems over the age of 6. The *DSM-5* estimated prevalence is 2.7%.

Anger is a normal emotion all humans experience. It can be a healthy indicator of internal stress, a sign that deep emotions are being tapped, or a cue that someone has offended us. In many instances, the anger turns from thoughts and feelings into behaviors and is acted out in some form. Anger can be extraordinarily destructive, and this destructiveness comes across verbally or physically. Intermittent explosive disorder is diagnosed when there are several discrete episodes of aggressive impulses that result in serious assaults or property destruction. Several good films depict intermittent explosive disorder.

In *Boy A* (2007), a young boy, Eric, is frequently beaten up at school and becomes isolated. Desperate for social contact, Eric connects with another young boy who has conduct disorder. The boys' behavior turns from "bad" (e.g., shoplifting, beating up kids) to despicable (e.g., killing a young girl). They are prosecuted and sent away, not as punishment but to protect others (and themselves). The prosecutor emphasizes that the two boys are evil and dangerous. Upon release, the newspaper announces that "evil comes of age" and shows a photo of Eric on the release day. Eric decides to changes his name to Jack and create a new persona. He is shy, awkward, and nice, and desperate to connect with others. He makes an effort but struggles to overcome his past demons and previous instincts; in one instance he impulsively explodes and attacks a bully who is mistreating someone. He is supported by a social worker who is portrayed as caring, resourceful, and insightful.

> ## Additional Questions for Discussion (*Boy A*)
>
> ➤ What diagnoses would you give Eric/Jack as you observe him progress throughout the film? Be sure to consider all the diagnoses discussed in this chapter as well as depressive disorders, anxiety disorders, and sexual dysfunctions.
> ➤ What is the significance and meaning behind the film's title?
> ➤ Can one ever fully escape one's past, especially if it was traumatic and/or violent?
> ➤ Does Eric's behavior at the end of the film seem realistic? Is it the best option for him? Considering what you know about his psyche, what alternate approaches might he have chosen?
> ➤ What is your take on Terry, the social worker portrayed in the film? Is it a flawless portrayal? Does he commit any ethical violations?
> ➤ Do you believe a child or adolescent can be described as evil? If so, what does "evil" mean? Is there any treatment for evil?
> ➤ Are some children simply "born bad?"

Acclaimed director Ang Lee's *Hulk* (2003) is a commentary on anger and, more specifically, intermittent explosive disorder. The whole film is about raw anger: anger being unleashed, the dangers and detrimental effects of anger, the build-up and development of anger, and family of origin issues in regard to anger. When Bruce Banner (Eric Bana) transforms into the Hulk, there is enormous destruction of property, and this occurs in intermittent episodes of rage as he shifts into the role of Hulk and then back to the scientist role after his anger subsides. If this film is viewed by someone eager to understand the psychological phenomenon of anger, the movie is educational as well as entertaining. A recent remake, *The Incredible Hulk* (2008), starring Edward Norton as Bruce Banner, also provides a useful perspective on this particular impulse control disorder.

"But you know what scares me the most? When I can't fight it anymore, when it takes over, when I totally lose control ... I like it."

Bruce Banner in *Hulk* (2003)

Two quintessential films about men who are angry with society (and people in general) and who impulsively decide to take matters into their own hands are *Falling Down* (1993) and *Noise* (2007). In the former film, Michael Douglas's character explosively attacks (sometimes with weapons) anyone who confronts or challenges him as he can no longer tolerate anything or anyone that brings forth any degree of disagreement, tension, or offense. In *Noise*, the protagonist is portrayed by Tim Robbins who becomes fed up with the sounds and noises of New York City. He decides to act as "the rectifier," becomes a vigilante, and proceeds to smash in the windows of cars that have alarms going off. We highly recommend both films.

In *Punch Drunk Love* (2002), Barry Egan (Adam Sandler) is a quirky, serious character who alternates between extreme passiveness (often to his sisters' requests) and brief explosions of anger. Interestingly, when he is confronted with danger, he either runs away or explodes with rage (illustrating the fight-or-flight response).

In *Manic* (2001), an adolescent Lyle (Joseph Gordon-Levitt) is sent to an inpatient unit for what appears to be intermittent explosive disorder: While angry, he had smashed a peer's head with a baseball bat. Though Lyle does begin to relate and connect with others as well as understand himself in a deeper way, he continues to explode periodically with his rage directed toward others. Lyle is sporadic in his anger management attempts – sometimes he stops his anger choosing not to fight and at other times he provokes fights. Lyle reflects that the cause of his anger is that his father was physically abusive and his peers made fun of him because of this. An authoritative psychologist (Don Cheadle) utilizes an intervention that involves telling Lyle he is "just like dad" with regard to his anger outbursts.

Mateo (Djimon Hounsou), a man dying of AIDS, frequently screams and destroys property in his apartment in the film *In America* (2003). Another man dying of AIDS, Roy (Keifer Sutherland) in *Behind the Red Door* (2001), has repressed rage resulting from his diagnosis and a family history of neglect and abuse. His outbursts emerge verbally and at seemingly random times (e.g., when his rice is not fully cooked).

The title character in *Antwone Fisher* (2002) exhibits explosive anger, attacking his fellow sailors in response to minor provocations. The viewer later learns that beneath the anger lies intense internal pain and unresolved abuse issues. The classic character of Bluto in *Popeye* (1980) could also be diagnosed with this disorder.

The female protagonist, portrayed by Julie Delpy, in *2 Days in Paris* (2007) has an intermittent explosive disorder. She shows numerous anger outbursts and explosiveness in both private and public settings. Another woman with impulsive and explosive behavior can be seen in *Stuck* (2007), starring Mena Suvari.

Kleptomania

Kleptomania is the recurrent failure to resist impulses to steal objects that are not needed for personal use or for their monetary value. Feelings of tension precede the theft act, and pleasure or relief occurs at the time of the theft.

The independent film *Klepto* (2003) uses kleptomania as a major plotline. In an opening scene, a young woman, Emily (Meredith Bishop), steals some CDs; after spotting a camera, she runs out of the store and is chased by an employee. She does not steal because she needs the particular items or money, but because stealing is a way to manage her stress. It quickly becomes clear that Emily loves the rush she experiences whenever she steals something. Those with kleptomania feel a sense of increasing tension prior to stealing and pleasure or relief at the time of theft or immediately thereafter. After the pleasurable rush, Emily feels worse as she realizes how out of control she is; in turn, this leads her to steal more. She stores boxes of unopened and unused stolen items in her car trunk. Emily realizes she cannot stop herself from stealing, exclaiming, "I'm a pill freak with a bad habit," referring to a large collection of bottles of medications. Emily is an interesting contrast with her mother who is a compulsive shopper who accumulates a $100,000 debt but is unable to stop buying things (for an example of similar psychopathology, see the "Spending/Shopping Addiction" section in the next chapter). Emily later finds out that her father was a thief who died in prison. Emily eventually gets treatment for her impulse-control disorder – she takes medication and sees a therapist who comes across as supportive and inquisitive.

> "I have a mental condition and I have to take things. I'm addicted to getting caught."
>
> Emily explaining her kleptomania in
> *Klepto* (2003)

It is uncertain whether the characters in the following films meet the full *DSM-5* criteria for kleptomania, but they are at least interesting to consider: *Niagara, Niagara* (1997), *Female Perversions* (1996), and *Mortal Transfer* (2001). In *Mortal Transfer*, one of the psychiatrist's patients is undergoing psychoanalysis and cannot resist her impulses to steal, including stealing things from her psychiatrist's desk. Kleptomania symptoms can also be seen in *Virgin* (2003), although the protagonist would undoubtedly carry multiple psychological diagnoses.

> "I steal to stop me from killing myself."
>
> Maddie Stevens in *Female Perversions*
> (1996)

Pyromania

Pyromania is deliberate and purposeful fire setting on more than one occasion, in which there is tension prior to the act, pleasure or relief after it, and a fascination and curiosity with fire itself.

In *House of Fools* (2002), one of the patients at a psychiatric hospital, Mamud, is a veteran with pyromania. After burning the curtains in the hospital, he quickly exclaims, "It wasn't me!" Mamud is restricted from having any fire-setting materials, and the other patients are instructed not to give him matches. Francie in *The Butcher Boy* (1997) sets fires, but he would not qualify for this diagnosis in-

Figure 18. *The Butcher Boy* (1997, The Geffen Film Company). Produced by Redmond Morris and Stephen Wolley. Directed Neil Jordan.

sofar as his aberrant behavior is better explained by other diagnoses. Figure 18 depicts Francie, an adolescent with multiple diagnoses and behavior problems, reading a letter from his mother and avoiding the task at hand while all those around him are hard at work. Francie would present a diagnostic challenge for any mental health professional working with him.

International Films: Disruptive, Impulse-Control, and Conduct Disorders

The French film *The Chorus* (2004, France) is about life at a boarding school for troubled children. The school is headed by a dictatorial headmaster, M. Rachin (Francois Berléand). The movie depicts defiance, conduct problems and running away, and children who draw obscene pictures of teachers and set traps for the teaching staff. Many of these children would qualify for a diagnosis of conduct disorder or oppositional defiant disorder. Clément Mathieu (Gérard Jugnot) is hired to teach these rowdy children. With the superintendent's approval, he turns his 4 o'clock study hall into a chorus class. Pierre Morhange (Jean-Baptiste Maunier), the most problematic student, has a beautiful voice and after initial hesitation joins the choir. The choir and Mathieu are eventually able to expose Rachin's cruelty.

The 400 Blows (1959, France) is regarded as one of the best films ever made, and it is a classic among the **French New Wave** movement. It was directed by Francois Truffaut. In the United States, the title is thought to reference corporal punishment; in French, it means "raising hell." The protagonist, Antoine, is a young boy with conduct disorder who is mischievous and gets into trouble frequently. His mother is harsh, unemotional, and does not appear to love her son; his father is playful and emphasizes humor in his interactions with his son. As the film progresses, Antoine's parents' behavior is inconsistent and unstable as well as immoral (e.g., he witness his mother's infidelity). He also receives strong negative and verbal/emotional abuse from a teacher. There are some pleasant times and positive interactions with his parents, and he makes some effort at school but is largely oppressed by the teacher. He

runs away from home on more than one occasion, steals a typewriter, steals money from his family, frequently lies, sets fires, plagiarizes and cheats, frequently misses school, and smokes.

Antoine is not a horrible child, and his behavior seems to be a result of a combination of poor parenting and childhood rebellion. After running away from home, he is caught and sent away to a reform school. It is clear he has been outright rejected and abandoned by both of his parents. He then runs away from this strict facility, and the film concludes with his simply running; he is shown running through the woods, streets, and alongside the ocean. This can be viewed as a poignant symbol of autonomy and individuality, of self-reliance, and of rebellion (i.e., a refusal to be controlled, a rejection of authority). Viewers might want to compare the core themes of this film, and the boy's personality, with Paul Newman's classic depiction of rebellion in *Cool Hand Luke* (1967).

The short film *The Antichrist* (2002, Poland) depicts four boys exploring a field in which explosions are occurring because of excavations. One boy, who has a number of oppositional defiant and conduct disorder symptoms, calls himself the Antichrist and challenges the other boys to engage in dangerous behavior. He catches a fish with his bare hands and then gleefully stabs it. He also buries himself alive, runs barefoot in thistles, and rides down a treacherous rocky hillside on his bicycle. It is highly likely that anyone similar to the child portrayed in this film would develop an antisocial personality.

The 2003 Brazilian film *City of God* looks at children and adolescents growing up in a poor, gang-infested area of Rio de Janeiro (called the "City of God") who must choose between a life filled with drug dealing, guns, and violence and a life based on the hope that they will be able to escape their circumstances. These young children quickly learn to show no fear, and they do not seem to care if they live or die. The film depicts very young children (referred to as "runts") running around with guns and talking about getting revenge by murdering their enemies. The film is especially disturbing because it is based on a true story (it is estimated that at least 100,000 people are involved in drug dealing in Rio), and conduct disorders are the norm for children and adolescents living in the City of God. The film contrasts two of the younger boys brought up in this culture: One, the protagonist, finds passion and meaning in photography and rejects gang life; the other, named Li'l Zé, achieves his life goal of rising to power to take over as drug boss in the City of God by killing his competition. The Rio police walk around in fear and largely ignore the drug dealers; before the dealers established their own power base, the police would come into homes and pillage.

An interesting and provocative dilemma emerges for the children of the City of God: A child can either choose an honest occupation and live in poverty or become rich by dealing drugs. If these children choose to deal drugs, there is a well-established career trajectory: First, they act as a drug delivery boy, then as a lookout, then dealer, soldier, and eventually manager. For many of these children, the life of a drug dealer is the more appealing option.

One of the most powerful cinematic portrayals of childhood psychopathology is found in the 1994 New Zealand film *Heavenly Creatures*, directed by Peter Jackson and starring Kate Winslet. The film is based on the true story of two teenage girls, aged 15 and 17, who conspire to murder the mother of one of the girls. The older girl went on to develop a significant reputation as an author of murder mysteries, writing under the name of Anne Perry. The girl's confusion and mental illness in *Heavenly Creatures* is artistically captured in film through her interactions with life-size clay figures that inhabit a medieval fantasy land.

Happy-Go-Lucky (2008, UK) is an outstanding film by renowned British director Mike Leigh about a young woman, Poppy (Sally Hawkins), who faces life's stressors with a refreshing yet realistic optimism and humor. A supporting character in the film is Poppy's driving instructor, Scott (Eddie Marsan), who has an intermittent explosive disorder. On the

surface, Scott is a fascinating contrast to Poppy's character as he always has a frown on his face and comes across as very tightly wound, controlling, edgy, and angry. His anger emerges in each driving lesson he gives Poppy, usually taking the form of yelling and threatening. His mental illness becomes apparent when the viewer observes Scott's inability to control his impulses when he learns Poppy has a boyfriend. He speeds up the car, endangers himself and Poppy, becomes abnormally demanding, and at one point, grabs Poppy's hair and shakes her repeatedly. He screams at her on a public street, unable to control his anger, which is palpable. However, Scott is not merely a one-dimensional character; the viewer sees glimpses of his desperation and profound loneliness.

> "The American dream never happened. The American nightmare is already here. I mean, look at the Washington Monument. It is 555 feet above the ground and 111 feet below the ground. 555 plus 111 is 666. 6-6-6, Poppy. 6-6-6"
>
> Scott, the explosive driving instructor, during one of his rants in *Happy-Go-Lucky* (2008)

In a remarkable Norwegian film, *Elling* (2002, Norway), the character Kjell, upon being released from a psychiatric hospital, has explosive bouts of anger whenever he is frustrated. His condition would likely be diagnosed as intermittent explosive disorder.

Critical Thinking Questions

➤ Many films portray children who are resilient at very difficult times and in challenging environments. How common is this? Is psychopathology the opposite of resilience? Can a child be mentally ill and resilient at the same time?

➤ Should adolescents who commit serious crimes like rape and murder be tried as adults? At what age should a child be held responsible for committing "adult crimes"?

➤ The film *Kids* (1995) deals with sex, drugs, violence, and AIDS. Is the film accurate in its suggestion that these issues are becoming increasingly salient for very young adolescents?

➤ Are "rainbow parties" real, or is this an urban legend perpetuated by the media?

➤ William Golding's 1954 novel *Lord of the Flies* and the films based on it (*Lord of the Flies* [1963, 1990]) suggest that without adult supervision, young children quickly become savages. Do you find this position plausible? Are the kids in *Gummo* (1997) simply savages?

➤ Films often portray step-parents as cold and sadistic. Is there any empirical evidence for this, or is it a simplistic and misguided stereotype?

➤ Some reviewers have criticized director Neil Jordan for Sinead O'Connor's portrayal of the Virgin Mary in *The Butcher Boy*. Did you find the role offensive?

➤ Do psychologists and other mental health professionals have anything to offer when asked to explain school shootings like those at Columbine and Sandy Hook?

➤ Would stricter gun control laws reduce the likelihood of school shootings and similar atrocities (like the one committed by Kevin)?

➤ Winona Rider is a very wealthy woman who was arrested in 2001 for shoplifting at a Beverly Hills Saks Fifth Avenue store. Why would someone with significant personal wealth want to steal?

➤ Is there any relationship between pornography and violence?

➤ Are fire-setting, bed-wetting, or cruelty to animals in childhood predictive of adult psychopathology?

➤ In a busy clinical practice, how often might a clinician expect to treat someone meeting criteria for pyromania or kleptomania? What is the best treatment approach for each condition?

Authors' Picks

If you have time to read just one book relevant to this chapter, make it:

Kazdin, A. E. (2008). *The Kazdin method for parenting the defiant child: With no pills, no therapy, no contest of wills.* Boston: Houghton Mifflin.

If you only have time for one article, read:

Webster-Stratton, C., & Taylor, T. (2001). Nipping early risk factors in the bud: Preventing substance abuse, delinquency, and violence in adolescence through interventions targeted at young children (0 to 8 years). *Prevention Science, 2*(3), 165–192. doi: 10.1023/A:1011510923900

Wedding and Niemiec's Top 10 Disruptive, Impulse-Control, and Conduct Disorders Films

Oppositional Defiant Disorder and Conduct Disorders

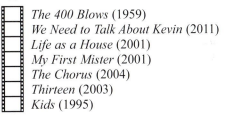

The 400 Blows (1959)
We Need to Talk About Kevin (2011)
Life as a House (2001)
My First Mister (2001)
The Chorus (2004)
Thirteen (2003)
Kids (1995)

Impulse-Control Disorders

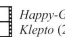

Happy-Go-Lucky (2008)
Klepto (2003)
Punch Drunk Love (2002)

Chapter 11

Substance-Related and Addictive Disorders

Nicole: You are sick, Whip.
Whip: Yeah, well, I embrace it. ... I choose to drink.
Nicole: You do?
Whip: Yes, I do.
Nicole: You choose it? Well, I don't see a whole lot of choice going on here!
*Whip: I choose to drink! And I blame myself! I am happy to! And you know why? Because I choose
to drink! I got an ex-wife and a son I never talk to! And you know why? Because I choose to drink!*

Denzel Washington in the role of pilot Whip Whitaker
acknowledging the role of choice in his addiction in *Flight* (2012)

➤ Whip's blood alcohol level (BAL) is found to be 0.17 after his crash. What BAL constitutes legal intoxication in your state or country?

➤ What would be the behavioral expectations for someone with a BAL of 0.17 who did not have a high tolerance?

➤ How do body mass and sex of the individual affect BALs?

➤ What signs of alcohol withdrawal do you see in this film?

➤ Could someone using alcohol and cocaine to the extent shown in the film actually fly a plane without his intoxication being detected?

➤ Did you expect Whip to admit to his alcoholism when on the witness stand?

➤ What is a functional alcoholic? How common is this?

➤ Is alcohol abuse/dependence linked with violence?

➤ What psychological disorders most highly correlate with alcohol use/abuse?

➤ How does abuse/dependence on alcohol affect the health of a society? Is it a public health problem?

➤ How common is it for alcoholics who hit "rock-bottom" to turn their life around?

➤ Why is maintenance of sobriety so challenging for individuals with alcohol (or drug) problems?

Patient Evaluation

Name: Whip Whitaker

Patient's stated reason for coming
"I need your help to make sure I never drink again when I leave this place."

History of the present illness
Whip Whitaker is a former airline pilot with a long history of alcoholism and cocaine abuse. He routinely flew planes while under the influence of alcohol and other drugs. He was sentenced on four counts of manslaughter following a recent dramatic crash that occurred while Whitaker was both drunk and high on cocaine; however, an investigation suggests that his quick responses actually saved the lives of most passengers on the plane, despite his intoxication.

Past psychiatric illness, treatment, and outcomes
There is no history of psychiatric illness in this patient or his family; however, he has been drinking heavily and using a variety of drugs for at least a decade.

Medical history
Nonsignificant.

Psychosocial history
Mr. Whitaker is the oldest of four children. He describes a happy childhood, and he excelled in both sports and academics in high school and college. He is a former Air Force pilot who transitioned from the Air Force to the airline industry. He has numerous friends, most of whom are involved with alcohol and drugs in some way. This patient is divorced from his wife and estranged from his 17-year-old son.

Drug and alcohol history
Mr. Whitaker began drinking beer in high school, and by the time he was in college, he drank beer and whiskey most evenings. He continued to drink heavily while in the Air Force and this is where he probably became addicted to alcohol. He smoked marijuana with his Air Force friends but did not use other drugs. However, Whitaker became a routine cocaine user after leaving the Air Force and reported almost daily use prior to the crash that eventually brought him to Rikers Island jail.

Behavioral observations

Mr. Whitaker came to the evaluation dressed in standard prison attire. He responded to all questions quickly and completely. He was friendly and seemed genuinely eager to understand why he developed a problem with alcohol and drugs and what he could do to ensure that he would no longer drink or drug after leaving prison.

Mental status examination

Mr. Whitaker was oriented to time, place, and person. He was able to complete serial sevens quickly and without any errors. There are no obvious impairments of language, memory, or speech. This patient was able to copy complex figures without difficulty. Mr. Whitaker earned a perfect score of 30 on the Mini-Mental State Examination.

Functional assessment

This patient functioned at a very high level prior to his crash and subsequent arrest and incarceration. He earned approximately $180,000/year as a senior pilot. He has excellent social skills and a good sense of humor. His parents are deceased, and he is divorced and no longer sees his teenage son; however, he still has numerous friends from his time as a pilot, and he has established several friends while incarcerated. His keen intelligence, excellent social skills, and sense of humor will serve him well when he leaves prison.

Strengths

Mr. Whitaker is sociable and engaging. He is very intelligent, and he has keen spatial intelligence. On the VIA Survey, a measure of character strengths, Mr. Whitaker's highest strengths were leadership, love of learning, social intelligence, zest, and fairness.

Diagnosis

Alcohol use disorder, in early remission, in a controlled environment, severe (F10.20).

Treatment plan

(1) Continued participation in the prison AA group; (2) Medical evaluation for the potential use of Naltrexone upon release from prison; (3) Supportive psychotherapy.

Prognosis

Good.

Flight

Flight (2012) is a powerful film that portrays the life of Whip Whitaker (Denzel Washington), a pilot for a major airline who is also a functional alcoholic. He is high on vodka and cocaine when a plane he is flying crashes due to mechanical malfunction. Quick thinking on his part allows him to flip the plane and fly it upside down to avoid a crash that would have resulted in the death of everyone onboard. Although he could have been exonerated and walked away a free man, Whip confesses to his extensive history of alcohol and drug abuse and is imprisoned for manslaughter. Figure 19 depicts one of Whitaker's many relapses; in this instance, he is enabled by his "supplier," played by John Goodman.

Whitaker has a poor relationship with his ex-wife and no relationship with his son. He makes attempts to reconnect with his son, but the boy – upset after years of disappointments and neglect – angrily refuses his father's overtures. When in prison, his son finally decides to reach out to Whitaker and offers to interview his father for a class project. In a poignant, concluding scene, his son tells him that the title of the project is "the most fascinating person I *never* met." The first question makes the now-sober Whitaker pause: "Who are you?" his son inquires.

> "It was as if I had reached my life-long limit of lies. I could not tell one more lie."
>
> A sober Whip Whitaker commenting on his rock-bottom turning point

Figure 19. *Flight* (2012, Parkes-MacDonald Productions, ImageMovers). Produced by Laurie MacDonald, Walter F. Parkes, Jack Rapke, Steve Starkey, and Robert Zemeckis. Directed by Robert Zemeckis.

Alcohol Use Disorder

The use of alcohol can be traced back at least 5,000 years, and the relationship among alcohol, drugs, and mysticism has been explored in books such as William James's *Varieties of Religious Experience* (1902) and Aldous Huxley's *Doors of Perception* (1954). Oliver Wendell Holmes Jr. once remarked, "There is in all men a demand for the superlative, so much so that the poor devil who has no other way of reaching it attains it by getting drunk."

In *DSM-5*, the diagnosis of alcohol use disorder requires the presence of at least two of 11 symptoms occurring within a 12-month period. These symptoms include using alcohol in larger amounts than intended or for longer periods than intended; the presence of a persistent desire to cut back on alcohol use; excessive time spent obtaining alcohol, drinking, or recovering from intoxication; craving; failure to fulfill major life obligations; and tolerance and withdrawal. **Tolerance** refers to the need to use increasingly large

amounts of a substance to obtain a desired effect (a buzz or the feeling of being high), or else to the fact that a given amount of a substance after continued use fails to produce the same effect it once did.

Alcohol and the Brain

Alcohol is quickly absorbed into the bloodstream and transported to the liver, which is capable of metabolizing about one ounce of 100-proof alcohol in an hour. If a person consumes only one drink per hour, the liver is able to keep up, and alcohol has less of an impact on the brain. However, at consumption rates greater than one drink per hour, the brain is quickly affected, with obvious consequences. In particular, there is rapid uptake of alcohol in the cerebellum, and this results in staggering, diminished coordination, and slower reaction times. Judgment is impaired, and alcohol can trigger aggression in some individuals. Although alcohol may initially facilitate sexual interactions by reducing inhibitions, at higher levels there is clear impairment of functioning. In the words of Shakespeare: "Lechery, sir, … [alcohol] provokes, and unprovokes; it provokes the desire, but it takes away the performance" (*Macbeth*, Act II, Scene 3).

The Lost Weekend

Billy Wilder's classic film *The Lost Weekend* (1945) is a powerful portrayal of alcoholism. The protagonist, Don Birnam (Ray Milland), is ready to sacrifice his brother's trust, his career as a writer, and the love of his girlfriend Helen (played by Jane Wyman) for one more drink. Early in the film, we see clear examples of denial, believed by many to be the characteristic defense mechanism of the alcoholic. Don Birnam minimizes the significance of his drinking as long as he can, but eventually he realizes that it is ruining his life. A scene in which Birnam watches an imaginary bat kill and eat a mouse is an effective illustration of the type of hallucinations characteristic of **delirium tremens**. Birnam eventually hocks his girlfriend's coat to get a gun and writes a suicide note. However, Helen arrives before he pulls the trigger, and the film ends with Birnam planning the novel he is going to write and, in a heavily symbolic gesture, dropping a cigarette in a glass of rye. Some of the symptoms that apply to Don Birnam's alcoholism are presented in Table 4. The symptoms of

Table 4. Criteria for alcohol use disorder

Selected criteria for alcohol use disorder from the *DSM-5*	Examples from *The Lost Weekend*
1. Alcohol is consumed in a larger amount or over a longer period than the individual intended.	Birnam is drinking when the film begins, and he drinks throughout the film.
2. People know that their use of alcohol is excessive but fail in their attempts to control their drinking.	Birnam tries repeatedly to go on the wagon and has "taken the cure" at least once without success.
3. A great deal of time is devoted to acquiring alcohol, drinking it, or recovering from its effects. In severe cases, almost all of the individual's waking hours are devoted to the substance.	Birnam is preoccupied with rye and has hidden it throughout his apartment. He thinks about little else, and he steals a purse and robs a liquor store to support his addiction.
4. Intoxication or withdrawal symptoms occur at work or in other inappropriate situations (e.g., while driving a car).	Birnam has quit writing altogether and has pawned his typewriter to buy whiskey.
5. Important social, occupational, or recreational activities are replaced by alcohol.	Birnam's relationship with his brother is seriously damaged by his drinking, and he avoids spending a weekend in the country with his family. He also comes close to destroying his relationship with his girlfriend.
6. Alcohol use persists, despite increasing awareness of the problems it causes.	Birnam describes himself as a "drunk," and he is acutely aware of his declining prowess as a writer.
7. Tolerance develops, and an increased amount of alcohol is required to produce the same effect. (Tolerance is less marked for alcohol than for some other drugs.)	The film shows Birnam drinking approximately two quarts of whiskey per day, far more than most people would be able to tolerate.
8. Withdrawal symptoms develop when the individual cuts back on their use of alcohol.	Birnam develops delirium tremens and hallucinates in the film.
9. After experiencing withdrawal symptoms, the individual begins to drink to avoid these unpleasant experiences rather than to produce the pleasant feelings initially associated with alcohol use.	When questioned by a bartender about drinking so early in the morning, Birnam remarks, "At night it's a drink; in the morning it's medicine."

dependence are the same for all psychoactive substances (alcohol or drugs).

"One's too many and a hundred's not enough."

A bartender chides Don Birnam in Billy Wilder's *The Lost Weekend* (1945)

Despite an ending that is somewhat too pat for contemporary viewers, the film is still a dramatic illustration of the destructive effects of alcohol. Ray Milland won an Academy Award for Best Actor for his portrayal of Birnam, and the film earned additional Academy Awards for best picture, best director, and best screenplay. Billy Wilder, the film's director, consulted with Alcoholics Anonymous before beginning work on the film.

Epidemiology of Alcoholism

The majority of American adults (about 65%) drink at least occasionally, and many adults consume alcohol on a daily basis. Men tend to tolerate alcohol more easily than women, in part because they typically weigh more, and the definition of a heavy drinker needs to be adjusted for males and females. However, it is generally accepted that individuals who average more than three drinks per day are heavy drinkers. Many individuals will consume far more than this average: 10% of all drinkers consume more than 50% of all alcohol consumed.

The *DSM-5* estimates the prevalence of alcohol use disorder is 8.5% among adults in the United States (i.e., approximately one in 12 people). The disorder occurs far more frequently among men than women, and there are marked differences across ethnic groups, with Native Americans and Alaska Natives having the highest risk. The prevalence is lowest for Asian Americans and Pacific Islanders.

Alcoholism is one of the most serious public health problems in the United States, costing billions annually in lost productivity, increased health care costs, and accidents. Alcohol abuse contributes to about 30% of all motor vehicle accidents, and it is responsible for about half of all traffic fatalities.

About 10% of adults seeking treatment by physicians are dependent on alcohol, and about a third of admissions to general hospitals are for alcohol-related problems. The mortality rate for alcoholics is 2–3 times greater than that of the general population, and the life span of alcoholics is 10–12 years shorter. In addition, the children of alcoholic parents are at increased risk for hyperactivity, low IQ, emotional problems, child abuse, and fetal alcohol syndrome (NIAAA, 2000). Despite the severity of these problems, less than 10% of those addicted to alcohol will receive treatment for their problems.

The Portrayal of Alcoholism in Films

Images of alcohol and drinking are ubiquitous in contemporary films, and one is hard-pressed to name adult films in which alcohol use is not portrayed. This may reflect the fact that alcohol affects everyone directly or indirectly.

The early success of *The Lost Weekend* (1945) led to other films with alcoholism as a central theme, including *Key Largo* (1948), *Harvey* (1950), *Come Back Little Sheba* (1952), *A Star Is Born* (1954), *Cat on a Hot Tin Roof* (1958), *Days of Wine and Roses* (1962), and the vicious alcoholism portrayed by Bette Davis as Baby Jane Hutson in *What Ever Happened to Baby Jane?* (1962). Other relevant older films include *Who's Afraid of Virginia Woolf?* (1966), *Arthur* (1981), *Barfly* (1981), *Tender Mercies* (1983), *Paris, Texas* (1984), *Under the Volcano* (1984), *Hoosiers* (1986), *Ironweed* (1987), *The Verdict* (1987), and *Clean and Sober* (1988).

"You can never lose your talent ... you can lose everything else, but can never lose your talent."

Jane's father referring to her talent for musical performance. In fact, Jane's alcoholism contributes to the deterioration and squandering of her talent in *What Ever Happened to Baby Jane?* (1962)

In contrast to the sobering representations of alcoholism in films such as *Clean and Sober* (discussed later in this section), some films portray the alcoholic as happy and carefree. *Harvey* (1950) and *Arthur*

(1981) are the two most obvious examples. Writing about *Arthur*, Vincent Canby (1981, p. 10) noted:

> Not since Nick and Nora Charles virtually made the dry martini into the national drink … has there been quite so much boozing in a movie without hidden consequences. Arthur drinks scotch the way people now drink Perrier…. When he goes giggling about town, sloshed to the eyeballs, he's not seen as a case history but as eccentric.

Unfortunately, the film presents Arthur as an appealing model driving around Long Island in his Rolls Royce. In the film, he has the good fortune to have a chauffeur; most of the teenage viewers emulating his example will not be so lucky.

Movies *reflect* social mores as interpreted by filmmakers, and this certainly applies to the use of alcohol. In the film *Revolutionary Road* (2008), alcohol plays an important role in anesthetizing the boredom and rigidity of gender roles of the 1950s. In turn, movies *affect* social mores in a cyclical manner. A film presentation of the ways in which families are affected by alcoholism is found in *When a Man Loves a Woman* (1994). Other powerful films about alcoholism and its treatment include *Leaving Las Vegas* (1995), in which Nicholas Cage willingly drinks through graphically depicted delirium tremens until his death; Steve Buscemi's *Trees Lounge* (1996); and *Drunks* (1997). This last film is an especially helpful introduction to Alcoholics Anonymous (AA) and is highly recommended to anyone who has not had an opportunity to visit an open AA meeting. In addition, students interested in the way in which alcoholism is portrayed in films should read an excellent book by Norman Denzin, *Hollywood Shot by Shot: Alcoholism in American Cinema* (1991).

The functional impact of alcoholism is well-portrayed in the film *The Prize Winner of Defiance, Ohio* (2005), starring Julianne Moore and Woody Harrelson as the parents of 10 children growing up in the 1950s. Harrelson gives a strong performance as Kelly Ryan, an alcoholic who spends his weekly paycheck on alcohol, to the point that the family cannot afford milk and risks foreclosure on their home. Kelly shows a childlike dependency, and he is unable to care for his children or take care of the house. He is enabled by a community that, true to the time and culture, had no diagnosis or solutions for alcoholism; a police officer arrives after a dramatic incident resulting from Kelly's alcohol abuse and simply talks about baseball; a priest takes it a

step further in the wrong direction and places blame on Kelly's wife, Evelyn, saying she has to try harder to give him a better home.

> "This has been going on for a very long time. Every night he drinks a six-pack and a pint of whiskey and by the end of the week there's nothing left of his paycheck. It's all gone to the liquor store."
>
> Evelyn Ryan describing her husband's alcoholism in *The Prize Winner of Defiance, Ohio* (2005)

Everything Must Go (2011) stars Will Ferrell as Nick, a married man who is an executive vice-president for a corporation. At the film's onset, Nick is both fired from his job and separated from his wife who throws all of his possessions on the front lawn. With frozen credit cards, no resources, and minimal support, he feels he has no choice but to live on his front lawn. He discovers that he can live on his front lawn for 5 days if he is having a yard sale so he hastily identifies some things he can sell. He befriends a young African American boy, Kenny, who helps him sell his personal items. The viewer soon learns Nick is addicted to alcohol. This has frequently led to serious work problems, which often requires treatment. His minimizing and denial is clear and he notes, "I had had a couple slip-ups." His recent stressors lead to another relapse, and he begins to drink beer on his lawn chair in his front yard. He drinks first thing in the morning, while driving, and throughout the evening, despite having little or no money. The film has a number of redeeming qualities as it taps into the human condition, depicts the suffering and consequences of alcohol dependence, and portrays a unique, unlikely friendship between Nick and Kenny.

In *Crazy Heart* (2009), Jeff Bridges plays Bad Blake, a 57-year-old, four-time divorced, small-time musician. Blake is an alcoholic who travels around the southwest performing in bars and restaurants. He spends his days and nights drinking and womanizing, ending each night isolated and broke. He develops a meaningful relationship with a young woman (Maggie Gyllenhaal) and her son, but his alcohol dependence seriously affects his relationship with both. She continues to either enable him and give him second chances, but the last straw occurs when he loses her son at a busy mall after he becomes distracted due to his drinking. Some lyrics from one of his songs are particularly poignant and seem to describe Blake's alcoholism, suffering, and related behaviors:

> Pick up your crazy heart and give it one more try; Falling feels like flying; Never see it coming till it's gone; Days and nights all feel the same.

When Blake does become sober and maintains his sobriety for an extended period of time, his transformation is evident: He returns to writing songs (which is his true passion), and he elevates his subjective well-being, increases his empathy levels, and becomes more generous. This film and the depiction of substance abuse/dependence can be compared and contrasted with other excellent films portraying alcoholic musicians, such as *Ray* (2004), *Walk the Line* (2005), and *Tender Mercies* (1983), as well as other traveling/wandering figures with substance abuse problems who try to reclaim their life (e.g., *Don't Come Knocking* [2005]). Robert Duvall, the down-and-out musician in *Tender Mercies*, has a minor role as a bartender in *Crazy Heart*.

Following Meg Ryan's outstanding portrayal of a woman with alcoholism in *When a Man Loves a Woman* (1994), several films have portrayed depressed women who are either dependent upon or abuse alcohol; powerful examples include *House of Sand and Fog* (2003), *Monster's Ball* (2001), *28 Days* (2000), and *Smashed* (2012). In *28 Days*, Sandra Bullock portrays Gwen Cummings, a writer who is remanded to a rehabilitation setting by a judge after a drunk driving accident. Bullock's character displays symptoms of intoxication and tolerance, including excessive drinking, blackouts, use of an "eye opener" in the morning, and drinking throughout the day. In addition to extreme denial, she is impulsive and enjoys taking risks. Her out-of-control behavior includes carrying a drink wherever she goes, creating a spectacle at her sister's wedding, and inadvertently starting a fire while drinking. Her withdrawal symptoms are depicted as shaky hands, cravings, agitation, and a strong desire to immediately replace alcohol with pain medication, nicotine, or any other drug she can get her hands on. A complicating factor not uncommon for alcoholics is a partner who drinks heavily; in this film, her boyfriend is an alcoholic and significant enabler who is very rejecting and critical of treatment.

Helen Hunt plays an alcoholic working two jobs to pay her bills while secretly drinking in *Pay It Forward* (2000). Even a very small amount of alcohol is associated with violence by Kim Bassinger's character in *Final Analysis* (1992).

Alcohol abuse is evident in several lead characters, such as the title character (Robert Duvall) in *The Apostle* (1997), William Forrester (Sean Connery) in *Finding Forrester* (2000), Willie (Billy Bob Thornton) in *Bad Santa* (2003), and Matt Damon's character, Rannulph Junuh, in *The Legend of Bagger Vance* (2000), who drinks heavily upon returning from war. Alcohol only exacerbates his isolation and loneliness. Alex and his "droogs" use alcohol to "sharpen up" before committing violent acts in *A Clockwork Orange* (1971).

Alcoholism is particularly common in Western films, and saloons, bar fights, whiskey bottles, drunken gunfighters, and town drunks are staples of the genre (Wedding, 2001). *High Noon* (1952), *Stagecoach* (1939), *Shane* (1953), *Rio Bravo* (1959), and *Unforgiven* (1992) are classic examples.

"Now it's thirty days later. I've been to a funeral, been on about nine million job interviews, I'm $52,000 in debt, and I've got this chip. Suddenly I've got this startling belief that I'm an alcoholic and a drug addict."

Daryl Poynter (Michael Keaton) referring to his 30-day sobriety chip from Alcoholics Anonymous in *Clean and Sober* (1988)

Clean and Sober (1988) stars Michael Keaton as Daryl Poynter, an alcoholic and cocaine addict, and Morgan Freeman as an addictions counselor known simply as "Craig." Some of the most interesting scenes in the film show Poynter at AA meetings and in group therapy. The film ends with Daryl getting his 30-day AA chip, acknowledging to the group that he is both an alcoholic and a drug addict, and realizing that each of us can be responsible only for his or her own behavior.

Some other films depicting alcohol use disorder include *My Name Was Bette: The Life and Death of an Alcoholic* (2011), a documentary about a nurse, wife, and mother whose life was destroyed by alcohol abuse; *There Will Be Blood* (2007), in which Daniel Day-Lewis's character pours whiskey into his adopted son's baby bottle; *Flight* (2012), in which Denzel Washington plays an alcoholic commercial pilot; *California Solo* (2012); and *Smashed* (2013). Teenage alcoholism is portrayed in *The Spectacular Now* (2013), and alcoholism in a very wealthy playboy is found in the somewhat disappointing remake of *Arthur* (2011). *The Last Ride* (2011) tells the story of Hank Williams and documents the damage done to his life and his career by his heavy drinking, and *Country Strong* (2010) stars Gwyneth Paltrow as a country singer who tries to reestablish her career after leaving a rehabilitation facility early; she fails, resumes drinking heavily and eventually commits suicide. *The Last Day of August* (2012) portrays a man who responds to his paralysis by retreating to the country and drinking heavily. *Bluebird* (2013) documents the ways that many people use alcohol to cope with personal crises (in this case the death of a child due to a bus driver's negligence and a mother's alcoholism). *Suddenly* (2013) is a film about a small town police officer who uses alcohol to cope with his PTSD; he is forced to turn in his badge because of his alcoholism, but he is given a shot at redemption when he is reassigned to duty to help the president of the United States who will be coming through town. *Family of Four* (2011) portrays an alcoholic mother who is usually able to keep her alcoholism hidden, and *Deep in the Heart* (2011) is a film based on the true story of Richard Wallrath, an alcoholic man who loses his family because of his drinking, but who later regains sobriety with the help of a 12-step program, establishes a successful business, and goes on to become a philanthropist, donating millions of dollars for 4-H and Future Farmers of America scholarships.

We want to highlight a number of critically-acclaimed films depicting drug and/or alcohol abuse that were released in 2013 as we were finalizing work on this new edition. These films include cocaine, methamphetamine, alcohol, sex, and gambling addiction in *Dallas Buyers Club* (2013), alcohol dependence in *Nebraska* (2013), the horrifying effects of prescription drug abuse by Meryl Streep's character in *August: Osage County* (2013), and drug and alcohol abuse in *American Hustle* (2013) and *The Wolf of Wall Street* (2013).

We strongly recommend that readers make time to watch *Bill W.* (2012), a biopic about the lives of William Griffith Wilson (Bill W.) and Dr. Robert Holbrook Smith (Dr. Bob), the two men who founded Alcoholics Anonymous (AA). Reviewing this film in *PsycCRITIQUES*, Fred Freese wrote:

AA members regularly identify each other among themselves as "friends of Bill"; and thousands of AA members converge on the city of Akron, Ohio, every June to celebrate Founders' Day. It was in Akron where Dr. Bob and Bill W. met and founded the AA organization in 1935. … Bill W. died of emphysema in 1970 at the age of 76. The organization he cofounded has grown to having over two million members worldwide … [and] spawned over 60 other recovery-oriented, anonymous self-help groups based on the twelve-step approach.

We also recommend that you secure a copy of the limited release film *Bob and the Monster* (2011). This documentary portrays the life of Bob Forrest, a rock musician whose career was almost ruined by his alcoholism and drug addiction. After several failed attempts at rehabilitation, Forrest succeeded in overcoming his various addictions, and today he is both successful and sober, working as an addictions recovery counselor who specializes in helping musicians, actors, and other celebrities achieve sobriety.

Drug Abuse

The use of mind-altering substances appears to have existed almost from the time that humans first became aware of the potent effects plants could have on human perception. Substance use disorders (alcohol or drugs) include substance abuse and substance dependence problems. **Substance abuse** is defined as a *pattern* of use characterized by *recurrent adverse consequences* related to the use of the substance. The diagnosis requires evidence of impairment according to one of the following four criteria: (1) failure to meet role obligations; (2) recurrent use in situations, such as driving, in which clear hazards are present; (3) recurrent legal problems; and (4) continued use, despite social or interpersonal problems related to the substance. In addition, the symptoms must never have met the criteria associated with the diagnosis of substance dependence.

In addiction or **substance dependence,** tolerance, withdrawal, and compulsive drug-taking behavior are present. The symptoms associated with dependence on different drugs are similar (but not identical) across drug categories. Dependence is characterized by the presence of symptoms like those listed in Table 5.

Table 5. Symptoms of substance dependence

Criteria	Examples from *Ray* (2004)
1. Tolerance, defined by (a) a need for ever increasing amounts of the substance to achieve intoxication or (b) diminished effect with use of a set level of the substance.	Throughout the film, Ray continues to use more and more heroin.
2. Withdrawal, defined by (a) specific effects associated with the particular substance being abused or (b) use of a substance to relieve or avoid the withdrawal symptoms.	Ray's withdrawal from heroin is life threatening. He refuses to use any medication to ease the physiological and psychological effects of his "cold turkey" withdrawal.
3. Using the substance in larger amounts or over a longer period than was intended.	He continues to use heroin more frequently throughout the movie, even when he intends to attend family functions.
4. A persistent desire to cut back or eliminate use of the substance.	Ray says he could quit whenever he wants, and he knows he should quit.
5. A great deal of time is devoted to acquiring the substance or recovering from its effects.	He is often intoxicated. He seems to have easy access to the drug.
6. Important social, occupational, or recreational activities are ignored because of the preoccupation with use of the substance.	He misses important family events when under the influence.
7. The substance use is continued despite recurrent physical or psychological problems resulting from its use.	He continues to use even though he is often scratching, unable to concentrate, and losing balance.

Opioids

The opioids are a class of drugs that includes opium, morphine, codeine, methadone, Percodan (a combination of aspirin and oxycodone), and heroin. They are highly addictive and lead to severe physical and psychological dependence.

Heroin is particularly dangerous and has taken the lives of countless people addicted to it, including stars such as Philip Seymour Hoffman, whom many consider one of the most talented actors of this generation. He overdosed and died alone in his Manhattan apartment at age 46 in February 2014. His films are described throughout this book, including several in this chapter.

These drugs are sometimes lumped together under the general rubric of narcotics. Opium is usually smoked; the other drugs are most often ingested or injected. In most countries, opioids are controlled substances. When used legally, these drugs are prescribed for pain or diarrhea, with the exception of methadone, which is used to treat opioid addiction. Fentanyl and meperidine are opioid analogs (chemical compounds that are similar to other drugs in their effects, but differ slightly in their chemical structure) that are legally prescribed for pain, but are also illegally sold as recreational drugs. Fentanyl is especially dangerous because it is at least 50 times more potent than morphine.

Numerous films depict the use of opioids. Robert De Niro can be seen smoking opium in both the opening and the ending scenes of Sergio Leone's *Once Upon a Time in America* (1984), and opium plays a significant role in both *Indochine* (1992) and Bernardo Bertolucci's *The Last Emperor* (1987).

Katharine Hepburn plays a morphine addict with an alcoholic son (Jason Robards) in the film adaptation of Eugene O'Neill's *Long Day's Journey into Night* (1962). Morphine abuse is also portrayed in the science fiction thriller *Pitch Black* (2000). An example of the ability to function despite being very high on drugs can be found in Quentin Tarantino's *Pulp Fiction* (1994). Vincent (John Travolta) shoots up before going out on a date with his boss's wife, Mia (Uma Thurman), who snorts cocaine before meeting him. The two wind up at "Jack Rabbit Slims" and maintain a coherent – if not stimulating – conversation. They even manage to win a dance contest. Later in the evening, Mia discovers the heroin in Vincent's coat pocket. Believing it to be cocaine, she proceeds to snort a line of the drug and goes into a coma. Vincent eventually manages to save Mia's life by plunging a syringe filled with epinephrine into her heart.

One of the most compelling, yet still disturbing, portrayals of heroin addiction is in the classic film *Requiem for a Dream* (2000). Most of the main characters are substance dependent – prescription diet pills for Sara (Ellen Burstyn) and multiple other substances including heroin for the teenagers Harry (Jared Leto), Marion (Jennifer Connelly), and Tyrone (Marlon Wayans). In this film, Harry's arm is eventually amputated because of drug-related untreated infections that lead to gangrene.

A young Leonardo DiCaprio stars in *The Basketball Diaries* (1995), a film based on the life of writer Jim Carroll that chronicles his descent from a high school basketball star to a desperate heroin addict who loses everything he once held dear. Eventually Carroll overcomes his addiction with the help of an older friend.

Opioid withdrawal occurs when use of opioid drugs is discontinued or when an opioid antagonist (any drug that blocks the effects of an opioid) is administered. Complete withdrawal usually takes 3–8 days. Opioid withdrawal can lead to the following symptoms: dysphoric mood, nausea or vomiting, muscle aches, lacrimation (crying) or rhinorrhea (runny nose), diarrhea, yawning, fever, or insomnia. Dramatic examples of opioid withdrawal can be seen in *Ray* (2004), *The Basketball Diaries* (1995), *Candy* (2006), and in the Frank Sinatra film *The Man with the Golden Arm* (1955).

The classic film about the heroin trade is William Friedkin's *The French Connection* (1971). Friedkin won an Academy Award for his directing, and Gene Hackman won the Academy Award as Best Actor for his role as police detective Jimmy "Popeye" Doyle. *The Connection* is a 1961 film about a group of junkies waiting for the arrival of a pusher. A more powerful and realistic presentation of teenage addiction and prostitution is *Christiane F.* (1981, Germany) which explores the drug culture of West Berlin. Other film examples of heroin addiction include *High Art* (1998), *Who'll Stop the Rain* (1978), *Mona Lisa* (1986), *Chappaqua* (1966), and *Lady Sings the Blues* (1972).

One of the most powerful drug films ever made is Gus Van Sant's 1989 film *Drugstore Cowboy*, starring Matt Dillon as Bob, the leader of a group of four addicts who rob drugstores to maintain their habit. The film is especially memorable because of a very realistic cameo played by William Burroughs as an old, burned-out, addicted, and defrocked priest living in a seedy motel. Bob sees in the priest the image of the man he (Bob) will eventually become. His decision to go straight and the dilemmas he faces (including attempts by his friends to seduce him back to the world they formerly shared) are realistic and illustrative of the challenges ex-addicts face trying to go straight.

Ray and Heroin Addiction

The Academy Award-winning film *Ray* (2004) is based on the first 35 years of the life of Ray Charles (Jamie Foxx), the legendary musical genius of rhythm and blues who lived until the age of 73. Charles's childhood years are marred with racial discrimination, extreme poverty, an absent father, the traumatic drowning of his younger brother, and the loss of his sight. A local café musician fosters Ray's early interest in music. At age 15, following the death of his mother, he leaves school and begins touring the South with a number of dance bands that play Black dance halls. Charles's second wife, Della Bea Robinson (Kerry Washington) struggles with his absence, addictions, and extramarital affairs. In the movie, she stays with him, but in reality, Della Bea left the marriage. Throughout the movie, Ray's iconic success in music is contrasted with a struggle for a personal identity, multiple failed and conflicting relationships, a need for constant sexual gratification, and an overall fear of being alone. Figure 20 shows Ray Charles as a boy being nurtured by his mother as he struggles to cope with the realities of his blindness.

Ray Charles begins his 20-year heroin addiction in his teenage years with an injection from an older musician. Ray immediately experiences the surge of pleasure and the "rush" that occurs as heroin crosses the blood–brain barrier, is converted to morphine, and binds rapidly to the brain's opioid receptors. Ray also experiences other heroin effects. Clouded mental functioning is shown in the film, but nausea, vomiting, and suppression of pain (other short-term effects) are not. A user's response to heroin or other opioids will vary depending on dose level and experience with the drug. During a state of opioid intoxication, the user tends to be euphoric,

Figure 20. *Ray* (2004, Bristol Bay Productions, Anvil Films, et al.). Produced by Howard Baldwin, Karen Elise Baldwin, Stuart Benjamin, and Taylor Hackford. Directed by Taylor Hackford.

drowsy, apathetic, and usually indifferent to his or her surroundings. Constipation is common. The user's pupils become markedly constricted, and hallucinations may occur. Judgment is often impaired, although an experienced user may function in routine occupational and social roles.

The long-term effects of heroin are quite devastating and include addiction, infections (from dirty needles), collapsed veins, abscesses, infection of heart lining and valves, and arthritis. The primary long-term effect for Ray is addiction. All opioids produce significant tolerance, and withdrawal symptoms are common when drug use is discontinued. In *Ray*, withdrawal is graphically depicted. As tolerance develops, heroin users frequently require doses in excess of 100 times the amount that was originally necessary to produce a state of euphoria. In *Ray*, viewers can clearly see tolerance develop. Typical of addicts, Ray Charles becomes more impaired as he continues to use heroin. Unlike most people with heroin addictions, Ray has extensive financial resources and does not have to engage in typical drug-seeking behavior such as theft or pros-

titution. Eventually, the FBI arrests him for possession of heroin. Ray seeks treatment only because it is a better alternative than prison.

? Questions to Consider While Watching *Ray*

➤ How does a heroin addiction differ from an alcohol addiction?

➤ How is it possible that Ray Charles could function as a performer while he was addicted to heroin?

➤ What examples of denial does the film illustrate?

➤ Does the fact that Ray is blind help or hurt his music? Does it in any way interact with his substance abuse?

➤ At what point is it clear that Ray has an addiction problem?

➤ Does Ray Charles have any other addictions?

➤ What factors contributed to his use of heroin?

➤ How does Ray Charles's heroin addiction compare with George Jung's cocaine addiction in *Blow* (2001)?

➤ How common is it for substance abusers to have a double life? Is a double life typical for musicians?

Sedative-Hypnotics

Sedative drugs produce a calm feeling of well-being in low doses and induce sleep in larger doses. These drugs include barbiturates such as amytal, pentobarbital, and seconal, as well as **anxiolytics** (anxiety-reducing drugs) such as the **benzodiazepines** (Valium, Librium, etc.). Xanax, a more recently developed anxiolytic with a short half-life, combines the anxiety-reducing properties of other benzodiazepines with a mild antidepressant effect. It has become one of the most widely prescribed drugs in the United States. Some of the problems associated with Valium addiction are portrayed in the autobiography and film *I'm Dancing as Fast as I Can* (1982).

Barbiturates are muscle relaxants that induce feelings of well-being in small doses; with larger amounts, the user falls into a deep and profound sleep. Although tolerance develops extremely rapidly with barbiturates, the dose that is lethal remains relatively constant. This puts the barbiturate abuser at high risk and is one of the reasons barbiturates are rarely prescribed for anxiety. However, they remain the medication of choice in some cases of epilepsy.

The effects of barbiturates mimic the effects of alcohol and include symptoms such as slurred speech and staggering gait. These effects may be especially pronounced when barbiturates are combined with alcohol, and this combination is likely to be lethal. Marilyn Monroe committed suicide using a combination of alcohol and sleeping pills. In addition, barbiturate withdrawal is generally more difficult and more painful than withdrawal from narcotics, and it is more likely to be life threatening.

Benzodiazepines have largely replaced barbiturates for the treatment of insomnia because they are less addictive and not as likely to be successfully used in suicide attempts. Benzodiazepines are especially widely prescribed in the United States, and many people feel they are prescribed too often.

Stimulants

Stimulant drugs excite the central nervous system (CNS), fight fatigue, suppress one's appetite, and enhance mood. Cocaine, amphetamines, methamphetamines (meth), 3,4-methylenedioxy-*N*-methyl-amphetamine (MDMA; or ecstasy), nicotine, and caffeine are all stimulants with varying consequences of addiction. These substances activate the reward systems of the brain resulting in a pleasurable feeling. Cocaine and methamphetamine effects are highly addictive and can lead to serious consequences such as tremors, psychosis, and convulsions. Lethal overdose generally causes death from respiratory failure. Drug cravings and stress lead to drug seeking behavior. **Methylphenidates** (Ritalin, Concerta, etc.) are also classified as stimulants, but are legally prescribed for attention-deficit/hyperactivity disorder.

Cocaine

Cocaine is usually snorted or, more rarely, injected intravenously. Sigmund Freud's recreational and therapeutic use of cocaine has been documented and is described in the film *The Seven Percent Solution* (1976), a historical fantasy in which Freud and Sherlock Holmes share their love of cocaine and pool their deductive talents to solve the puzzle of a missing patient.

The film *Blow* (2001), named for the street name of cocaine and based on the life of a cocaine smuggler, George Jung (Johnny Depp), chronicles the rise and fall of one of America's most powerful drug traffickers. This movie portrays the influence of the seductive forces of money and power on a seemingly typical adolescent of the 1960s who would rather smoke marijuana on a California beach than work. He discovers that it is easy to make money selling marijuana. While imprisoned for his marijuana dealing, he was introduced to the world of cocaine trafficking. This film shows the social realities of the illegal, but highly profitable, drug culture. George also displays the physiological and psychological symptoms of addiction and withdrawal.

"The official toxicity limit for humans is between one and one and half grams of cocaine depending on body weight. I was averaging five grams a day, maybe more. I snorted ten grams in ten minutes once. I guess I had a high tolerance."

George Jung in *Blow* (2001)

Other compelling films dealing with cocaine addiction include *The Bad Lieutenant* (1992), starring Harvey Keitel, Martin Scorsese's *Goodfellas* (1990), Brian De Palma's *Scarface* (1983), Alejandro Gonzalez Inarritu's *21 Grams* (2003), featuring a tormented woman played by Naomi Watts, and *The Wolf of Wall Street* (2013).

In Casey Affleck's mockumentary film, *I'm Still Here* (2010), Joaquin Phoenix announces his retirement from making films and instead turns to drugs and hip-hop music. The viewer sees a dramatic change in Phoenix who snorts cocaine any chance he gets, pays for prostitutes, slurs his words, and explodes angrily around his friends. Many viewers will assume this must be a hoax; however, many indicators show it to be "real" as well as a major identity crisis because these behaviors are maintained for about 18 months during the film's inception, production, and promotion. Just as the media rumors that this was a hoax began to subside, it was revealed to be a hoax and Phoenix admitted to this on the David Letterman Show, after having embarrassed Letterman 18 months earlier with his disheveled appearance, mumbling, and refusal to talk in the interview.

Crack cocaine, named after the sound made as the drug is consumed, takes the form of small "rocks" and is smoked. The effects of smoking crack cocaine occur almost immediately, but the high that is produced is relatively brief. Although crack is relatively inexpensive, crack addicts can quickly develop addictions that require hundreds of dollars each day to support. For many people, cocaine addiction leads to prostitution, theft, or violence. The day-to-day life of a crack dealer is portrayed by Djay (Terrence Howard) in *Hustle and Flow* (2005), a film about a man who tries to make money to support his family but begins to question what kind of life he ultimately wants to be leading. *Half Nelson* (2006) is a well-directed film in which Ryan Gosling portrays a drug-addicted teacher/coach of inner city students in a racially diverse neighborhood. He uses cocaine regularly – alone and with strange women – and smokes crack in the girl's locker room after a game. While he is a creative and engaging teacher, his drug addiction leads him to be distant, avoidant, angry, tired in class, and disengaged from his family.

MacArthur Park

The independent film *MacArthur Park* (2001), depicts Cody, a man addicted to crack and struggling to leave both his addiction and the park where he lives with other homeless crack addicts. He has a good reason to leave: His son recently tracked him down, and his son has a home where Cody could re-cover. This film depicts the obstacles of crack addiction Cody must overcome in order to leave.

"I'm not homeless; I just don't wanna go home."

Cody in *MacArthur Park* (2001)

The film explores a world of crack addiction where extensive drug abuse and dependence – as well as drug selling and producing – are depicted. The film's characters use large amounts of crack to cope with their pain and to avoid withdrawal effects. A variety of characters are depicted, and each has a different relationship with the park's drug world: Some are leaving the lifestyle; others are trying to leave, entering the world, deteriorating in it, or have no interest in leaving; still others are simply "lost causes."

The screenplay was written by Tyrone Atkins, a man who was homeless in Los Angeles' MacArthur Park and addicted to crack cocaine. Atkins wrote most of the story while in jail; after leaving jail, he returned to the park before entering a rehabilitation program.

Sweet Nothing

Another film illustrating the degradation associated with crack addiction is *Sweet Nothing* (1996), a true story based on a set of diaries discovered in an abandoned apartment in the Bronx. The film demonstrates the corrosive effects of the protagonist's addiction on his marriage, his relationship with his children, his friends, and his job. At one point, Angelo, the lead character, actually misses his father's funeral because he has an opportunity to get high, and this need supersedes all others. Angelo loses the ability to become sexually aroused by his wife, and we watch him become increasingly paranoid as the film progresses.

Cocaine has affected the lives and careers of numerous actors and directors. For example, Tommy Rettig (best known as Jeff, Lassie's master in the TV series) was sentenced to 5 years in federal prison for smuggling cocaine; Richard Pryor became badly burned as a result of an explosion related to smoking crack cocaine; and when Rainer Werner Fassbinder, considered by many to be Germany's finest director, died at the age of 37, his death was attributed to heart failure resulting from a combination of barbiturates and cocaine.

Amphetamines

Common amphetamines include **amphetamine** (Benzedrine), **dextroamphetamine** (Dexedrine), and **methamphetamine** (Methedrine). Amphetamines or their derivatives are commonly found in nasal decongestants and appetite suppressants. These agents are taken orally. Methamphetamine crystals ("ice"), a highly concentrated form of amphetamine, can also be smoked, injected or taken orally, producing a high that can last as long as 14 hours. Khat, a shrub grown in Africa and the Middle East, produces leaves that can be chewed to produce an amphetamine-like effect. The use of khat is referred to in *Black Hawk Down* (2001). In *Walk the Line* (2005), a drama based on the life of Johnny Cash, Joaquin Phoenix is masterful in the role of the musician. The film tells the story of Cash's rise in the music business, his history of amphetamine abuse, and his love for singer June Carter (Reese Witherspoon). Cash chronically abused prescription drugs, among other substances, often using them to manage tension and stress. Tolerance and withdrawal (both physiological and psychological) are well-portrayed, as is intoxication as Cash falls over on stage in the middle of his performance. The film parallels *Ray* (2004) in that both depict renowned musicians who overcome trauma, rise to the top of the music business, fall dangerously into drugs, are unfaithful in their marriages, lead a double life, recover from drug dependence, make a comeback in their music, and inspire millions.

Winter's Bone (2010) is a compelling film that dramatically but indirectly portrays the ways in which methamphetamine abuse affects a family and a community. Ree (played by Jennifer Lawrence, in her breakthrough performance) is a 17-year-old girl who is highly resilient and takes on the dangerous role of trying to discover what has happened to her father. The viewer never actually sees the father (alive) in the film, but we learn he is an addict who cooks and sells crystal meth for a living, The viewer also comes to understand how this drug can affect (and ruin) entire rural communities. Amphetamines are highly addictive, and tolerance for drugs like methamphetamine develops rapidly. There is a characteristic withdrawal syndrome that includes depression, fatigue, nightmares, insomnia or sometimes hypersomnia, increased appetite, and either psychomotor retardation or agitation. This "crashing" effect appears to be the price the user must pay for the euphoria that accompanies the initial drug use. Amphetamine-induced psychoses often produce symptoms that closely resemble those found with serious mental disorders such as schizophrenia.

The film *Dopamine* (2003) features a lead character who engages in heavy use of stimulants. He gets amphetamine pills from a drug dealer and stays up all night working; in one scene, he has lined up seven cups of coffee next to his computer. Two better films that offer more compelling portrayals of stimulant abuse are *Requiem for a Dream* (2000) and *Spun* (2002).

Requiem for a Dream

The unforgettable film *Requiem for a Dream* (2000) tells the stories of four lonely, desperate characters, each on the wrong track and each destroying his or her life with drugs. Uppers are not the only drug portrayed in the film, which notably contains one of the most vivid and disturbing portrayals of heroin addiction; essentially, these characters will take any drug available. Drugs take the place of food, sex, life goals, and just about everything else. The effect of drugs on the body and mind is unrelenting. Sara (Ellen Burstyn) takes drugs to lose weight so that she can appear in a live broadcast of a television show. Her son, Harry (Jared Leto), repeatedly steals Sara's television set (even though it is chained to the wall) and pawns it for drugs.

Director Darren Aronofsky uses extreme close-ups to demonstrate the effects of drugs. He shows characters swallowing pills, injecting substances, and snorting drugs followed by predictable physiological effects (e.g., pupil dilation), all with exaggerated sound effects. Vigorous camera work, editing, and split-screen techniques allow the viewer to experience the confusion and fast-paced world of addicts abusing "uppers."

In the end, each is alive but destroyed, well past the point of no return, living in a hospital, prison, psychiatric institution, or on the streets as a prostitute. In his review, Roger Ebert appropriately labels this film as "a travelogue of hell."

Spun

Spun (2002) is a devastatingly realistic portrayal of several methamphetamine addicts. Virtually every character is a meth addict – Mickey Rourke plays the cook, who sets up meth labs in various shady apartments until they blow up, and John Leguizamo plays Spider Mike, the addicted dealer. Another character dependent on methamphetamine is the cook's girlfriend, Nikki (Brittany Murphy), whose dog has turned green due to drug exposure in the meth lab. The lead character, Ross (Jason Schwartzman), is so preoccupied with using and having meth available at all times that he forgets he has chained a woman to his bed during sex. Ross wants to have another chance at a relationship with a different woman, Amy, who left Ross because of his methamphetamine abuse and moved on in her life; she is able to see through Ross's denial so patently evident in one of his comments, "You know what the best part is, Amy? I'm not hooked. I can stop anytime."

"Spoof, dope, crank, creep, bomb, spank, shit, bang, zip, tweak, chard. Call it what you will, it's all methamphetamine. That's what I'm here for."

An opening quote from an addict in *Spun* (2002)

These characters are depicted doing meth around the clock – off a girl's body, off a urinal, and "doing a round" while driving. Symptoms of intoxication are present in each character: Inappropriate laughter, jerky, quick body language and movement, and completely trashed living quarters; this is a world in which no one sleeps, everyone talks fast, and no one has meaningful relationships. The postintoxication impairment following the repeated pattern of getting high on meth and crashing to sleep after several days of being awake is called being "spun." All these characters surround themselves with meth – they all get spun. The consequences are clear: The meth addict will eventually be jailed, hospitalized, blown up, or (if lucky) he or she will find a way to escape the lifestyle.

As in *Requiem for a Dream* (2000), the camera speeds everything up to let the viewer experience in some small way what it is like to take methamphetamines. A character inhales meth, and a close-up shows his eyes bloodshot and wide open; car-

toon images accentuate thoughts and drug effects; other close-ups display spinning movements with pupils dilating and contracting.

Hallucinogens

Hallucinogens, sometimes referred to as psychedelics, are drugs that distort the perception of reality. Users report hallucinations involving all senses, **synesthesia** ("crossed" sensations, such as hearing sights and seeing sounds), and depersonalization. These drugs can also have profound effects on mood.

Hallucinogens can occur in the natural environment but are more often produced synthetically. Naturally occurring hallucinogens include **mescaline**, derived from the peyote cactus, and **psilocybin**, which is present in *Psilocybe* mushrooms. Some Native Americans use *Psilocybe* mushrooms in religious ceremonies.

Mescaline can also be produced in a laboratory. However, the best-known and most widely used of all synthetic hallucinogens is **lysergic acid diethylamide** (LSD). It is most often swallowed as a pill, but it can also be mixed with a fluid, licked off blotter paper, or swallowed in sugar cubes or gelatin sheets. LSD is colorless, tasteless, and extremely potent. It produces varied symptoms and can result in affective changes that range from euphoria to absolute terror. The most dramatic effects are often sensory in nature: When the drug experience is positive, it allows the user "to see a world in a grain of sand / And a heaven in a wild flower, / Hold infinity in the palm of your hand / And eternity in an hour" (William Blake, *Auguries of Innocence*). Unfortunately, the experience is not always this benign, and injury or death can result from bad decisions made while under the influence of the drug. Some users have also reported "flashbacks" in which they reexperience the sensory phenomenon associated with previous trips weeks or years after last using the drug. The drug is not addictive, but tolerance develops rapidly.

In a *Playboy* interview, the renowned director Stanley Kubrick made the following constructive observation about LSD:

> One of the things that's turned me against LSD is that all the people I know who use it have a peculiar inability to distinguish between things that are really interes-

ting and stimulating and things that appear to be so in the state of universal bliss that the drug induces on a "good" trip. They seem to completely lose their critical faculties and disengage themselves from some of the most stimulating areas of life. Perhaps when everything is beautiful, nothing is beautiful (Agel, 1970, *The Making of Kubrick's 2001*, excerpted from a 1968 Playboy interview, p. 346).

In the film *In the Name of the Father* (1993), prisoners cope with the monotony of prison life by licking LSD off the back of a jigsaw puzzle. The puzzle is a large world map, and the prisoners get high "one country at a time." The LSD experience is also portrayed in any number of films from the 1960s that document the youth culture of that period. In *Awakening the Beast* (1970), a psychiatrist tests his theory that drugs are the conduit for evil. He conducts research on four subjects who will take LSD as an experiment while he monitors their behavior for a book he is writing about addicts. He injects distilled water as a way of delivering the drug. In the film he observes: "Drugs are but an excuse to release the instinct in all of us."

Phencyclidine (PCP), also known as angel dust, is another powerful hallucinogen that has been used since the early 1960s. It can be taken in pill form or dusted onto marijuana and smoked. The drug produces symptoms even more marked than those associated with LSD and may result in analgesia, depersonalization, paranoia, rage reactions, or schizophrenia-like psychoses. Hallucinogen use is depicted in *Easy Rider* (1969) and *Fear and Loathing in Las Vegas* (1998).

The stylized, partly computerized characters of *A Scanner Darkly* (2006) portray a science fiction / fantasy world characterized by paranoia, drug abuse, and government control. Richard Linklater directs Keanu Reeves, Robert Downey Jr., Winona Ryder, and Woody Harrelson in this story about a family man who is unhappy so he leaves his life to become a narcotics agent. During his training, he learns that good agents do drugs in moderation. The made-up drug in the film is Substance D (D stands for despair, desolation, and death) to which 40% of the population is addicted. A number of intoxication and withdrawal symptoms are dramatized including tactile hallucinations (e.g., bugs crawling all over the body), shakiness, bloodshot eyes, extreme paranoia, dramatic anger, and a suicide attempt. One character develops an extensive hallucination in which a foreign creature spends eternity reading out his life sins without ever pausing.

Inhalants

Common substances that inhalant addicts abuse include glue, gasoline, paint thinners, spray paints, cleaners, and spray-can propellants. Methods used to inhale the vapors include soaking a rag with the substance, placing the substance in a paper or plastic bag, inhaling directly from the container, or spraying the substance into the nose or mouth. The chemicals inhaled reach the lungs and bloodstream very rapidly.

Love Liza

In *Love Liza* (2002), Wilson (masterfully portrayed by Philip Seymour Hoffman) is a computer technician who becomes addicted to inhaling gasoline following his wife's suicide. This is a fairly bizarre and atypical bereavement reaction. Wilson is an emotional wreck and puts all his energy and concerns into "huffing" gasoline. The method he uses is to soak a rag with gasoline and hold the rag over his face while he inhales. He is frequently shown bending over to smell gasoline at gas station pumps and the opening in his car's gas tank.

When intoxicated, Wilson's speech becomes slurred, distorted, inappropriate, and at times nonsensical. His interpersonal relationship skills dramatically diminish to a level that he appears confusing, rude, and distant to the person speaking with him. Cinematic elements enhance the effects of his blurred vision, and in one scene he experiences hallucinations. Wilson vacillates from complete euphoria from the gasoline highs, which lead to grossly inappropriate behavior such as swimming in a lake where remote-controlled boats are racing and cheerfully attempting to converse with other drivers on a highway, to severe agitation and anger outbursts evident when he is not huffing or is awakening from a blackout. Wilson becomes more isolated as the film progresses and would probably be completely isolated if it were not for a few dedicated and long suffering friends. His judgment is impaired in other ways such as when he supplies two young huffing adolescents who have been banned from gas stations with the intoxicant.

The consequences of his huffing include the loss of a new job, damage to important relationships, and his house burning down. Wilson is experiencing so much pain that he cannot bring himself to read his wife's suicide note; instead, he carries it around with him as a constant reminder of her death. Upon eventually reading it, he knows exactly what to do. Overall, this portrayal of a serious and severe addiction is realistic, honest, and not unduly melodramatic.

Cannabis

Marijuana is obtained from the hemp plant *Cannabis sativa*. The active ingredient in marijuana is the drug **tetrahydrocannabinol** (THC). The greater the THC content, the more potent the drug. The THC content of marijuana purchased illegally varies widely, but in general, THC levels have been increasing over the past 3 decades, and the marijuana used today is approximately five times stronger than that widely available on street corners and on college campuses in the 1960s. The resin of the *Cannabis sativa* plant can be used to produce **hashish**, a stronger form of the drug.

Marijuana has medicinal value, and it can be obtained legally for the treatment of some disorders. The drug enhances appetite and is often helpful in controlling the nausea associated with chemotherapy. Other physical effects include tachycardia, sedation, and psychomotor impairment. Like the hallucinogens, marijuana can produce markedly varied psychological effects, depending on the mood and situation of the user. Most often, the drug produces mild euphoria, giddiness, and a general sense of well-being. However, at a different time and in a different setting, the same drug can produce marked apprehension or paranoia.

Examples of marijuana use can be found in countless films. One especially memorable scene involves a group of characters (played by Dennis Hopper, Peter Fonda, and Jack Nicholson) sitting around a campfire and smoking marijuana in *Easy Rider* (1969).

The low-budget, antidrug exploitation film *Reefer Madness* (1936), formerly titled *Tell Your Children*, became a cult classic among young people who smoked marijuana in the 1960s. Many people be-

lieved the film was tongue-in-cheek; however, it was meant to be a serious film. It begins by dramatizing marijuana with introductory text referring to it as "ghastly," a menace to society, a "deadly narcotic," and "public enemy #1," followed by various mock newspaper headlines on the dangers and societal consequences of marijuana use. The film turns to a parent meeting in which an expert speaks of the dangers to concerned parents and the need for a united front against marijuana; the bulk of the film (which runs like a satirical story) revolves around a group of normal-looking drug dealers who get adolescents addicted to marijuana by throwing wild jazz parties. Everyone who uses marijuana has serious deleterious effects – laughing foolishly and uncontrollable, extreme shakiness, intense anger and edginess, pacing, terror and panic, and paranoia; the eventual effects include sexual abuse, suicide, and murder. Marijuana is clearly portrayed as a drug that directly changes one's character for the worse. The film ends with the same parent meeting noting that these are the dangers and consequences of addiction and concludes with a finger pointing at the camera and an admonition that the viewer's children could be next. Clearly this film does little to educate the viewer about marijuana, its side effects, or consequences; if it was ever taken at face value, it would mislead and confuse viewers. The film does document the misconceptions that people have had in the past and the power of group contagion and its ability to produce paranoia and hysteria.

Several Cheech and Chong movies celebrate marijuana use and ridicule its classification as a narcotic. Other movies emphasizing marijuana include the Coen Brothers' noir *The Big Lebowski* (1998) and the outlandish comedy *Half Baked* (1998). Kevin Spacey portrays a psychologist who is addicted to marijuana in *Shrink* (2009). He uses the drug in the opening scene and throughout the film – while driving, when he first wakes up after hearing the alarm clock, while showering, and while shaving. He uses it at good times and bad, for example, as a celebration after hearing about the success of his self-help book and as a way to cope with stress. He has regular interactions with his drug dealers and enjoys hanging out with them. In one scene, he smokes "laced" weed which ends up putting him in the hospital. He eventually decides to give up smoking and dumps all of his drugs down the toilet.

Polysubstance Dependence

Polysubstance refers to the use of three or more groups of substances (excluding nicotine and caffeine) with no particular substance predominating.

Naked Lunch (1991), the David Cronenberg film adaptation of the William Burroughs' book, is fascinating albeit not always tightly linked to the novel. William Lee, the protagonist, is a polydrug addict trying to go straight. Unfortunately, both he and his wife are addicted to bug spray, and Bill's job as an exterminator makes it almost impossible for him to avoid this particular drug. The cinematic representation of visual hallucinations in *Naked Lunch* is especially fascinating.

In the B movie, *Shadow Hours* (2000), a young man working as a gas station attendant is lured back into drug addiction by a wealthy, mysterious writer who advises the young man he must go into the abyss before he can get back to sobriety. The two men visit dance clubs, drug fests, strip clubs, fight clubs, sadomasochism clubs, and torture events.

Leonardo DiCaprio plays a wall street investor in Martin Scorsese's *The Wolf of Wall Street* (2013), a film based on the true life story of Jordan Belfort. Belfort uses dozens of different drugs, at almost every opportunity, and some critics have complained that the film glamorizes drug use.

"On a daily basis I consume enough drugs to sedate Manhattan, Long Island, and Queens for a month. I take Quaaludes 10–15 times a day for my 'back pain,' Adderall to stay focused, Xanax to take the edge off, pot to mellow me out, cocaine to wake me back up again, and morphine ... Well, because it's awesome."

Jordan Belfort (Leonardo DiCaprio) brags about his drug use in *The Wolf of Wall Street* (2013)

Tobacco

The drug most often portrayed on television and in films is tobacco. Epidemiological studies suggest it is also our most lethal drug. The US Centers for Disease Control and Prevention (CDC) estimates that tobacco accounts for 480,000 deaths annually in the United States, approximately one out of every five deaths (see http://www.cdc.gov/Tobacco/data_sta-tistics/fact_sheets/fast_facts/index.htm). Although fatality rates are only one index of the severity of a drug problem, it is clear that none of the drugs typically regarded as our most "serious" are ultimately as dangerous as cigarettes.

In part because of the pain of withdrawal, less than 5% of smokers are successful in their attempts to stop smoking, although about 35% try to stop each year (and 80% express the desire to stop). Some of the symptoms associated with nicotine withdrawal include dysphoric or depressed mood, insomnia, irritability/anger, anxiety, difficulty concentrating, restlessness, decreased heart rate, and increased appetite or weight gain.

The morbidity and mortality associated with tobacco use have been underscored by a series of reports issued since 1964 by the Office of the Surgeon General. Partially in response to the massive public education efforts spearheaded by the surgeon general, numerous Americans have stopped smoking. In addition, the American Medical Association and the American Public Health Association have been very vocal in their opposition to tobacco use.

Various films depict people smoking cigarettes, and it is actually difficult to find a standard drama or comedy where smokers are absent. *Coffee and Cigarettes* (2003), directed and written by Jim Jarmusch, explores the use of nicotine and another addictive substance, caffeine. Several separate vignettes about different characters are connected only by conversation and the use of coffee and cigarettes, with some characters using the substances more compulsively than others. There are comical interactions between musicians Iggy Pop and Tom Waits, between actors Alfred Molina and Steve Coogan, between Bill Murray and two members of the Wu-Tang Clan (where Murray drinks coffee straight from the pot), and between Cate Blanchett and herself. Gwyneth Paltrow's character, Margo, is addicted to nicotine and finds creative ways to hide her smoking habits in *The Royal Tenenbaums* (2001). Ironically, the satirical comedy *Thank You for Smoking* (2005), while being about a lobbyist who works for a marketing organization supported by major tobacco companies, does not portray a single character smoking in the film. Aaron Eckhart plays Nick Naylor, a master of spin, who is able to argue that cigarettes should be made available for patients with cancer. In one scene, he is abducted and covered with nicotine patches; however, what keeps him alive is the fact that he has a high tolerance from heavy smoking (though he is never shown smoking).

Substances Depicted in Films

Countless films depict characters abusing substances, and at times it is unclear what substance is being abused. Rather than labeling the character as a "drug addict," it is more important to decipher the particular substance being abused, as each substance has different characteristics (e.g., tolerance, withdrawal, and intoxication levels). Table 6 helps make this clarification with some of the best portrayals of substance abuse in films. The number of psi's (Ψ) provides a rating scale, further emphasizing the importance of each – see Appendix H for details on this scale.

Substance Abuse Recovery

Many films depict characters who are former substance abusers in full recovery (i.e., sustained full remission) and are not depicted as abusing or relapsing in the film. Support groups are a key component for many individuals' recovery from alcohol and drug abuse. The founding of AA, by Bill Wilson and Dr. Bob Smith, which has paved the way for countless support groups over the decades, is portrayed in *My Name Is Bill W.* (1986). The Louis Malle film, *The Fire Within* (1963) is about a depressed writer searching for intimate connections. He has been recovering from alcohol dependence

Table 6. Substances abused, with accompanying film examples

Abused substance	Film example(s)	Comments	Rating
Alcohol	*Leaving Las Vegas* (1995)	Nicholas Cage as an alcoholic giving up	ΨΨΨΨ
	Born on the Fourth of July (1989)	Tom Cruise as a bitter veteran	ΨΨΨΨ
	House of Sand and Fog (2003)	Jennifer Connelly relapsing	ΨΨΨΨΨ
	Smashed (2012)	Kate (Mary Elizabeth Winstead) and Charlie (Aaron Paul) have a relationship built around a mutual love of alcohol	ΨΨΨΨ
Heroin	*Pulp Fiction* (1994)	Uma Thurman mistakes cocaine for heroin in classic Tarantino scene	ΨΨΨΨΨ
	Quitting (2001)	Deterioration and withdrawals	ΨΨΨΨ
Sedatives/ hypnotics	*I'm Dancing as Fast as I Can* (1982)	Valium addiction	ΨΨ
Cocaine	*Traffic* (2000)	Dynamic, integrated drug film	ΨΨΨΨΨ
	Blow (2001)	Johnny Depp as a famous cocaine importer	ΨΨΨ
Crack cocaine	*MacArthur Park* (2001)	Gripping realism in LA	ΨΨΨ
Amphetamine	*Walk the Line* (2005)	Johnny Cash mixing uppers & song	ΨΨΨΨΨ
	Requiem for a Dream (2000)	Ellen Burstyn's role is unforgettable	ΨΨΨΨ
	Spun (2002)	Methamphetamine addiction and lifestyle	ΨΨΨ
Hallucinogens	*Fear and Loathing in Las Vegas* (1998)	Normalizes drug use	ΨΨ
Inhalants	*Love Liza* (2002)	Philip Seymour Hoffman depicts gasoline huffing	ΨΨΨ

Table 6. Continued

Abused substance	Film example(s)	Comments	Rating
Steroids	*The Wrestler* (2008)	Mickey Rourke pumping for a fight	ΨΨΨΨ
Cannabis (Marijuana)	*The Big Lebowski* (1998) *Shrink* (2009)	Jeff Bridges as "The Dude" Kevin Spacey as an addicted psychologist	ΨΨ ΨΨΨ
Nicotine (Tobacco)	*The Royal Tenenbaums* (2001)	Gwyneth Paltrow's character tries to hide her smoking habits	ΨΨΨΨΨ
Caffeine	*Coffee and Cigarettes* (2003)	Vignettes with both substances	ΨΨΨ
Combination	*Eyes Wide Shut* (1999)	Speedball (cocaine & heroin)	ΨΨΨΨΨ
Polysubstance	*Naked Lunch* (1991) *Dallas Buyers Club* (2013)	Bug spray and other substances Addiction to cocaine, meth, alcohol, gambling, and sex	ΨΨ ΨΨΨΨ

for a few months following a treatment called "the cure," which involved having him drink until he "bursts." He decides to continue to stay at the treatment center because he feels safer there – he is simply too frightened to face the world. Malle discloses that the film was transformative for him to make and that it helped him to "clear away the clouds" in his mind. He said it was never intended to be a commercial film. He shares the fact that the protagonist in many ways represents his alter ego.

Rachel Getting Married

Rachel Getting Married (2008) is a Jonathan Demme film that realistically portrays substance abuse recovery, emphasizing some of the family dynamics that can erupt when an addict returns home from rehabilitation. Kym (Anne Hathaway) leaves rehab for a few days to spend time with her family as they prepare for the wedding of her sister, Rachel. The family tries to accept her, although they cannot help but be hypervigilant, cautious, and tense at times. Kym has an explosive temper, and many issues emerge from the past (e.g., Kym's tragic incident years ago when she was supposed to be looking after her baby brother – instead, she drove off a bridge while high on drugs, and he died in the accident) and from the present (e.g., tension with her sister's best friend seemingly competing for Rachel's attention).

At times, Kym's sickness emerges, such as when she gives a rehearsal dinner speech that is tangential and self-involved (and embarrassing for her family) before taking time to comment on the bride and groom. Remarkably, Kym maintains her sobriety throughout the party-filled weekend and the tensions and issues that come up. However, after a physical and emotional fight with her mother, she drives her car off the road, perhaps as a suicide attempt (symbolically atoning for the egregious behavior years ago that killed her brother). It is never clear what drug(s) Kym is addicted to, but the film alludes to alcohol and other substances. Despite the dreary topic, the film illustrates the importance of humor and hope, two important character strengths for an addict or a family dealing with an addict. The film is also strong in its portrayal of support group meetings, which are accurately portrayed as real, supportive, and helpful for those who participate. Individuals share their personal stories, recite the 12 steps, and common 12-step adages (e.g., "keep coming back; it works if you work it"), prayers (e.g., the serenity prayer), and themes (e.g., life can feel boring without substances) are shared. Kym is persistent in her life with her family, which is critical for substance abuse recovery, and puts forth good effort; she is difficult yet endearing for both her family and the viewer.

The film *28 Days* (2000), discussed earlier in the chapter (see the section "The Portrayal of Alcoholism in Films"), also depicts 12-step support

Movies and Mental Illness

groups; in this case, it is AA. In addition to the serenity prayer, inspiring AA adages used include: "It works, if you work it, you're worth it"; "God never gives us more than we can handle"; and "We are better, together." An alcohol/drug counselor (Steve Buscemi) is a recovering addict (also common for alcohol/drug counselors) and shares his story as a source of inspiration.

Another film depicting a character trying to make it outside of an institution (although in this case it is a release from prison) is Sherry Swanson (Maggie Gyllenhaal) in *Sherrybaby* (2006). Sherry has been clean for two and a half years following a 6-year heroin addiction; however, she has strong urges within 4 days of her release. She tries to do what is right, but she has few coping resources, and she still craves heroin. She functions out of a survivor mentality – she is manipulative, lacks empathy, and displays poor social judgment; she has significant inner rage and aggression and frequently slams doors and curses. In one scene, her emotionally aloof father takes advantage of her and fondles her breasts during a vulnerable moment; the stress as-sociated with her father's sexual abuse, triggers an immediate relapse. The opening song of the film repeats the line "there's an angel on my left but the devil's on my right," which describes the inner struggles of the addict, particularly those who are trying hard to maintain sobriety.

Benicio Del Toro plays a recovery alcoholic and ex-con who becomes a born-again Christian in *21 Grams* (2003). In *A Mighty Wind* (2003), Eugene Levy's folk singing character, Mitch, has flat affect, slowed speech and thought, and presents with wide-eyed expressions, each assumed to relate to significant drug abuse in his past.

The 12 steps are a set of guidelines that have become a tradition for numerous support groups. These important beliefs have revolutionized the conceptualization and treatment of substance abusers and have contributed to saving the lives of countless addicts. Table 7 lists the 12-step approach used by AA; however, the word *alcohol* can be easily replaced by *drugs* (Narcotics Anonymous), *sex, gambling, money,* or *food,* depending on the person's addiction.

Table 7. The 12 steps and 12 traditions[1]

1. We admitted that we were powerless over alcohol – that our lives had become unmanageable.
2. Came to believe that a Power greater than ourselves could restore us to sanity.
3. Made a decision to turn our will and our life over to the care of God *as we understood Him.*
4. Made a searching and fearless moral inventory of ourselves.
5. Admitted to God, to ourselves, and to another human being the exact nature of our wrongs.
6. Were entirely ready to have God remove all these defects of character.
7. Humbly asked Him to remove our shortcomings.
8. Made a list of all persons we had harmed, and became willing to make amends to them all.
9. Made direct amends to such people whenever possible, except when to do so would injure them or others.
10. Continued to take personal inventory and, when we were wrong, promptly admitted it.
11. Sought through prayer and meditation to improve our conscious contact with God *as we understood Him*, praying only for knowledge of His will for us and the power to carry that out.
12. Having had a spiritual awakening as the result of these steps, we tried to carry this message to alcoholics and to practice these principles in all our affairs.

[1] The 12 steps are reprinted with permission of Alcoholics Anonymous World Services, Inc. Permission to reprint the Twelve Steps does not mean that AA has reviewed or approved the contents of this publication, nor that AA agrees with the views expressed herein. AA is a program of recovery from alcoholism only – use of Twelve Steps in connection with programs and activities which are patterned after AA, but which address other problems, or in any other non-AA context, does not imply otherwise.

Non-Substance-Related Disorders

Gambling Disorder

Gambling disorder is the only non-substance-related disorder included in the *DSM-5*, and its inclusion is controversial. Many authorities believe we can only become addicted to substances; others argue that we can just as surely become addicted to gambling or other behaviors like sex, shopping, exercise, and Internet gaming. The *DSM-5* panel did not believe there was sufficient peer-reviewed evidence to set diagnostic criteria and classify these addictive areas as mental disorders. Nevertheless, as in the last edition of *Movies and Mental Illness*, we continue to provide examples of some of these addictive behaviors in this edition as well, following the discussion of gambling disorder.

Gambling disorder is diagnosed when four or more of nine criteria are met over a 12-month period. Criteria include the need to gamble with increasing amounts of money; restlessness or irritability when attempting to cut back or stop gambling; repeated unsuccessful efforts to stop gambling; preoccupation with gambling; gambling to relieve guilt, depression, or anxiety; lying to conceal the full extent of one's involvement with gambling, and jeopardizing or losing a significant job, relationship, or opportunity because of gambling. The prototypical gambler with this diagnosis has made several unsuccessful attempts to stop gambling, gambles with increased amounts of money, "chases" losses, lies to cover up the problem, and escapes from personal problems or internal pain by gambling.

Gambling is fairly frequent in movies. Although not all of these films depict characters who would meet the criteria for a gambling disorder, one film is a particularly compelling example – *Owning Mahowny* (2002).

Owning Mahowny

This film is based on true events that occurred in Toronto between 1980 and 1982; the movie tells the story of a man who stole $10.2 million from his employer to support his gambling addiction. He eventually served a 6-year prison term for fraud.

Philip Seymour Hoffman stars as Dan Mahowny, a man described at the onset as having three lives: (1) a public life, (2) a private life, and (3) a secret life. Mahowny has a loving, dedicated girlfriend, and at work he is the youngest in his position as a loan officer, someone described as having an "impeccable record" and "excellent judgment." His secret life involves his very serious, self-destructive gambling problem.

Psychologist: "How would you rate the thrill you got from gambling, on a scale of one to 100?"

Dan Mahowny: "Um ... a hundred."

Psychologist: "And what about the biggest thrill you've ever had outside of gambling?"

Dan Mahowny: "Twenty."

Owning Mahowny (2002)

Mahowny accumulates a debt of $10,300 by placing bets with shady bookies. He decides to write fake loans to pay off his debt. He then begins to gamble with this money at casinos to pay off the debt more quickly. He flies to Atlantic City numerous times to gamble. Along the way, he tells various lies to his girlfriend Belinda (Minnie Driver) and his boss to keep his secret life hidden. While gambling, Mahowny appears to be in a trance – he is very focused and absorbed in the experience, and he loses track of time. His losses progressively increase; he loses $15,000 one night and then $100,000 another night, unsuccessfully attempting to chase losses by doubling up on his bets. His denial is obvious to the viewer, such as when he frequently convinces himself that he is "in the zone." Mahowny deteriorates psychologically and behaviorally, and his behavior becomes erratic, his appearance disheveled and unkempt, and his self-care is poor. At one point, he gives a friend money to hold, making him promise not to give it back to him no matter what; soon Mahowny is screaming at his friend to "give me my money and stay away from me." Scenes like this dramatically display the intensity and power of this addiction. Mahowny is alone and depressed, he does not get enough sleep, and and in one scene he falls asleep while driving. The film is a dramatic depiction of the despair of someone caught in the throes of a gambling addiction.

The casino realizes its potential profit and goes to great lengths to keep Mahowny gambling, following him; watching him; trying to entice him; offering him food, drinks, a free hotel stay, and women; and even sending him a "friend" to shadow him and keep him there. Mahowny rejects the women and alcohol; he is referred to as a "purist" in his gambling addiction because he does not mix sex, alcohol, or drugs with his gambling.

The addiction worsens when Mahowny takes his girlfriend on a special vacation and then neglects her; when she confronts him about this while he is gambling, he simply begs for a "few more minutes," ultimately choosing gambling over love and sex. This scene illustrates the huge disparity that has developed in their relationship; she continues to be focused on the relationship, while his addiction leaves him too engrossed in gambling to even care what happens to her.

Additional Questions for Discussion (*Owning Mahowny*)

➤ How common is it for someone to have a "secret life"?
➤ What is the difference between having a debt problem and having a gambling problem? How does each apply to Dan Mahowny?
➤ What addictions typically co-occur with gambling?
➤ What is the percentage of gamblers who are purists?
➤ At what point does Mahowny's behavior become unmanageable and out of control?
➤ In what ways does Mahowny lie to himself?
➤ What treatments and support groups are available for someone like Dan Mahowny?

In another movie based on a true story, *Two for the Money* (2005), a young, savvy football expert, Brandon Lang (Matthew McConaughy) is hired by Walter Abrams (Al Pacino) to work in a fast-paced business as a gamblers' advisor (helping gamblers make good bets on football games). Walter is a recovering pathological gambler of 18 years – though he is clearly experiencing similar highs from devoting his life to helping gamblers. Much of his life relates to gambling – he bets on his salesmen, he watches each football game closely, and his income is based on how successful his clients are. He sees the successes of Brandon, who seems to beat the odds and predict game outcomes at an 80% success rate, becomes attached to his new protégé, and obsesses about building an "empire" around Brandon. Walter is unable to quit, focused on riding the ex-

citement he experiences when working with Brandon. Walter displays typical gambler self-sabotaging behavior, taking increasingly high-risk bets. He continues despite clear evidence of a serious heart condition that he treats with medication. The film depicts a Gamblers Anonymous meeting in which one member speaks honestly of his struggles; however, Walter attempts to take advantage of the man by giving him his business card, tempting the man to reclaim his addiction. The deep sense of inherent defectiveness and shame common to this addictive behavior is portrayed in the film.

Oscar and Lucinda (1997), based on the 1988 Booker Prize–winning novel by Peter Carey, portrays two outcasts who connect through pathological gambling. Oscar Hopkins (Ralph Fiennes) copes with his anxiety disorder by gambling. He won his first bet on horse racing (this is common for those with the disorder) and is unable to stop gambling. He is quite distressed by his behavior, even breaking his own strict adherence to keeping the Sabbath holy and free of gambling. He rationalizes his gambling, arguing that belief in God is a gamble, so how could gambling not be accepted by God? Another rationalization is that he is not gambling for personal gain, because he gives away his winnings. When he has periods of sobriety during which he is able to stay away from gambling, he lives in constant fear that he will revert to his old habits and ways. Lucinda Lepastrier (Cate Blanchett) stays up all night gambling, tries to hide her behavior from others, and uses gambling as a way to cope with loneliness. Oscar and Lucinda make a pact to not gamble or lead one another in that direction, and they attempt to put their energy productively into a floor-washing competition. Soon they break the pact and make the ultimate gamble – their inheritance.

In *Dinner Rush* (2001), a cook at an upscale New York City restaurant is unable to control betting on sports teams. This significantly affects his work performance, interpersonal relationships, and his ability to focus. He exhibits the common gambler's behavior of attempting to chase his losses. The impact on his life and functioning is clear: He continues to upset more and more people around him, and eventually he puts his life in danger.

In *21* (2008), an MIT student is accepted into Harvard Medical School but is unable to pay the steep tuition, so he reluctantly takes part in an illegal card counting operation, lead by his teacher (Kevin Spacey). The teacher crosses a number of boundaries as he promotes this illegal activity, manipulates his students, fixes grades in his course, and orchestrates some nasty university politics. While the film is not particularly strong in portraying elements of pathological gambling, it does illustrate a common dynamic gamblers and other addicts experience – a double life. In addition to his normal life as a student, the protagonist creates a gambler's (or card counter's) life in which he spends time in exciting cities, takes on a variety of high-roller personas, and becomes invested in a new peer group. As is the case in many of these instances, all is well until the two lives converge. This film is based on a true story about six smart MIT students who took on the Las Vegas casinos and walked away with millions.

Sex Addiction

Sexual addiction is increasingly recognized as a growing problem in contemporary society. Patrick Carnes, one of the world's leading authorities on sexual addiction, has written extensively on the topic, addressing sexual compulsivity (*Don't Call It Love* and *Out of the Shadows*), Internet sex addiction (*In the Shadows of the Net*), and each of the paraphilias discussed in Chapter 14. There are movies that illustrate each of these clinical problems.

I Am a Sex Addict (2005) is an autobiographical documentary film that emphasizes the role of compulsivity in sexual addictions – for the director/actor, the acting out was compulsive sex with prostitutes and compulsive masturbation. The important role of 12-step recovery groups (e.g., Sex Addicts Anonymous) is highlighted, as are a number of unhealthy and healthy coping strategies. A better movie, *De-Lovely* (2004), documents the numerous compulsive homosexual affairs of Cole Porter and the conflict he felt about reconciling these affairs with his very genuine love for his wife.

Good films on sex addicts will not only reveal the behaviors of the addict but also the consequences and realities of the decisions they make. Characters who are presented as male sex addicts include Joe Taylor (Ewan McGregor) in *Young Adam* (2003), the title characters in *Alfie* (2004) and *Don Juan De-Marco* (1995) (played by Jude Law and Johnny Depp, respectively), and Sammy Horn (Michael Des Barres) in *The Diary of a Sex Addict* (2001; Spain).

Don Jon (2013) depicts the life of a man addicted to masturbation; he initially views this as a harmless habit, but eventually sees that it interferes with his ability to form a mature, adult loving relationship.

The classic Luis Buñuel film *Belle de Jour* (1967) portrays a married woman who takes a job as a prostitute. The film illustrates female sexual addiction and depicts the creation of a double life. As the protagonist sinks deeper into her new lifestyle and becomes more comfortable with her lies, she becomes unable to extricate herself. Other female sex addicts are depicted in *Swimming Pool* (2003), *Leap Year* (2010), and in one segment of *Personal Velocity* (2002), and Juliette Marquis plays the role of a confident, self-assured, and enthusiastic porn star in *This Girl's Life* (2003). A memorable female sexual addict can also be found in *Diary of a Nymphomaniac* (2008). This serious film reveals the loneliness, suffering, and emotional turmoil common to sexual addicts.

"I need sex. I see a man and I need him."

The insatiable sexual appetite described in *Diary of a Nymphomaniac* (2008)

On Line (2002) examines the serious problem of Internet addiction. In the film, a man is abandoned by his fiancée; consequently, he spends countless hours on the Internet, partly to help his roommate with a popular pornographic website designed to "link people together with their fantasy." At the end of the film, the viewer learns that the fiancée had been a person online with a webcam whom he had watched all day and had never personally met. His compulsive fantasy had become so ingrained that it shaped his personal reality. The film accurately portrays the intense loneliness, isolation, and lack of intimacy or connection that Internet addicts and Internet sex addicts experience.

An important feature of sex addiction is the secrecy of the behavior. The link between secrecy and sexuality is explored in *Far From Heaven* (2002), *Unfaithful* (2002), and *The Secret Lives of Dentists* (2002). Film directors Pedro Almodóvar, Peter Greenaway, and John Waters are especially known for their creative depiction of sexuality, sexual addiction, and paraphilias (the latter of which are a group of disorders discussed in Chapter 14).

Shame

Shame (2011) offers a memorable portrayal of sexual addiction. The film depicts Brandon (Michael Fassbender), the male protagonist, as someone whose suffering and sexual addiction is clear. The viewer can see all of the signs and symptoms associated with alcohol or drug abuse, such as intoxication, dependence, and withdrawal, but in this case sex is the "substance." Brandon becomes "high" on sex, dependent in that he needs more frequency in order to meet his needs, and experiences withdrawal symptoms when he does not get sex (e.g., negative isolation, irritability, explosiveness, loneliness, risk taking, and self-defeating behavior). He attempts to connect with others in a more meaningful way; however, when these attempts fail, he returns to the pursuit of meaningless, anonymous sex with women, multiple partners, and men to cope with his failures.

Brandon's longest relationship lasts 4 months. After going on a second date with a woman and beginning to connect with her, this connection becomes too substantive and "real" for him, and he becomes impotent. He then curls up in a fetal position, cannot look the woman in the eye, and refuses to speak to her. His pathology worsens when he is faced with the stressor of his younger sister dropping in to temporarily live with him in his apartment. He treats her badly, is constantly irritable toward her, and he becomes physically abusive, explosive, and dismissive. The ending scene might be viewed as ambiguous to someone unfamiliar with sexual addiction as it shows Brandon making eye contact with an attractive woman on the subway whom he had seen before; she is married yet their protracted eye contact is clearly flirtation. The final shot shows a somewhat serious looking close-up on Brandon's face as if to leave the viewer to wonder whether he has made a substantive change and he will resist temptation or if he will continue to pursue his addictive behavior. Yet, this also reveals one of the danger points of sexual addiction – Brandon is breaking a boundary by visually lingering and prolonging his eye contact. This is one step too far for the sexual addict. He does not display a coping strategy or quickly turn away, but instead he does what sex addicts call "rubbernecking." This suggests he has actually made no progress and his sexual addiction is still a problem for him.

Spending/Shopping Addiction

Maxed Out (2006) is a documentary that looks at the impulse control problem of compulsive spending. The film focuses on the problem of credit card debt, the cyclical patterns therein, and the factors that contribute to the development of this disorder. The film notes that a family living in today's world has less money for the essentials than a family living in the 1970s, that $9,200 is the average American credit card debt, and that 10 million people filed for bankruptcy over a recent 10-year period. Some of the consequences of excessive credit card debt include depression and suicide. Problems with impulse control often play a significant role in the development of compulsive spending and the accumulation of massive debt.

International Films: Substance-Related and Addictive Disorders

The film *Quitting* (2001, China), by Chinese director Zhang Yang, depicts heroin abuse and withdrawal, intermixing both through flashbacks. A young man, Hongsheng, at one time a famous actor, is living with his parents to help him deal with his heroin addiction. He is bitter and verbally abusive toward his parents. Through flashbacks, the viewer learns of his deterioration due to heroin dependence and the ramifications of its abuse; his career is in shambles, he loses several friends, develops a delusional obsession with John Lennon, hallucinates, and has several anger outbursts.

> "I was fighting with myself. I didn't know what I was fighting about."
>
> Hongsheng in *Quitting* (2001)

Vodka Lemon (2003, France/Italy/Switzerland/Armenia) is a slow but engaging comedy/drama with an interesting and subtle vibrancy, from exiled Iraqi Kurd director, Hiner Saleem. The film takes place in Armenia, post-USSR, and depicts the romance of a widowed man and woman after they meet during their daily, separate trips to visit the graves of their former spouses. The background of this minimalist film is alcohol. It seems that all of the townspeople drink alcohol as a coping strategy that is accepted as an established part of daily life. Everybody drinks all the time, hence the need for the only store in town – a "vodka lemon" shop where people purchase vodka by the bottle. No unruly behaviors or symptoms result from the extensive alcohol use, barring one exception, and it is unclear if this incident is alcohol related.

No Such Thing (2001, Iceland/US), a film by independent auteur Hal Hartley, tells the story of a young woman (Sarah Polley) who goes to investigate the story of a "monster" who has killed a film crew (including her cameraman–fiancé) in a remote Icelandic village. She tracks down the monster, who is an isolated, grotesque alcoholic, and befriends it, bringing it home to America despite the fact that the monster breathes fire, kills people at will, and is described as indestructible, beyond science and unable to even commit suicide. It is interesting to reflect on what the monster (and alcohol) represents, as well as the dichotomies that arise – hope/fear, good/evil, comedy/tragedy, denial/reality, and humanity/inhumanity.

The film *16 Years of Alcohol* (2003, UK) portrays Frankie, an alcoholic, who as a child of an alcoholic observed his father's infidelity, alcoholism, and violence, and grew up to repeat the same patterns. The film pays homage to another film that mixes violence and substance abuse, *A Clockwork Orange* (1971, US/UK); this film includes a scene in which an intoxicated gang of hoodlums severely beats up a bartender in a tunnel, very similar to what Alex and his droogs do in an early scene in the classic Kubrick film. Women with alcoholism are portrayed in *Rain* (2001, New Zealand) and *Walking on Water* (2002, Australia).

Gervaise (1956, France) is a fairly depressing film based on an Emile Zola novel about the deterioration of individuals and families as a result of alcohol addiction. Gervaise is a young, beautiful, and lame laundress who is left by her lover, Lantier, with their two boys. She then marries Coupeau, a roofer. Shortly thereafter, Coupeau falls off a roof, and although he recovers he is too fearful and lazy to return to work so he avoids work and turns to drinking full-time. His alcohol dependence threatens Gervaise, potentially ruining both their relationship and the new laundering business she has opened. He drinks day and night, prioritizes drinking over all other activities, becomes angry at any attempts to get him to slow down, makes poor decisions, displays a disregard for his children and the impact of his behavior on them, and he begins to treat Gervaise badly. He invites her former husband, Lantier, to join them at a special event party and then to live in their already-crowded home. Coupeau, in a fit of alcohol rage, ends up physically destroying the home and Gervaise's business. He later dies from alcoholism, but not before he has destroyed the family. In the final scene, the kind and gentle Gervaise is shown sitting haggard in the middle of the day at a pub, unkempt, unresponsive, and drunk for the first time in her life, paying no attention to her nearby daughter who is filthy and starving.

Gambling disorder is depicted in a number of international films. For example, the protagonist, Fugui, in *To Live* (1994, Hong Kong/China) is addicted to gambling and, chasing his losses, he loses everything. His family goes through major ups and downs and many of their hardships are due to his gambling disorder.

The movie *2046* (2004, China) is Kar Wai Wong's portrayal of pathological, or at least excessive, gambling in which the protagonist loses most of his money playing cards. As is typical with many addicts, the gambler in this film is addicted to both card playing and sex.

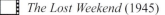

Critical Thinking Questions

➤ Can a case be made for the prohibition of alcohol and tobacco, or is this simply a societal experiment that has already been tried without success? On the other hand, would the legalization of some drugs lead to a decrease in drug addiction?

➤ What are the advantages and disadvantages of the 12-step approach?

➤ Compare the number of films depicting a character using only one substance with those depicting a character using multiple agents. Which is most likely to be a solitary addiction?

➤ Compare the social treatment of persons addicted to legal substances (alcohol, nicotine) with those addicted to illegal agents (cocaine, heroin, marijuana).

➤ What role, if any, did heroin play in Ray Charles's success? Were there any other addictions evident in the film *Ray* (2004)?

➤ Should intoxication from alcohol and drugs be a mitigating factor in sentencing prisoners for crimes they committed while high (e.g., murder in *Dead Man Walking* [1995])?

➤ How important is it for therapists treating alcoholism and drug abuse to have been in treatment for these problems themselves? Can a nonaddict ever truly understand the needs and problems of the addict?

➤ What are the arguments for and against the legalization of drugs in the United States?

➤ How many places do you suppose there are in the world similar to the park in *MacArthur Park* (2001)? Does every major city have such a place?

➤ Whom do you find to be the most sympathetic character in *Requiem for a Dream* (2000)? Does your choice change at different points of the film?

➤ Do most methamphetamine addicts behave in ways similar to the characters in *Spun* (2002)?

➤ What is the difference between "recovered" and "recovering" in addiction terminology?

➤ If an individual has one definite addiction, how likely are they to have a second addiction?

➤ What is the relationship between drugs and violence? Which drugs have the highest incidence of aggressive behavior? Identify films that support your answer.

If you have time to read just one book relevant to this chapter, make it:

 Jacobs-Stewart, T. (2010). *Mindfulness and the 12 steps: Living recovery in the present moment*. Center City, MN: Hazelden Foundation.

If you only have time for one article, read:

Degenhardt, L., Whiteford, H. A., Ferrari, A. J., Baxter, A. J., Charlson, F. J., Hall, W. D., ... Vos, T. (2013). Global burden of disease attributable to illicit drug use and dependence: Findings from the Global Burden of Disease Study 2010. *The Lancet, 382*(9904), 1564–1574. doi: 10.1016/S0140-6736(13)61530-5

Wedding and Niemiec's Top Substance-Related and Addictive Disorders Films

Substance Use Disorders

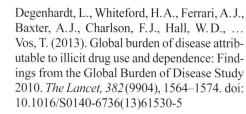

- *The Lost Weekend* (1945)
- *Days of Wine and Roses* (1962)
- *Leaving Las Vegas* (1995)
- *Crazy Heart* (2008)
- *Flight* (2012)
- *Clean and Sober* (1988)
- *Spun* (2002)
- *Requiem for a Dream* (2000)
- *Ray* (2004)
- *Long Day's Journey into Night* (1962)

Non-Substance-Related Disorders

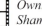

- *Owning Mahowny* (2002)
- *Shame* (2011)

Chapter 12

Neurocognitive Disorders

I have no short-term memory. I know who I am. I know all about myself. I just – since my injury I can't make new memories. Everything fades.

If we talk for too long I'll forget how we started and the next time I see you I'm not gonna remember this conversation. I don't even know if I've met you before. So if I seem strange or rude or something ... I've told you this before, haven't I?

Leonard Shelby in *Memento* (2000)

Patient Evaluation

Name: Leonard Shelby

Patient's stated reason for coming
"I need you to help me find out who killed my wife. I was told you could help me. Teddy sent me." (Patient stated this as he referred to notes on a crumpled piece of paper taken from his pocket).

History of the present illness
Mr. Leonard Shelby is a 29-year-old White male who suffered a severe head injury 3 years ago. He experienced a severe concussion on the left side of his head as he fought with an intruder who broke into his home, raped his wife, and tried to suffocate her. As a result, Mr. Shelby suffers from severe anterograde amnesia, a memory dysfunction that prevents him from converting short-term to long-term memory.

Past psychiatric illness, treatment, and outcomes
According to the available medical records, Mr. Shelby has lived "off and on" at the neuropsychiatric unit of a hospital for the last 2 years. He has also been placed in group care facilities on two occasions but left both times within a month. He also escaped from the hospital; each time he has fled, it has been "to find out who killed my wife and get revenge." The year immediately after the injury, this patient lived with his wife as they tried to cope with the wife's rape trauma and adapt to Mr. Shelby's head injury. Records indicate Mr. Shelby has killed at least three people, two of whom he believed had raped his wife.

Medical history
Medical records indicate Mr. Shelby has been prescribed several types of antidepressant and mood stabilizing medications; however, he is noncompliant with all medications whenever he is away from the hospital.

Psychosocial history
Mr. Shelby had been married for 8 years when his wife died. Medical records indicate Mr. Shelby killed his wife by giving her an overdose of insulin. Apparently, his wife was skeptical of his anterograde amnesia diagnosis and decided to "test" his short-term memory loss. She tested his memory by asking him to give her insulin shots repeatedly, thinking this extreme and life-threatening situation would force him to admit he was "faking." However, he was not faking, and his wife went into insulin shock and coma, from which she never recovered.

Mr. Shelby graduated from college with an undergraduate degree in finance. He does not have any children, and he is not currently in a relationship. He has been unemployed since his injury. For 8 years prior to the injury, he worked as an insurance claims investigator. He states he enjoyed this work and found it very fulfilling. He began to tell a story about a client he once worked with named Sammy Jenkins; he told parts of this story on three separate occasions during the interview. It may be significant that he has "Remember Sammy Jenkins" tattooed on his left arm.

Drug and alcohol history
There is no significant history of drug or alcohol abuse.

Behavioral observations
Mr. Shelby was 15 minutes late for the interview. He wore a sport coat and slacks that appeared unwashed. Interestingly, he took a photograph of the interviewer upon walking into the examination room, saying, "it's so I can remember you," as he wrote down the interviewer's first name and the words "Teddy recommended: Shrink" on the photograph.

Mr. Shelby used numerous compensatory strategies to assist his memory during this interview, including note cards, handwritten pieces of paper, photographs of people with names and notes written on them, and his own tattoos. The last, he stated, are for "vital information." He often repeated, "You really do need a system if you're gonna make it work." On two occasions, he began to take off his jacket and shirt to read the tattoos on his chest but the interviewer stopped him and encouraged him to read them later. Frequently, the pieces of paper oriented him to where he was and why he was being examined. He asked himself numerous questions, and he repeated many statements at different points during the interview. This pattern of repetition occurs every 10–15 minutes.

Mental status examination
Mr. Shelby was suspicious and guarded during the evaluation. Mood and affect were labile, quickly shifting from agitation to dysphoria. Anxiety was evident after some questions when the patient appeared to have lost his memory; when this occurred, he would fumble with his photographs and notes, or attempt to read his body tattoos. There was no evidence of flight of ideas, hallucinations, or delusions. There was no significant suicidal or homicidal ideation present, although the latter is a significant concern due to his history. Short-term memory is extremely limited. Anxiety and agitation exacerbate this patient's memory problems.

Mr. Shelby was oriented to person. He was not oriented to place, time, or situation. However, he was able to figure out each with the help of compensatory strategies. He showed the interviewer some of his notes and writings. Many were phrases and random thoughts, tasks to do, and ideas. The purpose of these notes is multifold: First, they serve as a compensatory strategy to help him stay "on track" long enough to complete tasks; secondly, they help him remember important past events and people, and third, they coach him along through his difficulties. He forgot my name several times during the interview, but as we concluded, he quickly referred to his photograph of me, mentioned my name, and smiled. Mr. Shelby was given the Mini-Mental State Examination twice, the first time without the use of notes and the second time with notes. He scored a 15/30 and a 23/30, respectively. Without the use of compensatory strategies, Mr. Shelby struggled with orientation, memory recall, and serial sevens. He was able to following simple commands, name objects in the room, write a sentence, and copy a complex drawing. When using compensatory strategies on the second examination, his notes helped him remember the date and place.

Functional assessment
Mr. Shelby has almost no ability to convert short-term memory to long-term memory. This has a severe and serious impact on every activity in his life. He has difficulty taking care of himself, and he needs to be reminded to eat meals, change his clothes, and perform other activities of daily living. His injury prevents him from working or going to school and limits his ability to maintain new relationships. Mr. Shelby does not have insight into his actions, speech, emotions, or thoughts, as he forgets them within 15 minutes.

Strengths
Mr. Shelby is creative, spontaneous, and intelligent. His personality is energetic, engaged, and interesting. He is disciplined and systematic in the organization of compensatory memory strategies. He is highly motivated, and perhaps this motivation can be channeled in prosocial directions. He is aware of his condition and appears to know that he suffers from a problem with the consolidation of memories. On the VIA Survey, a measure of character strengths, Mr. Shelby's highest strengths were perseverance, self-regulation, creativity, love, and fairness.

Diagnosis

Diffuse traumatic brain injury with loss of consciousness of unspecified duration, sequel (S06.2X9S); major neurocognitive disorder due to traumatic brain injury, with behavioral disturbance (F02.81).

Treatment plan

Mr. Shelby should be monitored closely on the neuropsychiatric unit. In addition, his notes, writings, and photographs should be reviewed frequently due to the high homicide risk that appears to rise quickly and for no obvious reason. A complete neuropsychological evaluation is recommended with periodic follow-up testing to assess changes in functional ability, and especially memory. An occupational therapist should also be consulted so the patient can be trained in additional compensatory strategies, particularly ones involving activities of daily living.

Prognosis

Poor.

Memento, Memory, and Viewer Empathy

Memento (2000) is a psychological thriller that centers on the life of Leonard Shelby (Guy Pearce), a man with anterograde amnesia that makes it impossible for him to transfer new experiences into long-term memory. The movie chronicles the psychological and social complications associated with this memory disorder, as well as this man's efforts to get revenge for past offences against himself and his wife. This is the second film of director Christopher Nolan (see also *Insomnia* (2002) and *Following* (1998), discussed in Chapters 8 and 14, respectively), who amazingly created this incredibly complex film in 25.5 days.

Memento is a cleverly edited film that begins at the end of the story and works backward: The color portions of the film progress backward in approximately 10-min segments, and these clips are juxtaposed with black-and-white clips that move forward in time.

Leonard has lost his wife and is struggling to avenge her loss by finding the killer. He does not remember that he is the person who killed her when she "tested" his amnesia by having him administer repeated doses of insulin until she went into shock and coma, and subsequently died. Leonard actually believes that Sammy Jenkins injected the insulin. Leonard also believes that Sammy Jenkins was malingering (with anterograde amnesia) when Leonard was a claims investigator. Leonard fuses his story with Sammy's and distorts reality. The film

cleverly gives the viewer clues to the truth that Leonard is both denying and forgetting. For example, in one scene, one frame of Leonard is superimposed on the character of Sammy Jenkins, and it is unclear who is actually in the hospital. Another example involves a flashback at the end of the film (the beginning of the story) of Leonard and his wife lying in bed together; the camera focuses briefly on the words "I've Done It" tattooed on his chest, as if to give the viewer one final piece of direct evidence.

The film does a brilliant job of depicting the suffering of someone with a memory disorder, and illustrates the painstaking discipline and detail-oriented approach necessary for someone to cope with such a disorder using compensatory strategies (e.g., tattoos and Polaroid photographs of people and places). Leonard's use of tattoos to record key facts in his life is illustrated in Figure 21.

As if Leonard is not facing enough as a man who has lost the ability to consolidate memories, he must also cope with others determined to take advantage of his illness, manipulating and lying to him. Ultimately, he has no one he can rely on or trust, including himself, as those who appear to help only "use" him (e.g., for drug deals, for murderous revenge, or to make some extra money, all at his expense). Eventually, he is confronted with a harrowing truth. A corrupt police officer, Teddy, tells him: "You don't want the truth ... you create your own truth." The viewer eventually comes to realize that Leonard has not known the truth from the beginning, and he is preparing to kill an innocent man.

Perhaps the most remarkable aspect of this film is its ability to force the viewer to experience the world as someone with anterograde amnesia experiences it. The viewer experiences the protagonist's struggles, distortions, lapses, questions, and emotions as he or she tries to put together the scenes going backward while making sense of the juxtaposed black-and-white scenes that are going forward. The viewer is constantly reevaluating and rethinking what has just been seen. The film demands both strong concentration and memory from the viewer, who almost immediately begins to appreciate the majesty of something most of us take for granted: the ability to convert new information into long-term memory. The viewer experiences the protagonist's confusion, as he or she tries to decide who is manipulating whom, and feels what the amnestic patient feels when trying to sort through conflicting distortions of time, place, person, and situation. The viewer questions his or her own memory, and must also adopt some cognitive strategy to keep all of the confusing aspects of the film straight. The viewer also begins to lose trust in the film's characters, particularly the "unreliable narrator" (Leonard) who comes by the role honestly due to his anterograde amnesia.

This film's complexity extends further to address existential themes about our search for meaning, the loss of identity, finding and operating out of the "shadow," the role of truth and lies (both to oneself and to others), the problem of coping with a cognitive disorder, and the ubiquitous power of denial.

Neurocognitive Disorders

This chapter describes conditions that result in a significant deficit in cognition or memory and consequently have an impact on the individual's ability to function normally. Neurocognitive disorders are unique in the *DSM-5* because the underlying pathology is almost always known, and the etiology of the disorder can usually be established (e.g., stroke, trauma, Alzheimer's disease). These disorders are always acquired rather than developmental, and they represent a decline from previous level of functioning.

Figure 21. *Memento* (2000, Newmarket Films, Team Todd). Produced by Jennifer Todd and Suzanne Todd. Directed by Christopher Nolan.

Neurocognitive disorders result in impairment in one or more of six cognitive domains: complex attention, executive functioning, learning and memory, language, perceptual-motor abilities, or social cognition. A deficit in **complex attention** might result in an individual who experiences significant distress in situations in which there are competing stimuli (e.g., multiple conversations occurring at the same time a television is playing). A person with deficits in **executive functioning** might need help in planning the day's activities or focusing on more than one task at a time. Deficits in **learning and memory** are clearly apparent in *Memento*; other examples might include repeating oneself often and or experiencing difficulty recalling three or four items after a brief delay on a mental status examination. Deficits in the **language** domain can be either expressive or receptive; patients with difficulties in this domain may use vague language and be unable to remember the names of celebrities, casual friends, or common household objects. Problems in the **perceptual-motor** domain result in difficulties navigating in unfamiliar territory, and difficulty using tools or driving a car. Perceptual-motor defects may worsen at sunset ("sundowning"). Finally, examples of problems in the **social cognition** domain include inappropriate social behavior (e.g., sexually touching the breast or leg of a nurse) or wandering in a cold, winter environment without proper clothing.

Neurocognitive disorders are first classified as major or mild; after that, specific codes are provided to indicate the presumed or known etiology of the disorder (e.g., major neurocognitive disorder due to Alzheimer's disease). The *DSM-5* recommends that deficits be documented by standardized neuropsychological testing whenever possible.

The overall prevalence for major cognitive disturbance is estimated to be 1%–2% at age 65 and as high as 30% by age 85. The overall prevalence for mild cognitive disturbance is 2%–10% at age 65 and 5%–25% by age 85. The *DSM-5* categorization of mild cognitive disturbance has been widely criticized because it pathologizes what many consider to be normal cognitive changes that accompany aging. Writing about the medicalization of ordinary life, Alan Francis notes:

In the early 1980s, about a third of Americans qualified for a lifetime diagnosis of mental disorder. Now about half do. … Some people think these are underestimates – more carefully done prospective studies actually double the lifetime prevalence. If you believe the results, our population is almost totally saturated with mental disorders. (Francis, 2013, p. 104)

Dementia

The term **dementia** refers to a collection of brain disorders characterized by memory disturbance, impaired judgment, and personality change. Insidious onset and gradual deterioration of cognitive abilities characterize the dementias. Although some authorities believe the term should be applied only to those conditions that are nonreversible, the more common practice to use the term descriptively, without any implications for prognosis. Hence, brain dysfunctions from causes as diverse as nutritional deficiencies and Cushing's syndrome can be diagnosed as dementias.

Dementia can be caused by any number of medical conditions, or they can be substance induced. Some of the more commonly known medical causes are cerebrovascular disease, head trauma, Parkinson's disease, HIV infection, Huntington's disease, frontotemporal lobar degeneration, and Creutzfeldt-Jakob disease. *Awakenings* (1990) offers excellent demonstrations of dementia and catatonia due to Parkinson's disease. The film is based on the experience of neurologist Oliver Sacks, best known as the author of *The Man Who Mistook His Wife for a Hat*.

The single leading cause of dementia is **Alzheimer's disease**, responsible for at least 60% of all cases of dementia. Alzheimer's is a public health problem of enormous dimensions, and one that is becoming an increasing problem as the average life span steadily increases. Advances in medical science and public health have resulted in dramatically longer lifespans around the world; unfortunately, for many of us our bodies will outlive our minds

The brains of patients with Alzheimer's disease are demonstrably different from those of age-matched controls, and they contain **senile plaques** and **neurofibrillary tangles.** Although some neuronal loss is universal with aging, the brain of the Alzheimer's patient shrinks at a more rapid rate. Psychological tests are often the best indicators of the presence of Alzheimer's disease, especially in the early stages, as these patients will often maintain excellent social skills and use these skills to disguise the marked problems they develop with their memory. Other early signs of the insidious onset of Alzheimer's disease include diffuse generalized anxiety and inappropriate social behavior. An official diagnosis of Alzheimer's cannot be made until after the individual has died and an autopsy has been performed.

The Alzheimer's Project (The Memory Loss Tapes) (2009) is a poignant and important documentary that integrates education with seven vignettes of individuals at various stages of Alzheimer's disease, along with their families. The vignettes help the viewer appreciate the variability in presentation and the extent of the degeneration caused by the disease. The film addresses both the suffering caused by Alzheimer's and challenges for the caregiver, including adult–child role reversal, wandering, loss of independence, and the grieving process.

Sunset Blvd. (1950) offers a classic portrayal of the lack of insight, confusion, and delusions that accompanied the dementia of an aging movie star. *The Iron Lady* (2011) is a biopic about the life of Margaret Thatcher; the sections of the film most relevant to this book show her as an elderly and demented woman having imaginary conversations with her deceased husband, Denis, played by Jim Broadbent. Jeffrey Tambor plays a demented client cheated by his attorney (Paul Giamatti) in *Win Win* (2011). Frank Langella plays Frank, a retired jewel thief with early dementia, in *Robot & Frank* (2012); Frank's son buys a robot to take care of his father, but this purchase has unforeseen consequences. *Quartet* (2012), directed by Dustin Hoffman, is a charming film about life in a home for retired musicians. Some of the residents appear to have mild dementia.

> "She was the greatest of them all. You wouldn't know, you're too young. In one week she received 17,000 fan letters. Men bribed her hairdresser to get a lock of her hair. There was a maharajah who came all the way from India to beg one of her silk stockings. Later he strangled himself with it!"
>
> Max Von Mayerling commenting on the life of Norma Desmond, a washed out movie star in *Sunset Blvd.* (1950)

Paul Giamatti portrays Barney Panofsky, a small-time television producer in *Barney's Version* (2010). Barney would likely be diagnosed with substance-induced neurocognitive disorder. There seems to be a clear relationship between Barney's alcohol dependence and not only his languishing life and poor relationship skills, but also his memory. At first, he displays subtle forgetfulness for something he should have remembered, but he soon begins to deteriorate into what is clearly a progressive dementia.

Iris

Iris Murdoch was one of the greatest writers and thinkers of the 20th century. She wrote 26 novels, six philosophical works, and several plays. The content and purpose of her intricate works can be simplified in one phrase: She wanted to teach humans how to be free and how to be good. Murdoch was a deep, complex, and gifted thinker. It is bitterly ironic to see such a brilliant and well-used brain deteriorate with dementia, as we observe in the film *Iris* (2001).

Some of the early signs of Iris' major cognitive disorder (i.e., dementia) are indicated in her experiences of memory loss – she would forget what she had just said and frequently repeat herself. She then began to talk to herself, exhibit blank stares and flat affect, display further language disturbance (i.e., babbling), and lose her ability to care for herself. Her writing, which had always flowed easily and extensively, came to be constricted and limited, and she would frequently sit at a table with blank pages in front of her. She stopped cleaning her house or caring about her appearance. The film depicts the development of increasingly serious symptoms, and shows Iris (Judi Dench) in serious danger on several occasions, e.g., jumping out of a moving car, trying to control the steering wheel when on the passenger side, and leaving her house to wander in the middle of traffic. The viewer sees Iris slowly retreat into a world of her own; at first, it is for brief periods and she comes back to reality, but she experiences increasingly longer periods of isolation and quiet. She does emerge from her world at times to say, "I love you," to her husband in powerful cinematic moments.

The film *Iris* also speaks deeply to the challenges and responses of the caretaker of someone with Alzheimer's. John Bayley (Jim Broadbent), Iris's loving husband, joins Iris in denying her disease at first, saying, "she disappears into a mystery world … [but] she always comes back." As he continues to watch his wife display more serious symptoms, his emotions catch up with him, and he screams out in anger. Several scenes show John Bayley deep in despair as he sits alone, helpless to do anything to stop the disease. He sadly repeats the phrase: "Love will soon be over." It is fascinating to watch him experience predictable stages of grief: denial, anger, questioning/challenging, sadness, and finally acceptance when he takes Iris to a nursing home.

"She's in her own world now,
perhaps that's what she always wanted."

John Bayley on his wife's illness in
Iris (2001)

Love and Dementia

Two other memorable films have portrayed husbands coping with their wives' dementia: Sarah Polley's *Away from Her* (2006) and Nick Cassavetes' *The Notebook* (2004). The first film portrays an Ontario couple who have been married for 44 years; the wife, Fiona (Julie Christie), is becoming increasingly forgetful, and she and her husband Grant (Gordon Pinsent) are acutely aware that whatever is happening, it is something far more serious than benign senescent forgetfulness. In addition to her forgetfulness, Fiona finds herself engaging in seemingly irrational behavior (e.g., putting a frying pan into the freezer after it is washed, being unable to retrieve the word *wine*). She realizes that she needs nursing home care, and she does not want to be a burden on her husband. The husband, a college English professor guilty about his history of infidelity during the marriage, eventually capitulates to this plan, agreeing that his wife needs to be in a setting in which she can confront her illness "with a little bit of grace." When Grant takes Fiona to the nursing home, he accompanies her to her room and they have sex ("I'd like to make love, and then I'd like you to go. Because I need to stay here and if you

make it hard for me, I may cry so hard I'll never stop.") No visitors are allowed for the first 30 days of residency in the nursing home, allegedly to facilitate the new resident's adjustment. (Visitor restriction is very unlikely in any nursing home.) During this time Fiona becomes romantically, albeit not sexually, involved with another resident in the facility. Part of the cinematic tension in the film involves the fact that it is never entirely clear whether Fiona's interest in Aubrey, the other resident, is simply due to her lost memories of her marriage and husband or a willful way to get back at Grant because of his history of extramarital affairs with his students. The film is also remarkable for the persistence and unconditional love of Grant – not dissimilar from John Bayley's – in visiting Fiona regularly despite her obvious intimate involvement with another man.

The Notebook (2004) stars Gena Rowlands and James Garner as a married couple coping with the wife's dementia. Allie Calhoun (Gena Rowlands) is in a nursing home; her husband (Duke) has moved in with her and spends each day reading to her out of a notebook. We later learn that she has written the story of their romance and life together so that she can continue to relive it even as her illness progresses. A series of flashbacks is used to tell the story of their initial love affair, separation, and eventual reunion. The film is sentimental and unduly romanticizes Alzheimer's, but at the same time it illustrates the dramatic loss of memory that is one of the defining features of the disease.

The Savages

Laura Linney and Philip Seymour Hoffman play a brother and sister confronting the dilemma of caring for an aging, demented father in *The Savages* (2007). The two siblings have never been close to their father, but when his girlfriend dies, decisions about his care are foisted upon them. They are initially notified of their father's condition when he begins writing on the wall with his own excrement; for many demented individuals, loss of bowel and bladder control become powerful metaphors for the loss of self associated with diseases like Alzheimer's. The movie illustrates how depressing some nursing homes can be – even very expensive ones

"People are dying, Wendy! Right inside that beautiful building right now, it's a fucking horror show! And all this wellness propaganda and the landscaping, it's just there to obscure the miserable fact that people die! And death is gaseous and gruesome and it's filled with shit and piss and rotten stink!"

Jon Savage confronting his sister in
The Savages (2007)

– and it provides a compelling example of the stress associated with the decisions children often must make when a parent develops dementia.

The tempo of life in a nursing home is captured in *Assisted Living* (2003), a pseudodocumentary filmed with real residents of a real nursing home in Kentucky. In one scene, Todd, an underequipped, pot-smoking orderly, amuses himself by pretending to be God on phone calls with a resident. Despite Todd's antics, it is also clear that he cares about many of the residents, and he goes out of his way to help one of the residents who is quickly deteriorating with Alzheimer's.

Dementia versus Depression

One of the most important tasks confronting clinicians working with older patients is the difficult discrimination between dementia and **clinical depression**. Appropriate diagnosis is critical in these cases so that a depressed patient will not go untreated because he or she is inappropriately believed to be suffering from Alzheimer's disease. In the majority of cases, the two disorders will present in ways that are different enough for the alert clinician to distinguish between them. For example, Alzheimer's has a more insidious onset, whereas depression may come on more rapidly. The patient with Alzheimer's will always have genuine cognitive deficits and experience difficulty with learning new tasks. The depressed patient will lack motivation and may have trouble concentrating but should be able to learn adequately, although slowly. The depressed patient is also more likely to experience loss of appetite and a fluctuating course, and he or she is far

more likely to have a history of affective illness. In addition, depressed patients tend to acknowledge and sometimes even exaggerate their problems. In contrast, patients with Alzheimer's are far more likely to cover up their difficulties, deny that they are having problems, and may be euphoric. Finally, in the later stages of the illness, patients with true dementias will often have abnormal brain images and electroencephalograms (EEGs).

Another important film portraying Alzheimer's disease is a made-for-TV movie, *Do You Remember Love?* (1985), in which Joanne Woodward plays a college professor who develops Alzheimer's disease. Woodward's portrayal is sensitive and moving. There is also a memorable scene between Jane Fonda's character and her mother in *Agnes of God* (1985). Fonda plays Dr. Martha Livingston, a psychiatrist who goes to visit her mother in a nursing home. The scene opens with the mother watching a children's cartoon program. The disoriented mother gets Martha confused with her younger sister, who had died years earlier in a convent.

Jessica Tandy very convincingly portrays an old woman who eventually develops Alzheimer's disease and is placed in a nursing home in *Driving Miss Daisy* (1989). Tandy won an Academy Award for her performance in this film.

Delirium

Delirium refers to the rapid onset of confusion and disorganized thinking (a "clouding" of cognition) and is often characterized by rambling, incoherent, or inappropriate speech. Emotions are often inappropriate as well; for example, the delirious individual may be extremely anxious or euphoric in situations in which these reactions would be inappropriate. Delirium can also cause illusions, hallucinations, or misinterpretations of sensory stimuli; for example, a doctor's look of concern may be perceived as extreme anger by the delirious patient. Most films depicting dementia will show some examples of delirium as well (e.g., *Iris*).

Using the *International Statistical Classification of Diseases and Related Health Problems* (ICD-10; World Health Organization, 1992), clinicians would code for substances that might be responsible for a patient's delirium, and they would indicate with the code whether or not the disorder was mild, moderate, or severe. The prevalence of delirium is highest in hospitalized, older individuals; the disorder will occur in as many as 60% of individuals in nursing homes and in up to 83% of all individuals will experience delirium at the end of their life.

Delirium most often (but not always) results from a disturbance of the metabolism of the brain, and causes can include infections, insufficient oxygen levels, ionic imbalances, vitamin deficiencies, and kidney disease. One common cause of delirium is either acute intoxication with – or withdrawal from – drugs. **Delirium tremens** is a common problem for alcoholics with a history of problem drinking. Patients experiencing the "DTs" become disoriented, hallucinate, and display marked tremors. Other symptoms may include intense fear, fevers, and sweating. The intensity of delirium tremens is vividly portrayed in Billy Wilder's film, *The Lost Weekend* (1945), and in Nicholas Cage's character in *Leaving Las Vegas* (1995).

Amnesia

Patients with amnesia display marked impairment of short-term memory with relatively intact long-term memory and preserved intellectual functioning. In its extreme form, the disorder results in the total inability to learn new information. A patient with an amnestic syndrome will be unable to recall a doctor's name, no matter how many times it is presented; simple learning tasks such as recalling the names of four objects become virtually impossible. The patient will be able to *repeat* the four items, suggesting intact understanding of the task and good receptive and expressive language skills; however, after dozens of trials the patient will still be unable to recall the four items from memory.

Patients with amnestic syndromes will sometimes **confabulate** and present detailed and plausible explanations for their obvious inability to acquire new information. The patient who cannot remember four numbers for more than a few seconds will explain that he was never any good at math, and the patient in a psychiatric hospital may say he is there because of problems with his kidneys. One of our patients with an amnestic syn-

drome was asked four times during a 1-hour, taped interview what he had had for breakfast that morning. The patient responded by supplying four different "menus" during the interview, each equally plausible. On each occasion, he had absolutely no recollection of being asked this question earlier in the interview.

One of the most commonly encountered amnestic syndromes is **Wernicke-Korsakoff syndrome**. Patients with this disorder have great difficulty with new learning, fail to recall recent experiences, exhibit gait disturbances secondary to cerebellar dysfunction, and display a variety of ocular disturbances, including impaired conjugate gaze. This condition is found in older alcoholics after many years of substituting the nutritionally empty calories of alcohol for the protein, carbohydrates, vitamins, and fat found in a normal diet. The disorder is particularly related to deficiencies in thiamin (vitamin B_1), and some public health experts have recommended "enriching" spirits with vitamins in the same way we enrich bread. Although this could be done with minimal cost, the distillers have not been enthusiastic about this procedure, despite its potential benefit to alcoholics.

A number of films have portrayed characters with amnesia, including *Spellbound* (1945), *Mirage* (1955), *Anastasia* (1956), and *Desperately Seeking Susan* (1985). *Eternal Sunshine of the Spotless Mind* (2004) is about a man who attempts to have memories of his girlfriend, Clementine, erased (after discovering that she has done the same with *his* memories). As his memories begin to fade, he realizes he still loves Clementine and he attempts to subvert the process. The 1983 film *The Return of Martin Guerre* creatively explores the limits of memory and the extent to which it can be influenced by motivation and need. Dissociative amnesia (see Chapter 7) needs to be differentiated from amnesia caused by a substance or general medical condition (including head injuries).

Head Trauma

The link between head injuries, amnesia, and movies is very strong, and numerous films have been produced in which someone experiences head trauma and becomes amnestic to their past – they can start over from scratch, they can try to rediscover life with a deeper appreciation, other people can manipulate them, etc.

Although not given a separate rubric in the *DSM-5* nomenclature, it is common to see references to **dementia pugilistica** (punch-drunk syndrome) in the professional literature and in the medical charts of aging boxers. These patients, after a lifetime of repeated blows to the head (with concomitant brain injuries), often develop difficulty with movement and a tremor similar to that found in **Parkinson's disease**. They develop slurred speech and diminished mental agility, and they become especially sensitive to the effects of alcohol. Dramatic mood swings (referred to as **emotional lability**) are common, and these individuals are quick to become angry, engage in fights, and become paranoid. Many of these symptoms can be seen in Robert De Niro's portrayal of Jake LaMotta in *Raging Bull* (1980).

The repetitive head blows associated with boxing have been shown to cause brain injuries that may not be detected by MRI. There is evidence that microstructural damage exists in professional boxers when compared with an age- and sex-matched control group (Zhang et al., 2003).

"You don't understand! I could've had class. I could've been a contender. I could've been somebody, instead of a bum, which is what I am."

Terry Malloy (Marlon Brando) in
On the Waterfront (1954)

This problem is so serious that the American Medical Association and other professional organizations have called for the elimination of professional boxing as an organized sport. Indeed, it is hard to find redeeming social value in a sport in which the express purpose is to damage the brain of an opponent. However, boxing remains a popular American pastime, and this popularity is reflected in films such as *The Great White Hope* (1970), *The Harder They Fall* (1956), *The Joe Louis Story* (1953), *Kid Galahad* (1937/1962), *On the Waterfront* (1954), *Requiem for a Heavyweight* (1962), the ever popular *Rocky* films (1976, 1979, 1982, 1985, 1990, 2006), and many others.

When visualizing brain injuries, it is useful to remember that the cranium is a closed, solid container, and the brain is soft and consists of a jelly-like substance that moves inside the skull when the head is struck. The brain is actually quite fragile, albeit well protected by the skull and meninges (the three layers of protective covering that are found between the skull and brain).

Head injuries are usually classified as **concussions, contusions,** or **open-head injuries**. Concussions occur when the brain is jarred, and amnesia and loss of consciousness are common consequences. Impaired memory and concentration, headaches, fatigue, anxiety, dizziness, and irritability characterize the postconcussion syndrome. Contusions occur when the brain is actually bruised, most often because of an impact between the brain and the skull. Contusions produce more serious neurological consequences than concussions and can result in death. Contusions are characterized as **coup injuries** if the damage is at the site of impact (e.g., at the point where a baseball bat hits the skull). **Contrecoup injuries** occur opposite the point of impact. They most often result from acceleration injuries (such as occur when a moving head hits a stationary steering wheel). Open-head injuries occur when the skull is hit with sufficient force to open it and expose the underlying neural tissue. Open-head injuries from missile wounds are common in wartime, and much of what we know about the organization of the brain is the result of examination of soldiers injured in battle.

The effects of head injuries often become apparent only hours or days after the initial injury. This occurred in the case of actress Natasha Richardson, daughter of Vanessa Redgrave and wife of Liam Neeson. Richardson died 2 days after suffering a head injury as a result of a skiing accident during a Quebec holiday. Paramedics at the scene were turned away because the actress reported that she felt fine and was in no distress.

The Vow (2012) depicts amnesia following a head injury from a car accident that had left the protagonist, Paige (Rachel McAdams), in a coma. Paige is unable to remember anything after a certain point in her past (i.e., around the time she moved to New York City and later met her future husband) up to the day of her injury. She is able to successfully recall everything prior to that point in time (e.g., high school friends and sweethearts, family interactions), and she is able to create new memories. This is based on a true story in which the woman was never able to regain the particular memories she lost. The film emphasizes the strengths of love and perseverance as her husband, Leo, works hard to support her and help her remember him.

Raging Bull

Raging Bull (1980) is a Martin Scorsese film starring Robert De Niro (who won an Academy Award for Best Actor for his role in this film), Cathy Moriarty, and Joe Pesci. This engrossing drama portrays the life of Jake LaMotta (De Niro), a prizefighter confronted with the need to find purpose and meaning in life once he leaves the ring. LaMotta's marriage fails, his wife takes their children with her, sexual jealousy drives a wedge between him and his brother, and he ultimately is forced to mutilate and then hock the jewels in the belt he re-

ceived for winning the world middleweight championship. The viewer is never certain whether La-Motta is a pathetic or a heroic figure, but the film ends with reconciliation between the two brothers and with the protagonist successfully performing a Broadway reading of the works of several notable authors. The recitation of one of Marlon Brando's monologues from *On the Waterfront* (a 1954 Elia Kazan film about the life of a down-and-out prizefighter) is Scorsese's way of paying homage to another great filmmaker and provides a dramatic conclusion for the film.

Raging Bull is replete with examples of La-Motta's poor judgment. Two especially vivid examples are his failure to defend himself in the final round of a fight with Sugar Ray Robinson (Johnny Barnes) and his decision to let two 14-year-old girls into his nightclub after each girl kisses him. Impaired judgment is common in aging prizefighters. It is also likely that LaMotta's history of repeated blows to the head (concussions) contributed to his sexual jealousy and paranoia and was responsible for the slurred speech he exhibits in the film as he ages.

Additional Questions for Discussion (*Raging Bull*)

➤ What actually happens to the brain of a fighter when he is "knocked out"? The American Academy of Neurology has supported a ban on professional boxing since 1983. Do you agree with this position?

➤ What are the characteristic features of chronic traumatic encephalopathy? What features of Robert De Niro's portrayal of Jake LaMotta suggest the disorder is present?

➤ Is the protective headgear used by amateur boxers effective in protecting against head injuries?

➤ In the film, LaMotta, as an old man, becomes sexually involved with two young girls. Is this an example of impaired judgment?

➤ LaMotta is incredibly jealous of his second wife, and he becomes convinced she is having multiple affairs. Is this paranoia the result of personality or cerebral impairment?

➤ What is the *Madonna–whore complex*? How is it illustrated in the life of Jake LaMotta?

Other Films Dealing with Head Trauma

In addition to *Memento* (2000), discussed in detail earlier in this chapter (see the section "*Memento*, Memory, and Viewer Empathy"), many films show characters who display serious neurological symptoms such as the amnesia that can result from a head injury. One of the best is David Lynch's challenging film *Mulholland Drive* (2001), which begins with an automobile accident. The amnestic female survivor, Rita (a name she took from a movie poster) finds refuge in the condominium of an aspiring Hollywood actress, Betty (Naomi Watts). The two women befriend each other and Betty takes a particular interest in helping Rita (Laura Harring) find answers to the questions regarding her identity. The already unique film takes a major surrealistic twist, and the viewer is left to either accept the events as they are portrayed or challenge them as illusions. Like Christopher Nolan in *Memento*, Lynch creates a rich atmosphere that allows the viewer to experience the confusion and discomfort of amnesia as he or she increasingly becomes disoriented to person, time, place, and situation. Lynch does not attempt to give answers or insights into amnesia but rather to depict the experience for a character and to give a particular experience to the viewer. It is the viewer who is challenged, like the amnestic character, to accept the film as an experience; this is perhaps more important than a pat explanation for what is happening in the film. This is reinforced at the film's conclusion (and final word) when a character on stage looks at the viewer and with a finger to her lips, says "Silencio."

In contrast to the unforgettable depiction of anterograde amnesia in *Memento*, *The Majestic* (2001) depicts retrograde amnesia. Jim Carrey plays disenfranchised screenwriter Peter Appleton, who, upon being accused of communist ties, goes for a drive away from his Hollywood home. His car topples over a bridge into a river and he subsequently develops retrograde amnesia after he hits his head on a rock in the river and is washed up on the shore of a small town. The townspeople mistake Peter for a former townsperson, Luke Trimble, who had gone to war many years ago, and the town proclaims Peter (now Luke) a hero, someone who had been lost for almost a decade after going to war. Not remembering his past, Luke identifies with many of the townspeople and rebuilds the local theater. He does not go through the pain, confusion, mental torture, and frustration that one would expect with retrograde amnesia. Instead, Luke readily accepts his new role and does not seriously challenge himself to figure out where he was over the previous 10 years. A theory of "double amnesia" is hypothesized, whereby he could have gone to war, experienced PTSD and memory loss, reestablished his life for years as a writer, and then, upon getting involved in an accident, experienced amnesia a second time.

Two 1991 films address the complexity of amnestic symptoms that result from head injuries: *Regarding Henry* and *Shattered*. *Regarding Henry* is a Mike Nichols film starring Harrison Ford as a high-powered attorney who suffers a major traumatic head injury. After coming out of a coma, he discovers that his life can never be the same. There are interesting scenes in a rehabilitation hospital, and the viewer gets some sense for the sequelae of a head injury. However, the film is flawed by an unrealistic presentation of the deficits following head injury and by the simplistic assumption that someone's personality could be *improved* by a head injury. In *Shattered*, an architect undergoes extensive reconstructive surgery of his face following an automobile accident. Amnesia symptoms mix with his memories (that may or may not be distorted) and the inconsistent stories relayed by various people in his life.

The Lookout (2007) presents the story of Chris Pratt (Joseph Gordon-Levitt), a talented and handsome high school hockey player who sustains a serious closed head injury after a car wreck that resulted from a school prank (drunk driving with the lights off on the night of the high school prom). The result of the injury is similar to that seen in *Memento,* in that Chris is unable to remember things for any extended period of time. As a result, he winds up as a bank's janitor, the only job he can handle. He displays classic signs of head injury, coping with these problems by repeating a kind of mantra for people with head injuries: "Ritual. Pattern. Repetition." One of the characteristics of head injuries is poor judgment, and the head-injured Chris Pratt displays extremely poor judgment as he gets caught up in plans to rob the bank at which he works. We also see his constant reliance on a notebook in which he frequently writes notes to himself, and he has put labels on almost everything in his apartment; these are actually valuable **compensatory strategies** (coping strategies) for people with head injuries. He also has problems with impulse control; for example, when meeting with his case worker, Chris blurts out "I want to fuck you." However, he is clearly acutely aware of his deficits, and at one point he notes, "I call tomatoes lemons, [but] I know it's not right."

Brain Tumors

Aberrant behavior and abnormal sensations and perceptions can result from brain tumors **(neoplasms)**. The specific behaviors that result will vary across individuals as a function of lesion site, size, type, and rate of growth. Brain tumors often, but not always, result in headaches and seizures. However, fewer than one out of a thousand people who have headaches will be found to also have a brain tumor.

An individual's premorbid personality will in part determine how he or she reacts to a brain tumor. About half of all patients with brain tumors first complain of psychiatric or behavioral symptoms, especially when the tumor involves the frontal or temporal lobes. Hallucinations, depression, apathy, euphoria, social impropriety, and personality change can all result from brain lesions.

Patients who have **frontal lobe lesions** are likely to display personality changes. They may be passive, apathetic, depressed, and slow to respond. Paradoxically, frontal lobe lesions also may result in irritability and problems with anger control. **Temporal lobe tumors** are often misdiagnosed as psychiatric disorders, and this is especially likely to occur in those cases that result in **psychomotor seizures**. These tumors can produce hallucinations, stereotyped movements, feelings of unreality, and intense fear. Reports of **déjà vu** (feeling you are reexperiencing a former experience) and **jamais vu** (feeling that familiar settings and situations are now very strange) are common with temporal lobe tumors. Patients with **parietal lobe lesions** often report abnormal sensory experiences (e.g., smelling burning rubber), may have difficulty with simple copying tasks, and may exhibit **anosognosia** (denial of illness). **Occipital lobe tumors** produce relatively few psychological symptoms, but these lesions may result in visual field defects.

Dark Victory (1939) stars Bette Davis as a 23-year-old socialite whose headaches and double-vision are eventually diagnosed as symptoms of a glioma by her physician, Dr. Frederick Stelle. Other symptoms include loss of feeling in her right hand, inability to distinguish objects by touch alone, and eventual blindness. The physician and patient fall in love, but he hides her diagnosis. Eventually she discovers she only has 6 months to live. *Dark Victory* is reported to be Bette Davis's favorite film; it was nominated for an Academy Award for Best Picture (then called "Outstanding Production"); however, it had formidable competition including *Mr. Smith Goes to Washington; Wuthering Heights; Stagecoach; Goodbye, Mr. Chips; The Wizard of Oz; Ninotchka; Of Mice and Men;* and *Gone with the Wind* (the winner).

In *The Bucket List* (2007), Morgan Freeman plays the role of Carter, a blue-collar mechanic with cancer that eventually becomes metastatic, spreads to his brain, and kills him. Before he dies, he develops a friendship with Edward, played by Jack Nicholson, and the two men share a series of adventures in which they collaboratively attempt to do everything on their "bucket lists" (things to do before you "kick the bucket"). Edward survives his cancer, lives to be 81, and has his ashes buried alongside Carter's at the top of the Himalayas.

Rhapsody in Blue (1945) is a biopic about the life of George Gershwin who died at the age of 38 from a glioblastoma multiforme. Gershwin's first symptom was passing out while playing the piano; other symptoms included blinding headaches and olfactory hallucinations (he complained about the acrid smell of burning rubber). In *The Green Mile* (1999), a film based on a novel by Stephen King, John Coffee (Michael Duncan) plays the role of a death row prisoner who is able to heal the prison warden's wife who has an inoperable brain tumor.

> "Brain cells. Why do healthy normal cells go berserk and grow wild? ... Nobody knows. But we call them cysts and gliomas and tumors and cancers. And we operate and hope to cure with a knife and half the time we don't even know the cause. Our patients have faith in us because we're doctors ... Someday, somebody will discover a serum that will be to these growths what insulin is to diabetes and anti-toxins to diptheria, and maybe earn his title of Doctor of Medicine."
>
> Dr. Frederick Steele describing his sense of professional impotence in *Dark Victory* (1939)

Stroke

A **cerebrovascular accident** (CVA), more commonly known as a stroke, occurs when there is inadequate supply of blood and oxygen to the brain. Strokes are characterized by sudden onset and are often fatal. Cerebrovascular disease is currently the third leading cause of death in the United States, following heart disease and cancer. Twenty individuals will experience CVAs for every one who develops a brain tumor.

Infarctions occur when arterial blood flow is blocked. This can occur when a piece of fat or cholesterol becomes lodged in a vessel. This sudden blockage of blood flow is called an **embolus.** Blood flow can also be impeded by the gradual buildup of **atherosclerotic plaque** along the inside of a vessel, resulting in a **thrombus.** Vessels sometimes burst, and the resulting cerebral hemorrhage can be life-threatening. Only about 20% of patients survive a cerebral hemorrhage. An **aneurysm** occurs when part of a vessel "balloons" and threatens to burst. Signs of a ruptured aneurysm include painful headaches, nausea, and vomiting.

Transient ischemic attacks (TIAs) are "ministrokes" that last for less than 24 hours. Many patients who experience TIAs will go on to have actual strokes. Other risk factors for CVAs include diabetes, heart disease, and the use of oral contraceptives in women who also smoke. The patient experiencing a TIA will become disoriented, confused, and sometimes amnestic.

In John Steinbeck's novel *The Grapes of Wrath,* Grandpa Joad dies from a stroke. We do not actually see the old man die in John Ford's film adaptation, *The Grapes of Wrath* (1940), but there is a memorable scene in which his relatives bury him alongside the road because they are too poor to do anything else. Tom Joad (Henry Fonda) writes a short, poignant note to leave at the grave: "This here is William James Joad, died of a stroke, old, old man. His folks buried him because they got no money to pay for funerals. Nobody kilt him. Just a stroke and he died."

David Lynch's *Blue Velvet* (1986) opens with a man watering his yard. As we watch, he has a stroke and falls to the ground. His dog comes over and proceeds to drink out of the hose, and at this point the viewer becomes aware that this will not be an ordinary movie.

Epilepsy

People with **epilepsy** experience uncontrollable attacks of abnormal neuronal activity. These brain "storms" can result from a variety of causes, and it is critical to remember that epilepsy is a *symptom* of a variety of brain disorders, not a disease in itself.

Head trauma is the most common cause of epilepsy, and about half of all penetrating head wounds will result in seizures. Prodromal symptoms and auras often precede seizures. **Prodromal symptoms** are "feelings" that a seizure is about to occur and usually appear several days before the seizure itself. In contrast, an **aura** signals the imminent arrival of a seizure and occurs only minutes before the seizure itself. Auras are often auditory or gustatory sensations.

Jacksonian seizures occur when there is a motoric response, such as twitching or jerking that is confined to one side of the body. A "Jacksonian march" results when minor motor movements in a finger or toe become more exaggerated and spread to other parts of the body on the affected side. If the initially isolated abnormal brain activity spreads to the other hemisphere, the entire body may stiffen or jerk; this attack is referred to as a **grand mal seizure.** Grand mal seizures typically last from 2 to 5 min and are sometimes referred to as **tonic-clonic** seizures because of their alternating periods of rigidity and jerking. In contrast, **petit mal seizures** (absence seizures), which are relatively common in young children, do not result in falling, jerking, or loss of muscle tone. The child experiencing a petit mal seizure will be, for a very brief period (usually 2–10 seconds), very unresponsive to the external environment.

Complex partial seizures (also referred to by the older terms *psychomotor* or *temporal lobe seizures*) are of considerable interest to anyone working in the field of mental health, because these disorders often mimic psychiatric diseases. The patient with complex partial seizures may hallucinate, engage in stereotyped motor behavior, experience feelings of unreality, or become extremely anxious. The sensations of déjà vu and jamais vu are often reported. The EEG is typically found to be normal in these patients, and about one in five will experience auditory or visual hallucinations. Unlike the hallucinations of the patient with schizophrenia, however, auditory hallucinations in the patient with a complex partial seizure will be localized within the head (rather than from an external source); and they will rarely contain bizarre, threatening, or accusatory material.

One of the world's leading experts on epilepsy was fond of relating a story about a patient who had a genuine seizure disorder that could be documented with electroencephalography. However, she only seized when she heard Mahalia Jackson singing "My Heart Has a Life of Its Own." The song could be sung by anyone else, and the patient would not seize. Likewise, she could listen to Mahalia Jackson sing anything else, and she would not experience seizures.

After several weeks in the hospital, someone asked the patient what was so special about Mahalia Jackson singing "My Heart Has a Life of Its Own."

"Didn't you know?" she replied. "That was the song they played at my mother's funeral as her casket was being lowered into her grave."

A character in independent auteur Hal Hartley's *Simple Men* (1992) suffers from epilepsy, and the diagnosis of temporal lobe epilepsy is made in *Happy Accidents* (2001) due to a character's petit mal seizures and heightened sense of emotion. Interestingly, the diagnosis is made by a psychologist who in addition to practicing outside of her competence loses additional credibility by stating that the man is delusional. The made-for-TV movie *First Do No Harm* (1997) stars Meryl Streep and depicts a young boy with a type of epilepsy where there is no known cause. The film explores particular types of diet in the treatment of epilepsy. The depiction of seizures in movies is fairly common and is portrayed for a variety of reasons: As a response to insulin-shock treatment in *A Beautiful Mind* (2001); electroconvulsive therapy (ECT) in *One Flew Over the Cuckoo's Nest* (1975); and brain surgery in *Molly* (1999).

International Films: Neurocognitive Disorders

The inspirational Argentinean film *Son of the Bride* (2002), which was nominated for an Academy Award for Best Foreign Film, follows a man too busy for his family until he suffers a heart attack. This brings him to reevaluate his life and his relationships, one of which is with his mother, who is suffering from Alzheimer's disease. He had always found his mother to be cynical, controlling, and demanding, and he managed this situation by distancing himself from her. He is inspired by his father who ritualistically and lovingly visits his wife every day, showing nothing but faithful love and devotion to her despite her rambling speech, distant stares, and frequent inability to recognize her family. This is a touching, realistic, and emotional portrayal of Alzheimer's disease and the family members' reactions and coping.

In the Finnish film *The Man Without a Past* (2002), a man is robbed and brutally beaten while sleeping outside. He suffers a severe head injury, and physicians pronounce him medically dead and walk out of the room; suddenly, the man wakes up, rises, and simply walks out of the hospital beyond the sight of staff. He has retrograde amnesia since the time of the injury and is forced to recreate his life. Although he is an outcast in society, he manages to cope with a greedy landlord, works at the Salvation Army, dates a woman, and finds a trusted companion in a dog and eventually a community. Pieces of memory return to him as he begins to find, reject, and come to terms with his past.

A Separation (2011, Iran) centers around marital tension. The film opens with a woman telling her husband that she has finally received her green card and wishes for the family to head to the United States to attain a much better life. Her husband insists he must stay in Iran to take care of his ailing father who suffers from Alzheimer's; he also insists on raising their daughter in Iran. While the film has several subplots, one of them involves the rigors and challenges of caretaking for a parent with dementia – the challenges of finding and maintaining a good caretaker, managing practical issues such as going to the bathroom, handling the logistics of busy work schedules within everyday life, attempting to block escapist behaviors of the person with Alzheimer's, and managing problems such as encopresis.

The sequelae of head injury secondary to a motor vehicle accident are portrayed in the French film *The Accidental Hero* (2002).

A Spanish film, *The City of No Limits* (2002), depicts a family patriarch (Max) who is dying of a brain tumor. Max displays paranoia and quirky behaviors. Medical doctors describe his psychological state as "verging on derangement." He stares at objects, carefully touches walls, speaks of video cameras watching him, calls a phone number that does not appear to exist, and tries to escape the hospital. He has a concerned and paranoid expression on his face, does not trust others, is constantly fearful, and is dishonest. Some of his comments appear random: "I'll never tell you where they are," and "Don't speak in front of them." He becomes preoccupied with escaping from the hospital to meet with someone named Rancel, wanting to warn him "before it is too late." He is not compliant with his medications. Though the viewer does not know his psychological condition prior to the brain tumor's onset, it is to be assumed most of these symptoms have emerged because of his tumor. Overall, Max's condition waxes and wanes: At times, Max is coherent and oriented; on other occasions, he confuses novels with reality. Important family secrets are uncovered due to Max's seemingly random and ridiculous comments.

The Belgian film *The Memory of a Killer* (2003) portrays a hit man in the early stages of Alzheimer's. He is repelled by his last assignment – he has been told to kill a 12-year-old girl forced into prostitution by her father – and he knows that his increasing forgetfulness puts him at great risk. The protagonist is all too familiar with the progression of Alzheimer's because he regularly visits his older brother who has the same disease.

Bille August, the Danish director of the heart-wrenching *Pelle the Conqueror* (1987), turned to the tragedy of Alzheimer's disease with the film *A Song for Martin* (2002). The film depicts the life story of a composer, Martin, who falls in love with his first violinist. The two divorce their spouses to be together, and the relationship is fairly idyllic until Martin begins to show early signs of forgetfulness, and eventually it becomes clear that he is the victim of a dementing illness. The film provides an excellent illustration of the demands Alzheimer's disease can place on a caregiver. Film critic Shelley Cameron called this film "one of the most moving portraits of human relationships ever chronicled."

A powerful, haunting Japanese film, *The Ballad of Narayama* (1983), deals with the village practice of taking old people to the top of a mountain on their 70th birthday where they are left to die. As the US population ages, nursing homes are increasingly serving as our own mountain top.

Amour

Amour (2012, France) is a remarkable film directed by Michael Haneke, and it presents one of the most compelling illustrations of dementia in film history. This movie is about the life and love of Georges and Anne, two retired music teachers sharing a good life in Paris. They are both in their 80s, and they have an adult daughter who occasionally visits. Their life begins to change dramatically after Anne experiences a minor stroke one morning during breakfast; this event marks the beginning of the end of their long and happy life together. The film documents mature love between a man and his wife, but it also illustrates the stress and tension associated with care-giving (see Figure 22). *Amour* stars Jean-Louis Trintignant and Emmanuelle Riva; Trintignant is best know for his role in *A Man and a Woman* (1966), and Riva is celebrated for her role in *Hiroshima Mon Amour* (1959). The movie will stay with you long after the viewing, and it will leave you thinking about – and talking with your friends about – both dementia and euthanasia.

Anne: "There's no point in going on living. That's how it is. I know it can only get worse. Why should I inflict this on us, on you and me?"

Georges: "You're not inflicting anything on me."

Anne: "You don't have to lie, Georges."

Georges: [looks down at the floor contemplatively] "Put yourself in my place. Didn't you ever think that it could happen to me, too?"

Anne: "Of course I did. But imagination and reality have little in common."

Georges: "But things are getting better every day."

Anne: "I don't want to carry on. You're making such sweet efforts to make everything easier for me. But I don't want to go on. For my own sake, not yours."

Georges: "I don't believe you. I know you. You think you are a burden to me. But what would you do in my place?"

Anne: "I don't want to rack my brain over this. I'm tired, I want to go to bed."

A husband and wife share their anxiety over her symptoms in *Amour* (2012)

Figure 22. *Amour* (2012, Artificial Eye, Sony Pictures Classics). Produced by Stefan Arndt, Veit Heidiuschka, Michael Katz, and Margaret Ménégoz,. Directed by Michael Heneke.

Critical Thinking Questions

➤ How could a psychologist distinguish between genuine amnesia and malingering?

➤ Which seems to be more accurate – cinematic portrayals of retrograde amnesia or of anterograde amnesia?

➤ Films like *Memento* (2000) and *Mulholland Drive* (2001) induce viewer confusion, disorientation, and distortion. Does this help to increase empathy for the character(s)? Does this empathy tend to generalize beyond the screen?

➤ Should people who have seizure disorders controlled by medication be allowed to drive?

➤ What are the most current, avant-garde treatment options for Alzheimer's disease?

➤ Is it helpful for people who have a family member suffering from Alzheimer's to watch films like *Iris* (2001), *Son of the Bride* (2002), or *Amour* (2012)?

➤ How likely is it that a nursing home would have a "no visitors" policy for the first 30 days as is portrayed in *Away from Her* (2006)?

➤ Should married people be allowed to have sex in nursing homes if it is clear that one of the partners is becoming demented and no longer able to give meaningful consent? Does it make a difference if they are not married?

➤ Is society obligated to provide care for old people who have dementias that dramatically limit the quality of their lives? What is the alternative?

➤ How will the aging of the baby boomers affect society? Is it possible to estimate how many people will develop Alzheimer's disease as the baby boom generation ages?

➤ Should helmets be mandatory for bicycle riders and motorcyclists?

➤ Was Georges' decision to end Anne's life justified in *Amour*? Is euthanasia a sensible solution to the ever more widespread problem of dementia?

➤ Do you have a living will?

If you have time to read just one book relevant to this chapter, make it:

Horstman, J. (2012). *Scientific American brain series. The Scientific American healthy aging brain: The neuroscience of making the most of your mature mind.* San Francisco: Jossey-Bass.

If you only have time for one article, read:

Loprinzi, P. D., Herod, S. M., Cardinal, B. J., & Noakes, T. D. (2013). Physical activity and the brain: A review of this dynamic, bi-directional relationship. *Brain Research, 1539,* 95–104. doi: 10.1016/j.brainres.2013.10.004

Wedding and Niemiec's Top 10 Neurocognitive Disorders Films

Head Trauma

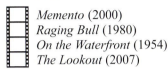

Memento (2000)
Raging Bull (1980)
On the Waterfront (1954)
The Lookout (2007)

Dementia

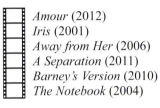

Amour (2012)
Iris (2001)
Away from Her (2006)
A Separation (2011)
Barney's Version (2010)
The Notebook (2004)

Chapter 13

Personality Disorders

Llewelyn Moss: If I was cuttin' deals, why wouldn't I go deal with this guy Chigurh?

Carson Wells: No, no, no. You don't understand. You can't make a deal with him. Even if you gave him the money he'd still kill you. He's a peculiar man. You could even say that he has principles. Principles that transcend money or drugs or anything like that. He's not like you. He's not even like me.

Dialogue about the psychopath Anton Chigurh in *No Country for Old Men* (2007)

➤ Do you think the diagnosis of antisocial personality disorder adequately explains the personality dynamics of Anton Chigurh?

➤ What advice would you give to a colleague who stated they were treating someone who fit the description of Chigurh given in the epigraph?

➤ What clues in the film explain why Chigurh acts the way he does?

➤ Is there a typical childhood for those with antisocial personality? What are some common themes?

➤ Is it possible for a person to experience absolutely no guilt and remorse for severe wrongdoings?

➤ Do most people with antisocial personality disorders engage in highly risky behavior?

➤ Is there any way Chigurh could ever have a positive prognosis? Can someone with a diagnosis of antisocial personality disorder recover?

➤ Can a person have several different personality disorders at the same time?

➤ Is antisocial personality disorder more common in men or in women? Why?

➤ How are personality disorders qualitatively different from other *DSM-5* disorders?

Patient Evaluation

Name: Anton Chigurh

Patient's stated reason for coming

"I am looking for someone. You're not the man I am looking for." He later added, "This guy wanted me to come speak with you," referring to a probation officer who accompanied him. The probation officer stated that this evaluation is "a recommendation of the court."

History of the present illness

Anton Chigurh is a 48-year-old man who has never married, lives alone, and does not appear to have any meaningful relationships. He has had a number of legal problems, most recently arrests for car theft and arson. He has been accused of murder but has been acquitted. The officers at the local jail know Mr. Chigurh well because he is arrested a couple of times each year. He has escaped from his jail cell on two previous occasions.

Past psychiatric illness, treatment, and outcomes

Mr. Chigurh reported a long history of rule-breaking behavior and problems with the legal system. He was raised in foster homes during his childhood and was placed in juvenile detention centers and psychiatric treatment centers for much of his adolescence. As a child, he tortured and killed dogs, cats, and rabbits. He stated he has been given a number of diagnoses over the years; these include schizophrenia, depression, and bipolar disorder. He denied problems controlling his impulses, saying any action he takes is conscious and deliberate, not impulsive. He does not report any pleasure resulting from his acts of arson. He denied feelings of guilt or remorse for his previous illegal activities. He stated he has never backed down from a fight and is often the instigator.

Medical history

Mr. Chigurh denied any significant medical history or use of prescription medications. He reports being physically healthy.

Psychosocial history

Mr. Chigurh says he is self-employed but would not explain his work any further. He noted he has never held a regular job with an employer for longer than 1 day. He dropped out of high school and did not attend any college class or receive a GED. He has committed a number of felonies and misdemeanors and has spent several months in jail as an adult. He is socially isolated, and he has no interest in making friends or initiating intimate relationships; however, he does state that he "knows" a lot of people who are acquaintances and work contacts.

Drug and alcohol history

Mr. Chigurh reported he used to use hallucinogens and "other stuff" on a daily basis over several years. He noted he has not used a single illegal drug for over 20 years. He has not used alcohol or smoked a cigarette for over 20 years. When asked about the turning point 2 decades ago, Mr. Chigurh refused to share much, stating: "Sometimes things happen."

Behavioral observations

Mr. Chigurh was very taciturn, and rarely spoke more than a sentence or two at a time; his voice tone was deep, and he was very clear and precise in his choice of words. His range of affect was limited – flat with mild agitation. Mr. Chigurh described his mood as "good." His eye contact was direct and penetrating to the point of inappropriate staring at the interviewer; it was uncertain as to whether he was trying to intimidate the interviewer or whether this was his typical style. His appearance was clean and casual. He was particularly insightful and appeared to understand the rationale behind each of the interviewer's questions; however, he refused to offer insights into his own behaviors or personal life.

Mental status examination

Mr. Chigurh was oriented to person, place, time, and situation, and he scored 30 out of 30 on the Mini-Mental State Examination. There was no evidence of cognitive difficulty or psychiatric disturbance on the mental status examination. Homicidality was indeterminate; he did not give a yes or no response but also did not reveal any details as to any harm he was intending to inflict. He denied suicidality. Hallucinations, delusions, and paranoia were not exhibited and were explicitly denied; however, he did make cryptic comments such as when the interviewer asked about his thoughts about the man who recently turned him in to the authorities, Mr. Chigurh replied, "I freed him. Sometimes people get lucky." Mr. Chigurh stated that since he answered a number of questions and took the mental status exam that the interviewer should play a game with him in return. For rapport-building purposes and because it was toward the end of the interview, the interviewer agreed to participate. Mr. Chigurh took out a coin and stated "Heads or tails, call it." He flipped the coin, and the interviewer guessed correctly; Mr. Chigurh then smiled and walked out of the room without saying another word.

Functional assessment

Mr. Chigurh reported he is functioning adequately in all areas of his life. By societal standards, he is not functioning well socially, psychologically, or personally. However, Mr. Chigurh shows no concern about these areas.

Strengths

Mr. Chigurh is quite intelligent and seems to be very aware of what is going on in his environment and the motives of those around him. He seems to be patient and highly self-controlled. He displayed a dry sense of humor. On the VIA Survey, a measure of character strengths, Mr. Chigurh's highest strengths were self-regulation, prudence, creativity, bravery, and perseverance. It is evident that he misuses these strengths to manipulate others.

Diagnosis

Antisocial personality disorder (F60.2).

Treatment plan

Mr. Chigurh is at high risk of harming again although no specific plan or intention has been shared. His violent and aggressive history, his diagnosis, and his lack of empathy for others support this belief. His enigmatic presentation and unsettling body language do not help his case. A release of information was signed that permits the interviewer to communicate regularly with Mr. Chigurh's probation officer. The interviewer will consult with a forensic psychologist colleague on this case and will contact the American Psychological Association ethics office for consultation on best approaches at present to prevent harm to others and for advice about how to respond to future scenarios that might emerge. The top treatment priority should be ensuring the safety of others who may come into contact with Mr. Chigurh.

Prognosis

Poor. This man shows no remorse, no interest in changing anything about himself, and no awareness that anything that he has done is wrong.

Psychopathy, Antisocial Personality, and *No Country for Old Men*

Javier Bardem's 2007 Academy Award–winning performance as Anton Chigurh is one of the most chilling portrayals of psychopathology and evil in cinema history. It is hard to imagine Chigurh not being named as one of the top 5 villains on the next list by the American Film Institute of the top 50 heroes and villains in cinema history (see Appendix A). His portrayal is as engaging as it is frightening. On one level, he is a man after money, simply doing a job; on another level, he is a cold-blooded, psychopathic serial killer; on still another, he symbolizes evil itself. It is fair to call him amoral – he is someone totally devoid of a moral code; on the other hand, some might say he is a man of principle, following his belief in one thing – fate. At times, Chigurh uses a coin toss to determine whom he will kill; at other times he simply kills anyone who gets in his way. He does not show a hint of goodness, morality, or care for anyone with whom he comes into contact; meaning and purpose are the furthest thing from his mind. He employs a unique weapon – a penetrating captive bolt pistol that is normally used to stun or kill cattle. A confrontation with a gas station proprietor, played by Gene Jones, is unforgettable (Figure 23); this scene underscores how difficult it is for most people to understand the motives and behavior of someone with an antisocial personality disorder.

The character of Chigurh is a fascinating film portrayal – he has a deep, harsh voice, penetrating eyes, and a steady, self-assured gait. He is usually fairly taciturn; when he does speak, he chooses his words carefully. His nationality and ethnicity are intentionally left unclear so he could potentially be from anywhere. His behavior is incredibly resourceful with a high level of "negative ingenuity" (creativity in the moment and for malicious purposes). He appears as unstoppable, and he adeptly "uses" everyone he encounters. There are no walls or locked doors that can slow him down or block him; his bolt gun blows through every lock he encounters. It seems to make no difference where a person goes if Chigurh is waiting there to deliver his or her fate. In one scene he is put on the defensive, yet he finds a way to disappear. This is another critical aspect of his character. Just as one does not necessar-

ily see "pure evil," but perhaps forms of evil, we do not see Chigurh, and he does not want to be seen. One character refers to him as a ghost. Indeed, the first shot of him (and several other shots) in the film is a shadow as he sits in the back seat, just before an escape and a brutal killing. He follows his subjects silently and then suddenly is present; just as quickly as he appears, he disappears. When asked if he was going to kill a man, Chigurh responds "That depends, can you see me?"

When reading these descriptions, it is probably clear that Chigurh is not a typical antisocial personality. He not only displays a pervasive pattern of breaking rules, irresponsibility, impulsiveness, and aggressiveness, but he is also a serial killer devoid of any hint of humanity. The diagnosis of psychopathic personality (not a formal *DSM-5* diagnosis, but something discussed later in this chapter in the section "Antisocial Versus Psychopathic Personality") provides a more accurate and apt description.

No Country for Old Men (2007) won a number of awards, including Academy Awards for Best Director, Best Picture, and Best Adaptive Screenplay. Directed by the Coen Brothers, the film merges a number of genre elements – thriller/suspense, crime drama, and western.

Anton Chigurh's character can be compared with the late Heath Ledger's Academy Award-winning performance as the Joker in *The Dark Knight* (2008). The Joker is an incredibly engaging – and more charismatic – villain who clearly fits the dimensions of the psychopathic personality. He displays no remorse or hint of human goodness and kills at will. Both of these characters would be on the severe end of this personality disorder dimension. Viewers are very curious about each of these characters and eagerly anticipate each scene in which they appear. There are a number of explanations for viewers' fascination with these two characters and those of other psychopaths such as Hannibal Lecter in *The Silence of the Lambs* (1991) and Alex in *A Clockwork Orange* (1971). Curiosity researcher Todd Kashdan offers three explanations (Kashdan, 2009):

1. **Exposure**: Movies are a safe place for the viewer to experience one's greatest fears and this opportunity is often relished since the viewer always knows at some level that what they are seeing is not real. These films combine curiosity and fear, producing a blended emotional state that can be a very pleasurable and positive experience. The viewer's anxiety amplifies the pleasure of the intrigue and the resulting positive experience is more intense and long-lasting.

Figure 23. *No Country for Old Men* (2007, Miramax Films, Paramount Vantage). Produced by Ethan Coen, Joel Coen, and Scott Rudin. Directed by Ethan Coen and Joel Coen.

2. **Thrill seeking**: Some viewers enjoy taking personal and emotional risks for the sake of the experience. Since much of life falls into the neutral category and there are typically few instances in which we can experience intense emotions (e.g., hatred), these movies let us fill out the full spectrum of experiences allowing the viewer to experience intense sensations.

3. **Social scripts**: We know that courage and overcoming fear can lead to positive outcomes. Some viewers get to tap into this positive social script, while for others who don't necessarily enjoy the experience, it is nothing more than a test of courage. There are few occasions in which we get to do this, so the viewer will often seek them out, even if he or she doesn't particularly enjoy the experience. This occurs when a viewer has an emotion profile of high curiosity and low pleasure.

Types of Personality Disorders

All of us have unique personalities and our own individual personality traits. On occasion, these personality traits get us in trouble. For some individuals, their personalities result in a persistent pattern of recurring interpersonal difficulties. When there is a persistent pattern of inflexible and maladaptive behavior that *continually* gets an individual in trouble or that causes him or her considerable subjective distress, a diagnosis of personality disorder may be appropriate.

People with personality disorders exhibit enduring, pervasive, and inflexible patterns of behavior that deviate markedly from societal expectations. Their behavior seems odd, unusual, or peculiar to most other people. However, to the individual, the experience is so ingrained that it is **ego-syntonic**; it does not bother them – that is, they have learned to be comfortable with their own pathology.

The list of 10 personality disorders in Table 8 is not arbitrary but is based on a conceptual model that groups all personality disorders into one of three relatively distinct clusters. **Cluster A** (for *odd or eccentric behavior*) includes the paranoid, schizoid, and schizotypal personality disorders. **Cluster B** (for *dramatic, emotional, or erratic behavior*) includes

Table 8. Characteristics of personality disorders with examples from both classic and contemporary cinema

Disorder cluster	Personality disorder	Characteristics	Classic film examples	More recent film examples
A	Paranoid	Distrust and suspiciousness about the motives of others	Lt. Cmdr. Philip Francis Queeg (Humphrey Bogart) in *The Caine Mutiny* (1954); Fred C. Dobbs (Humphrey Bogart) in *The Treasure of the Sierra Madre* (1948)	Paul (John Diehl) in *Land of Plenty* (2004); Dell Spooner (Will Smith) in *I, Robot* (2004)
	Schizoid	Detachment from social relationships and a restricted range of emotional expression	Will Penny (Charlton Heston) in *Will Penny* (1968)	Bartleby (Crispin Glover) in *Bartleby* (2001); Ed Crane (Billy Bob Thornton) in *The Man Who Wasn't There* (2001)
	Schizotypal	Acute discomfort in close relationships, cognitive or perceptual distortions, and behavioral eccentricities	Jack Arnold Alexander Tancred Gurney (Peter O'Toole) in *The Ruling Class* (1972)	Willy Wonka (Johnny Depp) in *Charlie and the Chocolate Factory* (2005); Charlie Fineman (Adam Sandler) in *Reign Over Me* (2007)
B	Antisocial	Disregard for, and violation of, the rights of others	Alex (Malcolm McDowell) in *A Clockwork Orange* (1971); Bruno Anthony (Robert Walker) in *Strangers on a Train* (1951)	Patrick Bateman (Christian Bale) in *American Psycho* (2000); Chris Wilton (Jonathan Rhys Meyers) in *Match Point* (2005); Andy Hanson (Philip Seymour Hoffman) in *Before the Devil Knows You're Dead* (2007); Richard Kuklinski (Michael Shannon) in *The Iceman* (2013)
	Borderline	Instability in emotions and interpersonal relationships, inadequate self-image, fear of abandonment, and marked impulsiveness	Alex Forrest (Glenn Close) in *Fatal Attraction* (1987)	Barbara Covett (Judi Dench) in *Notes on a Scandal* (2006); Margot (Nicole Kidman) in *Margot at the Wedding* (2007)
	Histrionic	Excessive emotionality and attention seeking	Blanche DuBois (Vivien Leigh) in *A Streetcar Named Desire* (1951)	Carolyn Burnham (Annette Bening) in *American Beauty* (1999); Countess Sofya Andreevna Tolstoy in *The Last Station* (2009); Cate Blanchett in *Blue Jasmine* (2013)
	Narcissistic	Grandiosity, a need for admiration, and lack of empathy for the problems and needs of others	Norma Desmond (Gloria Swanson) in *Sunset Blvd.* (1950)	Bud Fox (Charlie Sheen) in *Wall Street* (1987); Troy Duffy as himself in *Overnight* (2003); Ron Burgundy (Will Ferrell) in *Anchorman: The Legend of Ron Burgundy* (2004)

Table 8. Continued

Disorder cluster	Personality disorder	Characteristics	Classic film examples	More recent film examples
C	Avoidant	Social inhibition, feelings of inadequacy, and hypersensitivity to criticism or negative evaluation	Laura Wingfield (Jane Wyman) in *The Glass Menagerie* (1950)	Amélie Poulain (Audrey Tautou) in *Amélie* (2001); William Forrester (Sean Connery) in *Finding Forrester* (2000)
	Dependent	Submissive and clinging behavior and fears of separation	Bob "Bobby" Wiley (Bill Murray) in *What About Bob?* (1991)	Claire Richards (Renée Zellweger) in *White Oleander* (2002)
	Obsessive-Compulsive	Preoccupation with orderliness, perfectionism, and control	Felix Ungar (Jack Lemmon) in *The Odd Couple* (1968)	Al Fountain (John Turturro) in *Box of Moonlight* (1996)

the antisocial, borderline, histrionic, and narcissistic personality disorders. **Cluster C** (for *anxious or fearful behavior*) includes the remaining personality disorders: avoidant, dependent, and obsessive-compulsive. Students sometimes find it instructive to remember these three clusters using the helpful (but potentially offensive) mnemonic "weird, wild and wimpy" for clusters A, B, and C, respectively.

DSM-5 also presents a dimensional model of personality disorders to accompany the standard taxonomy presented in the core manual. This represents an attempt to "have it both ways." The core taxonomy preserves continuity with current practice (and is identical to the categorical classification of personality disorders found in *DSM-IV*); the newer, dimensional model "aims to address numerous shortcomings of the current approach to personality disorders" (American Psychiatric Association, 2013, p. 761). One of these shortcomings is the fact that patients who meet diagnostic criteria for one diagnosis often meet criteria for other personality disorders as well. This can be seen in Cate Blanchett's title character in Woody Allen's film *Blue Jasmine* (2013); Jasmine clearly meets the criteria for histrionic personality disorder; she just as clearly meets the criteria for narcissistic personality disorder.

The general criteria for the diagnosis of personality disorder, of any type, include the presence of "an enduring pattern of inner experience and behavior that deviates markedly from the expectations of the individual's culture" (American Psychiatric Association, 2013, p. 646). The pattern must be present in at least two of four areas: cognition, affectivity, interpersonal functioning, and impulse control. In addition, the pattern must be inflexible and pervasive.

Just as it is a challenge for clinicians to diagnose a personality disorder in a single meeting with a client, it is challenging to diagnose cinematic characters with personality disorders in films that take place over a short period of time. Films that show the developmental course of a character from childhood to adulthood and that depict the character in a variety of settings leave the viewer in a better position to make the diagnosis, e.g., *Red Dragon* (2002), *The Silence of the Lambs* (1991), *Hannibal* (2001), and *Hannibal Rising* (2007) – the four films documenting the life of Hannibal Lecter.

Morten Hesse and two colleagues reported an interesting study in which they found that psychology students with little formal training in psychopathology could achieve reasonable levels of agreement when using rating scales to diagnose personality disorders in film characters (Hesse, Schliewe, & Thomsen, 2005). The characters and films evaluated were Sarah Morton in *Swimming Pool* (2003), Aileen Wuornos in *Monster* (2003), Suzanne Stone in *To Die For* (1995), and Coleman Silk in *The Human Stain* (2003). These authors suggest that Morton's character would be diagnosed as "personality disorder, not other specified" (a *DSM-IV* diagnosis); the character of Aileen Wuornos would be diagnosed as having comorbid borderline and antisocial personality disorder; Stone's character would be diagnosed as someone with a narcissistic personality disorder (with histrionic features); while Silk's character was not believed to meet the criteria for any of the personality disorders.

A personality disorder diagnosis is inappropriate in any situation in which aberrant behavior results from transient situational factors (e.g., an individual who repeatedly gets his or her tax returns audited may become understandably paranoid about the government). Finally, it is critical that cultural variables be considered when a diagnosis of personality disorder is being considered. For example, the Italian film *Down and Dirty* (1976) includes a protagonist who appears to have an antisocial personality. However, his behavior must be understood in terms of the culture of southern Italy and the debilitating and corrosive effects of poverty.

Some personality disorders are more common in men (e.g., antisocial and narcissistic personality disorders), while others are found more often in women (e.g., borderline, histrionic, and dependent personality disorders). This is quite consistent with cinematic portrayals, as we will soon show.

Cluster A Disorders

These "odd and eccentric" disorders are rare and hence their depiction in cinema is uncommon (unlike other disorders such as dissociative identity disorder, which, though rare in reality, are often shown in movies).

Paranoid Personality Disorder

People with a paranoid personality are isolated and suspicious. They are convinced that others are talking about them behind their backs or plotting against them. The behaviors of others are carefully scrutinized for evidence of intent to harm, and overtures of friendship or good will by other people are rejected as manipulative gestures or parts of a plot. Ironically, because paranoid individuals behave in peculiar ways, a self-fulfilling prophecy occurs and people *do* begin to discuss the paranoid individual

behind his or her back. Paranoid people tend to have few or no friends. They personalize almost everything and misinterpret casual remarks to make them fit into their belief structure.

Land of Plenty (2004, US/Germany) is a Wim Wenders film about misguided post-9/11 patriotism and paranoia in the United States. A young woman, Lana (Michelle Williams), returns to the United States from Tel Aviv with a mission to meet her Uncle Paul and deliver a letter to him on behalf of her mother. Paul is a highly suspicious and paranoid man whose life is preoccupied with searching for individuals with bombs or who may be attacking the city of Los Angeles. He has an irritable disposition, often characteristic of those with this personality disorder. When he communicates to others, his verbiage is intense and convincing. Paul lives in a dilapidated van, uses a makeshift camera with a joystick and monitor, and covers the walls of his van with newspaper clippings. Some of these come from the garbage cans he digs in looking for evidence. He racially profiles Arabic men, and when he encounters a homeless man wearing a turban, he immediately concludes the man is a terrorist. He later watches a drive-by killing of the man – and since he was taping the man's every move, he is able to keep the tape to rewatch for his own amusement. Paul notes he had been exposed to Agent Orange in Vietnam; therefore, a physical disorder would need to be ruled out before any psychological diagnostic conclusions could be made.

"They're trying to infect our country. They're trying to destroy us. I won't let 'em do that."

Paul revealing his paranoia in
Land of Plenty (2004)

Lakeview Terrace (2009) stars Samuel L. Jackson as Able, a paranoid LAPD officer in this Neil LaBute film. LaBute offers good character development of this multifaceted man, allowing the viewer to build some stereotypes and negative impressions of Able who then reveals his honest, genuine concern for his children, his inner pain, and his rationale for his frustration with interracial couples. Tension mounts between Able and an interracial couple who move in next door as Able begins to terrorize them. Able displays a high degree of rigidity and irritability and insists on all rules being followed. He is oversensitive in interpersonal communications and is hypervigilant and skeptical everyone's motives. Subsequently, he is quick to react negatively to virtually any conversation. LaBute is known for using subtlety and metaphor in his films to parallel key themes. In this film, forest fires get closer and closer to Able's neighborhood as the film progresses; this adds to a sense unpredictable danger.

The dangers associated with having a leader with a paranoid or antisocial personality disorder become clear in *The Last King of Scotland* (2006), in which Academy Award winner Forest Whitaker portrays the leader of Uganda, Idi Amin. On the one hand, Amin is quite charismatic as he tries to convince the people that he is their rightful leader and the "father" of Uganda. He is also often fun-loving, friendly, jovial, and teasing. On the other hand, he is shown to be a ruthless dictator, explosive, and unpredictable, who murdered over 300,000 Ugandans during his reign. Paranoia was a significant part of this man's personality, and he used his paranoia to justify his horrendous actions.

> "But a man who shows fear. He is weak … and a slave"
>
> Idi Amin's ironic observation in
> *The Last King of Scotland* (2006)

A convincing portrayal of paranoid personality disorder is found in Detective Del Spooner (Will Smith) in *I, Robot* (2004). Spooner is a highly suspicious, judgmental, and angry person, particularly around robots, which are a mainstay in this world of 2046. Spooner's frustrated mistrust of robots leads him to push away a friendly robot delivering a package. His misperceptions bring him to randomly chase down and tackle a robot running with a purse, which he has assumed is a robbery even though no robots had ever committed a crime at this point in history. Much of the plot unfolds around Spooner's paranoia, which other characters recognize. One man (Dr. Alfred Lanning, played by James Cromwell) counts on Spooner's paranoia to save the human race from robots. As with many

films depicting a paranoid character (e.g., Jerry Fletcher, played by Mel Gibson, in *Conspiracy Theory* [1997]), the psychopathology is often distorted by the entertainment value of the plot, which results in a character's paranoia proving to be accurate and justified in the end.

Ben Stiller's character Chas Tenenbaum in *The Royal Tenenbaums* (2001) displays numerous paranoid characteristics that seem stable over time. He feels an underlying anger and rage toward his father, unrealistic fears, and displays excessive concern and hypervigilance regarding his environment and home.

Humphrey Bogart's role as Captain Queeg in *The Caine Mutiny* (1954) is a wonderful illustration of the paranoid personality. Queeg becomes preoccupied with trivial misdemeanors by sailors while he ignores the important parts of his job – such as maintaining the morale of his men. He eventually falls apart under pressure when he is called to the witness stand to testify in a court martial hearing for an insubordinate junior officer. There is a famous scene in which Queeg takes two ball bearings out of his pocket and begins to move them around nervously in his palm, and everyone in the court senses that this man is not well adjusted. Bogart plays another paranoid personality in *The Treasure of the Sierra Madre* (1948) in which he becomes obsessed with the idea that his partners are out to steal the gold all three men have agreed to split between them.

Schizoid Personality Disorder

The individual with a schizoid personality has little interest in and avoids close interpersonal relations. He or she is likely to be described as a loner who lacks meaningful ties to a family, community, or value system. These individuals are unlikely to display strong emotions or tenderness to others; they appear apathetic, diffident, and indifferent. They most often have little or no interest in sexual encounters, and few marry.

There are some excellent portrayals of schizoid personality in the cinema. Two examples come from two films titled *Bartleby* (1970, 2001); both are remakes of a Herman Melville short story, "Bartleby the Scrivener." The 2001 version is a fascinating, cult film about a quiet, passive man named Bartleby

(Crispin Glover) hired for a mundane office job. He thoroughly does his job at first but soon begins to refuse doing extra work, repeating the mysterious phrase, "I would prefer not to." This quirky behavior continues as he stares for hours at an air conditioning vent and displays no interest in socializing with his work peers. Schizoid individuals are often isolated from society, and an opening scene symbolizes Bartleby's isolation as he is depicted enclosed and caged on an overpass bridge above a busy, productive society represented by an expressway below. His speech is slow, eye contact is limited, and affect is flat and emotionless throughout the film. At times, he displays an incongruent, distant, random smile or two, but he does not engage others interpersonally with smiles or laughter. Often, there is no understandable reason for a person behaving in a schizoid manner, and the film parallels this idea, as no explanation is overtly given for Bartleby's behaviors, lack of emotions, or social apathy. The earlier, 1970 version portrays very similar schizoid traits for the lead character, and the plot is very similar to the new version. This older film is black and white, dark, slow, and gloomy.

Another classic example of schizoid personality is found in the Coen brothers' film noir *The Man Who Wasn't There* (2001), where even the title of the film suggests a schizoid quality. Billy Bob Thornton plays Ed Crane, an aloof, taciturn barber who appears disinterested in life and claims he dislikes most things and that his life has been one of "no excitement." He is unemotional with flat affect and a monotone voice. He moves slowly and stiffly, and even the way he smokes cigarettes is a slow, unconscious, steady ritual. His responses to others are dull with heavy sighs, and he is passive when criticized. He does not seem very bothered by the fact that his wife is cheating on him with his best friend. He allows himself to be exploited by a traveling salesman. The only relationship he seems to invest emotional energy in is with a young girl; he appears committed to helping her pursue her dream of becoming a musician. Also consistent with schizoid characteristics is that no one "really knows him;" this is reinforced by his inability to share anything of himself with others.

Eraserhead (1976) is a cult classic created by innovative director David Lynch. The film is surreal, not only in direction but also in characterization, lighting, sound, imagery, and story. The plot involves a young man, Henry, who visits his girl-friend's family, and he discovers a premature, alien-like fetus in the home. Henry has a schizoid personality disorder – he is a loner and socially awkward, with no idea how to interact with people (including his girlfriend), and he displays flat and inappropriate affect throughout the film. There are multiple themes of birth and fetuses, as well as umbilical cords, blood, and womb images in various scenes.

Crispin Glover plays another socially awkward, schizoid character in *Willard* (2003). Willard is isolated from others, and his only companions are the rats that congregate in his basement. After one rat, whom he names Socrates, saves him from a suicide attempt, he distances himself further from people and rallies the rats to help him get revenge.

In the film *Heavy* (1995), the lead character displays a schizoid reaction to his mother's death. He becomes frozen, emotionless, sexually disinterested, and isolated with flattened affect. To qualify for a diagnosis of schizoid personality disorder, his bereavement would need to be evaluated and his personality assessed prior to his mother's death. The film offers another interesting schizoid description about the lead character's isolation, through his belief that you can be as "big as an ox and no one sees you."

The figure of the loner is a staple in Western films, and many of these characters would meet the criteria for schizoid personality disorder. These individuals avoid close relationships, prefer solitary activities, lack close friends and confidants, and appear indifferent to the praise or criticism of others; the title character (Charlton Heston) in *Will Penny* (1968) is one example; the eponymous lead (Robert Redford) in *Jeremiah Johnson* (1972) is another.

Schizotypal Personality Disorder

People with schizotypal personality have "schizophrenia-like" characteristics but do not typically meet the diagnostic criteria for schizophrenia. They hold odd or peculiar beliefs, thoughts, and/or behaviors. They are often very superstitious, have unusual perceptual experiences, and are suspicious and paranoid.

In the *DSM-5*, schizotypal personality disorder is included *both* in the chapter on schizophrenia and in the chapter on personality disorders (where it is fully described). Its inclusion in the chapter on schizophrenia results from its clear presence on the "lower end" of the schizophrenia spectrum. In his *PsycCRITIQUES* review of the new *DSM-5*, Greg Neimeyer (2013) noted:

> The scope and scale of the challenges faced within (and between) the 13 different work groups that revised the *DSM-5* are scarcely imaginable. Numerous disorders were brought into this game of diagnostic musical chairs; when the music stopped, participants must surely have looked around to see who had found a seat and where they were located. At least one disorder seems to have found itself in two chairs: Schizotypal personality disorder is now listed twice, once under the Personality Disorders and again under the category Schizophrenia Spectrum and Related Disorders. The irony of this latter designation is not lost on those who have cut their eye-teeth on earlier versions of the DSM, where schizotypal personality disorder was fashioned from the long-defunct diagnosis of borderline schizophrenia. Quizzically, it now returns again to its homeland, though its tandem location obligates it to live out its current dissociative life in *A Tale of Two Cities*.

Adam Sandler's portrayal of Charlie Fineman in *Reign Over Me* (2007) is an impressive portrayal of someone with a schizotypal personality disorder. Charlie has lost his whole family – three daughters and his wife – in the 9/11 tragedy, but the viewer sees the character's deterioration and not his immediate reaction to the tragedy. Instead, the story picks up years later, and the viewer observes a man who would qualify for the diagnosis of schizotypal personality. Charlie exhibits eccentric and bizarre behavior, is odd in his appearance (e.g., he is unkempt, and he constantly wears headphones while riding around on a motor scooter), and seems childlike. He appears to be clueless socially and interpersonally – brutally cold and inappropriate at times (e.g., he eats with his new friend's family but sits on the counter while singing to himself with his headphones on). When he speaks with others it is only to ask random trivia questions. He repeatedly remodels his kitchen and spends his time in one of two activities: death metal drumming or playing solitary video games. The features of personality disorders in each cluster may merge and overlap at times. For example, Charlie appears to have no desire to connect with others (schizoid) and is highly suspicious of others (paranoid). Before making a diagnosis of schizotypal personality disorder, the clinician would need to discern how much of Charlie's personality features result from prolonged bereavement, or the extent to which they might be related to severe depression or PTSD, and the therapist would need to know what Charlie's personality was like prior to the tragedy.

An outstanding illustration of a schizotypal personality can be found in Johnny Depp's unique portrayal of Willy Wonka in Tim Burton's *Charlie and the Chocolate Factory* (2005), a portrayal that is much more clear in terms of this diagnosis than the portrayal by Gene Wilder in *Willy Wonka and the Chocolate Factory* (1971). Depp's Wonka has a quality of desperate aloofness in which his isolation, unusual perceptual experiences, and odd thinking are much more apparent. He lives alone, and his only friends are a culture of dwarfs (Oompa-Loompas). He is quirky when he does communicate – for example, he exhibits disorganized speech, uses note cards to compensate for his poor social skills, talks to himself in public, and is unable to say the word "parents." His appearance is colorful and eccentric. The film depicts a familial root for Wonka's personality in that he lived alone with his father who was distant and authoritarian. His father showed no concern when he decided to run away from home.

In *The Royal Tenenbaums* (2001), Owen Wilson plays Eli, a man who wears flamboyant outfits and uses unusual words. He has a quirky tone of voice, exhibits odd and eccentric behavior, and often does not have a firm grasp on reality. His apartment has numerous odd paintings covering the walls. It is uncertain to what extent these qualities result from his drug abuse; regardless, his behavior and interactions are quite schizotypal.

Denis Leary plays a truly fascinating man who has paranoid schizophrenia in *Final* (2001). He displays some interesting schizotypal traits as well, but to qualify for a diagnosis of schizotypal personality, these traits could not occur exclusively with the schizophrenia episodes.

The character Ernest (Maury Chaykin) in *Bartleby* (2001) displays many schizotypal traits. He has a poor use of logic and when he gets upset, he speaks in a verbal salad, mixes words, and is somewhat nonsensical. His appearance is disheveled. He is easily overwhelmed by stress. His behavior is often inappropriate for the situation, as he never appears to be working when he is at the office, he displays no reaction after spilling water and copier ink, and he is later repeatedly and genuinely scared by a pop-up spin toy. He presents with a constant paranoid, concerned look on his face and has blunted affect throughout the film.

A schizotypal personality is demonstrated in Flannery O'Conner's novel *Wise Blood* (1952) and in the 1979 John Huston film adaptation also titled *Wise Blood*. A Southern preacher works hard to convince people to join his "Church Without Christ." He has numerous peculiar beliefs, odd speech, constricted affect, strange behavior, and few close friends. These five characteristics would be sufficient to justify the diagnosis of schizotypal personality.

Hyler (1988) uses DeNiro's portrayal of Travis Brickle in *Taxi Driver* (1976) to illustrate the schizotypal personality. He feels this film is such a useful tool for teaching medical students about psychopathology that he has incorporated it into a computer program that can be used to teach students to perform and record a complete mental status exam (Hyler & Bujold, 1994).

> ### 💬 Additional Questions for Discussion (Cluster A Disorders)
>
> ➤ Where do you draw the diagnostic line for these disorders, and how can one differentiate a personality disorder like schizotypal personality disorder from a major mental illness (e.g., schizophrenia)?
>
> ➤ What are some etiological components for schizoid personality (such as for the title character in *Bartleby*)?
>
> ➤ Is there any validity to the argument that people who are odd and eccentric, as illustrated by these examples, are simply extremely creative people?
>
> ➤ What is the treatment of choice for someone with a Cluster A diagnosis?
>
> ➤ Do any of the characters in the films discussed above make meaningful changes in their personal, social, or occupational life? Are Cluster A disorders resistant to change?
>
> ➤ How does culture affect the presentation of personality? Would an undocumented worker in the United States be justified in behaving in a paranoid manner?

Cluster B Disorders

Each of the personalities in this cluster is often lively and colorful, fitting the description "dramatic, emotional, and erratic." Consequently, individuals with Cluster B disorders are common in movies, as they tend to make fascinating, stimulating cinematic characters. They are often attention grabbing, conflicted, manipulative, charming, and charismatic – many of the qualities the moviegoer typically loves or hates. In addition, they often have troubled pasts, and the viewer gets to observe them escape from present pain or make impressive changes, either way making for good drama.

The Talented Mr. Ripley (1999) is a wonderful example of a film's character (Tom Ripley, played by Matt Damon) who displays characteristics of each of the disorders in this cluster. Even the opening credits get at the complexity of this disorder, listing the following adjectives to replace "talented" in the title: mysterious, yearning, secretive, lonely, troubled, confused, loving, musical, gifted, intelligent, beautiful, tender, secretive, haunted, and passionate.

Antisocial Personality Disorder

People with antisocial personality break the law, can be physically aggressive, manipulate others, lie, take senseless risks, and have little or no sense of remorse or guilt about the consequences of their behavior. These individuals violate the rights of others and appear to experience distress only when their behavior results in punishment or incarceration. They are impulsive, thrive on the "pleasure principle," and have a great deal of trouble planning their future behavior or anticipating its consequences. Individuals with antisocial personality disorder find it difficult to learn from their mistakes and find themselves dealing with similar legal and interpersonal problems throughout their lives. To examine the drivers of deviant behavior and the influence of social factors in the context of the Ben Affleck film, *The Town* (2010), read the *PsycCRITIQUES* review of the film by Swenson and Schwartz-Mette (2011).

Daniel Day-Lewis is the only actor in history to win 3 Academy Awards for Best Actor (*Lincoln* [2012]; *There Will Be Blood* [2007]; and *My Left Foot* [1990]). In addition to being one of the world's most versatile actors, he is exemplary in the role of characters with antisocial personality, such as *Gangs of New York* (2002; a film for which he was nominated for Best Actor) and *There Will Be Blood*. In the latter film, he portrays Daniel Plainview, an ambitious prospector who calls himself "an oil man" and gets rich after purchasing a family's oil rich ranch. As the film progresses, Plainview becomes increasingly greedy, violent, and selfish. He abandons his son at an early age and eventually rejects every significant person in his life. His approach is to kill or eliminate/abandon anyone who gets in his way. He becomes a despicable character who, like the Joker and Anton Chigurh, represents a beastly, immoral, wretched human being.

"I have a competition in me.
I want no one else to succeed. I hate most people"
"There are times when I look at people
and I see nothing worth liking."
"I want to earn enough money to get away from everyone."

Plainview's description of himself in
There Will Be Blood (2007)

The Assassination of Jesse James by the Coward Robert Ford (2007) portrays the obvious antisocial characteristics of a well-known train robber, Jesse James (Brad Pitt), and it also illustrates James's calm manipulation and defiant recklessness, as well as a high level of paranoia. He becomes suspicious that his followers and fellow criminals are out to get him. His paranoia leads him to become more controlling, impulsive, and unpredictable, especially as the price on his head increases. James would likely be diagnosed with unspecified personality disorder with antisocial and paranoid traits.

Before the Devil Knows You're Dead (2007) is an intense Sidney Lumet melodrama in which the story defines the characters (in a drama the characters define the story). Two brothers struggling financially and craving a better life scheme to rob a "mom and pop" jewelry store; however, the owners are their own mom and pop. After things go wrong with the robbery, the antisocial tendencies of each brother strongly emerge, and their deceit, impulsivity, and recklessness run rampant. Lumet reveals how each character is ultimately a flawed human being, and each becomes terrible in their revenge, decompensation, or inaction.

People with antisocial personality disorder often have multiple sexual partners and tend to use others for sexual gratification, with little concern for the needs or feelings of their sexual partners. They

Questions to Consider While Watching *Before the Devil Knows You're Dead* **(2007)**

➤ It seems that each of the characters in the film could change. Why don't they? Is resistance to change common in those with antisocial personality?

➤ Do the actions and inactions of the characters played by Philip Seymour Hoffman, Albert Finney, and Ethan Hawke make them evil? If not, what would a person have to do to be considered simply evil rather than mentally ill?

➤ Philip Seymour Hoffman's character abuses drugs as a way of coping with a horrifying set of circumstances. How common is this among people with antisocial personality disorders?

➤ The film's unique title comes from a famous Irish toast: "May you have food and raiment; a soft pillow for your head; may you be 40 years in heaven; before the devil knows you're dead." What does this mean? Why is the title appropriate for this film?

can be superficially warm and charming but become distant and aloof after their sexual conquest. This is evident in Johnny, the intellectual, philosophical, and antisocial character portrayed by David Thewlis in *Naked* (1993). Robert Duvall plays a complicated, antisocial minister who philanders, abuses, and projects his problems onto other characters and God in *The Apostle* (1997). Duvall's character, Sonny, is driven but flawed. He is a "spiritual antisocial" in that he passionately preaches, and his manipulation and charm often take the form of genuinely wanting to help others have more meaningful lives; however, he externalizes his problems by blaming Satan and not taking responsibility for his life. He abuses alcohol, is unfaithful to his wife, threatens her with a gun, throws an object through a window, and, most seriously, grabs his wife roughly by the hair and attempts to drag her away from a baseball game and then hospitalizes his wife's boyfriend by hitting him on the head with a baseball bat. He lies to others about his past, despite their trust in him as their spiritual leader. Sonny certainly embodies the qualities of narcissism as well, with his grandiose speech and in his preaching, and he feeds off others' admiration and his ability to stake out a position on center stage. This film will remind some of the role of the much more psycho-pathic "preacher" played by Robert Mitchum in the classic film *The Night of the Hunter* (1955).

The fascinating film *Tape* (2001) takes place in one setting (a motel room) with only three charac-ters (played by Ethan Hawke, Robert Sean Leon-ard, and Uma Thurman). Despite this simplicity, the film is a complex look at a devious, antisocial per-sonality, Vince (Hawke), and his manipulation of two high school friends. Vince is a 28-year-old without a job who volunteers as a firefighter. He presents as unstable, using drugs, jumping and run-ning around the small motel room, "chugging" beers, and throwing the cans around. He has a his-tory of drug dealing and reports that he has "anger tendencies" and "unresolved issues." At times, he is sweet and soft spoken, but the viewer soon real-izes he is purposefully acting this way to manipu-late his friends. With extreme craftiness, he secretly tape records his friend John (Leonard) revealing some vulnerable information (about a date rape in high school) after Vince interrogates him in cross-examination style; displaying a total lack of empa-thy, he blackmails John and calls another old friend (Vince's ex-girlfriend and John's date rape victim), Amy (Thurman), with the hopes of continuing his plotted manipulation.

Jonestown: The Life and Death of Peoples Tem-ple (2006) utilizes old footage, tapes, writings, and interviews with several survivors and family mem-bers of those involved in what has been called the largest mass suicide in modern history. On Novem-ber 18, 1978, in Jonestown, Guyana, 909 members of Peoples' Temple killed themselves, along with their evangelical leader, Jim Jones. Members of the church adored Jones for his charisma and his mes-sages of integration, hope, equality, and justice. Many embraced him as godlike and considered him a savior. What was missed by those who died and many others was that Jim Jones was a vicious anti-social personality. He abused power and used the congregation to meet his own sexual needs (in one case explaining to a woman shivering while he had sex with her, "I'm doing this for you"). He fre-quently humiliated, shamed, and manipulated the congregants, finding pleasure in spanking or beat-ing people in front of the congregation as punish-ment for petty transgressions. Jones once staged a blind woman in a wheelchair and performed a fake healing. He convinced people to sell their homes for the church, and in return he promised that the

church would take care of elderly family members. He encouraged people to not think for themselves so that he could think for them; he reflected that he was happy to play whatever role the congregant needed – friend, brother, savior, or God. Jones ex-hibited significant pathological traits as a child; for example, he killed cats so that he could officiate at their funerals.

The true story of Danny Burrows (played by Ryan Gosling) in *The Believer* (2001) speaks to the serious love–hate relationship a young man has with himself as he adopts a dramatically contradictory role as a Jewish Nazi. In the opening sequence, the viewer sees Burrows, who presents as a stereotypic skinhead displaying Nazi symbols, seek out and beat a young Jewish man in the middle of the street. He embraces repugnant Nazi beliefs, ranking races by worthiness in the following order: Whites, Asians, Blacks, and Jews. At the same time, Burrows is highly intelligent and articulate, speaking charis-matically to adults many years older than he is about Nazi order, discipline, and values, articulating "kill your enemy" and "Judaism is a sickness" messages. His aggressiveness and impulsivity lead him to in-stigate numerous fights. Burrows displays little re-morse for any of his antisocial behaviors until, while ransacking a synagogue with a Fascist group, he be-gins to show concern for how people treat a scroll containing sacred Jewish writings. He brings the scroll home, takes painstaking care of it, and be-gins to teach his girlfriend Hebrew. From here, he must face his internal contradiction and deal with the consequences of the lifestyle he has created for himself.

Another film illustrating an antisocial personal-ity, which is based on a true story, is the film *Shat-tered Glass* (2003) about Stephen Glass (Hayden Christensen), the *New Republic* magazine writer who went to extensive lengths to fabricate and em-bellish stories. Both the film and Christensen do a remarkable job of depicting not only the elaborate deceit, fantasy, and double life associated with this personality disorder, but also the neurotic quality of the "antisocial in trouble." The latter phrase refers to anxiety mixed with a façade of change that comes about when a person with an antisocial personality disorder is caught or about to be caught. Glass's re-sponse is to become emotional, obsequious, and/or apologetic. His manipulations take many forms, from trying to emphasize his need for the editors' support and how important it is (when he is lying), to trying to play others against one another to the incessant repetition of the question "Are you mad at me?" Glass does not see the consequences of his actions as he continues to tell various lies and stories to cover up earlier lies, digging himself deeper into deception with each interaction; we later see the tremendous impact of his behavior on the *New Republic*.

Another "caught" antisocial is Edward Norton's character in *25th Hour* (2002), who has 24 hours before he must begin a prison term for trafficking marijuana. Since he has been caught, he is forced to face some of his shame, guilt, and anger. In one unforgettable scene, he externalizes intense anger, blaring out "fuck you" to every race, group, district, and borough in New York City, as well as his father and girlfriend. We can infer he is saying this to himself as well, especially since he is looking at himself in the mirror while talking, but the acceptance of personal responsibility seems to be missed – as it often is in the antisocial personality. This Spike Lee film brings up important issues of regret and choice and brilliantly leaves many questions unanswered.

Catch Me If You Can (2002) is another film about a character with an antisocial personality disorder. The film is based on the true story of Frank Abagnale Jr., a con man who used his charm and good looks to defraud banks of millions of dollars in the 1960s. The role of Abagnale is played by Leonardo DiCaprio, who successfully impersonates a Pan Am copilot, a physician, and an attorney. Abagnale is pursued for 6 years by FBI agent Carl Hanratty (Tom Hanks) before he is eventually captured, and he winds up consulting with the FBI on fraud crimes.

In the remarkable film *Dogville* (2003), Lars von Trier directs the depiction of a woman (Nicole Kidman) trying to escape the destiny her mob boss father has planned for her. She is clearly *not* antisocial, and she works hard to be accepted into the little community that she hides in after fleeing her father's control. However, she is exploited and abused by the community she works so hard to serve, and she eventually turns on them, murdering everyone in the little town with little apparent remorse.

An interesting contrast of antisocial personalities occurs in *Levity* (2003), a film in which Billy Bob Thornton plays a person with an antisocial personality trying to make amends for his actions

(a murder many years ago), and Morgan Freeman plays an antisocial preacher who uses a fake identity to hide from the police. Likewise, Tom Hanks is a charming person with an antisocial personality who cleverly uses sophisticated speech and extensive rationalizations to manipulate an old woman for his own purposes in *The Ladykillers* (2004).

A somewhat less dramatic illustration is found in the callous manipulation of naïve home buyers vividly portrayed by Jack Lemmon, who plays a desperate and unhappy real estate salesman in *Glengarry Glen Ross* (1992). The manipulation of others for personal gain without concern for the consequences of one's behavior is a characteristic feature of antisocial personality disorders. Natasha Richardson and Mia Farrow play two consummate con artists in *Widow's Peak* (1994), although the diagnosis of antisocial personality is incompatible with the character portrayed by Farrow for most of the film. Many films appear to depict antisocial behavior, but it is often unclear as to whether these characters would meet all the criteria for the disorder. *Compulsion* (1959) depicts two antisocial fraternity men, Artie and Judd, who are intent on showing that the perfect crime is "the true test of the superior intellect." They believe they should be able to manipulate the system to get away with murder simply because "we can." Each has an antisocial personality disorder, although Artie's case is more severe. He is cool, smooth, and calculating under pressure, and enjoys listening to the police discuss the murder of which he is the perpetrator, taking pleasure in their confusion and the chaos.

Some actors like Kevin Spacey make a career out of playing antisocial characters. Though Spacey can play a variety of characters with vastly different personalities, he has played an impressive range of roles that illustrate some dimension of the antisocial personality; for example, he portrayed an arrogant writer in *The United States of Leland* (2004), an unhappy man who becomes obsessed with "the pleasure principle" in *American Beauty* (1999), a devious serial killer in *Se7en* (1995), a con man in *The Usual Suspects* (1995), a brutal executive in *Swimming With Sharks* (1994), and an ineffectual, unethical and depressed therapist in *Shrink* (2009).

While the film *Enron: The Smartest Guys in the Room* (2005) describes the antisocial behavior of various executives in a corrupt organization, the film *The Corporation* (2004) demonstrates that the typical corporation meets the criteria for psychopathy (e.g., callous unconcern for others, failure to conform to social norms).

"The fatal flaw at Enron, if there was one you'd say it was pride, but then it was arrogance, intolerance, greed."

The underlying issues for the executives in *Enron: The Smartest Guys in the Room* (2005)

Antisocial Versus Psychopathic Personality

Though **psychopathic personality disorder** is not an actual diagnosis, it is a commonly used term, and there is often confusion when the labels antisocial personality, sociopath, and psychopath are all lumped together. Robert D. Hare, the world's leading authority on psychopathy, has been doing research on psychopaths for over 50 years. Hare explains that most psychopaths fit the criteria for antisocial personality; however, the reverse is not necessarily true. Hare adds that cross-cultural studies have noted that psychopathy is generalizable. He cites a number of criteria for psychopathic personality including shallow emotions, glibness, manipulativeness, a parasitic lifestyle, episodic relationships, persistent violation of social norms, egocentricity, lack of remorse/empathy, low frustration tolerance, and lying (Hare, 2006).

In movies, psychopaths and sociopaths are often described as people who have "no conscience." Consider *Pirates of the Caribbean* (2003, 2006, 2007, 2011, 2016) and contrast Johnny Depp's character as the antisocial pirate with many of the pirate zombies led by Geoffrey Rush's character. The latter are clearly psychopathic. Table 9 uses contemporary films to illustrate the difference between antisocial personality disorder and psychopathy.

People have been fascinated with the topic of serial killers since Jack the Ripper strangled and cut the throats of five London prostitutes in 1888. More recent serial killers include Albert De Salvo (the Boston Strangler), David Berkowitz (the Son of Sam killer), Henry Lee Lucas, John Wayne Gacy, Ted Bundy ("the Preppie killer"), Wayne Williams, Charles Manson, and Jeffrey Dahmer, a harmless-looking young man who killed dozens of other young men, ate their body parts, and kept other parts in his refrigerator. The FBI defines a serial killer as anyone who has committed three or more separate murders. It seems that if a serial killer is fairly well known, a movie will eventually follow: for example, *Dahmer* (2002), *Ted Bundy* (2002), *Gacy* (2003), *Monster* (2003), *B. T. K.* (2008), *The Night Stalker* (1987), *Summer of Sam* (1999), and *Zodiac* (2007).

"I believe what doesn't kill you makes you stranger."
"Do I really look like a guy with a plan? You know what I am? I'm a dog chasing cars. I wouldn't know what to do with it if I caught it. I just do things."
"Madness is like gravity, all it takes is a little push."

Comments made by the Joker revealing his psychopathology in *The Dark Knight* (2008)

James Iaccino has written a number of *PsycCRITIQUES* film reviews examining the portrayal of various serial killers according to different classification systems and serial killer typologies. Examples include an analysis of the female serial killer in *Scream 4* (2011) (Iaccino & Dondero, 2013a) and the mission-oriented and hedonistic serial killer who matches wits with Edgar Allan Poe in *The Raven* (2012) (Iaccino & Dondero, 2013b).

Anthony Hopkins plays one of the most terrifying serial killers ever filmed in *The Silence of the Lambs* (1991), *Hannibal* (2001), and *Red Dragon* (2002). *American Psycho* (2000) is a quality film depicting a serial killer if the film is taken literally by the viewer. Another possibility is that all of the murders committed by the fictional character Patrick Bateman are simply fantasies rather than reality; there are numerous cinematic elements to support this hypothesis, although few viewers leave the theater with this impression.

Contrary to media presentations and popular opinion, few if any serial killers are psychotic. (David Berkowitz was a salient exception.) In contrast, many are sexual sadists who derive sexual excitement from the murders they commit, and most are sociopaths who experience little remorse or regret after their crimes. Both John Wayne Gacy and

Table 9. Differentiation of antisocial personality from psychopathic personality through movies

Personality Type	Film	Personality characteristics
Antisocial	Jack Sparrow (Johnny Depp) in *Pirates of the Caribbean* (2003, 2006, 2007)	Manipulative and devious, though Jack Sparrow does show qualities of trust, care, allegiance, and teamwork
	Monty Brogan (Edward Norton) in *25th Hour* (2002)	History of not conforming to laws/rules, impulsive, irritable, and reckless disregard but shows remorse and care for others
	Johnny (David Thewlis) in *Naked* (1993)	Deceitful, impulsive, self-centered, lacks empathy, irresponsible; also shows fleeting concerns and care for others and for the betterment of society
	Euliss "Sonny" Dewey – The Apostle E. F. (Robert Duvall) in *The Apostle* (1997)	Heavily deceitful, impulsive, and dangerous in words and behaviors; also shows genuine care for others, love for God, and exhibits remorse
Psychopathic/ Sociopathic	The Joker (Heath Ledger) in *The Dark Knight* (2008) Barbossa (Geoffrey Rush) in *Pirates of the Caribbean* (2003, 2007)	Kills, tortures, manipulates, and creates mass confusion/terror, for his entertainment and pleasure. Kills at will for own gain, embodies the seven deadly sins, particularly greed
	Vann (Owen Wilson) in *The Minus Man* (1999)	Serial killer with no conscience and no reason or purpose, kills randomly
	Mickey Knox (Woody Harrelson) and Mallory Knox (Juliette Lewis) in *Natural Born Killers* (1994)	Torture and kill anyone who gets in their way or bothers them, without hesitation or regret
	Elijah Price (Samuel L. Jackson) in *Unbreakable* (2000)	Complete disregard for human life as he commits mass murder out of a self-serving need to find his "better half"
	Richard Kuklinski (Michael Shannon) in *The Iceman* (2013)	Based on a true story; Kuklinski murdered more than 100 people when reportedly working for the Gambino family.

Jeffrey Dahmer were homosexual pedophiles as well as serial killers.

Some serial killers commit multiple murders for utilitarian reasons – that is, they are "hit men" who kill for money. This is the kind of serial killer portrayed by Jack Nicholson in *Prizzi's Honor* (1985) and in *The Iceman* (2013), a film biography of the life of Mafia contract killer Richard Kuklinski.

Quality documentaries addressing the lives of sociopathic serial killers include *In Cold Blood* (1967) and *Henry: Portrait of a Serial Killer* (1986).

The latter is loosely based on the life and confessions (since called into question) of Henry Lee Lucas. Henry (Michael Rooker) shares a cheap room with Otis (Tom Towles), a man he had met in prison in Vandalia. The film is controversial because it presents graphic details of several murders, including one in which Henry and his roommate, Otis, pretend their car is not running and then kill a man who stops to help. In a subsequent scene, Henry and Otis videotape the murder of an entire family. The film portrays the triangular sexual tension that existed between Henry, Otis, and Becky (Tracy Arnold), Otis's sister, a woman down on her luck who has come to live with her brother. In the final scene of the movie, Henry decapitates Otis. The movie is especially powerful insofar as it seems to trivialize murder, as in the scene in which Henry and Otis murder two prostitutes, then go out and casually share an order of French fries.

A family of serial killers can be seen in Rob Zombie's horror films, *House of 1000 Corpses* (2003) and *The Devil's Rejects* (2005). Serial killers also are depicted in numerous other popular films, such as *Se7en* (1995) and the *Scream* films (1996, 1997, 2000, 2011).

Two particularly powerful films pose interesting questions relevant to this distinction: *Monster* (2003) and *American Psycho* (1999). *Monster*'s Aileen (Charlize Theron) might be a rare example of a serial killer who seems more antisocial than psychopathic. She is able to express and share love for another (her lover, played by Christina Ricci) and in the film she claims that her killings were in self-defense (as did serial killer Aileen Wuornos in real life). In *American Psycho*, Patrick Bateman (played by Christian Bale) is shown killing many people throughout the film. If we are to take this literally, then he is clearly a psychopathic personality. Interestingly, the film also suggests that all of the murders depicted in the film are in Bateman's thoughts/fantasies, which is supported by plot elements, by his extensive fantasy doodles, and cinematically at the end through close-up shots of Bateman's head. The viewer is left to believe that Bateman is very narcissistic and has heavy antisocial traits, but is not a psychopath.

The cinema is replete with examples of characters who illustrate the psychopathic personality. Some salient examples include Kurt Dussander (Ian McKellen) in *Apt Pupil* (1998), a film that depicts the rekindling of a suppressed psychopathic personality; *In Cold Blood* (1967); *The Boston Strangler* (1968); *Henry: Portrait of a Serial Killer* (1990); Fritz Lang's child serial killer in *M* (1931); Dennis Hopper as a sociopath in both *Blue Velvet* (1986) and *Speed* (1994); and Michael Shannon playing hit man Richard Kuklinski in *The Iceman* (2013). Charles Manson, as portrayed by Steve Railsback in the film *Helter Skelter* (1976), is another example of the indifferent disregard for social values and moral behavior that is found in people with psychopathic per-

sonalities. (Manson, responsible for the death of nine people in 1969, has never shown any remorse for his behavior or the deaths of his victims.)

"A door had been opened that couldn't be shut."

Kurt Dussander (Ian McKellen), a reclusive former Nazi henchman in hiding in *Apt Pupil* (1998)

The legendary director Stanley Kubrick frequently depicted psychopathic personalities in his films. Perhaps his most famous is the street hoodlum, Alex, in *A Clockwork Orange* (1971); other characters in his films with strong psychopathic tendencies include the senior drill instructor (Gunnery Sergeant Hartman) in *Full Metal Jacket* (1987), the deteriorating character of Jack Torrance (Jack Nicholson) in *The Shining* (1980), the deceptive computer, Hal, in *2001: A Space Odyssey* (1968), the obsessed pedophile in *Lolita* (1962), and the generals who confronted Kurt Douglas's character in the antiwar masterpiece *Paths of Glory* (1957).

A classic example of a psychopathic personality is found in Alfred Hitchcock's *Strangers on a Train* (1951). Bruno Anthony (Robert Walker), who repeatedly engages in unlawful behavior (including murder), is deceitful and glib and shows impulsivity, and there is never any reason to suspect he feels any remorse for the murder he commits or his plan to have his father murdered.

Borderline Personality Disorder

Borderline personality disorder is characterized by unstable but intense interpersonal relationships, labile mood, impulsive behavior, and erratic emotions. These individuals are easily angered, but their anger may pass as quickly as a summer storm, leaving no sign of its recent presence. Fear of abandonment is a pathognomonic characteristic of borderline personalities. These individuals become overly attached in almost all of their relationships: When they initially become romantically involved, their partners are apt to feel smothered by the intensity of the relationship and perplexed by the wild swings between affection and anger; when they enter therapy, therapists quickly become concerned about their excessive dependence and inappropriate adulation. These are the patients most likely to call in the middle of the night, insisting on an emergency consultation or late-night office visit. This is most apt to occur when the patient feels isolated or alone (e.g., when the therapist is about to take a vacation). They often vacillate between indiscriminate adulation and active hatred, sometimes within the space of a few hours.

Suicidal gestures and self-injury are common in people with borderline personality disorders. These gestures cannot be ignored, because completed suicide occurs in about 10% of borderline personality disorder cases. However, it is more common for the patient to behave in ways that are more attention seeking than life threatening, such as swallowing 20 Valium pills and then calling a crisis center, or making superficial cuts on the upper arm before calling a suicide hotline. Self-mutilation is also a common and serious problem with borderline personalities. The symptoms of borderline personality disorder overlap with those of both depression and bipolar disorders, and some borderline personality patients respond to treatment with either antidepressants or mood stabilizers. Women are diagnosed with borderline personality disorder much more often than men.

Glenn Close's character Alex Forrest in *Fatal Attraction* (1987) offers one of the best available depictions of borderline personality disorder. Michael Douglas plays Dan Gallagher, a happily married New York attorney who becomes sexually involved with Alex Forrest, a glamorous and sexually aggressive publishing executive. What starts out as a simple, one-night affair for Dan turns into a nightmare for him and his family as Alex becomes increasingly possessive and manipulative. Dan tries to extricate himself from the affair, but Alex resorts to verbal threats, telephone calls to his wife, a suicide gesture (slashing her wrists after Dan tells her the affair is over), and intimidation of his wife and child. The performance by Close dramatically illustrates many characteristics of patients with a borderline personality disorder: anger, impulsivity, emotional lability, fear of rejection and abandonment, inappropriate behavior, vacillation between adulation and disgust, and self-mutilation. Although people with borderline personality disorder can be dangerous to others (as displayed dramatically in *Fatal Attraction*), this

is not typically the case, and these individuals are probably more likely to be dangerous to themselves. If the individual has strong antisocial personality characteristics as well (which Alex Forrest does), the risk of danger to others rises.

Nicole Kidman portrays the title character in *Margot at the Wedding* (2007). Margot, a likely borderline personality, has separated from her husband, and she and her son are spending time at her sister's home for a wedding. As noted earlier in the chapter, it is difficult to diagnose a personality disorder with only a snapshot of the individual's life (e.g., a period of just a few days). Margot has very loose boundaries, labile affect, and is impulsive in her speech, and she shares the confidential news of her sister's pregnancy. Her mannerisms, speech, and behavior frequently reveal tension, anger, impulsivity, and reactivity. It is clear there has been significant tension over the years between the two sisters and a history of abuse which they discuss casually in front of their children. Margot roars with uncontrollable laughter when describing a rape. Margot also displays her fear of abandonment at the end of the film when she goes running uncontrollably after her son on a bus after just having sent him off, leaving her handbag and other items behind her on the ground. Most of her behavior and reactions are at least mildly inappropriate and have a significant impact on her life.

A more intense example of borderline personality disorder can be found in Rae (Christina Ricci) in *Black Snake Moan* (2006), a film that exposes the protagonist's character flaws through a mixture of tragic scenes and beautiful interpersonal scenes. Rae is an unstable young woman whose fear of abandonment intensifies when her boyfriend Ronnie (Justin Timberlake) leaves for war. She covers over her fear with alcohol, drug abuse, and casual sex with multiple men. Sex is the only way she knows to relate to others. She has a history of abuse and allows others to take advantage of her. She displays a high level of explosive behavior and transient dissociative symptoms, both characteristic of people with borderline personality disorders. Also interesting is that over time she reverts back to her same pervasive patterns of seductiveness and explosiveness.

Christina Ricci has become very successful at portraying borderline personality, as demonstrated by two other films. In *Prozac Nation* (2001), her character, Elizabeth "Lizzie" Wurtzel, displays an intense fear of abandonment, is emotionally labile, possesses and then rejects her boyfriend, sabotages her friends, experiences multiple crises, has a deep underlying self-hatred, and reports a history of self-injurious behavior. She also suffers from comorbid depression. Likewise, her character Amanda Chase in Woody Allen's *Anything Else* (2003) displays borderline personality qualities in her interpersonal relationships and her affective instability. She has some attention-seeking qualities, is dishonest, manipulatively takes advantage of a dependent man, uses drugs, and is defensive and self-righteous in explaining her decisions and behaviors.

Another Woody Allen character – albeit deeper and darker – displaying a borderline personality disorder is Maria Elena, played by Academy Award winner Penelope Cruz in *Vicky Cristina Barcelona* (2008). She is unstable, intense in relationships, sexually impulsive, affectively labile, has rage-like temper and revengefulness, and is briefly suicidal with dissociative symptoms.

A more manipulative illustration of borderline personality can be found in Barbara Covett (Judi Dench), in *Notes on a Scandal* (2006). Barbara, a veteran teacher, discovers a younger teacher, Sheba Hart (Cate Blanchett), having an affair with a 15-year-old student, and the two women engage in a battle of manipulation and deceit. Barbara is a lonely woman with no friends or intimate contacts and seems to crave touch and emotional connection; she feels an intense attraction toward Sheba, sexualizes her, and engages her in a touching/stroking game. People with borderline personality disorders often misread and distort the realities of interpersonal situations, particularly those involving intimacy, and Barbara misreads their friendship as evidence of a deeper, more intimate connection. At the same time, she has no qualms about taking advantage of Sheba's trust and loyalty, and she betrays Sheba's trust, just as Shakespeare's Iago betrays Othello. Barbara also displays the pathognomonic symptom of fear of abandonment, even with respect to her cat. The viewer peers into Barbara's internal world through voice-over narration associated with her thinking and her journaling. In watching this film, the viewer is reminded that people with personality disorders exhibit repetitive behavioral patterns over time, and we learn that Barbara had often been obsessed with younger teachers and that in the past her behavior

had led to a restraining order against her by another teacher; in a concluding scene, the viewer sees Barbara grooming her next victim.

The hospital staff in the film *Girl, Interrupted* (1999) apply the diagnosis of borderline personality disorder to the lead character, Susanna (Winona Ryder). It is difficult to justify this diagnosis, as Susanna only seems to display two behaviors fitting this diagnosis – a suicide attempt and sexual promiscuity. However, she is clearly depressed and has serious relationship problems. A rare depiction of male borderline personality can be found in Tom Ripley (Matt Damon) in *The Talented Mr. Ripley* (1999). Ripley has a tremendous fear of abandonment and even commits a murder to prevent himself from experiencing the pain of abandonment. Other potential examples of borderline personalities include Theresa Dunn (Diane Keaton) in *Looking for Mr. Goodbar* (1977), Marilyn Monroe in *My Week with Marilyn* (2011), and several of the female supporting characters in Martin Scorsese's *After Hours* (1985). Catherine Tramell (Sharon Stone) in *Basic Instinct* (1992) and *Basic Instinct 2* (2006) displays a number of borderline characteristics, not all of which meet explicit *DSM-5* criteria; for example, she is interpersonally manipulative, sexually exploitative and impulsive, seductive in therapy sessions (in the latter film), emotionally labile, angry, and vengeful.

Histrionic Personality Disorder

The defining feature of histrionic personality is dramatic attention-seeking behavior. These individuals are self-centered and preoccupied with their appearance. They feel uncomfortable in any situation in which they are not "center stage," and they can quickly turn their emotion on or off and with little provocation. They resent attention directed at others and will often engage in excessive behavior to have the focus of attention redirected to themselves. They initially seem to be spontaneous and interesting people, not unlike Rosalind Russell's portrayal of the title character in the film *Auntie Mame* (1958). However, true histrionic personalities soon find that others quickly tire of their desperate attempts to remain at the center of attention and are angered by their inability to engage in equitable social interaction.

Carolyn Burnham (Annette Bening) in *American Beauty* (1999) is very melodramatic and clearly a character with a histrionic personality. She is unhappy and understimulated in her marriage, and she is having an affair with a man whom she admires for superficial reasons – he is rich, successful, charming, and highly narcissistic. She ruins a rare intimate moment with her husband Lester (Kevin Spacey) when she shows obsessive concern that he might spill beer on the couch. She is exact in her appearance, dressing in elegant clothes that make her stand out. At work as a real estate agent, Carolyn attempts to sell a house by exaggerating the house's appearance to unimpressed customers. She shows excessive emotionality and breaks down when faced with the reality that bright smiles and superficiality do not sell houses, and she goes into an emotional fit, crying, slapping herself in the face, stomping on the floor, and yelling, "Shut up! Stop it! You're weak! You baby! Shut up! Shut up! Shut up!" In social situations, Carolyn displays a very loud laugh that can be heard across a crowded room. She is socially inappropriate and highly critical of family members, such as when she greets her daughter after her daughter's dance routine, "I watched you closely. You didn't screw up once," with a big smile on her face as if she has just made an important, helpful observation. Her daughter looks at her in disgust.

In addition, rapid shifting from one extreme emotion to another is common in people with histrionic personality disorders. Carolyn quickly switches from hysterical laughter to blatant seriousness with a man she desires, and later from tearful crying to anger and slapping her daughter's face. Histrionic personalities are often very suggestible as well. Carolyn displays a ridiculous level of awe for another real estate agent's mantra, "You cannot count on anyone except yourself," and she follows and teaches this as the most important lesson to learn in life. In summary, appearance and style are far more important than substance for the person with a histrionic personality disorder.

Another precisely accurate example of a histrionic personality is Katharine Hepburn's portrayal of a dying mother in *Long Day's Journey into Night* (1962). Family life centers around the mother, and her two sons and her husband dote on her. She is extremely concerned with her appearance, openly fishes for compliments, and makes frequent references to her lost beauty. If she were being clinically evaluated, Hepburn's character Mary Tyrone would be diagnosed as having histrionic personality disorder and as opioid-dependent (morphine) with physiological dependence.

In *White Oleander* (2002), Robin Wright Penn plays Starr (an appropriate name for a histrionic character), the first mother figure for a young adolescent, Astrid (Alison Lohman), whose biological mother has been incarcerated. Starr is a former stripper, recovering alcoholic, and born-again Christian who encourages Astrid to read the Bible and accept Jesus as her savior. At first, Starr is kind and overly helpful in her care for Astrid; soon the viewer realizes these are superficial overtures that develop into a dangerous murder attempt when Starr becomes threatened as she realizes that Astrid's emerging sexuality excites her husband.

The classic example of histrionic personality disorder is found in Blanche DuBois's character (played by Vivien Leigh) in Elia Kazan's *A Streetcar Named Desire* (1951) based on Tennessee William's play by the same name. Blanche is clearly attention seeking, and she likes to be the center of attention. Her behavior is seductive and sexually provocative, and the sexual tension between her and Stanley, her brother-in-law, played by Marlon Brando, is present from the earliest moments in the film. Her emotions are shallow and shift often (such as when she screams when a glass of cola overflows onto her dress). There is a theatrical quality to almost every interaction, and it is clear that she imbues even casual interactions with a significance that simply would not be there for most people. Woody Allen plays homage to *A Streetcar Named Desire* in *Blue Jasmine* (2013), a film in which Cate Blanchett plays the title role of Jasmine, a woman widowed and left broke after her husband's suicide, who still flies first class when she comes to San Francisco to stay with her sister. Jasmine – like Blanche DuBois – would also qualify for a diagnosis of narcissistic personality disorder. Her exhaustion and apprehension about an uncertain future are captured in Figure 24.

"Anxiety, nightmares and a nervous breakdown, there's only so many traumas a person can withstand until they take to the streets and start screaming."

The histrionic Jasmine reflects on her troubles in Woody Allen's *Blue Jasmine* (2013)

Figure 24. *Blue Jasmine* (2013, Gravier Productions). Produced by Letty Aronson, Stephen Tenenbaum, and Edward Walson. Directed by Woody Allen.

Narcissistic Personality Disorder

People with a narcissistic personality have an intense need for admiration, are often self-centered, and have an exaggerated sense of their own importance. They may spend a great deal of time fantasizing about success or power. They feel entitled to special treatment and expect that others will automatically comply with their expectations; this often leads to their appearing conceited and pretentious. Their preoccupation with themselves leads them to overlook or devalue the contributions of others. The name of this disorder is taken from the Greek myth of Narcissus, who fell in love with his own reflection. Mirrors are often used in films portraying narcissists to symbolize self-reflection and infatuation with self, and distorted or broken mirrors are used to represent a fractured sense of worth or esteem.

Although presenting as confident and secure, people with narcissistic personality disorder have low self-esteem and harbor unconscious feelings of insecurity, unworthiness, and self-doubt. Consider the film *Phone Booth* (2003), which is mainly worthwhile for the ending in which a highly narcissistic New Yorker is stripped of his defenses and completely unravels, admitting to all his deceits, manipulations, and cover-ups, from the expensive clothes he wears, to his deep relationship fears, to keeping a young male sidekick around to feel better about himself. Suddenly, all his grandiosity, entitlement, and conceit are gone. He had never admitted these deeper issues even to himself in a conscious way, and they remained present but deeply embedded. It took an extreme situation to trigger awareness and admission. Of course, most narcissists do not come to such insights about themselves, and when they do, it is not long before they return to their old patterns.

The narcissistic wound is also exhibited in *Overnight* (2003), a docudrama that tells the rags to riches to rags story of Troy Duffy, a bartender offered an attractive deal by Miramax for his screenplay. Nevertheless, it is Duffy's narcissism – his grandiose sense of self-importance, preoccupation with success, entitlement, and his willingness to exploit others to get his own way – that leads to his downfall and the likelihood he will never work in Hollywood again. The film does a good job of depicting a deeply troubled/wounded man who is completely unaware of his shortcomings.

Contemporary cinema is replete with examples of narcissistic personality disorders: Andy Garcia's fascinating character, Byron, in *The Man from Elysian Fields* (2001), is a narcissistic, struggling writer who eventually realizes his narcissism and subsequent self-inflicted destruction and makes a change by facing his pain; Michael Douglas's portrayal of narcissistic personalities in *Solitary Man* (2009) and *Wall Street* (1987, 2010); Nicholas Cage's corporate character Jack Campbell in *The Family Man* (2000) states that his only concerns are for money and power, nothing deeper; Ben Stiller's ridiculous character Derek in *Zoolander* (2001), is too self-absorbed to realize he has been brainwashed; and John Turturro's character Dante Dominio is a narcissistic opera singer and performer in *The Man Who Cried* (2000). Robert Downey Jr.'s superhero character in the *Iron Man* (2008, 2010, 2013) films has a strong need for admiration, is grandiose, feels superior and special, and approaches relationships in an egotistical way. The consequences of his narcissism emerge when he insists that no one in the world can mimic or replicate his amazing technology; this is disproven, and it almost results in his death. In *Watch Out* (2008) we see an extreme example of narcissism in the film's protagonist, who masturbates while admiring polaroid photos of himself and who at one point has sex with an anatomically correct blowup doll with a pasted image of his own face pasted over the doll's face. In *American Psycho* (2000), Christian Bale's character would clearly qualify for a diagnosis of narcissistic personality disorder, as well as antisocial personality disorder – and a number of other diagnoses as well.

"Underneath all that bravado beats the heart of a guy who's not nearly as cocky as he wants everybody to believe."

Liz (Susan Sarandon) calling out the narcissism of Alfie (Jude Law) in *Alfie* (2004)

In *Roger Dodger* (2002), Roger Swanson (Campbell Scott) is a classic narcissistic personality – a womanizer who is teaching a 16-year-old adolescent boy about how men think and see the world. He teaches the boy to see, think, and perceive sex everywhere he looks. Roger creates various "opportunities" for the boy to seduce women – at the bar, at a party, and then with prostitutes. He has no qualms about encouraging the boy to take advantage of a drunken woman who has passed out. Roger displays little true empathy for the boy as he thrusts him to manhood. Underneath Roger's inflated self-image and conceit is his rage at being rejected by his attractive boss (Isabella Rossellini) who has put an end to their love affair.

In *Lovelife* (1997), Alan (Jon Tenney) is a minor writer and professor who believes his work is very important. He seems to care only for himself and his writing. He treats women badly and exploits them through seduction, deceit, and manipulation, and he eloquently explains his approach and craft to a barfly. In denying his own arrogance, Alan believes he is compassionate and sensitive because he has to struggle to manage a relationship with two women (the real issue is that one of the women is not as fawning as the other). He believes women should be at his "beck and call" (one character describes him by saying, "he says what he wants and everybody jumps").

"I want somebody to think I'm the greatest thing that ever happened to them and without me they couldn't go on."

The narcissistic writer Alan in *Lovelife* (1997)

The film accurately portrays the underlying sensitivity to criticism and inherent low self-esteem of the narcissist (which frequently results in narcissistic injuries). Alan gets very upset, stubborn, and passive-aggressive when his girlfriend does not come to his lecture; he expresses an intense fear of abandonment as he makes a big production about his girlfriend leaving a party without him, he then grovels on his knees with the girl standing over him, and lies on a girl's lap to receive the motherly nurturance and attention he so deeply craves.

"Let's hurt someone!"

Chad (Aaron Eckhart) in
In the Company of Men (1997)

Director Neil LaBute created unforgettable and cruel narcissists in two of his bitterly satirical movies – *In the Company of Men* (1997) and *The Shape of Things* (2003). Though there are two male narcissists in the former movie, Chad (Aaron Eckhart) is more pathological as he convinces his friend that they should seduce a vulnerable, deaf woman and get her to fall in love with both of them, planning to subsequently dump her. Chad feels entitled to do this, blaming women for being rejecting, controlling, and manipulative, ostensibly believing he and his partner can restore dignity to men through revenge and the pain of the innocent. In *The Shape of Things*, a character named Evelyn (Rachel Weisz) transforms Adam (Paul Rudd), an anxious, insecure, shy person, into a physically attractive, stylish, confident man. Without any qualms, she shocks Adam, the viewer, and the audience to whom she is giving a presentation when she reveals that her relationship with Adam has been a class "project" in which she used a human subject to prove that people are like clay and can easily be molded and manipulated. When talking with Adam afterward, Evelyn has a strongly stubborn, confident, and resentful expression on her face. She believes she has made him a better person and thus should be thanked for her behavior. The characters in each film have strong antisocial qualities evident in their complete disregard for others and social convention and in their pathological manipulation. They are literally predators who consciously seek out their prey – a vulnerable, neurotic individual with poor esteem. The endings of both movies reveal just how pathological both characters are as they reveal their manipulative "game," totally devoid of empathy. A similar plotline depicting extensive female manipulativeness can be found in *My Summer of Love* (2004).

Female narcissists are less common, but include Madonna portraying a grandiose, striking Eva Peron in *Evita* (1997). Eva emphasizes physical appearance, presentation to others, and her posture as critically important features. She manipulates people throughout the film for her own advantage – to help her rise in her career and look better in front of oth-

ers. Annette Bening as Julia Lambert in *Being Julia* (2004) is another example of a female narcissist. Julia is a star of the theater who relishes her success and revels in her fame; however, feelings of self-loathing break through whenever she is rejected. She has been addicted to work most of her career, but taking a break and having an affair revitalize her, and her narcissism seems to shift. The character also has some histrionic qualities as throughout the film it is often difficult for the viewer to discern when Julia is acting and when she is feeling/expressing real emotions. In addition, Mena Suvari's adolescent character, Angela Hayes, in *American Beauty* has narcissistic traits clearly seen in her preoccupation in becoming a model, her lack of empathy for a new student who has been hospitalized, and her strong beliefs that she is somehow special and important.

Additional Questions for Discussion (Cluster B Disorders)

➤ Why are most film examples of borderline personality cases women and most examples of narcissistic personality disorders men? Is this an accurate clinical picture?

➤ What qualities of the Cluster B disorders make them the most common personality disorders found in jails and prisons?

➤ Do you agree with the distinction between the antisocial personality and psychopath/sociopath? State your case.

➤ Does society have a role in the creation of serial killers?

➤ One way of interpreting *Monster* is that Aileen Wuornos is a victim of circumstance. Would Aileen have developed into a murderer if she had not been a prostitute? What would have happened if she had never been abused?

➤ With which of these disorders is a client most likely to seek treatment? When and why? Who is least likely to ask for help?

➤ How close does Tom Ripley's character in *The Talented Mr. Ripley* come to meeting the criteria for each of the four disorders in this cluster?

➤ Richard Kuklinski, the hit man portrayed in the biopic *The Iceman*, refuses to kill women or children, although he has no compunctions about killing dozens of other people. Is this portrayal realistic and accurate?

Other classic narcissistic characters include Norma Desmond (Gloria Swanson) in *Sunset Blvd.* (1950) and an (initially) arrogant and self-serving Whitey Marsh (Mickey Rooney) in *Boys Town* (1938). In *The Doctor* (1991), William Hurt plays Jack MacKee, a self-centered and narcissistic physician who cares little for anything except himself and his career until he develops a tumor in his throat and discovers what it feels like to be a patient. Warren Beatty plays Bugsy Siegel, a narcissistic and self-centered gangster in the Barry Levinson film *Bugsy* (1991). Finally, Nicole Kidman plays the role of Suzanne Maretto, a narcissistic television personality who will stop at nothing to achieve her ambitions in *To Die For* (1995).

Cluster C Disorders

As is true in clinical settings, characters in films will have symptoms and personality characteristics that overlap with more than one disorder in each cluster. For example, it is clear that Robin Williams' milquetoast character in *One Hour Photo* (2002) has a personality disorder; however, he has characteristics of several disorders, most of which are found in Cluster C. He lives alone, being too scared to take the risks that relationships require (avoidant); he is obsessed with a pseudo family (dependent); and he is orderly and rigid in handling photos at work and hoarding photos at home (obsessive-compulsive). Add in some depression with psychotic features, a probable history of past sexual abuse, and voyeuristic elements and Williams' character becomes even more complex.

Avoidant Personality Disorder

People with **avoidant personality disorder** have a tremendous fear of being exposed as inadequate and inferior. They are hypersensitive to criticism and shape their lives around fear of rejection and disapproval. They generally avoid intimate relations, convinced that they would be ridiculed as inadequate lovers. They conceptualize the world (and especially interpersonal relationships and interactions) as unsafe and threatening. They have diminished self-esteem and describe themselves as inept, incompetent, and inferior. They are apt to spend much of their time at home and alone, in large part because of their concern that their personal deficiencies will be revealed if they venture out in public. These pervasive feelings of inferiority typically originate in childhood. In Adlerian terms, the person with an avoidant personality lacks the *courage to be imperfect*. However, it is important for clinicians to be sensitive to cultural differences that may affect a client's behavior. For example, in some Asian cultures, self-deprecation and extreme modesty about one's own achievements are normative behaviors and not indicative of a maladaptive personality trait.

This diagnosis overlaps substantially with the diagnosis of **social phobia, generalized type**. The overlap is so substantial that many clinicians find the distinction between the two diagnoses to be meaningless, and the two diagnoses may be simply different ways of conceptualizing the same (or similar) conditions. Keep this in mind as you read about the characters in the following films.

Avoidant personality can be distinguished from schizoid personality in that although both avoid interpersonal contact, the avoidant person actually craves the intimacy lacking in life. *Finding Forrester* (2000) is about a high school student, Jamal, who befriends a reclusive, retired professor and writer, William Forrester (Sean Connery), who seems to want more intimate connections. This film is about people who are trying to get "unstuck" from their avoidance patterns. In *Finding Forrester*, Connery's character does not leave his apartment and can only be seen by others when he is cleaning his windows. He wrote an award-winning book 50 years ago but has not been published since then. He seems to have given up, perhaps because of fear of rejection. He avoids other people and denies being interested in any life other than his own. When he does eventually go out, he has a panic attack when in a crowd. He is socially inappropriate, such as when he closes the door in the face of Jamal without saying goodbye. There is a fundamental sadness in William's isolation in his apartment; he actually does look for connection as a voyeur, watching others outside with interest and keeping his windows clean so he can continue observing the outside world. The viewer begins to wonder how much of William's isolation is loneliness. The protagonist frequently drinks alcohol alone, often while working. He avoids discussing personal issues such as his family history or his work. Clearly, he is reluctant to risk interpersonal sharing, and although this changes significantly as the friendship with Jamal develops, William keeps the secret of his cancer to himself.

Dependent Personality Disorder

Dependent personalities have extreme difficulty making decisions. They are submissive and look to others for structure, meaning, and direction in their lives. They tend to be passive and clinging. These people lack assertion skills and submit to the will of others. They sometimes submit to verbal, physical, or sexual abuse by their spouses and others. They lack self-confidence and feel they cannot manage on their own. They fear the loss of approval that may occur if they express their own opinions or beliefs. They invest tremendous time and energy in maintaining a relationship with the person upon whom they are dependent. When a close, dependent relationship ends, they almost immediately seek out another relationship that supports their chronic need for succor.

An amusing illustration of a dependent personality occurs in the 1991 film *What About Bob?* Bob, played by Bill Murray, is the patient of a psychologist played by Richard Dreyfuss. Bob pursues the beleaguered psychologist across the country when he tries to take a short family vacation. Almost all therapists have had overly dependent patients, although they are unlikely to have encountered a case as extreme as that of Bob. The film is an interesting starting point for a discussion of transference and countertransference.

"I've been seeing myself through him for years."

Dependent personality in *Lovelife* (1997)

In *Lovelife* (1997), a female bartender, Molly, maintains a high level of obsequiousness toward her narcissistic boyfriend, Alan, doing everything she can for him and losing her own identity in the process. Molly believes Alan can do "no wrong" and that he has no flaws; in addition, she subjects herself to his

unrelenting criticism. Like many other dependent personalities, she finds herself rejected by her boyfriend who takes up with another woman; when he loses that other woman, he shows up, and Molly takes him back.

In *White Oleander* (2002), Renée Zellweger plays Claire Richards, a foster mother with a dependent personality. Claire's submissiveness to her husband, her inability to confront or challenge his decisions, and her vulnerability to manipulation by others leads her to commit suicide. Jason Biggs' agreeable, people-pleasing character Jerry Falk in *Anything Else* (2003) is so dependent he has to be "tricked" into being alone, into asserting his needs, and into challenging himself.

Obsessive-Compulsive Personality Disorder

A person with **obsessive-compulsive personality disorder** (OCPD) has enduring, inflexible, and maladaptive personality traits that involve perfectionism, orderliness, and an excessive need for control. They display exacting attention to detail and may devote a great deal of time to making lists and plans. Time is seen not as the fabric of life but rather as an enemy and something to be conquered. All of this psychological energy is expended in a futile attempt to achieve a sense of control over the exigencies of life and the vicissitudes of fortune. Two films that are solid depictions of OCPD are *The Odd Couple* (1968) and *M*A*S*H* (1970). *The Odd Couple* presents a memorable performance by Jack Lemmon as Felix Unger, the neurotic roommate of Oscar Madison (Walter Matthau), who roams the house with a can of air freshener, determined to eliminate any unpleasant smells. In *M*A*S*H*, Major Frank Burns (Robert Duvall) spends the entire war fretting about the antics of "Hawkeye" Pierce (Donald Sutherland) and "Trapper" John McIntyre (Elliott Gould) and the inability of the system to set limits on their exuberant behavior. He is obsessed with rank and bitterly resents any undue familiarity by enlisted men or junior officers. He also works hard to ensure that the enlisted men do not fraternize with Korean women. He is self-righteous, moralistic, and rigid, despite the fact that he is having an ongoing affair with "Hot Lips" Hoolihan (Sally Kellerman). He becomes furious when he does not get his way, and he is totally ineffectual in responding to the cavalier attitudes of his tent mates.

Another classic film to portray OCPD is *Mommie Dearest* (1981), which stars Faye Dunaway as Joan Crawford. Joan pursues a life devoted to extrinsic values – appearance, fame, money, and possessions are what matter most to her. She senses she is missing one thing in her life – a child; following two divorces and many miscarriages, she finally adopts two children after using her power and lawyer boyfriend to pull some strings. Her attempts at being a good parent vanquish quickly, and her OCPD takes over. She is deeply perfectionistic of herself (e.g., her personal appearance, the cleanliness of her house, her relationships, and her children). She drives her daughter harder and harder, and her behavior becomes monstrous and abusive. She displays rigidity, perfectionism, and orderliness in almost every situation. In addition, there is an underlying anger that drives her behavior. Joan would likely be diagnosed with comorbid conditions of alcohol dependence and borderline personality disorder, the latter diagnosis supported by her deep fear of abandonment, emotional instability, sexual promiscuity, and push–pull messages in her relationships (e.g., in one scene with her boyfriend, she alternates between of begging and threatening).

Ben Stiller portrays a character with OCPD in *Greenberg* (2010). Rastogi (2011), in her *PsycCRITIQUES* review of the film, finds that Greenberg shows that he meet the criteria for OCPD, as evidenced by those scenes in which his sensitivity to imperfections becomes pathological and affects his daily life. He copes with this by writing complaint letters to institutions: for example, he writes to American Airlines detailing a problem with the button on his reclining seat on an airplane, and he writes to government officials because too many Los Angeles drivers are honking their horns.

It is important to understand the difference between OCPD and obsessive-compulsive disorder. The first reflects a maladaptive personality style; the second indicates the presence of a serious mental disorder characterized by recurrent and persistent thoughts, images, or impulses (obsessions) and repetitive behaviors or mental acts (compulsions) that the individual cannot avoid or suppress. For example, an obsessive-compulsive personality may need to be constantly cleaning the house and "picking up." This is maladaptive (when excessive) but may not significantly impair the person's life, and may be mildly adaptive in some roles. However, the patient with an **obsessive-compulsive disorder** – for example, Nicholas Cage's character Roy Waller in *Matchstick Men* (2003) – spends much of the day focused on their obsession or engaged in compulsive behavior. This individual is significantly distressed by his or her problem, and realizes that the behavior or thoughts are abnormal and out of control. In contrast, people with OCPD are far less likely to be troubled by their condition.

John Turturro plays Al Fountain, a man with OCPD, in *Box of Moonlight* (1996). Turturro's character is rigid, overly conscientious, and rule-driven in both his work as a manager and in his family life with his wife and children. Al is rigid about the way his child learns using flashcards and obsessively asks about their use; he seems unable to handle joking, and has to rehearse a social situation before its occurrence. He is awkward and rigid at his job, bossing others around, seems robotic and machine-like, and is stiff in behavior (e.g., walking). The depiction of the effect of these OCPD traits on the family and coworkers is very clear: Family members are avoidant, passive, or hesitant around him, and his coworkers make fun of him behind his back.

Al takes time off work and away from his family to loosen up as he goes on a journey to search out his past. Along the way, two Jehovah's Witnesses quickly and accurately get at his pain and sense of loss over the years (perhaps confronting the etiology of his OCPD), but they soon turn reli-

> **Additional Questions for Discussion (Cluster C Disorders)**
>
> ➤ How close does Robin Williams' character in *One Hour Photo* (2002) come to meeting the criteria for each of the disorders in this cluster?
> ➤ Since anxiety is a strong component of these disorders, can medication be an important part of treatment?
> ➤ Is the treatment the same for a person with OCD as it is with OCPD?
> ➤ What advantages are associated with being OCPD, avoidant, or dependent?

gious and begins proselytizing, which only alienates him. In a couple of scenes, Al sees things going backwards – for example, water being poured and a child riding a bike. Does this represent his life going backwards? It is a fascinating cinematic example of the lack of progress that occurs when one is so stuck in routine that it seems as if one is going backwards. Moreover, it is a metaphor for time, one of the biggest enemies to someone with OCPD.

Films Portraying Various Personality Disorders

Some readers may want to see films that depict several personality disorders in one viewing for educational and clinical purposes. These films present interesting dynamics in their portrayal of interactions between different pathologies. Some examples follow.

Bartleby (2001) displays a classic example of schizoid personality in the lead character, Bartleby, portrayed exquisitely by Crispin Glover. Surrounding Bartleby, in a colorful office, are coworkers who are narcissistic (Joe Piscopo as Rocky, a self-inflated womanizer), schizotypal (Ernie, a disheveled man who often speaks in word salad), histrionic (Vivien, seductive and attention seeking), and dependent (the boss, unable to separate himself from a "fired" employee).

In *White Oleander* (2002), we see a young girl under the care of various mother figures, each with their own personality flaws. The child goes from her biological mother, Ingrid (an antisocial manipulator), to Starr (a dangerous histrionic), to Claire (a dependent personality with low self-esteem), and eventually to Rena (an antisocial personality who forces her foster children to sell clothes on the street to make money). The eyes of each mother seem to say it all, from the penetrating eyes of Ingrid to the downtrodden eyes of Claire.

The Royal Tenenbaums (2001) portrays the ultimate dysfunctional family, with pathologies that include narcissism, dependency, incest, suicidal behavior, paranoia, addiction, depression, and antisocial behavior, along with a schizotypal friend.

Woody Allen's *Anything Else* (2003) portrays an older man with a narcissistic personality disorder who befriends a young person with a dependent personality disorder in a relationship with someone with a borderline personality.

French director Jean Pierre-Jeunet purposefully creates films with very interesting and quirky personalities who play their roles on elaborate, often fantastical, set designs. For examples, see *Amélie* (2001), *The City of Lost Children* (1995), and *Delicatessen* (1992).

International Films: Personality Disorders

Cluster A

The character Joseph (Dominique Pinon) in *Amélie* (2001) meets the criteria for a paranoid personality, as he is so suspicious of his ex-girlfriend dating and meeting other men that he sits all day in the café where she works and watches her closely. He carries a small tape recorder in his pocket and records her various laughs, comments, and conversations with his own play-by-play and time of day voice-over. The viewer sees this is a pattern (thus providing additional weight for the diagnosis) as he continues similar suspicious behavior with the next woman he begins to go out with and then again with the first girlfriend when the new girlfriend dumps him. Anger and quick defensive reactions are common in the paranoid personality and are clearly part of Joseph's personality.

Cluster B

A classic in film history is *Breathless* (1960, France) by Jean-Luc Godard, one of the leading directors of the French New Wave cinema of the 1960s. This movement involved filmmakers who shifted toward being more abstract and experimental in writing style and narrative structure, and emphasized psychological and social issues such as psychopathology and alienation rather than hard sciences and technology. In *Breathless*, the protagonist, Michel Poiccard (Jean-Paul Belmondo), is a young hoodlum and an antihero. He steals, gets in police chases in which he glibly kills one of the officers, and spends his time on the run from the authorities. He becomes truly fascinated by an American girl (Patricia Franchini, played by Jean Seberg) and tries to convince her to escape to Rome with him. This character is devoid of empathy and is characterized by selfishness, rudeness, blaming, and objectification of women.

Polish director Krzysztof Kieslowski created *The Decalogue* (1989), an extraordinary work composed of ten 1-hour films portraying a variety of tenants in a apartment complex. Each film relates loosely to one of the Ten Commandments. There are a number of antisocial characters scattered throughout the films, such as the mother who uses deceit and manipulation in an attempt to keep her daughter's child from her, and the young vagabond who wanders the streets and randomly strangles a taxi cab driver. *Perfume: The Story of a Murderer* (2006, Germany) is an interesting film from independent director Tom Tykwer, about a boy who grows up with a superior olfactory sense. He becomes obsessed with this ability, smelling anything in the environment, near or far. As the character, Jean-Baptiste Grenouille (Ben Whishaw), matures to adulthood, he develops a mission to "preserve scent" and to "keep smell" as he searches for the ultimate perfume. Along this journey, he directly and indirectly begins to cross boundaries (e.g., he inappropriately grabs the arm of a woman on the street without speaking to her and carefully smells her arm) and kill people – in one scene, he obsessively smells a woman after accidentally killing her by covering her mouth to prevent her from screaming; he then strips her naked and smells her whole body carefully. Recklessness, irresponsibility, and lack of remorse are key features of this character.

The Robber (2010, Germany) is based on a true story of a solo bank robber who is also an accomplished marathon runner. His one connection in life is his ex-girlfriend. His antisocial personality is dramatically portrayed in a scene in which he kills his parole officer and experience no remorse. He displays flat affect and does not consider the consequences of his actions on others. *Animal Kingdom* (2010, Australia) is a well-directed story of a diabolical crime family; the family includes numerous psychopathic killers and drug addicts. The plot involves a 17-year-old boy whose mother has just died of a drug overdose; he is sent to live with this crime family consisting of his grandmother and uncles. Upon learning how deeply pathological, manipulative, and dangerous they are, the young man realizes he must either join them or escape.

Tsotsi (2005, South Africa/UK) is a movie about an African gangster who kills others when needed and brutally beats a fellow gang member to a pulp. One day Tsotsi (Presley Chweneyagae) robs a woman and steals her car but discovers there is an infant in the back seat. He reluctantly decides to care for the baby, and this experience slowly transforms his character. Through flashbacks the viewer learns of Tsotsi's painful past – his longing for a connection with his mother, his physically abusive father, his observation of his father abusing animals, and the neglect his father orchestrated in intentionally keeping Tsotsi separate from his mother despite living in the same household. The viewer begins to feel some sympathy for this brutal character, and this experience for the viewer intensifies when Tsotsi's caring and nurturing of an infant leads him to make a connection with a caretaking mother in his village, renew a friendship with the man he beat up, and sacrifice his livelihood by returning the infant to its mother.

Another young person with an antisocial personality disorder is portrayed in a film that won the Palm d'Or at Cannes, *The Child* (2005, France). A somewhat endearing, petty street thief, Bruno (Jérémie Renier), becomes much less likeable when he sells his newborn for money. The film shows an interesting depiction of selling a baby: Bruno makes a phone call, goes into a seemingly abandoned house, walks up several flights of stairs, places his baby on his jacket in a room, walks into the next room and closes the door. He makes a call on his cell phone, saying "it's done," waits a short time, and then goes back into the first room and picks up his jacket and money.

Luis Buñuel is regarded as one of the greatest directors in cinema history. In the filming of *That Obscure Object of Desire* (1977, France/Spain), the lead actress walked off the set and Buñuel jokingly remarked that her role should be played by two women. This comment became a reality and marked his signature style of surrealism. In the film, Mateo (Fernando Rey) pursues a young Spanish woman, Conchita (who is played by two actress who do not look alike). The use of two actresses is helpful in depicting the character's borderline psychopathology. Conchita displays a mix of teasing, controlling, avoiding, manipulating, taunting, and erratic fighting. When she attempts to get the couple to agree they will never leave each other, it is clear fear of abandonment is the underlying issue. Conchita is seductive, reeling Mateo back to her – but then refusing to be intimate with him. Her push–pull behavior becomes so significant that the viewer begins to wonder when Mateo will leave the relationship.

Love Exposure (2008, Japan) is a little-known film that is surprisingly accurate in its depiction of borderline personality disorder. A dramatic woman, Kaori, falls in love with a priest and attempts to seduce him by wearing provocative clothing. She admits she goes to confession so she can be close to him in a tiny room. In the confessional, she puts his hand to her chest (so he can feel both her rapidly beating heart and her breast) and speaks of being in love with someone who cannot return her love. After the confession, she asks for his cell phone number and calls him immediately after she leaves the church. She invites him to a park where she jumps on him. He initially rejects her sexual overtures, but she persists. The two eventually move in together and hide out from the churchgoing community. Shortly thereafter, she becomes controlling, angry, and aggressive, and moves out of the home to be with a younger lover. Several scenes later, she reappears, admitting she has slept with many men in the interim. She is emotional labile with him – expressing sadness, hopelessness, anger, and joy – cycling around and around. She desires immediate satisfaction of all her whims, and she insists that they be married immediately. She also has an intense fear of abandonment, as shown by her statement: "Don't leave me! I won't let you!" She once again gets her lover to abandon his role as a priest; predictably, once they are living together, she becomes labile and agitated and walks out of their relationship.

Kaori: "Father, listen to my confession! If you turn away from me, I'll kill myself. Please listen to me."

Priest: "What can I do?"

Kaori: "I'm in love with you. I know I really am a hopeless woman. What can I do about it? Please listen to my confession."

The manipulative verbiage of Kaori, a borderline personality in *Love Exposure* (2008, Japan)

The intriguing movie *Swimming Pool* (2003, France/UK) portrays a young woman, Julie (Ludivine Sagnier), who is seductive, provocative, and has a desire for excitement. She presents as nonchalant and laid back, but she is also someone who can be easily hurt or angered. She is sexually impulsive and promiscuous, having sex with a different man each night. She throws herself at older men, even when they express disinterest. One night she appears with a bruise on her face around her eye, and the viewer is left to speculate as to what sort of danger she had been involved in while staying out the whole night. She is manipulative and jealous when her roommate begins to dance with a man. Julie acts out in anger when she is rejected. Her instability leads to a dissociative episode where she thinks she sees her mother (who is deceased) and expresses happiness at the prospect of her mother's return, screams when she is told that her mother is not there, and then faints. Julie also experiences a loss of memory, in which she is unable to remember killing her lover.

Zaza (Michel Serrault), the gay transvestite performer in *La Cage aux Folles* (in English *Birds of a Feather*; 1978, France), provides a wonderful example of a histrionic personality. She is dramatic and flamboyant, and almost everything she does is exaggerated. When her partner Renato (Ugo Tognazzi) tells her that he plans to invite his ex-wife to an important dinner with his son's future in-laws, Zaza is highly insulted and announces her intention to commit suicide. Neither Renato nor the viewer thinks for a minute that she is serious about her threat.

Cluster C

Sheila McCarthy plays Polly Vandersma, an insecure, socially awkward, temporary worker with avoidant traits in the popular Canadian film *I've Heard the Mermaids Singing* (1987). She is naïve, socially inhibited, and seems to have a fragile self-esteem and self-concept. The voice-over narration done by McCarthy provides insights into her thinking and feeling when she is interacting with others.

Audrey Tautou's whimsical and endearing title character in *Amélie* (2001, France) has many avoidant personality characteristics. Amélie wants contact with others, especially intimate love, though she is unable to take the risk. The emphasis in the film is on her thoughts and the challenge involved in meeting a man; the key theme, which the movie cleverly portrays cinematically, is her constant avoidance of actually meeting a man who comes into her life. After doing a good deed, Amélie appears nervous and looks away, ignoring an opportunity for human interaction; she simply does not know how to interact socially. The film is rare in its sophisticated exploration of the causes of Amélie's anxiety and avoidant behavior. It notes that, from birth, she was trapped between a neurotic mother (who had "shaky nerves" and was anxious about everything) and an iceberg father, who avoided all feelings. In addition, she had no playmates or social life and therefore became used to isolation, fantasy, and imagination. Other contributing etiologies are presented when she is tricked by a neighbor into feeling guilty as the "cause" of natural disasters, when her mother is dramatically killed in front of her, and when she has ongoing problems in relating and communicating with her father.

A common pattern for people with avoidant personality is the problem of self-sacrifice – devoting oneself to helping others and losing sight of one's own struggles and self-care. Amélie epitomizes self-sacrifice as she devotes herself to being a regular "do-gooder," helping others find joy and become "unstuck" from their life patterns. Amélie is personally stuck in her avoidant pattern and does not know it. Eventually, she learns to reach out to others for support and develops the courage necessary to face her fears.

Audrey Tautou portrays a Cluster C character, Michèle, in another French film, *God Is Great and I Am Not* (2002), in which she has a quirky element of dependent personality (but probably not the disorder) insofar as she repeatedly compromises her beliefs by conforming and converting to the religion of her partner at the time. She is shown trying to dedicate herself to Catholicism and Buddhism before finding a Jewish man and converting to Judaism. Her fear of being alone leads her to become suicidal after the end of an intimate relationship.

In the Spanish period film *Mad Love* (2002), a woman compulsively attaches to her husband despite continuous evidence of his philandering. She becomes preoccupied and worried about his whereabouts, yet she maintains a high level of excitement when he returns from a journey that has obviously involved infidelities. In one scene, he resists a warm embrace despite her clinging and affectionate behavior, and she asks him to lie to her about where he has been. Even when she is rejected by him, she obsessively continues to love him and believe they will be reunited upon her death.

"I want to love you even if you loathe me."

A classic dependent quote from "Joan the Mad" in *Mad Love* (2002)

Critical Thinking Questions

➤ Why do many of the films portraying personality disorders exhibit some of the most compelling and memorable characters?

➤ Why is the public so fascinated and drawn to characters who are so diabolically evil (e.g., the Joker, Anton Chigurh, or Hannibal Lecter)? Is it appropriate for these characters to receive so much attention in the media and many of the major movie awards?

➤ Is it useful to treat life-long personality characteristics as *diseases* (i.e., should personality disorders be included in the *DSM-5*)?

➤ It is difficult to treat personality disorders, and treatment may last for several years. Should insurance companies be required to cover the treatment of these conditions?

➤ Is the concept of *evil* meaningful when discussing people with antisocial personality disorders?

➤ How does a personality feature (such as suspicion) differ from a personality disorder (such as paranoid personality disorder) or a disease (such as paranoid schizophrenia)? Are the differences qualitative as well as quantitative?

➤ *Fatal Attraction* (1987) originally ended with a suicide by Alex Forrest, using a knife that had Dan Gallagher's fingerprints on it. However, viewers did not like this ending, and it was replaced with the memorable bathtub scene. Would the original ending have been more consistent with a diagnosis of borderline personality disorder?

➤ What problems can therapists anticipate when they are treating clients with borderline personality disorders?

If you have time to read just one book relevant to this chapter, make it:

 Widiger, T.A., & Costa, P.T., Jr. Eds. . (2013). *Personality disorders and the five-factor model of personality* (3rd ed.). Washington DC: American Psychological Association. doi: 10.1037/13939-000

If you only have time to read one chapter, read:

Ryder, A. G., Dere, J., Sun, J., & Chentsova-Dutton, Y. E. (2014). The cultural shaping of personality disorder. In F. T. L. Leong, L. Co-mas-Díaz, G. C. Nagayama Hall, V. C. McLoyd, & J. E. Trimble (Eds.), *APA handbooks in psychology. APA handbook of multicultural psychology: Vol. 2. Applications and training* (pp. 307–328). Washington DC: American Psychological Association. doi: 10.1037/14187-018

Wedding and Niemiec's Top 10 Personality Disorders Films

- *That Obscure Object of Desire* (1977)
- *No Country for Old Men* (2007)
- *The Talented Mr. Ripley* (1999)
- *Sunset Blvd.* (1950)
- *The Odd Couple* (1968)
- *A Streetcar Named Desire* (1951)
- *American Beauty* (1999)
- *A Clockwork Orange* (1971)
- *Blue Jasmine* (2013)
- *The Iceman* (2013)

Chapter 14

Paraphilic Disorders

Why is that day marked in red?

Arturo asks Laura about the significance of February 29th, in *Leap Year* (*Año Bieiesto*; 2010)

?   **Questions to Consider While Watching *Leap Year* (*Año Bieiesto*)**

➤ Are the depictions of sex in this film pornographic? Why or why not?

➤ Laura masturbates while watching the happily married couple next door making love. How common is it for masturbation to be paired with voyeurism?

➤ We see the sadomasochism intensify throughout the film for both Arturo and Laura. Is this kind of escalation commonplace with the paraphilias?

➤ How commonplace is rough sex? When does it become pathological?

➤ How common is it for lonely people to use casual sex as an anodyne to assuage their loneliness?

Patient Evaluation

Name: Laura

Patient's stated reason for coming
"I'm depressed; I'm lonely; I miss my father; I have sex with too many men too often, and for no good reason."

History of the present illness
Laura is a 25-year-old Mexican journalist who presents with a chronic history of dysthymia that has become worse since her father's death on February 29th, 4 years ago. She attempts to assuage the pain of loneliness with casual and sometimes violent sex. She reports that her current relationship is sadomasochistic and involves spanking, cutting, and occasional strangulation. She recently asked her lover to insert a loaded pistol into her vagina, but he refused. She sometimes uses the pistol to masturbate, and she has become obsessed with the idea that her lover will murder her on the leap year anniversary of her father's death.

Past psychiatric illness, treatment, and outcomes
Laura has been depressed for all of her adult life by self-report, but she has never been formally diagnosed or treated with psychotropic medication.

Medical history
Unremarkable. Laura is slightly obese, and she does not exercise. She was treated for gonorrhea when she was 19 years old, but there is no history of other sexually transmitted diseases.

Psychosocial history
Laura is a college graduate who is working on a freelance basis as a journalist. She lost one job recently, but quickly found another. She has a small circle of casual friends, and an on-going relationship with her mother and her brother who is her only sibling. She lives in a small apartment in Mexico City, and rarely goes out other than to visit bars where she meets and picks up sexual partners. She reports having had "hundreds" of lovers, but no serious relationship until recently when she met and became romantically involved with a man named Arturo. This relationship is sadomasochistic, with Laura being the masochistic partner. This is her first sadomasochistic relationship, and it is one that has become characterized by degradation and escalating levels of violence and abuse. She encourages her lover to slap her, urinate on her, choke her, burn her with cigarettes, and include knives and guns as a part of their sexual activity.

Drug and alcohol history
Laura denies use of drugs other than alcohol. She visits local bars almost nightly where she drinks until meeting an appropriate sexual partner. She minimizes both the amount of alcohol consumed when in bars and the clear risks associated with unprotected sex with multiple partners. For the past several months, she has been in a committed (on her side) relationship with a man who appears to be abusing her and exploiting the relationship. She drinks at home with her partner almost every time they are together; however, she denies drinking to the point of drunkenness.

Behavioral observations
Laura is articulate but soft spoken. She was appropriately dressed and on time for the interview; however, she displayed markedly depressed affect and admitted to recent suicidal ideation. She looked exhausted, and this affect coincides with her reported symptoms of fatigue and insomnia.

Mental status examination
Laura is oriented in all spheres. She was slow and deliberate in answering questions on the Mini-Mental State Examination; however, she was able to answer all questions correctly and obtained a perfect score of 30.

Strengths
Laura is an educated, articulate, and intelligent woman. She has considerable personal insight, and she recognizes and understands that she has been depressed since her father's death 4 years ago. She understands that risks are associated with both sadomasochism and unprotected sex with multiple partners. On the VIA Survey, a measure of character strengths, Laura scored highest on curiosity, creativity, perseverance, humility, and forgiveness.

Diagnosis
Sexual masochism disorder (F65.51). Rule out major depressive disorder and persistent depressive disorder.

Treatment plan
(1) Personal insight–oriented psychotherapy on a weekly basis for continued assessment of her depression and suicidal ideation; a self-care plan to manage suicidal ideation will need to be a priority in treatment. I will support and enhance her strengths of character to increase her well-being and better manage her moods; (2) Group psychotherapy with other individuals coping with paraphilias; (3) Counseling about the physical and psychological risks associated with multiple sexual partners. I will also insist that Laura gets rid of the gun she keeps in her apartment, either giving it away or having her mother or brother keep it for her for the time being.

Prognosis
Guarded.

Leap Year (Año Bieiesto) and Sadomasochism

Leap Year (Año Bieiesto) is a powerful film about a 25-year-old woman who lives in Mexico City. Laura is a journalist who spends every evening in bars where casual meetings with new men inevitably lead to one-night stands. She is deeply dissatisfied with her loneliness, and she frequently masturbates while watching a happily married couple kiss in a nearby apartment. She thinks there may be potential for a more substantive relationship when she meets Arturo, a sadist who introduces her to the world of sadomasochistic sex. She initially has reservations, but soon joins in with abandon, embracing the role of the masochist. This low-budget film was directed by Michael Rowe, an Australian expatriate living in Mexico City, and many reviewers have compared it to Bernardo Bertolucci's *Last Tango in Paris* (1972). Almost the entire movie takes place in Laura's apartment. It is a difficult film to watch, but the viewer comes away with a deep appreciation for the depth of Laura's loneliness and a better understanding of how it might lead to a masochistic relationship. Figure 25 depicts the unequal, degrading but surprisingly symbiotic relationship between Arturo the sadist and Laura the masochist.

The Range of Normal Sexual Behavior

Few areas of human behavior are as complex, varied, and interesting as sexual behavior, and filmmakers, social scientists, and the public are all fascinated by the multitude of possibilities inherent in our sexuality. It is important to appreciate that the range of normal sexual behavior is exceptionally

Figure 25. *Leap Year (Año Bisiesto)* (2010, Machete Producciones, Instituto Mexicano de Cinematografía [IMCINE]). Produced by Edher Campos and Luis Salinas. Directed by Michael Rowe.

broad, and many behaviors that seem unusual or disturbing to most people do not qualify for a *DSM-5* label (e.g., rape, incest). As a rule, remember that complex or elaborate sexual fantasies are commonplace and do not suggest that any type of psychological disturbance is present. A psychological problem exists when a person acts on his or her fantasies with unwilling partners or behaves in ways that distress other people.

Filmmakers have been quick to exploit our fascination with sexual behavior, and contemporary cinema is replete with examples of sexual psychopathology. A serious student can learn a great deal about abnormal psychology from selective viewing.

Paraphilic Disorders

According to the *DSM-5*, the term *paraphilia* "denotes any intense and persistent sexual interest other than sexual interest in genital stimulation or prepa-

ratory fondling with phenotypically normal, physically mature, consenting human partners" (p. 685). The paraphilic disorders included in the *DSM-5* are voyeuristic disorder, exhibitionistic disorder, frotteuristic disorder, sexual masochism, sexual sadism disorder, pedophilic disorder, fetishistic disorder, and transvestic disorder. Sexual desire has many faces, and there are numerous other ways it can manifest (e.g., necrophilia); however, these eight disorders are the most common paraphilias, and they are included in the *DSM-5* because clinicians frequently encounter them in clinical practice, and because many of them are illegal and sometimes can result in prosecution and incarceration. Clients frequently present with two or more paraphilias; these sometimes are logically related (e.g., the person with a foot fetish may also have a shoe fetish), but often are quite disparate (e.g., a pedophile may also be a sadist).

It is important to note that at some time in their lives most people have had fantasies or have engaged in a behavior that may fit one or more of the categories listed above. However, sexual fantasies per se are not a psychological problem – and do not warrant a diagnosis – unless a person has acted on his or her fantasies or is significantly distressed by them. The male who has fantasies about peeping through a window and watching his neighbor undress, for example, is not engaging in deviant behavior. In fact, fantasies of this type are common among males. The behavior would be deviant if the man could be aroused *only* by the fantasy, or if he acted out and actually spied on his neighbor.

Voyeuristic Disorder

A **voyeur** is a "peeping Tom" who experiences arousal and derives sexual satisfaction from spying on unsuspecting people, usually strangers, as they are getting undressed, using the toilet, or having sexual relations. Although it is normal to want to look at the bodies of others (e.g., at the beach), the voyeur goes to great lengths to find surreptitious hiding places from which he or she can watch others without being detected. Arousal is always associated with the clandestine aspects of the situation; voyeurs report little interest in watching pornographic films, visiting topless or nude beaches, or attending topless bars – all experiences where public voyeurism has been sanctioned. Voyeurism is the most common illegal sexual behavior, and the *DSM-5* estimates that the highest possible lifetime prevalence is 12% in men and 4% in women. The diagnosis requires a minimum age of 18 years, because viewing associated with sexual curiosity in puberty is both age appropriate and developmentally normal.

As is the case with exhibitionism and obscene phone calls, it is rare for the voyeur to attempt to initiate sexual relationships with the victim. The voyeur will most often masturbate while viewing the arousing scene or sometimes later, when replaying the scene in memory. Although it is rare for voyeurs to progress to crimes of sexual violence, more than two thirds of males who commit sex-related murders report early experiences with voyeurism (Ressler, 1986).

Pulp Fiction (1994) depicts a sadist who derives sexual pleasure from watching Marsellus Wallace being raped, and *Psycho* (1960) includes a classic scene in which Norman Bates watches Marion

Crane undress, spying through a peephole in the hotel office. In Gus Van Sant's 1998 remake of the film, Norman is obviously masturbating while spying on Marion. (It is interesting to note that Alfred Hitchcock used a 50-mm lens on a 35-mm camera to film every scene in which Norman spies on Marion; this method replicates human vision, and filming in this way draws in the viewer and makes him or her a fellow voyeur.)

In David Lynch's *Blue Velvet* (1986), Jeffrey watches from a closet while Frank (Dennis Hopper) inhales amyl nitrate and abuses Dorothy. The scene in which a confused and naked Dorothy is walking on a Wilmington street was based on a childhood memory of the director who had been with his brother when they saw a naked woman walking toward them.

In *American Beauty* (1999), the character of Ricky Fitts is clearly a voyeur, and he films his neighbor Jane through her window (and eventually persuades her to undress while he films her). Finally, *The Truman Show* (1998) is a classic example of extreme voyeurism in which Ed Harris's character devotes his life to filming and viewing every moment in the life of Jim Carrey's character. Films like *Porky's* (1981) depict adolescent boys drilling holes in the wall to watch girls showering, while a more serious film, *Sex, Lies and Videotape* (1989), introduces Graham Dalton (James Spader), a character who is otherwise impotent and can only become aroused when listening to videotapes in which women he has interviewed talk about the personal details of their sex lives.

An interesting variation of voyeurism is **troilism**, or sexual gratification derived from watching other people have sex (or allowing others to watch oneself engage in sexual activity – behavior more logically linked to exhibitionism than voyeurism). This practice is sometimes referred to as **scoptophilia**. Variations on these themes include the **ménage à trois** ("family of three"), swinging, and couples that have monogamous sex in each other's presence. Swinging or mate swapping is probably widespread, although AIDS and other sexual diseases have presented serious obstacles to this form of sexual expression. A failed attempt at swinging is portrayed in Paul Mazursky's 1969 film *Bob and Carol and Ted and Alice*, starring Robert Culp, Eliot Gould, Dyan Cannon, and Natalie Wood. The film celebrates social permissiveness and the mores of the late 1960s more than sexual freedom; in the final scene, Bob, Carol, Ted, and Alice, all in bed together, reaffirm their commitment to monogamy.

Other films depicting voyeurism include *Lovelife* (1997) and the Canadian film *The Adjuster* (1991). Most films that have dealt explicitly with voyeurism have been misleading presentations that perpetuate common myths. For example, *Peeping Tom* (1960) presents the story of a voyeur (raised by a sadistic psychologist who constantly filmed Tom as he was growing up) who tortures his victims and then photographs them as they are dying. This is an example of sexual sadism, not voyeurism. The pain of voyeurism is evident in the film *Voyeur Confessions* (2001).

Some films depict a strong voyeuristic component without depicting explicit sexual fantasy or gratification. (Note: if there is no sexual arousal, a diagnosis of voyeuristic disorder is *not* made.) Christopher Nolan's debut film, *Following* (1998), tells a creative story about a man who enjoys picking out one person in a crowd and then following this individual for a day. The voyeur is a lonely writer who convinces himself he follows people to get character ideas for his stories. His habit has qualities of an addiction insofar as it becomes "irresistible" to him, he is unable to keep it under control, he obsesses about it, and he employs various cognitive justifications for maintaining this inappropriate and disturbing behavior.

Another nonsexual (perhaps impotent) voyeur is displayed in Hitchcock's classic film *Rear Window* (1954). Voyeurism is clearly portrayed; James Stewart's character watches his neighbors incessantly, and he cannot pull away from his window. His whole life revolves around looking into others' lives, and he satisfies his psychological needs in this way. He also resists and rejects a beautiful, caring woman. If the viewer assumes Stewart's character is wrong about the murder and that all his behavior was pure voyeurism with no positive, beneficial outcome, it is hard to avoid the conclusion that this is a film about voyeurism. Brian De Palma's *Body Double* (1984) pays homage to Hitchcock, and portrays an interesting connection between a male voyeur and a female exhibitionist.

Exhibitionistic Disorder

The exhibitionist's preferred form of sexual gratification is exposing his genitals to unsuspecting strangers. Masturbation often occurs during or after the exposure. The exhibitionist will almost never attempt to have intercourse with the person intimidated and would likely be personally intimidated and frightened by an opportunity for an adult sexual encounter. Although reports of exhibitionism in a neighborhood usually result in increased concern about the possibility of rape, exhibitionism and rape are dramatically different behaviors and are almost never linked.

The *DSM-5* requires that exposing one's genitals to unsuspecting persons occur for at least 6 months before the diagnosis of exhibitionistic disorder can be made, and specifiers are used to stipulate whether the behavior occurs with prepubescent children, physically mature individuals, or both. The prevalence of exhibitionistic disorder in males is estimated to be at most 2%–4%, and the disorder in females is dramatically lower (*DSM-5*).

Exhibitionism can occur at any age, but typically develops in males in their mid-20s. Despite the popular image of a "dirty old man in a raincoat," the incidence of exhibitionism falls off rapidly after the age of 40 and is rare in older males who are cognitively intact. Many exhibitionists have never had meaningful or satisfying adult sexual relationships; others have normal psychosexual development histories.

Reports of true exhibitionism in females are quite rare, although exposing their breasts or legs in public may arouse some women. Exhibitionism in females can also be used as a way of establishing dominance in a nonsexual encounter with males. The potential for psychological manipulation through exposure was dramatically portrayed during Sharon Stone's interrogation scene in *Basic Instinct* (1992). Brief scenes of exhibitionistic behavior are depicted in *Natural Born Killers* (1994) and *Morvern Callar* (2002).

The Good Mother (1988) raises interesting questions about the boundaries between healthy sexuality and exhibitionism. Diane Keaton plays Anna Dunlap, the divorced mother of a 6-year-old daughter. Anna falls in love with an artist and starts to live a bohemian life that includes nudity in front of her daughter. Her new lover at one point innocently lets the daughter touch his penis when he is getting out of the tub, and she expresses natural childhood curiosity. When the ex-husband learns about this event, he sues for custody, and Anna is forced to renounce her lover to maintain visitation rights with her daughter.

Frotteuristic Disorder

The **frotteur** is someone who derives sexual pleasure from brushing or rubbing against others in a seemingly inadvertent but clearly sexual manner. This rubbing typically involves a man's pelvis or erect penis. Frotteurs frequent crowded stores, escalators, buses, and subways, where their behavior can be attributed to crowding. The *DSM-5* lists frotteurism as an independent paraphilia, although many authors view it as a variation of exhibitionism. In *All Out!*, clinical psychologist Albert Ellis's autobiography, he describes being an enthusiastic teenage frotteur (Ellis & Ellis, 2010).

The film *Dummy* (2003) portrays an unemployed man who is a frotteur. The man is balding and wears thick glasses. He is included in the film purely for laughs. Though his behavior is not depicted cinematically, the character clearly meets the *DSM-5* criteria for frotteurism.

Sexual Masochism Disorder

The **sexual masochist** becomes sexually excited when he or she is humiliated, beaten, bound, or made to suffer. It is important to appreciate that the diagnosis of sexual masochism is made only when patients actually engage in these behaviors. As is the case with other paraphilias, masochistic fantasies are both common and harmless, and moderate sadomasochistic behavior (e.g., scratching and biting) can be a rewarding part of normal sex play.

Masochists allow themselves to be abused in a variety of ways, including bondage, whipping, handcuffing, spanking, cutting, and burning. They are often verbally abused as well as physically mistreated. Humiliation may be necessary for arousal to occur – for example, a masochist may be forced to wear a diaper, or his partner may defecate or urinate on the masochist. Whips, chains, leather, and rubber accouterments often play an important role in the sexual activity of the masochist, who is happiest with a (mildly) sadistic partner. A woman who caters to the sexual preferences of masochistic men is referred to as a **dominatrix**. Masochists may be gay or straight, although the majority of sadomasochistic encounters are heterosexual. Among homosexuals, masochists appear to outnumber sadists (Innala & Ernulf, 1992). There are no good estimates of prevalence of the disorder; however, the *DSM-5* cites data from Australia suggesting about 2% of males and 1% of females had been involved in bondage and discipline, sadomasochism, or dominance and submission during a 12-month period.

Secretary (2002) is an intriguing film about a young woman (Maggie Gyllenhaal) who is depressed and seriously self-injurious. She takes a job as a secretary working for a successful attorney, Mr. Grey (James Spader). She begins to enjoy his harsh criticism of her mistakes, and a sadomasochistic relationship develops. Grey enjoys spanking her, yelling at her, and engaging in other sadistic behavior, but he prohibits her from injuring herself (paradoxically using his sadism to control her masochism). The film opens with her nicely dressed at work, arms tied to a long bar behind her neck. She picks up items with her teeth or by turning her torso horizontally. Through a variety of sadomasochistic behaviors, she matures, stops her self-abuse, and develops a meaningful relationship with her boss, eventually marrying him.

Quills (2000) depicts the last years of the Marquis de Sade (Geoffrey Rush), who spent years in an institution. The protagonist engages in a variety of paraphilias that give his life meaning and pleasure. In Lars von Trier's *Dogville* (2003), Nicole Kidman plays the role of Grace, a woman who becomes involved in a masochistic relationship with an entire community in her efforts to become accepted by the community and escape her mob pursuers. Peter O'Toole plays T. E. Lawrence in *Lawrence of Arabia* (1962), and the film hints at his masochism. Paul Schrader's biopic, *Mishima: A*

Life in Four Chapters (1985), accurately presents Mishima as a bisexual masochist; the final scene in the film shows Mishima committing ritualistic suicide *(seppuku)* by disemboweling himself before having himself beheaded by one of his followers.

Extreme masochism is present in the documentary *Sick: The Life and Death of Bob Flanagan, Supermasochist* (1977), a film about a Los Angeles performance artist who used masochism to cope with his cystic fibrosis. Flanagan was involved in a love relationship Shree Rose, a woman who collaborated in his need to embrace pain as a way of coping with his illness.

> "I want a wealthy collector to finance an installation in which a video camera will be placed in the coffin with my body, connected to a screen on the wall, and whenever he wants to, the patron can see how I'm coming along."
>
> One of Bob Flanagan's last wishes in
> *Sick: The Life and Death of Bob Flanagan,*
> *Supermasochist* (1977)

The Piano Teacher

In *The Piano Teacher* (2001), Erika Kohut (Isabelle Huppert) is a highbrow, successful pianist. She performs concerts for standing-room-only crowds and gives demanding lessons to her students. Erika clearly presents as a sexually repressed and conservative woman with a stern, controlling presence. The film takes its time in getting to important themes and core issues, allowing the viewer to be gradually introduced to her world and values. The viewer sees her go to a porn shop briefly in which she chastises a young male student before she leaves. In another scene, she goes into a booth in the shop to watch a video. These scenes progress to acting out sexually with a male student in a public restroom; in this scene, she is mildly sadistic and very controlling. A relationship begins, and it is only then that her deepest fantasies (and true diagnosis) are revealed. She is in fact masochistic. In one scene, she sets up a blockade so her nosey, controlling mother is unable to burst into her room. Erika gives her lover a letter revealing her fantasies about sadomasochistic behavior. As he reads the letter he

learns about her desires to be reminded of her powerlessness, to be gagged, and to be hit if she disobeys any of his commands or rules. Next, she reveals her stash of ropes and other sadomasochistic toys. He responds by telling her that he feels both love and repulsion, and that she is "sick" and needs treatment.

> "The urge to be beaten has been in me for years."
>
> *The Piano Teacher* (2001)

The film makes inferences about etiology, mostly surrounding a forceful, controlling mother who needs to know every last detail about her adult daughter. The mother is physically controlling, aggressive, and quick to criticize everything from Erika's attire and her piano playing (although Erika is an expert pianist) to a benign conversation she has with a young man. She instructs her daughter, "No one must surpass you, my dear." Erika's father had reportedly died from an unspecified mental illness in an asylum.

? Questions to Consider While Watching *The Piano Teacher*

➤ Was Erika's letter to her lover a true expression of love?
➤ Why is Erika afraid of being seduced?
➤ How did Erika's mother contribute to her paraphilia?
➤ Is it typical for masochists to occasionally adopt the role of a sadist?
➤ How common is it for people to adopt fantasy roles during sex?

Autoerotic asphyxia, using self-strangulation to produce excitement or to intensify erections or ejaculation, is an unusual but not uncommon paraphilia, often related to masochism. It is estimated that autoerotic asphyxiation results in 250–1,000 deaths per year in the United States (Uva, 1995). Blanchard and Hucker (1991) were able to review the cases of 117 males who died during autoerotic asphyxial activity. Autoerotic asphyxia is especially significant because most of the deaths that result from this practice are assumed to be accidents.

Most of what we know about the practice of autoerotic asphyxia is derived from police reports following death investigations. The victims tend to be young White males. Bondage accouterments are often employed, along with mirrors and cameras. Transvestism is a common practice in these cases. There is often evidence that ejaculation occurred before death. *With asphyxiophilia* is included as a specifier for the diagnosis of sexual masochism disorder in *DSM-5*.

Sexual Sadism Disorder

Sexual sadism presents the mirror image of sexual masochism. The sadist derives sexual pleasure from the suffering and humiliation of his or her victims. Partners may be consenting or nonconsenting. If the partner is consenting, the diagnosis requires that sexual sadism be "repeatedly preferred or exclusive" and that "bodily injury that is extensive, permanent, or possibly mortal is inflicted in order to achieve sexual excitement."

The terms **sadism** and **masochism** were first used by a German sexologist, Richard von Krafft-Ebing, in the 19th century. Krafft-Ebing, who wrote *Psychopathia Sexualis*, the first medical school textbook on sexuality (first published in 1886), took the term *sadism* from the name of the French author Marquis de Sade. De Sade's novels and short stories are replete with abuse, torture, and murder, all of which are linked with sexual gratification. One of his works, *The 120 Days of Sodom*, was made into the controversial and repugnant movie *Salò, or the 120 Days of Sodom* (1976), the final film of Italian director Pier Paolo Pasolini.

Sadomasochistic sex often involves elaborate sex toys such as chains, whips, rubber and leather garments, and spike heels. Flagellation and bondage are common practices.

Although some sadists are also rapists, it is important to understand that rapists do not derive sexual pleasure from the rape itself. Rape is an act of violence in which sexual arousal may play virtually no role. In contrast, the sexual sadist derives intense sexual pleasure from the suffering of the victim.

It is important to distinguish between *minor* sadism and masochism (sex play involving bondage and discipline or dominance and submission) and *major* sadism and masochism involving torture and the risk of death and bodily injury (Arndt, 1991).

There is some evidence that at the minor level, there are more women who dominate males; at the extreme level, men are more likely to abuse women.

The Girl With the Dragon Tattoo (2011) depicts rape scenes in which the rapist is clearly sadistic, and *Tesis* (1996, Spain), *Vacancy* (2007) and *8MM* (1999) all deal with **snuff films**, a particularly odious form of sadism in which people are filmed while being murdered, most often after or while being raped. Other films depicting sexual sadism include *Belle de Jour* (1967, France), *Venus in Furs* (1969), *Last Tango in Paris* (1962), *The Night Porter* (1972), *The Story of O* (1972), *In the Realm of the Senses* (1976, Japan), *Tie Me Up! Tie Me Down!* (1990), and *New Tokyo Decadence – The Slave* (2007, Japan).

Current interest in sadomasochism is reflected in the popularity of the 2011 erotic romance novel *Fifty Shades of Grey*, the fastest selling paperback of all time. The novel is part of a trilogy that has sold more than 90 million copies worldwide, and which has been translated into 52 languages. A film based on the novel will be released in 2015.

Films depicting sexual sadism are fairly common in the United States, and they play for large audiences in Europe and Asia as well. Many of these films are heavy-handed and crude and have little social value. A salient exception is David Lynch's *Blue Velvet* (1986).

Blue Velvet

Blue Velvet opens with Bobby Vinton's song of the same name and scenes of a bucolic Midwest neighborhood. This idyllic scene is soon interrupted, and the viewer is never really allowed to relax again until the film concludes.

The plot of the story involves a student, Jeffrey Beaumont (Kyle MacLachlan), who is home from college to care for his father who has just had a stroke. While walking in a field near his house, Jeffrey discovers a severed ear. It turns out to be the ear of the husband of a cabaret singer, Dorothy Vallens (Isabella Rossellini). Dorothy's husband and son are being held hostage to force her to comply with the sexual demands of a local gangster, Frank Booth (Dennis Hopper). Dorothy, one of the most complex characters in the film, discovers Jeffrey in her apartment after he goes there in a foolish attempt to solve the crime. In a controversial scene, Dorothy discovers Jeffrey and uses a knife to force him to have sex with her. She displays many of the features of masochism previously discussed; these become more prominent later when Frank arrives and proceeds to savagely abuse her. Frank, both obsessed with Dorothy and fixated on the song "Blue Velvet," has cut off a piece of Dorothy's blue velvet bathrobe. It is a fetish that Frank carries with him and uses during other sexual encounters. Hopper is unforgettable as Frank Booth, who is addicted to inhalants as well as sadistic sex.

"I have a part of you with me. You put your disease in me. It helps me. It makes me strong."

A masochistic and troubled Dorothy in
Blue Velvet (1986)

One troubling aspect of the film is that both Dorothy and Jeffrey seem attracted to sadomasochistic sex after they have been exposed to it. A subplot involves Jeffrey's involvement with Sandy, the daughter of a corrupt local detective. The relationship with Sandy seems pale and insipid after the intensity of a sexual encounter with Dorothy.

The film won the National Society of Film Critics award for Best Film of 1986, and Lynch was selected as Best Director of the year by the same group. It is a brutally honest film, and not one that will appeal to all viewers. However, it is a film rich in psychopathology and one worth seeing by anyone interested in the complex world of the sexual psychopath.

Pedophilic Disorder

The **pedophile** is someone who is sexually aroused by children and who has acted on these desires or who is markedly distressed by them. The pedophile can be attracted to girls, boys, or both, although heterosexual pedophilia appears to be somewhat more common than homosexual pedophilia. The *DSM-5* stipulates that the child must be prepubescent (generally age 13 or younger) for a diagnosis of pedophilia to be appropriate. In addition, the diagnosis is not used unless the perpetrator is at least 16 years old and at least 5 years older than the child involved. Specifiers are used to indicate whether the sexual attraction to children is exclusive or nonexclusive, and whether the individual involved is sexually attracted to male children, female children, or both.

The true prevalence is unknown, but it is clear that this disorder is far more common among men than among women. Pedophilia is a difficult condition to treat, and in most clients it will be a lifelong condition that can be controlled but not eliminated.

Although not a formal diagnostic label, the term **ephebophilia** is sometimes used to describe a person who is attracted to postpubescent adolescents; the ephebophile's attraction is exclusive and specific to this age group (ages 14–17). The phrase **Lolita syndrome** is also used to describe men attracted exclusively to female adolescents. Though often illegal, ephebophilia is not seen as pathological and is even normative in some societies in which adolescent girls routinely marry older, adult men. Ephebophilia illustrates the conflict that often exists between biology and societal norms.

Ephebophilia is portrayed in the coming of age film *Towelhead* (aka *Nothing is Private*; 2007), the first film directed by Alan Ball (who also produced and cowrote *American Beauty*, a film that deals with the emerging sexuality of two young girls). In *Towelhead*, several adults abuse Jasira, a 13-year-old girl, including her mother's boyfriend, who feigns paternal concern while he is shaving Jasira's pubic hair. *Towelhead* is a derisive term for someone of Arab descent; the protagonist's father is a strict Lebanese American who is ill prepared to deal with his daughter's sexual maturation or the challenges of menstruation.

Venus (2006) stars Peter O'Toole as a septuagenarian actor with prostate cancer who becomes romantically and erotically involved with a woman 53 years younger than he is; the movie makes this relationship seem entirely plausible.

While an adolescent achieves sexual maturation (puberty) around 13, most mental health professionals believe adolescents are not prepared to deal with the demands of sexual intimacy at such an early age and recommend a slow transition to adult sexuality; however, there is wide variation in the ages at which different cultures define the age of consent for sexual intercourse, and the minimum age of consent varies across countries from age 12 to 18.

Hard Candy (2005) illustrates the ways in which the Internet has opened new avenues for pedophiles to exploit their victims. The film involves an online relationship between a 14-year-old student and a 32-year-old photographer who is a pedophile. The two eventually meet, and both understand from innuendo that they are meeting to have sex; however, in a curious twist, the precocious 14-year-old winds up in control of the situation and proceeds to castrate the older man (who may have been involved in the disappearance of a child whose photo is included in his files), and the man eventually commits suicide.

While most cases of ephebophilia (and most movies with this theme) involve older men who are attracted to young girls, two films have successfully explored relationships between older women and teenage boys. *Private Lessons* (1981) is a movie about a French maid who seduces a 15-year-old boy; the film depicts grooming, boundary violations, and sexual abuse of a minor. *The Reader* (2008) is a more powerful, engaging and compelling film in which Kate Winslet plays Hanna Schmitz, a 36-year-old woman who becomes involved with a 15-year-old boy. They have an affair one summer, and then she drops out of his life, only to reappear 8 years later when she is on trial for war crimes committed as a concentration camp guard. The title of the film comes from the fact that Hanna and her adolescent lover begin each of their trysts with him reading to her. Kate Winslet won an Academy Award for her role in this film.

"She had favorites. Girls, mostly young. We all remarked on it, she gave them food and places to sleep. In the evening, she asked them to join her. We all thought – well, you can imagine what we thought. Then we found out – she was making these women read aloud to her. They were reading to her. At first we thought this guard ... this guard is more sensitive ... she's more human ... she's kinder. Often she chose the weak, the sick, she picked them out, she seemed to be protecting them almost. But then she dispatched them. Is that kinder?"

A witness describes Hanna Schmitz's behavior in *The Reader* (2008)

Another nondiagnostic variation of pedophilia is the rare condition called **infantophilia**; this term is applied to adults with a primary sexual attraction to children from birth to age 5. The movie *Bliss* (1997) includes a scene illustrating infantophilia.

Many pedophiles report being sexually abused as children (Freund, & Watson, 1990). Pedophiles who have been attracted to children since adolescence are identified as **fixated pedophiles**. In con-

trast, if an individual has satisfying adult sexual experiences, but then reverts to a sexual preoccupation with children, the person is classified as a situational or **regressed pedophile**.

Hundreds of thousands of children are sexually abused in the United States each year; however, a recent report released by the Institute of Medicine suggests the incidence of child sexual abuse in the United States actually is declining for reasons that are not fully understood. This report noted that more than 3 million referrals for child abuse and neglect are received by child protective services each year that involve around 6 million children; about three-quarters of reported cases in 2011 were classified as neglect, about 15% as physical abuse, and about 10% as sexual abuse (Institute of Medicine, 2014).

Most people consider the practice of pedophilia reprehensible, perhaps because children are among the most vulnerable members of the human family. However, the widespread availability of "kiddie porn," despite the social opprobrium associated with pedophilia, suggests that sexual interest in children is as common as most of the other paraphilias. Empirical data document the extent of sexual attraction to children by adults. For example, Briere (1989) surveyed undergraduate males and found that 21% acknowledged being sexually attracted to children, 9% had sexual fantasies involving children, and 7% would consider having sex with a child if certain they could avoid being detected or punished.

Pedophiles and ephebophiles seduce their victims using play, food, or gifts, which are followed by appropriate touching eventually leading to inappropriate touching and assault. The seduction of an adolescent is powerfully and realistically portrayed in *Blue Car* (2003), in which a young, vulnerable girl is seduced by her teacher. Most viewers are not aware that the teacher is manipulating the adolescent from the very beginning of the film. The seduction of adolescents is also depicted in *American Beauty* (1999), *Lolita* (1962), *Lolita* (1997), *Y Tu Mamá También* (2001), and *Manic* (2003). In *The Magdalene Sisters* (2002), a priest has sex with a vulnerable, emotionally and physically abused adolescent girl.

Child sexual abuse is portrayed in the powerful and riveting documentary, *Capturing the Friedmans* (2003). In *Capturing the Friedmans*, a father (Arnold) and his son (Jesse) are accused of pedophilia. When their house is searched, child pornography is found hidden throughout the home. The movie does not fully indict or acquit either individual. In *Hap-*

piness, Dylan Baker plays a married psychiatrist who is also a pedophile who masturbates to teen magazines and fantasizes about raping the friends of his 11-year-old son.

Mysterious Skin (2004) tells the story of two boys growing up in a small Kansas town. Both boys are molested by their Little League coach, but they respond in very different ways. Brian repressed the experience and only remembered waking up with a nosebleed; he accounts for the missing 5 hours in his life by developing a deep conviction that he has been abducted by aliens. Neil responds by becoming a teenage prostitute, working at first in local parks before moving to New York where his clients are mainly older White men. The film presents an evenhanded and unsensationalized examination of the effects of childhood sexual abuse.

Two films offer especially sensitive portrayals of the problem of pedophilia: *Little Children* (2007) and *The Woodsman* (2004). Director Todd Field's *Little Children* is a powerful film that shows how difficult it is to find and maintain long-term love relationships. Kate Winslet plays Sarah Pierce, a disen-

chanted stay-at-home mother whose husband is addicted to online pornography. One of the characters in the film, Ronnie, lives with his mother after completing a prison term for exposing himself to a little girl. Ronnie's mother is convinced that he will become attracted to adult women if he only starts to date one; however, the date she arranges for him turns into a disaster when he asks his date to drive him by a playground so he can masturbate. Before his mother dies from cancer, she writes him a short note, simply asking him to "be a good boy." He responds to his grief by castrating himself, and his life is saved by Sarah, who is able to set aside her previous repugnance and aversion to relate to Ronnie as a genuinely suffering human being. One of the most memorable scenes in the film occurs when Ronnie visits a public swimming pool, frightening both the mothers and the children, almost all of whom know he has been identified as a pedophile (Figure 26). *The Woodsman* stars Kevin Bacon as a pedophile who has just been released from prison after serving a 12-year sentence; the film shows him continuing to struggle with his demons, at the same time he is

Figure 26. *Little Children* (2006, Bona Fide, Standard Film Company). Produced by Albert Berger, Todd Field, and Ron Yerxa. Directed by Todd Field.

"Little Red Riding Hood! That's it! That's it. The Woodsman, he cuts open the wolf's stomach, the girl comes out without a scratch ... [But have you ever seen] a seven-year-old sodomized in half? She was so small, just broken. I saw 20-year vets on that job. Hard guys, they just broke down and cried. I was there, I cried ... There ain't no fucking woodsman in this world."

A police sergeant describing the stress involved in working with children victimized by pedophiles in The Woodsman (2004)

trying to establish a mature sexual relationship with a woman with whom he works. The movie underscores the complexity of the problem without providing pat solutions or a feel-good ending.

Fetishistic Disorder

An individual has a **fetish** when an inanimate object habitually arouses him or her. A diagnosis is justified only if the sexual arousal associated with the object or fantasies about it is intense, recurrent, and lasts for at least 6 months. Sex often involves masturbation with the fetish, or the fetish may be incorporated into sexual activity with one's partner. The term *fetish* is used to refer to both the object itself and the inordinate attraction to it. However, the true fetish involves inanimate objects such as panties, silk stockings, garter belts, high heel shoes, or rubber items of clothing or body parts not normally associated with sexual activity (e.g., hair, feet, or the stumps of amputated limbs). Normally the link to sexuality can be surmised, but occasionally a patient will report sexual arousal to stimuli as obscure as file cabinets or baby buggies, and it is difficult to determine (a) how arousal initially could have been paired with the stimulus or (b) the potential symbolic value of the fetish. The fetish is often used for masturbation, but it may also be worn, worshipped, put in the rectum, hoarded, fondled, or sucked (Chalkey & Powell, 1983).

The *DSM-5* requires at least a 6-month history of sexual arousal from nonliving objects or a specific focus on nongenital body parts for the diagnosis. In addition, clinically significant distress must be present or impairment in important life tasks

(e.g., keeping a job). Specifiers are used to indicate whether the fetish involves body parts (e.g., feet) or nonliving objects (e.g., bras and panties). As with most other paraphilias, fetishes occur far more often in men than in women.

Some authorities have speculated that fetishism is related to the same psychological impulses that trigger transvestism and kleptomania (an overwhelming desire to steal, usually trivial or inexpensive objects). The differences among the three conditions seem trivial in comparison with the similarities that link the disorders. The person with a sexual fetish longs to relate to the object sexually, the transvestite longs to wear it, and the kleptomaniac longs to steal it. Anxiety frequently precedes the unusual behavior, and masturbation is common.

A number of films have included either leading or secondary characters with a fetish. Our favorite is *Claire's Knee*, a French film directed by Eric Rohmer and released in 1971. This charming movie details the obsession of a soon-to-be-married writer for his friend's daughter – or, more exactly, the daughter's right knee. He becomes increasingly attracted to her because he cannot have her, and he has difficulty speaking when she is around. He focuses on her knee as the fulcrum for her beauty; in one scene, he massages her knee with considerable erotic glee, but does not move his hand anywhere else. The erotic elements in the film are handled with delicacy and good taste, and the writer's fixation on the girl's knee soon seems entirely plausible.

Peter Greenaway's *Pillow Book* (1997) portrays a woman with a fetish for calligraphy. She melds calligraphy with sex, and the calligraphic pen symbolizes the instrument of pleasure. She develops a passion for calligraphy and experiences withdrawal without it. She searches for the ideal mate to write on her; she rules out the old for not having enough energy, and the young for their distracted nature. She captures and tests out a graffiti writer and other random people to write on her in her search. "You're not a writer, you're a scribbler," she tells one candidate.

Another not-to-be-missed film demonstrating a sexual fetish is Steven Soderbergh's *Sex, Lies and Videotape* (1989). This intelligent film, which won the Best Picture and Best Actor awards at the 1989 Cannes Film Festival, was written, directed, and edited by Soderbergh. The film describes how the lives of three people (a man, his wife, and her sister, with whom he is having an affair) are changed forever by the arrival of the man's college roommate, Graham

Dalton. Dalton is an impotent male who can achieve orgasm only by masturbating while he is watching the videotapes he makes of women discussing the intimate details of their sexual lives. Dalton has decided to live his life with absolute honesty, and he shares the details of his sexual life with Ann, the rejected wife. The two eventually become lovers, and there is a dramatic confrontation between Dalton and his old roommate (Ann's husband). Dalton is transformed through his relationship with Ann, and eventually he is able to move out of his isolation and into an emotionally satisfying and sexually mature relationship.

An equally powerful film is *Equus* (1977). This movie stars Richard Burton as Martin Dysart, a disillusioned psychiatrist who has lost all traces of passion in his life. The film revolves around Dysart's treatment of Alan Strang (Peter Firth), a young man arrested for blinding six horses. This cruel act is linked to Strang's fascination with horses; he finds them both threatening and sexually exciting. The film offers some insight into how an animal fetish might develop.

Some films utilize fetishes solely for comic purposes and offer little insight into the paraphilias, as in *Sex and Zen* (1993), and the depiction of a woman who proclaims to have a "Santa fetish," in *Bad Santa* (2003).

Crash (1996) is a controversial No One 17 and Under Admitted (NC-17) David Cronenberg film about people who have developed fetishes for cars and car wrecks. The film is based on a novel by J. G. Ballard, and the opening scene shows a woman rubbing her breasts against the wing of a plane and then licking metal while an apparently anonymous lover enters her from behind. She later relates this experience to her husband, who in turns shares his day's sexual adventures. The husband later becomes involved in a serious car accident in which the driver of the other car is killed. This man's wife, Helen, survives the accident but is hospitalized and has to walk on crutches while she recovers. Shortly after leaving the hospital, she becomes sexually involved with James, the man who had been driving the car that had killed her husband. Helen arouses James by telling him stories about all the men with whom she has had sex in cars. Both individuals find themselves sexually aroused by crashes and the accouterments of highway deaths (ambulances, flares, fire trucks, etc.). They are increasingly drawn into a deviant subculture that shares their sexual fascination with metal, cars, and crashing. This group is led by an unusual man who amuses himself and others by reenacting the 1955 death of James Dean in his sports car named "Little Bastard." In addition to its main theme of fetishism, the film involves exhibitionism, voyeurism, troilism (pleasure in having sex in front of others), and homosexuality. The film ends with a suggestion of necrophilia – James deliberately drives his wife's sports car off the road at high speed, and she is thrown from the car. He determines she is alive, and then embraces her unconscious and injured body while muttering, "Maybe the next one, darling, maybe the next one."

> ### Additional Questions for Discussion
>
> ➤ Are the fetishes described in *Crash* simply too far-fetched to be believed?
> ➤ Metal, leather, and plastic are all common fetishes. What is it about these particular materials that make them sexually arousing for some patients with a paraphilia?
> ➤ How common is it for a husband and wife to share fantasies about sex with other partners?
> ➤ How is it possible for sexual arousal (a positive experience) to so often become linked with pain (a very negative experience for most people)?

Transvestic Disorder

Unlike transsexuals, **transvestites** are comfortable with their anatomic sex. However, transvestites derive pleasure and satisfaction from cross-dressing and being identified as a female, and cross-dressing and fantasies about cross-dressing play a prominent role in the sexual lives of transvestites. The transsexual male may cross-dress, but this is not done for purposes of sexual arousal but, rather, because female clothes are important in establishing a female identity. In contrast, the transvestite is likely to be a masculine, heterosexual male who becomes sexually excited when he dresses up in women's clothes. The transvestite does not desire to *be* a woman, but merely wants to be admired as one, or to experience the sexual excitement associated with wearing women's clothes. Brown (1994) maintains that the majority of wives who discover their husband's cross-dressing after marriage come to accept the behavior, and suggests there are no ill effects on children from these marriages. The children of transvestites engage in appropriate sex-role behavior as adults and are unlikely to cross-dress themselves.

As with transsexualism, transvestites may be heterosexual or homosexual, although most are clearly heterosexual. Transvestites cannot be asexual, since sexual arousal is part of the definition of the syndrome. The *DSM-5* used specifiers to document "with fetishism" when arousal is triggered by the feel of women's garments, and "with autogynephilia" when arousal results from the thoughts and images associated with thinking of oneself as female.

The cross-dressing behavior of the transvestite almost always begins in childhood, although few little boys who dress up in the clothes of their mother or sister will grow up to be confused about their sexual identity. While transsexualism is found among both males and females, the diagnosis of transvestism is almost inevitably reserved for males, and there are very few case studies of women who become sexually aroused by wearing men's clothes.

Many transvestites cross-dress only on special occasions, and they may attempt to suppress the behavior, yielding to the impulse only when anxious, during periods of stress, or when separated from a sexual partner. The preferred objects of clothing include nightgowns, panties, bras, hose, and high heels. These garments are often the stimuli associated with fetishes, and in the *DSM-5,* transvestism is referred to as **transvestic fetishism.** It is similar to other forms of fetishism in that sexual arousal is associated not with an individual but, rather, with inanimate objects (women's clothing).

The topic of cross-dressing (but not necessarily transvestism) is surprisingly common in films, where it is generally treated with humor and almost never as a serious issue. One comedy that addresses cross-dressing is the popular film *Tootsie* (1982), in which an unemployed actor played by Dustin Hoffman pretends to be a woman in order to get an acting job. The counterpart to this film is Blake Edward's *Victor/Victoria* (1982) in which Julie Andrews portrays a starving cabaret singer who gets her big break when she manages to land a job singing as a male female impersonator. Both films are sensitive analyses of the complex relationships linking gender and role.

Other films that have explored cross-dressing include *Some Like It Hot* (1959) directed by Billy Wilder and starring Marilyn Monroe, Tony Curtis, Jack Lemmon, and George Raft. This is the classic example of this genre. More recently, *Mrs. Doubtfire* (1993) starred Robin Williams as a man who passes himself off as a "nanny" to spend more time with his children. The movie *Yentl* (1983) stars Barbra Streisand as a woman who must dress in male clothes and pretend to be a man in order to achieve an education. *To Wong Foo, Thanks for Everything, Julie Newmar* (1995) is an entertaining film that examines the lives of three transvestites whose car breaks down in a small town filled with bigots. This film stars Wesley Snipes and Patrick Swayze. In Jane Campion's *Holy Smoke* (1999), Harvey Keitel's authoritarian character falls into a sexual obsession and begins to cross-dress as he regresses and deteriorates.

"I'm the Latina Marilyn Monroe. I've got more legs than a bucket of chicken!"

Miss Chi-Chi Rodriguez in *To Wong Foo, Thanks for Everything, Julie Newmar* (1995)

Unfortunately, some otherwise good films, such as Brian De Palma's *Dressed to Kill* (1980), starring Michael Caine and Angie Dickinson, link transvestism with violence and sociopathy. There is no evidence that transvestites are more likely than the average individual to be homicidal, although, like others whose sexuality may be viewed as deviant by the majority culture, they are significantly more likely to be victims of crime.

Incest

Incest refers to sexual relations between persons too closely related to marry. Russell (1983, 1984) has reported that the incidence of incest for stepdaughters and stepfathers is as high as 16%, and stepfathers are seven times more likely to abuse their children than biological fathers. Barnard et al. (1989) report that one out of six women who have stepfathers experienced sexual abuse at some point during childhood.

Stanley Kubrick's *Lolita* (1962) is the classic example of incest in a contemporary movie. The film takes liberties with Vladimir Nabokov's novel, but the changes were made with the permission of the great writer, who served as screenwriter for the movie. A psychoanalyst has argued that Nabokov himself was a pedophile as a result of childhood sexual abuse by an uncle (Centerwall, 1992). Considered quite daring when it was released more than 4 decades ago, the film portrays the love of Humbert (James Mason) for Lolita (Sue Lyon). Shelly Winters plays Lolita's mother, and Peter Sellers has two roles in the film. Like many actual incestuous stepfathers, Mason's downfall comes from the restrictions he places on his daughter's emerging sexuality and his paranoia about her sexual experience with anyone but him. *Lolita* was remade in 1997 with Jeremy Irons playing the role of Humbert.

There are vivid scenes of bathroom seduction by a stepfather (Karl Malden) in Barbra Streisand's film *Nuts* (1987). The classic example of the combination of pedophilia and sociopathy is found in the 1931 Fritz Lang film *M*, in which Peter Lorre plays a child molester stalking the streets of Berlin. A riveting presentation of the fate of child molesters when they are caught and incarcerated is found in the 1977 prison drama *Short Eyes*.

AKA (2002) is a creative film that depicts a father who sexually abuses his son. In *Dolores Claiborne* (1995), a father sexually abuses his daughter in various ways; one scene occurs when the father makes his daughter masturbate him while riding on a ferry in cold weather, claiming her hands are needed to keep him warm. Incest also figures conspicuously in other excellent films including *Angels and Insects* (1995; brother–sister), *La Luna* (1979, Italy; mother–son), *The Dreamers* (2003, Italy; brother-sister), *Oldboy* (2003, Korea; father–daughter), *Antonia's Line* (1995, Netherlands; brother–sister), *The Royal Tenenbaums* (2001; brother–sister), *Aguirre, the Wrath of God* (1972, German; father-daughter), *Dogtooth* (2009, Greece; brother–sister), and *Chinatown* (1974; father–daughter).

The drama in the controversial film *Priest* (1994) in part derives from the fact that a young girl tells her priest that she is being abused by her father (who attends mass every Sunday), and the priest is deeply troubled by his inability to break his vow of confidentiality to protect the child. The plot is complicated further by the fact that this same priest is involved in a sexual relationship with a gay friend, while his superior has broken his vows of celibacy and become sexually involved with the housekeeper.

Other Paraphilias Not Specifically Classified in the DSM-5

Telephone Scatologia

Most American women and a considerable number of men have experienced obscene phone calls (although it appears this will be replaced with offences committed on the Internet). The practice of making obscene calls for sexual gratification is generally referred to as **telephone scatologia**. Clinical assessment of 19 male adolescent sexual offenders who had committed exhibitionism or telephone scatologia showed that the majority were maladjusted, had committed numerous sexual offenses, and came from multiproblem families. Several of them appeared to be sexually deviant. Antisocial traits, sexual deviance in the family, homosexual conflicts, repressed sexuality, and sexual deviance were considered to be contributing factors (Saunders & Awad, 1991)

People who engage in telephone scatologia are generally males with low self-esteem. They often feel sexually inadequate, and the outrage of their victims gives them a feeling of power. These feelings of power are similar to those that accompany exhibitionism; however, the man making obscene phone calls is far less likely to be apprehended, and the practice provides similar thrills with far fewer risks. Obscene phone callers seldom seek out contact with the individuals they call.

Another variation of telephone scatologia involves "dial-a-porn" services. These "900" numbers allow one to engage in paraphilic behavior without risk and with a seemingly enthusiastic partner. The lead character in Spike Lee's *Girl 6* (1996) and a woman supporting her family in Robert Altman's *Short Cuts* (1994) work as phone sex operators handling such calls. In the latter film, the woman moans, groans, and sighs at the same time she is changing the diapers on her baby and cooking her family's supper. Adam Sandler's character Barry Egan connects with a phone sex company in *Punch Drunk Love* (2002).

Philip Seymour Hoffman portrays a lonely man who is addicted to telephone scatologia in *Happiness* (1998). He initiates innocuous phone conversations, and then probes for more intimate details while he masturbates.

Miscellaneous Paraphilias

Other paraphilias include **coprophilia** (feces), **urophilia** (urine), **klismaphilia** (sexual pleasure from enemas), **partialism** (exclusive focus on part of the body), **necrophilia** (sex with corpses), and **zoophilia** (animals). Alfred Kinsey investigated zoophilia (bestiality) and found that in some rural areas up to 65% of boys had experienced sexual contact with animals. One quirky character in *The Ballad of Narayama* (1984, Japan) has sex with a neighbor's female dog.

Necrophilia is believed to be extremely rare, although estimating the prevalence of the disorder is difficult for obvious reasons. In *Kill Bill: Vol. 1* (2003) a hospital aide sells the right to have sex with patients in comas; this behavior would probably be considered to be a form of necrophilia. Public interest in necrophilia was heightened by the arrest of Jeffrey Dahmer, someone who murdered his victims, had sex with their corpses, mutilated their bodies, and ate various body parts. Dahmer was tested with the **Minnesota Multiphasic Personality Inventory** (MMPI), a psychological test widely used to assess psychopathology. A computerized assessment of Dahmer's test results reported: " [This patient] is likely to have significant psychological problems … He typically deals with frustration by acting out in an extrapunitive way … [He is] quite conflicted over sexual issues." *Dahmer* (2002), a film based on the life of Jeffrey Dahmer, has little value as either entertainment or pedagogy.

John Waters is a director whose films are often designed to shock the viewer, and he has produced interesting cult films with sexual themes (e.g. *Pink Flamingos*, 1972); another of his films, *A Dirty Shame* (2004), about a woman who becomes a sex addict after a head injury, portrays a large number of fetishes, but the viewer actually learns little about fetishism from watching this somewhat insipid movie. The film stands in marked contrast to Molly Parker's sensitive portrayal of necrophilia in *Kissed* (1966). Parker's character, Sandra Larson, first becomes fascinated with death observing dead sparrows and chipmunks; she buries the animals but later digs them up and rubs her body with them. Sandra eventually gets a job in a funeral home; she has sex with the corpses but treats the sex act as a quasireligious ritual. This film makes necrophilia seem more plausible than most of us believe it to be, and perhaps a little less reprehensible.

Necrophilia is sometimes portrayed or alluded to in vampire movies. One of the best of these is *Bram Stoker's Dracula* (1992), directed by Francis Ford Coppola. There are a number of case studies of people who are aroused by the sight of blood; this phenomenon is frequently referred to as **vampirism**.

International Films and Paraphilic Disorders

Edouard Molinaro's *La Cage aux Folles* (*The Birdcage*; 1978) is a comedy that portrays the relationship between two middle-aged homosexual lovers, Renato and Albin. Renato owns and manages La Cage aux Folles, a nightclub in the south of France in which all the performers are male transvestites who perform as women. Albin, whose stage name is Zaza, is the star performer at La Cage aux Folles, as well as Renato's lover and longtime companion. Albin cross-dresses both on and off stage and has adopted an exclusive feminine identity.

It is important to understand that this film is a farce and not an accurate presentation of either homosexual relationships or transvestites. Albin's role as a drag queen is as exaggerated as his feminine mannerisms, and probably served to perpetuate many of the stereotypes about homosexuality that existed when the film was released in 1978. However, despite reliance on stereotypes, the film can be credited for its presentation of an enduring, loving relationship between its two lead characters. Both men are secure in their sexual identity, even though it does not conform to conventional norms, and they know the life they have made for themselves is the right one for them. At one point Renato remarks, "Yes, I use make-up. Yes, I live with a man. Yes, I'm an old fag. But I know who I am. It's taken twenty years and that deputy isn't going to destroy it."

The film also highlights the sanctimonious hypocrisy of many of those people who are so quick to limit sexual expression in others and illustrates the perils inherent in denial of one's true sexual identity. The film is best viewed as the hilarious farce it is, and one does the film a disservice by insisting that it portray too strong a social message.

Breakfast on Pluto (2005, Ireland/UK), Neal Jordan's adaptation of a novel by Patrick McCabe, is an Irish film that presents the life of "Kitten," an orphan and a transvestite who enjoys dressing up in women's clothes from a very early age. This film is less a gender identity study than the story of societal abuse, ostracization, tragedy, and/or diagnostic pathology. It is about an individual who happens to cross-dress and have gender issues and overcomes enormous stressful and tragic experiences, including but not limited to serious life threats, prostitution, homelessness, job loss, and his house being burned down. Kitten perseveres through all of this. Transvestites also are portrayed in the award-winning film *All About My Mother* (1999, Spain) and in *House of Fools* (2002, Russia).

Breaking the Waves (1996) is a powerful Danish film that examines troilism in a situation in which a formerly virile man paralyzed from an industrial accident insists that his wife have intercourse with other men so he can derive vicarious satisfaction from her stories. The wife, a devout Catholic, goes along with her husband's demands because she is convinced that these voyeuristic pleasures are the only thing keeping her husband alive.

Korean director Chan-wook Park's unforgettable film *Oldboy* (2003) presents a man caught up in a terrible situation in which he unwittingly and unavoidably becomes involved in an incestuous relationship with his daughter, someone he has not seen for 15 years. Another film from Korea is the comedy *Sex is Zero* (2002), a cult film in Korea about the sexual energies and promiscuity of adolescents and college students. The film depicts a number of normal and abnormal sexual behaviors, including rubbing against others on a subway (differentiated from frotteurism), sex with a blow-up doll, men gawking at women doing aerobics and sunbathing, compulsive masturbation, priapism, and young males' obsession with female breasts. The film's director claims that 80% of what happens in the film is based on real experiences.

Pedro Almodóvar's *Tie Me Up! Tie Me Down!* (1990) is a provocative investigation of the relationship between a mildly masochistic woman and the man who kidnaps her and holds her hostage, hoping she will eventually come to love him. The theme is ancient, present in other movies, such as William Wyler's 1965 film *The Collector*. However, few directors have developed the concept with as much skill as Almodóvar, who previously directed another complex psychological investigation of the relation-

ships between men and women, *Women on the Verge of a Nervous Breakdown* (1988). *Tie Me Up! Tie Me Down!* tells the story of Ricky, a young man released from a mental institution, whose only ambition is to find a woman, Marina, he had slept with once when he had escaped from the institution. Marina, an actress and a former drug addict, now stars in pornographic movies and has no memory of her tryst with Ricky. Their interactions after the kidnapping present the viewer with an odd mix of sexual violence and comedy, and the film constantly jumps between the themes of love and control. Love eventually wins out, and Ricky and Marina develop a healthy, satisfying relationship. The movie's description sounds misogynistic, but Almodóvar very skillfully demonstrates the power Marina maintains throughout her captivity.

Sexual sadism is depicted in Ang Lee's *Lust, Caution* (2007, China/Taiwan/Hong Kong), which is set at the time immediately prior to the Chinese revolution (i.e., during the Chinese resistance to the Japanese). A group of mainland Chinese attempt to take down Mr. Yee, a spy from Hong Kong. Yee is very cautious and careful, looking out for anything suspicious; he accounts for his unusual behavior by explaining that he is afraid of the dark. He is sexually sadistic, and at the end of each sexual act he becomes further aroused when he hurts his sexual partner. Sadomasochistic behavior is also portrayed in Lars von Trier's film, *Antichrist* (2009, Denmark), a movie about a couple whose toddler falls out of a window to his death while the couple is having sex. Their sexual behavior and treatment of one another deteriorates and becomes deviant and dangerous, including sadomasochistic sex that is mostly related to grief and punishment rather than sexual pleasure. Roger Ebert described the film as a movie built around "torture porn." The David Cronenberg film, *A Dangerous Method* (2011, UK/Germany) addresses the split in the relationship be-

> "All the way in. I take him in like a slave. I play my part faithfully, so I, too, can get to his heart. Every time he hurts me till I bleed and scream. Then he is satisfied. Then he feels alive."
>
> A sexual masochist describes her relationship with a sexual sadist in *Lust, Caution* (2007)

tween Freud and Jung as well as Jung's alleged affair with a patient, Sabina Sprielrein, who suffered from a severe mental illness. During her treatment, Sabina spoke of the abuse and humiliation she endured from her father. She seemed to have internalized her father's criticism, and her self-deprecating behavior is clearly apparent throughout the film (e.g., her sexual masochism).

Warm Water Under a Red Bridge (2001), a Japanese film directed by Shohei Imamura, tells the story of a woman who retains water in her body that she can only release by "doing something wicked" like stealing things or having sexual intercourse. The woman's water is a symbolic life force; fish flourish and plants grow larger when exposed to it. This fictional character's diagnosis, if any, is unclear. Despite its unusual plot, this is a film well worth seeing.

There is a fascinating portrayal of autoerotic asphyxia in another Japanese film, Nagisa Oshima's *In the Realm of the Senses* (1976). This movie documents the sexual obsessions of two Japanese lovers who are preoccupied with sexual pleasure. The woman increasingly resorts to strangulation to prolong the erections of her lover; eventually and predictably, he dies during one of these episodes. In one graphic scene, the woman severs off the man's penis. The film is based on the true story of a woman who accidentally strangled her lover and then wandered around in a daze, carrying her lover's severed penis with her. Oshima was tried for obscenity in Japan when the film was released, but he was eventually acquitted. His stature as a filmmaker was vindicated by the critical and commercial success of the film in Europe and the United States.

A Short Film About Love (1988), a Polish movie directed by Krzysztof Kieslowski, is about Tomik, a shy and withdrawn 19-year-old voyeur who uses a telescope to spy on an older woman who lives in a nearby apartment. He becomes increasingly obsessed with the woman and eventually confesses that he has been watching her have sex with her numerous lovers. She is at first outraged, then intrigued. She later repositions her bed so he can observe her more easily when she is having sex with one of her lovers. Eventually the teenager has brief physical contact with her, but it is an unsatisfying, humiliating experience, and he flees from her apartment and attempts suicide by slitting his wrists. He survives, and while he is in the hospital recovering, the woman, Magda, becomes increasingly obsessed with him, using binoculars to watch his apartment to see when he will return. The first part of the film is presented from his perspective; the second from hers. The film is reminiscent of Hitchcock's masterpiece *Rear Window* (1954).

Many of the foreign films discussed are classics and highly recommended. The films are engaging and provocative, and they will help viewers understand the complex, complicated, and endlessly fascinating varieties of human sexual experience.

⚙ Critical Thinking Questions

➤ How do you explain the popularity of the sadomasochistic novel *Fifty Shades of Grey*?

➤ How common are paraphilic disorders among criminals? What percentage of inmates would be diagnosed with a paraphilic disorder?

➤ Have you met someone with voyeuristic disorder or exhibitionistic disorder? Were there any clues from their behavior that made you wonder about this prior to learning they had this condition?

➤ Is pedophilia more common among certain groups, cultures, sexual orientations, or professions? Is there a relationship between pedophilia and the priesthood?

➤ Homosexuality was deleted from the *Diagnostic and Statistical Manual* of the American Psychiatric Association in 1973. What brought about this decision? What have been its effects?

➤ Body piercing of the genitals and nipples became common in the 1990s, whereas it was quite rare in the 1950s. Would these behaviors have been viewed as sexual deviance in the 1950s? How do culture and context influence the process of labeling pathology?

➤ Why is it that women's clothes (e.g., dresses and slips) are distinctly feminine, while men's clothes (e.g., pants and belts) are far less likely to be regarded as exclusively male?

➤ What psychological theories have been put forward to explain the development of fetishes and other paraphilias?

➤ Should it be a crime to possess child pornography if someone only uses it to masturbate and never actually acts out with children?

➤ Incest is not included as a diagnostic label in the *DSM-5*. Should it be labeled and treated as a mental illness?

➤ What is the age of consent for sexual activity in your state? Is it too conservative or too liberal?

➤ If you had a client who found she was aroused by incorporating guns or knives into foreplay, what advice would you give her?

➤ What should parents do when they discover their children are watching hard core pornography on the Internet?

If you have time to read just one book relevant to this chapter, make it:

 Golden, G. H. (2009). *In the grip of desire: A therapist at work with sexual secrets.* New York: Routledge/Taylor & Francis.

If you only have time for one article, read:

Taborda, J. G. V., & Michalski-Jaeger, C. A. (2012). Sexual disorders and crime. *Current Opinion in Psychiatry, 25*(5), 370–374. doi: 10.1097/YCO.0b013e328356b7d9

Wedding and Niemiec's Top 10 Paraphilic Disorders Films

- *Leap Year* (2010)
- *Lolita* (1962)
- *Secretary* (2002)
- *The Piano Teacher* (2001)
- *Towelhead* (2007)
- *The Reader* (2008)
- *The Woodsman* (2004)
- *Blue Velvet* (1986)
- *Breaking the Waves* (1996)
- *Hard Candy* (2005)

Chapter 15

Violence and Physical and Sexual Abuse

When I woke up, I went on what the movie advertisements refer to as a roaring rampage of revenge. I roared and I rampaged and I got bloody satisfaction. I've killed a hell of a lot of people to get to this point. But I've only one more ... the last one ... the one I'm driving to right now. The only one left. And when I arrive at my destination, I am gonna kill Bill ...

Beatrix Kiddo, "the bride," in *Kill Bill: Vol. 1* (2003)

➤ What is the murder rate in the United States? In your hometown?

➤ Is Beatrix Kiddo's ("the bride's") revenge justified?

➤ What would you say to someone intent on getting revenge via murder?

➤ Following a 4-year coma, how long should it typically take to work through muscle atrophy in the legs? Can a person "will" their toes to move as the bride does in *Kill Bill: Vol. 1*?

➤ What is the role of violence in these two films? Does it change from one film to the next?

➤ Director Quentin Tarantino works hard to develop characters who are violent and dangerous. What is he trying to express in doing so?

➤ Tarantino blocks out the bride's real name for much of both films. What is the psychological relevance of this?

➤ There are several seriously violent characters in this film. How do their motives and worldviews differ from one another? How are they similar? How is their worldview different from that of a nonviolent person?

➤ One scene involves a deviant hospital worker prostituting coma patients for money. How frequently does something like this occur?

➤ Tarantino engages the viewer in feeling compassion for a serial killer. How does he do this? Do you feel manipulated by this?

Patient Evaluation

Name: Beatrix Kiddo

Patient's stated reason for coming
"I have only one thing on my mind ... revenge. As soon as I get out of here, I'm gonna kill Bill!"

History of the present illness
Ms. Beatrix Kiddo is a 34-year-old White woman being evaluated to assess her mental status and to develop treatment recommendations. She was caught by police 3 days ago driving a stolen vehicle owned by a man who was murdered in the hospital in which she was staying. She is a suspect in several murder investigations, including a mass murder of over 50 people. She is currently in isolation at the county jail. She did not provide details regarding any homicides; however, she was adamant about her plan to kill five people, of which, according to Beatrix, only one remains. The person who remains is her ex-boyfriend and former boss, "Bill."

Past psychiatric illness, treatment, and outcomes
Beatrix does not have a history of psychiatric problems. She denied posttraumatic stress symptoms. She denied depression, anxiety, hallucinations, and delusions.

Medical history
Beatrix was hospitalized in a coma for 4 years following a severe head injury from a gunshot to her head. She awoke from the coma suddenly, immediately remembering the events that lead her to the hospital. Shortly thereafter she overheard a conversation noting she was raped several times while in the coma by a hospital worker who had been prostituting her to various men. She has been out of the coma for about 2 weeks.

Beatrix has no history of taking psychiatric medication. She denied a history of other injuries, illnesses, or medical disorders, other than "occasional bumps and bruises from kung fu training and fighting."

Psychosocial history
Beatrix would not disclose her complete occupational history; however, she did state she "helped rid the world of scum." Following this job, she worked at a music store and became engaged. On the night of the wedding rehearsal, her fiancé

and his family were killed, and she states she was beaten and shot by the five people mentioned earlier and she was shot in the head by "Bill." She believes this was revenge taken on her for leaving her previous job. She was pregnant at the time she was shot. She states this caused her to lose the baby and put her in a coma. This disclosure brought tears to her eyes.

Beatrix has never been married. She graduated from high school and then traveled around the world receiving training in various forms of specialized martial arts. Beatrix states she does not have any friends, but paradoxically also states that she makes friends easily.

Drug and alcohol history
Beatrix denied any significant substance use history. She occasionally drinks alcohol (twice per month) and smokes marijuana (once per month).

Behavioral observations
Beatrix presented as pleasant, charming, and engaging. She was quite relaxed throughout the interview. She expressed considerable intensity when she spoke of the revenge she hoped to achieve. Mood and affect were euthymic. Speech was normal, evenly paced, and coherent. She seemed to be very clear in her choice of words as she frequently placed emphasis on particular words. No tangential or circumstantial speech was noted. No psychotic processes were evident. No dissociative symptoms were observed. She appeared guarded throughout the evaluation, but she cooperated fully, and the results of the examination are believed to be valid. There were no inconsistencies in her story that might indicate dishonesty, malingering, or other form of manipulation.

Mental status examination
Beatrix was oriented to place, person, time, and situation. She appears to be very intelligent, both socially and intellectually. She scored 30 out of a total of 30 possible points on the Mini-Mental State Examination. No cognitive, attention, concentration, or memory problems were noted, despite the severe head injury and coma in her fairly recent past.

Functional assessment
Beatrix is very bright and clever. She clearly knows how to take care of herself and get her needs met. She does not appear to experience any aftereffects from the head injury and coma, other than an intense anger and preoccupation with revenge. Though she ruminates and plans revenge, this does not get in the way of getting her needs met. She states she lacks "mercy, compassion, and forgiveness," but that she has a high dose of rationality. She does present as rational; however, this rationality is not congruent with the allegations of serial killing and her revenge plans involving murder.

Strengths
Beatrix is direct, assertive, and succinct in her communication. She is talented in martial arts and well-skilled in self-defense.

Diagnosis
Adjustment disorder with disturbance of conduct (F43.24); antisocial personality disorder (F60.2).

Treatment plan
(1) It is recommended Beatrix not be released at this time due to her significant threats to harm others. (2) Request personality and projective psychological testing to provide a more complete evaluation (e.g., Minnesota Multiphasic Personality Inventory-2 [MMPI-2]. (3) Request hospital records from her 4-year hospitalization following her head injury. (4) Offer the option of individual psychotherapy to work with decision making, provide support, and discuss coping strategies.

Prognosis
Guarded.

Violence, Revenge, and *Kill Bill*

Beatrix Kiddo (aka "the bride," played by Uma Thurman) is not a typical prototype of a violent figure. She is a middle-aged woman who was in a relationship, does not abuse substances, and does not have a poor socioeconomic background. Research has shown repeatedly that substance abuse increases the likelihood of violent acts; other risk factors for violence include being young, male, single, and of lower socioeconomic status. Nevertheless, Thurman is engaging, fascinating, and compelling in her role as the vengeful character in *Kill Bill: Vol. 1* (2003) and *Kill Bill: Vol. 2* (2004), both of which involve dramatic depictions of violence (e.g., see Figure 27). Some viewers will argue these are two of the most artistic action films ever made. Others will see the violence as overly graphic and gratuitous. Still others will speak of the role of violence influencing today's culture and today's youth, and argue that despite the artistry, the violent imagery that defines these films cannot be beneficial for youth or adults.

Others will speak to the glorification of murder and the purposeless nature of revenge. Some will say the violence is justified as it is always either in self-defense or directed solely at those individuals who killed her family and left her for dead. Finally, some will note the film is not to be taken "literally," and that it is to be seen for entertainment, distraction, appreciation, and even inspiration (e.g., the theme of a woman's courage and bravery). Each of the above perceptions is valid and at least partially accurate.

In an interview, David Carradine (who played the character Bill) stated: "The essence of a Tarantino movie is not the violence, not the action. It's the inside look at the mind, the heart, of violent people." This insight emphasizes looking more deeply at all cinematic characters and looking beyond violent acts to better understand them. There are a variety of violent characters in the film; each is portrayed as unique, with different backgrounds, motivations, thought processes, and actions. Rather than one-dimensional "bad guys," Tarantino develops all of his characters, showing their flaws,

Figure 27. *Kill Bill: Vol. 1* (2003, A Band Apart). Produced by Lawrence Bender and Katsuji Morishita. Directed by Quentin Terantino.

strengths, nuances, and everyday interactions behind their violent presentation.

Some people will be offended by the frequency and intensity of the violence in these films. This is not unjustified, for in many ways these are quintessential violent movies. Scores of people are killed, arms are chopped off, blood sprays, and eyes are ripped out of their sockets, at times in cartoonish ways. The bride is buried alive, she is raped while in a coma, and other characters are tortured as the killer watches them suffer and die. One of the most violent sequences occurs in *Kill Bill: Vol. 1* and is presented completely in animation; this episode presents the traumatic history of one assassin, who as a girl watched her father and mother brutally murdered in front of her. Tarantino does not do this for gratuitous purposes – there are real depths to these characters, an intricate story to be told, and beautiful cinematic artistry to appreciate. The dramatic mixture of violence and cinematic genius is reminiscent of Stanley Kubrick's classic, *A Clockwork Orange* (1971), which was criticized for being overly violent and degrading women, neither of which was Kubrick's intent.

Many of Tarantino's other films involve similar themes and use violence as a communication medium: examples include *Reservoir Dogs* (1992), *Pulp Fiction* (1994), and *Jackie Brown* (1997). He also wrote the screenplay for *From Dusk Till Dawn* (1995). Most recently, Tarantino (along with Robert Rodriguez) wrote and directed two full-length horror films that were shown together as *Grindhouse* (2007) and were touted as a homage to gory exploitation films. Individually, these violent films are titled *Death Proof* and *Planet Terror*; they portray, respectively, a stunt race car driver (Kurt Russell) who stalks and kills women until he encounters a group of women who turn the tables on him, and an army of flesh-eating zombies created by a bioweapon mishap.

Most people who read this book will have an interest in films and likely be aware of the death of David Carradine in Bangkok, Thailand, on June 4, 2009. Carradine was found hanging by a rope in his hotel room closet, and speculation about his death has included suicide, murder by Kung Fu gangs he was investigating, and autoerotic asphyxiation. Two of Carradine's ex-wives have reported that he practiced erotic self-bondage. Whatever the cause of his death, he was a gifted actor who was perfectly cast in the *Kill Bill* films.

Violence and Movies: When is Violence Gratuitous?

In the majority of current action and horror movies, the purpose of the violence is to stimulate, dazzle, and entertain the viewer for a brief period. This helps the viewer escape from their present reality and magically enter a more exciting world. Ultimately, the violence in this type of action film (usually a Hollywood product) is unrealistic, unnecessary, and/or gratuitous. It is merely a means to an end – the overriding purpose is to sell movie tickets, not to enhance the cinematic art, to relay an important message to the viewer, or to engender insights.

We have identified seven exceptions to this type of escapism violence. We have grouped films around these thematic exceptions, which at least begin an argument that violence in films can have a meaningful purpose. However, this does not mean that the purpose outweighs the negative effects associated with violence.

Depicting a Particular Reality

Often violence is the most succinct and honest way to portray the reality of a particular situation, problem, or conflict. In *Elephant* (2003), the reality of violence in schools is depicted. Director Gus Van Sant portrays the typical everyday life of several students who are unaware of the danger and violence about to take place. *Hotel Rwanda* (2004) depicts another terrible reality: The genocide that took place in Rwanda in which nearly 1 million Rwandans were killed. The film focuses on the heroic behavior of a hotel owner, Paul Rusesabagina, who saved well over 1,000 people's lives, and the multiple threats of violence he had to face in order to do so.

Rendition (2007) attempts to show the realities of politics and "Washington." The film is a depiction of "extraordinary rendition" – the detaining of suspected terrorists with minimal evidence (e.g., a phone record) and interrogating/questioning them on foreign soil without judicial oversight. In this film, an Egyptian man traveling in South Africa to attend a conference is detained without due process of law and is then tortured by means of waterboarding and other methods. The film also portrays Islamic extremists, brainwashing, and the training of suicide bombers.

"Sometimes I wonder will God ever forgive us for what we've done to each other? Then I look around and I realize God left this place a long time ago"

Realistic cynicism portrayed by Leonardo DiCaprio in *Blood Diamond* (2006)

Blood Diamond (2006) is an intense action film with a deeper purpose – to depict and raise awareness about "conflict diamonds." The film takes place in Sierra Leone in 1999, where a civil war has ravaged the country, leaving millions of refugees; the irony is they were fighting over diamond fields when most of them had never even seen a diamond. The film notes that whenever something of value is found in Africa, many innocent villagers end up dying – this was the case with ivory, rubber, gold, oil, and diamonds. It is further noted that the Americans who purchase two thirds of the world's diamonds are usually unaware of the violence associated with the diamonds they buy. As one character puts it: "In America, it's bling-bling but out here it's bling-bang." Leonardo DiCaprio gives a standout performance as a diamond smuggler who transforms and sacrifices himself to help the victims of the diamond trade. The film concludes by noting that 40 countries signed the Kimberley Process in January 2003 in an effort to stem the flow of conflict diamonds, and that it is up to the consumer to demand conflict-free diamonds. It also notes there are still 200,000 child soldiers living in Africa, and the viewer gets to see horrifying examples of their training.

Sometimes films portray actual historical events – for example, *Schindler's List* (1993). War films depict not only historical events, but can be generalized to illustrate the atrocities and violence of present-day wars. For example, *Saving Private Ryan* (1998) reveals the realities of war, deglamorizing it, while not denigrating the sacrifices made by the men involved. Antiwar films reveal similar realities emphasizing the futility of war. *No Man's Land* (2001), a film that won an Academy Award for Best Foreign Film, is one good example; likewise, Stanley Kubrick made three excellent antiwar

films: *Paths of Glory* (1957), *Dr. Strangelove or: How I Learned to Stop Worrying and Love the Bomb* (1964), and *Full Metal Jacket* (1987).

Showing the Ridiculous and Futile Nature of Violence

The purpose of the film *Series 7: The Contenders* (2001) is to demonstrate the futility and folly of violence. The film is a tongue-in-cheek fictional reality television show where six people are randomly chosen from their government-issued numbers and forced to hunt and kill the others while cameras film them for the television audience. The narrator excitedly describes "real people, real murders" and states that "the rules are as simple as life and death." Dawn, a pregnant woman, is "the longest running contender;" she continues with each new episode enhancing the theme of "kill or be killed." Her success fails to impress her family, and her sister labels her as an "animal, whore, addict, murderer, and thief."

Revealing the Psyche of Violent People

As discussed earlier in the chapter, most of Quentin Tarantino's films embody this theme. Serial killer movies (discussed in more detail in Chapter 13) sometimes attempt to attain this level, but they rarely succeed. In *American Psycho* (2000), assuming the violence is all in Patrick Bateman's mind, the purpose of the violence is to depict the inner psyche and violent fantasies of a disturbed man. The film illustrates a fundamental contradiction as Bateman spends hours daydreaming about violent acts while his body, attire, job, business cards, selection of social outings, and overall presentation are virtually perfect. Thus, the film gets at what no one else in Bateman's world would be privy to – his mind. *Sweeney Todd: The Demon Barber of Fleet Street* (2007) is in part a musical which allows the music to contain or "hold" the violence, almost sectioning it off from the rest of the film. The barber's (Johnny Depp) revenge and killings seem to reveal more about his psyche and deterioration than anything else.

The Act of Killing (2012) is a powerful documentary that lingers with the viewer long after he or she has seen the film. The movie deals with death squads in Indonesia that are reported to have killed more than a million people. Death squad leaders describe horrendous acts of torture and murder; these stories are told while their companions listen and laugh at the details of these accounts, all of which are viewed as heroic acts of bravery by the individuals relating the stories. The viewer is reminded of Hannah Arendt's comment about Otto Adolf Eichmann, after Eichmann was hanged for war crimes and crimes against humanity: "It was as though in those last minutes he was summing up the lesson that this long course in human wickedness had taught us – the lesson of the fearsome, word-and-thought-denying *banality of evil*" (Arendt, 2006, p. 365). Evil is a topic that has been recently addressed by many psychologists and social scientists (e.g., Baron-Cohen, 2011; Bartlett, 2005; Mikulincer & Shaver, 2012; Pinker, 2011; Taylor, 2009; Zimbardo, 2007).

Showing How Violence Is a Cyclical Trap

In *American History X* (1998), one of the purposes of the violence is to show its cyclical nature. This film relates the following sequence of events: A man gets involved in a violent group, he gets out of the group but not before the consequences of his involvement emerge, and he tries to challenge and resolve these new conflicts, but ultimately must face the fact that it is too late and violence ensues, completing the circle. The message: Do not get involved with violence in the first place. Mel Gibson's *Apocalypto* (2006) is graphically violent depicting the self-destruction of the Mayan culture.

"I'm going to peel off his skin and make him watch me wear it."

Comment made by a violent Mayan in *Apocalypto* (2006)

A History of Violence (2005), directed by David Cronenberg, depicts Tom Stall (Viggo Mortensen), an everyday family man who owns a café in a small town. He is involved in a hold-up by two criminals; however, he instinctively springs to action, killing both men and saving all his customers and workers. The media proclaim him a hero, and this news attracts three thugs from Philadelphia who claim Tom

has led a previous life filled with violence and that they have come to take him back. The film reinforces research that suggests a history of violence is the best predictor of future violent behavior. It also emphasizes that one can never fully escape one's past, and that once violence starts, it finds a way to cycle back. One of the comments Tom's wife makes after learning about his history illustrates a common misconception in films. She asks: "What are you, some multiple personality schizoid?!" She is confusing two mental disorders in her statement, and she assumes that violence must mean mental illness of some kind (in the case of Tom Stall, it does not).

No one is able to escape the shadow part of his or her character in *Crash* (2004). This Academy Award for Best Picture winner integrates a number of stories in an eclectic mix of races and ethnicities in Los Angeles that provides a meaningful look at the pain of racism, the dangers of discrimination, and the possibility of redemption. Even the Buddhist who practices nonviolence eventually resorts to highly violent and threatening acts. The film depicts the vicissitudes of the human condition, and illustrates that violence leads to more violence, which can be verbal, emotional, or physical.

In Wim Wenders' *The End of Violence* (1997), Bill Pullman plays Mike Max, an action/violence film director who hides out from society and starts a new life after he is almost murdered. While this character promotes violence in his movies, he also fears violence, as documented by his high level of paranoia, leading him to believe his enemies can come from anywhere – land, water, and sky. A contrasting character (Ray Bering, played by Gabriel Byrne) tries to prevent violence as a secret government officer working a program that oversees the city with thousands of cameras watching over every interaction. The cyclical nature of violence is evident both in the man who directs violent movies only to be attacked and thereby become a victim of violence and in the man trying to prevent violence through spying, who is himself killed.

Projecting a Dangerous Future

The message associated with these films is clear: If society keeps heading in a particular direction, a dangerous future is inevitable. *A Clockwork Orange* (1971), in a very artistic way, speaks to this theme with regard to youth violence, the role of the prison system, and the predominant psychological approach at the time, behaviorism. Rather than denigrating such a film and labeling it as offensive, it is more helpful to see the film as a message and motivator to promote change in the present. In *Sin City* (2005), the graphic, stylized violence and surreal settings created with computer animation present a violent and dangerous future. The violence and societal control seen in films such as *Equilibrium* (2002) and *The Island* (2005) clearly depict an unpleasant and dangerous future.

Showing the Potential Danger of Authority Roles and Group Contagion

Group contagion occurs when an individual's identity is merged with that of a group and the individual begins to accept and conform to the values and beliefs of the group. This process of **deindividuation** can be linked with increases in aggressive behavior as people feel more anonymous acting within a group rather than alone. These social psychology themes can clearly be seen in *A Clockwork Orange* (1971), *Fight Club* (1999), *Amores Perros* (2000), and gang-related movies such as *South Central* (1992). It also occurs in larger numbers in the persecution of religious figures, where crowds and major groups of people turn against Gandhi in *Gandhi* (1982) and Jesus in *The Passion of the Christ* (2004).

These themes are also present with gang behavior, which is frequently portrayed in movies. *City of God* (2003), a Brazilian drama/documentary about a poor area of Rio de Janeiro, portrays how gangs can take over much of a major city through group violence, leaving the individual with few options other than joining the drug lords or dying. In *South Central* (1992), the gangs portrayed take over the city at night, implement rules that allow them to keep their power, emphasize controlling the "hood" by killing, and enforce the idea that "nothing goes on without we saying so." The film emphasizes three alternatives to gang-life: (1) Kill the enemy; (2) Turn against oneself and go crazy; or (3) Change. The film also speaks to anger and hate in the lead character, Ali, who must change and influence others to break his own "hate cycle," thus removing his "badge of shame." This theme is also found in a nongang film, *Antwone Fisher* (2002), in which a

young African American man must face his own anger about abuse that can be traced back to the time of slavery.

Gang-related films often explore issues of racism and the link between racism and violence; this is the case in *South Central* (1992) as well as in *8 Mile* (2002), which stars the rapper Eminem. Gangs of violent skinheads promoting hate are depicted in four especially powerful films: *American History X* (1998), *The Believer* (2001), *MacArthur Park* (2001), and *Hate* (1995).

In the psychologically complex film *Fight Club* (1999), men gather one-on-one to physically and brutally fight one another until one of the combatants can no longer stand. An entirely underground fight club movement grows and moves from city to city. The violence is depicted as a way of expressing anger and repressed rage, as an alternative to the monotony of everyday life, as an antidote to consumerism and depression, and as a way of feeling "really alive."

Demonstrating Obstacles People Must Face with Courage and Sacrifice

Jesus and Gandhi look directly in the face of violent crowds in *The Passion of the Christ* (2004) and *Gandhi* (1982), respectively. Both show the enormous sacrifice and courage that is often necessary to confront oppression and defeat violence.

The Impact of Violence in Films

In the United States, children are exposed to an average of almost 11 hr of media each day, and they spend more time learning from these experiences than they do learning from school teachers and in formal classes (Warburton, 2012). According to the American Academy of Pediatrics, the typical American youngster will have witnessed about 200,000 acts of violence on television by the age of 18, and is likely to have witnessed several thousand additional acts of violence in films such as *The Hunger Games: Catching Fire* (2013) or any of the many *Halloween* films. Contemporary films and television programs are replete with violence, and it is difficult to avoid violence in the media or to briefly catalogue the most egregious examples of violence in recent films.

Several studies have examined the role of violence in television and movies and explored its impact on aggression, attitudes, and behavior. Likewise, hundreds of articles have emphasized the impact of movie violence on children and adolescents, and authors often attempt to link this violence with violent acts committed by teens. However, while viewing violent movies does appear to contribute to increases in acts of aggression, the degree of influence is unclear, as many other factors are involved (e.g., video games, parental upbringing, level of poverty, education level, etc.)

Often the person committing the violent act in movies is mentally ill, and as many as 70% of movie characters with mental illness are dangerous. This certainly contributes to the misconception that all people with mental disorders are violent. Some films are able to appropriately make the distinction between violence and mental illness, such as Roman Polanski's *Repulsion* (1965), and Martin Scorsese's *Taxi Driver* (1976) and *Raging Bull* (1980) (Zimmerman, 2003).

War and Mass Murder

Numerous films have been devoted to the problems of genocide or mass murder. Some of the most compelling are *The Diary of Anne Frank* (1959), *Judgment at Nuremberg* (1961), *Little Big Man* (1970), *The Killing Fields* (1984), *The Official Story* (1985), *Salvador* (1986), *The Mission* (1986), *Natural Born Killers* (1994), *Welcome to Sarajevo* (1997), *Windhorse* (1998), *City of God* (2002), *The Last Samurai* (2003), *Congo: White King, Red Rubber, Black Death* (2003), *Hotel Rwanda* (2004), *Beyond the Gates* (2005), *The Last King of Scotland* (2005), *God Grew Tired of Us* (2005), *Pinochet's Last Stand* (2006), *Defiance* (2008), *Darfur Now* (2008), *Shake Hands with the Devil* (2007), *Katyn* (2007), *We Need To Talk About Kevin* (2011), *Avatar* (2009), and *The Hunger Games* (2012). Some classic films depicting the horror of World War I include *All Quiet on the Western Front* (1932), *Gallipoli* (1981), *Johnnie Got His Gun* (1971) and *Paths of Glory* (1957). Mass murder is also portrayed in almost every film depicting World War II and the Holocaust; some salient examples include *The Shop on Main Street* (1966), *Sophie's Choice* (1982), *Europa Europa* (1990), *Schindler's List* (1993), *Life Is Beautiful* (1997), the documentary *The Last Days* (1998), *The Pianist* (2002), *The Boy in the Striped Pajamas* (2008), and *Inglourious Basterds* (2009). Films about the Vietnam War are also compelling indictments of the horror and futility of war; especially memorable films include the documentary *Hearts and Minds* (1974), *The Deer Hunter* (1978), *Coming Home* (1978), *Apocalypse Now* (1979), *Platoon* (1986), *Full Metal Jacket* (1987), *Casualties of War* (1989), *We Were Soldiers* (2002) and the documentary *Kim's Story* (1996) about the life of the 9-year-old child who was photographed running down a country road naked and in pain from napalm burns. The photograph won a Pulitzer Prize, and the film tells the story of Kim Phuc's life after the war ended.

The Hurt Locker (2008) was the surprise winner for the Oscar for Best Picture and depicts the impact of the Iraqi war on an elite team of soldiers as well as the deaths of numerous individuals during the war.

> "We crushed their necks with wood. We hung them. We strangled them with wire. We cut off their heads. We ran them over with cars. We were allowed to do it … we murdered people and were never punished. The people we killed, there's nothing to be done about it. They have to accept it. Maybe I'm just trying to make myself feel better, but it works: I've never felt guilty, never been depressed, never had nightmares."
>
> A former military leader in *The Act of Killing* (2012), proudly describing the murders he committed

The Act of Killing (2012) is a chilling film that documents mass murders committed in Indonesia after a military coup in 1965. The death squad leaders who are interviewed appear proud and almost gleeful as they describe despicable atrocities and the murder of more than a million suspected communists. One of the military leaders depicts how he would decapitate his victims in Figure 28. The murders are regarded as present day heroes in Indonesia. This is a film you will not soon forget.

Figure 28. *The Act of Killing* (2012). Produced by Anne Köhncke, Signe Byrge Sørensen, and Michael Uwemedimo. Directed by Joshua Oppenheimer.

School Shootings

Regrettably, there is an entire genre of films devoted to the topic of mass murders in US schools. One of the most compelling of these films is *We Need To Talk About Kevin* (2011), a film depicting a mother's attempt to love a child who is almost from birth, hateful and vicious. Kevin eventually kills his father and sister, along with several dozen classmates, sparing his mother because "you never want to kill your audience." Gus Van Sant deals with school shootings in his film *Elephant* (2003), and Michael Moore tries to make sense out of the 1999 Columbine High School shootings by Eric Harris and Dylan Klebold, in his film *Bowling for Columbine* (2002). Much of Moore's film is an indictment of lax gun control laws in the United States, and the film includes interviews with Charlton Heston, former president of the National Rifle Association. *Beautiful Boy* (2010) is a film that depicts the difficulties a married couple face after learning that their college age son had shot 17 professors and students before taking his own life. They eventually find a videotape their son had left for them with a simple message: "Mom and Dad, I'm sorry. Please don't hate me."

Physical and Sexual Abuse in Films

Domestic Violence and Films

Domestic violence is a serious, ubiquitous, and underreported problem in our society. Violence sufficient to cause death or serious injury will occur in about one in 25 families, and hitting, slapping, or punching will occur in approximately one in four families. It is unfortunate that some men feel that marriage gives them special license to hit, hurt, or rape their spouse. (Whether or not a man can be charged with raping his wife is one of the themes explored in the 1959 film *Anatomy of a Murder*.)

Two out of three female victims of violence know their attackers; however, they frequently will not report their abuse because they desire to protect their assailants or because they fear reprisals (White, Koss, & Kazdin, 2011).

The film *Personal Velocity* (2002) studies three very different, vulnerable, and courageous women, each in separate segments. One segment addresses issues of domestic violence; Delia (Kyra Sedgwick) is physically abused by her husband. She is slapped hard in the face at the kitchen table in front of her children for saying the wrong thing, and she is frequently beaten. Delia develops enough motivation to leave when she realizes the pain of what her children are going through; this helps her to "break through the inertia." When speaking to her child, she says she stayed with her husband because he needed her more; this speaks to the irrational self-sacrificing of the victim. In looking back, Delia admits that she and her husband never talked about their problems. In a later scene, a memory of her husband triggers a catharsis. Delia struggles to create a new life, depending on compassionate people, such as a counselor at a women's shelter and an old acquaintance who houses Delia and her children.

One type of domestic violence that does not get a lot of attention due to its often intangible nature is that of psychological/emotional abuse. Psychological/emotional abuse is a common phenomenon depicted in films that would be too extensive to list here. One poignant example that illustrates emotional abuse occurs in the film *Waitress* (2007). Jeremy Sisko portrays Earl, the husband of Jenna (Keri Russell). Earl is an extraordinarily needy and psychologically abusive husband. He controls her every move, does not allow Jenna to have a car, collects her tip money as soon as he sees her, and watches her every action with suspicion. He sometimes tells her he will pick her up from work and then decides to simply leave her waiting for hours while at other times he greets her by honking his car's horn, embarrassing her in front of her coworkers. He is fueled by significant jealousy and becomes upset when she tells him she is pregnant, fearing the baby will take away her attention; he subsequently insists she verbally admit that she will put him ahead of the baby and prioritize taking care of him (he, of course, is fully capable of taking care of himself). He also forces her to repeat verbatim sentences on a number

of occasions – usually involving her proclaiming her dedication and allegiance to caring for him – to produce a temporary sense of reassurance. He forces himself upon her sexually but only cares about his personal gratification. Jenna eventually confronts Earl in a classic scene that should not be missed.

Rape and Films

Rape is included in this section rather than in the chapter on sexual and gender identity disorders because rape is an act of violence and an act of sexual abuse, *not* an act of sexual passion. Incest is discussed in the chapter "Gender Dysphoria and Sexual Dysfunctions" (Chapter 9).

The statistics on rape are sobering. The United States has one of the highest rates of rape in the world – four times higher than Germany, 13 times higher than England, and 20 times higher than Japan. It is estimated that one out of three women will be sexually assaulted in her lifetime, and one out of seven will be raped by her husband. Among rape victims, 61% are under the age of 18, and 78% know their attacker. One in four college women have either experienced rape or have been exposed to attempted rape, and the majority of both men and women involved in acquaintance rape had been drinking or using drugs at the time of the rape. About a third of the victims of rape develop a rape-related posttraumatic stress disorder sometime in their lifetime. It is estimated that only about 16% of rapes are reported to the police in the United States, usually because women feel that nothing can be done or because they feel it is a private matter between them and their assailants. When compared with women who have not experienced rape, rape victims are found to be more than nine times more likely to attempt suicide.

Rohypnol (flunitrazepam), a powerful benzodiazepine often referred to as the "date rape drug" is about 10 times more powerful than diazepam (Valium). It is used to treat insomnia and to take the edge off the crash that accompanies withdrawal from binge use of other drugs. Women who have passed out after unwittingly taking Rohypnol have found that the profound sedation and memory impairment that accompany its use have made it very difficult for them to prosecute their assailants. Rohypnol is used to facilitate a rape in the film *Virgin*

(2003); the rape has horrific consequences for the woman.

Rape has been a recurrent theme in contemporary American films. There were significant rape scenes in *A Clockwork Orange* (1971), Ken Russell's *The Devils* (1971), and *My Old Man's Place* (1972). Paul (Marlon Brando) rapes a passive and indifferent Jeanne (Maria Schneider) in *Last Tango in Paris* (1973). There is a vicious and unforgettable rape scene in *Blue Velvet* (1986). Farrah Fawcett takes control of the situation and exacts revenge on a rapist in *Extremities* (1986); Dustin Hoffman gets revenge following his wife's graphic rape in Sam Peckinpah's violent film *Straw Dogs* (1971); and two independent women inadvertently kill a man who tries to rape one of them in *Thelma & Louise* (1991). Vietnamese women are raped in several of the Vietnam War films, most notably in *Casualties of War* (1989). Harrison Ford is wrongly accused of rape in *Presumed Innocent* (1990). Date rape occurs in the 1995 film *Higher Learning*; gang rape is portrayed in *Last Exit to Brooklyn* (1989); and there are homosexual rapes in *Deliverance* (1972) and *American History X* (1998). A nun is raped in *Bad Lieutenant* (1992), but the nun forgives her assailant and refuses to press charges against him. Two children play a game of rape in *Welcome to the Dollhouse* (1996). Ingmar Bergman takes up the theme of the rape of innocence in *The Virgin Spring* (1959), and two rapes occur in the gritty Dutch film *Antonia's Line* (1995), one of which involves a man who rapes his sister who has an intellectual disability. *Dead Man Walking* (1995) presents the viewer with difficult choices about the appropriateness of capital punishment in a case of rape and murder, and we are forced to think about whether or not drug intoxication is a mitigating circumstance in this case and others similar to it. Russell Crowe's wife is raped and killed in Ridley Scott's *Gladiator* (2000).

Attempted rape of a man by a woman is discussed extensively in the film adaptation of Michael Crichton's novel, also titled *Disclosure* (1994). When Tom Sanders (Michael Douglas) rebuffs Meredith Johnson (Demi Moore), the new female boss, she lies and manipulatively accuses her new subordinate of sexual harassment. A Black man is wrongfully accused of rape in *To Kill a Mockingbird* (1962), and the routine rape of slave women in the antebellum South is vividly portrayed in *12 Years a Slave* (2013).

Victims of Physical and Sexual Abuse

Every act of violence or abuse has both a perpetrator and a victim. Both are depicted in films, but for emphasis of story, character development, or artistic integrity, one is often emphasized over the other. The cultural phenomenon *Slumdog Millionaire* (2008), which received eight Academy Awards (including for Best Picture, Best Director, and Best Adapted Screenplay), depicts abuse and torture of children and of the protagonist as an adult. This film is a classic underdog story in which the protagonist overcomes a number of adversities in his quest for love.

In *Precious* (2009), Gabourey Sidibe portrays Claireece "Precious" Jones, an illiterate, obese, African American, 16-year-old, who is pregnant for the second time by her father. She lives in Harlem with her viciously abusive and dangerous mother, Precious struggles to cope with constant degradation and abuse (physical, psychological, and emotional) from her mother through fantasies and dissociation. She gradually builds self-esteem through the help of a teacher at an alternative school.

Peter Jackson's film *The Lovely Bones* (2009), based on the bestselling novel, is about a young teenage girl who is raped and murdered by a pedophile in her neighborhood. The focus in the film is on the perpetrator's chilling acts of violence, his subsequent cover-up behaviors, his craving, obsession, intent, plan to kill again, and the impact of the death on the girl's family.

In the psychological film *Doubt* (2008), Philip Seymour Hoffman portrays Father Brendan Flynn, a priest accused of sexual misbehavior by the school's superior, Sister Aloysius Beauvier (Meryl Streep). As a study of the psychology of doubt, the film is remarkable, as it gives no clear answer as to the priest's innocence or culpability, and the viewer leaves the theater – with doubt. The film is included in this section not for its depiction of abuse, but rather because it illustrates the issues underlying the accusation of abuse.

In the intense, realistic film *Mysterious Skin* (2004), two boys are sexually molested by their coach, and their lives go in completely different directions. Brian, as a child, has nightmares, nosebleeds, blackouts, and enuresis, along with nervous, skittish behavior as he enters adolescence. He realizes he has lost time and believes it is linked with a UFO experience. He is described as asexual. Neil, on the other hand, is hypersexual, and likes the attention and grooming of his coach, and he sets up other children to be groomed by the coach. As an adolescent, he cruises parks, has sex with men for money and takes pride in being written about on dirty bathroom stalls. He has minimal sexual boundaries, uses drugs, gets a sexually transmitted disease, and becomes the victim of severe violence during one of his "tricks." *Antwone Fisher* (2002) is based on the true story of a young man, Antwone Fisher (Derek Luke), who enlists in the Navy and begins to have problems with anger and assault. He is sent to a Navy psychiatrist (Denzel Washington) and eventually opens up his traumatic past, which includes a history of significant physical and sexual abuse.

Some films depict entire groups, cultures, or ethnicities that are victims of physical or sexual abuse. *The Magdalene Sisters* (2002), based on a true story, depicts the lives of a large group of young girls sent away for behavior problems who are forced to endure daily physical hardships, abuse, and humiliation. Each adolescent sent to this Catholic workhouse is abused by nuns who seem oblivious to the pain they inflict.

Another type of abuse not often discussed is harassment. Charlize Theron portrays Josey Aimes, a woman who attempts to support her children by working in a blue-collar mining job in *North Country* (2005). She and the other women experience significant harassment (verbal, physical, emotional, and sexual) by the men, including finding semen on her clothes in her locker, confronting words written with feces on the walls in the woman's locker room, and the placement of a vibrator in her lunch pail. Other depictions of violence in the film include rape and physical abuse by one's partner.

Mystic River and Sexual Abuse

In *Mystic River* (2003), director Clint Eastwood depicts three boyhood friends (Sean Penn as Jimmy, Tim Robbins as Dave, and Kevin Bacon as Sean) who reunite following the death of Jimmy's daughter. At the film's onset, the three boys are approached by a man in a car who intimidates them and identifies himself as a cop. Only Dave gets in the car with the man who turns out to be a pedophile. Dave is sexually abused and escapes from his abductor after 4 days. The story moves ahead about

30 years, and the viewer sees the adult Dave, now married with a son. Dave has never fully recovered from the abduction.

Tim Robbins, who won an Academy Award for Best Supporting Actor for his role as Dave, provides a stunning portrayal of a sexual abuse survivor. Dave is passive, timid, unassuming, and unemotional, yet appears to have a happy family life. In what can be viewed as an unfortunate consequence, Dave sees a man abusing a young boy, and his own abuse history is triggered; trying to free the boy and (metaphorically) himself, Dave snaps, kills the man and allows the boy to escape. Consequently, Dave is plagued with confusion and pain that he is unable to share with his wife; he tells her a different story, and he becomes a suspect in the murder of Jimmy's daughter who had died the same night. Dave becomes more distant (thus appearing more guilty), increasingly quirky, and begins to talk to himself. In one dramatic scene, he seems to hallucinate, hearing voices in his head.

The Accused and Rape

The Accused (1988) is based on a true story of gang rape on a pool table in a blue-collar bar. The crime was especially despicable insofar as more than a dozen spectators stood by clapping and cheering while a woman was repeatedly raped. No one attempted to stop the rape or assist the victim. The complacency of the bystanders in the film is in part attributed to the fact that Sarah Tobias (Jodi Foster) had been drinking heavily and smoking pot earlier in the evening, had openly flirted with one of the men, was provocatively dressed, and had engaged in a sensuous dance immediately before being raped. Her defense is weakened further by the fact that she had jokingly referred to one of the men earlier in the evening, telling her girlfriend, "I should take him home and fuck his brains out." The attorneys for the defense argue that Tobias is simply "trailer park trash" who was an enthusiastic and willing participant in everything that occurred.

Some of the most vivid scenes in the film occur during an insensitive gynecological examination by a woman doctor who asks detailed questions about Sarah's sexual history ("Have you ever made love to more than one man at a time?") and recent experiences. The insensitivity is compounded by the questions of the assistant district attorney, who wants to know how Sarah was dressed and when was the last time she experienced intercourse before the rape.

Tobias loses the first legal round, when the three rapists are convicted but have their sentences reduced from rape to "reckless endangerment." However, she is eventually successful in convicting several of the men who witnessed the rape and did nothing. The film concludes with two sobering facts: (1) in the United States, a rape is reported every 6 min, and (2) one out of every four rape victims is attacked by two or more assailants.

Neglect and Abandonment

An interesting portrayal of an attempt to resolve neglect can be found in Ben Affleck's directorial debut, *Gone Baby Gone* (2007). In this multilayered, complex film, a young girl, who is the neglected child of a cocaine addict, is missing. As the plot develops, we learn that a retired police captain (Morgan Freeman) has kidnapped the girl, rationalizing it by arguing that he is trying to give her a better life and that she was otherwise destined for a terrible future. We also learn that the captain has a personal agenda in that his only child was murdered years ago. The girl seems to be treated exceptionally well, and she has a happy life with her new

Questions to Consider While Watching *Gone Baby Gone*

➤ Should all children who are neglected be taken from their homes? When is "some neglect" too much neglect?

➤ Where do you believe the child in this film should be placed? Is this where you believe the child will have the best future? Do parental rights override the child's right to a happy, safe, and secure future?

➤ Whatever you believe, can you make a clear argument and provide a rationale for the other side of the debate?

➤ What is the role of integrity and psychological courage in this film?

➤ It has been said that the subtext of this film (and the book) is to raise questions and to document that society does not have any idea how to raise children in a healthy way. Do you agree with this? Why or why not?

caretakers. The film concludes with the girl and the protagonist watching television and the camera shifts so that they are then watching the viewer – leaving the viewer with the question of how best to handle a situation in which there are multitudes of parents who neglect their children and potentially high quality parents who would like to have children but cannot.

International Films: Violence and Physical and Sexual Abuse

Violence

Rashomon (1950, Japan) is a classic Akira Kurosawa film in which a bandit, a wife, and a samurai tell three conflicting stories about the rape of the wife and the murder of her husband. The film is considered a classic and is often shown in both film studies programs and social psychology classes. The German director Werner Herzog commented that *Rashomon* was "as close to perfect as a film can get."

Osama (2003, Afghanistan) is based on a true story, and it is the first movie made in Afghanistan after the fall of the Taliban. It depicts the heavy discrimination, violence, and oppression of women under Taliban rule. Violence is also depicted in the everyday reality of everyone living in a poor section of Rio de Janeiro in *City of God* (2003, Brazil). Gangs and drugs are a normal part of existence for these children. This type of film is often a shock to viewers who live a very different life and are unaware of the daily poverty and dangers other people face. The Oscar-winning film *The White Ribbon* (2009, Germany) depicts themes surrounding the abuse and oppression of children. The film depicts not only secrecy, group contagion, and innocence transgressed but also a variety of reactions from the children to the abuse (e.g., denial; trance states; flat affect, automaton behavior; protecting the perpetrator; group bonding, etc.)

2LDK (2003, Japan) demonstrates the ridiculous and futile nature of violence. A competition develops between two girls rooming together following an audition for an acting role. Growing anger, resentment, and negative and hateful thoughts develop in each girl. These emotions are artfully shown as the girls speak and act one way with voice-overs revealing their true but opposite thoughts. Eventually they come face-to-face and exchange physical assaults in the forms of electrocution, cleaning fluid, and attacks with a fire extinguisher. Violence is used to reveal the psyche of a violent thief in Peter Greenaway's *The Cook, the Thief, His Wife, & Her Lover* (1989, France/UK). In addition to being intensely controlling, the thief is revealed to be psychotic.

Das Experiment (2001, Germany) illustrates the potential dangers associated with authority roles and group contagion. This film depicts a research study in a prison setting in which subjects are divided into either prisoners who waive their civil rights or guards who are instructed to maintain peace and order. This film bears some initial structural similarity to one of the most well-known psychological experiments ever conducted, Philip Zimbardo's Stanford Prison Experiment. However, the depiction of violence goes well beyond what actually occurred in Zimbardo's study. The violence in this film, though at times exaggerated, is used to show the danger of group contagion and the power of the authority role. Shortly into the study, the guards collude and decide they need to humiliate the prisoners to regain control. Prisoners are stripped, ridiculed, called names, denigrated, urinated on, and even beaten and left to bleed to death. One guard captures and rapes a female psychologist. The prisoners experience depression, extreme helplessness, psychosis, and panic attacks. It is difficult for anyone from the United States to see this film and not be reminded of the shocking reports of prisoner abuse that occurred at Abu Ghraib prison in Baghdad or at the detention facility at Guantanamo Bay, Cuba.

A Prophet (2009, France/Italy) is an intense film that reveals the culture of prison and the subgroups, often based on racial divides, one finds in prison settings. Malik, 19, is an Arab sent to a French prison where he becomes a mafia kingpin. In the prison system, violence is the method of communication, of payment, of respect, of control, and of redemption.

The Warrior (2001, UK/France/Germany) takes places in feudal India. A warrior, working for a lord as an executioner, destroys entire villages and kills the defenseless and the poor on behalf of the lord. The film illustrates the challenges associated with breaking the vicious cycle of violence.

Abuse

Men who abuse their wives are also likely to abuse their children. Domestic violence can be found in the intriguing film *3-Iron* (2004, South Korea). Alcohol or other drugs are commonly involved in cases of domestic violence, and this relationship is clearly present in *Once Were Warriors* (1994, New Zealand). This remarkable film documents the life of a New Zealand Maori family and the devastating effects of alcoholism and domestic violence on every member of the family, including the husband/ father/perpetrator. The film is especially effective in portraying the effects of domestic violence on the children in the family: One son responds by returning to his Maori roots, while a sensitive, poetry-writing daughter responds by committing suicide.

> ### Additional Questions for Discussion (*Once Were Warriors*)
>
> ➤ What role does alcoholism play in the violence we witness in this family?
> ➤ To what extent is violence an important part of Maori culture?
> ➤ Should a therapist be sensitive to the fact that family violence may believed to be appropriate and justified in some cultures?
> ➤ If you were Beth's therapist, would you actively encourage her to leave Jake, or would you leave this decision to Beth (knowing she has always decided to stay with him in the past)?

Some of the most troubling portrayals of rape occur in those films in which rape is presented as a woman's fantasy, or in those films in which a woman who is being raped becomes aroused by the experience or attracted to the rapist. These themes are found in two otherwise remarkable movies, Pedro Almodóvar's *Tie Me Up! Tie Me Down!* (1990, Spain) and Lina Wertmuller's *Swept Away* (1974, Italy).

If there was ever a character who is a victim of abuse, it would be Lilya in *Lilya 4-Ever* (2002). This poignant Danish/Swedish film develops the character of Lilya, a 16-year-old girl who seems to encounter just about every form of abuse and exploitation a person can experience. She is lied to and abandoned by her mother, rejected by her family, manipulated and sold into prostitution by a man she had hoped to live with, gang raped, physically and sexually abused, and forced to work as an unpaid prostitute. She is completely tossed away by society as the viewer clearly sees at the onset of the film when Lilya is depicted walking the streets, bloodied and beaten up, with no safe place or person to turn to. Nevertheless, Lilya does not take on the victim role of helplessness and fear, but instead pushes forward. Her resiliency is commendable and inspirational, but she eventually reaches a breaking point and begins to contemplate suicide.

The impact of sexual abuse in childhood on adult life is portrayed in two excellent films, *The Celebration* (1998, Denmark/Sweden) and *Don't Tell* (2005, Italy/UK/France/Spain). The former depicts a dramatic announcement and confrontation of the father/perpetrator during his 60th birthday celebration in the presence of a host of extended family members. This film was done according to a film movement and style called **Dogme 95**, popularized and set forth by Lars von Trier, in which filmmakers abide by certain rules for a more pure film, such as no nondiegetic sound (sound that is added after filming) and no special effects. *Don't Tell* is a powerful depiction of the secrecy and shame surrounding sexual abuse, the role of secrets, and the horror that lies behind facades of normalcy. The film also depicts the enabling role of a spouse: "It's a vice. He doesn't want to hurt you. He's sick" (says the mother as she enables her abusing spouse and rationalizes his behavior).

Christian: "I've just never understood why you did it."

Father: "It was all you were good for."

Christian, referring to his father's sexual abuse, and the father's arrogant reaction in *The Celebration* (1998)

---

5 x 2 (2004, France) explores the relationship of a couple in five stages, beginning at their divorce and flashing backward to when they first met. There are two ambiguous rape scenes in the film; however,

most viewers would dismiss the ambiguity and clearly regard the behaviors depicted as rape. One occurs when the couple meets up after having been separated for a year and go to a hotel room to have sex. She is reluctant and passive, and he is animalistic; she wants him to stop after they begin, but he continues and rapes her. In another scene, immediately following his neglect of her on their wedding night, she meets a stranger who after some pleasant dialogue forces himself on her and prevents her from getting away, and she gives in to him. A classic cycle of violence is experienced by the femme fatale in the quirky film, *Terribly Happy* (2008, Denmark).

Many films depict the neglect of children by their parents. One particularly striking film in which neglect plays an important role is the Russian film *The Return* (2003). Two boys are abandoned and neglected by their father for 12 years, then suddenly and without warning the father returns. He is quick to leave them again for business, but then changes plans and takes his sons on a trip. The boys are pushed physically and emotionally to survive his challenges (e.g., they are left to do the work of figuring out how to set up a tent, push a car out of the mud, and row a boat in challenging waters) and continued abandonment (e.g., one boy is left in the middle of nowhere in the pouring rain because he asked too many questions about fishing). The father is an enigma throughout the film: Taciturn in speech with comments of "get in" and "get out," cryptic in his behavior, and secretive about his occupation. Among many other themes, one theme is clear: Many issues arise from abandonment and neglect by a parent, and one cannot simply "return" and expect everything to be normal. A mother neglecting her children due to her mental illness and her desperate quest for a man appears in *Something Like Happiness* (2005, Czech Republic).

Nobody Knows (2004, Japan) is based on real events concerning four children (the oldest being 12) who are abandoned by their mother and left to raise themselves. This is one of the most detailed depictions of the realities and struggles of abandonment in cinema history.

⚙ Critical Thinking Questions

➤ Some movies (e.g., *Pulp Fiction* [1994] and *The Act of Killing* [2013]) depict people who commit extremely violent acts but do not suffer the consequences. What kind of meaning and impact does this have on the viewer?

➤ Do therapists have an obligation to respect cultural values and practices that may be harmful or degrading (e.g., slapping children for misbehaving or female genital mutilation)?

➤ What is the relationship between pornography and violence against women?

➤ Should alcohol or drugs be considered mitigating circumstances in cases of rape or murder (e.g., *Dead Man Walking* [1995])?

➤ Is it possible to develop accurate "psychological profiles" that can help identify people likely to rape and murder?

➤ Are there common factors that characterize the childhood experiences of those individuals who grow up to become serial killers?

➤ How do the media perpetuate violence in American society?

➤ Should a woman's dress or provocative behavior be treated as extenuating circumstances in a rape case?

➤ What conformity studies in social psychology can be used to understand the behavior of the bystanders in The Mill bar who do nothing to help Sarah Tobias in *The Accused* (1988)?

➤ What steps could police officers and hospitals take to ensure rape victims are treated humanely and compassionately?

➤ In *Mystic River* (2003), how different would Dave (Tim Robbins) be on an emotional and behavioral level if he had not gotten in the car?

➤ Can mental professionals help prevent the kind of school shootings and mass murders that occurred at Sandy Hook Elementary School?

➤ How would you respond as a parent if you discovered e-mails suggesting your son was contemplating a mass murder?

Authors' Picks

If you have time to read just one controversial book relevant to this chapter, make it:

   Pinker, S. (2011). *The better angels of our nature: Why violence has declined.* New York: Viking.

If you only have time for one article, read:

Stöckl, H., Devries, K., Rotstein, A., Abrahams, N., Campbell, J., Watts, C., & Moreno, C.G. (2013). The global prevalence of intimate partner homicide: A systematic review. *The Lancet, 382* (9895), 859–865. doi: 10.1016/S0140-6736(13)61030-2

Wedding and Niemiec's Top 10 Violence and Physical and Sexual Abuse Films

Rashomon (1950)
Once Were Warriors (1994)
A Clockwork Orange (1971)
Hotel Rwanda (2004)
City of God (2003)
Kill Bill: Vol. 1 and Vol. 2 (2003, 2004)
Schindler's List (1993)
The Accused (1988)
American Psycho (2000)

Chapter 16

Treatment

She was fifteen years old, going on thirty-five, Doc, and she told me she was eighteen, she was plenty willing, I practically had to take to sewing my pants shut ... I don't think it's crazy at all and I don't think you do either. No man alive could resist that ... and that's why I got into jail to begin with. And now they're telling me I'm crazy over here because I don't sit there like a goddamn vegetable. Don't make a bit of sense to me. If that's what being crazy is, then I'm senseless, out of it, gone-down-the-road, wacko. But no more, no less, that's it.

Randle P. McMurphy responds during a psychiatric interview in *One Flew Over the Cuckoo's Nest* (1975)

➤ Is the stereotype of psychiatric treatment presented in *One Flew Over the Cuckoo's Nest* still accurate? Was it at the time?

➤ Can you identify the theoretical position that links Billy's suicide with an intrusive, overly protective parent?

➤ How common is it for prisoners to evade punishment in the criminal justice system by entering the mental health system?

➤ The orderlies and aides in the film appear indifferent and apathetic. What are the entry-level wages for similar positions in your state?

➤ How would Paul Newman's title character in *Cool Hand Luke* (1967) have fared if he had been transferred to the mental health system in today's society?

➤ Chief Bromden chooses to murder McMurphy rather than have him beaten by the system. Is this a true mercy killing? Is it justified?

➤ How likely is it that McMurphy's lobotomy would have altered his personality? What is the neurological basis for the personality changes that accompany lobotomy?

➤ If you were an attendant working at the hospital when the ward psychiatrist recommended a lobotomy, would you have tried to stop it? What political and social tools could you have used?

➤ How is the treatment portrayed in *One Flew Over the Cuckoo's Nest* different from the treatment provided in psychiatric hospitals today?

Patient Evaluation

Name: Randle P. McMurphy

Patient's stated reason for coming
"I figured the funny farm couldn't be any worse than a chain gang."

History of the present illness
Randle Patrick McMurphy is a 35-year-old White man, never married, who presents with a long history of minor legal problems dating back to his adolescence. He was awarded a distinguished service cross for leading an escape from a Communist prison camp during the Korean War, but he also received a dishonorable discharge for insubordination, and he has been involved in a series of street brawls and barroom fights since his discharge from the military. He was recently arrested for statutory rape and sentenced to 2 years of hard labor in the Rivermead Correctional Facility. While at Rivermead, his behavior became increasingly erratic and "goofy," and he was sent to the state hospital for observation, evaluation, and treatment.

Past psychiatric illness, treatment, and outcomes
Mr. McMurphy has been arrested on several occasions for public drunkenness and disturbing the peace. He was typically allowed to "sleep off" these episodes in the county jail; however, because of a conviction of statutory rape of a 15-year-old girl, he was sentenced to 2 years in prison. He denies any history of psychiatric or psychological treatment, although he was seen sporadically by high school counselors for truancy and problems relating to authority figures, and he has received some counseling by parole officers over the years.

Medical history
Mr. McMurphy had the usual childhood illnesses and met development milestones at the expected times. He broke his arm in a schoolyard altercation at age 15. He states (proudly) that he has had gonorrhea at least five times. He denies any history of hospitalization or other significant medical treatment.

Psychosocial history

Mr. McMurphy's parents separated shortly after his birth, and he was raised by a widowed aunt (his mother's sister). There were no other children in the home, and the elderly aunt was an ineffectual disciplinarian. Mr. McMurphy made good grades in high school, apparently with little effort; he left high school in the middle of the 11th grade after a high school girlfriend became pregnant. "It was time for Randle Patrick to hit the road," he says. He joined the Navy at age 18 and served for 3 years; however, he received a dishonorable discharge before completing his last tour of duty due to a history of frequently being absent without leave (AWOL). Since being discharged from the Navy, he has traveled widely and has worked at a series of jobs, including gardener, handyman, bouncer, massage parlor manager, car salesman, apple picker, state fair carney, and mechanic. He has never married, and his relationships with women tend to be short-term and relatively inconsequential.

Drug and alcohol history

Mr. McMurphy is candid about his history of drug use: "I've tried them all at least once." He has experimented with LSD and peyote, has snorted cocaine, and frequently uses amphetamines and barbiturates. However, alcohol remains his drug of choice, and beer and whiskey have been responsible for most of the legal problems Mr. McMurphy has experienced over the past decade. He smokes approximately one pack of unfiltered cigarettes each day.

Behavioral observations

Mr. McMurphy arrived on time for the examination. He was casually dressed. He was cheerful and talkative and seemed proud and happy to have been taken off the prison work detail. He cooperated fully with all tasks and seemed to take pride in his good performance on cognitive tasks.

Mental status examination

Mr. McMurphy's speech was rapid but not pressured. He appears to be quick-witted and mentally agile. Mood was within normal limits. There were no indications of thought disorder present. There is no evidence of suicidal ideation. Mr. McMurphy reports there were several sadistic guards at the prison: "I'll nail their balls to the wall if I ever get the chance." However, this appears to be braggadocio, and McMurphy is not believed to be a danger to self or others.

This patient was fully oriented to time, place ("the looney bin"), and person. He performed all tasks on the Mini-Mental State Examination quickly and without difficulty, earning a perfect score of 30. When asked to write a sentence, the patient surprised the examiner by writing a line from Shakespeare: "A man can die but once, and let it go which way it will, he that dies this year is quit for the next." When asked to explain the significance of the line, McMurphy simply remarked, "I read it somewhere and liked it." This does not appear to be evidence of suicidal thinking.

Functional assessment

Although he never finished high school, this patient is believed to have superior intelligence. He is a group leader, and he has quickly become the dominant figure on the ward and the center of most ward activity. He has an exuberant charisma that most of the other patients find very attractive. He has worked in a wide variety of jobs and appears to be a "quick study." There are no significant work limitations, although his history of alcohol abuse may make him a high risk for some jobs (e.g., he would not be a good security guard); he may function best in a highly structured environment. He has limited social support; he is unmarried and is not aware of any living relatives. He has few hobbies and formerly spent most of his leisure time in bars. He is disliked and resented by the ward staff, who regard him as a troublemaker and the instigator of most of the recent disciplinary problems that have occurred on the ward.

Strengths

Mr. McMurphy's engaging personality is his greatest asset. He appears to be a natural leader; both men and women are attracted to his high energy, quick wit, and ebullience. On the VIA Survey, a measure of character strengths, his highest strengths were creativity, curiosity, zest, leadership, bravery, and social intelligence.

Diagnosis

Rule out antisocial personality disorder (F60.2), rule out alcohol use disorder (F10.20), rule out pedophilic disorder (F65.4).

Treatment plan
There is no clear evidence of psychopathology in this individual, and I am unable to ascertain why he was transferred from the state prison to the state hospital. He does not appear to be appropriately placed, and I will investigate other treatment alternatives.

Prognosis
Good.

One Flew Over the Cuckoo's Nest

One of the great joys associated with teaching abnormal psychology and related courses and using *Movies and Mental Illness* as a text is the opportunity to introduce a new generation of students to films we watched – and loved – as college students. *One Flew Over the Cuckoo's Nest* (1975) is one of those films; two others are *Psycho* (1960) and *A Clockwork Orange* (1971).

Films such as *One Flew Over the Cuckoo's Nest* attempt to show the human injustices that existed and are occasionally still found in the mental health system. In this classic film, once McMurphy moves from the prison system into the mental health system, he loses almost all civil rights, such as his right to refuse treatment. The issues addressed by the film are not the usual problems of large institutions such as lack of facilities, cleanliness, staff, or organizational communication. Instead, the film addresses fundamental issues of autonomy and paternalism. The treatment team has ultimate control over McMurphy's treatment and discharge. A rigid, controlling nurse, Nurse Ratched, widely regarded as one of the greatest villains in cinema history, engages in an ongoing power struggle with a patient whom she perceives as a threat to her control of the unit. She

Figure 29. *One Flew Over the Cuckoo's Nest* (1975, United Artists). Produced by Michael Douglas and Saul Zaentz. Directed by Miloš Forman.

uses her position and knowledge of the system to gain control over McMurphy. McMurphy's lobotomy is the ultimate abuse of psychiatric power. The relative power of doctors, nurses and patients is underscored in the film, as illustrated in Figure 29.

Treatment Modalities Portrayed in Films

Individual Psychotherapy

Individual psychotherapy is the most common treatment modality depicted in movies. Sometimes it is quite accurate; at other times, it is preposterous. Gabbard and Gabbard (1999) estimated that through 1998, over 450 films dealing with psychiatry have been created; from the films we have viewed, we conclude that most of these involve the modalities and topics discussed in this chapter.

There are a number of misconceptions of psychologists and mental health professionals perpetrated by films. We have previously outlined several of these cinematic biases and errors that confuse the public (for a discussion of these, see Niemiec and Wedding, 2006). Here are seven of these common misconceptions; we believe US cinema has shown some improvement in each of these over the last several years:

1. Psychiatrists are the main professionals who perform psychotherapy.
2. Psychoanalysis is the dominant practice in psychotherapy.
3. Psychologists are patently unethical.
4. Psychologists are cavalier about boundary violations.
5. Almost all therapists are men.
6. Almost all therapists are White.
7. Research is of little value.

The most frequently portrayed theoretical orientation continues to be **psychoanalysis**, though it is only one of many approaches to therapy. Both the frequency of cinematic depictions of psychotherapy and many of the stereotypes can be credited to director Woody Allen, who has portrayed psychoanalysts in dozens of his films. Interestingly, the psychologist portrayal in the film *Anything Else* (2003) is one of his most stereotypic (e.g., he is a therapist

who refuses to respond to important patient questions). One of the least stereotypic portrayals occurred the previous year when Allen directed *Hollywood Ending* (2002), a film about a man hired to direct a picture being produced by his ex-wife. The protagonist develops a case of psychosomatic blindness, and his therapist is portrayed as someone who accurately diagnoses the conversion disorder and offers helpful suggestions.

Almost all of Woody Allen's films present ethical and moral challenges, often in the context of therapy. For example, in *Another Woman* (1988), Marion Post (Gena Rowlands) is a philosopher and a college professor who rents a private office so she can focus on writing a book. Her new office is adjacent to the office of a psychiatrist, and she discovers that she can overhear therapy sessions through an office vent. She initially successfully blocks the sound, but she soon discovers that eavesdropping is seductive, and she becomes particularly intrigued by therapy sessions with Hope (Mia Farrow), a pregnant woman whose marriage is on the rocks. Listening in on Hope's therapy sessions, Marion begins to examine and understand her own life and her refusal to embrace it fully. In *Deconstructing Harry* (1997) Allen pays homage to Ingmar Bergman's *Wild Strawberries* (1957). It is arguably his most autobiographical film, and it presents multiple examples of therapy boundary violations. For example, Harry's psychotherapist (Joan, played by Kirstie Alley) discharges Woody Allen's character (Harry Block – a blocked writer) so she can become his lover. Joan later marries Harry and has a son with him. She sees therapy patients in her home office, and one comic episode involves her screaming and berating her philandering husband (who is in an adjoining room) while trying to conduct therapy with a troubled client who is simply wondering if he should continue working at a dead-end job. Writing about this film, Miguel Floriano (2008) notes:

> In one of the most memorable scenes ... we see Joan (Kirstie Alley) arguing with her husband Harry because he has slept with one of her twenty-year old patients who has subsequently spilt the beans in a therapy session. The affronted wife is trying to strangle him, screaming that she is going to kill him, when a patient arrives for a consultation. Suddenly, she says she is sorry and gets up. The camera remains on the patient who, horrified, hears voices from off the set. "You fucked-up fuck! I can't believe you did this! Fucking asshole! You fucked my patient – You don't fuck somebody's patient! Fuck you!" Then she returns to the office, sits down and begins to write in her

notebook. She asks poor Mr. Farber to pick up where they had left off but while he is trying to do this she struggles to open a bottle of pills. She jumps up again and carries on with the argument at full volume "And with my patient! That is a sacred trust! My patient!" Harry attempts to defend himself: "But who else do I meet?" Joan sits down again and asks Mr. Farber to continue, but before he can she screams to the other end of the house "Get your shit and your goddam clothes and get the fuck out of here! … And I mean tonight, motherfucker." This is when Mr Farber bursts into tears like a child. (p. 22)

Other orientations illustrated by films include a humanistic and supportive approach in *Lantana* (2001), and what appears to be **transactional analysis** in *Good Will Hunting* (1997). (Note the titles of the books in his study when Sean Maguire [Robin Williams] pins Will Hunting [Matt Damon] to the wall.) Interestingly, one of the most widely used, popular and empirically validated approaches, **cognitive behavior therapy**, is very rarely depicted in films.

"My father was an alcoholic. Mean fuckin' drunk. He'd come home hammered, lookin' to wail on somebody. So, I had to provoke him so he wouldn't go after my mother and little brother."

Will Hunting describing his childhood in a therapy session with Sean Maguire in *Good Will Hunting* (1997)

Antwone Fisher (2002) depicts multiple sessions of individual psychotherapy. Antwone (Derek Luke) and his psychiatrist, Dr. Jerome Davenport (Denzel Washington), slowly work through the topics of anger, physical abuse, sexual abuse, and trauma. The film is framed around the psychotherapy sessions, and the plot deepens whenever Antwone opens up in a deeper way. The sessions can be divided into phases of resistance and exploration: At first Antwone refuses to share anything; later he begins to open up, sharing his physical abuse, next his sexual abuse, and finally his feelings as he witnessed the murder of his best friend. These four therapy phases are appropriately juxtaposed with relevant narrative components.

The psychiatrist is also influenced by the therapy sessions with this patient. Dr. Davenport had not realized the full extent of his isolation, and he was not aware of how he also needed to change.

Davenport is humble enough to recognize his own weaknesses as he watched his patient's courage and resilience grow.

In addition to those in *Antwone Fisher*, other balanced individual psychotherapy portrayals can be seen in *Good Will Hunting* (1997), *K-Pax* (2001), *The Sixth Sense* (1999), *Gothika* (2003), and *Elling* (2002), while unbalanced individual psychotherapy portrayals can be seen in *Normal* (2003), *Lantana* (2001), and *Vanilla Sky* (2001) (Niemiec & Wedding, 2006). A very good albeit brief portrayal of an Asian American therapist whose suggestions are the catalyst for a major turning point in an adolescent's life can be seen in *The Squid and the Whale* (2005).

Successful individual treatment is seen in films such as *Sybil* (1976) and *Ordinary People* (1980). In *Ordinary People*, Conrad Jarrett (Timothy Hutton), following the accidental death of his brother, begins therapy with a psychiatrist (played by Judd Hirsch) who demonstrates warmth and caring and allows his young patient to examine painful family relationships within the safety of individual therapy. In *Equus* (1977), Richard Burton plays a psychiatrist who treats a very disturbed young man played by Peter Firth. During psychotherapy, the true depth of the psychological disturbance is revealed. In some instances, as in *Best Boy* (1979), a rehabilitation program is portrayed.

David and Lisa (1962), a film based on a novel by psychiatrist Theodore Isaac Rubin, is a dated but still sensitive portrayal of a young man with a severe case of what is likely obsessive-compulsive disorder and a phobia about being touched; he becomes curious about Lisa, a young woman who presents as autistic (displaying repetitive behaviors, limited communication, sing-song responses with rhymes). The film presents David's parents in stereotypical roles (e.g., the mother is overly enmeshed in her son's life, while the father is cold and distant), and the ending is trite. These concerns aside, this film is still worth viewing, and it portrays mental health professionals, and especially Dr. Swinford (Howard Da Silva), in a sympathetic light.

Films frequently present images of mental health professionals behaving unethically. For example, breaches in confidentiality are evident in *Equus* (1977), and sexual relationships between clients and mental health professionals are depicted in *Prince of Tides* (1991), *Mr. Jones* (1993), *Tin Cup* (1996),

Deconstructing Harry (1997), and *Bliss* (1997). A psychiatrist rapes his son's best friend in Todd Solondz's *Happiness* (1998).

The relationship between a psychologist and her patient in *Numb* (2007) is especially troubling because the boundary violations are so patently wrong (e.g., the therapist calls her patient at home, meets with him in a restaurant, is inappropriately self-disclosing, and proclaims her love for him in a crowded restaurant).

In *Prime* (2005), Meryl Streep plays Lisa Metzger, a Jewish social worker who discovers that her client Rafi Gardet (Uma Thurman) has taken a younger lover – who is identified later in therapy as Lisa's son, David Bloomberg. Rafi describes her sexual life with David in lurid detail, at one point describing his penis as "beautiful." Streep knows she should reveal this obvious dual relationship, but postpones doing so because she is intrigued and fascinated by what she is learning about her son.

Kevin Spacey plays psychologist Henry Carter, in *Shrink* (2009). Carter is a flawed character who is addicted to marijuana (see Chapter 11), which he routinely smokes before sessions with clients and between sessions. He eventually quits smoking, and he is able to make a meaningful impact in therapy with a young adolescent girl who has experienced a significant loss in her life.

Mumford (1999) is a Lawrence Kasdan film that depicts a man named Mumford with dubious credentials who sets up shop as a psychologist in a small town – also named Mumford. It turns out that Mumford is a former IRS agent and cocaine addict, and he is an imposter pretending to be a psychologist. He commits numerous boundary violations such as going for long walks with a patient whom he finds especially attractive and telling other townspeople intimate details about the lives of his patients; how-

---

"What kind of doctor are you?"
"PhD. Psychologist."
"Oh, not a real doctor."
"That's right. The fake kind."

Mumford responding with sarcasm to a common misconception in *Mumford* (1999)

---

ever, the movie also suggests that psychotherapy is primarily "the purchase of friendship," and that credentials and training really are not all that important as long as one is a sympathetic listener.

Group Psychotherapy

Manic (2003) depicts group psychotherapy on an inpatient unit for adolescents. It is accurate and appropriate as a portrayal of group intervention, perhaps helped by the inclusion of some actual psychiatric patients. The psychiatrist (Don Cheadle) has his hands full with severely depressed individuals; patients who are self-injurious, threatening, and violent; and patients with explosive personalities. He attempts to include everyone in group discussions, and he cleverly reframes patient experiences in a positive, balanced way.

In stark contrast, the group therapy sessions portrayed in the film *Wilbur Wants to Kill Himself* (2002) are disappointing and unrealistic. One of the psychiatrists is overly supportive, obsequious, and flirtatious with patients, while the other psychiatrist smokes during sessions, sets himself apart from the group, and makes jokes about not wanting to be there.

Advocacy

Out of all of the various mental health professions portrayed in film, the field of social work might be the most commonly portrayed in a positive light. Valentine and Freeman (2002) studied 27 movies that include social workers – usually child welfare workers – across a variety of settings. They found that social workers are most typically placed in one of three roles: advocate, supervisor, or clinician. All three of these roles can be seen in the social worker in the excellent film *Elling* (2002, Norway). In this movie, a social worker is assigned to two adults – one with social anxiety disorder and the other with intermittent explosive disorder – who have recently been released from a psychiatric hospital. The social worker supervises their progress, advocates for them, and counsels them as they integrate back into regular society. He is authoritarian at times but is also motivational and compassionate, helping them to connect with numerous community services. He uses exposure and systematic desensitization to help his clients face their anxiety.

Psychiatric Hospitalization

Mental health treatment settings are most often portrayed in films as capacious institutions, and their depiction is almost always negative. Psychiatric hospitals are usually filmed as dark, gloomy, and unwelcoming places with considerable background noise (often screaming), staff nurses dressed in white, and patients with nothing to do other than to walk the halls of the institution acting odd. It is immediately obvious to the viewer when a movie scene takes place in such an institutional setting. From a cinematic perspective, this stereotyped presentation makes sense inasmuch as the viewer is more likely to remember a majestic, foreboding hospital exterior than a simple clinical office. These hospitals typically have stunning architecture, curious corridors, and an interesting dayroom.

Most films that depict the treatment of a person with mental illness during a time period predating the last 15–20 years show a psychiatric hospital. In most cases these institutions are dreary and foreboding, and these hospitals are certainly not places that one would seek out for care. Martin Scorcese's film *Shutter Island* (2010) offers this classic portrayal of a psychiatric institution. In this film (set in the 1950s), the sickest patients are treated, and some sordid aspects of the history of psychiatry are revealed, such as extreme isolation, allowing patients to lie in their own filth, and use of extensive restraints. Then, it is correctly noted that Thorazine, the first new and truly effective psychopharmacological agent, was introduced in the early 1950s. A psychiatrist, played by Ben Kingsley, explains that the role of the psychiatrist is to heal, to listen and to care for patients, and not to judge them.

"Insanity is not a choice."

Ben Kingsley as a psychiatrist in
Shutter Island **(2010)**

Some movies with these dreary though memorable settings include *The Snake Pit* (1948), *One Flew Over the Cuckoo's Nest* (1975), *Don Juan DeMarco*

(1994), *Twelve Monkeys* (1995), *Sling Blade* (1996), *Instinct* (1999), *Girl, Interrupted* (1999), *A Beautiful Mind* (2001), *Analyze That* (2002), and *Asylum* (2005).

One Flew Over the Cuckoo's Nest (1975) is a classic film that depicts the violation of human rights in mental institutions, but it was certainly not the first. *The Snake Pit* (1948) was one of the earliest films to raise consciousness about the treatment of persons with mental illness. It depicted the institution metaphorically as a zoo in which patients were fenced in, and as a place for visitors to tour, and a place where patients were "herded" into their own cages (rooms). One important difference between the two films is that the character of Virginia in *The Snake Pit* is truly mentally ill, whereas Randle Patrick McMurphy in *One Flew Over the Cuckoo's Nest* is not. *Chattahoochee* (1989) also describes the plight of those who disagree with institutional authority and power, and *Nuts* (1987) portrays a woman's struggle not to be committed to an institution.

Beautiful Dreamers (1990) is based on a true story from the life of Walt Whitman. Whitman was especially interested in the care of people with mental illness because he had a younger brother who was both physically and mentally ill. In the film, Rip Torn plays the role of Walt Whitman. Whitman visits a hospital in London, Ontario, where he is appalled by the treatment of the patients. He finds a sympathetic and congenial psychiatrist, Dr. Maurice Bucke, and the two of them work together to introduce more humane approaches to treatment. In real life, Dr. Bucke became Whitman's official biographer.

The film *K-Pax* (2001) moved away from some of the stereotypes of the psychiatric hospital environment. It depicts an institution in New York that has adequate light, numerous windows, and meaningful activities for both staff and patients. The patients contact and communicate easily with one other. Although the film loses this focus at times, such as when the patients begin to run about in a frenzy, their excitement is not "crazy" and random but grows out of support for one another. Overall, *K-Pax* portrays a less dehumanizing environment than did many older films.

As the closing of psychiatric hospitals continues, there will be fewer institutions to portray in films, and eventually the only portrayals of massive psychiatric institutions in movies will be in period films.

"Okay, I know you're thinking, 'What is this? Kid spends a few days in the hospital and all his problems are cured?' But I'm not. I know I'm not. I can tell this is just the beginning. I still need to face my homework, my school, my friends. My dad. But the difference between today and last Saturday is that for the first time in a while, I can look forward to the things I want to do in my life. Bike, eat, drink, talk. Ride the subway, read, read maps. Make maps, make art. Finish the Gates application. Tell my dad not to stress about it. Hug my mom. Kiss my little sister. Kiss my dad. Make out with Noelle. Make out with her more. Take her on a picnic. See a movie with her. See a movie with Aaron. Heck, see a movie with Nia. Have a party. Tell people my story. Volunteer at 3 North. Help people like Bobby. Like Muqtada. Like me. Draw more. Draw a person. Draw a naked person. Draw Noelle naked. Run, travel, swim, skip. Yeah, I know it's lame, but, whatever. Skip anyway. Breathe ... Live."

Craig contemplates life after he leaves the hospital in *It's Kind of a Funny Story* (2010)

It's Kind of a Funny Story (2010) is about the psychiatric hospitalization of a teenage boy, Craig (Keir Gilchrist), who seeks help after seriously contemplating suicide by jumping off the Brooklyn Bridge. Because there are too few patients on the adolescent ward, Craig is assigned to an adult ward. While in the hospital he bonds with other patients, and especially with Bobby (Zach Galifianakis), a man hospitalized because of a series of suicide attempts. Bobby becomes Craig's mentor, introducing him to the other patients and hospital life. The close and symbiotic relationship that develops between Craig and Bobby is illustrated in Figure 30.

A Clockwork Orange

Stanley Kubrick's *A Clockwork Orange* (1971) does not take place in a psychiatric institution, but instead at a specialized hospital running a research program for the prison system. This film remains a prototype in the cinematic exploration of the ethical issues associated with behavior therapy. In the film, Malcolm McDowell plays Alex, the leader of

Figure 30. *It's Kind of a Funny Story* (2010, Alliance Films, Misher Films, et al.). Produced by Ben Browning and Kevin Misher. Directed by Anna Boden and Ryan Fleck.

a vicious gang. Alex and his friends are psycho-pathic personalities: They thrive on violence and commit both rape and murder without any evidence of remorse. However, at the same time that audiences are repulsed by Alex's violence, they find themselves attracted by his high-spirited personality and his love of classical music.

Alex is captured after being set up by his friends, who have come to resent his authority. He is convicted of murder and sentenced to 14 years in prison; however, he is given the option of early release if he is willing to participate in a conditioning experiment. In scenes almost as horrifying as the earlier rape scenes, Alex is injected with a nausea-inducing drug and repeatedly forced to watch scenes depicting rape and violence while Beethoven symphonies are played in the background.

The conditioning proves to be highly successful, and Alex cannot even think about a violent incident without becoming ill. He is released from prison, but finds himself totally unable to cope with life on the streets. He eventually attempts suicide. While he is recovering in the hospital, a reform movement occurs in the government, and Alex is portrayed as a guinea pig who was abused by the previous administration. The treatment is reversed, and Alex is once again able to fantasize happily about rape and murder. The film dramatically presents the conundrum faced by society as it contemplates treatments that attempt to

improve society by limiting personal freedom (e.g., mandatory injections of drugs such as **Depo-Provera** that reduce testosterone levels and diminish sex drive in men convicted of sexual crimes).

Treatment Interventions

Hypnosis

It is interesting to discuss hypnosis in a book about movies because the film viewer goes in and out of light trance states throughout the movie-viewing experience. However, we have grown so accustomed to the habit of viewing movies and television shows that we rarely realize when we have entered a trance state. Hypnosis has been portrayed in numerous films, but it is rarely given an accurate or realistic portrayal.

Hypnosis has remained a popular intervention for over 100 years and is an empirically validated intervention for many psychological and medical disorders. Hypnosis continues to fight a battle against public misconception, part of which unfortunately is perpetrated by movies (also by stage hypnotists).

The portrayal of hypnosis in films has a history almost as long as movies themselves. The portrayal, however, is predominately a negative, stereotypic one. Barrett (2006) explored the role of hypnosis in over 230 films and found the majority of the portrayals to be negative, with hypnosis being applied to seduce the subject, to bring the subject to kill, to make the subject harm himself or herself, or to get the subject to commit a crime. She reports there are very few realistic portrayals – exceptions include *Mesmer* (1994, Austria/Canada, directed by Roger Spottiswoode) and *Equus* (1977, UK/US, directed by Sidney Lumet). In the latter film, an accurate explanation of hypnosis by a psychiatrist is depicted.

Robert Wiene's *The Cabinet of Dr. Caligari* (1920; Germany) is a classic silent film that portrays Dr. Caligari using hypnosis to control the life and behavior of a sleepwalker in a carnival side-show who can predict the future. He accurately predicts the imminent death of one of the characters in the film. Like so many films, this movie erroneously suggests that hypnotists have absolute control over the people they hypnotize.

Torture and hypnosis are used in tandem to brainwash British scientists in *The Ipcress File*

> **Additional Questions for Discussion (*A Clockwork Orange*)**

➤ Can Alex accurately be described as evil? Is the concept of evil meaningful for mental health professionals?

➤ How accurate are the behavior modification practices portrayed in the film? What behavioral treatments most resemble those applied to Alex?

➤ Are fantasies about rape or murder significant mental health problems? Under what conditions does their presence warrant intervention?

➤ What diagnostic label in *DSM-5* would be most appropriate for Alex? For the others in his gang?

➤ Is Alex treatable? If so, what theoretical orientation, treatment approach, and interventions are likely to be of most help for Alex?

➤ Can you think of real-life examples of situations in which health professionals have exploited prisoners?

(1965); Ipcress stands for "Induction of Psycho-neuroses by Conditioned Reflex under strESS." Kenneth Branagh's *Dead Again* (1991) has Derek Jacobi playing an antique dealer who dabbles in hypnotherapy, using hypnosis to regress patients to the point that they can reexperience events from their past lives. Hypnosis also is used to treat the title character in *Donnie Darko* (2001). Life coach Tony Robbins uses hypnosis to help the character Hal appreciate real beauty rather than shallow outward appearances in the Farrelly brothers film *Shallow Hal* (2001). Robbins also uses a trigger phrase when he decides Hal needs to "break out" of the hypnotic spell: "Shallow Hal wants a gal." The character Prot is hypnotized by Jeff Bridges' character, a psychiatrist, in *K-Pax* (2001).

When directing *Heart of Glass* (1976, Germany), Werner Herzog actually had almost all of the actors hypnotized so they could realistically play their roles as hypnotized subjects. The character of Will Hunting (Matt Damon) ridicules the therapist trying to hypnotize him, breaking into the song "Afternoon Delight" in the middle of a therapy session. (Will is eventually treated by Robin Williams' character – a community college psychology professor – who proves to be an effective therapist.)

In Chan-wook Park's remarkable film *Oldboy* (2003), a man who has kept the protagonist (Dae-su) imprisoned for 15 years uses hypnosis (and hypnotic "triggers" delivered over a cell phone) to get Dae-su and his daughter to become lovers (without ever realizing that they were related); when Dae-su discovers what has happened, he cuts out his tongue. Eventually he seeks out this same hypnotist to help him overcome his torment over his incestuous relationship with his daughter. Dae-su must communicate with the female hypnotist through writing because he can no longer speak. She treats Dae-su using a quick hypnotic induction to split him into two distinct personalities: "The beast," someone who remembers the incestuous relationship with the daughter, and an innocent Dae-su who remembers nothing. The hypnotist suggests that the beast walk away, growing older by 1 year with each step. At the age of 70, the beast is instructed to die. This happens, and the innocent Dae-su wakes up in the snow, remembering nothing.

A common misconception is that hypnosis represents a form of mind control through which a person can be programmed to do things against his or her will. This myth is perpetuated by films like *The Manchurian Candidate* (1952) and its 2004 remake. In the more recent film, a character, upon hearing the designated cue word, immediately comes under the hypnotist's spell (cinematically accompanied by changes in ambient light) and is at once fully controlled by the voice of the hypnotist. Through flashbacks, other characters are shown killing while in a trance. One character is depicted going fully against his own values when he smothers his long-time lover following a trance suggestion. Of course, this is cinematic nonsense.

> "I was a damn good shrink. Nineteen years I worked with a lot of people through a lot of shit. OK, I slept with a patient or two. It's not like I didn't care about them. I loved being a doctor. I used to not charge half my patients. Then the fucking state comes along, they send in some bitch undercover, and I'm fucked. Life isn't fair, is it?"
>
> Robin Williams reviews his life as a hypnotherapist in *Dead Again* (1991)

In films like Kenneth Branagh's *Dead Again* (1991) and Woody Allen's *The Curse of the Jade Scorpion* (2001), hypnosis is used as a blatant form of manipulation for malevolent purposes. In the former film, a hypnotist (who is also an antiques dealer) takes advantage of vulnerable people by asking them questions in the trance state about where rare antiques can be found in their home or at their work sites; he then gives the suggestion that the person will have total amnesia for the experience. In the latter film, hypnosis is used to steal jewels; here too, subjects are told they will be totally amnestic for the hypnosis episode. Films like these convince viewers that hypnosis can be used to make people do things that are illegal, unethical, and immoral. Likewise, some films suggest that hypnosis may be painful and destructive. *The Butterfly Effect* (2003) perpetrates this misconception by having a young

> "Just think of your mind as a movie. You can pause, rewind or slow down any details you want."
>
> A hypnotherapist's advice in *The Butterfly Effect* (2003)

man replay his past under hypnosis; when he does, we see him squirming in pain, his nose bleeds, and he falls onto the floor only to become amnestic for the experience.

Professionals are often depicted as incompetent in their use of hypnosis, such as the psychologist in *Donnie Darko* (2001) who uses hypnosis with a patient who has schizophrenia; this diagnosis would actually be a contraindication for hypnosis. The patient in *Donnie Darko* begins to masturbate while in a trance.

Even when the intent to use hypnosis is justified and well intentioned, it is most often depicted in an overly dramatic manner; for example, in many films the hypnotic technique of "age regression" is employed, and the patient is shown reliving very painful experiences or past traumatic events. The psychiatrist played by Jeff Bridges in *K-Pax* (2001) explains hypnosis, performs an induction, and begins to explore his patient's past. The patient screams in agony and nearly goes into shock. In reality, hypnosis is very rarely this dramatic.

The film *Office Space* (1999) presents an interesting dilemma in which a psychologist induces a trance, deepens the trance – and then has a heart attack and dies before he can bring the patient out of the trance state. In reality, the trance would wear off shortly if not immediately, but since this is a comedy, the character stays in the trance for days.

In most of these films, the subject is depicted as helpless and under the control of the hypnotist. These depictions ignore the well-established therapeutic truism that "all hypnosis is self-hypnosis."

Medications

The first genuinely effective antipsychotic medication was **chlorpromazine** (Thorazine), first used as an antihistamine. Several compounds with similar properties were also synthesized. Thorazine was believed to be a miracle drug that would empty all of our mental hospitals. These medications did enable many patients to live once again in the community; unfortunately, they were often indiscriminately prescribed, and dosages were usually excessive. Because of a lack of knowledge about the drug and its consequences, excessive sedation and **extrapyramidal side effects** (muscle cramps of the head and neck; restless pacing or fidgeting; and stiffening of muscular activity in the face, body, arms, and legs)

were common. In *One Flew Over the Cuckoo's Nest* (1975), the patients receive excessive dosages of medications that sedate them and put them at high risk for debilitating side effects.

Today there are several different classifications of pharmacological agents. **Antipsychotic medications** are given to treat thought disorders, such as schizophrenia, and some mood and anxiety disorders. **Antidepressants** are given for the mood disorders, and **mood stabilizers** such as **Depakote** and **lithium** are common medication choices for bipolar disorders. **Anxiolytic** (antianxiety) medications are carefully prescribed for patients with anxiety disorders. Some of these drugs, such as Xanax, Valium, and Librium, can be addictive. These drugs are also the ones most often used in combination with alcohol and recreational drugs. The 1982 movie *I'm Dancing as Fast as I Can* stars Jill Clayburgh as the award-winning TV producer Barbara Gordon, who becomes addicted to Valium but eventually recovers.

> "You know, our bodies are capable of incredible things when they're subjected to anxiety and stress. I found my ex-best friend's cufflinks in my wife's purse one time. I couldn't get an erection for a year and a half."
>
> Inappropriate self-disclosure by a psychiatrist in *Garden State* (2004)

In *Don Juan DeMarco* (1994), Marlon Brando plays a psychiatrist who wants to wants to treat his patient (Johnny Depp) solely with psychotherapy; however, he is pressured by other physicians to treat Depp's character with psychotropic medications. David Cronenberg's *Dead Ringers* (1988) is a film about two identical twins who are gynecologists. They routinely switch roles at work without anyone knowing, and the more aggressive twin (Elliot) often shares his (unwitting) lovers with his more timid brother (Beverly). The twins routinely take amphetamines to get up and barbiturates to come down, each prescribing medications for the other. Jeremy Irons brilliantly plays the role of each brother. Cronenberg coauthored the script and based the film on the true story of Stewart and Cyril Marcus, identical twins who were highly successful New York gynecologists and the authors of a leading textbook in gynecology. The brothers died in 1975 in their Manhattan apartment as a result of their attempts to withdraw from barbiturate addiction.

In the film *Garden State* (2004), the overly sedated protagonist, who has been taking various medications for a mood disorder for over a decade, decides on his own to discontinue taking medication after learning of the death of his mother. He prospers without the medication, meets a wonderful woman, learns to be assertive when dealing with his controlling psychiatrist father, and feels genuinely happy for the first time in years. While this film is meant to be inspirational and liberating, it also imparts an inappropriate and confusing message to countless people who are taking similar medications.

Electroconvulsive Therapy (ECT)

In the 1950s, both electroshock and insulin shock became accepted treatment methods to induce seizures, and many psychiatrists were convinced that seizures could be used to protect patients from mental illness. By the 1960s, electrical stimulation, called **electroconvulsive therapy** (ECT), was well established as the safest way to induce seizures.

Originally, ECT was used for many psychiatric illnesses, including schizophrenia. However, more effective pharmacological approaches were ultimately developed for most of these disorders. Today, severe depression, mania, and occasionally some types of thought disorders are treated with ECT, but only when other approaches have failed. The procedure is accompanied by the administration of short-acting general anesthesia and muscle paralytic agents that prevent the muscle contractions associated with seizures. Then a very mild electrical stimulus is passed through the brain, which causes the seizure. A series of 8–10 treatments is usually administered before clinically significant results are obtained.

McDonald & Walter (2001) examined the portrayal of ECT in 22 American movies from the middle of the 20th century to the onset of the 21st century and concluded that ECT was initially portrayed as a severe but helpful treatment; however, it progressed to being represented as a negative and cruel treatment. In one study, after viewing ECT portrayed in movies, medical students were more likely to talk friends and family out of receiving ECT, and one third reported a decrement in their support for ECT (Walter, McDonald, Rey, & Rosen, 2002).

In the past, ECT was used frequently and indiscriminately, often with excessive voltage. In films such as *One Flew Over the Cuckoo's Nest* (1975) and *An Angel at My Table* (1990), ECT is pictured as a painful, lengthy treatment, with the hapless patient strapped to a table by sadistic attendants. In reality, contemporary use of ECT takes about 5–10 min from start to finish and rarely results in a visible seizure. There are also very clear practice guidelines that help physicians identify when ECT is appropriate and when it is not. In *One Flew Over the Cuckoo's Nest,* ECT was used as punishment for patients who challenged the authority of Nurse Ratched. Its use was just as inappropriate when used to treat New Zealand novelist Janet Frame, as portrayed in *An Angel at My Table*. Another controversial film biography, *Frances* (1982), depicts the 1930s Hollywood actress Frances Farmer and her confinement in mental institutions for rebellious behavior. Frances, played by Jessica Lange, received both shock treatment and a lobotomy.

In *A Beautiful Mind* (2001), John Nash receives **insulin shock therapy** and not ECT, although many viewers do not make this distinction. When insulin shock therapy is used, insulin is injected, the body goes into a state of shock and convulsions ensue. *A Beautiful Mind* shows Nash receiving multiple treatments over several weeks.

Treatment of Different Disorders

Treatment of Anxiety Disorders

There are numerous approaches to the treatment of anxiety, and all of them are at least partially efficacious. Education can be a critical first step in therapy, and it is often tremendously therapeutic for the patient with an anxiety disorder simply to realize that he or she is not going insane and that these disorders are commonplace and often readily respond to treatment. In addition, patients need to realize that their symptoms are not life-threatening, that they will not pass out or fall down no matter how bad they feel, and that many people experience similar symptoms but assign different labels (**attributions**) to these sensations (e.g., a tingling sensation in your stomach before you give a speech can be interpreted as anticipatory excitement and a signal that you are going to do a good job).

It is also critical to carefully assess a patient's prior use of alcohol or drugs as ways of coping with his or her anxiety symptoms. Many of these patients have learned to use substances to modulate their anxiety levels: For example, alcoholism is common in veterans with posttraumatic stress disorders (as portrayed in *Born on the Fourth of July*). In addition, it is necessary to assess the consumption of coffee, soft drinks, and nicotine. All three exacerbate the symptoms of anxiety.

Psychotherapy may be helpful with some patients with anxiety. In particular, behavior therapy appears to be the treatment of choice for many phobic disorders, and some patients have been helped by behavioral methods after years of insight therapy. Almost all behavior therapies will involve exposure to the feared stimulus or situation. **In vivo exposure with response prevention** is an empirically validated approach (and the treatment of choice for OCD and other anxiety disorders) involving a graduated exposure hierarchy of anxiety-arousing stimuli where the patient is prevented from avoiding the stimulus and must use anxiety management coping skills instead. **Flooding** and **implosion** are related techniques that involve massive exposure to the feared stimuli. Niemiec and Ferland (2006) discuss how the film *Batman Begins* (2005) illustrates flooding; in this film, Bruce Wayne faces his fear of bats and takes on the name *Batman,* in part, to demonstrate his mastery of his fear. Mindfulness and hypnosis may also be used as adjunctive therapies in the treatment of anxiety.

VanDyke and Anderson (2013) argue that the popular, animated movie *The Croods* (2013) is a good model for illustrating key principles involved in the treatment of anxiety, such as fear acquisition and extinction, safety learning, avoidance, modeling, and the reevaluation of situations.

Movies themselves can be powerful stimuli when developing an **exposure hierarchy** for a person with an anxiety disorder. Particular movies can be tailored to the individual's fears, obsessions, and dysfunctional belief patterns. The individual will typically be asked to watch a film or a particular scene (often repeatedly) while practicing anxiety management techniques. For example, a person with a contamination fear of dirt might be asked to watch a war film where dirt, dust, and blood are prominent, such as *Saving Private Ryan* (1998), and the individual will be trained to use coping skills to manage their anxiety as it rises during parts of the film. The individual who is homophobic and afraid of contamination with the AIDS virus might be asked to watch *Kissing Jessica Stein* (2002) and *The Birdcage* (1995), and those afraid of getting in an accident or seeing an accident could watch action films containing multiple crashes such as the *Lethal Weapon* series (1987, 1989, 1992, 1998). Other films that could potentially be used for desensitization purposes include *Cast Away* (2000), *Philadelphia* (1993), and *Super Size Me* (2004), for fear of isolation, contamination, and throwing up in public, respectively. Children or adolescents afraid of being rejected might be asked to watch *A Bug's Life* (1998), *Shrek* (2001), or *Hercules* (1997), and those afraid of the dark might watch particular scenes from *Harry Potter and the Sorcerer's Stone* (2001) or its sequels. The use of films in therapy is explored further in Wedding and Niemiec (2003).

Cognitive therapy, which includes the practice of **cognitive restructuring**, is often employed in the treatment of anxiety disorders. Cognitive therapy helps patients identify and understand the internal statements and irrational thoughts that may trigger arousal in certain situations and settings (Beck & Emery, 1985). Medication may also be used as a treatment or, more commonly, as an adjunct to therapy. Widely used classes of drugs include **β-blockers** (often used to treat social phobias), **tricyclic antidepressants** (often used for panic disorder and agoraphobia), and **selective serotonin reuptake inhibitors** (SSRIs) (for OCD and comorbid depression issues). **Benzodiazepines** are also widely used in the treatment of anxiety symptoms, and include diazepam (Valium), chlordiazepoxide (Librium), and alprazolam (Xanax). In addition, there is growing interest in the use of over-the-counter herbal remedies such as **kava-kava** (available from health food stores) and **valerian root** in the treatment of mild to moderate anxiety.

Treatment of Mood Disorders

Lithium carbonate is often the treatment of choice for the bipolar disorders. This agent is a naturally occurring element that has been found to be effective in correcting the chemical imbalance associated with this illness. No one is sure how or why lithium works, but it is believed that it either alters the neurotransmitters or inhibits viruses that affect DNA. If lithium carbonate is not effective, other mood stabilizers can be used (**Depakote**).

Cognitive behavior therapy (CBT), which addresses a client's defective thinking process, is particularly helpful for patients with depression. This approach to psychotherapy forces the patient to examine the evidence for his or her negative beliefs, and the therapist encourages patients to reframe their beliefs based on the evidence presented in therapy. Once beliefs change, patients begin to perceive the world in a more balanced way, which has an impact on future behaviors. This technique has been very successful and is generally believed to be as efficacious as antidepressants in the treatment of mild to moderate depression.

Side Effects (2013) is an interesting film that deals in part with the optimal treatment of depression using anxiolytic medications; the surprise ending suggests life – like therapy – is seldom as simple as we might like.

Treatment of Alcoholism

The first stage of treatment is **detoxification,** or "drying out." This process can vary from several days to a month in duration and is usually extremely unpleasant for the person involved. Vitamins are routinely prescribed in the treatment of addictions. At one time, tranquilizers (primarily Librium and Valium) were often administered to help an individual cope with the physiological distress that accompanies detoxification; however, this approach to treatment has always been controversial and is less common now.

Antabuse (disulfiram) blocks the metabolism of alcohol and may help some alcoholics avoid resumption of drinking after detoxification. An individual taking Antabuse will become violently ill if exposed to even a very small amount of alcohol and will experience nausea, vomiting, sweating, and accelerated respiration and heart rate. Antabuse is most useful in the first months of sobriety, when the craving for alcohol is most intense.

Alcoholics Anonymous, a self-help fellowship founded in 1935, is widely regarded as an important part of treatment for most alcoholics. More than a million people in the United States belong to this self-help group, and there are more than 1.5 million members worldwide. Almost every town of any size has a local chapter of Alcoholics Anonymous, and many large cities have meetings in different chapters every evening of the week. These meetings involve self-disclosure, social support, and a commitment to the disease model of alcoholism. The well-known 12 Steps of Alcoholics Anonymous are presented in Table 7 of Chapter 11 on p. 202. The founding of Alcoholics Anonymous is described in the film *My Name Is Bill W.* (1989).

Al-Anon is a related group for families and friends of alcoholics. The program is modeled on Alcoholics Anonymous and uses a 12-step model. **Alateen** is a similar affiliated group designed to serve teenage children of alcoholic parents.

Although most providers in the substance abuse community are quick to praise the good work done by Alcoholics Anonymous, there is little empirical evidence supporting the program. In addition, some individuals find the quasireligious philosophy of the organization distasteful.

Alcoholics Anonymous meetings have been portrayed in numerous films including *The Lost Weekend* (1945), *Days of Wine and Roses* (1962), *Clean and Sober* (1988), *When a Man Loves a Woman* (1994), *Drunks* (1995), *28 Days* (2000), and, more recently, *Flight* (2012). Almost all of these films offer sympathetic portrayals of Alcoholics Anonymous meetings and participants. Participation in Alcoholics Anonymous saves the life of Kate (Mary Elizabeth Winstead) in *Smashed* (2012). This film depicts Kate drinking in her car before going to teach her first-grade class; she throws up in front of her students and then feigns pregnancy as an excuse for vomiting. She starts each day with a beer in the shower, and in one episode she becomes enraged when she can not buy beer or wine in a convenience store because of "Blue Laws;" she publically urinates on the floor and then runs out of the store after

---

"The last time I seen my father, he was blind and diseased from drinking. And every time he put the bottle to his mouth, he don't suck out of it, it sucks out of him until he shrunk so wrinkled and yellow even the dogs didn't know him."

Chief Bromden describes his father's alcoholism in *One Flew Over the Cuckoo's Nest* (1975)

stealing a bottle of wine. Her out-of-control behavior is clearly enabled by her husband who continues to drink heavily, even after Kate stops. We see Kate relapse after losing her job, but she eventually achieves sobriety, rejecting her ex-husband's request that she return to the life they once shared.

Treatment of Drug Addiction

Before treatment can begin, **detoxification** must occur. In general, the severity of detoxification from narcotic drugs depends on the health status of the addict and the purity of the drugs he or she has been taking. Withdrawal from barbiturates tends to be more serious than withdrawal from heroin, cocaine, or alcohol. Detoxification is potentially life threatening and should occur in a structured medical setting. The film *Quitting* (2001) depicts the challenges and pain of detoxifying outside of a structured hospital environment. Anxiolytics such as Valium, Librium, and Xanax are sometimes used to reduce the severity of the effects of detoxification.

Methadone is a synthetic narcotic that is taken orally rather than injected. It is administered on a daily basis, usually in an outpatient setting. The drug itself is addicting; however, it is longer lasting, and with daily use the addict is able to avoid the symptoms of withdrawal that typically occur a few hours after use of drugs such as heroin. In addition, the drug blocks the reinforcing effects of other narcotics. With methadone treatment, there is a reduction in intravenous drug use and a concomitant reduction in crime. In addition, the likelihood of needle sharing and AIDS is dramatically reduced. Despite these benefits, methadone maintenance programs remain controversial, and there are some clear disadvantages to methadone maintenance therapy, including the development of a large underground market for methadone, the fact that many people drop out of methadone treatment because of side effects (sweating, impotence, constipation, and insomnia), and the fact that many people are philosophically offended by the idea of giving addicts another addictive drug in the name of treatment.

Some programs have used **narcotic antagonists** such as **naloxone** or **naltrexone** to treat opioid addiction. These drugs block the reinforcing effects of narcotics; in effect, the addict may still take drugs but they no longer produce a high. However, be-

cause of the potential for precipitating withdrawal reactions, these programs are complex and costly and require medical supervision.

Programs such as **Narcotics Anonymous** (NA), modeled after Alcoholics Anonymous, advocate total abstinence from drugs. These programs are often associated with therapeutic communities in which a highly structured program and frequent group therapy are core components of treatment. Former addicts who serve as powerful role models for residents often staff these programs. Therapy is often confrontational and may involve spouses and significant others. The film *Clean and Sober* (1988) presents an excellent example of the kind of treatment that occurs in a **therapeutic community**, with Morgan Freeman in the role of a recovered addict and counselor.

Antidepressant medications are sometimes used to assist in the treatment of amphetamine or cocaine addiction. However, in general, all treatment programs for stimulant addiction have unimpressive success records. Methamphetamine addiction is explored in *Spun* (2002), *The Salton Sea* (2002), and *Winter's Bone* (2010). This last film is especially effective in documenting the relationship between rural poverty in the Ozarks and the proliferation of underground methamphetamine labs.

The success of smoking cessation programs has been more notable. Nicotine gum and transdermal nicotine patches hold considerable promise as important aids in comprehensive treatment packages. Behavior modification and hypnosis are two other techniques that have helped many individuals overcome their addiction to nicotine.

Despite the success of some treatment programs, it is clear that the only real solution to the drug problem is prevention. Prevention will involve limiting the flow of drugs to the United States and educating the public about the deleterious effects of drug use.

Ethical Issues and the Right to Humane Treatment

Movies illustrate the ongoing struggles for civil and human rights that have occurred in the mental health system. They also reflect the prevailing stigma that still affects persons with mental illness. Our language characterizes individuals with these illnesses as crazy, nuts, or wacky. The people who treat them are called shrinks, do-gooders, or bleeding hearts (Trachtenberg, 1986). The media often portray patients as clowns, buffoons, or harmless eccentrics (Hyler, Gabbard, & Schneider, 1991). In *The Dream Team* (1989) and *The Couch Trip* (1988), a little bit of freedom proves adequate to cure mental illness. Other films, such as *Psycho* (1960) and its remakes and sequels, depict individuals with mental illnesses as homicidal maniacs. In John Carpenter's *Halloween* series, an escaped psychiatric patient serially kills teenagers who have engaged in sexual experimentation. When Tommy Lee Wallace directed *Halloween III* (1982), the central villain was portrayed as a madman toy maker who made wicked Halloween masks programmed to harm children. However, the original madman on the loose from a mental hospital returned in *Halloween IV* and *V* (1988, 1989). These films and others have misled the public about the dangerousness of psychiatric patients.

One Flew Over the Cuckoo's Nest was not the first movie to portray patients' lack of control over treatment. One of the first movies to address mental illness seriously was *The Snake Pit* (1948), a film directed by Anatole Litvak that stars Olivia de Havilland as Virginia Stuart Cunningham. The movie portrays a woman trying to overcome her illness in a crowded mental institution. The horrifying conditions portrayed in the film actually mobilized state legislators to improve the level of care provided in institutions. This movie was especially effective in portraying the lack of power females have traditionally had in inpatient psychiatric settings. In *The Snake Pit*, Virginia truly has a mental illness and is taken for treatment by a caring husband. However, many women who did not have mental illnesses were placed in psychiatric hospitals and kept there as a convenience for husbands who had grown tired of them (Geller & Harris, 1994).

Another powerful film, *Chattahoochee* (1990), not only depicts the horrible conditions in a Florida state hospital during the 1950s but also one patient's campaign to change these conditions. In this film, Korean War veteran Emmett Foley (played by Gary Oldman) loses many of his rights because of his protests against authority. This film, based on a true story, begins when Emmett Foley becomes depressed by unemployment and tries to provoke the police into killing him after he shoots up the neighborhood. He wants his wife to receive his life insurance (which she would be denied if he committed suicide). Instead, he is sent to Chattahoochee, a prison for people with mental illness. The conditions in Chattahoochee are deplorable. With the support of his friend Walker Benson (Dennis Hopper), he begins a letter-writing campaign to protest the abuse he has experienced. His writing privileges are taken away, and he starts writing in a Bible and surreptitiously slipping pages to his sister. A state commission is formed, hearings are held, and conditions improve as a result.

The Jacket (2005) stars Adrien Brody playing the role of Jack Starks, a veteran who sustains a head injury in the Iraq war, enters into a coma, and is taken for dead; however, a hospital attendant notices eye movement, and eventually Brody's character comes out of his coma, although he still has a profound retrograde amnesia. He is wrongly accused of killing a police office, but is found to be not guilty by reason of insanity. He is sent to a psychiatric institute "for the criminally insane" run by Dr. Thomas Becker (Kris Kristofferson), a sadistic psychiatrist. Therapy consists of putting Brody in a wet, hot straitjacket and keeping him in a morgue-like room, ostensibly to recreate the sensation of being in the womb. The hospital staff are presented as controlling and abusive, and the film perpetuates the myth that psychiatric hospitals are dangerous places run by inhumane and uncaring staff; in fact, the exact opposite is true, and the individuals who work in these settings include some of the finest people we know.

Ian McKellen is masterful in his role as a sadistic psychiatrist, Dr. Peter Cleave, in *Asylum* (2005). The film is based on a Patrick McGrath novel and takes place in an old, gothic psychiatric hospital. A new psychiatrist, Dr. Max Raphael (Hugh Bonneville), has arrived to take over management of the hospital – the job Peter Cleave craved – and his wife and young son accompany him. The son befriends a patient, a man who has been institutionalized because he murdered his wife; his diagnosis is "severe personality disorder with features of morbid jealousy." Natasha Richardson plays Stella, the boy's bored mother, and she is soon involved in a torrid affair with the patient. Although we liked the film, we were troubled by the subtext suggesting that psychiatric hospitals are dangerous places staffed by indifferent attendants and cruel professionals.

> "I want you to understand what's going to happen next. The shock will wear off, and it will be replaced by a devastating grief. In time, you will come to terms with what you have done and you'll just be very, very sad. And that sadness will stay with you for the rest of your life."
>
> Psychiatrist Max Raphael tells his wife what to expect after the accidental drowning of their son in *Asylum* (2005)

International Films: Treatment

David Cronenberg's film *A Dangerous Method* (2011, UK/Germany) is a provocative and entertaining depiction of historical fiction that depicts the relationship between Sigmund Freud and Carl Jung, as well as the early history of psychoanalysis. The film also features Sabina, a patient with psychosis, who was treated by both Freud and Jung prior to becoming a respected physician and scholar. Jung is portrayed as a serious and curious clinician who interacts with patients in a calm, concerned, and deliberate way. He prioritizes work over family – in one scene he stops a conversation about his wife's pregnancy so he can describe his work. Freud is stereotyped as someone obsessed with dreams and sex, and he is frequently shown smoking cigars. The first meeting of these two men is reported to have lasted over 13 hours. Freud, the founder of psychoanalysis, interprets almost all dreams and conflicts in terms of sexuality. Jung challenges Freud's theories, especially his emphasis on sex, and suggests there are other ways to "peek" into the workings of the human mind, such as trying to determine the meaning behind "coincidences." The film addresses a number of topics that are of interest to mental health professionals interested in psychoanalysis or Jungian psychology: hysteria (a

> "Whatever you do, give up any idea of trying to cure them."
>
> Freud's advice to Jung in *A Dangerous Method* (2011)

common diagnosis in psychiatry at the time), repression, aggression, suppression of instincts, synchronicity, anima/animus, the shadow, the pleasure principle, dream analysis, mysticism, and the rigors of science.

Additional Questions for Discussion (*A Dangerous Method*)

➤ How does this film educate viewers about the personalities of Freud and Jung? What characteristics describe each of these men?

➤ Is there any truth to the boundary violations we see Jung commit in the film?

➤ Do all psychotherapists cross a "boundary" at some point in their careers with patients? What percentage do you believe make substantive boundary violations such as having sex with a patient?

➤ How accurate is the portrayal of psychoanalysis and the characterization of these legendary psychiatrists?

➤ How might a film that included the life and work of Alfred Adler be very different?

In the film, Jung has erotic, ecstatic, and sadomasochistic sex with Sabina. In his *PsycCRITIQUES* review of the film, Taylor (2012) notes:

> There is no evidence that any of the sexual scenes in the film actually ever happened. We have only Sabina's ravings to any and all that she and Jung were lovers. Cronenberg made sure that the statement that the most intimate, erotic parts of the movie remain "highly speculative" is buried deep in the credits at the end.

There is no doubt that movies are notorious for depicting psychologists and psychiatrists who cross boundaries, especially sexual ones. In fact, it is far easier to spot a psychotherapist who crosses boundaries than one who does not throughout an entire film, especially if the character is the protagonist.

King of Hearts (1966) is a charming French film that has achieved cult status. The movie stars a young Alan Bates as a Scottish soldier sent into a small French village during World War I to disarm a bomb. He discovers that the villagers have all fled, and the inmates of a local psychiatric hospital are running the town. While we enjoyed the film, it does perpetuate the myth that people with mental illness are simply harmless eccentrics.

House of Fools (2002, Russia/France) is a film reminiscent of *King of Hearts* but based on a true story. It takes place in a psychiatric institution in a war-torn country (Chechnya). When the town is about to be taken over by the enemy, the staff evacuate, the patients stay, and the soldiers find refuge in the hospital. The movie raises questions about the folly of war, and it uses the hospital as a metaphor for the insanity of a world at war.

Intimate Strangers (2004) is a French film built around the idea that accountants and psychotherapists have a lot in common. A woman in a troubled marriage is looking for the office of a psychiatrist she is visiting for the first time when she mistakenly enters the office of a timid accountant just down the hall. She begins to share intimate details about her troubled marriage (e.g., her husband wants her to have sex with other men so he can watch), but the accountant initially does not interrupt – he is in a profession in which people needing tax advice about issues like divorce often reveal very personal facts about their private lives. After some time, it becomes clear that the woman believes she is confiding in a psychiatrist, but by this time the accountant is so intrigued by her story that he is loath to reveal his true identity. When he does explain the misunderstanding, the patient is upset – but continues to come for therapy sessions because she is benefiting from them and the patient and "therapist" have a good connection with one another. In their review of this film for *PsycCRITIQUES: Contemporary Psychology – APA Review of Books*, John C. Norcross and his son, Jonathan Norcross, remark:

> This film, drawing on the Freudian tradition, can be encountered on a number of levels. As a public portrayal of insight-oriented psychotherapy, the film fails miserably. The film inaccurately depicts psychoanalytic treatment ... and reinforces four pervasive stereotypes: That anyone can do psychotherapy; that psychotherapy largely consists of a patient's monologue with occasional open-ended questions from the psychotherapist; that an erotic transference will inevitably develop between an attractive female patient and a distinguished male therapist; and that ... commonsense methods are superior to psychoanalytic treatment in modifying behavior ... On the other hand, as a public representation of the intimacy of psychotherapy, the film succeeds admirably. *Intimate Strangers* provides a riveting example of the constructive power of (quasi) psychotherapy and ...

the centrality of an affirming, empathic relationship to a successful outcome. Love heals both the patient and the psychotherapist. Moreover, the film underscores that therapy can be one rare and privileged place where people can gradually live without secrets and lies.

The film *16 Years of Alcohol* (2003, Scotland) demonstrates the links between alcohol abuse and violence and hints at the genetics of alcoholism (e.g., one of the earliest and most vivid memories of the protagonist, Frankie, was watching his drunken father copulating with a stranger he had met at a pub). *Candy* (2006, Australia) offers a compelling portrayal of heroin addiction and treatment. The title is both the name of the female lead (Abbie Cornish) and a euphemism for heroin. Candy is deeply in love with a bohemian poet named Dan (Heath Ledger, in his first role after *Brokeback Mountain*). Their addiction is supported and celebrated by a chemistry professor friend, Casper, played by Geoffrey Rush. Candy starts by snorting heroin with Dan, but soon moves to mainlining. She overdoses the first time she injects the drug, and almost dies in a bathtub. Dan and Candy's sexual and social lives suffer as they become more and more involved with heroin, and Candy turns to prostitution to secure the money needed to support their habits. Candy becomes pregnant, but miscarries because of her addiction. Both Candy and Don try methadone as a way of coping with their addiction, but eventually go cold turkey to overcome their habit, spending days lying on a dirty mattress. Both overcome their addiction, but Candy relapses after initiating an affair with a drug-using neighbor. Candy eventually tries to reunite with Dan, but he rejects her, knowing their relationship was only based on a mutual love of heroin. The film is divided into three distinct segments, named to describe the protagonists' descent into addiction: "Heaven," "Earth," and "Hell."

"They say for every ten years you've been a junkie, you'll have spent seven of them waiting. On the one hand it was nice having all that time to think. On the other, anxiety was a full time job."

Dan (Health Ledger) reflects on life as an addict in *Candy* (2006)

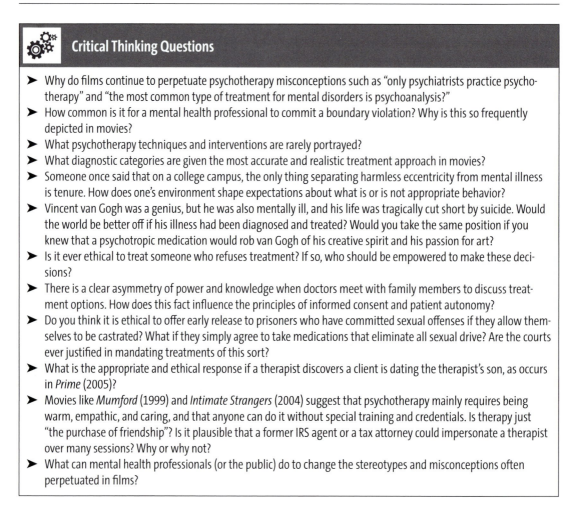

Critical Thinking Questions

➤ Why do films continue to perpetuate psychotherapy misconceptions such as "only psychiatrists practice psycho-therapy" and "the most common type of treatment for mental disorders is psychoanalysis?"

➤ How common is it for a mental health professional to commit a boundary violation? Why is this so frequently depicted in movies?

➤ What psychotherapy techniques and interventions are rarely portrayed?

➤ What diagnostic categories are given the most accurate and realistic treatment approach in movies?

➤ Someone once said that on a college campus, the only thing separating harmless eccentricity from mental illness is tenure. How does one's environment shape expectations about what is or is not appropriate behavior?

➤ Vincent van Gogh was a genius, but he was also mentally ill, and his life was tragically cut short by suicide. Would the world be better off if his illness had been diagnosed and treated? Would you take the same position if you knew that a psychotropic medication would rob van Gogh of his creative spirit and his passion for art?

➤ Is it ever ethical to treat someone who refuses treatment? If so, who should be empowered to make these decisions?

➤ There is a clear asymmetry of power and knowledge when doctors meet with family members to discuss treatment options. How does this fact influence the principles of informed consent and patient autonomy?

➤ Do you think it is ethical to offer early release to prisoners who have committed sexual offenses if they allow themselves to be castrated? What if they simply agree to take medications that eliminate all sexual drive? Are the courts ever justified in mandating treatments of this sort?

➤ What is the appropriate and ethical response if a therapist discovers a client is dating the therapist's son, as occurs in *Prime* (2005)?

➤ Movies like *Mumford* (1999) and *Intimate Strangers* (2004) suggest that psychotherapy mainly requires being warm, empathic, and caring, and that anyone can do it without special training and credentials. Is therapy just "the purchase of friendship"? Is it plausible that a former IRS agent or a tax attorney could impersonate a therapist over many sessions? Why or why not?

➤ What can mental health professionals (or the public) do to change the stereotypes and misconceptions often perpetuated in films?

Authors* Picks

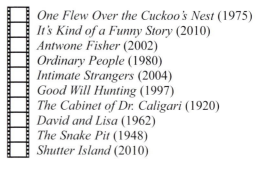

If you have time to read just one book relevant to this chapter, make it:

Wedding, D., & Corsini, R. J. (2014). *Current psychotherapies* (10th ed.). Belmont, CA: Thompson Brooks/Cole. (Selected chapters)

If you only have time for one article, read:

Kazdin, A. E. (2008). Evidence-based treatments and delivery of psychological services: Shifting our emphases to increase impact. *Psychological Services*, *5*, 201–215.

Wedding and Niemiec's Top 10 Treatment Films

- *One Flew Over the Cuckoo's Nest* (1975)
- *It's Kind of a Funny Story* (2010)
- *Antwone Fisher* (2002)
- *Ordinary People* (1980)
- *Intimate Strangers* (2004)
- *Good Will Hunting* (1997)
- *The Cabinet of Dr. Caligari* (1920)
- *David and Lisa* (1962)
- *The Snake Pit* (1948)
- *Shutter Island* (2010)

Appendices

Appendix A

The American Film Institute's Top 50 Heroes and Villains[5]

Heroes

1. **Atticus Finch**
   To Kill a Mockingbird
2. **Indiana Jones**
   Raiders of the Lost Ark
3. **James Bond**
   Dr. No
4. **Rick Blaine**
   Casablanca
5. **Will Kane**
   High Noon
6. **Clarice Starling**
   The Silence of the Lambs
7. **Rocky Balboa**
   Rocky
8. **Ellen Ripley**
   Aliens
9. **George Bailey**
   It's a Wonderful Life
10. **T. E. Lawrence**
    Lawrence of Arabia
11. **Jefferson Smith**
    Mr. Smith Goes to Washington
12. **Tom Joad**
    The Grapes of Wrath
13. **Oskar Schindler**
    Schindler's List
14. **Han Solo**
    Star Wars
15. **Norma Rae Webster**
    Norma Rae
16. **Shane**
    Shane
17. **Harry Callahan**
    Dirty Harry
18. **Robin Hood**
    The Adventures of Robin Hood
19. **Virgil Tibbs**
    In The Heat of the Night

Villains

1. **Dr. Hannibal Lecter**
   The Silence of the Lambs
2. **Norman Bates**
   Psycho
3. **Darth Vader**
   The Empire Strikes Back
4. **The Wicked Witch of the West**
   The Wizard of Oz
5. **Nurse Ratched**
   One Flew Over the Cuckoo's Nest
6. **Mr. Potter**
   It's a Wonderful Life
7. **Alex Forrest**
   Fatal Attraction
8. **Phyllis Dietrichson**
   Double Indemnity
9. **Regan MacNeil**
   The Exorcist
10. **The Queen**
    Snow White and the Seven Dwarfs
11. **Michael Corleone**
    The Godfather: Part II
12. **Alex De Large**
    Clockwork Orange
13. **HAL 9000**
    2001: A Space Odyssey
14. **The Alien**
    Alien
15. **Amon Goeth**
    Schindler's List
16. **Noah Cross**
    Chinatown
17. **Annie Wilkes**
    Misery
18. **The Shark**
    Jaws
19. **Captain Bligh**
    Mutiny on the Bounty

[5] Reprinted with permission of the American Film Institute (http://www.afi.com/100years/handv.aspx)

20. **Butch Cassidy and the Sundance Kid**
Butch Cassidy and the Sundance Kid
21. **Mahatma Gandhi**
Gandhi
22. **Spartacus**
Spartacus
23. **Terry Malloy**
On the Waterfront
24. **Thelma Dickerson & Louise Sawyer**
Thelma & Louise
25. **Lou Gehrig**
The Pride of the Yankees
26. **Superman**
Superman
27. **Bob Woodward & Carl Bernstein**
All The President's Men
28. **Juror #8**
12 Angry Men
29. **General George Patton**
Patton
30. **Luke Jackson**
Cool Hand Luke
31. **Erin Brockovich**
Erin Brockovich
32. **Philip Marlowe**
The Big Sleep
33. **Marge Gunderson**
Fargo
34. **Tarzan**
Tarzan the Ape Man
35. **Alvin York**
Sergeant York
36. **Rooster Cogburn**
True Grit
37. **Obi-Wan Kenobi**
Star Wars
38. **The Tramp**
City Lights
39. **Lassie**
Lassie Come Home
40. **Frank Serpico**
Serpico
41. **Arthur Chipping**
Goodbye, Mr. Chips
42. **Father Edward**
Boys Town
43. **Moses**
The Ten Commandments
44. **Jimmy "Popeye" Doyle**
The French Connection
45. **Zorro**
The Mark of Zorro
46. **Batman**
Batman
47. **Karen Silkwood**
Silkwood
48. **Terminator**
Terminator 2: Judgment Day
49. **Andrew Beckett**
Philadelphia
50. **General Maximus Decimus Meridus**
Gladiator

20. **Man**
Bambi
21. **Mrs. John Iselin**
The Manchurian Candidate
22. **Terminator**
The Terminator
23. **Eve Harrington**
All About Eve
24. **Gordon Gekko**
Wall Street
25. **Jack Torrance**
The Shining
26. **Cody Jarrett**
White Heat
27. **Martians**
The War of the Worlds
28. **Max Cady**
Cape Fear
29. **Reverend Harry Powell**
The Night of the Hunter
30. **Travis Bickle**
Taxi Driver
31. **Mrs. Danvers**
Rebecca
32. **Clyde Barrow & Bonnie Parker**
Bonnie and Clyde
33. **Count Dracula**
Dracula
34. **Dr. Szell**
Marathon Man
35. **J.J. Hunsecker**
Sweet Smell of Success
36. **Frank Booth**
Blue Velvet
37. **Harry Lime**
The Third Man
38. **Caesar Enrico Bandello**
Little Caesar
39. **Cruella De Vil**
One Hundred and One Dalmatians
40. **Freddy Krueger**
A Nightmare on Elm Street
41. **Joan Crawford**
Mommie Dearest
42. **Tom Powers**
The Public Enemy
43. **Regina Giddens**
The Little Foxes
44. **Baby Jane Hudson**
Whatever Happened to Baby Jane?
45. **The Joker**
Batman
46. **Hans Gruber**
Die Hard
47. **Tony Montana**
Scarface
48. **Verbal Kint**
The Usual Suspects
49. **Auric Goldfinger**
Goldfinger
50. **Alonzo Harris**
Training Day

Appendix B

Syllabus for Sample Course that Integrates Films

Movies and Mental Illness: Understanding Psychopathology[6]

Course Description

This course focuses on the portrayal of mental illness in films. Representations of psychopathological states in films will be examined within the context of contemporary social issues such as stigma and discrimination. Major mental disorders will be highlighted.

Objectives

Upon completion of this course the student will be able to:
1. Discuss the social influence of films.
2. Discuss the significance of film in the public perception of mental illnesses.
3. Compare behavioral symptoms of major mental disorders.
4. Identify discrimination and stigma associated with mental disorders.
5. Analyze the portrayal of various mental illnesses in films.

Required Text

Wedding, D., & Niemiec, R. M. (2014). *Movies and mental illness: Using films to understand psychopathology* (4th ed.). Cambridge, MA: Hogrefe.

Learning Experiences

Seminar, dyad presentation, videos, and written papers

Students should watch the films outside of class, preferably in small groups. All films selected are well known and will be easily available through DVD rental outlets or on the Internet. Please come to class prepared to discuss whether the film presented an accurate portrayal of the condition being discussed each week.

---

[6] Adapted from the syllabus Danny Wedding used in an abnormal psychology course he taught at Yonsei University in Seoul, Korea, where he was the 2008–2009 Fulbright-Yonsei Distinguished Scholar.

(a) Tuesdays 10 am – 12	(b) Thursdays 9–10 am	Topic	Readings and Films to View Before Coming to Class
Sep 2	Sep 4	(a) Introduction to the class (b) Films and psychopathology	(b) Chapter 1: Films and Psychopathology
Sep 9	Sep 11	(a & b) Neurodevelopmental disorders	(a) Chapter 2: Neurodevelopmental Disorders (b) *Temple Grandin* (2010)
Sep 16	Sep 18	(a & b) Schizophrenia spectrum and other psychotic disorders	(a) Chapter 3: Schizophrenia Spectrum and Other Psychotic Disorders (b) *A Beautiful Mind* (2001)
Sep 23	Sep 25	(a & b) Bipolar and depressive disorders	(a) Chapter 4: Bipolar and Depressive Disorders (b) *The Beaver* (2011) or *Silver Linings Playbook* (2013)
Sep 30	Oct 2	(a & b) Anxiety and obsessive-compulsive disorders	(a) Chapter 5: Anxiety and Obsessive-Compulsive Disorders (b) *The Aviator* (2004)
Oct 7	Oct 9	(a & b) Trauma and stressor related disorders	(a) Chapter 6: Trauma and Stressor Related Disorders (b) *The Dry Land* (2010) or *The Hurt Locker* (2008)
Oct 14	Oct 16	(a & b) Dissociative disorders	(a) Chapter 7: Dissociative Disorders (b) *Psycho* (1960)
Oct 21	**Oct 23**	**(a) Review session (b) Midterm Examination**	**No readings or film**
Oct 28	Oct 30	(a & b) Somatic symptom, feeding, eating, elimination and sleep-wake disorders	(a) Chapter 8: Somatic Symptom, Feeding, Eating, Elimination, and Sleep-Wake Disorders (b) *Insomnia* (2002) or *Modify* (2005)
Nov 4	Nov 6	(a & b) Sexual dysfunctions and gender dysphoria	(a) Chapter 9: Gender Dysphoria and Sexual Dysfunctions (b) *Boys Don't Cry* (1999)
Nov 11	Nov 13	(a & b) Disruptive, impulse and conduct disorders	(a) Chapter 10: Disruptive, Impulse-Control, and Conduct Disorders (b) *We Need To Talk About Kevin* (2011)
Nov 18	Nov 20	(a & b) Substance-related and addictive disorders	(a) Chapter 11: Substance-Related and Addictive Disorders (b) *Flight*
Nov 25	Nov 27	(a & b) Neurocognitive disorders	(a) Chapter 12: Neurocognitive Disorders (b) *Memento* (2000) or *Amour* (2012)
Dec 2	Dec 4	(a & b) Personality disorders	(a) Chapter 13: Personality Disorders (b) *No Country for Old Men* (2007) or *Blue Jasmine* (2013)
Dec 9	Dec 11	(a & b) Paraphilic disorders; violence, physical and sexual abuse	(a) Chapter 14: Paraphilic Disorders (a) Chapter 15: Violence and Physical and Sexual Abuse (b) *Leap Year* (*Año Bieiesto*, in Spanish, 2010) OR *Kill Bill: Vol 1 or 2* (2003, 2004)
Dec 16	Dec 18	(a & b) Treatment	(a) Chapter 16: Treatment (a) *One Flew Over the Cuckoo's Nest* (1975)

Take Home Final Exam

Appendix C

Recommended Websites

Movies in General

Movies and Mental Illness – Blog
http://www.moviesandmentalillness.blogspot.com

Internet Movie Database (the largest movie database)
http://www.imdb.com

Movie Review Query Engine (over 76,000 movie titles; over 748,000 reviews)
http://www.mrqe.com

American Film Institute
http://www.afi.com

Independent Movies
http://www.indiewire.com

Hogrefe Publishing (contains free movie filmographies, files, and information on *Movies and Mental Illness* and *Positive Psychology at the Movies*; search the site for "movies")
http://www.hogrefe.com

Voice Awards
http://www.samhsa.gov/voiceawards/

Other Recommended Movie Databases

Rotten Tomatoes (movie database)
http://www.rottentomatoes.com

Literature, Arts, and Medicine Database
http://litmed.med.nyu.edu/Annotation?catid=3&action=listcat

AMC Filmsite
http://www.filmsite.org

Films Featuring Mental Disorders
http://en.wikipedia.org/wiki/List_of_films_featuring_mental_disorders

Films Involving Disabilities
http://www.disabilityfilms.co.uk/

Atkinson on Film
http://www.atkinsononfilm.com, http://www.psychflix.com

Susan Nicosia: Movies and Mental Illness: Psychology, Psychiatry and the Movies
http://www.imagiscape.ca/research/art/Movies%20and%20Mental%20Illness%20Filmography.htm

Hollywood Entertainment Corporation
http://www.reel.com

Internet Movie Network
http://www.movieweb.com

Appendix D

12 Misconceptions About Mental Illness and Mental Health Professionals Perpetuated by Movies

Misconception	Film examples
Love alone conquers mental illness.	*Mozart and the Whale* (2005) *Stateside* (2004) *Wilbur Wants to Kill Himself* (2002) *Matchstick Men* (2003) *Benny & Joon* (1993)
People with mental illness are violent.	*Keane* (2004) *Edmond* (2005) *The Killing of John Lennon* (2006) *The Assassination of Richard Nixon* (2004) *Peacock* (2010) *Nightmare on Elm Street* (1984)
People with mental illness are wild and crazy.	*Michael Clayton* (2007) *Mozart and the Whale* (2005) *Black Snake Moan* (2006) *The Big White* (2005) *I'm a Cyborg, But That's OK* (2007)
People referred to as delusional or psychotic are actually telling the truth, as well as being mentally healthy and grounded in reality.	*Flightplan* (2005) *K-Pax* (2001) *Happy Accidents* (2000) *The Jacket* (2005)
Parents cause schizophrenia, autism, etc. (the myth of the schizophrenogenic parent).	*Clean, Shaven* (1993) *Shine* (1996)
All mental illness has a traumatic etiology.	*The Fisher King* (1991) *The Snake Pit* (1948) *The Three Faces of Eve* (1957) *K-Pax* (2001) *Nurse Betty* (2000)
Schizophrenia is the same as dissociative identity disorder, gender identity disorder, etc.	*Me, Myself & Irene* (2000) *Dressed to Kill* (1980)
Psychiatric hospitals are dangerous places, or at the least, unhelpful; the patients are not sick, they are harmlessly eccentric or misdiagnosed.	*One Flew Over the Cuckoo's Nest* (1975) *Asylum* (2005) *The Jacket* (2005) *King of Hearts* (1966) *House of Fools* (2002)
Psychiatric treatment (e.g., ECT, medications) blocks creativity and intelligence.	*A Beautiful Mind* (2001) *A Clockwork Orange* (1971)
It is liberating to discontinue psychiatric treatment on one's own (e.g., medications).	*Garden State* (2004)
The treatment of mental illness involves boundary violations by a therapist (these are usually sexual).	*The Prince of Tides* (1991) *Numb* (2007) *Mr. Jones* (1993) *Final Analysis* (1992) *Tin Cup* (1996) *A Dangerous Method* (2011)
Psychological diagnoses are routinely made up by psychologists and patients and touted as a standard condition.	*Me, Myself & Irene* (2000): Advanced delusionary schizophrenia with involuntary narcissistic rage *Asylum* (2005): Severe personality disorder with features of morbid jealousy *Transamerica* (2005): Gender dysphoria *The Ringer* (2005): Highly functioning developmental disability *Shrink* (2009)

Appendix E

Portrayals of Psychotherapists in Movies[7]

See Niemiec & Wedding (2006) for more details.

Balanced Portrayals

Antwone Fisher (2003)
David and Lisa (1962)
Don Juan DeMarco (1994)
Donnie Darko (2001)
Elling (2002)
Equus (1977)
Girl, Interrupted (1999)
Good Will Hunting (1997)
Gothika (2003)*
Hope Springs (2012)
Hollywood Ending (2002)
Identity (2003)
Intimate Strangers (2004)
K-Pax (2001)
Klepto (2003)
Lars and the Real Girl (2007)
Manic (2003)
Ordinary People (1980)
Psycho (1960)
Stateside (2004)
Transamerica (2005)*
What Happens in Vegas (2008)

Unbalanced Portrayals

Analyze This (1998)
Antichrist (2009)
Anything Else (2003)
Asylum (2005)

Basic Instinct 2 (2006)
Batman Begins (2005)
Bliss (1997)
Changeling (2008)
The Chorus (2004)
A Dangerous Method (2011)
Deconstructing Harry (1997)
The Departed (2006)
Dirty, Filthy Love (2004)
Final Analysis (1992)
The Great New Wonderful (2005)
Happiness (1998)
Happy Accidents (2000)
Harvey (1950)
High Anxiety (1977)
I Am Sam (2001)
The Island (2005)
Jesus of Montreal (1989)
Mr. Jones (1993)
Normal (2004)
Numb (2007)
One Flew Over the Cuckoo's Nest (1975)
Prime (2005)
Shrink (2009)
Shutter Island (2010)
Stay (2005)
Temple Grandin (2010)
The Silence of the Lambs (1991)
The Snake Pit (1948)
Twelve Monkeys (1995)
Vanilla Sky (2001)
What About Bob? (1991)
Wilbur Wants to Kill Himself (2002)

---

[7] The film has both balanced and unbalanced portrayals.

Appendix F

PRISM Awards for Feature Films[8]

1997 *Trainspotting*

1998 *Gridlock'd*

1999 *Down in the Delta*

2000 *The Insider*

2001 *The Hughleys*

2002 *Blow*

2003 *Skins* and *Never Get Outta the Boat* (Festival Award)

2004 *City of God* and *Happy Hour* (Festival Award)

2005 *Ray* (Wide Release) and *A Love Song for Bobby Long* (Limited Release) and *Relative Evil* (Direct to DVD)

2006 *Walk the Line* (Wide Release), and *Down to the Bone and Pure* (tie, Limited Release), and *Self Medicated* (Direct to DVD)

2007 *Sherrybaby* (Limited Release) and *Thank You for Smoking* (Wide Release) and *Jelly Smoke* (Bipolar Disorder)

2008 *You Kill Me* (Limited Release) and *Georgia Rule* (Wide Release) and *Michael Clayton* (Bipolar Disorder)

2009 *Rachel Getting Married* (Substance Use) and *Stop-Loss* (Mental Health)

2010 *The Soloist* (Mental Health) and *Crazy Heart* (Substance Use)

2011 *Black Swan* (Mental Health) and *The Fighter* (Substance Use)

2012 *Take Shelter* and *Shame* (Mental Health) and *Warrior* (Substance Use)

2013 *Silver Linings Playbook* (Mental Health) and *Flight* (Substance Use)

---

[8] The PRISM awards are presented by the Entertainment Industries Council to recognize accurate portrayals of substance abuse, addiction, and mental health. Used with permission of the Entertainment Industries Council, Inc., www.eiconline.org and www. prismawards.com.

Appendix G

SAMHSA Voice Awards[9]

2013
FEATURE FILMS

- *Being Flynn* for addressing behavioral health problems, suicide, homelessness, friends and family support, and recovery;
- *The Perks of Being a Wallflower* for addressing the impact of trauma, friends and family support, resilience, and recovery; and
- *Silver Linings Playbook* for addressing bipolar disorder, the impact of trauma, peer support, and recovery.

DOCUMENTARIES

- *Bill W.* for addressing substance use disorders, peer support, and recovery;
- *Of Two Minds* for addressing bipolar disorder, friends and family support, and recovery; and
- *Running From Crazy* for addressing mental disorders, suicide, family support, and recovery.

2012
FEATURE FILMS

Take Shelter

Plagued by a series of terrifying visions, young husband and father Curtis LaForche (Michael Shannon) questions whether to shelter his family from a coming storm, or from his own mind. When he begins having terrifying dreams about an encroaching apocalyptic storm, he chooses to keep the disturbance to himself, channeling his anxiety into the obsessive building of a storm shelter in his family's backyard. His seemingly inexplicable behavior concerns and confounds his wife, Samantha (Jessica Chastain) and provokes intolerance among coworkers, friends, and neighbors. But the resulting strain on his marriage and tension within the community do not compare to Curtis' private fear of what his dreams may truly signify. Faced with the proposition that his disturbing visions signal disaster of one kind or another, Curtis eventually confides in Samantha, testing the power of their bond, against the highest possible stakes.

DOCUMENTARIES

Bob and the Monster

Six years in the making, this award-winning documentary follows outspoken indie-rock hero Bob Forrest from his life-threatening struggle with addiction to his transformation into one of the most influential and controversial drug counselors in the United States. The film combines contemporary footage, animation, and compelling interviews with archival performances and personal videos from Bob's past to reveal the complex layers of this troubled but hopeful soul.

Testimony from Bob's peers, including Courtney Love, Anthony Kiedis, Flea, John Frusciante, and members of Jane's Addiction, Fishbone, and Guns N' Roses, adds texture to the film, but it is the depth of Bob's music that illuminates this unforgettable and inspirational story.

[9] This content is used courtesy of the Substance Abuse and Mental Health Services Administration (SAMHSA), US Department of Health and Human Services (HHS), from http://beta.samhsa.gov/voice-awards/award-winners, accessed on 4/24/2014. Inclusion of this content in *Movies and Mental Illness* does not constitute an official endorsement of this product by SAMHSA or HHS.

Demi Lovato: Stay Strong

In this 1-hr documentary film on Demi Lovato, the young singer reflects on the rough ride that led her to purging and self-harming. Demi lets the MTV audience inside her most private moments during her very public recovery from her eating disorder. With cameras following, she returns for the first time to the treatment facility she retreated to in November 2010, speaks candidly to her recovering peers about her experiences, and thanks the counselors and staff who she says kept her alive. Demi also lets the audience witness firsthand her evolution as an artist, as she ditches her Disney past and tries on a new persona as confessional singer-songwriter, performing an album full of deeply personal material in front of sold-out crowds for the first time.

Unguarded

Award-winning filmmaker Jonathan Hock has mastered the art of telling stories about the struggles and triumphs of American hometown heroes. In this documentary, Chris Herren of Fall River, MA, was a high school basketball standout who battled the pressures of making it big from an early age. After dropping out of Boston College, he landed on Jerry Tarkanian's notorious Fresno State team, where players were likely to be found on both police blotters and All-American lists. Mr. Herren failed drug tests at Boston College and Fresno State, but he was so talented that he was drafted into the National Basketball Association anyway, ending up with the Boston Celtics.

At the moment he started to realize his childhood dream of becoming a star for his home team, Mr. Herren fell into a 10-year spiral of addiction, bouncing from team to team and country to country. Ultimately, he found redemption and personal fulfillment through the game.

2011
FEATURE FILMS

It's Kind of a Funny Story

Directed by Ryan Fleck and Anna Boden, and adapted from Ned Vizzini's 2006 novel of the same name, *It's Kind of a Funny Story* is a comedy drama set in Brooklyn, New York.

It's 5 a.m. on a Sunday. Craig Gilner (Keir Gilchrist) is bicycling up to the entrance of a mental health clinic; this bright 16-year-old is stressed out from the demands of being a teenager. Before his parents (Lauren Graham and Jim Gaffigan) and younger sister are even awake, Craig checks himself into Argenon Hospital and is admitted by a psychiatrist. But the youth wing is temporarily closed – so he finds himself stuck in the adult wing.

One of the patients, Bobby (Zach Galifianakis), soon becomes both Craig's mentor and protégé. Craig is also quickly drawn to another 16-year-old displaced to the adult wing, the sensitive Noelle (Emma Roberts), who just might make him forget his longtime unrequited crush Nia (Zoë Kravitz). With a minimum 5 days' stay imposed on him by the adult wing's staff psychiatrist, Dr. Eden Minerva (Viola Davis), Craig is sustained by friendships on both the inside and the outside as he learns more about life, love, and the pressures of growing up.

The Beaver

Directed and starring by two-time Academy Award winner Jodie Foster, *The Beaver* is an emotional story about a man on a journey to rediscover his family and restart his life.

Overwhelmed with his own demons, Walter Black (Mel Gibson), once a successful toy executive and family man, struggles with major depression. No matter what he tries, Walter can't seem to get himself back on track until a beaver hand puppet enters his life.

The Fighter

Directed by David O. Russell and based on a true story, *The Fighter* is about two brothers who, against all the odds, come together to train for an historic title bout that has the power to reunite their fractured family and give their hard-luck town what it's been waiting for – pride.

Mickey Ward (Mark Wahlberg) is a struggling boxer long overshadowed by his older brother and trainer, Dicky (Christian Bale), a local legend battling his own demons and using drugs to cope. Their explosive relationship threatens to take them both down, but the bond of blood may offer a chance for redemption.

The King's Speech

Directed by Academy Award-winner Tom Hooper and based on the true story of King George VI, *The King's Speech* follows the royal monarch's quest to find his voice.

After the death of his father King George V (Michael Gambon) and the scandalous abdication of King Edward VIII (Guy Pearce), Bertie (Colin Firth), who has suffered from a debilitating speech impediment all his life, assumes the crown. With his country on the brink of war and in desperate need of a leader, his wife, Elizabeth (Helena Bonham Carter), arranges for her husband to see an eccentric speech therapist, Lionel Logue (Geoffrey Rush).

After a rough start, the two delve into an unorthodox course of treatment and eventually form an unbreakable bond. With the support of Logue, his family, his government, and Winston Churchill (Timothy Spall), the King will overcome his stammer and deliver a radio address that inspires his people and unites them in battle.

DOCUMENTARIES

Dad's in Heaven With Nixon

When Janice Murray first saw her newborn son, Chris, in the spring of 1960, the whites of his eyes were bright scarlet – a sure sign of oxygen deprivation. When he turned 4 and still wasn't talking or developing normally, a wide array of medical "experts" told Janice that Chris's prospects were bleak. Virtually all of them concluded that he was never going to talk, and their solution to the daunting challenge that Janice faced was brutally unanimous – put him in an institution. But Janice refused to consider giving up on reaching her son.

Dad's in Heaven With Nixon is the story of Chris's journey from the darkness of brain damage, coupled with what was eventually diagnosed as autism, to the light that is his life today – as a happy, independent, and fulfilled person, as well as an acclaimed artist. It is also the story of a mother's enduring love and her fierce, primal determination to ensure that her silent, isolated, and seemingly aloof little boy reached the potential she was convinced he had.

Finally, the film is the story of tragedy and triumph in one family. Chris's grandfather and father

both had bipolar disorder – proud individuals who stubbornly refused to seek help for an illness that caused devastating damage for both men and their families. Against all odds, Chris not only survived, but ultimately thrived – an inspiring and shining example of the wonder and power of the human spirit.

If God Is Willing and da Creek Don't Rise

This film continues the story of the rebirth of the Big Easy, begun in Spike Lee's epic, Emmy- and Peabody-winning documentary *When the Levees Broke: A Requiem in Four Acts.* Alongside the city's storied ability to celebrate life with unmatchable ebullience, it documents the successes and failures in the ongoing efforts to restore housing, health care, education, economic growth, and law and order to a battered but unbowed community.

If God Is Willing and da Creek Don't Rise visits Houston, where an estimated 150,000 New Orleans evacuees remain. The film also looks at other areas along the Gulf, including Gulfport and Biloxi, Mississippi, where rebuilding has progressed more quickly. In addition, it assesses the impact of the more recent BP Gulf Coast oil spill and captures the reaction of area residents.

More than 300 people share their stories in *If God Is Willing and da Creek Don't Rise*, including former Louisiana Governor Kathleen Babineaux Blanco, New Orleans Mayor Mitch Landrieu, former New Orleans Mayor Ray Nagin, historian Douglas Brinkley, activist actors Brad Pitt and Sean Penn, Houston Mayor Anisse Parker, and community organizer Tanya Harris. In addition, longtime New Orleans residents, whose compelling testimonies were a key part of *When the Levees Broke,* provide updates on their lives.

Lost Angels

Thomas Napper's empathetic but tough-minded documentary invites us into a part of Los Angeles that many choose to ignore – downtown's Skid Row. As we meet the distressed area's residents, including a former Olympic runner, a transgendered punk rocker, and an eccentric animal lover and her devoted companion, their remarkable stories paint a multifaceted portrait of life on the streets. There are undeniable problems – mental illness and addiction are common themes – but there is also hope and a surprising sense of community.

Passionate, polemic, and generous in spirit, *Lost Angels* finds a unique vitality to life on Skid Row and a stirring humanity in those who call it home.

Wartorn 1861–2010

Civil war doctors called it hysteria, melancholia, and insanity. During the World War I, it was known as shell-shock. By World War II, it became combat fatigue. Today, it is clinically known as posttraumatic stress disorder (PTSD), a crippling anxiety that results from exposure to life-threatening situations such as combat.

With suicide rates among active military servicemen and veterans currently on the rise, the HBO special *Wartorn 1861–2010* brings urgent attention to the invisible wounds of war. Drawing on personal stories of American soldiers whose lives and psyches were torn apart by the horrors of battle and PTSD, the documentary chronicles the lingering effects of combat stress and posttraumatic stress on military personnel and their families throughout American history, from the Civil War through today's conflicts in Iraq and Afghanistan.

2010
FEATURE FILMS

Adam

Romance can be risky, perplexing, and filled with the perils of miscommunication – and that's if you aren't Adam, for whom life itself is this way. In this heartfelt romantic comedy, Hugh Dancy stars as Adam, a handsome but intriguing young man with Asperger's Syndrome who has all his life led a sheltered existence – until he meets his new neighbor, Beth (Rose Byrne), a beautiful, cosmopolitan young woman who pulls him into the outside world with funny, touching, and entirely unexpected results. Their implausible and enigmatic relationship reveals just how far two people from different realities can stretch in search of an extraordinary connection.

Precious: Based On The Novel Push by Sapphire

Set in Harlem in 1987, it is the story of Claireece "Precious" Jones (Gabourey Sidibe), a 16-year-old African American girl born into a life no one would want. She's pregnant for the second time by her absent father and must wait hand-and-foot on her mother (Mo'Nique), a poisonously angry woman who abuses Precious emotionally and physically. School is a place of chaos, and Precious has reached the ninth grade with good marks and an awful secret: She can neither read nor write. Precious may sometimes be down, but she is never out. Beneath her impassive expression is a watchful, curious young woman with an inchoate but unshakeable sense that other possibilities exist for her. Threatened with expulsion, Precious is offered the chance to transfer to an alternative school, Each One/Teach One. Precious doesn't know the meaning of "alternative," but her instincts tell her this is the chance she has been waiting for. In the literacy workshop taught by the patient, yet firm Ms. Rain (Paula Patton), Precious begins a journey that will lead her from darkness, pain, and powerlessness to light, love, and self-determination.

The Dry Land

James (Ryan O'Nan) returns from Iraq to face a new battle – reintegrating into his small-town life in Texas. His wife (America Ferrera), his mother (Melissa Leo), and his friend (Jason Ritter) provide support, but they can't fully understand the pain and suffering he feels since his tour of duty ended. Lonely, James reconnects with an army buddy (Wilmer Valderrama), who provides him with compassion and camaraderie during his battle to process his experiences in Iraq. Their reunion also exposes the different ways that war affects people – at least on the surface. This moving, taut story of redemption and reconstruction extends beyond a PTSD narrative. O'Nan is heartbreaking as he explores the depths of his internal struggle, and Ferrera fearlessly tackles her role of a young wife in turmoil. *The Dry Land* is about one man's fight within his own terrain – his country, home, and mind – and his journey to rebuild what he's lost.

Temple Grandin*

Starring Claire Danes, Julia Ormond, Catherine O'Hara, and David Strathairn, *Temple Grandin* paints a picture of a young woman's perseverance and determination while struggling with the isolating challenges of autism at a time when it was still quite unknown. The film chronicles Temple's (Danes) early diagnosis; her turbulent growth and development during her school years; the enduring support she received from her mother (Ormond), her aunt (O'Hara), and her science teacher (Strathairn); and her emergence as a woman with an innate sensitivity and understanding of animal behavior. Undaunted by educational, social, and professional roadblocks, Grandin turned her unique talent into a behavioral tool that revolutionized the cattle industry and laid the groundwork for her successful career as an author, lecturer, and pioneering advocate for autism and autism spectrum disorder education. This visually inventive HBO film offers insights into Grandin's world, taking the audience inside her mind with a series of snapshot images that trace her self perceptions and journey from childhood through young adulthood to the beginning of her career and beyond.

*Note: This award was given in the "Television" category because the film was initially produced and released by HBO.

DOCUMENTARIES

No Kidding, Me Too!

Directed by actor and mental health advocate Joe Pantoliano, *No Kidding, Me Too!* is an empowering film that seeks to fight the stigma associated with mental illness. It is shot using candid, and often humorous, discussions with Pantoliano and his family on their struggle with his own clinical depression, as well as the compelling stories of five other people from all walks of life: Maj. Joe who has been living with PTSD, a brain surgeon with bipolar disorder, a psychologist with attention-deficit/hyperactivity disorder, and three high school students managing bipolar disorder and clinical depression. Each frankly discusses the struggles they endured

before being diagnosed, including attempts at self medication and other destructive behavior, as well as the hope and encouragement they discover when managing their own recovery and realizing they are not alone.

This Emotional Life

This Emotional Life is a three-part series that explores improving social relationships, learning to cope with depression and anxiety, and becoming more positive, resilient individuals. Prof. Daniel Gilbert, Harvard psychologist and best-selling author of *Stumbling on Happiness*, talks with experts about the latest science on what makes us "tick" and how we can find support for the emotional issues we all face. Each episode weaves together the compelling personal stories of ordinary people and the latest scientific research, along with revealing comments from celebrities like Chevy Chase, Larry David, Alanis Morissette, Robert Kennedy Jr., and Richard Gere. The series also features an Iraq war veteran and his family who share their knowledge and experience with the challenges facing America's veterans.

Coming Home: Military Families Cope With Change

Part of Sesame Workshop's Talk, Listen, Connect initiative for military families, *Coming Home: Military Families Cope with Change* is a primetime family television special that tells the stories of military families coping with the challenges of combat-related injuries – both visible and invisible. Featuring John Mayer, Queen Latifah, and Sesame Street characters, *Coming Home* explores the different ways these heroic families are coming together to find a "new normal" and gives a voice to young children as they play a central role in their families' adjustment process. The special, which was developed in collaboration with the US Department of Defense, encourages them to ask questions, talk about how they feel, and be what they are – kids. Queen Latifah hosts, meeting real families dealing with combat-related injuries including the loss of a leg, traumatic brain injury, and PTSD.

2009 FEATURE FILMS

Helen

Helen is the story of a university music professor who seems to have it all. Happily married to David (Goran Visnjic), Helen (Ashley Judd) also enjoys a loving relationship with her teenage daughter, Julie (Alexia Fast). Yet, she suffers from a deep, debilitating depression that penetrates the very fabric of her well-being. David and Julie love and support her unconditionally, but at times she becomes inaccessible and withdrawn. When she befriends one of her music students, Mathilda (Lauren Lee Smith), Helen understands they share a common bond. While continuing to struggle with her own issues, Helen tries desperately to help her student. *Helen* is a portrait of a marriage and a story of friendship – of courage, devotion, and the triumph of love.

Lars and the Real Girl

This heartfelt comedy revolves around a lovable introvert whose emotional baggage has kept him from fully embracing life. After years of near solitude, Lars Lindstrom (Ryan Gosling) invites Bianca, a friend he met on the Internet, to visit him. He introduces Bianca to his brother, Gus (Paul Schneider) and his sister-in-law, Karen (Emily Mortimer). They are stunned to learn that Bianca is a life-sized doll, not a real person, although Lars is treating her as though she is alive. They consult the family doctor, Dagmar (Patricia Clarkson), who explains that this is a delusion Lars has created – and recommends that they should all go along with it. What follows is an emotional journey for Lars and the people around him.

Michael Clayton

This suspenseful thriller is about a powerful attorney who is backed into a career corner that offers little room to fight free. Attorney Michael Clayton (George Clooney) is a "fixer," the go-to guy when his powerful New York law firm wants a mess cleaned up. But now he is handed a crisis even he may not be able to fix. Arthur Edens (Tom Wilkinson), the firm's top litigator in a $3 billion case, has an apparent mental breakdown during a deposition and goes from advocate to whistleblower. When Clayton is dispatched to bring him home, he soon learns that Edens not only has doubts about defending the lawsuit, but also that the company in question may be acting to ensure a positive outcome no matter what the cost. And the more Clayton tries to undo the damage, the more he's up against forces that value corporate survival over human life – including his own.

The Soloist

From Academy Award–nominated director Joe Wright, *The Soloist* is a poignant and ultimately soaring tale based on an incredible true story of a disenchanted journalist's transformative odyssey through the hidden streets of Los Angeles. It is here that he discovers and builds a most unlikely friendship with a man with schizophrenia, bonding through the redemptive power of music.

Columnist Steve Lopez (Robert Downey Jr.) is at a dead end. The newspaper business is in an uproar, his marriage to a fellow journalist has fallen apart, and he can't remember what he loved about his job in the first place. While walking through Los Angeles' Skid Row one day, he sees the mysterious, bedraggled figure Nathaniel Ayers (Jamie Foxx) pouring his soul into a two-stringed violin. At first, Lopez approaches Ayers as just another story idea in a city of millions, but as he unearths the mystery of how this alternately brilliant and distracted street musician – once a dynamic prodigy headed for fame – wound up living in tunnels and doorways, an unexpected quest begins. Imagining he can change Ayers' life, Lopez embarks on a quixotic mission to get him off the streets and back to the world of music. But even as he fights to save Ayers' life, he begins to see that it is Ayers – with his unsinkable passion, his freedom-loving obstinacy, and his valiant attempts at connection and love – who is profoundly changing him.

DOCUMENTARIES

Autism: The Musical

Autism: The Musical counters today's growing statistics with one woman's optimistic pledge to lead a group of children with autism in defying diagnosed expectations by writing, rehearsing, and performing their own full-length musical. Following five Los Angeles children over the course of 6 months, director Tricia Regan captures the struggles and triumphs of their family lives and observes how this musical production gives these performers a comfort zone in which they can explore their creative sides. Both on- and off-stage, *Autism: The Musical* is a call-to-action, bringing attention to a modern-day challenge, all the while celebrating the way the human spirit can overcome any challenge.

In a Dream

In a Dream, directed by Jeremiah Zagar, is an exploration into the life of his father, the remarkable mosaic artist Isaiah Zagar. Over the past 4 decades, Zagar has covered more than 50,000 square feet of Philadelphia with stunning mosaic murals made out of tiles and mirrors. This documentary chronicles Zagar's work and his tumultuous relationship with his wife, Julia. It follows the Zagars as their marriage implodes and a harrowing new chapter in their life unfolds. It is an exploration of the fallout that ensues when the line between art and life is blurred beyond distinction.

True Life: I Have Schizophrenia

On *True Life: I Have Schizophrenia*, we meet three young people who are living with schizophrenia and get a glimpse into the everyday challenges they face. Twenty-five-year-old Josh refuses treatment because, for the most part, he feels his voices are his companions and doesn't see his illness as a problem. Most of the symptoms 23-year-old Ben suffers from are controlled with medication, but the varied side effects of the meds keep him primarily in the house, only comfortable hanging out with his family. Amber, 19, was only diagnosed a year ago. Her

response to medication has been very successful. *True Life: I Have Schizophrenia* shines a light on mental illness and gives viewers a glimpse of what it's like to go through life working on recovery.

2008 FEATURE FILMS

Canvas

10-year-old Chris Marino (Devon Gearhart) just wants to be like other kids, but his mother Mary Marino's (Marcia Gay Harden) bouts of paranoia and delusion make that challenging for him. His dad, John Marino (Joe Pantoliano), a construction worker, struggles to cover Mary's doctor bills and find the right medicine to treat her schizophrenia, which leaves little time or energy to give to his son. When Mary's behavior takes a turn for the worse, father and son watch helplessly as she is hospitalized. Unable to face his wife's illness or console his son, John quits his job and works compulsively day and night to build a sailboat. Ridiculed at school and feeling abandoned, Chris begins to act out and makes plans to move in with an aunt in Alaska. After a dramatic confrontation, father and son decide to complete the boat together. In the end, they are able to come to terms with Mary's illness, and fulfill a special promise made long ago.

Home of the Brave

Home of the Brave tells the story of four American soldiers nearing the end of their tours of duty in Iraq. Shortly after learning their unit will soon return home, they are sent on one final humanitarian mission, and the unit is ambushed. With many lives lost, the surviving troops suffer both physical and psychological injuries. Now, as they return to the United States, the four soldiers, Will Marsh (Samuel L. Jackson), Tommy Yates (Brian Presley), Vanessa Price (Jessica Biel), and Jamal Aiken (Curtis "50 Cent" Jackson), must face memories of the past as they look toward the future and return to civilian life.

Reign Over Me

In *Reign Over Me*, former college roommates Charlie Fineman (Adam Sandler) and Alan Johnson (Don Cheadle) meet up again by chance on a Manhattan street corner. Five years after losing his family on 9/11, Charlie – once a successful dentist – has retreated from his life, and Alan is stunned to see the changes in his formerly gregarious friend. At the same time, Alan – who should be enjoying his beautiful wife, children, and career – is overwhelmed by his responsibilities. Their rekindled relationship becomes a lifeline for the two men, who are both in need of a trusted friend at this pivotal moment in their lives.

DOCUMENTARIES

Cracking Up

The documentary *Cracking Up* raises the question: When it comes to mental illness, is laughter the best medicine? It depicts a year in the life of 11 individuals who opted to participate in counselor and comedian David Granirer's Stand Up for Mental Health program in Vancouver, BC, Canada. The program, which is now being offered in other parts of the province, as well as in Ontario, is intended to help individuals diagnosed with mental illness increase their self-esteem and fight some of the stigma that exists in society. Granirer's approach uses laughter as therapy, and he coaches participants to face their illness through the use of standup comedy. The film depicts each of the comics' journeys from their first stab at standup in a classroom setting to their sold-out finale show.

Stephen Fry: The Secret Life of the Manic Depressive

This two-part documentary features comedian, actor, author, and filmmaker Stephen Fry, who interviews celebrities including Robbie Williams, Carrie Fisher, and Richard Dreyfuss, as well as members of the public, who talk frankly about the impact that manic depression – or bipolar disorder – has had on their lives, the stigma attached to it, and how they got help.

During the two programs, Stephen talks in detail about his own experiences with bipolar disorder. He recounts his suicide attempt after walking out of the West End play *Cellmates* in 1995, and the continuing severe mood swings he has to endure. He also meets ordinary people and their families coping with the condition and talks to them about some of the possible triggers. They all speak candidly about how bipolar disorder has affected their day-to-day lives.

Through My Eyes

Through My Eyes is a documentary film produced by Emmy Award–winner Linda Midgett. It is a half-hour program intended to educate teens about mental health issues. *Through My Eyes* features Mecklenburg County, North Carolina, teens and their families sharing their own emotional and mental health challenges, and how they are able to draw on their successes to overcome these challenges. The film also aims to reduce stigma, raise awareness, and improve community-wide support for youths who struggle with challenges such as anxiety disorders, depression, eating disorders, ADD, and ADHD.

2007 No awards were presented this year

2006
FEATURE FILMS

Proof

In this feature film, Catherine (Gwyneth Paltrow) is the devoted daughter of Robert (Sir Anthony Hopkins), a brilliant mathematician whose life and work have been impacted by mental illness. Upon her father's death, Catherine comes face-to-face with her long-held fears about her own possible predisposition toward mental illness. Additionally, a mathematical proof discovered after Robert's death (one that was written at the height of his illness), and the question of who actually wrote the proof, bring up issues of sanity, intelligence, credibility, and trust. The movie is based on David Auburn's Tony- and Pulitzer Prize–winning stage drama of the same name.

Jellysmoke

Jacob (Michael Ealy), a young man with bipolar disorder adjusting to life after release from a psychiatric hospital, becomes romantically involved with a woman and tries to keep his disorder a secret despite the resurgence of his mania. Most of the feature film shows him grappling with his growing symptoms (and the subsequent impact on his relationship), resulting in his readmission to the hospital. As the movie ends, he is living in supported housing and reestablishing contact with the woman he loves.

DOCUMENTARIES

Legacy of the Harp

This six-part documentary profiles people with mental illness who have also experienced drug addiction, homelessness, and incarceration, but who reclaimed their own lives and are now helping others recover.

I Have Tourette's, But Tourette's Doesn't Have Me

This documentary highlights children with Tourette's disorder. The interviews with the kids themselves give the viewer an inside look at what it's like to have Tourette's, show how they cope with their illness and their peers, and relate their optimism in the face of their illness.

Shadow Voices: Finding Hope in Mental Illness

This hour-long documentary deals with the stigma associated with mental illness, recovery, and hope. The film offers an inside look at what it is like to live with a mental illness. It includes interviews with consumers, experts, and advocates.

Appendix H

Films Illustrating Psychopathology

Table of Contents

Key to Ratings

ΨΨΨΨΨ   A must-see film that combines artistry with psychological relevance
ΨΨΨΨ   Highly recommended both as art and as professional education
ΨΨΨ   A good film relevant to your education as a mental health professional
ΨΨ   Mildly interesting and somewhat educational; possibly worth your time
Ψ   Description provided for your information only; don't bother with the film

Neurodevelopmental Disorders

Adam (2009) Drama/Romance ΨΨΨΨ
Beth gradually falls in love with Adam, a high functioning man with autism spectrum disorder, but she eventually decides she can't make a permanent commitment to
Adam. The film is sympathetic in its portrayal of Adam,
and is genuinely helpful in illustrating some of the challenges faced by highly intelligent people coping with autism.

Antonia's Line (1995) Comedy ΨΨΨΨ
A film with unforgettable characters, including Loony
Lips and Dede, two people with intellectual disabilities
who fall in love and get married. The film is a joyful celebration of life and family.

Any Day Now (2012) Drama ΨΨΨ
Two gay men in a loving, committed relationship have to
fight to maintain custody of the special needs son they
adopt. Based on a true story.

Being There (1979) Comedy ΨΨΨΨ
Peter Sellers plays the role of a gardener with what appears to be borderline IQ who finds himself caught up in
a comedy of errors in which his simple platitudes are mistaken for wisdom. This film is a precursor to *Forrest
Gump*.

Ben X (2007) Drama ΨΨΨ
A young man with an autism spectrum disorder loses himself in videogames while plotting revenge on his classmates who torment him.

Best Boy (1979) Documentary ΨΨΨΨ
Ira Wohl's moving tribute to his cousin (who has an intellectual disability) examines the options facing the young
man when his father dies and his aging mother is no longer able to care for him. This film won an Academy
Award for Best Documentary film.

**Best Man: "Best Boy" and All of Us Twenty Years
Later** (1997) Documentary ΨΨΨ
A sequel to the 1979 film documenting that director Ira
Wohl's cousin has a rich, full and meaningful life, despite
his cognitive limitations.

Beyond Borders (2009, Belgium) Drama ΨΨΨ
Short film that interweaves three stories – those of a boy
with an intellectual disability (Down syndrome), a woman
with multiple sclerosis, and a blind man. The common
theme that binds them is the importance of positive relationships.

Big White, The (2005) Drama/Crime Ψ
Black comedy starring Robin Williams, Holly Hunter,
Giovanni Ribisi, and Woody Harrelson. Margaret (Hunter)
is diagnosed with Tourette's disorder, which appears to
be adult onset (i.e., it doesn't match *DSM-5* criteria); she
has little self-control over her verbal outbursts.

Bill (1981) Biography ΨΨ
Mickey Rooney won an Emmy for playing a man with an
intellectual disability who was forced to leave an institution after 46 years in this made-for-TV movie.

Black Balloon, The (2008, Australia) Drama/Romance
ΨΨΨΨ
A teenage boy in a dysfunctional family copes with the
challenges of caring for his brother with autism spectrum
disorder while his mother is bedridden because of pregnancy. The film provides excellent illustrations of the
combined stresses of adolescence and caregiving.

Boy Who Could Fly, The (1986) Fantasy ΨΨ
Love story about the affection that develops between a
teenage girl whose father has just committed suicide and
a new neighbor who is autistic.

Breaking and Entering (2006) Drama ΨΨΨ
A Bosnian boy robs an architect who secretly follows the
young thief home and eventually becomes involved with
the boy's mother. The architect and his live-in girlfriend
are raising her adolescent daughter who has a pervasive
developmental disorder, but the stress of caring for the
child interferes with the adults' relationship. The film also
depicts seasonal affective disorder.

Charly (1968) Drama ΨΨ
Cliff Robertson won an Oscar for his role as a man with
an intellectual disability who is transformed into a genius,
only to find himself eventually reverting to his previous
level of disability. (Compare this film with *Molly* [1999].)

Child Is Waiting, A (1963) Drama ΨΨ
Burt Lancaster and Judy Garland star in this film about
the treatment of children with intellectual disabilities living in institutions.

City of Lost Children, The (1995, France) Fantasy/Drama
ΨΨΨΨ
A mad scientist is aging prematurely so he tries to capture children to steal their dreams. The circus strongman
named One, who has a developmental disability, teams
up with a bold, bright young girl to save the children.

Dangerous Woman, A (1993) Drama ΨΨ
Debra Winger plays a woman with a mild intellectual disability who becomes involved with an itinerant alcoholic.

Day in the Death of Joe Egg, A (1972) Comedy ΨΨ
British black comedy that examines the issue of mercy killing.

Dead Mother, The (1993, Spain) Drama/Thriller ΨΨΨ
Child with characteristics of autism and a developmental disability witnesses her mother's murder by a petty thief who kidnaps the child, now a woman, 2 decades later.

Dodes'ka-den (Clickety-Clack) (1970, Japan) Drama ΨΨΨ
Akira Kurosawa film about a boy with an intellectual disability living in the slums of Tokyo. This was Kurosawa's first color film. Although now regarded as a classic, this film was not well received by the public or by critics when it was released, and its failure led to Kurosawa's attempt to commit suicide by slashing his wrists in 1971. Kurosawa survived the suicide attempt, and eventually died in 1998 in Tokyo.

Dominick and Eugene (1988) Drama ΨΨΨΨ
This is a coming-of-age film about two brothers. Eugene, who is finishing medical school, is the primary caregiver for his brother Dominick who has an intellectual disability and works as a Pittsburgh trash collector. Dominick's income supports the brothers but Eugene wants to move to California for his residency.

Extremely Loud and Incredibly Close (2011) Drama ΨΨΨΨ
An 11-year-old boy with what might be an autism spectrum disorder searches for meaning after his father dies in the 9/11 bombings of the World Trade Center.

Forrest Gump (1994) Fantasy ΨΨΨΨΨ
Traces the life of Forrest Gump, who triumphs in life despite an IQ of 75 and a deformed spine. The film will make you examine your stereotypes about intellectual disability.

Forrest Gump: "Lieutenant Dan, what are you doing here?"
Lieutenant Daniel Taylor: "I'm here to try out my sea legs."
Forrest Gump: "But you ain't got no legs, Lieutenant Dan."

Forrest Gump (1994)

Front of the Class (2008) Drama ΨΨΨΨ
This film is based on the life of Brad Cohen; it deals with his courage as a child dealing with Tourette's disorder and an ignorant and unsympathetic father. Cohen later went on to become a gifted and award winning teacher.

Girlfriend (2010) Drama ΨΨΨ
A young man with Down syndrome inherits money and uses it to pursue a single mother he has loved since high school.

Harvey Krumpet (2003) Animation/Comedy ΨΨΨ
Short film about a character who faces innumerous tragedies and challenges, including Tourette's disorder.

Her Name Is Sabine (2007, France) ΨΨΨΨ
Striking documentary depicting the impact of a psychiatric institution on a woman with autism.

Horse Boy, The (2009) Documentary ΨΨΨΨ
A family travels to Mongolia to find a shaman who can help their son who has an autism spectrum disorder.

House of Cards (1993) Drama Ψ
Tommy Lee Jones is wasted in an insipid movie about a young girl who becomes autistic and withdrawn.

I Am Sam (2001) Drama ΨΨΨ
Sean Penn portrays a man with a mild intellectual disability who fights for custody rights for his daughter.

I Think We're Alone Now (2008) Documentary ΨΨ
This documentary profiles two individuals in love with the pop singer Tiffany. One of the two is identified as someone with Asperger's syndrome; the other is a hermaphrodite from Denver.

Jack Goes Boating (2010) Drama ΨΨΨ
Philip Seymour Hoffman directs and plays the role of Jack, a limo driver with limited intellectual ability and social skills, who becomes romantically involved with Connie and learns to swim so he can take her on a boat ride.

Jefftowne (1998) Documentary ΨΨ
A man with Down syndrome lives with his 93-year-old adoptive parent and spends his time socializing.

Junebug (2005) Comedy/Drama ΨΨ
An autistic painter has a minor but highly stereotypic role in an otherwise good film.

King's Speech, The (2010) Drama ΨΨΨΨΨ
Colin Firth plays the role of Bertie (George VI) who must accept the responsibilities of being King of England when his older brother abdicates the throne. His role as national leader is complicated by his childhood-onset fluency disorder (stuttering), a problem treated successfully by speech therapist Lionel Logue (Geoffrey Rush).

King George VI: If I'm King, where's my power? Can I form a government? Can I levy a tax, declare a war? No! And yet I am the seat of all authority. Why? Because the nation believes that when I speak, I speak for them. But I can't speak.

Bertie contemplates his dilemma as a leader in
The King's Speech (2010)

Larry (1974) Biography ΨΨ
Dated but still interesting film about a man discharged from a psychiatric hospital and forced to cope with the outside world. The film suggests the patient himself isn't really ill but still acts strange because he has grown up in a world where everyone acts a little odd.

Mary and Max (2009) Animation/Comedy/Drama ΨΨΨΨ
Philip Seymour Hoffman provides the voice of Max, a morbidly obese 44-year-old man living in Manhattan, who develops an unlikely but lasting friendship with Mary, an 8-year-old girl living in Melbourne. Max is a man with autism spectrum disorder who functions at a very high level.

Me, Too (2009, Spain) Drama ΨΨΨ
Daniel has Down syndrome and graduates from a university. After he begins a new job he promptly falls in love with a coworker.

Memory Keeper's Daughter, The (2008) Drama ΨΨ
A physician's wife has twins, one of whom has Down syndrome. He instructs the nurse to put the child in an institution for the feeble-minded; she ignores his instructions and raises the child on her own.

Monica and David (2009) Documentary ΨΨΨΨ
Two young people with Down syndrome marry and live together with her parents and create a meaningful life.

Mozart and the Whale (2005) Comedy/Drama ΨΨ
Based on a true story about two high functioning people with autism spectrum disorder who meet and develop a life long relationship.

Molly (1999) Drama Ψ
This film tries hard to be *Rain Man* with a female autistic character (Elisabeth Shue) but ends up being highly stereotypic, unrealistic, and unhelpful in educating the public about autism.

My Left Foot (1989, Ireland/UK) Drama/Biography ΨΨΨΨ
Based on the true story of Christy Brown, a successful artist/author who triumphed over cerebral palsy. Brown grew up as part of a large, poor, working class Irish fam-

ily. At that time, the world was ill-equipped to understand or care for people with cerebral palsy. A prisoner in his own body, Brown never gave up. He painted and wrote several novels and books of poetry.

My Name is Khan (2010, India) Drama ΨΨΨΨ
In a film that represents a new perspective in Bollywood filmmaking, a man with autism spectrum disorder travels across the United States with a message for the president that although he is routinely discriminated against, he is not a terrorist. The portrayal of autism (formerly Asperger's disorder) is very strong in the film.

Niagara, Niagara (1998) Drama ΨΨ
Two teenagers on the lam encounter multiple problems en route. Reminiscent of *Bonnie and Clyde*, the film is chiefly memorable because it is one of the few films in which Tourette's disorder is sympathetically and realistically portrayed.

Of Mice and Men (1992) Drama ΨΨΨ
John Malkovich as Lenny, a farmhand with an intellectual disability. This is a wonderful film, but see the 1939 original as well.

"He's a nice fella. Guy don't need no sense to be a nice fella."

A comment on Lenny's personality in
Of Mice and Men (1992)

Other Sister, The (1999) Comedy ΨΨ
This film portrays a young woman's struggles to be an independent adult and to distance herself from an overly protective family. She is successful in her special school, enters the local community college against her father's wishes, and develops friendships.

Pauline and Paulette (2001, Belgium) ΨΨΨΨ
Following the death of their older sister Martha, two sisters unwillingly become responsible for their sister Pauline who has a developmental disability.

Praying with Lior (2008) Documentary Biography ΨΨΨ
A young man with Down syndrome prepares for his Bar Mitzvah.

Pushing Tin (1999) Drama/Comedy ΨΨ
John Cusack portrays an air traffic controller with adult attention deficit disorder.

Radio (2003) Drama ΨΨΨ
Cuba Gooding Jr. plays a man with a developmental disability who when given a chance by the coach (Ed Harris)

of the local football team, inspires and influences many lives. With regard to the portrayal of disabilities, the pros outweigh the cons in this heart-warming, true story.

"I know you're in there somewhere."

Charlie Babbitt responds to his brother
Raymond in *Rain Man* (1993)

Rain Man (1993) Drama ΨΨΨΨ
Dustin Hoffman plays an autistic man who is also a savant, initially exploited by an older brother. Hoffman read widely about autism and worked with autistic people when preparing for this role.

Ringer, The (2005) Comedy ΨΨ
A man desperate for money decides to fix the Special Olympics by entering to beat the reigning champion.

Rudely Interrupted (2009, Australia) Documentary ΨΨΨΨ
A popular rock band from Australia made up of musicians with a variety of disabilities – Asperger's, Down syndrome, blindness, and deafness – go on a world tour.

Shorty (2003) Documentary ΨΨΨΨ
A 55-year-old man with Down syndrome who is passionate about football is about to be inducted into the Hampden-Sydney College Athletic Hall of Fame.

Silent Fall (1994) Drama ΨΨΨ
A retired child psychiatrist works with a boy with autism who witnessed his parent's murder.

Sling Blade (1996) Drama ΨΨΨΨΨ
Billy Bob Thornton wrote the screenplay, directed the film, and played the lead in this remarkable film, which examines the life of a 37-year-old man with an intellectual disability who has been incarcerated in a mental hospital for the past 25 years after killing his mother and her lover. The fact that the protagonist winds up committing a third murder after being released perpetuates the misconception that people with developmental disabilities are potentially dangerous.

"I reckon I got no reason to kill no one. Uh, huh."

Karl Childers in *Sling Blade* (1996)

Snow Cake (2006) Drama ΨΨ
Sigourney Weaver portrays a high functioning woman with autism spectrum disorder. This film received an "honorable mention" at the Voice Awards.

Somersault (2004, Australia) Drama Ψ
A small part of this coming-of-age tale involves a young boy with an autism spectrum disorder.

"Trust me. We know how different she is."
"Different but not less."

A teacher and mother having a conversation
about a young Temple Grandin

Temple Grandin (2010) Biography ΨΨΨΨΨ
This engaging film introduces the viewer to Temple Grandin, a woman with autism spectrum disorder who also has a PhD in animal husbandry. Although Temple Grandin is extraordinary and atypical, the film conveys a tremendous amount of information about autism spectrum disorder.

There's Something About Mary (1998) Comedy ΨΨ
Ted (Ben Stiller) tries to track down and rekindle love with Mary (Cameron Diaz). Mary has a brother with a developmental disability who plays a significant role in the story.

Tim (1979) Drama ΨΨ
In this Australian film, an older woman has an affair with a man with an intellectual disability.

Thumbsucker (2005) Comedy/Drama ΨΨΨ
An adolescent boy self-soothes by secretly sucking his thumb. He is unable to stop and is diagnosed with attention deficit disorder. His life is transformed after he begins treatment with stimulant medication.

To Be and To Have (2005, France) Documentary/Drama ΨΨΨΨ
A creative teacher adapts his style to children of different ages, learning levels, and types of problems, ranging from autism spectrum, communication disorders, and ADHD.

Unforgotten: 25 Years After Willowbrook (1996) Documentary ΨΨΨΨΨ
Geraldo Rivera follows up on the original Willowbrook State School expose and contrasts the grim reality of institutional life with the current success of some survivors, including Bernard Carabello, a man abandoned by his parents at age three because he had cerebral palsy, who spent 18 years at Willowbrook.

Up Syndrome (2000) Documentary ΨΨΨ
A film about a young man with Down syndrome who deals with the struggles all young people confront: finding meaningful work, finding someone to love, and establishing meaning in life.

Village, The (2004) Drama/Suspense Ψ
Director M. Night Shyamalan's film about a village surrounded by forest containing the highly feared "those we don't speak of." One character is stereotyped as dangerous with a developmental disability.

What's Eating Gilbert Grape? (1993) Drama ΨΨΨ
Johnny Depp stars in this interesting portrayal of the dynamics of a rural Iowa family and small town America. Depp's life revolves around the care of his brother (who has an intellectual disability) and his morbidly obese mother.

Schizophrenia Spectrum and Other Psychotic Disorders

11'09"01 – September 11 (2002) Drama ΨΨΨ
Eleven renowned directors from around the world look to their own cultures to create a short film in tribute to the tragedy of September 11, 2001. This fascinating collection of films includes an allegory from Japan's Shohei Imamura about a man who returns from war believing he is a snake.

12 Monkeys (1995) Science Fiction/Suspense ΨΨ Terry Gilliam film about a time traveler (Bruce Willis) trying to save the world from a deadly plague. Brad Pitt co-stars as a character with paranoid schizophrenia. At times, the film seems to take on a cinematic representation of a nightmare.

13 Moons (2002) Drama ΨΨ
Three priests, a bail bondsman, a musician, and two clowns cross paths on nighttime city streets. One character, a drug addict needing an organ transplant, is blatantly psychotic throughout the film.

Aguirre, the Wrath of God (1972, West Germany/Peru/Mexico) Adventure ΨΨΨΨ
Werner Herzog film about Spanish conquistadors searching for the mythic treasure of El Dorado deep into the Amazon of Peru. The narcissistic leader deteriorates into psychosis.

Alone in the Dark (1982) Suspense Ψ
A psychotic patient besieges a psychiatrist's family during a citywide blackout.

Amadeus (1984) Biography/Musical ΨΨΨ
The film opens with the court composer Salieri, now old, mad, and suicidal, wondering if he murdered Mozart. Salieri is obsessed with the genius of Mozart and can never forgive his rival for his talent or himself for his mediocrity.

Angel at My Table, An (1990) Biography/Drama ΨΨΨΨ
Jean Campion's biography of New Zealand novelist Janet Frame, who was misdiagnosed with schizophrenia and mistreated with electroconvulsive therapy (ECT).

Angel Baby (1995) Drama ΨΨΨ
Australian film about two mentally ill people who meet in an outpatient clinic, fall in love, and try to face life together. Unfortunately, their lives fall apart as a consequence of an ill-fated decision to mutually discontinue their medication.

Angel in Red (1991) Suspense Ψ
A psychotic pimp goes gunning for his former employee after she turns to a rival pimp for protection.

Angels of the Universe (2000; Iceland) Biography/Drama ΨΨΨ
Paul is a musician and artist in love with a woman from a different social stratum; when she leaves him, he becomes psychotic and is hospitalized. The scriptwriter based the film (and his book on which the film is based) on his experiences with his brother, a man with mental illness.

Assassination of Richard Nixon, The (2004) Biography/Drama ΨΨΨ
Sean Penn portrays Sam Bicke, an aloof, taciturn, delusional furniture salesman who attempted to kill President Nixon. The film promotes the misconception that people with mental illness are always violent.

Asylum (2005) Thriller/Drama ΨΨ
A husband takes a job at a psychiatric institution and his wife begins to have an affair with a dangerous patient. The film perpetrates the misconception that patients in psychiatric hospitals are violent and dangerous.

Bee Season (2005) Drama Ψ
A father (Richard Gere) becomes over involved in his daughter's spelling bee competitions and looks to Jewish mysticism for support.

Benny & Joon (1993) Comedy ΨΨΨ
A generally sympathetic portrayal of schizophrenia, with a vivid example of decompensation on a city bus; the film trivializes the problem of schizophrenia by suggesting love alone is enough to conquer the problem.

Berlin Alexanderplatz (1980) Drama ΨΨΨΨΨ
This film, a 15-hr Fassbinder masterpiece, traces the gradual moral and mental disintegration of a man who leaves prison resolved to live a good life. The film explores exploitation of women, violence, homosexuality, and mental illness.

Betrayed (1988) Political/Thriller Ψ
Debra Winger plays an undercover agent who falls in love with a seemingly simple farmer, actually a right-wing, paranoid fanatic.

Betty Blue (1986) Drama ΨΨΨ
Artistic, erotic French film about two young lovers and their passions that lead from poverty to violence and destruction. One particularly shocking scene depicts self-mutilation resulting from psychosis.

Bill of Divorcement, A (1932) Comedy ΨΨ
A mentally ill man is discharged from a psychiatric hospital and returns home to his wife and daughter. Katharine Hepburn's debut as a film actress.

Birth (2004) Drama/Mystery ΨΨΨ
A rare depiction of what was previously referred to as shared psychotic disorder (folie à deux) featuring Nicole Kidman.

Black Swan (2010) Drama/Mystery/Thriller ΨΨΨΨΨ
Natalie Portman won an Academy Award for Best Performance by an Actress in a Leading Role for her performance as a troubled ballerina who becomes obsessed with her dual role as both the white and black swan in Tchaikovsky's *Swan Lake*. The film depicts bulimia and anorexia and presents a differential diagnosis challenge because of a plot that includes fantasies, delusions, hallucinations, mother/daughter conflict, seduction by a director, a lesbian encounter, ecstasy abuse and possible murder.

Boxing Helena (1994) Drama ΨΨ
Eminent surgeon is rebuffed by a beautiful woman. His obsessions of her turn delusional as he captures her and eventually amputates her arms and legs while paradoxically fawning over her. Interesting dynamic of his forcing the woman to be physically dependent upon him emerging from his psychological dependence on her. Directorial debut of Jennifer Chambers Lynch, daughter of distinguished filmmaker David Lynch.

"I am still haunted by my love for her ... those dreams."

A character in *Boxing Helena* (1994) leaves the viewer to ponder how much of the film is delusion, reality, or a dream

---

Bubba Ho-tep (2002) Comedy/Thriller Ψ
Two rest home residents who believe they are Elvis Presley and John F. Kennedy team up to fight evil.

Bug (2006) Drama/Horror ΨΨΨΨ
A William Friedkin film that offers a nice example of a shared delusional disorder (in this case the belief that the government implanted microscopic insects underneath her boyfriend's skin).

Butcher Boy, The (1997) Comedy ΨΨΨΨ
Dark comedy about a boy with schizophrenia, Francie Brady, living in Ireland in the 1960s. Francie's behavior ranges from absurd and humorous to delusional and dangerous.

"He took me, with the stink of filthy roadhouse whiskey on his breath, and I liked it. I liked it! With all that dirty touching of his hands all over me. I should've given you to God when you were born, but I was weak and backsliding, and now the devil has come home."

Francie Brady's mother laments her past in
The Butcher Boy (1997)

Camille Claudel (1988) Biography ΨΨΨ
Biographical film of the mistress of Rodin, who spent the last 30 years of her life in an asylum.

Canvas (2006) Drama ΨΨΨΨ
A remarkable portrayal of schizophrenia and its impact on the family, starring Marcia Gay Harden. Winner of a Voice Award for its outstanding depiction of mental illness.

Caveman's Valentine, The (2001) Crime/Drama ΨΨ
Depicts a homeless composer with schizophrenia living in a cave in New York City.

Confessions of a Superhero (2007) Documentary ΨΨΨ
A film that explores the lives of four individuals trying to make a living by posing as superheroes on Hollywood's walk of fame; the primary characters in the film impersonate Batman, Superman, Wonder Woman and The Hulk.

Dangerous Method, A (2011, United Kingdom) Biography/Drama ΨΨΨ
This David Cronenberg film documents the early days of psychoanalysis and some of the interactions between Freud and Jung. The film also features Sabina, a patient with psychosis, who prior to becoming a physician and scholar, was treated by both Freud and Jung. In the film, Jung has erotic and sadomasochistic sex with Sabina.

Dead Man on Campus (1998) Comedy Ψ
Two roommates try to find a roommate who is likely to commit suicide so that they can have their flailing grades excused. The film perpetrates misconceptions that people with mental illness are violent, that people with mental illness are always psychotic, and that those who are paranoid are the most likely to commit suicide.

Dead of Night (1945) Horror ΨΨΨΨ
Five short episodes loosely linked together. The last of these, "The Ventriloquist's Dummy," stars Michael Redgrave, who has to be hospitalized after he becomes convinced that he and his dummy are exchanging personalities (in fact, they are).

Delusions of Grandeur (1973) Comedy Ψ
In 17th-century Spain, a wily servant saves his king from the intrigues of a tax collector.

Derailroaded (2005) Documentary/Biography ΨΨ
Portrays the music and life of cult-rock icon "Wild Man Fischer," a man with schizophrenia; the film is both funny and informative, and it is not exploitative.

Deranged (2012, Korea) Drama ΨΨ
A parasite infects the residents of Seoul, causing them to commit suicide, while a pharmaceutical salesman searches for a cure. Not to be confused with a far horror inferior film by the same name released the same year.

Dogtooth (2010, Greece) Drama ΨΨΨ
An intriguing film about a bizarre family in which the parents teach their children a unique language and prevent them from having any contact with the outside world. The film features brother–sister incest and depicts extensive psychological abuse of children.

Don Juan DeMarco (1995) Drama ΨΨΨ
Marlon Brando plays a compassionate psychiatrist to Johnny Depp' character who thinks he is the legendary Don Juan.

"I am the world's greatest lover!"

Don Juan DeMarco (1995)

Donnie Darko (2001) Drama ΨΨΨ
Although this movie about a delusional high school student who frequently hallucinates a "demon bunny" instructing him that the end of the world is near sounds trivial, the film is fairly complex with important comments on fear, the pain of mental illness, and the nature of reality. It is a cult classic.

Don't Say A Word (2001) Suspense/Mystery ΨΨ   Michael Douglas plays a psychiatrist whose daughter is kidnapped for the ransom of a 6-digit code locked in the brain of a very disturbed psychiatric patient (Brittany Murphy).

Dressed to Kill (1980) Thriller Ψ
Popular film in which Michael Caine plays Angie Dickinson's psychiatrist. The film confuses transsexuality and schizophrenia, but it is exciting, if not always accurate.

Edmond (2005) Thriller ΨΨ
Interesting and memorable story about a man (William H. Macy) who slowly loses touch with reality and never fully returns.

Entertainer, The (1960) Drama Ψ
This film, starring Laurence Olivier and Albert Finney, portrays Olivier as a third-rate vaudevillian whose delusions of grandeur alienate people around him.

Face to Face (1976, Sweden) Drama ΨΨΨΨ
Two psychiatrists are portrayed, one of whom (Liv Ullmann) is depressed, delusional and suicidal, and a brief affair with another physician doesn't help. The poster for the film shows two faces superimposed on a strikingly realistic Rorschach plate.

Fan, The (1982) Horror Ψ
A Broadway star played by Lauren Bacall is terrorized by an embittered fan.

Fan, The (1996) Drama Ψ
Robert De Niro and Wesley Snipes are wasted in this tired film about a baseball fan who is obsessed with a Giants center fielder.

Final (2001) Drama ΨΨΨ
Well-acted performance by Denis Leary who plays "Bill" in this Campbell Scott film. Bill awakens from a coma in an isolated, bright room of a psychiatric hospital. He has frequent paranoid delusions, anger outbursts, and hallucinations as his therapist helps him remember flashbacks of his car accident and his father's death. Interesting portrayal of the doctor–patient relationship, presenting many questions about boundaries, ethics, and relational dynamics.

Fisher King, The (1991) Drama/Fantasy/Comedy ΨΨΨ
Terry Gilliam film in which Robin Williams plays a homeless, mentally ill man who is befriended by a disillusioned former disc jockey. The movie is funny but confusing, and it misleads the public with its suggestion of a traumatic etiology for schizophrenia.

Flightplan (2005) Suspense/Drama ΨΨ

While on a long flight, a woman (Jodie Foster) frantically claims she has lost her child, however, other passengers do not remember a child traveling with her. For much of the film, the viewer is left questioning whether Jodie Foster has a psychotic disorder. The film suggests that individuals referred to as delusional or psychotic are actually telling the truth and their delusions may well be reality-based.

Frailty (2001) Drama/Suspense ΨΨΨ

Bill Paxton plays a serial killing, religious zealot with a delusional disorder who believes he's on a mission from God to fight off demons (his human victims).

"Now you stay down here until you see the truth. Pray to god, Fenton. Pray for a vision. Only he can help you now!"

Frailty (2001)

Gothika (2003) Suspense ΨΨ

Halle Berry plays Dr. Miranda Grey who works to unravel the mystery of her patient's (Penelope Cruz) psychopathology and is confronted by disturbing secrets and the supernatural.

Goya in Bordeaux (1999) Drama/Biography ΨΨΨ

Spanish film, depicting the famous painter, Francisco de Goya on his deathbed, who recalls major events of his life, hallucinates, and experiences severe migraines. Addresses themes of psychosis and creativity, integrity versus despair, and the interrelationship of life and death.

Grizzly Man (2005) Documentary ΨΨΨ

Werner Herzog film about Timothy Treadwell, a well-known naturalist who lived with grizzly bears for 13 summers. The viewer wonders if Treadwell had a psychotic or bipolar disorder as he became increasingly wild, and his behavior increasingly bizarre.

Happy Accidents (2001) Romance/Sci-Fi Ψ

A man states he is from the future – the year 2470.

He Loves Me, He Loves Me Not (2002) Drama ΨΨΨΨΨ

A must-see film for depiction of delusional disorders that is so unique that it could only be done cinematically. First, the viewer sees reality from the young woman's perception and flashes back to the beginning giving the viewer the vantage point of the man she loves. This French film stars *Amélie*'s Audrey Tautou.

House of Fools (2002) Drama ΨΨΨ

Based on a true story: the staff in a mental institution flee due to conflicts in Chechnya, leaving the patients to fend for themselves. Soon soldiers occupy the hospital and the viewer is left with various questions of war, politics, mental health treatment and which one is really "crazy." Loaded with psychopathology examples, including a fire starter, all the schizophrenia subtypes, and a woman who believes she is the fiancée of singer, Bryan Adams (who appears in the film).

Housekeeping (1987) Drama ΨΨΨ

An eccentric aunt comes to care for two sisters in the Pacific Northwest after the suicide of their mother. The girls can't decide if their aunt is simply odd or seriously mentally ill. The viewer confronts a similar dilemma.

I'm a Cyborg, But That's OK (2006, South Korea) Drama/Romance ΨΨΨ

Despite the odd title, this is a fascinating film about a psychotic woman who believes she is a cyborg and is admitted to psychiatric institution.

I Never Promised You a Rose Garden (1977) Drama ΨΨΨ

Accurate rendition of the popular book by the same name. The patient has command hallucinations that tell her to kill herself. There is a sympathetic portrayal of psychiatry and treatment; a breakthrough occurs when the protagonist first realizes she is able to feel pain.

Images (1972) Drama ΨΨΨ

Robert Altman's examination of the confused life of a woman with schizophrenia. A difficult film, but interesting, with a heuristic presentation of hallucinations.

Inner Senses (2002, Korea) Horror Thriller ΨΨ

A psychotic woman is treated by a psychologist who falls in love with her and who soon comes to share her hallucinations.

Julien Donkey-Boy (1999) Drama ΨΨ

Director Harmony Korine breaks the narrative flow in this film about the horrors of schizophrenia, based on and dedicated to his uncle whom he wanted to take out of a psychiatric institution to be in the film. The film is sometimes shocking and insightful and at other times comedic. Werner Herzog plays the role of the abusive father who contributes to his son's illness.

Keane (2004) Mystery/Thriller ΨΨΨ

An engaging depiction of a man who begins to mentally deteriorate because he believes his daughter is missing. The film leaves the viewer wondering what is real and what is psychosis. Unfortunately, a powerful scene in which the protagonist randomly chases and attacks another man will stick out in the viewer's mind as a terrifying link between violence and mental illness.

Killing of John Lennon, The (2006, UK) Biography/Drama ΨΨΨ

Inside look into the mind of the delusional Mark Chapman leading up to the day he murdered John Lennon. Chapman was obsessed with Holden Caulfield from *The Catcher in the Rye* and believed he was the protagonist; he read from the book at the murder scene and trial. This film promotes the misconception that people with mental illness are violent and that Salinger's classic work somehow had something to do with Lennon's murder.

King of Comedy, The (1983) Drama ΨΨΨΨ

Martin Scorsese film about a fan who develops a delusional relationship with a talk show host after the two of them are forced to share a taxicab.

K-Pax (2001) Drama ΨΨΨΨ

Multilayered film in which Kevin Spacey plays Prot, a man claiming he's from a far away planet who is able to give convincing evidence for his case to astrophysicists. The viewer is left to hypothesize whether the character has schizophrenia, dissociative fugue, or is an enlightened spiritual being; whichever the case, the portrayal and diagnostic criteria are convincing for each.

La Dolce Vita (1960, Italy) Drama ΨΨΨ

Vintage Fellini film with an interesting vignette in which hundreds of Roman citizens develop a mass delusion following reports of a sighting of the Virgin Mary.

Love Object (2004) Thriller Ψ

A young man dealing with work stress copes by purchasing a $10,600 lifelike, silicone doll that he begins to believe is subtly torturing him as he deteriorates into psychosis.

Lunatics: A Love Story (1992) Comedy ΨΨΨ

A former mental patient spends 6 months hidden away in his apartment. The lead character has been described in reviews as agoraphobic, but a more serious diagnosis seems appropriate, especially in light of the patient's delusions and hallucinations.

Lust for Life (1956) Biography ΨΨΨΨ

Kirk Douglas as Vincent van Gogh and Anthony Quinn as Paul Gauguin. The film portrays the stormy relationship of the two men and van Gogh's hospitalization and eventual suicide. Contrast with *Vincent* (1987) and Robert Altman's *Vincent & Theo* (1990).

Madness of King George, The (1994) Historical Biography ΨΨΨ

Nigel Hawthorne as King George III in an adaptation of a stage play examining the reactions of the court and family as the king becomes increasingly demented (due to porphyria, a genetic metabolic disorder).

"One may produce a copious, regular evacuation every day of the week and still be a stranger to reason."

An observation by a court doctor
in *The Madness of King George* (1994)

Magic (1978) Thriller ΨΨ

Anthony Hopkins' talents are largely wasted in this Richard Attenborough film about a ventriloquist obsessed with his dummy. Not nearly as good a film as the 1945 movie *Dead of Night*.

Man From Earth, The (2007) Drama/Sci-Fi Ψ

A mysterious, successful professor attempts to convince his friends he can live forever and that he has met a variety of historical figures (e.g., Buddha).

May (2002) Thriller Ψ

Macabre psychological study of an isolated, socially awkward girl who sinks into psychosis as she tries to make a "best friend" by assembling the best parts of other people's bodies. Promotes the misconception that people with mental illness are violent.

Misery (1990) Horror ΨΨ

Kathy Bates plays an apparently delusional woman who becomes convinced she is justified in capturing a novelist and forcing him to rewrite his latest novel to meet her tastes.

Montenegro (1981) Drama ΨΨ

A Dusan Makavejev film about a bored housewife slowly becoming psychotic. She becomes sexually liberated and then murders her lover. Despite its psychopathological theme, the film is really about politics and social class.

Number 23, The (2007) Drama Ψ

A dogcatcher becomes obsessed with the number 23. Jim Carrey's considerable talents are largely wasted in this film, a movie that disappoints both artistically and pedagogically. The movie conflates obsessive-compulsive disorder, paranoia, paranoid personality disorder, and sexual sadism.

Observe and Report (2009) Comedy Drama Ψ

A mall security guard with bipolar disorder abuses drugs and is noncompliant with his medication. He is grandiose and delusional, believing that he is going to be able to solve the mall's problems of theft and a flasher.

Out of the Shadow (2004) Documentary ΨΨΨΨ
Realistic and moving depiction of schizophrenia and its impact on the family.

Outrageous! (1977) Comedy ΨΨ
Canadian film about a gay hairdresser and a woman with schizophrenia who is pregnant.

People Say I'm Crazy (2003) Documentary ΨΨΨ
Cinema verite–styled documentary of the daily life of a man with paranoid schizophrenia. Interesting for discussions on differentiation of schizophrenia, schizoaffective disorder, and mood disorders. Deeply honest, enlightening, and inspiring.

"I cannot trust my own perceptions."

John Cadigan, who directs and plays himself in
People Say I'm Crazy (2003)

Perfect Strangers (2003) Drama/Suspense ΨΨ
A mysterious man (Sam Neill) invites a woman he has just met to his private island home and then kidnaps her. The two become romantically involved, and she nurses him back to health after he is injured. His obsessions transfer to the woman who frequently hallucinates after her lover dies.

Pi (1988) Drama ΨΨΨΨ
Darren Aronofsky's first film features an eccentric and misanthropic mathematician who has built a supercomputer in his apartment, which he hopes to use to make predictions about the stock market. Max is paranoid and experiences delusions; however, he is also being pursued by both Wall Street business spies and Hasidic Jews who plan to use Max's genius to find hidden meaning in the Torah.

Possessed (1947) Drama ΨΨΨ
Joan Crawford stars in a suspenseful film depicting catatonic schizophrenia with examples of waxy flexibility and numerous other symptoms of severe mental illness.

Promise (1986) Drama ΨΨ
A made-for-TV movie, starring James Garner, about a man who honors a commitment made to his mother to care for his brother with schizophrenia. Excellent illustrations of the symptoms of schizophrenia.

Proof (2005) Drama ΨΨΨ
Gwyneth Paltrow portrays the daughter of a famous mathematician (Anthony Hopkins). She begins to develop similar symptoms of schizophrenia similar to those shown by her father as she attempts to solve a rare proof that has baffled other mathematicians.

Rampo Noir (2005, Japan) Horror Ψ
Four short, surreal horror films that are adaptations and tributes to the Japanese poet Rampo. Portrayals of hell, mental illness, and psychosis.

Red Dragon (2002) Thriller/Drama Ψ
Ralph Fiennes, as the serial killer in this prequel to *Silence of the Lambs*, deepens in his delusional framework as he becomes convinces he is a dragon. In one scene, he eats a painting of a dragon in order to internalize it.

Repulsion (1965) Horror ΨΨΨΨΨ
Powerful film about sexual repression and psychotic decompensation. Memorable examples of hallucinations (e.g., arms reaching out from walls); the film culminates in an unforgettable murder scene. This was Roman Polanski's first English-language film.

Revolution #9 (2001) Thriller/Drama ΨΨΨΨΨ
A psychological drama about a man coping with paranoid schizophrenia. Michael Risley's character is paranoid and delusional (e.g., he thinks the director of a perfume commercial is controlling his thoughts). The film offers an accurate and unflinching portrayal of how relationships are affected by a disease like schizophrenia.

Ruling Class, The (1972) Comedy ΨΨΨ
Brilliant British black comedy in which a member of the House of Lords inadvertently commits suicide and leaves his fortune and title to his son who is delusional and has schizophrenia (Peter O'Toole). The son at first believes he is Jesus and later Jack the Ripper.

Saint of Fort Washington, The (1993) Drama ΨΨΨ A man with schizophrenia is evicted from his home winds up in a shelter, where a street-wise Vietnam veteran befriends him. Good portrayal of the life of people who are both mentally ill and homeless.

Santa Sangre (1989) Horror/Thriller ΨΨΨΨ
A disturbing film about a young man forced to witness the mutilation of his mother and the suicide of his father. We never know if these events are real or simply delusions of a patient. The film is complex and visually stunning.

Save the Green Planet (2003, Korea) Drama/Thriller ΨΨ
A young man pursues individuals he perceives are aliens from Andromeda to keep them from destroying the planet.

Scissors (1991) Suspense Ψ
The paranoid delusions of a traumatized young woman take on a frightening reality when she finds her assailant dead.

Scotland, PA (2001) Comedy ΨΨ
Dark comedy that's a subtle parody of Macbeth, about greed, power, love, and "going crazy." A young couple who take over the work at a restaurant after killing the owner, begin to deteriorate with rumination, guilt, and poor coping as police detective (Christopher Walken) investigates the murder case.

Shine (1996) Biography/Drama ΨΨΨΨΨ
True story of David Helfgott, an Australian prodigy whose brilliant career is interrupted by the development of an unspecified mental illness that is probably schizophrenia. The film not so subtly suggests that David's domineering father was directly responsible for his mental illness and conveys the misleading but endearing message that love and hope can conquer mental illness.

"David, if you go you will never come back to this house again. You will never be anybody's son. The girls will lose their brother. Is that what you want?... You want to destroy the family... if you love me you will stop this nonsense."

David Helfgott's father admonishes him about leaving home in *Shine* (1996)

Shock Corridor (1963) Drama ΨΨ
Journalist feigns insanity in order to get a story from a man admitted to a psychiatric hospital; later the journalist begins to lose touch with reality.

Shutter Island (2010) Drama ΨΨΨΨ
A Martin Scorsese film staring Leonardo DiCaprio as Teddy Daniels, a federal marshal investing a missing person case at a hospital for the criminally insane in 1954. Although an interesting and intriguing film, it teaches the viewer little about mental illness.

Sixth Sense, The (1999) Drama ΨΨΨ
Bruce Willis plays a Philadelphia child psychologist treating a child who sees himself surrounded by dead people. If this child were seen at a clinic, he would probably be diagnosed with childhood schizophrenia. The film has a surprise ending and offers some insight into a troubled marriage, but it offers little to help us understand child psychopathology.

Snake Pit, The (1948) Drama ΨΨΨ
One of the first films to document the treatment of patients in a mental hospital.

Soloist, The (2009) Drama/Biography ΨΨΨΨ
Outstanding portrayal of schizophrenia in which Jamie Foxx portrays a brilliant, isolated musician, Nathaniel Ayers and the development of his friendship with an LA Times reporter (Robert Downey Jr.).

Some Voices (2000, Great Britain) Comedy ΨΨ
Ray has just been released from a psychiatric hospital, and he is cared for by his restaurateur brother. The film depicts the difficulties Ray experiences when he stops taking his medication.

Something Like Happiness (2005, Czech Republic) Comedy/Drama ΨΨ
Three adult friends from childhood support one another as they try to find happiness along different paths; one is admitted to a psychiatric hospital.

Sophie's Choice (1982) Drama ΨΨΨ
Meryl Streep won an Academy Award for her portrayal of a concentration camp survivor infatuated with Nathan, who is described as having paranoid schizophrenia but who may suffer from a bipolar disorder. Based on William Styron's novel.

Special (2006) Drama/Mystery ΨΨΨ
A man obsessed with comic books decides to take an experimental drug. The medication suppresses self-doubt and the man quickly believes he has superpowers – including telepathy, the ability to go through walls, and superhuman crime fighting.

Spider (2002) Drama ΨΨΨΨΨ
Ralph Fiennes plays a patient with schizophrenia, disorganized type, who is released from the hospital to a group home. It's a dark, bleak, psychologically complex film and a brilliant portrayal of the isolation and inner world of schizophrenia. Directed by David Cronenberg. The DVD cover reads: "The only thing worse than losing your mind, is finding it again."

Spiderman (2002) Fantasy/Drama ΨΨ
Sam Raimi classic based on the Marvel comic book series. The Green Goblin (Willem Dafoe) hears voices and seems to be mentally ill. The film perpetuates the myth that people who are mentally ill are also violent.

Stateside (2004) Drama ΨΨ
A young, spoiled, rich man turns his life around after he joins the Marines and falls in love with a woman with schizophrenia. Winner of a Voice Award.

Stay (2005) Mystery/Suspense Ψ
Ewan McGregor portrays a psychiatrist who tries to prevent one of his patients (Ryan Gosling) from committing suicide.

Story of Adèle H., The (1975, France) Biography ΨΨ
François Truffaut story about the sexual obsession of the daughter of Victor Hugo for a young soldier she can never marry.

Stroszek (1977, West Germany) Comedy ΨΨ
Offbeat Werner Herzog comedy about three Germans who come to America in search of the American dream. They fail to find it in Railroad Flats, Wisconsin. One of the three has schizophrenia.

Summer of Sam (1999) Drama/Documentary ΨΨΨ
This Spike Lee film succeeds artistically and presents interesting insights into ethnic dynamics and the process of scapegoating; however, it provides little insight into the motives or the mental illness that drove serial killer David Berkowitz, the highly publicized "Son of Sam," to commit multiple murders. The emphasis is on the fear and psychological trauma of people living in New York City who know a serial killer is still on the loose.

Sweetie (1989) Comedy ΨΨΨΨ
Director Jane Campion paints a memorable and realistic picture of a woman with schizophrenia and the difficulties her illness presents for her and her family.

Sylvia and the Phantom (1945) Drama ΨΨΨ
French film about a young woman who must distinguish between reality and fantasy, hallucination and phantom, love and illusion. Her many seducers include a narcissist, a lover, a criminal, and a phantom.

Synecdoche, New York (2008) Comedy/Drama ΨΨΨ
Interesting mix of delusion, physical illness, and existential angst in Charlie Kaufman's surrealistic film starring Philip Seymour Hoffman.

Take Shelter (2011) Drama Thriller ΨΨΨΨ
An Ohio farmer named Curtis (Michael Shannon) develops a delusional disorder and hallucinates about an impending disaster. He assumes his symptoms signify the onset of mental illness because his mother was diagnosed with paranoid schizophrenia at age 30.

Tarnation (2003) Documentary ΨΨΨΨ
Poignant, disturbing, dramatic, and realistic film chronicles the life of a family plagued by mental illness. *Tarnation* illustrates schizophrenia and depersonalization disorder as well as the effects of brain damage and traumatic abuse. The film integrates home movies, photographs, short videos, diaries, and pop culture artifacts into a striking visceral experience. If you can find this independent film, you should watch it.

Taxi Driver (1976) Drama ΨΨΨΨΨ
Robert De Niro becomes obsessed with Jodi Foster and determines to rescue her from prostitution.

Tenant, The (1976) Horror ΨΨΨ
Roman Polanski film about an ordinary clerk who moves into an apartment in which the previous owner commit-ted suicide. The new owner assumes the personality of the old owner, becomes paranoid, and commits suicide in the same way as the previous owner.

> "Someday a real rain will come and wash all the scum off the streets."
>
> *Taxi Driver* (1976)

Through a Glass Darkly (1962) Drama ΨΨΨΨΨ
Powerful and memorable Bergman film about a recently released mental patient who spends the summer on an island with her husband, father, and younger brother. This movie won an Academy Award for Best Foreign Film.

Truman Show, The (1998) Drama ΨΨΨΨΨ
This Peter Weir film stars Jim Carrey as Truman Burbank, who unbeknownst to him, has had his entire life broadcasted on a popular television show where all of the people in his life are actors and his home and town are part of an elaborate production studio. This film provides a fascinating setup for a discussion of delusional disorders.

Virgin (2003) Drama Ψ
A 17-year-old is raped by a man she is infatuated with, and subsequently she is ostracized, engages in kleptomania, and experiences delusions.

Who's Afraid of Virginia Woolf? (1966) Drama ΨΨΨΨ
A Mike Nichols film, with Elizabeth Taylor and Richard Burton, who appear to have a shared psychotic disorder involving a son who never really existed; the film also portrays alcoholism and interpersonal cruelty. Elizabeth Taylor and Sandy Dennis both won Academy Awards for their performances in this film.

> "Now that we're through with Humiliate the Host ... and we don't want to play Hump the Hostess yet ... how about a little round of Get the Guests?"
>
> *Who's Afraid of Virginia Woolf?* (1966)

World Traveler (2001) Drama ΨΨ
Julianne Moore has a supporting role as an alcoholic with a delusional disorder.

Zebraman (2004, Japan) Drama/Crime Ψ
A passive teaching supervisor becomes the superhero Zebraman to escape his miserable, mundane life. The more he accepts his character, the stronger his powers become.

Bipolar and Depressive Disorders

American Splendor (2003) Comedy/Drama/Documentary/Animation ΨΨΨΨ
Small time comic book writer and curmudgeon, Harvey Pekar, reaches cult status including several appearances on the David Letterman Show. This film integrates a narrative about a depressed couple trying to get along and manage life's stressors, comic book animation, and documentary of the real Harvey Pekar.

"Right now I'd be glad to spare some growth for some happiness."

Harvey Pekar in *American Splendor* (2003)

Anna Karenina (1935) Drama ΨΨΨΨ
Greta Garbo leaves her husband (Basil Rathbone) and son to follow a new love (Fredric March); when she sees him kissing another woman, she commits suicide by stepping into the path of an oncoming train. Based on the novel by Tolstoy.

Another Year (2010, United Kingdom) Drama ΨΨΨΨ
Mary is a depressed woman who cannot sleep and who uses wine to cope. Her unhappiness is contrasted with the happy life of her friends Tom (Jim Broadbent) and Gerri (Ruth Sheen), a psychotherapist. Mary's problems only worsens when she tries to seduce Tom and Mary's attorney son, Joe, who simply isn't interested.

Art of Failure: Chuck Connelly, The (2008) Documentary ΨΨ
Quirky, neo-expressionist painter of the 1980s, inspired by Andy Warhol and Jackson Pollack. The film depicts an agitated depression but it also presents a caricature of the "troubled artist."

Beaver, The (2011) Drama ΨΨΨ
Mel Gibson plays the role of Walter Black, a profoundly depressed and suicidal man in a dysfunctional family who uses a beaver puppet as an alter ego. Eventually he cuts off his arm to rid himself of the puppet, reunite his family and put together a meaningful life. This film was nominated for a PRISM Award, but lost out to *Take Shelter* and *Shame*.

Bell Jar, The (1979) Biography Ψ
An unsuccessful attempt to capture the spirit of Sylvia Plath's autobiographical novel *The Bell Jar*. Plath eventually committed suicide by putting her head into an oven and turning on the gas.

Biutiful (2010, Spain) Drama ΨΨΨ
Javier Bardem portrays a flawed character who struggles to find meaning despite anxiety and depression due to a general medical condition (prostate cancer).

Blue Sky (1994) Drama ΨΨΨΨ
Jessica Lange won an Academy Award for her role as a military wife with a bipolar disorder.

"You take water, for example. Sometimes it's water, sometimes it's ice. Sometimes it's steam, vapor. It always the same old H2O. It only changes its properties. Your mother's like that. She's like water."

Hank (Tommy Lee Jones) commenting on his bipolar wife's erratic behavior in *Blue Sky* (1994)

Broken Flowers (2005) Drama ΨΨ
Bill Murray is a depressed Lothario who moves from one casual affair to the next until he gets a letter telling him that he has a 19-year-son and he begins a quest to find the anonymous former girlfriend who wrote the letter.

Boy Interrupted (2009) Documentary ΨΨΨΨ
Two filmmakers tell the story of their son, Evan, a gifted child with bipolar disorder who committed suicide by jumping from the window of a skyscraper after leaving a note to his parents. This is a sensitive and moving film, and one hopes that producing the movie helped the parents at least partially heal after the loss of their son.

Cache (2005, France), Mystery/Thriller ΨΨ
A married couple begins to receive videotapes at their doorstep that depict surveillance of their house. The film provides an interesting commentary on the psychology of guilt.

Crooked Beauty: Navigating the Space Between Beauty and Madness (2010) Documentary ΨΨΨΨ
Director and producer Ken Paul Rosenthal mixes photographs, interviews and music to tell the story of activist and artist Jacks Ashley McNamara, a woman coping with depression and bipolar disorder. The film is recommended for therapists and anyone interested in mental illness.

Crossover (1983) Drama Ψ
A male nurse is plagued by self-doubts after one of the psychiatric patients commits suicide.

Cure for Terminal Loneliness, A (2007) Drama ΨΨ A short film about a lonely and depressed man discovers that the cure for loneliness is reaching out to love another person.

Death in Venice (1971) Drama ΨΨΨ
A depressed older composer becomes infatuated with a young boy; the film is based on a novel by Thomas Mann.

Devil and Daniel Johnston, The (2005) Documentary/Biography ΨΨΨΨ
Portrait of a musical genius who vacillates between madness and brilliant creativity.

Don McKay (2009) Drama ΨΨ
A depressed school janitor receives a letter from a high school telling him she is dying from cancer, and he returns to the small town he left years earlier to confront the past he left behind.

Eye of God (1997) Drama ΨΨ
Some of the scenes in this film address a boy who witnesses his mother's suicide, experiences acute stress disorder, and kills himself at age 14.

Faithless (2000) Drama ΨΨΨΨ
Liv Ullmann directed this film about a woman who has an affair with a deeply depressed man.

Field, The (1990) Drama ΨΨ Ψ
Dramatic presentation of the suicide by drowning of a young man who finds he cannot live up to his father's expectations.

Flying Scotsman, The (2006, Germany/UK) Drama ΨΨΨ
Champion cyclist who constructed his bike out of pieces of washing machines suffers with depression and suicidal thoughts. This film received an Honorable Mention at the Voice Awards.

Fox and His Friends (1975) Drama ΨΨΨΨ
Werner Fassbinder's scathing indictment of capitalism revolves around the life of a poor gay circus performer who wins money, only to lose it through the exploitation of those he assumes are his friends. He responds by committing suicide.

Garden State (2004) Drama/Comedy ΨΨΨ
A young man flies to his hometown in New Jersey for his mother's funeral. He has been estranged from his family for several years. Without his "bipolar" medication for the first time, he begins to experiment with life and finds love.

Good Morning, Vietnam (1987) Comedy/Drama/War ΨΨ
Robin Williams as an Air Force radio announcer in Vietnam. Williams has a funny, frenetic style that could be described as hypomanic.

Hairdresser's Husband, The (1992) Comedy/Drama ΨΨΨ
A woman chooses to commit suicide rather than face the incremental loss of love that she believes will accompany aging. This is a beautiful movie, despite the somewhat grim ending.

Harold and Maude (1971) Comedy ΨΨΨ
An acting-out teenager and an iconoclastic old woman bond and support one another's eccentricities, including Harold's repeated feigned suicide attempts.

Helen (2008) Drama ΨΨΨ
A music professor (Ashley Judd) is plagued by suicidal depression, and she finds comfort from another woman coping with her own problems.

Hello Ghost (2010, Korea) Drama ΨΨ
Ghosts plague a man after a series of failed suicide attempts; by letting the ghosts occupy his body to clear up unfinished business, he gets them to leave him alone, and he learns about himself in the process. Adam Sandler is producing and staring in a remake of this Korean film; it is scheduled for release in 2015.

Henry Poole Is Here (2008) Comedy Drama ΨΨ
A depressed, isolated and alcoholic man receives a terminal diagnosis and moves to the suburbs to wait to die; however, his life becomes complicated – and richer – after the face of Jesus appears on the stucco wall of his house and a mute child begins to speak after touching the image.

Hitchhiker's Guide to the Galaxy, The (2005) Comedy ΨΨ
One of the major characters, a robot, exhibits a number of symptoms of depression.

Horse Feathers (1932) Comedy ΨΨ
Groucho Marx plays a manic college president who displays flight of ideation and pressured speech.

Hospital, The (1971) Comedy/Drama ΨΨΨ
George C. Scott is first rate as a disillusioned and suicidal physician despondent in part because of the ineptitude he sees everywhere about him. There is an especially memorable scene in which Scott is interrupted as he is about to commit suicide by injecting potassium into a vein. "People are sicker than ever. We cure nothing. We heal nothing."

House of Sand and Fog (2003) Drama ΨΨΨΨ
Jennifer Connelly and Sir Ben Kingsley play opposite one another in a gripping and deeply poignant story about two seemingly very different people, each with a legitimate claim to ownership of the same house. The film accurately portrays depression, alcohol abuse, suicide attempts, and suicide.

Hours, The (2002) Drama ΨΨΨΨ
Well-acted and well-crafted tapestry integrating three stories from different times – Nicole Kidman as the renowned
novelist, Virginia Woolf, struggling to write her novel
Mrs. Dalloway; Julianne Moore, who is reading the novel
decades later; and Meryl Streep who embodies many of
Mrs. Dalloway's characteristics. Each of the four main
characters (the three women and Ed Harris) struggles with
some form of mood disorder.

> "Dearest, I feel certain that I am going mad again. I feel
> I can't go through another one of these terrible times
> and I shan't recover this time. I begin to hear voices and
> can't concentrate so I am doing what seems to be the
> best thing to do. You have given me the greatest possible
> happiness. You have been in every way all that anyone
> could be. I know that I am spoiling your life and without
> me you could work and you will, I know. You see I can't
> even write this properly. What I want to say is that I
> owe all the happiness of my life to you. You have been
> entirely patient with me and incredibly good. Everything
> is gone from me but the certainty of your goodness. I
> can't go on spoiling your life any longer. I don't think
> two people could have been happier than we have been.
> Virginia"
>
> Virginia Woolf's suicide note

Imaginary Heroes (2004) Drama ΨΨ
A young boy commits suicide by shooting himself, and
each member of the family responds to the tragedy in a
different way.

Informant, The (2009) Drama Comedy ΨΨ
Steven Soderbergh film based on a true story about a bipolar whistleblower.

Inside Moves (1980) Drama ΨΨ
A man who has failed in a suicide attempt makes new
friends in a bar and regains the will to live. Mainly notable as the comeback film for Harold Russell, the double
amputee from *The Best Years of Our Lives* (1946).

Into the Wild (2007) Biography ΨΨΨΨ
Sean Penn directed this film that is based on a true story
about an Emory student who graduates, gives away the
money he had saved for law school, and moves to Alaska.
It is a useful pedagogical exercise to speculate about potential diagnoses for this young man.

It's a Wonderful Life (1946) Drama ΨΨΨ
A Christmas tradition. The film actually presents Jimmy
Stewart as a complex character who responds to the stress
of life in Bedford Falls by attempting suicide.

I've Loved You So Long (2008, France) Drama
ΨΨΨ
A female physician moves in with her sister after serving
a 15-year prison sentence for killing her own son. The
two women struggle with learning to love one another
and reunite as a family, and the facts about the boys death
only come clear at the end of the film.

Jellysmoke (2005) Drama/Romance ΨΨΨ
A young man with bipolar disorder is released from a psy-
chiatric institution and struggles to adapt to his new life.
Winner of a Voice Award.

> "You see, George, you've really had a wonderful life.
> Don't you see what a mistake it would be to throw it
> away?"
>
> Clarence in *It's A Wonderful Life* (1946)

Juliet of the Spirits (1965) Drama ΨΨΨ
Frederico Fellini film about a bored, lonely, depressed,
and menopausal homemaker who hallucinates about the
life of the exotic woman next door.

Last Days (2005) Drama ΨΨΨ
Slow moving Gus Van Sant film depicting the final days
of Nirvana singer/guitarist Kurt Cobain. Various manic
and depressive symptoms are displayed.

Last Days of Disco, The (1998) Drama Ψ
One of the characters has bipolar disorder and is stereotyped as "looney" and "crazy"; however, he is depicted
as compliant with lithium treatment, and his life is stable
and balanced. Interesting contrast to the frequently portrayed stereotypes of bipolar disorder.

Last Picture Show, The (1971) Drama ΨΨΨΨ
Peter Bogdanovich adaptation of Larry McMurtry's novel
describing the events – and personalities – involved in the
closing of the town's only movie theater. There is a striking presentation of the symptoms of depression in the
coach's wife.

Life Upside Down (1964, France) Drama ΨΨΨ
French film about an ordinary young man who becomes increasingly detached from the world. He is
eventually hospitalized and treated, but with little
success.

Little Miss Sunshine (2006) Comedy ΨΨΨ
Steve Carell plays a renowned gay Proust scholar who
has just been released from the hospital after a suicide attempt.

Lincoln (2013) Biography/Drama/History ΨΨΨΨ
Steven Spielberg directs Daniel Day-Lewis in the title role. Lincoln's well-documented clinical depression is apparent in many of the scenes, as is the challenge of life with Mary Todd Lincoln, played by Sally Field. The film provides numerous examples of Lincoln's depressed affect.

"It's nighttime. The ship moves by some terrible power at terrific speed. And though it's imperceptible in the darkness, I have an intuition that we're headed towards a shore. No one else seems to be aboard the vessel, and I'm keenly aware of my aloneness."

Abraham Lincoln shares a dream with his wife

Lonely Guy, The (1984) Comedy Ψ
Steve Martin plays a depressed and suicidal New Yorker.

Lonesome Jim (2006) Drama ΨΨΨ
Steve Buscemi directed this engaging film about a depressed and discouraged writer who returns to his childhood home in Indiana after failing to make his mark in New York City.

Maborosi (1995, Japan) Drama ΨΨΨΨ
A Japanese film about the effects of a man's seemingly irrational suicide on the wife who is left behind to care for their 3-month-old infant.

Maddened by His Absence (2012, France) Drama ΨΨΨ
A man returns to France for the funeral of his father and attempts to reunite with his wife, someone he left nine years earlier after the death of their child in an auto accident.

Manic (2003) Drama/Action ΨΨΨ
Adolescent inpatient unit has patients with intermittent explosive disorder, disorder, major depression, self-injurious behavior, and night terrors.

Melancholia (2011, Denmark) Drama ΨΨΨΨΨ
A memorable Lars von Trier film starring Kirsten Dunst playing the role of Justine, a profoundly depressed woman who has just been married. She and her husband attend an elaborate but unhappy wedding reception; that evening Justine spurns her husband's sexual overtures and leaves him to have sex with a coworker on a golf course. Meanwhile, the end of civilization approaches as the planet Melancholia draws close.

Meet Bill (2007) Comedy/Drama ΨΨ
Aaron Eckhart portrays a man whose depression worsens when he discovers his wife is having an affair.

Melinda and Melinda (2004) Comedy/Drama ΨΨ This Woody Allen film alternates between two versions of a story, one tragic, one comic. In the tragic version, we find a depressed and suicidal Melinda.

Michael Clayton (2007) Drama ΨΨΨΨ
Tom Wilkinson plays the role of a brilliant attorney whose bipolar-manic episodes make it almost impossible for him to function as an attorney.

Michael Clayton: "You are the senior litigating partner of one of the largest, most respected law firms in the world. You are a legend."
Arthur Edens: "I'm an accomplice!"
Michael Clayton: "You're a manic-depressive!"
Arthur Edens: "I am Shiva, the God of death."

George Clooney reasons with a bipolar Tom Wilkinson in *Michael Clayton* (2007)

Mind the Gap (2004) Drama ΨΨΨ
The lives of five isolated, lonely and desperate people are intertwined in complex ways: eventually each live intersects with the other four. One poignant segment portrays a suicidal African American man who gets life-saving advice from a priest.

Mishima: A Life in Four Chapters (1985) Biography ΨΨΨ
A fascinating film about one of the most interesting figures in contemporary literature, Yukio Mishima. Mishima, a homosexual, traditionalist, and militarist, committed ritual suicide *(seppuku)* before being beheaded by a companion.

Monsieur Ibrahim (2003) Drama/Comedy ΨΨΨ
An elderly widower and troubled teen form a unique friendship while living in Paris in the 1960s. A secondary character, the boy's father, suffers from agitated, masked depression, and eventually abandons his son (who had already been abandoned by his mother) and commits suicide.

Monster's Ball (2002) Drama ΨΨΨΨ
Emotionally jarring film about two lost, self-hating people who begin to experience emotion and face their pain through their relationship. Stars Billy Bob Thornton and Halle Berry, the latter who won an Academy Award for Best Actress for her role in this film.

Morning (2010) Drama ΨΨΨΨ
A Seattle couple grieves the loss of their child to drowning.

Mosquito Coast, The (1986) Adventure ΨΨΨ
Harrison Ford is an eccentric American inventor who flees the United States for Central America because of his paranoia. His diagnosis is never clearly stated, but Ford appears to be bipolar (although almost continually manic in the film).

My First Wife (1984) Drama ΨΨ
A moving and well-directed Australian film about a man who falls apart after his wife decides to leave him.

Network (1976) Drama ΨΨΨ
A veteran anchorman who has just been told he is being fired announces on national TV that he will commit suicide on the air in two weeks. Ratings soar. He eventually reneges on his promise but becomes the leader of a national protest movement.

> "... I'm as mad as hell, and I'm not going to take this anymore!"
>
> Newscaster Howard Beale in *Network* (1976)

Nightmare Alley (1947) Crime ΨΨ
Tyrone Power's favorite film. Power plays a carnival huckster who teams up with an unethical psychologist to dupe the public. Memorable carnival "geek" scenes include biting the heads off chickens.

Nine Lives (2005) Drama ΨΨΨ
This film is directed by Rodrigo Garcia, the son of the novelist Gabriel Garcia Marquez. It consists of nine relatively brief vignettes about the lives of nine women, one of whom is suicidal.

Off the Map (2003) Drama ΨΨΨ
Sam Elliott plays Charley, a veteran living in New Mexico with his wife and 11-year-old daughter. The family is eccentric (e.g., the wife tends her garden in the nude) but happy until Charley develops a crippling depression.

Outcry, The (1957) Drama ΨΨΨ
Antonioni film about a man who becomes depressed and confused when he is rejected by his lover.

Perks of Being a Wallflower (2012) Drama ΨΨΨΨ
In a film that effectively captures the *angst* of high school, Logan Lerman plays Charlie, a lonely high school student. He is depressed until he makes friends with two other students. Charlie becomes suicidal and is hospitalized; while in the hospital his depression is traced to a history of sexual abuse by his aunt.

Pollock (2000) Drama ΨΨΨ
Ed Harris portrays the troubled painter Jackson Pollack, who struggles with alcoholism and bipolar disorder.

Prozac Nation (2001) Drama ΨΨΨ
A dramatic and realistic portrayal of depression and borderline personality disorder in a Harvard undergraduate.

Rabbit Hole (2010) Drama ΨΨΨΨ
Nicole Kidman stars in this powerful drama about a couple trying to cope with the loss of their 4-year-old son who was killed when he chased his dog into the street. The dog was chasing a rabbit. Group therapy seems to provide little solace for the couple, and their relationship is clearly threatened by their loss.

> "God had to take her. He needed another angel."
> "Why didn't he just make one? Another angel? I mean, he's God, after all. Why didn't he just make another angel?"
>
> Nicole Kidman's character responds to an insensitive remark in a group therapy session in *Rabbit Hole* (2010)

Rain (2001) Drama ΨΨ
Coming-of-age New Zealand film about a young girl whose mother is a depressed alcoholic.

Respiro (2002) Drama ΨΨΨ
An Italian film about a woman with a serious bipolar disorder who has to flee and hide in a cave to avoid coerced psychiatric treatment.

Running with Scissors (2006) Biography ΨΨ
Annette Bening plays the role of a bipolar mother who turns over her son's life to her psychiatrist.

Rust and Bone (2012, France) Drama ΨΨΨΨ
A whale trainer loses her legs and becomes profoundly depressed; the film offers a dramatic illustration of the ways in which an accident of this sort can trigger despair and withdrawal from the world, and the ways in which a relationship can buffer the pain of loss.

Scent of a Woman (1992) Drama ΨΨΨ
Al Pacino plays Colonel Slade, a depressed blind veteran who seems to have lost all meaning in his life until he is challenged by a younger man.

September (1987) Drama ΨΨ
A Woody Allen film in which Mia Farrow plays a depressed woman recovering from a suicide attempt.

Seven Pounds (2008) Drama ΨΨΨΨ
Will Smith plays a character who attempts to use his suicide to gain redemption for an accident he caused that resulted in the deaths of seven people.

Seventh Veil, The (1945) Drama ΨΨ
Psychological drama about a gifted musician who loses the ability to play the piano and becomes depressed and suicidal. Hypnotherapy makes it possible for Ann Todd to play again, as well as to sort out her complex interpersonal relationships.

Shawshank Redemption, The (1994) Drama ΨΨΨΨΨ
An outstanding film, memorable in part because of the suicide of one character who finds himself unable to adjust to life outside an institution.

Shopgirl (2005) Drama ΨΨ
A depressed salesgirl learns about the meaning of love through an affair with a much older man (played by Steve Martin, who also wrote the screenplay and the novella upon which the film was based).

Sherlock Holmes (2009; 2011) Action/Adventure ΨΨ
Robert Downey Jr. portrays the infamous detective but with significant flairs of mania and some symptoms of depression.

Silver Linings Playbook (2012) Drama/Comedy ΨΨΨΨΨ
Pat Solatano (Bradley Cooper) is struggling with bipolar disorder. His wife has left him, he has lost his job, he has just been discharged from a psychiatric hospital, and he is living with his parents. His life changes for the better after he meets Tiffany (Jennifer Lawrence), a woman with problems of her own.

"The world will break your heart ten ways to Sunday. That's guaranteed. I can't begin to explain that. Or the craziness inside myself and everyone else. But guess what? Sunday is my favorite day again. I think of what everyone did for me, and I feel like a very lucky guy."

Pat appreciates that he is making progress in his recovery from bipolar disorder in *Silver Linings Playbook* (2012)

Single Man, A (2009) Drama ΨΨΨ
Colin Firth plays the role of a depressed gay man living alone and contemplating suicide after the death of his lover.

Son's Room, The (2001, Italy) ΨΨΨ
A psychoanalyst and his wife and daughter all grieve in their own way following the loss of the man's son in a scuba diving accident.

Spanglish (2004) Comedy Ψ
An offbeat comedy about a talented cook and his manic wife who hires a Latina housekeeper.

Station Agent, The (2003) Drama/Comedy ΨΨΨΨ
Heartwarming, honest story of three lonely and disparate characters who form a unique friendship with one another. The three characters are a schizoid dwarf whose only desire is isolation, a woman who has repeated conflicts with her husband and attempts suicide, and a talkative man from New Jersey. Good mix of both healthy and unhealthy coping approaches to loneliness and depression.

Suicide Club (2002, Japan) Drama/Suspense ΨΨΨ
Fifty-four young girls collectively jump in front of an oncoming subway train, which triggers individual and group suicides around the country. This mysterious Japanese film raises questions of cause, documenting links between suicide and adolescence, violence, and consumerism.

Suicide Room (2011, Poland) Drama ΨΨΨ
Dominik kisses another boy while drunk, and he is relentlessly tormented via social media as a result. He withdraws from school and begins to self-mutilate, tutored by a girl he meets in an online chat room devoted to suicide.

Summer Wishes, Winter Dreams (1973) Drama Ψ
Joanne Woodward is a bored, depressed housewife searching for meaning and purpose in her life. The film includes dreams that may be hallucinations, and a possible somatoform disorder.

Sunset Limited (2011) Drama ΨΨΨ
A depressed and suicidal college professor (Tommy Lee Jones) is rescued by a deeply religious blue collar worked (Samuel Jackson), and the two men engage in dialogue about life's meaning and purpose. The college professor exhibits classic signs of depression.

Sylvia (2003) Drama ΨΨ
Gwyneth Paltrow portrays the life of respected American poet, Sylvia Plath, who committed suicide in 1963. The film focuses on the relationship between Plath and her husband, poet Ted Hughes.

"Sometimes I dream the tree, and the tree is my life. One branch is the man I shall marry, and the leaves my children. Another branch is my future as a writer, and each leaf is a poem. Another branch is a good academic career. But as I sit there trying to choose, the leaves bring to turn brown and blow away, until the tree is absolutely bare."

Sylvia Plath (Gwyneth Paltrow) contemplates her life in *Sylvia* (2003)

Taste of Cherry (1997) Drama ΨΨΨΨ
An Iranian film about a man who wants to commit suicide but who can't find anyone to help him.

Tenant, The (1976) Horror ΨΨΨΨ
Roman Polanski film in which a man rents an apartment previously owned by a woman who committed suicide. The man begins to assume the personality of the woman and becomes suicidal himself.

Tout de Suite, À (2004) Drama ΨΨ
A naïve teenager runs away from home with her Moroccan boyfriend who has just killed a man in a bank robbery. She winds up abandoned in Morocco, depressed and exploited.

Two Lovers (2008) Drama ΨΨΨ
Joaquin Phoenix and Gwyneth Paltrow star in this film about a troubled, depressed and suicidal man who torn between his love for two women. The film begins and ends with suicide attempts.

Umberto D. (1952) Drama ΨΨΨΨΨ
Classic Vittorio De Sica film about an indigent old man in Rome who is being evicted and must face the prospects of homelessness and isolation. The old man fails a suicide attempt and finds a reason for living through his devotion to his dog.

Vincent (1987) Biography/Documentary ΨΨΨ
An interesting examination of the life of Vincent van Gogh. The focus is on the artist's work rather than his mental illness.

Vincent & Theo (1990) Biography ΨΨΨ
This Robert Altman film deals sensitively with van Gogh's troubled relationships with Gauguin and Theo, the incident with the prostitute and his ear, van Gogh's hospitalization, and finally his suicide.

Virgin Suicides, The (1999) Drama ΨΨ
Sofia Coppola's directorial debut about a repressed family with five daughters, who in response to their mother's control, repression, and forced isolation, decide to commit suicide.

Visioneers (2008) Drama Ψ
Zach Galifianakis plays the protagonist in a drab film about office workers who explode because their lives lack meaning and purpose.

Visitor, The (2007) Drama ΨΨΨΨ
This film illustrates the apathy and indifference that can sometimes accompany depression. Richard Jenkins plays the role of Professor Walter Vale, a man coping unsuccessfully with the death of his wife.

War Within, The (2005) Drama ΨΨ
An examination of the motives behind the behavior of a suicide bomber.

Wilbur Wants to Kill Himself (2002) Drama/Comedy ΨΨ
Disappointing and highly stereotypic movie of both suicide and boundary-crossing psychotherapists. Perpetrates the misconception that love can conquer mental illness (in this case, multiple, severe suicide attempts).

Winter Passing (2005) Drama ΨΨ
A depressed young woman living in New York City uses alcohol, drugs, and casual sex to cope. She travels to the Upper Peninsula of Michigan to visit her father, an alcoholic novelist, to see if she can obtain copies of the letters he wrote to her recently deceased mother years earlier.

Woman Under the Influence, A (1974) Drama ΨΨΨΨ
A John Cassavetes film in which Gena Rowlands plays a homemaker who has to be hospitalized because of a mental illness that appears to be bipolar disorder. Peter Falk plays her mystified husband.

Wristcutters: A Love Story (2006) Fantasy ΨΨ
A young man commits suicide and then finds himself in purgatory, surrounded by other individuals who have all committed suicide in one way or another.

Wrong Man, The (1956) Drama/Crime ΨΨΨ
Hitchcock film in which a man and his wife (Henry Fonda and Vera Miles) become depressed in response to an unjust accusation of murder.

Anxiety and Obsessive-Compulsive Disorders

40 Year Old Virgin, The (2005) Comedy ΨΨ
Screwball comedy depicting issues relevant to those suffering from social phobia, such as fear of embarrassment, dating/sex fears, social inadequacy, and avoidance behavior.

Adaptation (2002) Comedy/Action ΨΨΨΨ
Multilayered Spike Jonze film in which Nicholas Cage plays twin brothers, one of whom is a neurotic screenwriter struggling to write a story based on a book about orchids.

Analyze That (2002) Comedy/Action ΨΨ
The follow-up film to *Analyze This*, in which a panic-disordered mob boss (Robert De Niro) malingers to get released from prison, tries to maintain an ordinary job, and

is convinced to return while stringing along his psychiatrist (Billy Crystal).

Analyze This (1999) Comedy/Action ΨΨ
The original Billy Crystal/Robert De Niro comedy where De Niro plays the lead thug in a New York mafia group who develops panic attacks. De Niro sees a psychiatrist (Billy Crystal) for treatment.

Arachnophobia (1990) Comedy/Horror ΨΨ
A story about a doctor with a paralyzing fear of spiders. (Actually, the spiders in this film are pretty intimidating, and fear appears to be a perfectly reasonable response.)

As Good As It Gets (1997) Romance ΨΨΨΨ
Jack Nicholson won his third Academy Award for Best Actor for this film, in which he portrays a homophobic, racist novelist with an obsessive-compulsive disorder.

Aviator, The (2004) Drama/Biography ΨΨΨΨΨ
Directed by Martin Scorsese, this film depicts Howard Hughes Jr.'s (Leonardo DiCaprio) early years (1920–1940s) and the progression of his obsessive-compulsive disorder. Winner of five Academy Awards and a Voice Award.

Batman Begins (2005) Action/Drama ΨΨΨΨΨ
Sophisticated Christopher Nolan film telling the story of Bruce Wayne, a young boy with a phobia who watches his wealthy parents being murdered and subsequently becomes a superhero. Wayne's phobia of bats is conquered through systematic exposure. The movie demonstrates the importance of facing up to what one fears the most.

Broken English (2007) Comedy/Drama/Romance ΨΨ
Parker Posey portrays an organizer/secretary/event planner who is bored and passes each day searching for a lover on the Internet. She chooses men who are unavailable because of a fear of commitment. When she gets close to a genuine commitment herself, she has panic attacks.

Bubble (2005) Crime/Drama ΨΨ
Minimalist Steven Soderbergh project about three characters in a poor town, working at a factory. One suffers from anxiety and panic attacks.

Cars that Ate Paris, The (1974, Australia) Comedy Ψ
Early Peter Weir film that takes place in a secluded town in rural Paris, Australia, where the main source of income is the revenue from salvaged valuables from car wrecks. Panic attacks and exposure are depicted.

Casualties of War (1989) War ΨΨΨ
Brian De Palma film about five GIs who kidnap, rape, and murder a young Vietnamese girl. The film deals with themes of guilt, stress, violence, and, most of all, the dehumanizing aspects of war.

Cat Ladies (2009) Documentary ΨΨ
This film will introduce you to four ladies who share their lives with numerous cats. The film is a good introduction to a special subset of hoarding disorder: animal hording.

Columbus Circle (2010) Drama ΨΨ
A wealthy agoraphobic woman is forced to confront her fears when new neighbors move in.

Copycat (1995) Suspense/Thriller ΨΨ
Sigourney Weaver plays a criminal psychologist who struggles with agoraphobia symptoms as she helps police track down a serial killer (Harry Connick Jr.).

Coyote Ugly (2000) Comedy/Drama ΨΨ
A young woman moves to New York City to try to make it as a songwriter. She takes a job as a "coyote" bartender at a wild, interactive bar and the experience helps her overcome her social anxiety.

Creepshow (1982) Horror ΨΨ
A man with an insect phobia winds up being eaten alive by cockroaches. Directed by George Romero, who also directed the classic film *Night of the Living Dead*. Stephen King wrote the screenplay, and the film is actually better than it sounds.

Croods, The (2013) Animation ΨΨΨ
A family living in a cave assuages their anxiety by adopting a strict and restrictive set of rules; when they are forced to leave their cave they learn to cope with the world by facing their fears and relying on each other.

Cyrano de Bergerac (1990, France) Romance ΨΨΨ
Gerard Depardieu stars as the inimitable Cyrano, a man obsessed with the size of his nose and convinced it makes him forever unlovable.

Da Vinci Code, The (2006) Drama/Mystery ΨΨ
This is a Ron Howard film about a murder inside the Louvre. Clues in Da Vinci's paintings lead to the discovery of a religious mystery protected by a secret society for two thousand years – which could shake the foundations of Christianity. Tom Hanks' character experiences somatic anxiety symptoms including shortness of breath and discomfort in social situations.

Departed, The (2006) Crime/Drama/Mystery ΨΨ
Engaging Martin Scorsese film starring Leonardo Di-Caprio, Matt Damon, Jack Nicholson, and Martin Sheen portraying Irish mafia, undercover detectives, and corrupt federal agents. DiCaprio's character experiences panic attacks, and anxiolytics are prescribed.

Devil (2010) Horror Ψ
Five people are trapped on an elevator; one is claustrophobic and another is the Devil.

Dirty, Filthy Love (2004, UK) Drama/Comedy ΨΨΨΨ
An outstanding movie about Mark Furness whose life falls apart as a result of his affliction with obsessive compulsive disorder and Tourette's disorder. Treatment, support groups, and severe symptoms of OCD and Tourette's are shown in the film.

"I'm not sure there is any help for you."

The dummy's comment to his ventriloquist Steven in *Dummy* (2002)

Dummy (2002) Comedy/Drama ΨΨ
A predictable film starring Adrian Brody as Steven, an aspiring ventriloquist, who is unemployed, naïve, passive, and socially awkward until he finds meaning and social support through his "dummy." Interesting metaphor of the socially phobic person finding his "inner voice." All ventriloquism in the film is actually performed by Adrian Brody. The DVD features interviews and comic classes with champion ventriloquist Jeff Dunham.

Elling (2001) Drama ΨΨΨΨΨ
Norwegian film about two men released from a psychiatric hospital and must prove themselves capable of coping with everyday life. Oscar nominee for Best Foreign Film.

Everything Is Illuminated (2005) Comedy/Drama ΨΨ
A young Jewish American travels to the Ukraine to find the woman who saved his grandfather from the Nazis. He stores everything in small plastic bags and claims to have a phobia of dogs, but ends up sharing both the backseat of a car and then a bed with a dog.

Feardotcom (2002) Thriller/Horror Ψ
Various characters access a deadly website that makes their deepest fears or phobias come true (e.g., one has a phobia of beetles and soon is covered by them).

Gigantic (2008) Drama Comedy Romance ΨΨ
A mattress salesman develops an obsession about adopting a Chinese child; however, his new love interest isn't

convinced that it is a good idea. Watch for multiple references to the concept of learned helplessness.

High Anxiety (1977) Comedy ΨΨ
Mel Brook's spoof of Hitchcock classics about a psychiatrist who works at "The Psycho-Neurotic Institute for the Very, Very Nervous." The film is better if you've seen the Hitchcock films on which the parody builds.

House of Games (1987) Crime ΨΨ
Lindsay Crouse plays the lead role as a psychiatrist who has just written an important book on obsessive-compulsive disorders. She becomes obsessed with confidence games and is slowly drawn into the criminal life.

In the Bedroom (2001) Drama/Suspense ΨΨΨΨ
Introspective film with a talented cast that examines grief, despair, and revenge after the murder of someone deeply loved. Marisa Tomei's character develops an acute stress disorder following the trauma. The film makes good use of silence; these scenes underscore the tension, unspoken feelings, and underlying pain associated with the death of a loved one.

Inside Out (1986) Drama ΨΨ
A little-known but interesting film in which Elliott Gould plays a man with agoraphobia. He is able to obtain food, sex, and haircuts in his home, but finds that he cannot meet *all* his needs without leaving his house.

"What does your therapist think of all this?" "Oh, I would never tell my therapist." "Why not?" "Because it's private."

Dialogue in *Kissing Jessica Stein* (2002)

Kissing Jessica Stein (2002) Comedy ΨΨΨ
Quality independent film about a neurotic, young woman who in exploring her sexuality and intrapersonal life is able to extend beyond her rigidity and generalized anxiety.

Lady in a Cage (1964) Drama/Suspense ΨΨ
Olivia de Havilland plays an upper class woman trapped inside her home elevator. The film melodramatically portrays claustrophobia and panic.

"Take it all but in the name of humanity, let me out of this cage."

Cornelia Hilyard in *Lady in a Cage* (1964)

Matador, The (2005) Comedy ΨΨ
Pierce Brosnan plays a narcissistic, antisocial "hit man." He suffers from panic attacks (without agoraphobia) that affect his ability to work.

> "Look, Doc, I spent last Tuesday watching fibers on my carpet. And the whole time I was watching my carpet, I was worrying that I, I might vomit. And the whole time, I was thinking, 'I'm a grown man. I should know what goes on my head.' And the more I thought about it ... the more I realized that I should just blow my brains out and end it all. But then ... I start worrying about what that was going to do to my goddamn carpet. Okay, so, ah-he, that was a GOOD day, Doc. And, and I just want you to give me some pills and let me get on with my life."
>
> Roy Waller in *Matchstick Men* (2003)

Matchstick Men (2003) Comedy ΨΨΨΨ
Nicholas Cage plays Roy Waller, a con man with OCD, agoraphobia with panic, tics, and antisocial personality in this interesting Ridley Scott film. Upon meeting his estranged daughter things begin to change for Waller.

Nothing (2003) Comedy ΨΨΨ
A Vincenzo Natali film about two men who make things disappear by hating and wishing. The film is based on the relationship two good friends, a travel agent who works from home and suffers from severe agoraphobia and a self-absorbed loser who is treated with contempt.

Obsession (1976) Thriller Ψ
Brian De Palma version of Hitchcock's *Vertigo*. The De Palma film doesn't live up to the original.

Open Water (2003) Suspense Ψ
A young couple on a scuba diving trip are left behind to fend for themselves. Sharks circle, distant boats do not see the divers, and fish bite at them. While the film depicts the terror someone would experience if abandoned in the open water, it is not a notable depiction of an anxiety disorder.

Panic Room (2002) Crime/Suspense Ψ
Jodie Foster plays a claustrophobic woman who becomes imprisoned in the panic room of her house when burglars enter.

> "Sergeant, I want you to arrange for the immediate transfer of this baby out of my regiment. I won't have any of our brave men contaminated by him."
>
> *Paths of Glory* (1957)

Phobia (1980) Horror/Mystery Ψ
Canadian film about the systematic murders of phobic psychiatric patients.

Phoebe in Wonderland (2008) Drama ΨΨΨ
Felicity Huffman plays the role of a young girl with an obsessive-compulsive disorder and Tourette's disorder who engages in repetitive hand washing; there is an unflattering portrayal of a psychiatrist in the film.

> "You are all so ready to label, medicate, and move on as if a name means something, as if all the answers are in a bottle. I've seen that solution. I have seen it all around me, and it is a life of side effects and dulled minds. Your profession just doesn't like kids to be kids."
>
> A mother berates a child psychiatrist in *Phoebe in Wonderland* (2008)

Play It Again, Sam (1972) Comedy/Romance ΨΨΨ
Early Woody Allen film depicting social anxiety. A neurotic film critic's wife leaves him, and he is crushed. His hero is a tough guy (Humphrey Bogart) whose apparition begins showing up to give him advice. He actually tries dating again and is unsuccessful until he learns to relax.

Raiders of the Lost Ark (1981) Adventure ΨΨ
Steven Spielberg film with Harrison Ford as anthropologist Indiana Jones, who is forced by the situational demands of heroism to overcome his snake phobia.

Red Eye (2005) Horror/Thriller Ψ
Wes Craven film portraying a character who hates to fly but finds herself on the red eye flight to Miami trapped with a villainous and charming middle-man in a plot to assassinate a Homeland Security official.

Roommate, The (2011) Drama/Thriller Ψ
A freshman at UCLA finds life gets complicated after her roommate becomes obsessed with her.

She's One of Us (2003, France) Drama ΨΨ
A socially awkward and anxious woman struggles in her social interactions. Watch for echoes of Dostoyevsky's "Dream of a Ridiculous Man."

Something's Gotta Give (2003) Comedy ΨΨ
Jack Nicholson plays a 63-year-old man obsessed with younger women; he has a genuine heart attack that is followed by a series of panic attacks.

Stranger than Fiction (2006) Comedy ΨΨΨ
An IRS auditor (Will Ferrell) suddenly finds himself the subject of a novel being read by the author that only the auditor can hear. The narration affects his entire life – his work, relationships, living situation, and livelihood – including his obsessive behavior (e.g., counting toothbrush strokes and steps).

Unmarried Woman, An (1978) Drama/Comedy ΨΨΨ
Tender, sensitive, and funny film about Jill Clayburgh learning to cope with the stress of being a single parent after her husband abandons her. Her friends, a psychiatrist, and an affair with Alan Bates all help.

> "I have this acrophobia. I wake up at night and I see that man falling."
>
> John Ferguson describing his symptoms in
> *Vertigo* (1958)

Vertigo (1958) Thriller ΨΨΨΨΨ
Wonderful Hitchcock film in which James Stewart plays a character whose life is dominated by his fear of heights. He attempts a self-created behavior modification program early in the film without success.

Waiting for Ronald (2003) Short Film/Drama ΨΨΨ
This short film about a man who leaves a supervised residence to live with a friend in the community depicts OCD with a hand-washing compulsion.

War of the Worlds (2005) Action ΨΨ
Directed by Steven Spielberg and starring Tom Cruise, Dakota Fanning, and Tim Robbins, this film depicts the impact of an alien invasion on a blue-collar father and two children. Cruise's character responds to tragedy with shock; his daughter develops a phobia; and Robbins' character has a psychotic break.

What About Bob? (1991) Comedy ΨΨ
Bill Murray plays an anxious patient who cannot function without his psychiatrist, played by Richard Dreyfuss. Not a great film, but a fun movie that explores the doctor–patient relationship and the obsessive-compulsive personality.

Whole (2003) Documentary ΨΨ
Fascinating documentary about individuals who have a strong desire to have one of their limbs amputated, despite being totally healthy. Presents interesting differential diagnostic questions. Is this OCD, body dysmorphic disorder, an identity disorder, or self-mutilation? One psychiatrist, who interviewed 53 people with this condition, proposed the rubric *body integrity identity disorder.*

> "As a four limb person, I don't feel incomplete. It's more of a feeling that my body doesn't belong to me."
> "The relief from the 50 years of torment I had was indescribable."
> "I'm complete now."
>
> Comments from individuals who want or have had healthy limbs removed in *Whole* (2003)

Without a Paddle (2004) Drama/Comedy Ψ
Three friends go canoeing after the death of a friend. One is painfully neurotic with numerous phobias including fear of small spaces, the dark, and cellophane wrap. He copes with difficult situations by pretending he is a *Star Wars* character.

Woman, a Gun, and a Noodle Shop, A (2009, China/Hong Kong) Drama/Comedy ΨΨΨ
Zhang Yimou film depicting a number of quirky characters, including one with severe anxiety.

Young Adult (2011) Drama ΨΨ
Charlize Theron plays a young woman who returns to her hometown, hoping to recapture her youth and her former boyfriend (who is now married). Among other problems, Theron's character suffers from trichotillomania.

Zombieland (2009) Horror Comedy Ψ
Four people team up to avoid zombies on a trip to California. One character has multiple phobias including a fear of clowns and a fear of rags used to wipe off tables.

Trauma and Stressor-Related Disorders

Alive (1993) Action/Adventure/Drama ΨΨ
The survivors of a plane crash in the Andes survive for more than 70 days by eating the passengers who died. The film is a vivid portrayal of traumatic stress and its consequences.

> "Oh, God! why did they do this to us? We only wanted to live, you and I. Why should they send us out to fight each other? If they threw away these rifles and these uniforms, you could be my brother, just like Kat and Albert. You'll have to forgive me, comrade. I'll do all I can. I'll write to your parents."
>
> Paul attempts to comfort a man he has killed in *All Quiet on the Western Front* (1930)

All Quiet on the Western Front (1930) Drama ΨΨΨΨΨ
This remarkable film illustrates the horror of war and celebrates pacifism as its only solution. The film poignantly documents that it is young men who fight our wars and shows the folly of jingoism and blind patriotism.

Best in Show (2000) Comedy ΨΨ
A couple entering their beloved dog in a competitive dog show continuously fight; their fights escalate in response to the tension and anxiety associated with the show. They later cure themselves of their "adjustment" problem by blaming their dog for being self-deprecating and purchase a new dog who does not mind watching them have sex.

Best Years of Our Lives, The (1946) Drama ΨΨΨΨ
Sam Goldwyn film about servicemen adjusting to civilian life after the war. One of the sailors has lost both hands.

Big Parade, The (1925) Romance/War ΨΨΨΨ
This epic film about World War I gives the viewer a sense of the stress of combat and the trauma of returning to civilian life minus a leg or an arm.

Birdy (1984) Drama/War ΨΨΨΨ
Nicolas Cage tries to help his friend, Matthew Modine, who is a catatonic inpatient in a military hospital. Both men are Vietnam veterans, but Modine's problems seem to predate the war.

Black Rain (1989) Drama ΨΨΨ
Black-and-white film by Japanese filmmaker Shohei Imamura about the aftermath of the bombing of Hiroshima and its long-term psychological effects.

> "Who's gonna love me, Dad? Whoever's going to love me?"
>
> Ron Kovic in *Born on the Fourth of July* (1989)

Born on the Fourth of July (1989) Drama/War/Biography ΨΨΨΨ
Oliver Stone film about the anger, frustration, rage, and coping of paralyzed Vietnam veteran Ron Kovic (Tom Cruise). Kovic was thrown out of the 1972 Republican convention, but went on to address the Democratic convention in 1976. The film has especially memorable VA hospital scenes.

Boy and the Bus, The (2013, UK) Drama/Family ΨΨΨ
Short film about a boy coping with the loss of his mother and new living environment. He takes up "racing" a bus by running across the land.

Brave One, The (2007) Crime/Thriller Ψ
Jodie Foster plays newlywed a radio talk show host. She survives a brutal attack that leaves her fiancé dead. Following the attack, she is extremely anxious, yet she forces herself to get revenge.

Brothers (2009) Drama ΨΨΨΨ
A powerful film in which one brother (Tobey Maguire) is tortured for months in Afghanistan and forced to beat another POW to death; when he returns to the states, his PTSD threatens to unravel his family, he develops symptoms of paranoia, and he becomes convinced that his wife has been having an affair with his brother.

Casualties of War (1989) War ΨΨΨ
Brian De Palma film about five GIs who kidnap, rape, and murder a young Vietnamese girl. The film deals with themes of guilt, stress, violence, and, most of all, the dehumanizing aspects of war.

Coming Home (1978) Drama/War ΨΨΨΨ
Jon Voigt plays a paraplegic veteran who becomes Jane Fonda's lover in this sensitive antiwar film. Fonda's Marine Corps husband winds up committing suicide. Interesting analysis of the various ways different people respond to the stress of war.

Deer Hunter, The (1978) War ΨΨΨΨ
Robert De Niro in an unforgettable film about how Vietnam affects the lives of three high school buddies. The Russian roulette sequences are among the most powerful scenes in film history. Psychopathology themes include drug abuse, PTSD, and depression. The movie won five Academy Awards, including one for Best Picture, and De Niro has described it as his finest film.

Dry Land, The (2010) Drama ΨΨΨ
An Iraq war veteran returns to his Texas home, only to discover that you can't go home again. The film presents a vivid and accurate picture of the symptoms of posttraumatic stress disorder (PTSD).

Enduring Love (2004) Drama/Mystery ΨΨΨ
Several men try to save a boy in a hot air balloon that is out of control. All but one let go and the one who hangs on dies; the resulting PTSD and a character with delusional disorder are portrayed.

Experiment, The (2010) Drama ΨΨΨ
This interesting film is a remake of *Das Experiment, a 2001* film based on Philip Zimbardo's infamous Stanford Prison Experiment. Both films document the effects of stress and show how life in an abnormal environment affects human behavior. Watching the film may help you understand some of the more egregious abuses that oc-

curred at Abu Ghraib. (Zimbardo testified as an expert witness for the defense and wrote a book, *The Lucifer Effect*, based on this experience.)

Falling Down (1994) Drama ΨΨΨ
Good presentation by Michael Douglas of the cumulative effects of stress on a marginal personality. The film does not give us enough information to clearly diagnose the character played by Douglas, but he does display significant symptoms of paranoia.

Fearless (1993) Drama ΨΨΨΨ
Jeff Bridges in an engaging film that portrays some of the symptoms of anxiety in airline crash survivors. Interesting vignettes show group therapy for PTSD victims.

Fever Pitch (2005) Comedy Ψ
Jimmy Fallon's character has an obsession with the Boston Red Sox and struggles to adjust to a new relationship that impacts his passion. American remake of the 1997 UK film of the same title, based on the Nick Hornby novel, in which the main character's (Colin Firth) obsession is with the Arsenal soccer team.

Final Cut, The (2004) Drama/Thriller Ψ
Some PTSD symptoms are displayed in a man (Robin Williams) who creates "rememories" for people at funerals using a microchip implanted in the people's heads while they were living.

Fisher King, The (1991) Drama/Fantasy/Comedy
ΨΨΨΨ
Jeff Bridges plays a former talk show personality who unwittingly encourages a listener to go on a shooting spree. Bridges' withdrawal, cynicism, and substance use can all be interpreted and understood in the context of a PTSD.

"If you ladies leave my island, if you survive recruit training, you will be a weapon. You will be a minister of death praying for war. But until that day you are pukes. You are the lowest form of life on Earth. You are not even human fucking beings. You are nothing but unorganized pieces of amphibian shit! Because I am hard, you will not like me. But the more you hate me, the more you will learn. I am hard but I am fair. There is no racial bigotry here. I do not look down on niggers, kikes, wops or greasers. Here you are all equally worthless. And my orders are to weed out all non-hackers who do not pack the gear to serve in my beloved Corps. Do you maggots understand that?"

Gunnery Sergeant Hartman in
Full Metal Jacket (1987)

Full Metal Jacket (1987) Drama ΨΨΨ
This Stanley Kubrick film captures the horror of war – but also the stress of basic training. The latrine homicide/suicide scene in which Private Pyle kills his drill sergeant and then himself is unforgettable.

Glengarry Glen Ross (1992) Drama ΨΨΨ
A hard-hitting and powerful presentation of job-related stress and interpersonal conflict in the real estate business. Wonderful cast, with Jack Lemmon playing a figure whose despair over his job is reminiscent of Willy Loman in Arthur Miller's *Death of a Salesman*.

Hamburger Hill (1987) War ΨΨ
A graphic presentation of the stress and horror of war.

Hammer, The (2011) Biography ΨΨΨ
Matt Hamill becomes the first deaf wrestler to win a National Collegiate Championship, but not without significant social struggles and duress.

Home of the Brave (2006) Action/Drama ΨΨΨ
Soldiers returning from the war in Iraq attempt to reintegrate back home but struggle with the memories and ramifications of having served in war. Winner of a Voice Award.

Hurt Locker, The (2008) Drama ΨΨΨΨ
A soldier who is an expert at dismantling improvised explosive devices (IEDs) in Iraq finds civilian life insipid and boring. The opening quotation captures the theme of the film: "The rush of battle is often a potent and lethal addiction, for war is a drug."

"You love playing with that. You love playing with all your stuffed animals. You love your Mommy, your Daddy. You love your pajamas. You love everything, don't ya? Yea. But you know what, buddy? As you get older... some of the things you love might not seem so special anymore. Like your Jack-in-a-Box. Maybe you'll realize it's just a piece of tin and a stuffed animal. And the older you get, the fewer things you really love. And by the time you get to my age, maybe it's only one or two things. With me, I think it's one."

Staff Sergeant James thinking about defusing
bombs as he speaks to his young son,
The Hurt Locker (2008)

In Country (1989) Drama ΨΨ
Bruce Willis plays a Vietnam veteran with PTSD who is unable to relate meaningfully to the world around him until he visits the Vietnam memorial.

Invisible War, The (2012) Documentary ΨΨΨΨ
An examination of rape in the military, a problem of epidemic proportions. The film will help students appreciate the psychological sequelae of rape.

Jacob's Ladder (1990) Drama ΨΨ
Complex film about a Vietnam veteran who has dramatic hallucinations of indeterminate etiology (possibly the result of military exposure to experimental drugs).

Last Kiss, The (2006) Drama ΨΨΨ
Cautionary tale, particularly for those around age 30 about midlife issues, falling in love, rites of passage, fear of commitment, and the importance of honesty. The film also portrays adjustment disorder.

M*A*S*H (1970) Comedy/War ΨΨΨ
Wonderfully funny Robert Altman film about military surgeons and nurses who use alcohol, sex, and humor to cope with the stress of war. The portrayal of Hawkeye Pierce, half-drunk but always ready for surgery, is troubling for mental health professionals.

Manchurian Candidate, The (2004) Drama/Suspense ΨΨΨ
The new version of this classic film stars Denzel Washington as a Gulf War veteran with PTSD, paranoia, and memories he cannot understand, which lead him to unravel a conspiracy involving brain washing and political maneuvering.

Manchurian Candidate, The (1962) Drama/Suspense ΨΨΨ
Original version stars Frank Sinatra as the veteran who experiences flashbacks and PTSD symptoms.

Martha Marcy May Marlene (2011) Drama ΨΨΨΨ
A woman disengages from her family and spends two years in a cult; she eventually becomes disenchanted, but when she eventually manages to escape to her sister's house, she experiences an acute stress disorder and behaves oddly and inappropriately. A related short film, *Mary Last Seen,* depicts the ways in which cult members manipulate newcomers.

Melvin Goes to Dinner (2003) Comedy ΨΨΨ
Interesting dialogue film about an unplanned get-together between four people. They discuss religion, God, faith, ghosts, affairs, and sex. The character Melvin probably has an adjustment disorder.

Men, The (1950) Drama ΨΨΨ
Marlon Brando in his first film plays a paralyzed World War II veteran full of rage about his injury and his limitations.

Mother Ghost (2002) Drama ΨΨΨ
A man (Mark Thompson) begins to have significant adjustment problems after his mother's death (she died a year ago) resulting in marital conflict, increased alcohol use, and other personal problems. Interesting interaction and therapy with a radio psychologist (Kevin Pollack) on the air.

My House in Umbria (2003) Drama ΨΨ
A made for TV movie in which Dame Maggie Smith plays one of four survivors of a railway bombing

Ordinary People (1980) Drama ΨΨΨΨ
This film was Robert Redford's debut as a director. It deals with depression, suicide, and family pathology and presents a sympathetic portrayal of a psychiatrist, played by Judd Hirsch. Conrad, the protagonist, would meet *DSM-5* criteria for PTSD as well as depression.

Outrage, The (1964) Drama ΨΨΨ
Three versions of the details of a rape and murder are related in this updated remake of Akira Kurosawa's *Rashomon.* Paul Newman plays the outlaw in the film.

Pan's Labyrinth (2006, Spain/Mexico) ΨΨΨΨ
The imaginative, young Ofelia manages the trauma of her situation and the tyrant behavior of her stepfather by creating a world of fantasy.

Paths of Glory (1957) War ΨΨΨΨ
Kirk Douglas in an early Stanley Kubrick film about the horrors and stupidity of World War I. There is a memorable scene in which a general repeatedly slaps a soldier, trying without success to bring him out of his shell-shocked state. The scene was repeated in the 1970 film *Patton.*

Pawnbroker, The (1965) Drama ΨΨΨ
Rod Steiger plays a concentration camp survivor who watched his wife being raped and his children being murdered; he copes by becoming numb. Interesting flashback scenes. Steiger lost the 1965 Academy Award for Best Actor to Lee Marvin in *Cat Ballou.*

Patton (1970) War/Biography ΨΨΨΨ
George C. Scott is perfect in the role of the controversial general who was relieved of his command after slapping a crying soldier who had been hospitalized for combat fatigue, or what would now be called PTSD. The film won an Academy Award for Best Picture and George C. Scott won the Oscar for Best Actor.

"I want you to remember that no bastard ever won a war by dying for his country. He won it by making the other poor dumb bastard die for his country."

General George S. Patton Jr. in *Patton* (1970)

Princess and the Warrior, The (2000) Drama ΨΨΨΨ
A nurse at a psychiatric hospital is hit by a truck and saved by a crook who cuts a hole in her throat and breathes for her. Upon recovering, the nurse goes on a journey of purpose to find this man. A minor character has PTSD. One intensely graphic and chilling scene depicts a kind-hearted adolescent with **pica**; believing the nurse has rejected him, the teenager eats glass.

San Francisco (1936) Romance/Disaster ΨΨΨ
This is one of the greatest disaster films ever made, and the special effects give the viewer some appreciation for the acute stress one would experience in a real earthquake. Clark Gable and Spencer Tracy have memorable roles in this film.

Secret Lives of Dentists, The (2002) Drama ΨΨ
A married couple, both dentists, is unable to adjust to both living and working together. One begins an affair while the other stews in anger.

Shoah (1985) Documentary ΨΨΨΨΨ
Widely praised 9-hr documentary about the Holocaust. The film offers some insight into the behavior of both the German officials and their victims and illustrates antisocial personalities and PTSDs.

Story of Us, The (1999) Comedy/Drama ΨΨ
Bruce Willis and Michelle Pfeiffer star as a couple on the brink of separation after 15 years of marriage. Directed by Rob Reiner.

Stuck (2007) Horror ΨΨ
A nurse's aid driving home from a party is high on ecstasy when she hits a homeless man who becomes lodged in her windshield. She hides the man, still stuck, in her garage while she makes love with her boyfriend, eventually deciding it is better to kill the victim than to risk a potential driving-under-the-influence charge.

Tennis, Anyone…? (2005) Comedy ΨΨ
Two small time actors cope with life and find meaning despite the significant stressors in their lives.

Twelve O'Clock High (1949) War ΨΨΨ
Gregory Peck in an interesting presentation of the stress of combat and the ways in which leaders can influence the behavior of those they lead.

Upside of Anger, The (2005) Comedy/Drama ΨΨΨ
Joan Allen portrays a woman with an adjustment disorder who discovers her husband has gone off to Sweden with another woman leaving his home and family. She befriends a jovial alcoholic to cope with her anger and the family disruption.

Walking on Water (2002) Drama ΨΨ
Australian film about a man who becomes haunted by intrusive memories and deteriorates into self-destructive behavior after suffocating a gay friend who was dying of AIDS.

Dissociative Disorders

3 Women (1977) Drama ΨΨΨΨ
Strange but engaging Robert Altman film about two California women who seem to exchange personalities.

Altered States (1980) Science Fiction ΨΨ
Not entirely satisfying film based in part on the sensory deprivation experiments of Dr. John Lilly. The scientist (William Hurt) combines isolation tanks with psychedelic mushrooms to induce altered states of consciousness. Good special effects.

"This is poetry, and don't you deny it. Come back to me when you've written something really perverse, really depraved."

An editor reviews Isabelle's work in *Amateur* (1994)

Amateur (1994) Drama/Comedy ΨΨ
Hal Hartley film in which a man who is amnestic as a result of a traumatic head injury takes up with a nun who has left the convent to write pornographic novels. Almost every character in the film has a complex double identity and is uncertain about who he or she *really* is.

Anastasia (1956) Drama ΨΨΨΨ
Yul Brynner, Helen Hayes, and Ingrid Bergman star in this film about an amnestic woman who is believed to be the lost princess Anastasia, daughter of the last czar of Russia.

Black Friday (1940) Horror ΨΨ
Boris Karloff and Bela Lugosi star in this film about transplanting a gangster's brain in a college professor's cranium.

Butterfly Effect, The (2003) Drama/Suspense ΨΨ
A young man (Ashton Kutcher) tries to change his traumatic past with unpredictable and increasingly problematic consequences. When he reflects on blackouts, he enters the memory and is able to change it for the long-term but must face the consequences of the change each time. The film attempts to depict chaos theory.

Dark Mirror, The (1946) Thriller Ψ
Olivia De Havilland plays both parts in a story of twin sisters, one of whom is a deranged killer.

Dead Again (1991) Mystery/Romance ΨΨΨ
Emma Thompson costars with her husband, Kenneth Branagh (who also directed the film). The movie illustrates traumatic amnesia and its treatment through hypnosis. The hypnotist, an antique dealer, is not the most professional of therapists!

Despair (1979) Drama ΨΨΨΨ
Fassbinder film based on a novel by Vladimir Nabokov. A Russian Jew émigré in Germany who runs a chocolate factory kills another man who looks like him, and tries to pass it off as his own suicide. When his plan fails, he becomes psychotic.

Devils, The (1971) Drama/Historical ΨΨΨ
Ken Russell film adapted from Aldous Huxley's book *The Devils of Loundun*. The film traces the lives of 17th-century French nuns who experienced highly erotic dissociative states attributed to possession by the devil.

Double Life of Veronique, The (1991) Fantasy/Drama ΨΨ
The lives of two women turn out to be linked in complex ways the viewer never fully understands.

Double Life, A (1947) Crime ΨΨ
Ronald Coleman plays an actor who is unable to sort out his theatrical life (in which he plays Othello) and his personal life.

Dr. Jekyll and Mr. Hyde (1932) Horror ΨΨΨΨ
Fredric March in the best adaptation of Robert Louis Stevenson's classic story about the ultimate dissociative disorder. Stevenson was an alcoholic, and the mysterious liquid that dramatically transforms Jekyll's personality may be a metaphor for alcohol.

Exorcist, The (1973) Horror ΨΨ
Linda Blair stars as a 12-year-old girl possessed by the devil in William Friedkin's film based on the William Peter Blatty novel. One of the most suspenseful films ever made.

"It's only after we've lost everything [that] we are free to do anything."

A premise of *Fight Club* (1999)

Fight Club (1999) Drama/Suspense ΨΨΨΨ
A disillusioned, insomniac (Edward Norton) meets a dangerous, malcontent part of himself in the character of Brad Pitt. Norton then establishes "fight clubs" in which men can unload their aggressions onto one another.

Forgotten, The (2004) Drama ΨΨ
A woman grieving over the loss of her 9-year-old son is told by her husband and her therapist that her son never existed, and that all her memories were created in response to a miscarriage. The mother isn't buying it.

Frankie & Alice (2010) Drama ΨΨ
Halle Berry plays the role of Alice, a Los Angeles woman with dissociative identity disorder (DID) and three personalities: (1) Francine L. Murdoch, Black woman, age 32, IQ 132; (2) Alice, White woman, age unknown, IQ 102. (3) Genius, Black female, age 8–12, IQ 156. The film is based on a true story.

Girl Cut in Two, A (2007, France) Drama ΨΨΨ
A Claude Chabrol film about a weatherwoman is being pursued by two suitors: an older, married novelist and the young heir to a pharmaceutical fortune. She falls in love with the older man who introduces her to sexual adventure, but she eventually marries the younger man.

Great Dictator, The (1940) Comedy ΨΨ
A satire of Adolph Hitler, with Charlie Chaplin in the role of a Jewish barber who suffers amnesia and eventually finds himself assuming the personality of Adenoid Hynkel, the dictator of Tomania.

Identity (2003) Suspense/Thriller ΨΨΨ
A serial killer with a dissociative identity disorder (DID) is at his final hearing before receiving the death penalty. This story juxtaposes with another tale of several people suddenly stuck at an isolated motel and living in terror as they are killed one by one. These two components are cleverly weaved together as the people represent DID alters being killed off.

Interpersonalities (2008) Mystery ΨΨΨ
Short film that depicts a number of character interactions, including a psychiatrist, which are based on various alters of the protagonist's personality.

Last Temptation of Christ, The (1988) Religious ΨΨΨ
Challenging and controversial Martin Scorsese film in which Jesus, while on the cross and in great pain, has a dissociative episode in which he imagines himself as an ordinary man who married Mary Magdalene and lived a normal life.

Lizzie (1957) Drama ΨΨ
Eleanor Parker, a woman with DID is treated by psychiatrist Richard Boone.

Method (2003) Suspense/Thriller Ψ
An actress studying and playing the role of a past serial killer tries too hard to "feel her character," and she dissociates and takes on her model's past behavior.

Mirage (1965) Drama ΨΨ
A scientist who makes an important discovery develops amnesia after viewing the death of a friend.

My Girl (1991) Drama/Comedy ΨΨ
The film centers on an 11-year-old girl whose mother has just died and whose grandmother has Alzheimer's disease. The child responds by developing a series of imaginary disorders. Strong performances by Dan Aykroyd and Jamie Lee Curtis.

Nurse Betty (2000) Drama/Mystery ΨΨΨΨ
Neil LaBute film about a woman (Renée Zellweger) who witnesses a traumatic event and develops a dissociative fugue. She travels to Los Angeles to find a character in a soap opera. Zellweger's character presents an interesting springboard for a debate about the differences between dissociative fugue and delusional disorder.

Numb (2007) Drama ΨΨ
Matthew Perry portrays a character who develops a depersonalization disorder that he overcomes by falling in love.

Overboard (1987) Comedy ΨΨ
Goldie Hawn plays a haughty millionaire who develops amnesia and is claimed by an Oregon carpenter as his wife and forced to care for his children.

Paris, Texas (1984) Drama ΨΨΨ
Wim Wenders film about a man found wandering in the desert with no personal memory.

Peacock (2009) Drama ΨΨΨ
A timid and unassuming bank clerk is found to be living a double life when a train crashes into his home. Cillian Murphy is extraordinary, playing both the male and female personalities.

Persona (1966) Drama ΨΨΨΨΨ
Complex, demanding, and absolutely fascinating Bergman film starring Liv Ullmann as an actress who suddenly stops talking after one of her performances. A nurse treats Ullmann, and the two women appear to exchange "personas."

"I have not spoken since I was six years old. Nobody knows why, least of all myself."

Ada's thoughts at the beginning of *The Piano* (1993)

Piano, The (1993) Drama ΨΨΨΨΨ
Jane Campion film about a woman who had voluntarily stopped speaking as a child. She communicates with written notes and through playing the piano, a pleasure forbidden to her by her New Zealand husband. There are scenes of extraordinary sensuality between characters played by Harvey Keitel and Holly Hunter and a dramatic suicide attempt.

Poison Ivy (1992) Drama Ψ
A newcomer into a pathological family plans to take over the role of wife and mother. The father is an alcoholic and the mother is a hypochondriac.

Prelude to a Kiss (1992) Comedy/Romance ΨΨ
The ultimate example of a dissociative disorder. A beautiful young woman and a sad old man kiss on her wedding day and exchange bodies. The film makes this extraordinary event seem almost plausible.

Primal Fear (1996) Drama ΨΨΨ
Richard Gere stars in this suspenseful drama about a man who commits heinous crimes, ostensibly as a result of a dissociative disorder. The film raises useful questions about the problem of malingering and differential diagnosis.

Psycho (1960) Horror/Thriller ΨΨΨΨΨ
Wonderful Hitchcock film starring Anthony Perkins as Norman Bates, who vacillates between his passive, morbid personality and his alter ego as his dead mother. In the final minutes of the film, a psychiatrist offers a somewhat confused explanation for Bates's behavior. The shower scene is one of the most famous scenes in film history.

"Mother, my mother, uh, what is the phrase? – She isn't qu-quite herself today."

Norman Bates in *Psycho* (1960)

Raising Cain (1992) Thriller/Drama Ψ
Confusing De Palma film about a child psychologist with multiple personalities who begins to kill women and steal their children for experiments.

Return of Martin Guerre, The (1982) Historical ΨΨΨ
Gerard Depardieu as a 16th-century peasant who returns to his wife after a 7-year absence. His true identity is never made clear. This film, the basis for the American movie *Sommersby,* was based on a true story.

Secret Window (2004) Drama/Suspense ΨΨΨ
Mort Rainey (Johnny Depp) finds his wife cheating on him in a motel; the film jumps forward 6 months to a scene in which Mort is an isolated writer in a house in the woods and now separated from his wife. He is visited and threatened by an odd psychopath (John Turturro). Based on the Stephen King short story, "Secret Window, Secret Garden."

Sisters (1973) Thriller/Horror ΨΨ
De Palma film about Siamese twins separated as children; one is good, the other quite evil. The use of Siamese twins is a Hitchcock-like twist on the theme of multiple personality.

Sommersby (1993) Drama ΨΨ
Richard Gere returns to wife Jodie Foster after a 6-year absence during the Civil War. Gere is remarkably changed, so much so that it appears he is a different man.

Spellbound (1945) Thriller ΨΨΨΨ
Ingrid Bergman and Gregory Peck star in this Hitchcock thriller. Peck is an amnestic patient who believes he has committed a murder; Bergman is the psychiatrist who falls in love with him and helps him recall the childhood trauma responsible for his dissociative state.

Steppenwolf (1974) Drama ΨΨ
Film adaptation of Herman Hesse's remarkable novel about Harry Haller (played by Max von Sydow), a misanthropic protagonist who wrestles with the competing forces of good and evil within himself.

Stigmata (1999) Suspense/Horror Ψ
A beautician begins to have episodes of visions, seizures, and stigmata wounds on her body after her mother sends her a sacred rosary from Brazil.

Suddenly, Last Summer (1959) Drama ΨΨΨ
Adaptation of a Tennessee Williams story about an enmeshed and pathological relationship between a mother (Katharine Hepburn) and her homosexual son and a dissociative amnesia in a cousin who witnessed the son's death. Among its other virtues, the film includes a fascinating discussion of the benefits of lobotomy.

"He-he was lying naked on the broken stones ... It looked as if-as if they had devoured him!... As if they'd torn or cut parts of him away with their hands, or with knives, or those jagged tin cans they made music with. As if they'd torn bits of him away in strips!"

Suddenly, Last Summer (1959)

Sullivan's Travels (1941) Comedy/Drama ΨΨΨΨ
Joel McCrea plays a movie director who goes out to experience life as it is lived outside a Hollywood studio. He winds up getting a head injury, becoming amnestic, and being sentenced to six years on a chain gang.

Sybil (1976) Drama ΨΨΨ
Made-for-TV movie in which Joanne Woodward, the patient in *The Three Faces of Eve*, plays the psychiatrist treating a woman with 16 different personalities.

Thérèse: The Story of Saint Thérèse of Lisieux (2004) Drama ΨΨΨ
The story of Saint Thérèse, the Carmelite nun who wrote *Story of a Soul*, and suffered from various somatic symptoms.

Three Faces of Eve, The (1957) Drama ΨΨΨΨ
Joanne Woodward won an Academy Award for her portrayal of a woman with three personalities (Eve White, Eve Black, and Jane); based on the book by Thigpin and Cleckley.

Unknown White Male (2005) Drama ΨΨΨΨ
An excellent exploration of the fugue state based on a true story about a man who discovers himself on a Coney Island subway with no recollection of who he is or how he got there.

Voices Within: The Lives of Truddi Chase (1990) Drama ΨΨ
Made-for-TV movie about a woman with multiple personality disorder; based on the best selling-book *When Rabbit Howls*.

Whatever Happened to Baby Jane? (1962) Drama ΨΨΨ
Bette Davis and Joan Crawford star as two elderly sisters who were formerly movie stars. Jane (Bette Davis) had been a child star, but her fame was eclipsed by the renown of her talented sister, now confined to a wheelchair. Jane torments her sister and experiences a dramatic dissociative episode in the final scene in the movie.

X-Men: The Last Stand (2006) Action/Science Fiction ΨΨ
Superheroine mutant Jean Grey is portrayed as someone with a DID; the actress playing the role researched DID to make her character more realistic.

Zelig (1983) Comedy ΨΨ
Quasi-documentary about Woody Allen as Zelig, a human chameleon whose personality changes to match that of whomever he is around. He is treated by psychiatrist Mia Farrow, whom Zelig eventually marries. Watch for Susan Sontag, Saul Bellow, and Bruno Bettelheim.

Somatic Symptom, Feeding, Eating, Elimination, & Sleep-Wake Disorders
(Note: Physical illnesses, diseases and deformities are also depicted in this section.)

2 Days in Paris (2007) Romance ΨΨΨ
Julie Delpy film about a couple, each with distinct psychological problems – him with a somatic symptom disorder and her with an intermittent explosive disorder.

3 Needles (2005) Drama Ψ
Brutal and disturbing film depicting the transmission of HIV and the misconceptions that arise (e.g., the belief that having sex with a virgin will cure the disease).

12 Angry Men (1957) Drama ΨΨΨΨΨ
Henry Fonda stars in this fascinating courtroom drama that illustrates social pressure, the tendency toward conformity in social settings, and the stress associated with noncompliance with societal norms.

50/50 (2011) Comedy/Drama ΨΨΨ
Based on a true story about a man who has a rare cancer with a 50% survival rate. Psychology students will appreciate the interactions between the patient and his neophyte therapist, with whom he becomes romantically involved.

61 (2001) Biography/Drama Ψ
Billy Crystal film with a subplot focused on the impact of stress on the body of Roger Maris during his quest to beat Babe Ruth's home run record.

Agnes of God (1985) Mystery ΨΨΨ
Good performances by Anne Bancroft, Meg Tilly, and Jane Fonda. Fonda plays a court-appointed psychiatrist who must make sense out of pregnancy and apparent infanticide in a local convent. Good examples of *stigmata,* an example of conversion.

Bandits (2001) Comedy ΨΨ
Loosely based on a true story about two criminals who rob banks in a non-violent way. One of the men (Billy Bob Thornton) is hypochondriacal. In interviews, Thornton stated it was not much of a "stretch" to play this role – he has acknowledged phobias for both antique furniture and plastic cutlery.

Barbarian Invasions, The (2003) Drama/Comedy ΨΨΨΨ
Friends and family gather to support a stubborn, outspoken man suffering from a terminal illness. The film vacillates from light to heavy, from the somber to the humorous. This Canadian film won an Academy Award for Best Foreign Film.

Best Little Girl in the World, The (1981) Drama ΨΨ
Good made-for-TV movie in which a psychiatrist treats a girl who is suffering from anorexia nervosa.

Blue (1993) Drama ΨΨΨΨ
British filmmaker Derek Jarman's last film; he died from AIDS shortly after the movie was completed. Jarman reviews his life and analyzes the ways in which his life has been affected by his disease.

Blue Butterfly (2004) Adventure/Drama ΨΨΨ
The mother of a terminally ill boy convinces an entomologist to take her son to the Costa Rican rainforest. The boy's brain cancer disappears and both lives are changed forever. The film is based on a true story.

Bone Collector, The (1999) Suspense/Thriller ΨΨ
Denzel Washington is a crime scene specialist with quadriplegia.

Brief History of Time, A (1992) Biography ΨΨΨ
A documentary about the life of Stephen Hawking, a theoretical physicist coping with amyotrophic lateral sclerosis.

Bubble Boy (2001) Comedy Ψ
Outlandish comedy about a boy born without immunity who must live in a bubble.

Bucket List, The (2008) Comedy ΨΨΨ
Jack Nicholson and Morgan Freeman meet as roommates in a hospital. Both are newly diagnosed with cancer and are given less than one year to live. Each makes a list of experiences they want to have before they "kick the bucket." These two very different men spend their last few months together in pursuit of their dreams.

Cactus (1986) Romance ΨΨΨ
Australian film about a woman who loses one eye and considers giving up sight in the other in order to more fully understand the world of her blind lover.

Center Stage (2000) Drama ΨΨ
A woman fights her way to the top role as a dancer and performs well despite encouragement to drop out. One dancer has bulimia and the portrayal is accurate and well done; however, the film is clichéd and predictable.

Children of a Lesser God (1986) Romance ΨΨΨ
The film examines the complications involved in a love relationship between William Hurt, a teacher in a school for the deaf, and Marlee Matlin, a young deaf woman who works at the school. Much of the conflict in the film revolves around Matlin's refusal to learn to lip-read. Matlin won an Academy Award for Best Supporting Actress for her role in this film.

Chinese Roulette (1976) Drama ΨΨ
Fassbinder film about a disabled girl and the ways in which she dominates and manipulates her family.

Chrystal (2004) Drama Ψ
Independent film in which one subplot involves a woman suffering from significant chronic pain caused by a motor vehicle accident.

Cinema Paradiso (1988) Drama ΨΨΨΨ
A young boy is mesmerized by a movie theater in a small, post–World War II, Italian town, and befriends a crusty yet warm-hearted projectionist who goes blind after a fire accident. Classic Giuseppe Tornatore film.

Control (2003, Hungary) Crime/Mystery/Comedy ΨΨ
Themes of good versus evil come to life in this farcical film depicting a variety of odd characters interacting in the vast, underground Budapest subway system. One character has narcolepsy.

Common Threads: Stories from the Quilt (1989) Documentary ΨΨΨ
This HBO film examines the lives of five individuals linked by a common illness – AIDS. The movie won the Academy Award for Best Documentary Feature in 1989.

Crash of Silence (1953) Drama ΨΨ
Mother agonizes over whether to keep a hearing impaired daughter at home or send her to a special school.

Crazy Sexy Cancer (2007) Documentary ΨΨ
Young woman faces the stress of her illness by transforming her lifestyle and attitude.

Cure, The (1995) Drama ΨΨ
Two adolescent boys become best friends. One has AIDS from a blood transfusion, leading the boys to set off in search of a miracle cure.

Dance Me to My Song (1998, Australia) Drama ΨΨΨ
A woman with debilitating cerebral palsy competes with her caretaker for a love interest.

Dancer in the Dark (2000, Denmark) Drama ΨΨΨ
Björk portrays Selma, an immigrant, factory worker and single mother with limited intelligence whose vision is deteriorating. Her impending blindness affects her work, her relationships, and her personal life. Her son Gene will probably suffer the same fate unless she can pay for an operation.

Darius Goes West (2007) Documentary ΨΨΨ
Depiction of a man with Duchenne's muscular dystrophy and his journey with friends to get his wheelchair customized by MTV's "Pimp My Ride."

Deaf Smith and Johnnie Ears (1973) Western ΨΨ
A deaf Anthony Quinn teams up with Franco Nero to cope with the challenges of life in rural Texas.

Diary of a Country Priest (1951, Italy) Drama ΨΨΨΨ
A depressed priest grapples with stomach cancer and his loss of faith.

Diving Bell and the Butterfly, The (2007, France) Drama, Biography ΨΨΨΨΨ
Jean-Dominique Bauby, editor of *Elle*, emerges completely paralyzed from a 3-week coma following a stroke. He cannot speak or move his body except for his left eye. Bauby responds to his situation with creativity and bravery. Much of the film is presented in the first person to help the viewer identify with his experience.

Doctor, The (1991) Drama ΨΨΨ
William Hurt plays a cold and indifferent physician whose approach to treatment changes dramatically after he is diagnosed with throat cancer.

Dreamland (2006) Drama Ψ
Coming of age story of a young woman in a remote desert trailer park who makes many sacrifices supporting her family and a friend who has multiple sclerosis and chronic pain.

"Why don't you ask me probing questions about my childhood?"

Stephanie Anderson queries her therapist in
Duet for One (1986)

Duet for One (1986) Drama ΨΨ
Julie Andrews plays a world-class violinist who learns to cope with multiple sclerosis. Good illustration of the effects of chronic illness on psychological health. Max von Sydow plays the role of Andrews' therapist.

Dummy (1979) Drama ΨΨ
Made-for-TV movie about a hearing impaired and mute teenager who is charged with murder and defended by a deaf attorney.

Deuce Bigalow: Male Gigolo (1999) Comedy Ψ
Rob Schneider takes a job as a male escort – one of his "calls" is for a woman with Tourette's disorder and the other is a woman with narcolepsy. The latter falls asleep in the middle of her bowling stride.

Early Frost, An (1985) Drama ΨΨΨ
Excellent made-for-TV movie (available on video) that explores the pain and anguish involved as a young man

explains to his family and friends that he is gay and has AIDS.

Eating (1990) Comedy ΨΨΨ
An extended conversation that examines the relationship among life, love, and food.

Elephant Man, The (1980) Drama ΨΨΨ
David Lynch film about the life of John Merrick, a seriously deformed man who is befriended by a London physician. The film is effective in forcing the viewer to examine his or her prejudices about appearance.

"I am NOT an animal! I am a human being!"

John Merrick in *The Elephant Man* (1980)

Emmanuel's Gift (2005) Documentary ΨΨΨ
Emmanuel was born in Ghana in 1977 with a deformed leg and was destined to become a beggar. However, his mother instilled confidence and hope. This is an inspirational film that challenges negative stereotypes of people with disabilities.

Eye, The (2002) Suspense/Thriller ΨΨΨ
A young, blind woman regains her sight through a cornea transplant. She immediately begins to see ghosts which she identifies as the souls of the dead. Pang brothers film in the tradition of *The Sixth Sense* and *The Ring*.

Freud (1962) Biography ΨΨΨ
Montgomery Clift in an interesting account of the early year's of Freud's life. The film illustrates paralysis, false blindness, and a false pregnancy, all examples of somatic symptom disorders.

Gaby: A True Story (1987) Biography ΨΨΨ
A true story about a woman with cerebral palsy who goes on to become a respected author. Contrast this story with the life of Christy Brown told in *My Left Foot*.

Godsend (2004) Suspense/Thriller Ψ
Disappointing film starring Robert De Niro as a genetics researcher cloning human beings. He clones a child who begins to experience night terrors, hallucinations, delusions, and murderous behavior.

Hannah and Her Sisters (1986) Comedy/Drama ΨΨΨ
Mickey (Woody Allen) is a hopeless hypochondriac who was formerly married to Hannah (Mia Farrow). Mickey spends his days worrying about brain tumors, cancer, and cardiovascular disease.

"A week ago I bought a rifle, I went to the store - I bought a rifle! I was gonna, you know, if they told me I had a tumor, I was gonna kill myself. The only thing that might-ve stopped me - MIGHT'VE - is that my parents would be devastated. I would have to shoot them also, first. And then I have an aunt and uncle - you know - it would've been a blood bath."

Mickey contemplates his options if he is found to have a brain tumor in *Hannah and Her Sisters* (1986)

Heart Is a Lonely Hunter, The (1968) Drama ΨΨ
Alan Arkin stars in this adaptation of Carson McCuller's sad, poignant novel about a simple friendship between two men. One of the men is deaf; the other has an intellectual disability. If you have to choose between the film and the novel, read the novel.

"Guess I'm a little cranky, lack of sleep, ya know."

Insomnia (2002)

Hollywood Ending (2002) Comedy ΨΨΨ
Woody Allen film about a struggling film director (Allen), Val, who develops a conversion disorder (hysterical blindness) and has to direct the film blind.

Home of the Brave (1949) Drama/War ΨΨ
An African American soldier develops a conversion disorder following his return from combat.

Honkytonk Man (1982) Drama Ψ
Clint Eastwood produced, directed, and starred in this film about a country and western singer with leukemia who hopes to make it to Nashville before he dies.

Hunchback of Notre Dame, The (1939) Horror ΨΨΨΨΨ
Charles Laughton plays Quasimodo in this film adaptation of the Victor Hugo novel. The film is a classic in the genre examining the relationship between body image and self-concept.

I Sent a Letter to My Love (1981) Drama ΨΨΨ
French film about a sister caring for her paralyzed brother. They each seek romance by writing to a newspaper personals column; without realizing what is happening, each winds up corresponding with the other.

Ikiru (*To Live*, 1952, Japan) Drama ΨΨΨΨΨ
A city bureaucrat learns that he is dying of cancer and wants to find some meaning in his life. He becomes as-

sertive in promoting projects for the public good. Until this time, he had lived a very mundane life.

In America (2003) Drama ΨΨΨΨ
Irish family immigrates to the United States to Hell's Kitchen. They befriend a Nigerian painter who is suffering with AIDS.

In for Treatment (1979) Drama ΨΨΨ
Dutch film about the indignities suffered by a cancer patient who has to deal with an impersonal health care system.

Inception (2010) Drama ΨΨΨΨΨ
This remarkable movie was made by Christopher Nolan, who directed *Memento* in 2000. The film stars Leonardo DiCaprio as a thief who has learned to infiltrate the dreams of corporate executives so he can steal their best ideas. The film will teach you little about sleep or sleep disorders per se, but you will leave the theater thinking about the relationship between dreams, sleep, reality, consciousness, and the unconscious. Highly recommended.

Insomnia (2002) Drama/Mystery ΨΨΨΨ
Al Pacino stars as Will Dormer, a cop tracking down a minor writer (Robin Williams) in a murder investigation. Dormer deteriorates with insomnia as he battles guilt, stress, and an Alaskan environment where the sun doesn't set. Directed by Christopher Nolan.

Italian for Beginners (2002) Comedy/Drama ΨΨΨ
In a hodge-podge of interrelated stories, one character has pancreatic cancer and suffers extraordinary pain.

It's My Party (1996) Drama ΨΨΨΨ
Sensitive film about a man with AIDS who throws one last party before killing himself. Much of the film centers on the issue of voluntary suicide and the ethics of euthanasia.

I Want Someone to Eat Cheese With (2007) Comedy Ψ
Portrayal of binge-eating disorder, the challenges of keeping a diet, and Overeaters Anonymous support group meetings.

Jacquot (1993) Biography ΨΨ
Moving film about the life of French director Jacques Demy, who died from a brain tumor shortly after the film was released.

Johnnie Belinda (1948) Drama ΨΨ
Jane Wyman (who was Ronald Reagan's wife at the time) earned an Academy Award for her performance as a deaf-mute woman who is stigmatized and raped. The film is dated but still offers insights into the ways in which people who are hearing impaired are perceived.

Kurt Cobain: About a Son (2006) Documentary ΨΨ
Sensitive portrayal of the infamous grunge rock star using only interviewed audio recordings. Documents Cobain's suffering with severe stomach problems and the stress associated with his illness.

La Symphonie Pastorale (1946) Drama ΨΨΨΨ
French adaptation of André Gide novel about a Swiss minister who falls in love with his blind protégée and abandons his wife to be with her. When the blind girl later regains her sight, she is tormented by the decisions he has made because of her.

Leap of Faith (1992) Drama ΨΨ
Steve Martin plays itinerant evangelist Jonas Nightengale, whose faith healing stunts require technological support from backstage assistant Debra Winger. Contrast Martin's role with that of Burt Lancaster in *Elmer Gantry* (1960) and the documentary *Marjoe* (1972).

Life Is Sweet (1990) Drama ΨΨΨ
Mike Leigh film about a dysfunctional British family. One of the twin girls binges and purges on chocolate bars.

Life on a String (1991) Drama ΨΨΨ
Lyrical movie about a blind Chinese musician who believes his sight will be restored when he breaks his thousandth banjo string. He grows old and wise while he waits.

Light That Failed, The (1939) Drama ΨΨ
Adaptation of Kipling novel about a great artist who goes blind as a result of an injury while in Africa.

Living End, The (1992) Comedy ΨΨ
Two HIV-positive men hit the road and explore what it means to live purposively with their disease.

"Let go. It's all right. You can let go now."

Bruce Davison comforts his dying lover in
Longtime Companion (1990)

Longtime Companion (1990) Drama ΨΨΨ
This film explores the ways in which AIDS has affected a group of gay friends and traces the love and loss that is shared between two men as one of them dies from the disease.

Lost in Translation (2003) Drama ΨΨΨ
Two Americans (Bill Murray and Scarlett Johansson) stranded in Japan find solace, excitement, and friendship in one another. Both characters suffer with severe insomnia symptoms.

Loverboy (2004) Drama ΨΨ
An overly protective mother illustrates the rare but fascinating phenomenon of factitious disorder by proxy.

Machinist, The (2004, Spain) Mystery/Drama ΨΨΨΨ
Christian Bale lost 80 pounds to play the gaunt Trevor Reznik who suffers from severe insomnia that causes what appear to be symptoms of psychosis (1 year later Bale gained the weight back to play the muscular Batman in *Batman Begins*).

"I'll be rejected if I meet a good person."

Lyle defending his façade of anger in *Manic* (2003)

Man Without a Face, The (1993) Drama ΨΨ
Mel Gibson directs and stars in this film about a man whose face becomes terribly disfigured after an automobile accident. He becomes reclusive but finds redemption in his relationship with the 12-year-old boy he tutors.

Marvin's Room (1996) Drama ΨΨΨΨ
A compelling examination of the way in which chronic illness affects caregivers and families.

Mask (1985) Drama ΨΨΨ
Cher stars in this film about her character's son, Rocky Dennis, a spunky teenager whose life has been dramatically affected by craniodiaphyseal dysplasia, a disorder that distorts the shape of his skull and face. This is a feel-good movie that succeeds. The thwarted love relationship between Rocky and a blind girlfriend underscores our tendency to judge people by their appearance.

Matrix Reloaded, The (2003) Action ΨΨΨ
Keanu Reeves is Neo in this first sequel of the daring Trilogy by the Wachowski brothers. Neo suffers from insomnia though on a more important level, his insomnia functions as a metaphor for being "awake" and "alive." He also experiences nightmares and frequently worries at night about decisions he needs to make the next day.

Miracle Worker, The (1962) Biography ΨΨΨ
Patty Duke and Anne Bancroft star in this well-known film about the childhood of Helen Keller and the influence of a gifted teacher.

Modify (2005) Documentary ΨΨΨ
An interesting documentary that highlights the many ways in which humans elect to change and improve the bodies with which they were born.

Motorcycle Diaries (2004, Argentina) Drama ΨΨΨΨ
Based on the true coming of age story of "Che" Guevara. Two men travel the countryside of South America seeing indigenous cultures while logging observations and experiences in a diary. They help out in communities and at a hospital in Peru with leprosy patients. The struggle with asthma is depicted.

My Own Private Idaho (1991) Drama ΨΨ
River Phoenix stars as a young male prostitute who has narcolepsy. He is befriended by Keanu Reeves, and the two leave Portland and travel together. Interesting presentations of dreams that occur during narcoleptic episodes.

My Flesh and Blood (2004) Documentary ΨΨΨ
Moving documentary about Susan Tom, who adopted 11 special needs children and raised them on her own. The children suffer in a variety of ways; their problems include cystic fibrosis, severe burns, developmental disabilities, the absence of legs, and a genetic skin disorder that causes severe pain.

My Life (1993) Drama ΨΨΨ
Michael Keaton learns he is dying from cancer and makes a series of videotapes for his still-unborn son, including one in which he teaches his son how to shave.

My Life Without Me (2003) Drama ΨΨΨ
A 23-year-old woman is diagnosed with ovarian cancer and decides not to tell her family but instead live her life more fully and prepare them for when she is gone. One of her bucket list goals is to have an affair.

Music Within (2007) Drama/Comedy ΨΨΨ
The true story of Richard Pimentel, a brilliant public speaker, who returned from Vietnam disabled by a severe hearing impairment. He became a passionate advocate for the disabled and is in part responsible for the creation of the 1990 American with Disabilities Act.

Oasis (2002, Korea) Drama ΨΨΨΨ
A quirky young man is released from prison after serving 2.5 years for accidentally killing someone while driving. He becomes curious and interested in the victim's daughter who has cerebral palsy. Both individuals are isolated and outcast from their families, and they find friendship and comfort in one another.

One Last Thing (2005) Comedy Ψ
A boy with terminal cancer gets a last wish from the Wish Givers Foundation. He gets to spend a week alone with a supermodel.

Open Hearts (2003) Drama ΨΨΨ
Danish film about a random car accident that leaves a man paralyzed from the neck down. He lashes out in anger un-

able to accept the reality of his losses. His girlfriend begins an affair with the driver's husband.

"My whole life disappeared with you that morning."

Grieving in *Open Hearts* (2003)

Pact of Silence, The (2003, France) Drama ΨΨ
A Jesuit priest tries to make sense out of a nun's psychosomatic fits that turn out to be related to the experiences of the nun's incarcerated twin sister.

Passion Fish (1992) Drama ΨΨΨΨ
The stress of disability and the demands a person with a disability can make on caregivers are nicely chronicled in this film about a querulous paraplegic actress and her caretaker/companion.

Patch Adams (1998) Comedy ΨΨ
Robin Williams plays a medical student, nicknamed Patch, who defies the medical institution and crosses boundaries in using humor and holistic medical practices with various patients throughout a hospital. Some humorous and touching scenes occur on the children's cancer ward and with other suffering patients.

Phantom of the Opera, The (1925) Horror ΨΨΨ
A disfigured music lover, played by Lon Chaney, lives in the bowels of the Paris opera house, unable to achieve romantic love because of his hideous face. He is eventually hunted down and killed by an angry mob.

Joe Miller: "What do you love about the law, Andrew?"
Andrew Beckett: "I ... many things ... uh ... uh ... What I love the most about the law?"
Joe Miller: "Yeah."
Andrew Beckett: "It's that every now and again – not often, but occasionally – you get to be a part of justice being done. That really is quite a thrill when that happens."

Philadelphia (1993)

Philadelphia (1993) Drama ΨΨΨ
Tom Hanks won an Academy Award for his portrayal of an AIDS-afflicted attorney who is fired from a prestigious law firm once the partners know of his illness. There is a particularly moving scene in which Hanks plays an opera and explains to Denzel Washington why he loves the music so passionately.

Pieces of April (2003) Drama/Comedy ΨΨΨ
A young woman, estranged from her family, is determined to impress them with a Thanksgiving dinner. She has a particularly tenuous relationship with her cynical mother who is dying of cancer.

Places in the Heart (1984) Drama ΨΨΨ
Sally Field won an Academy Award for Best Actress for her role in this film about a widowed woman struggling to keep her farm and her family in a small Texas town during the Depression. The film is memorable for bringing together John Malkovich as a blind World War I veteran and Danny Glover as a hapless drifter. The standoff between a blind Malkovich and the local chapter of the Ku Klux Klan is especially memorable.

Promises in the Dark (1979) Drama ΨΨ
Melodrama about a young woman dying from cancer.

Proof (1992) Drama ΨΨΨ
Australian drama about a blind man who takes photographs to document his life and its meaning.

Poison Ivy (1992) Drama Ψ
A newcomer into a pathological family plans to take over the role of wife and mother. The father is an alcoholic and the mother is a hypochondriac.

Primo Amore (2004, Italy) Drama/Romance ΨΨΨ
A goldsmith falls for an art-school model and becomes obsessed with controlling her diet and appearance. This film provides an interesting examination of eating disorders, and it can be viewed as a metaphorical commentary on society's beliefs about the female body.

Queen Margot (1994) Drama ΨΨ
Period film set in 1572 France at a time of heavy religious warfare (Catholic versus Protestant). The king in the film appears to have a somatoform disorder.

Rat Race (2001) Comedy Ψ
Several characters travel long distances in a competition for monetary reward. One character, played by Rowan Atkinson, has narcolepsy.

Rails and Ties (2007) Drama ΨΨΨ
Engineer Tom Stark (Kevin Bacon) cannot avoid crashing his train into a parked car occupied by a suicidal mother and her 11-year-old son who escapes the car unscathed. Stark's wife Megan (Marcia Gay Harden) is dying of cancer. The film depicts the relationship between the Starks and the young boy who help one another cope with life and death.

Return to Oz (1985) Adventure/Family Ψ
A follow-up to the classic story, this film depicts Dorothy returning for more adventures in Oz after evading ECT and "dangerous psychiatric treatment" and struggling with a sleep disorder.

Rory O'Shea Was Here (2005) Comedy/Drama ΨΨΨ
Depicts the quest for independence and friendship between two young men, one coping with muscular dystrophy, the other with cerebral palsy.

Safe (1995) Comedy/Drama ΨΨΨΨ
A rare film almost exclusively focusing on a woman (Julianne Moore) with a somatoform disorder, various treatment approaches, and the effects on her family. This satirical film was cleverly directed by Todd Haynes.

Secret of Dr. Kildare, The (1939) Drama ΨΨΨ
The good Dr. Kildare works hard to cure a patient's conversion disorder (blindness) in this interesting film.

Savage Nights (1992, France) Drama/Biography ΨΨΨΨ
This controversial film was directed by French filmmaker Cyril Collard, who died from AIDS three days before *Savage Nights* was selected as the best French film of the year. The movie deals with the existential decisions made by a bisexual antihero who continues to have unprotected sex even after learning he has AIDS.

Seabiscuit (2003) Drama ΨΨ
Tobey Maguire plays a disc jockey with bulimic symptoms in order to keep his weight down and compete in horse-racing championships. Bulimic symptoms are fairly common among jockeys, though this is not an emphasis in the film.

Secondhand Lions (2003) Family ΨΨ
A young adolescent (Haley Joel Osment) is forced to live with his two rich uncles (Robert Duvall and Michael Caine), one of whom often sleepwalks.

Send Me No Flowers (1964) Romance/Comedy Ψ
Rock Hudson plays a hypochondriac convinced he will die soon. Hudson sets out to find a suitable replacement so his wife will be able to get along without him.

Shadowlands (1993) Biography ΨΨΨ
Wonderful Richard Attenborough film about the late-life romance of C. S. Lewis (Anthony Hopkins) and Joy Gresham (Debra Winger). Lewis must come to grips with the meaning of pain, suffering, and loss when Joy develops cancer.

"You aim to do to me what they did with John Wesley Hardin. Lay me out and parade every damn fool in the state past me at a dollar a head, half price for children, and then stuff me in a gunny sack and shovel me under."

John Bernard Books confronts the undertaker
in *The Shootist* (1976)

Shootist, The (1976) Western ΨΨ
John Wayne's last film, about an aging gunfighter dying from cancer. Also stars Jimmy Stewart, Lauren Bacall, Ron Howard, Harry Morgan, John Carradine, Hugh O'Brian, and Richard Boone. John Wayne, a heavy smoker, died from lung cancer after making this film.

Shop on Main Street, The (1965) Drama ΨΨΨΨ
Czechoslovakian film about a man appointed as the "Aryan controller" of a button shop in World War II. He befriends and hides the Jewish owner of the shop, who does not understand the situation because she is deaf. She assumes the new arrival has been sent as her assistant; when he later hides her to avoid deportation to the death camps, she smothers. Overcome with remorse, he kills himself. Selected as the Best Foreign Film of 1965.

Simple Men (1992) Comedy ΨΨ
Deadpan comedy from auteur director Hal Hartley, that depicts a character suffering with epilepsy.

Smile (2005) Drama ΨΨ
Well-intentioned film depicting the suffering experienced by those with physical deformities such as cleft palates.

Sorry, Wrong Number (1948) Thriller ΨΨ
Barbara Stanwyck and Burt Lancaster in a murder film. Stanwyck is a rich heiress who is bedridden with psychosomatic heart disease and paralysis.

Starved (2006) Documentary ΨΨΨ
This film follows the lives of five women with eating disorders.

Storytelling (2001) Comedy/Drama ΨΨ
Two separate stories explore issues of race, sex, and exploitation. In the first story, a teenager allows herself to be exploited by her teacher after getting bored with her boyfriend who has cerebral palsy. In the second story, a shoe-store worker dreams of being a documentary filmmaker and uses a disillusioned teenager and his family as his subjects.

Tell Me That You Love Me, Junie Moon (1970) Comedy ΨΨ
Otto Preminger film in which three unusual roommates come together as a family. Liza Minnelli is disfigured; another has epilepsy; the third is wheelchair-bound.

Terms of Endearment (1983) Comedy ΨΨΨ
Shirley MacLaine, Debra Winger, and Jack Nicholson star in this poignant but funny movie about relationships, caring, and cancer.

Test of Love, A (1984) Drama ΨΨ
An Australian film based on a true story of a teacher's successful attempt to reach out to a girl with a disability.

Thin (2006) Documentary ΨΨΨ
Four women with anorexia or bulimia allow their treatment experiences – the struggles, progress, relapse, and symptoms – to be documented on film.

Twelve O'Clock High (1949) War ΨΨΨΨ
Gregory Peck plays the role of General Frank Savage, an effective leader who develops a conversion disorder (psychosomatic paralysis) in response to his role in the death of several of his subordinates. The film is based on a true story.

Unconscious (2004) Drama ΨΨ
A Spanish film that satirizes psychoanalysis; the movie includes examples of hypochondriasis and conversion disorder.

Up in Arms (1944) Musical/Comedy/War Ψ
Danny Kaye plays a hypochondriac in the Army.

Unbreakable (2000) Drama/Suspense ΨΨΨ
Samuel L. Jackson plays Elijah, a comic book collector, who was born with a rare genetic bone disease, which makes him highly susceptible to injury. Bruce Willis, on the other hand, plays a security officer who is in a train wreck and is the one survivor and does not have a scratch on him. Second mainstream film by master story-teller, M. Night Shyamalan.

Unfinished Life, An (2005) Drama ΨΨ
A physically abused woman escapes her abuser with her daughter and moves in with her father-in-law (Robert Redford) and a man (Morgan Freeman) he is taking care of. The latter was mauled by a bear, needs daily injections, walks with crutches, and cannot take care of himself.

Vanilla Sky (2001) Drama/Suspense ΨΨΨ
Cameron Crowe film in which Tom Cruise plays a wealthy businessman in NYC who has a car accident and must re-establish his life with a severe facial deformity. This changes his interactions especially with a woman he is falling in love with (Penelope Cruz). He begins to break down further as his dead friend (Cameron Diaz) reappears.

Waking Life (2001) Drama/Animation ΨΨΨ
This unique, creative film follows a character searching for answers to life's most important questions in a world that seems surreal and dream-like. The film is a surrealistic blend of animation and drama with a heavy philosophical and existential bent. The film questions whether we are sleepwalking through our days and our lives, and whether we are more awake when we interact with others or when we dream.

> "Got you in a halo, huh. I call that thing a crown of thorns. I thought they was gonna screw it into my brain."
>
> A paralyzed patient describes his rehabilitation in *The Waterdance* (1992)

Waterdance, The (1992) Drama ΨΨΨ
Realistic film about the way spinal cord injuries have changed the lives of three men who meet in a rehabilitation hospital.

Whales of August, The (1987) Drama ΨΨ
Vincent Price and Ann Sothern support Lillian Gish and Bette Davis in a remarkable film about what it means to grow old. Davis plays the blind and embittered sister who is still loved by Gish.

Whatever Happened to Baby Jane? (1962) Drama ΨΨΨ
Bette Davis and Joan Crawford portray two elderly sisters. Crawford is wheelchair-bound as a result of an automobile accident possibly caused by her sister. Davis is obviously demented and terrorizes her younger sister. Surprise ending.

White Heat (1949) Crime ΨΨΨ
James Cagney plays a ruthless gangster who has debilitating migraine headaches that only his mother can cure. The film ties into the psychoanalytic ideas of the day and features a famous ending in which Cagney blows up an oil tank.

> "Cody Jarrett. He finally made it to the top of the world. And it blew up in his face."
>
> *White Heat* (1949)

Wind Will Carry Us, The (1999, France/Iran) Drama ΨΨ
A man and his film crew travel to a remote Iranian village to film the special ceremony that occurs after an old woman dies. Directed by Abbas Kiarostami.

Whose Life Is It Anyway? (1981) Drama ΨΨΨ
Richard Dreyfuss plays a sculptor paralyzed from the neck down after a car crash. He argues convincingly for the right to die.

Woman's Tale, A (1991) Drama ΨΨΨ
An Australian film directed by Paul Cox about the final days in the life of a 78-year-old woman dying of cancer.

World's Fastest Indian, The (2005, New Zealand) Drama ΨΨΨ
Heart disease threatens the life of New Zealander Burt Munro, who spent years building a 1920 Indian motorcycle. Despite the stress of physical illness, Munro pushes forward in an attempt to break a land speed record at the Bonneville Salt Flats.

Wrestler, The (2008) Drama ΨΨΨΨ
Randy "the Ram" is a professional wrestler who is forced to retire due to multiple physical problems following use of steroids and body enhancers. He breaks down (vomits and faints) with a heart attack after a challenging match fighting with glass, a staple gun, and barbs. He attempts a comeback in both his personal life and in wrestling. Directed by Darren Aronofsky.

Yesterday (2004, South Africa) Drama ΨΨΨΨΨ
A woman named Yesterday focuses largely on the present and future as she takes care of her daughter, her dying husband, and her own HIV.

Sexual Dysfunctions and Gender Dysphoria

Adventures of Priscilla, Queen of the Desert (1994) Comedy ΨΨ
Terence Stamp plays an aging transsexual who joins with two friends to travel from Sidney to Alice Springs in the Australian outback to perform a lip-synching routine. Much of the film revolves around the prejudice and homophobic hostility the three transsexuals encounter.

"Being a man one day and a woman the next isn't an easy thing."

Bernadette complaining about life as a transsexual in *Adventures of Priscilla, Queen of the Desert* (1994)

AKA (2002) Drama ΨΨΨ
Fascinating artistry where most of the screen is split into three sections where the viewer is simultaneously shown past and present, different character reactions, different camera angles, and even the internal thoughts and behaviors of a character. The lead character, sexually abused by his father, escapes on a journey exploring his sexual and psychological identity. As in *Memento*, the viewer must pay close attention throughout the film.

All About My Mother (1999, Spain) Drama/Comedy ΨΨ
Pedro Almodóvar film about a nurse who tragically loses her beloved son and in her grief and travels meets a trans-

vestite prostitute and a pregnant nun (Penelope Cruz). Winner of an Academy Award for Best Foreign Language Film.

Any Day Now (2012) Drama ΨΨΨ
A drag queen and his attorney lover try to adopt a boy with special needs but come up against societal bias and legal limitations

(A)sexual (2011) Documentary ΨΨΨ
An examination of the 1% of the population not attracted to either males or females.

Beautiful Boxer (2003, Thailand) Action/Drama ΨΨ
A male to female transsexual makes use of kickboxing skills to pay for a sex change operation.

Birdcage, The (1996) Comedy ΨΨΨ
Mike Nichols and Elaine May's remake of *La Cage aux Folles*. This film is almost as good as the original, thanks to strong performances by Robin Williams and Gene Hackman.

"Al, you old son of a bitch! How ya doin'? How do you feel about that call today? I mean the Dolphins! Fourth-and-three play on their 30 yard line with only 34 seconds to go!"

A transvestite trying to act masculine in *The Birdcage* (1996)

Breakfast on Pluto (2005) Comedy ΨΨΨ
Neil Jordan's film about an Irish Catholic abandoned child who is raised by a parish priest but later becomes a flamboyant transsexual.

Boys Don't Cry (1999) Drama ΨΨΨΨ
One of the best films to ever depict the pain and problems that can emerge from gender identity disorder. A brutal, powerful film.

Crying Game, The (1992) Drama ΨΨΨΨ
This Neil Jordan film explores homosexuality, transsexualism, interracial sexuality, and the ability of two human beings to love one another deeply in an asexual relationship. Too complex to explain simply, the film must be seen to be fully appreciated.

Flawless (1999) Drama/Comedy ΨΨ
Philip Seymour Hoffman plays a drag queen named Rusty who is saving money for a gender modification operation; Robert De Niro is the homophobic neighbor who takes voice lessons from Rusty following a stroke.

Gun Hill Road (2011) Drama ΨΨΨ
A man returns from prison to discover that his teenage son is transsexual. He has to reevaluate his personal val-

ues and beliefs about the trans community in order to hold his family together.

La Cage aux Folles (1978, France) Comedy ΨΨΨ
A gay man and his transvestite lover manage a popular St. Tropez nightclub. Much of the humor revolves around sex roles and the folly of trying very hard to be something you're not.

> "I told them my father was a Cultural attaché. What will they think when they find out he lives with a drag queen?"
>
> Renato's son in *La Cage aux Folles* (1978)

Marie Antoinette (2006) Drama/Biography Ψ
The Queen finds herself in a loveless and asexual relationship with her husband, Louis XVI.

Mrs. Doubtfire (1994) Comedy ΨΨ
Robin Williams cross-dresses as an English nanny to have time with his children.

> "Well, I hope you're up for a little competition. She's got a power tool in the bedroom, dear. It's her own personal jackhammer. She could break sidewalks with that thing. She uses it and the lights dim, it's like a prison movie. Amazed she hasn't chipped her teeth."
>
> Daniel Hillard, disguised as Mrs. Doubtfire, tries to discourage Stu, his ex-wife's new lover in *Mrs. Doubtfire* (1994)

Mystery of Alexina, The (1985) Drama ΨΨ
A story about the psychological sequelae of the decision to raise a male child as a female.

Normal (2003) Drama ΨΨΨ
A man (Tom Wilkinson) after 25 years of marriage tells his wife (Jessica Lange) he is a woman trapped in a man's body, and he wants gender modification surgery.

Oh in Ohio, The (2006) Comedy ΨΨ
A married couple becomes open to new sexual experiences with different partners after a decade of insipid sex. Sexual desire and sexual disorders are depicted.

Princesa (2001) Drama Ψ
Brazilian transvestite moves to Italy and works as a prostitute in order to earn money for his sex change operation.

Sessions, The (2012) Comedy Biography ΨΨΨΨ
Helen Hunt plays the role of a sexual surrogate working with Mark, played by John Hawkes, a talented 38-year-old Berkeley student who has spent most of his life in an iron lung.

Soldier's Girl (2003) Drama/Biography ΨΨΨ
Based on the true story of Barry Winchell who entered the military and fell in love with a transsexual dancer at a club. Military peers find out about the secret relationship and the situation ends tragically.

> "The imagination is the most powerful force known to mankind. And it is my imagined self, the one who is beautiful and loving and worthy of being loved, that has been my guiding force. My inspiration. I can only hope to become the person Barry imagined me to be. I pray for the courage it will take to become a real, live soldier's girl."
>
> *Soldier's Girl* (2003)

Southern Comfort (2001) Documentary ΨΨ
Female to male transgender faces hate and prejudice in this award-winning film.

That's the Way I Like It (1998, Singapore) Drama ΨΨ
A young man who has always tried to please his parents announces that he is in fact a woman who plans to get surgery to make his body conform to his identity. The man attempts suicide but eventually lives and completes his surgery.

Tomboy (2011, France) Drama ΨΨΨΨ
A 10-year-old girl moves into a new neighborhood and is mistaken for a boy. She embraces the mistake and adopts a masculine identify, mystifying her younger sister and upsetting her parents.

> Director: "I'd like to make her look a little more attractive. How far can you pull back?"
> Cameraman: "How do you feel about Cleveland?"
>
> *Tootsie* (1982)

Tootsie (1982) Comedy/Romance ΨΨΨΨ
Funny Dustin Hoffman film in which an unsuccessful actor finds success when he impersonates a woman. He learns from the process, and the audience learns some important lessons about gender, sex roles, and human relationships.

Transamerica (2005) Comedy ΨΨΨΨ
A presurgical male to female transsexual takes a cross-country journey with the son she just met for the first time.

Victor/Victoria (1982) Musical/Comedy ΨΨ
Blake Edwards film with Julie Andrews as a down-on-her-luck singer who becomes a sensation when she pretends to be a male-female impersonator.

Wild Tigers I Have Known (2006) Drama ΨΨΨ
A coming of age film about a 13-year-old boy struggling with issues of sexual identity.

World According to Garp, The (1982) Comedy/Drama ΨΨ
John Lithgow plays transsexual Roberta Muldoon in a film in which troubled sexuality is commonplace.

Yentl (1983) Musical ΨΨ
Barbra Streisand directed and produced this film, and she has the lead role as a young woman in Eastern Europe who has to pass herself off as a man in order to get an education. Interesting examination of sex roles; terrific performance by Streisand.

Zerophilia (2005) Comedy/Romance Ψ
A young man discovers that he has "zerophilia," which means he can switch sexual identities and experience pleasure as either a man or a woman. The film is a less than satisfying exploration of sex roles.

Disruptive, Impulse-Control, and Conduct Disorders

400 Blows, The (1959) Drama ΨΨΨΨΨ
Francois Truffaut's first feature film based on his own experiences as a young boy. The film depicts ineffectual parenting and inept teachers, and Antoine is portrayed as more rebellious than bad.

> Psychiatrist: "Your parents say you're always lying."
> Antoine Doinel: "Oh, I lie now and then, I suppose. Sometimes I'd tell them the truth, and they still wouldn't believe me, so I prefer to lie."
>
> Strange behavior explained in
> *The Four Hundred Blows* (1959)

Afterschool (2008) Drama ΨΨΨ
A high school boy, addicted to violent online pornography, films the death of two classmates from a drug overdose.

Ali Zaoua: Prince of the Streets (2000) Drama ΨΨΨ
Four young homeless boys, living in poverty on the streets of Morocco, rebel against their gang leader's oppressive rule.

Behind the Red Door (2001) Drama ΨΨ
Keifer Sutherland plays a man dying of AIDS who exhibits explosive anger.

Beautiful Boy (2010) Drama ΨΨΨ
A couple with a strained marriage have to cope with additional stress after they learn that their 17-year-old son killed 17 professors and other students at his university before taking his own life.

Beautiful Ohio (2006) Drama Ψ
Independent film about two brothers growing up in the Midwest, one is gifted but also has severe oppositional tendencies.

Carrie (1976) Horror ΨΨ
This Brian De Palma film is based on a Stephen King novel and depicts the cruelty of adolescents and some of the stresses associated with caring for a mentally ill mother. Sissy Spacek's performance is remarkable.

Chorus, The (2004, France) Drama ΨΨΨΨ
A newly hired boarding school teacher tries to transform troubled kids into positive problem solvers through music and positive rewards. The headmaster, who believes in restriction and punishment, reluctantly agrees to let the new teacher try more positive approaches.

City of God (2003, Brazil) Drama/Foreign ΨΨΨ
Painful, sobering and graphic examination of the violence associated with gang life, drug trafficking, and poverty in Rio de Janeiro. This film depicts young children and adolescents who grow up in an environment in which guns and murder are commonplace.

Dangerous Lives of Altar Boys, The (2002) Drama/Comedy ΨΨ
High school outcasts express rebellion in a variety of ways, including abuse of an authoritarian nun (played by Jodie Foster).

Don't Come Knocking (2005) Drama ΨΨΨ
A former Western movie star drowns his sorrow in alcohol and self-pity until he discovers he has a son and sets out to find him. The son is oppositional-defiant.

Elephant (2003) Drama ΨΨΨΨ
Well-crafted, foreboding, eerie Gus Van Sant film addressing the tragedy of recent school shootings. Powerful parallels with the Columbine tragedy. Winner of the Palm award at Cannes for Best Picture and Best Director.

Elling (2001) Drama ΨΨΨΨ
Norwegian film about two men released from a psychiatric hospital who must prove themselves capable of coping with everyday life. One man suffers from intermittent anger episodes. Oscar nominee for Best Foreign Film.

Equus (1977) Drama ΨΨΨ
Richard Burton examines the meaning and purpose of his own life as he attempts to unravel the psychosexual roots

that led an adolescent to blind six horses. Wonderful soliloquies by Burton.

"And most importantly, have fun, man!"

Final words of an adolescent to his co-assassin preparing to enter a school building in *Elephant* (2003)

Every Man for Himself and God Against All (1975) Biography ΨΨΨΨ
Werner Herzog film based on a true story about a man who spent an isolated childhood virtually devoid of stimulation. This movie should be contrasted with Truffaut's film *The Wild Child* and the more recent film *Nell*.

Face to Face (1976, Sweden) Drama ΨΨ
Bergman film in which Liv Ullmann plays a suicidal psychiatrist estranged from her husband and 14-year-old daughter. During a coma that results from an overdose of sleeping pills, Ullmann dreams about a childhood experience in which she was punished by being locked in a closet.

Fanny and Alexander (1983, Sweden) Drama ΨΨΨΨ
Bergman film about two young children and the ways in which their lives change when their father dies and their mother remarries. The film is sensitive, tender, and haunting and shows how the world looks through the eyes of a 10-year-old.

Firestarter (1984) Drama/Suspense Ψ
Early Stephen King film in which Drew Barrymore portrays a young girl with pyrokinetic, telekinetic, and telepathic powers. Barrymore is able to set fires simply by staring at whatever she wants to set on fire.

Forbidden Games (1951) War/Drama ΨΨΨΨ
This beautiful French film is about two children who create and share a private fantasy world. The movie juxtaposes the innocence of childhood with the horror of war.

Great New Wonderful, The (2005) Drama ΨΨ
Several stories of New Yorkers converge, including one depicting a child with a serious behavior disorder.

Gummo (1997) Independent ΨΨΨ
This extremely disturbing and unforgettable film directed by Harmony Korine depicts life in a small, rural town after its destruction by a tornado. Despite the lack of a coherent plot, the film gets high marks for its honesty and realism. Various types of psychopathology are presented with an emphasis on conduct disorders.

Happy-Go-Lucky (2008, UK) Comedy ΨΨΨ
Poppy, an optimistic realist, interacts with a driver education instructor with intermittent explosive disorder in this Mike Leigh film.

Hate (1995, France) ΨΨ
Conduct disorders abound among adolescent gangs in a French suburban ghetto in this film about racism and oppression.

Holes (2002) Family ΨΨΨ
One of the better non-animated Disney films about troubled youth who are sent to a work camp to dig deep holes in the middle of the desert to help three criminals find a lost treasure. Sigourney Weaver has a memorable role in this film.

Hulk (2003) Action/Drama ΨΨΨ
Ang Lee converts the famous *Incredible Hulk* comic series to film and in doing so creates a wonderful representation of anger and intermittent explosiveness.

Innocents, The (1961) Horror ΨΨΨ
Deborah Kerr plays a governess hired to care for two precocious children. Is she hallucinating or delusional, or are there really ghosts in the house? Interesting sexual tension develops between Kerr and the boy. Based on the Henry James novella *Turn of the Screw*.

Island on Bird Street (2000) Drama ΨΨΨ
Polish film about an adventurous, high-spirited boy who escapes from Nazi control; inspired by Robinson Crusoe, he creates a hide-out and waits for his father's return.

"If you deflower a girl... you're the man. No one can ever do that again. You're the only one. No one, no one, has the power to do that again."

Telly describes his fascination with virgins in *Kids* (1995)

Kids (1995) Drama ΨΨΨ
Gritty and disturbing film about urban adolescents, sex, drugs, and violence. The main character is a teenager with AIDS who preys on young adolescent girls, taking particular pride in seducing virgins.

Klepto (2003) Drama/Comedy ΨΨΨ
Rare film in which the struggles associated with kleptomania are depicted.

Leolo (1992, France/Canada) Comedy ΨΨΨΨ
Leo, an adolescent boy growing up in a very dysfunctional family in Montreal, is unable to accept the reality

of his genetic heritage and concocts a fantasy in which he was accidentally conceived by sperm that crossed the Atlantic in a Sicilian tomato. (The film is better than this brief synopsis suggests.)

Life as a House (2001) Drama ΨΨΨ
Touching film about the transformation of the relationship between a rebellious, addicted adolescent (Hayden Christensen) and his terminally ill father (Kevin Kline).

Lilya 4-Ever (2002, Sweden/Denmark Drama ΨΨΨ
Heartbreaking film about a girl, rejected by her family and society, who seems to meet with tragedy just when it appears she is headed in the right direction. Lilya is physically, emotionally, and sexually abused in the film.

Little Man Tate (1991) Drama ΨΨΨ
Jodi Foster directed this film about a child prodigy and the tensions that arise between his mother and the psychologist to whom the child's education is entrusted. Foster acknowledged that the film is partly autobiographical.

Lord of the Flies (1963) Drama ΨΨ
Film adaptation of William Goldman's novel about a group of schoolchildren who quickly shed the thin veneer of civilization and become savages. Both the film and book raise interesting questions about nature and nurture. Remade in 1990.

Los Olvidados/The Young and the Damned (1950, Mexico) Drama ΨΨΨ
Luis Buñuel film about juvenile delinquency in the squalid slums of Mexico City.

Magdalene Sisters, The (2002) Docudrama ΨΨΨ
Troubled adolescent girls are sent to a dehumanizing boarding home where they are abused, mistreated and exploited by the nuns who run the home. One particularly abused adolescent sexually acts out with a priest and later becomes psychotic.

Marnie (1964) Thriller/Romance ΨΨ
Hitchcock film about a sexually frigid kleptomaniac who dominates her new husband. As in other Hitchcock films, the protagonist's problems are found to be rooted in childhood trauma. Watch for the use of a word association test.

Monsieur Ibrahim (2003) Drama ΨΨΨ
Heart-warming French film about an adolescent boy raised by a critical, neglecting father; he develops a meaningful friendship with a local store-owner.

Mortal Transfer (2001) Mystery/Drama ΨΨΨ
French film depicting one of a psychoanalyst's patients undergoing psychoanalysis and struggling with her kleptomania.

My First Mister (2001) Drama ΨΨ
Adolescent girl struggles with severe isolation, depression, self-injurious behavior, and other acting out behaviors until she befriends a 49-year-old man. The teen has a host of behavioral problems including "huffing," auto-erotic asphyxiation, isolation from her family, and prostitution.

My Flesh and Blood (2004) Documentary ΨΨΨ
Moving story of Susan Tom, who adopted 11 special needs children and raised them on her own. One has cystic fibrosis and severe anger and oppositional behaviors directed at most people around him.

Nell (1994) Drama ΨΨΨ
Jodi Foster plays a feral child raised in isolation in the North Carolina woods. She is terrified of the doctor who discovers her and eventually learns her own odd language. The doctor consults an expert on child psychology. Interesting examination of Rousseau's concept of the "natural savage."

Noi the Albino (2003) Drama ΨΨΨ
A film about a troubled but gifted teen who struggles with conduct problems in Iceland. The movie provides a realistic evaluation of a gifted adolescent who is out of place in both school and life.

Noise (2007) Comedy ΨΨΨ
Street noise is a stress stimulus for David Owen (Tim Robbins) who becomes the Rectifier, a vigilante who takes noise personally. He damages noisy cars and destroys car alarms. He also seriously damages his relationships and loses his job and family.

Pelle the Conqueror (1986) Drama ΨΨΨΨΨ
Moving film about lust, passion, dreams, aging, hope, pragmatic romance, and, most of all, the love between a father and his son. The film won the Grand Prix at the Cannes Film Festival and an Academy Award for Best Foreign Film.

Pieces of April (2003) Comedy ΨΨΨ
Previously troubled adolescent estranged from her family tries to create a pleasant, memorable experience for her dysfunctional family's Thanksgiving dinner. Well-acted by Katie Holmes and Patricia Clarkson.

Pixote (1981) Drama ΨΨΨΨΨ
A powerful film about the squalid, depressing lives of street children in Sao Paulo. In the film, the child Pixote,

commits his first murder at the age of 10. Ironically, the child star actually was shot and killed by the police five years after the film was released.

Popeye (1980) Drama ΨΨ
The archetypal Bluto, a character with an intermittent explosive disorder, is foiled by the heroic Popeye, played by Robin Williams.

Punch Drunk Love (2002) Drama/Comedy ΨΨΨ
Adam Sandler in a serious role about a man who alternates from an awkward passivity to explosive anger. Falling in love changes him. Quirky cinematic elements are added by director Paul Thomas Anderson.

Ratcatcher, The (1999) Drama ΨΨΨ
Young adolescent living in Glasgow has to cope with trash-covered streets, lice, and dead rats. He acts out as he tries to cope with poverty.

Rebel Without a Cause (1955) Drama ΨΨΨ
Dated but still interesting examination of teenage alienation, violence, and family pathology. James Dean is the rebellious protagonist. All three stars (Dean, Natalie Wood, and Sal Mineo) met violent deaths (a car wreck, a drowning, and a murder).

"Boy, if, if I had one day when I didn't have to be all confused, and didn't have to feel that I was ashamed of everything"

Rebel Without a Cause (1955)

Salaam Bombay! (1988) Drama ΨΨΨ
Remarkable story about the way indigent children manage to survive to adulthood on the mean streets of Bombay.

Splendor in the Grass (1961) Drama ΨΨ
A teenage girl unable to come to grips with adolescent sexuality winds up in a psychiatric hospital.

Squid and the Whale, The (2005) Drama ΨΨΨΨ
This excellent film depicts a family of four going through a divorce. The two children act out in significant ways.

Thirteen (2003) Drama ΨΨΨΨ
Important film about the rise and fall of teen friendships, sexual promiscuity, self-hate, rebellion, and the intense need adolescents fill to fit in and be accepted. Holly Hunter plays the recovered alcoholic mother struggling with the delicate balance between giving her daughter appropriate levels of freedom and setting limits.

Cole Sear: "We were supposed to draw a picture, anything we wanted. I drew a man who got hurt in the neck by another man with a screwdriver."
Malcolm Crowe: "You saw that on TV, Cole?"
Cole Sear: "Everyone got upset. They had a meeting. Mom started crying. I don't draw like that any more."
Malcolm Crowe: "How do you draw now?"
Cole Sear: "Draw … people smiling, dogs running, rainbows. They don't have meetings about rainbows."

A child figures out how to play the system in
The Sixth Sense (1999)

Tin Drum, The (1979) Drama/War ΨΨΨΨ
Political allegory about a child who decides to stop growing. Based on a Gunter Grass novel, the film won an Academy Award for Best Foreign Film. The film recently received considerable attention because a scene in which the child has oral sex with an adult was judged to be obscene under Oklahoma law.

To Kill a Mockingbird (1962) Drama ΨΨ
Robert Duvall makes his film debut as Boo Radley, a man with an intellectual disability who kills another man in order to protect two children.

"She did something that in our society is unspeakable. She kissed a black man. Not an old uncle, but a strong, young Negro man. No code mattered to her before she broke it, but it came crashing down on her afterwards."

To Kill a Mockingbird (1962)

United States of Leland, The (2004) Drama ΨΨ
Interesting story about Leland P. Fitzgerald (Ryan Gosling), an adolescent who kills a boy with autism but can't explain why. His emotions are blunted, his social behavior is quirky, yet his thoughts are often insightful and perceptive. Kevin Spacey co-stars.

Weather Man, The (2005) Drama ΨΨ
A meteorologist struggles in his personal life which includes supporting his depressed daughter.

Welcome to the Dollhouse (1996) Comedy ΨΨΨ
Interesting examination of families, emerging sexuality, and the cruelty of adolescents.

Wild Child, The (1969, France) Drama ΨΨΨΨ
François Truffaut's engaging film about the life of a feral child, the "Wild Boy of Aveyron." Based on a true story and the journal of Jean Itard, the doctor who set out to educate the child. Truffaut himself plays the role of Itard.

Willy Wonka and the Chocolate Factory (1971) Family ΨΨ

Five lucky children win a free tour of a wonderful chocolate factory. Four of the five children (excluding the hero, Charlie) are either oppositional, obsessed, or enormously selfish.

Wish You Were Here (1987) Drama ΨΨ

A teenage girl coming of age in Great Britain in the early 1950s must come to grips with her emerging sexuality.

Substance-Related and Addictive Disorders

Alcoholism

16 Blocks (2006) Drama ΨΨΨ

A corrupt, burnt out, alcoholic cop risks his job and life by confronting authority in order to save a criminal from being killed. He drinks on the job, is unshaven, overly fatigued, has poor stamina, slowed movement, and colleagues repeatedly comment about his alcohol abuse.

16 Years of Alcohol (2003, UK) Drama ΨΨ

The impact of parental alcoholism on a boy who eventually becomes an alcoholic. A transformation occurs when he becomes a member of AA and works at letting go of his anger and violent patterns.

28 Days (2000) Drama ΨΨΨ

A writer (Sandra Bullock) is court-ordered into a drug/alcohol rehabilitation center after a drinking and driving accident. The film depicts symptoms of alcoholism and its impact on a family.

Arthur (1981) Comedy Ψ

Dudley Moore as a drunken millionaire who falls in love with Liza Minnelli. A genuinely funny film, but upsetting in its cavalier approach to alcoholism and drunk driving.

Susan: "A real woman could stop you from drinking."
Arthur: "It'd have to be a real BIG woman."

Arthur (1981)

Bad News Bears (2005) Comedy Ψ

Richard Linklater remake portraying a despicable alcoholic (Billy Bob Thornton) who attempts to coach a little league baseball team that has minimal talent.

Barfly (1987) Comedy/Romance/Drama ΨΨΨ

Faye Dunaway and Mickey Rourke play two alcoholics whose lives briefly touch. Good examination of skid row alcoholism; based on a story by cult poet Charles Bukowski.

Basketball Diaries, The (1995) Drama ΨΨΨ

Adolescent basketball stars succumb to drug abuse in this film that stars Leonardo DiCaprio and Mark Wahlberg. Adapted from a Jim Carroll novel.

Be Here to Love Me: A Film About Townes Van Zandt (2004) Documentary Biography ΨΨΨΨ

An examination of the all-too-short life of Townes Van Zandt and the ways in which that life was affected by abuse of both alcohol and drugs. In one scene Van Zandt describes passing out in military school as a young man after sniffing glue.

Being Flynn (2012) Drama ΨΨ

Robert De Niro plays the role of Flynn, an aging and homeless poet, conman and alcoholic.

Beloved Infidel (1959) Biography Ψ Ψ

Gregory Peck plays F. Scott Fitzgerald and Deborah Kerr is columnist Sheila Graham, who tries to save Fitzgerald from his alcoholism.

Bob and the Monster (2011) Documentary ΨΨΨΨ

This film traces the life of Bob Forrest, documenting his struggles with drugs and alcohol and his eventual recovery. Today Forrest is a drug and alcohol counselor working with some of Hollywood's biggest names.

Born on the Fourth of July (1989) Drama/War/Biography ΨΨΨΨ

Tom Cruise plays paralyzed and alcoholic Vietnam veteran Ron Kovic in Oliver Stone's film. Stone won an Oscar as best director for this film.

"You're a T6 – paralyzed from the mid-chest down ... you'll be in a wheelchair for the rest of your life."

Ron Kovic's grim prognosis in
Born on the Fourth of July (1989)

Capote (2005) Drama/Biography ΨΨΨ

Philip Seymour Hoffman portrays the writer Truman Capote, and a segment of his life in which Capote gets material from a man who killed a family of four in Kansas for a new non-fiction book. Capote becomes depressed when he is unable to prevent the man from being hanged. He abuses alcohol and never writes again.

Cat Ballou (1965) Comedy/Western Ψ
Light-hearted film, with Jane Fonda playing a school-teacher turned outlaw. Lee Marvin got an Oscar for his role as an alcoholic gunman. The film perpetuates the myth of the down-and-out drunk whose shooting skills return after he has had a few drinks. Marvin won an Oscar as Best Actor for his role in this film.

"Big Daddy! Now what makes him so big? His big heart? His big belly? Or his big money?"

Cat on a Hot Tin Roof (1958)

Cat on a Hot Tin Roof (1958) Drama ΨΨΨ
Paul Newman, Elizabeth Taylor, and Burl Ives in a sub-dued adaptation of Tennessee Williams' play about "mendacity." Alcohol plays a prominent role in the life of almost all the characters' lives.

Changing Lanes (2002) Drama ΨΨ
A successful lawyer from a corrupt firm collides with an alcoholic insurance salesman who is on his way to court for a custody hearing and misses the court appearance. The role of Alcoholics Anonymous and the ongoing struggle associated with recovery are depicted.

Charlie Wilson's War (2007) Drama/Biography ΨΨ
Mike Nichols film about a legendary congressman who's also an alcoholic.

Children of Men (2006) Thriller/Drama Ψ
Alcohol abuse and marijuana abuse are depicted in this film about saving the human race.

Come Back, Little Sheba (1952) Drama ΨΨΨ
Burt Lancaster and Shirley Booth in a film about alcoholism and marriage. Booth won an Academy Award for Best Actress for her role.

Come Fill the Cup (1951) Drama ΨΨ
James Cagney and Jackie Gleason star in this serious examination of the problems of alcoholism in an ex-newspaperman.

Crazy Heart (2009) Drama ΨΨΨΨΨ
Academy Award–winner Jeff Bridges, plays Bad Blake, a 57-year-old, four-time divorced, small-time musician. Blake is an alcoholic who travels around the southwest for small-time gigs, spending his days and nights drinking and womanizing, ending each night isolated and poor. He develops a meaningful relationship with a young woman and her son, but his alcohol dependence seriously affects his relationship with both. The film is an interesting comparison with other musician/addiction films, such as *Ray* and *Walk the Line*.

Crazy Wisdom: The Life & Times of Chogyam Trungpa Rinpoche (2011) Documentary Ψ
This documentary explores the complicated life of Chogyam Trungpa Rinpoche, someone known as the "bad boy of Buddhism." Rinpoche smoked, abused alcohol, and slept with his female followers and sometimes the wives of his followers.

Dark Obsession (1989) Drama/Mystery ΨΨ
Five drunken British military officers are involved in a hit-and-run accident in which the victim dies. The five men take a vow of silence; one is troubled by the decision. Interesting analysis of responsibility for one's behavior while intoxicated.

Days of Wine and Roses (1962) Drama ΨΨΨΨ
Blake Edwards film starring Jack Lemmon and Lee Remick. Lemmon teaches Remick how to drink. Lemmon is saved by AA; Remick is unable to stop drinking, despite the consequences.

"You see, the world looks so dirty to me when I'm not drinking. Joe, remember Fisherman's Wharf? The water when you looked too close? That's the way the world looks to me when I'm not drinking."

Kristen describes why she continues to drink in Days of Wine and Roses *(1962)*

Drunks (1995) Drama ΨΨΨΨ
This film is the best available introduction to Alcoholics Anonymous. It is highly recommended for any student who will be working with substance abuse issues.

Educating Rita (1983) Drama ΨΨ
Michael Caine as an alcoholic college professor who takes on the task of educating a working-class woman.

Everything Must Go (2011) Comedy Drama ΨΨΨ
Will Ferrell's character Nick loses his wife and his job and copes by setting up a yard sale on his front lawn. He spends each day drinking beer from morning to night, but eventually makes contacts who help him put his life back together again.

Factotum (2005) Comedy ΨΨ
A struggling writer works multiple odd jobs and sleeps with multiple partners. He consistently drinks on the job and while writing. He loses several jobs, but is unable to stop drinking. The film accurately portrays alcohol dependence.

Fire Within, The (1963, France) Drama ΨΨΨΨ
French filmmaker Louis Malle's remarkable account of alcoholism, suicide, and the existential choices that confront us all.

Flight (2012) Drama ΨΨΨΨ
Denzel Washington plays Whip Whitaker, a handsome and talented airline pilot who abuses alcohol, cocaine and other drugs. His skill as a pilot allows him to land a damaged plane in a field, saving the lives of almost all the passengers and crew. The film is misleading in its premise that someone can be very intoxicated and still perform well-rehearsed skills at a very high level.

For One More Day (2007) Drama ΨΨ
A child of divorced parents grows up feeling guilty about his mother's death. As an adult, he becomes depressed and an alcoholic. His suicide attempt is interrupted by his deceased mother who gives him one last day to spend with her. Based on Mitch Album's novel.

Gervaise (1956, France) Drama ΨΨΨΨΨ
French film based on Emile Zola's novel *L'Assomoir*, depicting the fatal degeneration of a family, mainly because of alcohol.

"Mrs. Robinson, you're trying to seduce me. Aren't you?"

The Graduate (1967)

Graduate, The (1967) Drama/Comedy ΨΨΨ
A telling indictment of the shallow values of the time (e.g., "plastics"). Mrs. Robinson's alcoholism impairs her judgment and ruins her life.

Great Man Votes, The (1939) Drama ΨΨ
John Barrymore plays an alcoholic college professor fighting to maintain custody of his children.

Harvey (1950) Comedy/Drama ΨΨΨ
Elwood P. Dowd's (Jimmy Stewart) imaginary friend is a six foot white rabbit named Harvey with whom he has a good relationship. Dowd drinks daily, goes to taverns, and has hidden bottles behind books. He always gets two drinks, one for himself and one for Harvey, and therefore has two drinks at a time.

Henry Fool (1997) Comedy/Drama ΨΨ
Hal Hartley film about a taciturn garbage man who befriends a roguish alcoholic.

Iceman Cometh, The (1973) Drama ΨΨ
Lee Marvin in an adaptation of Eugene O'Neill's play about alcoholism and the pathos of dreams unfulfilled.

I'll Cry Tomorrow (1955) Biography ΨΨΨ
Singer Lillian Roth (Susan Hayward) attempts suicide as a way of coping with her alcoholism before AA support helps her find her way.

Ironweed (1987) Drama ΨΨΨΨ
Jack Nicholson and Meryl Streep in compelling roles as homeless alcoholics. The film, a very realistic portrayal of life on skid row, should be contrasted with another excellent film made the same year, *Barfly*.

Julia (2008) Drama ΨΨ
Tilda Swinton stars as Julia, a manipulative but charismatic woman with a long history of alcoholism.

Key Largo (1948) Crime ΨΨΨ
Claire Trevor won an Academy Award for Best Supporting Actress for her role as an alcoholic singer forced to beg gangster Edward G. Robinson for a drink during a hurricane in Key West.

Last Night at the Alamo (1983) Drama ΨΨΨ
Fascinating examination of bar culture in a small Texas town. Unforgettable characters, most of whom are coping with alcoholism and adultery.

Leaving Las Vegas (1995) Drama ΨΨΨΨ
Nicholas Cage delivers a stunning performance as an alcoholic who has no interest in quitting. He develops a relationship with a prostitute (Elisabeth Shue) who is the first to truly understand him. Gripping alcohol dependence portrayal with painful delirium tremens on screen.

Legend of Bagger Vance, The (2000) Drama/Inspiration ΨΨΨ
Matt Damon plays Rannulph Junuh, a talented golfer whose game has deteriorated because of his war experiences. He isolates himself, drinks heavily, and plays cards all night. He returns to golf in a promotional event against the top two golfers in the game with the help of an inspirational caddy and mentor, Bagger Vance (Will Smith).

Libertine, The (2004) Drama ΨΨ
John Wilmot, the second Earl of Rochester in 17th century Europe, a poet and author and close friends of Charles II (John Malkovich), desperately uses alcohol to cope with banishment. He drinks constantly for 5 years and the long-term consequences of alcohol use are shown.

Lonely Passion of Judith Hearne, The (1987) Romance ΨΨ
Maggie Smith plays a lonely alcoholic who mistakenly believes she has a last chance to find love and meaning in her life.

Long Day's Journey into Night (1962) Drama ΨΨΨΨ
Alcohol is a part of daily life for this deeply troubled family. Numerous examples of family pathology, conflict between father and sons, and denial.

Lost Weekend, The (1945) Drama ΨΨΨΨ
Billy Wilder classic starring Ray Milland as a writer struggling to overcome his alcoholism. Some scenes were filmed at Bellevue Hospital in New York City, and the examples of delirium tremens are very convincing. Polanski borrowed scenes from *The Lost Weekend* as models for his film *Repulsion*.

"It shrinks my liver, doesn't it, Nat? It pickles my kidneys, yeah. But what it does to the mind? It tosses the sandbags overboard so the balloon can soar. Suddenly I'm above the ordinary. I'm competent. I'm walking a tightrope over Niagara Falls. I'm one of the great ones."

Don Birnam talking to his bartender about what it feels like to be drunk in *The Lost Weekend* (1945)

Love Song for Bobby Long, A (2004) Drama ΨΨ
A young woman returns to her hometown, New Orleans, for a funeral and finds two drunken dwellers living in her deceased mother's home. Bobby Long (John Travolta), an English professor, and his former assistant have no intentions of moving.

Misfortunates, The (2009, Belgium) Drama ΨΨΨ
A 13-year-old boy grows up with an alcoholic father and several alcoholic uncles.

My Beautiful Laundrette (1985) Drama ΨΨ
The two lead characters are homosexuals, although this fact is almost incidental to the story about alcoholism, street gangs, race relations, and social class.

My Favorite Year (1982) Comedy ΨΨΨ
A great actor (modeled after John Barrymore and Errol Flynn) who has become a pathetic drunk must confront one of the greatest challenges of his career – a live television performance.

My Name Is Bill W. (1989) ΨΨΨ
Made-for-TV movie about the founding of Alcoholics Anonymous.

My Name Was Bette: The Life and Death of an Alcoholic (2012) Documentary ΨΨΨΨ
This film is a sensitive examination of the life and death of Bette VanderAkker, a nurse and mother who died from alcoholism. The film was made by Bette's daughter, and it provides considerable insight into the problem of alcoholism in women.

National Lampoon's Animal House (1978) Comedy ΨΨ
One of the best of a hundred or so college films that portray fraternity life as a series of beer busts interspersed with an occasional class. At one point, John Belushi, not the brightest of the fraternity brothers, chugs a fifth of Jack Daniels.

Night of the Iguana, The (1964) Drama ΨΨ
Richard Burton and Ava Gardner star in John Huston's adaptation of Tennessee Williams' play. Burton plays a very convincing alcoholic and erstwhile clergyman.

No Such Thing (2001, Iceland/US) Ψ
Hal Hartley film about a belligerent, foul-mouthed monster who is also an alcoholic.

"Think of an idea to change our world ... and put it into action."

A student assignment in *Pay It Forward* (2000)

Pay It Forward (2000) Drama/Inspiration ΨΨ
Haley Joel Osment plays a seventh grader implementing a class assignment that has profound effects on the people around him. His mother (Helen Hunt) is a struggling alcoholic.

Prize Winner of Defiance, Ohio, The (2005) Drama ΨΨΨΨ
A stay-at-home mother (Julianne Moore) in the 1950–60s, confronts her alcoholic and dependent husband (Woody Harrelson) with unswerving optimism. The film shows the social expectations of women who stay in relationships with abusive husbands.

Proud and the Beautiful, The (1953) Romance ΨΨ
A film about a woman who helps an alcoholic physician overcome his problems and regain some sense of dignity. Filmed in France and Mexico.

Sideways (2004) Comedy ΨΨΨ
Two men tour California's wine country. One is a depressed alcoholic craving a relationship; the other is going to be married later that week, but he begins an affair with a woman he meets on the trip.

Skin Deep (1989) Comedy ΨΨ
A funny Blake Edwards film about an alcoholic writer who continues to deny his alcoholism long after it has become apparent to everyone else.

Smash-Up, the Story of a Woman (1947) Drama ΨΨ
Melodramatic Susan Hayward film about a movie star who must come to grips with her alcoholism.

Some Like It Hot (1959) Crime/Comedy ΨΨ
Marilyn Monroe portrays a performer constantly sneaking drinks; she is nearly fired for alcohol abuse.

Streamers (1983) Drama ΨΨΨ
Robert Altman film about three soldiers waiting to go to Vietnam. The film deals with themes of homosexuality, violence, and racism, but also illustrates the alcohol abuse that is pervasive in military life.

Sweet Bird of Youth (1962) Drama ΨΨ
Paul Newman in an adaptation of Tennessee Williams' play about a has-been actress (played by Geraldine Page) addicted to alcohol and drugs who takes up with a young, vital Newman.

Taxi Blues (1990, Soviet Union) Drama ΨΨΨ
Alcoholic jazz musician becomes friends with an anti-Semitic taxi driver. This Russian film won the prize for Best Director at Cannes. Fascinating examination of the role of alcohol in the daily lives of the protagonists in Moscow society.

Tender Mercies (1983) Drama ΨΨΨΨΨ
Sensitive and optimistic film in which Robert Duvall plays a successfully recovering alcoholic songwriter. Duvall won an Oscar for this almost perfect performance.

Tree Grows in Brooklyn, A (1945) Drama ΨΨΨ
Elia Kazan film about a poor Irish family living in Brooklyn at the turn of the century. The family's problems are complicated by the father's alcoholism.

Trees Lounge (1996) Comedy ΨΨΨΨ
Steve Buscemi wrote and directed this compelling film, and he plays the lead character, a 31-year-old unemployed auto mechanic. Few contemporary films present a more vivid picture of the problems associated with alcoholism.

Under Capricorn (1949) Drama Ψ
A little-known Hitchcock film starring Joseph Cotton and Ingrid Bergman. Bergman is a wealthy socialite whose life is ruined by her alcoholism.

Under the Volcano (1984) Drama ΨΨΨΨΨ
John Huston directing Albert Finney; excellent portrayal of chronic alcoholism.

Verdict, The (1982) Drama ΨΨΨΨ
Paul Newman in a wonderful role as a disillusioned alcoholic lawyer who becomes genuinely involved with a brain-injured client who is the victim of medical malpractice. He wins the case but continues to drink. Interesting analysis of codependency.

> Edward J. Concannon: "Why wasn't she getting oxygen...?"
> Dr. Robert Towler: "Well, many reasons, actually ..."
> Edward J. Concannon: "Tell me one?"
> Dr. Robert Towler: "She'd aspirated vomitus into her mask..."
> Edward J. Concannon: "She threw up in her mask. Let's cut the bullshit. Say it: She threw up in her mask."
>
> *The Verdict* (1982)

Vital Signs (1986) Drama ΨΨ
Ed Asner in a surpassingly good made-for-TV movie about a father and son, both surgeons, fighting the twin problems of alcoholism and drug abuse.

Vodka Lemon (2003, France/Armenia) Comedy ΨΨΨ
Minimalist film about grieving widows who befriend one another in a culture where everyone seems to drinks vodka.

What Price Hollywood? (1932) Drama ΨΨ
Alcoholic director helps Hollywood waitress become a star. The figure of the alcoholic director may have been modeled after John Barrymore.

When a Man Loves a Woman (1994) Drama ΨΨ
Meg Ryan as a middle-class alcoholic. This is a melodramatic and somewhat predictable film, but an interesting introduction to AA and Al-Anon. The film explores the role of codependency and a husband's role in his wife's alcoholism.

Drug Abuse

21 Grams (2003) Drama/Mystery ΨΨΨΨ
Complicated, well-integrated stories of an ex-con and recovering alcoholic (Benicio Del Toro), a cocaine addict (Naomi Watts), and a terminal man awaiting a transplant (Sean Penn), all brought together by an accidental death.

> "They say we all lose 21 grams at the exact moment of death ... everyone. The weight of a stack of nickels. The weight of a chocolate bar. The weight of a hummingbird."
>
> *21 Grams* (2003)

Answer Man, The (2009) Drama ΨΨ
The author of the hit self-help book *Me and God* helps a single mother and a young man who has just been released from a drug rehabilitation facility find meaning in their lives.

Awakening of the Beast (1969) Drama Ψ
Cult film involving four subjects who take LSD as an experiment to provide data for a book a psychiatrist is writing about the effects of drugs.

Bad Lieutenant (1992) Drama ΨΨΨ
Harvey Keitel stars in one of his most powerful roles as a police lieutenant addicted to cocaine, alcohol, and prostitutes. The film illustrates stark abuse of power and the deterioration of family life that accompanies addiction. Keitel's character has a hallucination in which Jesus Christ comes to him.

Big Lebowski, The (1998) Comedy ΨΨ
Coen brothers film portraying The Dude (Jeff Bridges), a cannabis-smoking, unemployed drifter in this entertaining, film noir comedy.

Bird (1988) Biography ΨΨ
Clint Eastwood directed this biographical film of the life of jazz great and drug addict Charlie "Bird" Parker. Parker was an addict for all of his adult life, and his addiction killed him at the age of 34.

Blow (2001) Drama ΨΨΨ
Johnny Depp stars as George Jung, a man who claimed to have imported about 85% of all cocaine in America in the late 1970s.

Candy (2006, Australia) Drama ΨΨΨ
"Candy" is both the name of the female lead in the film (Abbie Cornish) and a slang term for heroin. The film accurately portrays heroin addiction and withdrawal. Geoffrey Rush is very convincing as a chemistry professor who supports the habits of his young friends and who eventually dies from an overdose.

Chappaqua (1966) Drama Ψ
Heroin addict checks in for treatment. The film is most notable for short roles by William Burroughs, Ravi Shankar, and Allen Ginsburg.

Christiane F. (1981) Drama ΨΨΨΨ
Powerful and frightening examination of the life of a teenage drug addict in West Berlin. Based on a true story, the film is still gripping almost 3 decades after it was made.

Clean and Sober (1988) Drama ΨΨΨΨ
Good portrayal of AA, cocaine addiction, and alcoholism.

> "The best way to break old habits is to make new ones."
>
> *Clean and Sober* (1988)

Cocaine Fiends, The (1936) Drama Ψ
Another "word of warning" film that portrays the dangers of cocaine. Made in the same year as *Reefer Madness*. The message in this film is exaggerated and histrionic but somewhat more realistic in its estimate of the dangers of the drug.

Coffee and Cigarettes (2003) Comedy ΨΨΨ
Various conversational skits (starring a variety of talents, including Bill Murray, Roberto Benigni, Cate Blanchett, Iggy Pop, and Steve Buscemi) linked through the characters' consumption of coffee and tea and smoking. Portrayals of compulsive use of each, side effects, and the desire to quit or avoid the substance.

Connection, The (1961) Drama ΨΨΨ
Heroin addicts in New York wait for their pusher.

Dead Ringers (1988) Drama ΨΨΨ
A David Cronenberg film about two twin brothers who are renowned gynecologists. They are also addicted to amphetamines and barbiturates. Based on a true story about two twin physicians who died from barbiturate withdrawal.

Dopamine (2003) Drama/Comedy ΨΨ
Independent film explores the chemistry behind male–female relationships. One character uses amphetamine pills and large quantities of caffeine. Interesting debate on how physical attraction emerges.

> "Most people don't know how they're gonna feel from one moment to the next. But a dope fiend has a pretty good idea. All you gotta do is look at the labels on the little bottles."
>
> Addict reflecting on the pleasures of drugs in
> *Drugstore Cowboy* (1989)

Drugstore Cowboy (1989) Drama ΨΨΨΨ
Matt Dillon leads a group of junkies who rob pharmacies to support their habit. William Burroughs plays a junkie priest.

Easy Rider (1969) Drama ΨΨΨ
Classic film of the late 1960s with Jack Nicholson as an alcoholic lawyer and Peter Fonda and Dennis Hopper as marijuana-smoking, LSD-using free spirits. The film is dated but still worth seeing.

> "The governor of Louisiana gave me this. Madame Tinkertoy's House of Blue Lights, corner of Bourbon and Toulouse, New Orleans, Louisiana. Now, this is supposed to be the finest whorehouse in the south. These ain't no pork chops! These are U. S. Prime!"
>
> Jack Nicholson plans for his trip to New Orleans in *Easy Rider* (1969)

Fear and Loathing in Las Vegas (1998) Drama/Fantasy ΨΨ
Terry Gilliam's adaptation of Hunter S. Thompson's Gonzo journalism classic. The book is better than the film; although the movie does not glorify drug use, it clearly models the behavior and tacitly condones the practice of driving while intoxicated.

Half Baked (1998) Comedy Ψ
Exaggerated comedy about smoking "weed." Interesting for its classification of different types of marijuana smokers: "you should have been there smoker," the "scavenger," the "enhancer," the "medicinal," the "after school special," the "father, I'm 40 and still cool," the "MacGyver smoker," the "straight-up potheads," and the "I'm only creative if I smoke" smokers.

Half Nelson (2006) Drama ΨΨΨ
A drug-addicted teacher/coach (Ryan Gosling) at an inner city school uses cocaine regularly and smokes crack in the girl's locker room after a game. He has a history of failed rehabilitation, and tries to rebuild relations but struggles with anger and is disengaged from his family.

Hatful of Rain, A (1957) Drama ΨΨ
Melodramatic film about the life and problems of a drug addict. This was one of the earliest films to honestly examine the problem of drug addiction.

High Art (1998) Drama/Comedy ΨΨ
Realistic, well-acted independent film about several people whose lives intersect for drugs, support, and conversation in a New York City apartment.

Hustle and Flow (2005) Drama ΨΨΨΨ
In this Sundance Audience Choice Award film, an aspiring Memphis disc jockey works to get his first record made as he approaches mid-life. He is a pimp, drug user, and dealer who questions his life's purpose and the decisions he has made along the way.

I Don't Buy Kisses Anymore (1992) Comedy/Romance Ψ
Lightweight but entertaining film about an obese male who falls in love with a woman using him as a subject for her master's thesis.

I'm Dancing as Fast as I Can (1982) Drama ΨΨ
Jill Clayburgh plays the role of a high-powered documentary filmmaker who becomes addicted to Valium and requires hospitalization in a special program for addicts. Based on a true story.

I'm Still Here (2010) Drama/Documentary ΨΨ
Casey Affleck film that is a mockumentary about Joaquin Phoenix, his drug use, and and his announced (but fake) retirement from films to concentrate on making rap/hip-hop music.

Jungle Fever (1991) Drama/Romance ΨΨΨ
Interesting film about race relations and sexual stereotypes, with a subplot involving Gator, the crackhead brother of the protagonist, who is destroying his middle-class family.

Kurt Cobain: About a Son (2006) Documentary ΨΨ
Cobain discusses his chronic pain and irritable bowel syndrome, as well as his suicidal ideation and heroin addiction.

La Femme Nikita (1990) Action/Drama ΨΨ
Sociopathic and drug-addicted woman is sentenced to die for murder and then is transformed into a government agent. Most memorable for the drugstore robbery that opens the film.

Lady Sings the Blues (1972) Biography/Musical ΨΨ
Diana Ross plays heroin addict Billie Holiday.

Long Day's Journey into Night (1962) Drama ΨΨΨΨΨ
Katharine Hepburn plays a morphine-addicted, histrionic mother with an alcoholic son (Jason Robards). One of O'Neill's greatest plays; one of Hepburn's greatest roles. Hepburn's character is a good illustration of a histrionic personality disorder.

Love and Diane (2002) Documentary ΨΨ
A mother recovers from an addiction to crack as she attempts to start a new life and connect with the children she had abandoned.

Love Liza (2002) Drama/Comedy ΨΨΨΨ
Philip Seymour Hoffman skillfully plays a man who huffs gasoline in response to his wife's suicide. A rare and illuminating depiction of inhalant abuse and intoxication.

Luna (1979) Drama Ψ
Disappointing Bernardo Bertolucci film, with Jill Clayburgh playing the mother of a drug addict son. The film hints at an incestuous relationship between mother and son.

MacArthur Park (2001) Drama ΨΨΨΨ
A crack addict struggles to leave drug dependence and his home in the park to live with his estranged son. A quality independent film.

> "What the fuck do I need to be sober for so I can see how fucked up shit really is, please. High is how I am gonna be. I'm high till I die"
>
> A crack addict in *MacArthur Park* (2001)

Man with the Golden Arm, The (1955) Drama ΨΨ
Frank Sinatra and Kim Novak in a dated but interesting portrayal of drug addiction. Good example of the challenge of "cold turkey" withdrawal.

Maria, Full of Grace (2004) Drama ΨΨΨ
Fascinating, independent film depicting the realities and dangers young girls from Colombia face as they take jobs as "mules," smuggling drugs into the United States by swallowing them in large latex packages. While this film is not directly about substance abuse, it depicts the drug trade and problems related to ingesting drugs for illegal purposes.

Mask (1985) Biography ΨΨΨ
Bogdanovich film with Cher as the mother of deformed but spunky teenager Rocky Dennis. Sympathetic portrayal of motorcycle gangs. Cher struggles with her angry father and her compulsive use of alcohol and drugs as she works hard to be a good mother.

Mighty Wind, A (2003) Comedy ΨΨ
Hilarious Christopher Guest parody of folk music. One character displays significant remnants of years of drug abuse.

Naked Lunch (1991) Drama/Science Fiction/Fantasy ΨΨ
This film is based on the novel by William Burroughs and deals with drug abuse, paranoia, and homicide.

New Jack City (1991) Action/Crime ΨΨ
Wesley Snipes and Ice-T in a realistic movie about the business of drugs. Good introduction to cocaine addiction and Narcotics Anonymous.

> "If the First Amendment will protect a scumbag like me, it will protect all of you."
>
> Larry Flint on free speech in
> *The People vs. Larry Flint* (1996)

People vs. Larry Flynt, The (1996) Biography/Drama ΨΨΨ
A good movie about a controversial figure, the film forces the viewer to examine his or her views on pornography and free speech. The film is included in this section because of the effects of drugs on the lives of Flynt and his wife, Althea (Courtney Love), after he is shot and becomes addicted to narcotics.

Pineapple Express (2008) Drama Ψ
Two enthusiastic marijuana users quickly find themselves embroiled in the complex world of drug dealing.

Platoon (1986) War ΨΨΨΨ
Vietnam veteran Oliver Stone directed *Platoon,* one of the most realistic of dozens of war movies. There is an interesting juxtaposition of "boozers" (those who use alcohol to escape) and "heads" (those who take refuge in marijuana and other illegal drugs).

Postcards from the Edge (1990) Comedy/Drama ΨΨΨ
Mike Nichols' adaptation of a Carrie Fisher story about life as the daughter of a famous actress. The mother is alcoholic; the daughter abuses multiple drugs, including cocaine and sedatives. There are brief scenes of therapy and a terrific cast.

Pulp Fiction (1994) Drama ΨΨΨΨΨ
Quentin Tarantino film about drugs, crime, depravity, the underworld, and life in urban America. One especially memorable scene involves Vincent Vega (John Travolta) smashing an adrenaline-filled needle into Mia Wallace's (Uma Thurman) chest to revive her after she inadvertently overdoses on heroin.

> "What now? Let me tell you what now. I'm calling a couple of hard, pipe-hittin' niggers, who'll go to work on this soon-to-be-dead hillbilly rapist here with a pair of pliers and a blow torch. You hear me talkin', hillbilly boy? I ain't through with you by a damn sight. I'm a gonna get medieval on your ass."
>
> Marsellus Wallace planning revenge in
> *Pulp Fiction* (1994)

Quitting (2001) Drama ΨΨΨΨ
Slow-moving but interesting Chinese film about a one-time famous actor who deteriorates due to a heroin addiction. The emotional and psychological withdrawals depicted are memorable. This is an important film on addiction and withdrawal.

Ray (2004) Drama ΨΨΨΨΨ
This award winning film depicts 20 years in the life of Ray Charles when he was addicted to heroin. Physical disability (blindness) and childhood psychological traumas shape the personal life of this renowned artist.

Reefer Madness (1936) Drama Ψ
Campy film depicting the dangers of marijuana. Ironically, countless college students have gone to see this film high on the very drug the film condemns.

Requiem for a Dream (2000) Drama ΨΨΨΨ
Greatly disturbing film about four drug addicts whose lives deteriorate. Unforgettable performances and critically acclaimed. Excellent direction by Darren Aronofsky.

"I'm somebody now, everybody likes me."

Requiem for a Dream (2000)

Rose, The (1979) Musical ΨΨ
Bette Midler portrays Janis Joplin and her problems with Southern Comfort and drugs.

Rush (1991) Crime/Drama ΨΨΨ
Two undercover narcotics agents find addiction to be an occupational hazard.

Scarface (1983) Crime ΨΨΨ
Brian De Palma movie starring Al Pacino as a Cuban immigrant mobster who becomes addicted to the cocaine he is marketing. This long film, which tends to be loved or hated, is based on a 1932 Howard Hawks classic with the same name.

Seven Percent Solution, The (1976) Mystery ΨΨ
Sigmund Freud treats Sherlock Holmes' cocaine addiction. Creative idea and historically accurate in documenting Freud's early enthusiasm for cocaine.

Shadow Hours (2000) Drama Ψ
A wealthy man manipulates a young gas station attendant into drug relapse and fraternizing with three types of "night owls": (1) those who find their prince charming or princess before midnight, (2) vampires – prostitutes, drug dealers, and (3) Mr. Hydes – those that can't sleep.

Sherrybaby (2006) Drama ΨΨΨ
A woman leaves prison following a 6-year history of heroin addiction and neglect of her daughter; despite the history of abuse, she eagerly wants to re-unite with her daughter and attempt to start anew.

Sid and Nancy (1986) Biography ΨΨΨΨ
Compelling biography of Sid Vicious of the Sex Pistols; offers insight into the worlds of drugs and rock and roll.

Side Effects (2013) Drama ΨΨΨ
A severely depressed woman who has made several suicide attempts is prescribed a new medication; she subse-

quently murders her husband, apparently as a result of the medication. She is sent to a psychiatric hospital, and the doctor who prescribed the medication sees his practice ruined. However, things turn out to be much more complicated than the viewer first believes.

"Dog had a litter of about 8, and my Mother was bending over killing each one of these little puppies in the bathtub. I remember I said 'why?'... She said 'I'm just killing what I can't take care of.' Then my momma said to me, she looked at me and she said, 'I wish I could do that to you.'"

A recollection by the cook in *Spun* (2002)

Spun (2002) Drama/Comedy ΨΨΨ
A well-done, intense film about methamphetamine addiction.

Stardust (1975) Drama Ψ
British film about a rock star whose success is tarnished by drug addiction and mental illness.

Sweet Nothing (1996) Drama ΨΨΨ
An effective examination of the futility, desperation, and violence associated with crack addiction. This is a true story based on diaries found in a Bronx apartment in March of 1991.

Synanon (1965) Drama ΨΨ
Interesting only insofar as the film documents the treatment methods practiced in this highly praised treatment program.

Tideland (2005) Drama/Fantasy Ψ
A disappointing Terry Gilliam film about a young girl with drug addicted parents; the mother dies from a drug overdose and the father takes his daughter to hide in the country at his mother's home.

Traffic (2000) Drama ΨΨΨΨ
This Steven Soderbergh film thematically intersects the lives of a newly hired government drug czar (Michael Douglas), his daughter who experiments with crack, police officers struggling with drug cartels, and a suburban wife of a drug lord.

"I've been known to sniff it, smoke it, swallow it, stick it up my arse and inject it into my veins. I've been trying to combat this addiction, but unless you count social security scams and shoplifting, I haven't had a regular job in years."

Trainspotting (1996)

Trainspotting (1996) Drama/Comedy ΨΨΨ
A realistic and disturbing film about the heroin scene in Edinburgh. The film presents accurate depictions of cold turkey withdrawal. There is one memorable scene in which a young mother's baby dies while she is high, and she immediately needs a fix to cope with her grief. Several scatological scenes seem gratuitous and unnecessary.

Veronika Voss (1982) Drama ΨΨ
Rainer Werner Fassbinder film about a German movie star who becomes addicted to morphine. Fassbinder himself died from abuse of alcohol and heroin.

Wasted (2002) Drama ΨΨ
Teens, covering up inner pain, fear, and loneliness, battle their heroin addiction.

What's Love Got to Do with It? (1993) Musical/Biography ΨΨ
Excellent film biography of singer Tina Turner includes some memorable scenes of husband Ike strung out on cocaine.

Who'll Stop the Rain? (1978) Crime/Drama ΨΨ
Also known as *Dog Soldiers,* this film explores the world of drug smuggling and addiction.

Winter's Bone (2010) Drama ΨΨΨΨ
Jennifer Lawrence is wonderful as the 17-year-old Ree Dolly, who struggles to find her methamphetamine-addicted father and keep her Ozark family together.

Megan: What are we ever gonna do with you, baby girl?
Ree: Kill me I guess.
Megan: That idea's been said already. Got any others?
Ree: Help me. Nobody's said that idea yet, have they?

Ree Dolly (Jennifer Lawrence) uses her social intelligence to get out of a difficult situation in *Winter's Bone* (2010).

Gambling and Other Non-Substance-Related Addictions

21 (2008) Drama ΨΨ
A young man is accepted into Harvard medical school but in order to afford the tuition joins a group of card counters led by their teacher. Kevin Spacey plays the ringleader.

2046 (2004, China/Hong Kong) Fantasy/Drama ΨΨ
One character has a compulsive gambling problem in this film that blends present and future; the movie is directed by War Kar Wai, who films without a script. "Love is all a matter of timing – it's no good meeting the right person too soon or too late."

Basic Instinct (1992) Suspense/Thriller ΨΨ
Psychological thriller about a novelist (Sharon Stone) who is a sex addict that entangles an investigator (Michael Douglas) in a complex mystery of murder, sex, and fascination.

Psychologist: "Nick, when you recollect your childhood, are your recollections pleasing to you?"
Nick: "Number 1, I don't remember how often I used to jerk off, but it was a lot. Number 2, I wasn't pissed off at my dad, even when I was old enough to know what he and mom were doing in the bedroom. Number 3, I don't look in the toilet before I flush it. Number 4, I haven't wet my bed for a long time. Number 5, why don't the two of you go fuck yourselves; I'm outta here."

Nick feels threatened by a psychological interview in *Basic Instinct* (1992)

Belle de Jour (1967) Drama ΨΨΨΨ
Luis Buñuel film with Catherine Deneuve playing a bored housewife who amuses herself by working in a brothel from two until five every afternoon, at least until her sexual obsessions begin to complicate her life. Buñuel may be filming what is just an erotic dream.

Bookies (2003) Drama ΨΨ
Three college roommates, obsessed with gambling, secretly launch a "bookie" operation.

Burn After Reading (2008) Comedy Ψ
Clever, dark comedy by the Coen brothers in which George Clooney's character has a sexual addiction.

California Split (1974) Comedy ΨΨ
Robert Altman movie starring George Segal and Elliott Gould as two compulsive gamblers. Not as strong a film as *The Gambler*.

Carnal Knowledge (1971) Drama ΨΨ
This Mike Nichols film traces the sexual lives of two college roommates, played by Jack Nicholson and Art Garfunkel, as they age and become increasingly disenchanted with sex, love, and the possibilities inherent in relationships.

Casino (1995) Drama ΨΨ
Martin Scorsese film explores the mafia's relationship to Las Vegas and gives an inside look at casinos and gambling addictions. A strong cast includes Robert De Niro, Joe Pesci, Sharon Stone, and James Woods.

Choke (2008) Drama ΨΨ
A sex addict and medical school dropout feigns choking to raise money for care of his mother with Alzheimer's disease.

Closer (2004) Comedy/Drama ΨΨΨ
A quality film with good dialogue and superb acting by Jude Law, Natalie Portman, Julia Roberts, and Clive Owen. Important issues related to sexuality are portrayed, including deceit, infidelity, the failure to self-disclose, dependency, the impact of guilt and shame, and relationship testing. One scene depicts an amusing online conversation between two men sending erotic instant messages.

Comfort of Strangers, The (1990) Drama ΨΨ
Sexual conflict and disorders abound as two couples find themselves entangled with one another in Venice.

Cooler, The (2003) Drama ΨΨΨ
Unlucky, depressed man (William H. Macy) walks around the casino as "the cooler," someone paid to bring bad luck to successful gamers by appearing near their gambling tables. He is paying off his enormous gambling debts owed to the casino owner Alec Baldwin.

Crime of Father Amaro, The (2002, Mexico) Drama ΨΨΨ
A young priest, newly ordained, goes to a small, Mexican town to serve a parish. He witnesses his pastor having sex with women and he falls for a woman whom he secretively uses for sex until she becomes pregnant.

Damage (1992) Drama ΨΨΨ
A Louis Malle film starring Jeremy Irons as a man who develops a sexual obsession for his son's fiancée. Both the father and the son's girlfriend seem powerless to control their erotic attachment despite its inevitable consequences.

De-Lovely (2004) Musical/Comedy/Biography ΨΨ
The story of the life of Cole Porter and his sexual addiction.

Diary of a Nymphomaniac (2009, Spain) Drama ΨΨ
A 28-year-old woman has an insatiable appetite for sex and eventually ends up in a brothel.

Diary of a Sex Addict, The (2001) Drama ΨΨ
Depiction of a classic sex addict who denies, rationalizes and continues a series of affairs until he finally can deceive no longer. He continues his compulsive behavior, even after the consequences of this behavior are almost fatal. The film offers a realistic portrayal of a sex addict.

> Therapist: "Which one is really you? The family man or the other guy?"
> Patient: "Both"
>
> *The Diary of a Sex Addict* (2001)

Dinner Rush (2001) Drama/Comedy ΨΨ
In New York City sits an upscale restaurant frequented by highbrow customers, self-centered art critics, hoodlums from Queens, and casual customers. One of the cooks has a gambling problem.

Dirty Shame, A (2004) Comedy Ψ
A woman becomes promiscuous after a head injury.

Don Jon (2013) Drama ΨΨ
A young, unmarried man finds that his addiction to online pornography gets in the way of meaningful sexual interactions; each week he confesses the same sins (masturbating to pornography and sex outside of marriage) to his priest.

Far From Heaven (2002) Drama ΨΨΨ
Julianne Moore, living in a conservative area in a conservative time, finds out her husband is a homosexual. Interesting film that explores racism, stereotypes, and secrets.

Felicia's Journey (1999, Canada, United Kingdom) Drama ΨΨ
A pregnant young woman leaves Ireland for England to find her boyfriend; upon arrival, she is befriended by a middle aged caterer who has a history of exploiting women in similar situations.

Gambler, The (1974) Drama ΨΨΨΨ
James Caan plays a university professor of literature who can't control his compulsive gambling. One of the best film portrayals of pathological gambling.

Good Thief, The (2002) Drama ΨΨ
Nick Nolte plays a junkie gambler.

Harold and Maude (1972) Comedy ΨΨΨ
A cult film that examines sexual and romantic attraction across generations; this movie will force you to reexamine your feelings about age and death.

House of Games (1987) Crime ΨΨ
A David Mamet film about a psychiatrist specializing in the treatment of gambling addiction. Fascinating introduction to the world of the con.

Hysteria (2011) Romantic Comedy ΨΨ
Maggie Gyllenhaal and Hugh Dancy star in this amusing story about two gynecologists who very properly masturbate their Victorian clients, initially using digital stimulation and later using a mechanical vibrator they invent. (The

word "hysteria" comes from the Greek term for "wandering uterus," and it was once believed only women could develop hysteria. The term is not found in the *DSM-5*.)

I Am a Sex Addict (2005) Biography/Comedy Ψ
A recovering sex addict describes how his life and marriages have been changed by his addiction to prostitutes.

Kiss of the Spider Woman (1985) Prison ΨΨΨΨ
A homosexual and a political activist share a prison cell and grow to understand and appreciate each other. William Hurt won an Academy Award for his performance.

Last Tango in Paris (1973) Drama ΨΨΨΨΨ
Marlon Brando stars in a classic Bernardo Bertolucci film about a man who begins a casual sexual liaison on the day his wife commits suicide. The two lovers never exchange names. The film includes themes of depression, sexuality, loneliness, and cynicism.

Lianna (1983) Drama ΨΨΨ
Sensitive film portraying the emotional life of a woman who leaves her husband and two children after she becomes romantically involved with a lesbian professor teaching a night course in child psychology.

Magenta (1996) Drama Ψ
Happily married physician crosses boundaries sexually with his sister-in-law, creating havoc in his family.

Maverick (1994) Western/Drama ΨΨ
Mel Gibson and Jodi Foster star as charming gamblers and cons in a game of high stakes poker.

Maxed Out (2006) Documentary ΨΨ
Interesting statistics and depiction of the struggles and realities of American credit card debt. The film depicts the consequences of "spending" addictions and impulse control disorders.

"Well, I'll tell you the truth now. I ain't a real cowboy, but I am one helluva stud."

Joe Buck in *Midnight Cowboy* (1969)

Midnight Cowboy (1969) Drama ΨΨΨΨΨ
Jon Voight leaves Texas to make his fortune in New York City working as a stud; instead, he winds up hanging out with Ratso Rizzo, who dies before the two can escape to Florida. This film is a fascinating and complex character study.

Oscar and Lucinda (1997) Drama/Romance ΨΨΨΨ
Pathological gambling and concomitant anxiety disorders are clearly depicted in this film set in mid-1800s England, starring Ralph Fiennes and Cate Blanchett

Owning Mahowny (2003) Drama ΨΨΨ
Philip Seymour Hoffman, one of today's finest character actors, plays a pathological gambler. Great portrayal of the addictive cycle and elements of denial, deterioration, and self-destruction. The film is based on a true story.

Personal Best (1982) Sports ΨΨΨ
Fascinating film that explores the sexual relationship that develops between two women competing for a position on an Olympic team.

Reflections in a Golden Eye (1967) Drama ΨΨ
A John Huston film in which Richard Burton plays the role of a repressed homosexual Army officer serving on a small Georgia military base. Elizabeth Taylor is his sadistic and sexually liberated wife. The film was banned by the Catholic Film Board.

Romance (1999, France) Drama Ψ
A young school teacher is ignored sexually by her boyfriend, so she engages in a desperate search for love and sexual fulfillment.

Rounders (1998) Drama ΨΨ
Matt Damon stars as a poker player who has gambled away his life savings to a Russian mobster, gives up gambling, and is lured back into the game by his friend (Edward Norton).

Sailor Who Fell from Grace with the Sea, The (1976) Drama ΨΨΨΨ
Interesting story of adult romance and child psychopathology; based on a novel by Yukio Mishima.

Shame (2011) Drama ΨΨΨΨ
This Steve McQueen film stars Michael Fassbender as Brandon, a man with a seemingly unquenchable need to have sex with multiple women (and occasionally men). Although not an official diagnosis in the *DSM-5*, many clinicians believe sexual addiction is a bona fide psychological disorder.

Swept Away (1975) Drama/Comedy ΨΨΨ
Lina Wertmuller's examination of sex roles. A rich woman and a poor deckhand are marooned on an island and find sexual excitement and satisfaction in the new roles each assumes.

That Obscure Object of Desire (1977) Drama ΨΨΨΨΨ
Surrealistic film by Luis Buñuel about violence, love, and sexual obsession in a middle-aged man. The film is complex, intriguing, and full of symbolism, including two actresses playing the same character. This was the last film Buñuel ever directed.

This Girl's Life (2003) Drama Ψ
A female porn star starts a business by getting women concerned about their husbands' fidelity to pay her to attempt to seduce them.

To Live (1994) Drama ΨΨΨΨ
This epic film by Zhang Yimou follows a Chinese family through tragic and wonderful times. One of the early struggles of the lead character, Fugui, is gambling; he loses his family home and his fortune gambling with dice.

To Our Loves (1983, France) Drama ΨΨΨ
A French film exploring the sexuality of a 15-year-old girl and the way it affects her family.

Two for the Money (2005) Drama ΨΨΨ
A young, savvy, football game predictor (Matthew McConaughey) gets hired by a pathological gambler (Al Pacino) to work in a fast-paced business as an advisor to gamblers betting on football games. Based on a true story.

Unbearable Lightness of Being, The (1988) Romance ΨΨΨ
A highly sensual film about a Prague neurosurgeon and his inability to separate sex and love. The film is based on the novel of the same name by Milan Kundera.

We Don't Live Here Anymore (2004) Drama ΨΨΨ
Two couples (played by Peter Krause, Naomi Watts, Mark Ruffalo, and Laura Dern) find both their marriages failing, in part due to adultery. The movie includes themes of deceit, manipulation, lack of integrity, and the excitement of secrecy. Each couple battles against boredom and idleness, using sex to escape the emptiness of their lives.

Young Adam (2003) Drama ΨΨ
Ewan Macgregor as a sexual addict who becomes intimately involved with his boss' wife, her sister, and a woman he meets at a ship's port.

Neurocognitive Disorders

50 First Dates (2004) Comedy Ψ
Adam Sandler plays a veterinarian and womanizer who falls in love with a woman (Drew Barrymore) with a fictional cognitive disorder in that she has no long-term memory as she awakens each morning forgetting everything from the day before (so she repeats the same activities each day, enabled by her family). A flawed *Memento*.

Accidental Hero, The (2002, France) Drama ΨΨ
A boy comes to more fully appreciate his mother after she is involved in a serious car accident and experiences a profound retrograde amnesia.

Alzheimer's Project, The (The Memory Loss Tapes) (2009) Documentary ΨΨΨΨ
Poignant and important HBO series integrated into a deeply meaningful film revealing seven vignettes of individuals at various stages of Alzheimer's disease and their families. The film addresses both the suffering caused by the disease and the challenges of the caregiver, such as themes of the adult-child role reversal, wandering, loss of independence, and the emotional grieving process. To watch the film online, see http://www.hbo.com/alzheimers/memory-loss-tapes.html

Amour (2012, France) Drama ΨΨΨΨ
Georges and Anne are two retired music teachers living in Paris. When Anne has a stroke, Georges promises to keep her out of the hospital and out of a nursing home. She becomes increasingly debilitated, and this forces Georges to make difficult decisions about their relationship and future. This film can be a wonderful springboard for class discussions of aging, long-lasting love, the impact of neurocognitive disorders, and of euthanasia.

Assisted Living (2003) Comedy/Drama ΨΨ
This movie was filmed in an actual nursing home. A pot-smoking janitor interacts with the residents and slowly learns to care.

Awakenings (1990) Drama ΨΨΨ
Robin Williams as neurologist Oliver Sacks treats patient Robert De Niro in a Bronx hospital. The film documents the use of L-Dopa in the treatment of patients with advanced Parkinson's disease. Good portrayal of the daily life of a mental hospital.

Away from Her (2006, Canada) Drama ΨΨΨΨ
Sarah Polley's directorial debut about a woman (Julie Christie) who realizes she has Alzheimer's disease and convinces her husband (Gordon Pinsent) to take her to a care facility. He visits her regularly despite discovering that she has fallen in love with another man.

Ballad of Narayama, The (1983) Drama ΨΨΨ
This Japanese film tells the story of a small village where by tradition all old people are taken up to the top of a mountain and left to die.

Barney's Version (2010) Drama ΨΨΨ
Paul Giamatti portrays a small time television producer who struggles with intimacy, alcohol dependence, and an early onset memory disorder.

City of No Limits, The (2002) Drama ΨΨ
A family patriarch becomes paranoid and delusional because of a brain tumor; as a result, he shares long hidden family secrets.

"This is not a hospital. They are not doctors or nurses. Didn't they tell you? They all believe that the city has got no limits."

A dying character's confusion and paranoia in
The City of No Limits (2002)

Dark Victory (1939) Drama ΨΨΨ
Bette Davis, George Brent, and Humphrey Bogart star, but watch for Ronald Reagan. Davis has a fatal brain tumor. She spends what little time she has left with her brain surgeon husband. The "dark victory" refers to living life well, even when facing death. Remade (not very effectively) with Susan Hayward in *Stolen Hours* (1963).

Death Be Not Proud (1975) Biography ΨΨ
A made-for-TV film based on John Gunther's moving account of his son's struggle with a brain tumor, which killed the boy at the age of 17. The book provides considerable insight into the neurology of brain lesions.

Do You Remember Love? (1985) Drama ΨΨ
Joanne Woodward won an Emmy for her portrayal of a middle-aged college professor who develops Alzheimer's disease.

Harder They Fall, The (1956) Sports ΨΨΨΨ
Humphrey Bogart in his last film, made the year before his death. The movie is very critical of the sport of boxing and the exploitation of fighters by promoters. A slow-witted boxer has a brain clot and is almost killed in his last fight.

Iris (2001) Drama/Biography ΨΨΨΨ
Based on the life of the famous British novelist and philosophical writer, Iris Murdoch (played by Judi Dench), who deteriorates because of her Alzheimer's disease. Oscar-winner, Jim Broadbent plays John Bayley, Iris' extraordinarily loving husband. A powerfully realistic and emotional film.

Jacket, The (2005) Drama/Thriller ΨΨ
Adrien Brody portrays a man with retrograde amnesia who is mistreated in a psychiatric hospital in this avant-garde film.

Lookout, The (2007) Drama ΨΨΨ
A high school student suffers a brain injury, and his life is changed forever. The film is a good introduction to many of the symptoms experienced by someone with a traumatic brain injury.

Lorenzo's Oil (1992) Drama ΨΨΨ
True story of the Odone family and their desperate struggle to save their son's life. The boy has a rare neurological disease that they are told is ultimately fatal. Good illustration of the effects of chronic illness on family functioning.

Majestic, The (2001) Drama ΨΨ
Jim Carrey plays a disenfranchised screenwriter who develops amnesia after his car topples over a bridge. He washes on the shore of a small town whose citizens take him in as a lost war hero.

Man Without a Past, The (2002) Drama ΨΨΨ
A man is severely beaten while sleeping outside and is proclaimed dead. He awakens with amnesia and begins to create a new life for himself before eventually discovering parts of his old life.

Memento (2001) Suspense/Mystery ΨΨΨΨΨ
Christopher Nolan directs this one-of-a-kind, exquisitely crafted masterpiece about a man suffering from anterograde amnesia. The film demands the viewer have very good short-term memory as the major plot progresses backwards scene by scene while juxtaposing past events (going forward) in black-and-white. This is a film not to be missed.

Natalie: But even if you get revenge you're not going to remember it. You're not even going to know that it happened.
Leonard Shelby: My wife deserves vengeance. Doesn't make a difference whether I know about it. Just because there are things I don't remember doesn't make my actions meaningless.

Leonard contemplates his need to avenge his
wife's murder in *Memento* (2001)

Memories of Me (1988) Comedy ΨΨ
Henry Winkler directs Billy Crystal, a high-powered surgeon who has just had a heart attack, and Alan King, his actor father who may have Alzheimer's. It turns out that an aneurysm is present, and father and son eventually learn to care for one another.

Memory of a Killer, The (2003) Drama ΨΨ
A hit man in the early stages of dementia attempts to do one last job before retiring.

Mercy or Murder? (1987) Drama ΨΨ
Made-for-TV movie about a Florida man who went to prison after killing his wife because she had advanced

Alzheimer's disease. The film raises interesting questions that society will increasingly be forced to confront.

Million Dollar Baby (2004) Drama ΨΨΨ
A female prize fighter (Hilary Swank) is paralyzed from the neck down after being sucker punched by an angry opponent between rounds; she pleads with her trainer (Clint Eastwood) to end her life before she loses the memory of the crowd's applause.

Mulholland Drive (2001) Mystery/Drama/Suspense ΨΨΨΨ
David Lynch film about a woman who experiences a head injury from a car accident, becomes amnestic, and finds refuge in an aspiring Hollywood actress' condominium. This is characteristic Lynch in its non-linearity and themes of reality versus illusion, identity confusion, and nightmarish dream sequences.

My Girl (1991) Drama/Comedy ΨΨ
Eleven-year-old girl is a hypochondriac with a mortician for a father and a grandmother who has Alzheimer's disease.

Notebook, The (2004) Drama ΨΨΨ
Gena Rowlands and James Garner play a couple coping with her ever worsening Alzheimer's disease. Based on the best-selling novel by Nicholas Sparks.

On Golden Pond (1981) Drama ΨΨΨΨ
Sensitive portrayal of an aging couple (Henry Fonda and Katharine Hepburn) cherishing and struggling with his increasingly apparent dementia.

On the Waterfront (1954) Drama ΨΨΨΨΨ
Classic Elia Kazan film starring Marlon Brando as Terry Malloy, a prizefighter of limited intelligence who is exploited by almost everyone around him. Brando won an Oscar as Best Actor for his performance as Terry Malloy, who took a dive and spent the rest of his life regretting it.

"You was my brother, Charley, you should've looked out for me just a little bit so I wouldn't have to take them dives for the short-end money."

On the Waterfront (1954)

Pride of the Yankees, The (1942) Biography ΨΨΨ
Gary Cooper stars in this Samuel Goldwyn film about legendary Yankees' first baseman Lou Gehrig, who had to give up baseball due to amyotrophic lateral sclerosis, which came to be known more widely by the eponym "Lou Gehrig's disease."

"Some people say I've had a bad break, but I consider myself to be the luckiest man on the face of the earth."

Lou Gehrig giving up baseball in
The Pride of the Yankees (1942)

Private Matter, A (1992) Biography ΨΨ
Provocative made-for-TV movie starring Sissy Spacek as a TV personality who gets national attention after her decision to abort a child likely to be affected by the drug thalidomide.

Random Harvest (1942) Drama ΨΨΨ
A shell-shocked, amnestic soldier (Ronald Coleman) is hospitalized in an asylum after World War I. He wanders away and becomes romantically involved with a cabaret singer (Greer Garson), eventually marrying her and establishing a new career as a writer. Three years later he is hit by a car – he can then remember all the details of his privileged life prior to World War I, but nothing of his new life with Greer Garson's character! She eventually tracks him down but doesn't reveal her identity upon the advice of a psychiatrist who cautions her that the shock would be too much for him to take. She becomes his personal secretary, and – not surprisingly – he falls in love with her all over again.

Raging Bull (1980) Biography/Sports ΨΨΨΨΨ
Powerful film depicting the psychological, moral, and mental decline of a prizefighter. Robert De Niro won an Oscar for his portrayal of Jake LaMotta.

Regarding Henry (1993) Drama ΨΨ
Attorney has his life permanently altered following a head injury; his values change as well as his personality.

Safe House (1998) Thriller ΨΨ
An ex-intelligence operative begins to develop Alzheimer's disease.

Savages, The (2007) Drama ΨΨΨ
A brother and sister find themselves becoming closer as they attempt to cope with the challenges associated with caring for their father who is suffering from Alzheimer's disease.

Sea Inside, The (2004) Biography/Drama ΨΨΨΨΨ
A sensitive and moving story about a Spanish citizen's quest to end his life.

Separation, A (2001, Iran) Drama ΨΨΨΨ
The wife wants to move to America; the husband insists on staying in Iran so they can take care of his father, a man coping with Alzheimer's disease.

Shattered (1991) Mystery/Suspense ΨΨ
A man in a near-fatal car accident experiences amnesia and undergoes reconstructive facial surgery. He begins to find inconsistencies in stories from loved ones about his past and his own memories, only to face a shocking truth.

Song for Martin, A (2002) Drama ΨΨΨ
An interesting portrayal of the ways in which a married couple deeply in love is affected by his Alzheimer's disease.

Son of the Bride (2002) Drama/Comedy/Romance ΨΨΨΨ
Moving drama from Argentina with many inspirational and comic moments about a man too busy for his family until he reevaluates his life following a heart attack. A major sub-story is the man's aging father, who steadfastly expresses unconditional love to his wife who is deteriorating with Alzheimer's disease.

Tuesdays with Morrie (1999) Drama/Inspiration ΨΨ
Made-for-TV movie based on the best-selling Mitch Albom book about a journalist who befriends and finds inspiration from a man dying of ALS.

Vow, The (2012) Drama ΨΨ
A recently married couple are in an automobile accident and the wife sustains a serious head injury. She awakes from her coma profoundly amnestic with no memories of her marriage or husband. She returns home to live with her parents where she resumes a relationship with a former boyfriend.

Waltz with Bashir (2008, Israel) Animation/Biography ΨΨΨΨ
An exploration on the construction and shifting nature of memory. Ari Folman served in the Israeli army during the Lebanon War of 1982 but has no recollection of the events and he attempts to reconstruct them in this film. The opening animation and the closing, unanimated, scene are especially vivid. Watching this film will help you understand more about PTSD and how trauma can cause amnesia.

Personality Disorders

25th Hour (2002) Drama ΨΨΨΨ
A Spike Lee film about a young man (Edward Norton) about to go away to prison for 7 years for marijuana trafficking. In making the most of his final hours, he meets with his "recovering alcoholic" father, girlfriend, friends, and an "underground" boss and his henchmen. Look for tributes to 9/11 throughout the film (it was the first film to use Ground Zero as a film scene).

A Heart in Winter (1992) Drama ΨΨΨ
This film depicts a complicated love triangle in which the character of Stéphane meets *DSM-5* criteria for schizoid personality disorder.

Accidental Tourist, The (1988) Comedy ΨΨΨ
William Hurt plays a withdrawn, unemotional writer whose isolation is compounded when his 12-year-son is senselessly murdered in a fast-food restaurant.

Alfie (2004) Comedy ΨΨΨ
Jude Law stars as a man with a narcissistic personality who prides himself in being a womanizer and not committing in relationships. Law's asides to the audience provide insight into his narcissistic thinking. By the end of the film, Alfie begins to face the impact of his behavior on others.

Amélie (2001, France) Comedy/Romance ΨΨΨΨΨ
Audrey Tautou stars as Amélie, an avoidant woman who wants an intimate relationship with others but is unable to be direct. Upon deciding to change her life by making a difference in others' lives, she adopts extreme and creative measures to bring joy to others and make connections. Brilliantly directed by Jean Pierre-Jeunet.

American Beauty (1999) Comedy/Drama ΨΨΨΨΨ
Kevin Spacey has the lead role in this remarkable film about a very dysfunctional family and the ennui that accompanies life in suburbia. Annette Bening plays a woman with a classic Histrionic Personality Disorder. Almost every character exhibits some degree of psychopathology. The film is a compelling examination of what Freud called the psychopathology of everyday life.

American Gangster (2007) Crime/Drama ΨΨΨ
An honest detective (Russell Crowe) tries to bring down a heroin kingpin (Denzel Washington) in this Ridley Scott film.

American History X (1998) Drama/Suspense ΨΨΨ
Edward Norton plays an antisocial, white supremacist who decides to change his life when he sees his younger brother is following his example.

Anatomy of a Murder (1959) Drama ΨΨΨΨ
Jimmy Stewart as an attorney defending a man accused of murder. His case rests on the contention that the defendant could not help behaving as he did because the man he murdered had allegedly raped his wife. The film raises interesting questions about the irresistible impulse defense.

Anchorman: The Legend of Ron Burgundy (2004) and **Anchorman 2: The Legend Continues** (2013) Comedy Ψ
A narcissistic anchorman (Will Ferrell) competes with an ambitious female journalist as well as rival newscasters.

Animal Kingdom (2010, Australia) Drama ΨΨΨΨ
A 17-year-old boy is sitting on a couch with his mother and watches as she overdoses on heroin and dies. He goes to live with his extended family, a group of criminals and drug addicts.

Anything Else (2003) Comedy ΨΨ
Woody Allen film about a young man with dependent personality who falls for an erratic young woman (Christina Ricci).

"See where I'm standing? That's where I'm from."

Sonny in *The Apostle* (1997)

Apostle, The (1997) Drama ΨΨΨΨ
Robert Duvall directs, writes, and stars as a philandering but dedicated minister who flees his hometown after committing a violent act. His redemptive journey takes him to a small town where he builds a ministry until his past catches up with him.

Apt Pupil (1998) Drama/Suspense ΨΨΨ
A high school student becomes fascinated with his discovery of a man (Ian McKellen) who was formerly a Nazi henchman. Kurt Dussander is living (and hiding out) in a local town. The student manipulates him to tell him detailed stories of his previous work.

"To the whole world I am a monster."

An escaped Nazi in *Apt Pupil* (1998)

Arsenic and Old Lace (1944) Comedy ΨΨ
Frank Capra film about Cary Grant's two aunts who practice mercy killing by giving their gentlemen guests poisoned elderberry wine. Grant worries about the fact that mental illness not only runs in his family, it gallops!

Assassination of Jesse James by the Coward Robert Ford, The (2007) Crime ΨΨΨ
The humanization and glorification of infamous outlaw, Jesse James (Brad Pitt) is depicted, along with the young, timid Robert Ford who shot him. James was an antisocial personality who was (understandably) paranoid.

Bad Santa (2003) Comedy Ψ
This Terry Zwigoff film stars Billy Bob Thornton as a rule-breaking, crass alcoholic who works as Santa Claus at a department store. The female costar has a "Santa fetish."

Bad Seed, The (1956) Drama Ψ
Interesting examination of whether or not evil is congenital.

Bartleby (2001) Comedy ΨΨΨΨ
This dark comedy brilliantly casts Crispin Glover as the aloof, quirky clerk, Bartleby, who repeats the same phrase, "I would prefer not to," when asked to work. Ironically colorful set design and a hodge-podge of quirky personalities as supporting cast. This is clearly a "love it or hate it" film, based on a short story by Herman Melville. Bartleby's character is a classic depiction of a person with a schizoid personality.

Bartleby (1970) Comedy ΨΨΨ
Original black-and-white version of the Herman Melville short story, Bartleby the Scrivener. More slow, dark, and dreary than its recent counterpart, yet still an excellent depiction of schizoid personality.

Basic Instinct (1992; 2006) Thriller/Drama Ψ
Sharon Stone as Catherine Tramell, a seductive and manipulative woman with many borderline traits.

Before the Devil Knows You're Dead (2007) Drama/Crime ΨΨΨ
Sidney Lumet directs Philip Seymour Hoffman, Ethan Hawke, Marisa Tomei, and Albert Finney in a film about a heist (of one's own family) gone terribly wrong.

Being Julia (2004) Drama/Comedy ΨΨΨ
Annette Bening portrays an actress with qualities of each of the Cluster B personality disorders, in addition to a work addiction.

Believer, The (2001) Drama ΨΨΨ
Fascinating character study of Danny Burrows who is living his life in an impossible contradiction as a Jewish Nazi. As he faces his true self, his ruthless antisocial characteristics begin to crumble. Based on a true story of events that occurred in Burrows' life in the Fall of 1965.

Bitter Moon (1992) Drama ΨΨΨΨ
Roman Polanski film in which a couple becomes entangled with a woman who meets several criteria for borderline personality.

Black Snake Moan (2006) Drama ΨΨΨ
Samuel L. Jackson plays a broken man who rescues a promiscuous, erratic woman (Christina Ricci) left for dead on the road. Both characters face and share their dark sides.

Blue Jasmine (2013) Comedy/Drama ΨΨΨΨΨ
Woody Allen pays homage to *Streetcar Named Desire* (1951) in this intriguing film. It is one of the best examples we know of a histrionic personality disorder.

> "Anxiety, nightmares and a nervous breakdown, there's only so many traumas a person can withstand until they take to the streets and start screaming."
>
> A histrionic Jasmine – who had just flown first class – contemplates life's challenges in *Blue Jasmine* (2013)

Box of Moonlight (1996) Drama ΨΨΨ
A rigid, orderly, rule-obsessed man, played by John Turturro, takes extra time off from his job and family to rediscover his lost adolescence. The title becomes a beautiful, transformational metaphor in the film.

Breach (2007) Thriller/Drama ΨΨΨ
A pathological, manipulative CIA official (Chris Cooper) leads a double life in this intriguing thriller. Based on the true story of the worst FBI spy in US history, someone who eventually cost the US government billions of dollars.

Breathless (1960, France) Drama/Crime ΨΨΨΨΨ
Classic antisocial hoodlum in a classic film by French New Wave director, Jean-Luc Godard. The pacing of the film justifies the title, as does the lead performance of the anti-hero.

Bruce Almighty (2002) Comedy Ψ
Whimsical comedy about a man (Jim Carrey) given the opportunity to "be God" for a day.

Butley (1974) Drama ΨΨΨΨ
Alan Bates in a Harold Pinter film adaptation of a London play about the life of a British university professor. Bates's wife and lover are both leaving him, and his colleagues are estranged. Bates seems to fail in every interpersonal encounter.

Caine Mutiny, The (1954) Drama ΨΨΨ
Humphrey Bogart is the ship's paranoid captain, who decompensates under the pressure of testimony when he is called to the witness stand. Humphrey Bogart plays the role of Captain Queeg.

Catch Me If You Can (2002) Drama ΨΨΨ
Steven Spielberg directs Leonardo DiCaprio who plays the role of a manipulative con man with an antisocial personality. He repeatedly changes his identity while defrauding banks and keeping FBI agent (Tom Hanks) one step behind him. Based on the true story of Frank Abagnal Jr.

Character (1997, The Netherlands) Drama ΨΨΨ
Best Foreign Film winner (Dutch) about a young man's personal and financial struggle to be free of his antisocial father. His mother appears to have a schizoid personality disorder.

> "That boy, I'll strangle him for nine tenths and the last tenth will make him strong."
>
> Dreverhaven describing his son in *Character* (1998)

Charlie and the Chocolate Factory (2005) Drama/Comedy ΨΨΨΨΨ
Tim Burton remake of the classic story is well-casted with beautiful set designs. Johnny Depp's portrayal of an eccentric, isolated, and perceptually disturbed Willy Wonka is one of the best depictions of schizotypal personality captured on film.

Child, The (2005, France) Drama/Crime ΨΨΨ
Bruno, who leads a gang of petty thieves, decides to sell his newborn for money.

Citizen Kane (1941) Drama ΨΨΨΨΨ
Orson Wells and Joseph Cotton star in this classic film that is a staple in film history courses. For our purposes, the film offers a dramatic illustration of narcissistic personality disorder.

Come Back to the 5 & Dime, Jimmy Dean, Jimmy Dean (1982) Drama ΨΨ
A Robert Altman film in which Sandy Dennis plays a local woman in a small Texas town who is convinced she bore a son by James Dean when he was in town filming *Giant*.

Compulsion (1959) Drama/Crime ΨΨΨ
Two young fraternity brothers believe their perfect crime of murder is "the true test of the superior intellect." Their defense attorney (Orson Welles) gives a memorable speech in an attempt to save their lives.

Conspiracy Theory (1997) Drama ΨΨ
Mel Gibson plays a cab driver with virtually no personal life, who is obsessed with a woman, and who writes a newsletter on conspiracies. His paranoia takes him to every possible place and situation, including one conspiracy that turns out true.

Conversation, The (1974) Drama ΨΨΨ
A Francis Ford Coppola film in which Gene Hackman plays a surveillance expert with a paranoid personality.

Corporation, The (2004) Documentary ΨΨ
Interesting, albeit one-sided, review of corporations that documents the similarities between them and the characteristics of a psychopathic personality disorder.

Criminal (2004) Drama/Crime Ψ
John C. Reilly portrays an antisocial con-artist who takes an apprentice. The film suffers from a contrived ending, standard fare for "con" films.

Crush, The (1993) Drama/Suspense Ψ
Alicia Silverstone plays a 14-year-old temptress who is obsessed with a 28-year-old man who is simply not interested in her. This is an interesting portrayal of a character who is likely to qualify for a diagnosis of Antisocial Personality Disorder (as soon as she turns 18).

Dark Knight, The (2008) Action/Crime ΨΨΨ
Christopher Nolan's follow-up to *Batman Begins* stars Heath Ledger in incredible form as "the Joker," a clever and fearless psychopath who battles Batman (Christian Bale).

Decalogue, The (1989, Poland) Drama ΨΨΨΨΨ
Ten, 1-hr films loosely based on the ten commandments, originally made for Polish television by director Krzysztof Kieslowski. This set of films was hailed as one of the most significant productions in recent history, and the late Stanley Kubrick once said it is the only film masterpiece he knows. Multiple psychological disorders are portrayed in various characters living in an apartment complex.

Dementia 13 (1963) Horror Ψ
Third rate film about an ax murderer; interesting primarily because it is Francis Ford Coppola's first "serious" film.

Detachment (2012) Drama ΨΨΨ
Adrien Brody stars as Henry Barthes, a substitute teacher who drifts from job to job, avoiding meaningful attachments to his students or other teachers. Students may want to debate the merits of a diagnosis of either schizoid personality disorder or avoidant personality disorder.

Henry Barthes: You know it's funny, I spend a lot of time trying to not have to deal ... to not really commit. I'm a substitute teacher, there's no real responsibility to teach. Your responsibility is to maintain order, make sure nobody kills anybody in your classroom, and then they get them to their next period.

Henry Barthes explains his passivity in
Detachment (2012)

Divine Secrets of the Ya-Ya Sisterhood (2002) Drama/Comedy ΨΨ
A group of friends teach a young woman (Sandra Bullock) about her troubled mother. Ellen Burstyn and Ashley Judd play the erratic, labile, and abusive mother.

Dogville (2003, Denmark) Drama ΨΨΨ
Nicole Kidman stars as a woman on the run who finds refuge in a small, isolated town. If a town could be diagnosed, this one would clearly be "antisocial" as group contagion results in manipulation, deceit, and abuse. Unique set design of a town without any houses or doors and is set as if on a theater stage.

Dot the I (2003, UK/Spain/US) Drama/Romance Ψ
A love triangle set in London with various twists of deceit and sabotage that leave the viewer wondering who is manipulating whom.

Dream Lover (1994) Drama Ψ
A sociopathic woman plots to marry a man and then have him committed to an insane asylum.

Employee of the Month (2004) Comedy/Drama Ψ
Dark comedy with Matt Dillon experiencing a day when everything in his "perfect" life goes wrong. Watch for numerous Buddhist references to the fact that "everything is an illusion."

End of Violence, The (1997) Drama ΨΨΨ
Wim Wenders film about a paranoid personality played by Bill Pullman.

Enron: The Smartest Guys in the Room (2005) Documentary ΨΨ
Depicts the antisocial personalities of the Enron corporation leaders and the back-story of their rise to power and eventual downfall.

Equilibrium (2002) Action ΨΨ
This film depicts a futuristic society in which everyone must take a drug to block the disease called "human emotion."

Eraserhead (1976) Drama ΨΨΨ
This early David Lynch film has become a cult classic. It depicts Henry Spencer as someone with a schizoid personality: He is an awkward loner who doesn't know how to interact with others; he has flat and frequently inappropriate affect; he has few friends; and he is seemingly indifferent to praise or criticism.

Eulogy (2003) Comedy Ψ
Dark comedy about a dysfunctional family of self-serving, self-absorbed, hypocrites.

Evita (1997) Drama/Musical ΨΨ
Madonna portrays Argentina's first lady, Eva Peron, and depicts her rise from poverty and scandal to fame, fortune, and the adulation of a nation. Eva (Evita) does what it takes to climb the ladder of success, eventually marrying military leader Juan Peron. She speaks out on his be-

half, mobilizes the people of Argentina, frees him from jail, and helps him get elected. Antonio Banderas plays her alter ego with running commentary, warnings, criticism, and song.

Family Man, The (2000) Family/Comedy ΨΨ
Corporate executive (Nicholas Cage) obsessed with money, fame, and power gets an opportunity to see how his life would have turned out if he had married his college sweetheart. The film includes obvious parallels with *It's a Wonderful Life*.

Fatal Attraction (1987) Thriller/Romance ΨΨΨ
Glenn Close displays classic characteristics of borderline personality disorder, including fears of abandonment, unstable interpersonal relationships, impulsivity, suicidal gestures, inappropriate and intense anger, and affective instability. This remarkable film is flawed by a contrived and artificial ending.

Fargo (1996) Comedy ΨΨΨΨΨ
Dark comedy from the Coen brothers about a car salesman (William H. Macy) whose plot to kidnap his wife has gone horribly awry. Frances McDormand has a memorable role as police chief Marge Gunderson.

Finding Forrester (2000) Drama ΨΨ
A high school student befriends an aloof, retired professor and writer who has avoided people for years. Their relationship is "rocky," taking many turns, yet each individual has a profound impact on the other.

Five Easy Pieces (1970) Drama ΨΨΨ
Jack Nicholson, raised in an upper class and gifted family, is a talented pianist who left his affluent life to work in the oil fields. The plot is thin, but the character Nicholson plays is complex and fascinating.

Fracture (2007) Thriller/Drama Ψ
Anthony Hopkins and Ryan Gosling star in this courtroom suspense film in which Hopkins kills his wife and gets away with it.

Freaks (1932) Horror ΨΨΨΨ
Fascinating film about a "normal" trapeze artist who marries a midget and then tries to poison him. When his friends find out, they kill her strong-man lover and turn her into one of them.

From Dusk Till Dawn (1995) Horror Ψ
Quentin Tarantino and George Clooney portray psychopaths who rendezvous at a biker bar that turns out to be run by vampires. The film presents as two very different movies combined – the first is Tarantino-like in character interaction and dialogue, and the second half is a horror show. Robert Rodriguez directs the film.

From the Life of the Marionettes (1980) Drama ΨΨΨ
Bergman film in which an executive rapes and kills a prostitute.

Ghost Dog: The Way of the Samurai (1999) Crime/Drama ΨΨΨ
Jim Jarmusch film about a reclusive man who lives with pigeons and believes he is indebted to a mob boss who once saved his life.

Girl, Interrupted (1999) Drama ΨΨ
A depressed, young woman (Winona Ryder), sent to a psychiatric hospital and labeled with Borderline Personality Disorder, encounters a dangerous patient (Angelina Jolie) with an Antisocial Personality Disorder.

Godfather, The (1972; 1974; 1990) Crime/Drama ΨΨΨΨΨ
The classic trilogy directed by Francis Ford Coppola about a New York Mafia family who are kind and generous to those who support the family and ruthless to those who oppose it.

God Is Great and I Am Not (2003) Comedy ΨΨ
Audrey Tautou plays a dependent woman who obsessively conforms to the religion of any man she is dating.

Gone with the Wind (1939) Romance/Drama ΨΨΨΨΨ
In the classic love story, Scarlett O'Hara meets full criteria for histrionic personality disorder; however, some have argued that these surface features are the result of the social forces of her culture & time and that her deeper character structure would not be considered histrionic.

Greenberg (2010) Drama Comedy Romance ΨΨ
A neurotic and self-centered man (Ben Stiller) discharged from a psychiatric hospital goes to housesit for his brother. Greenberg is obsessed with imperfections and meets almost all of the *DSM-5* criteria for obsessive-compulsive personality disorder.

Grey Gardens (2009) Drama/Biography ΨΨΨ
Drew Barrymore and Jessica Lange portray the infamous mother and daughter, Edie and Edith Beales. Lange's character was a first cousin to Jackie Onassis-Kennedy, and displays dependent personality and extreme symptoms of what might be agoraphobia. The extreme avoidance and pathology of the characters results in a deteriorating mansion that is nothing but a dilapidated cesspool of filth and cat urine.

Grifters, The (1990) Crime ΨΨΨΨ
Anjelica Huston stars in this fascinating introduction to the world of the con. Contrast this film with a movie almost as good, David Mamet's *House of Games* (see "Treatment" section).

Guy (1997) Drama ΨΨ
Fascinating story about a documentary filmmaker (Hope Davis) who chooses one person (Vincent D'Onofrio) at random and relentlessly follows him, filming his daily life for several days despite the victim's resistance and threats. Her obsession of filming him becomes his obsession with being filmed. The movie addresses narcissism and suggests that obsessions are a core part of human nature.

Heavy (1995) Drama ΨΨΨ
An obese, schizoid man loses his mother (with whom he has lived) and becomes even more withdrawn as he grieves.

I, Robot (2004) Action/Suspense ΨΨ
Surprisingly high quality action film about an agent who battles robots threatening to take over the world. Will Smith's role illustrates paranoid personality traits.

> "I did it because I could."
>
> *In the Company of Men* (1997)

In the Company of Men (1997) Comedy ΨΨΨ
Misogynistic satire of two men (with varying levels of narcissism) who deliberately seduce the same vulnerable girl, lead her on, and then abandon her. Directed by Neil LaBute.

Iron Man (2008) Drama ΨΨΨ
In this film and its sequel (2010), Robert Downey Jr. plays a grandiose, egotistical man who meets criteria for a diagnosis of narcissistic personality disorder.

Jobs (2013) Biography Ψ
Ashton Kutcher plays Steve Jobs in a disappointing film; however, it is a useful pedagogical exercise to watch the film and to see if Jobs meets the *DSM-5* diagnostic criteria for narcissistic personality disorder.

Jonestown: The Life and Death of Peoples Temple (2006) Documentary/Biography ΨΨ
Discussion and explanation of the events that led up to the largest mass suicide in modern history, brought about by the manipulative tactics of the antisocial preacher Jim Jones.

Kalifornia (1993) Thriller ΨΨ
Early Brad Pitt performance as a quirky, ruthless, psychopathic killer who teams up with his naïve sweetheart (Juliette Lewis), a woman with a borderline IQ. There is not a hint of remorse or empathy in Pitt's character.

Knife in the Water (1962) Drama ΨΨΨ
One of Roman Polanski's earliest films. A man and his wife on a sailing holiday pick up a hitchhiker. There is mounting sexual tension between the older man and his younger rival. The younger man eventually makes love to the wife after a complex turn of events that occur when the couple becomes convinced the young man has drowned.

La Cage aux Folles (1978) Comedy ΨΨΨ
Zaza (Albin), a transvestite nightclub performer, is a wonderful example of a histrionic personality. He is dramatic and flamboyant and threatens suicide when things do not go his way.

Ladies Man, The (2000) Comedy Ψ
Tim Meadows plays a narcissistic talk-show host and "player." Spin-off of a successful Saturday Night Live skit.

Ladykillers, The (2004) Comedy ΨΨ
Tom Hanks leads a group of thieves in a caper to steal money from a casino by digging underground from an oblivious, good-hearted, elderly woman. Good portrayal of how people with antisocial personalities can use language to manipulate. Directed by the Coen brothers.

Lakeview Terrace (2009) Drama/Thriller ΨΨΨ
Samuel L. Jackson portrays a police officer who terrorizes his next door neighbors because they are an interracial couple. His character would meet criteria for a paranoid personality.

Land of Plenty (2004, US/Germany) Drama ΨΨΨΨ
Wim Wenders film about misguided patriotism and paranoia in post-911 times in America; the protagonist is a classic paranoid personality disorder; this condition has rarely been portrayed so well.

Last King of Scotland, The (2006) Drama/Documentary/Biography ΨΨΨ
Forest Whitaker in an unforgettable, terrifying role as Idi Amin, the charming, charismatic, and paranoid ruler of Uganda who killed over 300,000 people during his reign.

Last Station, The (2009) Drama/Biography/Romance ΨΨΨ
A film about the last year in the life of novelist Leo Tolstoy. Tolstoy's wife, Countess Sofya Andreevna Tolstoy, is upset because her husband's new will leaves all of his writings – and all of his royalties – to the Russian people rather than to her and her children. She meets all of the *DSM-5* criteria for the diagnosis of histrionic personality disorder.

Last Supper, The (1996) Comedy Ψ
Dark comedy of five liberal graduate students seeking revenge against reactionary and conservative dinner guests. The film depicts elements of antisocial and compulsive behavior.

Le Boucher (1969, France) Thriller ΨΨΨ
Claude Chabrol film in which a butcher who is also a murderer commits suicide when the woman he loves realizes he is a criminal.

Leave Her to Heaven (1945) Romance/Crime ΨΨ
Protagonist commits multiple murders, watches her brother-in-law drown, and terminates her pregnancy by throwing herself down a flight of stairs with no sense of shame or remorse. Dated but interesting portrayal of an antisocial personality.

Lemony Snicket's A Series of Unfortunate Events (2004) Comedy/Drama ΨΨΨ
Jim Carrey plays a comical psychopath who adopts multiple disguises in an attempt to inherit a family fortune that rightfully belongs to three orphans whose parents have died in a fire.

Levity (2003) Drama ΨΨΨ
Billy Bob Thornton plays a "recovered antisocial," who, after his release from prison, tries to make amends with a family member (Holly Hunter) of a boy he killed decades ago. Morgan Freeman plays an antisocial preacher.

Lord of War (2005) Action/Drama Ψ
Nicholas Cage portrays Uri, an antisocial man who sells illegal arms to various countries. Based on actual events.

Love Exposure (2008, Japan) Drama ΨΨΨ
The character Kaori has a borderline personality disorder: She falls hopelessly in love with a priest and attempts to seduce him in a confessional booth, claiming "Father, listen to my confession! If you turn away from me, I'll kill myself. Please listen to me." The two eventually become lovers. The priest is a widower with a son who takes surreptitious photos of women's panties so he will have sufficient sins to confess to his demanding father.

Lovelife (1997) Comedy ΨΨ
Film about a group of friends and their struggles in relationships, many with symptoms of disorders that prevent them from connecting – the depressed intellectual, the dependant woman, and the neurotic voyeur – but the standout is the narcissist professor.

Mad Love (2002, Spain) ΨΨ
Spanish film about a princess who marries and later becomes queen and is nicknamed "Joan the Mad" because of her worries about her philandering husband.

Man from Elysian Fields, The (2001) Drama ΨΨΨΨ
A married man (Andy Garcia) becomes an escort and his life falls apart as a result of this decision.

Man Who Cried, The (2000) Drama ΨΨ
Slow-moving film of a young woman (Christina Ricci) who left a very poor Russian family years ago to make it as a dancer in the theater. Sub-par film with an all-star cast including Johnny Depp (in another vagrant role), Cate Blanchett, and John Turturro as a grandiose opera singer.

Man Who Wasn't There, The (2001) Drama ΨΨΨΨ
This Coen brothers film noir is a fascinating character analysis of Ed Crane (Billy Bob Thornton) who is an aloof, taciturn, and unemotional barber struggling to find purpose.

Margot at the Wedding (2007) Comedy/Drama ΨΨΨ
Nicole Kidman portrays Margot, a woman with a borderline personality disorder who displays loose boundaries, lability, anger, impulsivity, inappropriate affect, and fears of abandonment during a short visit to her sister's house.

Marriage of Maria Braun, The (1978) Drama/War ΨΨΨ
This Fassbinder film, an allegory about postwar Germany, portrays the dehumanizing effects of war and its aftermath as we watch the commercial success and personal failures of Maria Braun. There is an explosive finale.

Master, The (2012) Drama ΨΨΨ
A Navy veteran coping with alcoholism and PTSD is drawn into the inner circle of a charismatic cult leader played by Philip Seymour Hoffman, but begins to doubt the sincerity of the leader. Several of the cult followers meet criteria for dependent personality disorder. The film was inspired by the life of Scientology founder L. Ron Hubbard.

Match Point (2005) Drama/Crime ΨΨΨΨ
Very engaging and dark Woody Allen film about a young man who inadvertently murders someone and then demonstrates significant antisocial traits that keep him from getting caught.

Me and You and Everyone We Know (2005) Comedy Ψ
A number of odd and quirky characters exhibit subclinical syndromes and features of personality disorders.

Minus Man (1999) Drama ΨΨ
Owen Wilson stars as a charming, kind, drifting serial killer. The film does not explain his behavior, which he claims is spontaneous.

Mommie Dearest (1981) Drama/Biography ΨΨΨΨ
Biographical film based on the book by Joan Crawford's adopted daughter. Faye Dunaway plays Crawford. The film suggests the great star was tyrannical, narcissistic, alcoholic and probably bipolar. Other diagnoses include borderline personality disorder and obsessive-compulsive personality disorder.

> "What are wire hangers doing in this closet? Answer me! I buy you beautiful dresses, and you treat them like they were some dishrag. You do! Three hundred dollar dress on a wire hanger!"
>
> Joan Crawford in a manic state berates her daughter in *Mommie Dearest* (1981)

Monster (2004) Docudrama ΨΨΨΨ
Graphic, disturbing film based on the life of Aileen Wuornos, a prostitute and drifter turned serial killer. Charlize Theron won an Oscar for her powerful performance as Wuornos.

My Summer of Love (2004) Drama/Romance Ψ
Coming-of-age tale of a girl who falls in love with a girl her age who turns out to be a burgeoning case of antisocial personality disorder (compare this film with Neil Labute's *The Shape of Things*).

My Super Ex-Girlfriend (2006) Comedy/Romance Ψ
Uma Thurman portrays G-Girl, a superheroine with great powers but one who also exhibits borderline traits, fear of abandonment, hostility, all-or-none thinking, and revengeful behavior.

My Week with Marilyn (2011) Biography Drama ΨΨ
Marilyn Monroe, as depicted in this film, meets many of the criteria for borderline personality disorder, including an extreme fear of abandonment, impulsivity, insecurity, an unstable self-image and intense but labile interpersonal relationships.

Naked (1993) Drama ΨΨΨΨΨ
Fascinating story about an "existential antisocial," Johnny, wandering the streets of London exchanging philosophical beliefs with various quirky characters. Comedy, love, drama, and violence flow throughout this film. Written and directed by renowned British director Mike Leigh.

No Country For Old Men (2007) Drama/Crime ΨΨΨΨΨ
Javier Bardem gives one of the most chilling portrayals of psychopathology in cinema history in the role of Anton Chigurh, an evil man who plays with the destiny of everyone he encounters.

Notes on a Scandal (2006) Drama ΨΨΨΨ
Judi Dench and Cate Blanchett engage in a battle of manipulation and deceit in a movie that depicts ephebophilia, emptiness, objectification, obsession, and borderline traits.

Odd Couple, The (1968) Comedy ΨΨΨΨ
Jack Lemmon is magnificent as the obsessive-compulsive Felix Unger, who uses air freshener and leaves notes on the pillow of housemate Walter Matthau.

One Hour Photo (2002) ΨΨΨ
Robin Williams in a quirky, dramatic, and disturbing role as the personality disordered Sy, the Photo Guy. Sy collects photographs from a customer's family and finds meaning through their lives until he discovers they are not the perfect family.

> "The things we fear the most have already happened to us."
>
> Sy, the Photo Guy in *One Hour Photo* (2002)

Orphan (2009) Drama/Horror ΨΨ
A young couple decides to adopt a 9-year-old Russian girl after the mother miscarries; however, the child does not measure up to the fantasies of the parents.

Overnight (2003) Documentary/Drama ΨΨ
A rags to riches to rags story about a narcissistic bartender, Troy Duffy, who is offered an attractive deal by Miramax for his screenplay only to have his pathology eventually sabotage this opportunity.

Paper Moon (1973) Comedy/Drama ΨΨ
Fun Peter Bogdanovich film, with Ryan O'Neal and daughter Tatum working together as a pair of con artists in the early 1930s.

Pacific Heights (1990) Drama/Suspense ΨΨΨ
Michael Keaton plays a classic antisocial personality who becomes a tenant of a Victorian home and refuses to leave or pay rent, reaping significant havoc.

Perfume: The Story of a Murderer (2006, Germany) Drama/Crime ΨΨΨΨ
A young man with a phenomenal sense of smell becomes obsessed with capturing the perfect scent, but he takes his obsession too far. Directed by Tom Tykwer.

Phone Booth (2003) Action/Suspense Ψ
A one-dimensional, narcissistic New Yorker begins to unravel as he is manipulated and forced to stay on the phone on the busy streets of Manhattan with a serial killer (Kiefer Sutherland). Worth seeing for the ending that cinemati-

cally shows the deep wounds underlying many narcissistic personality disorders.

Plumber, The (1979, Australia) Mystery/Drama ΨΨ
In this early Peter Weir film, a strange and mysterious plumber seems to be manipulating a woman as he repeatedly returns to her house to check pipes and fix the plumbing. The film raises important questions about trust and class.

Pumpkin Eater, The (1964) Drama ΨΨ
Most memorable for the scene in which Anne Bancroft, responding to the stress of eight children and an unfaithful husband, breaks down in Harrods.

Rampage (1992) Drama/Thriller ΨΨΨ
A film that explores the insanity defense, sociopathy, and mass murder. Directed by William Friedkin, who was also the director for *The Exorcist*.

Reign Over Me (2007) Drama ΨΨΨΨ
Adam Sandler portrays a man with a schizotypal personality who is lost in pathological grief. An old friend (Don Cheadle) works hard to re-orient him back to the world around him. Winner of a Voice Award.

"Charlie, before you go, I'd like to say something. Look, the fact is you had a family and you suffered a great loss, and until you discuss that and we can really talk about that, this is all just an exercise. I can be patient, Charlie, but you need to tell someone your story. It doesn't have to be me, but someone."

Psychologist Angela Oakhurst works with Charlie Fineman in *Reign Over Me* (2007)

Remains of the Day (1994) Romance/Drama ΨΨΨΨ
Anthony Hopkins plays a butler whose rigid personality will not allow him to experience intimacy or genuine love. Few films have been more effective in presenting this reserved, over-controlled, and limiting personality type.

Rick (2003) Comedy/Drama ΨΨΨ
Satirical comedy starring Bill Pullman as Rick, a narcissistic corporate executive who is self-serving, misanthropic, and cruel. The film has strong independent cinema elements.

Robber, The (2010, Germany) Biography ΨΨΨ
This film is based on the true story of Johann Rettenberger, a world-class marathon runner who robber banks in his spare time.

Roger Dodger (2002) Comedy ΨΨΨ
Manhattan executive teaches his 16-year-old nephew about women in one night by taking him to the streets of New York. Great portrayal of narcissism.

Royal Tenenbaums, The (2001) Comedy ΨΨΨΨ
Dark comedy classic about the highly dysfunctional Tenenbaum family. The parents (Gene Hackman and Angelica Huston) raise three genius children (Ben Stiller, Gwenyth Paltrow, and Luke Wilson) who develop significant problems including paranoia, depression, incest, and suicidal thoughts. The family is reunited when the narcissistic father returns home claiming he is dying of stomach cancer. We are left to see the dysfunctional dynamics of the family take place in comical form. A schizotypal personality is also portrayed (Owen Wilson) – a cinematic rarity.

Saw (2004) Horror Ψ
Jigsaw, a serial killer and torturer, manipulates people whom he believes are ungrateful to test how far they will go to save themselves, such as cutting through one's own foot with a rickety saw in order to set oneself free.

Séance on a Wet Afternoon (1964) Crime ΨΨΨΨ
A British film in which Kim Stanley plays a medium who persuades her husband (Richard Attenborough) to kidnap a child so they can then use her power of clairvoyance to "find" the missing child.

Servant, The (1963) Drama ΨΨΨ
Joseph Losey film in which a wealthy British gentleman and his manservant wind up switching roles. There are strong homosexual overtones in the relationship between the two men, and a complex relationship develops with two women. The film is an interesting examination of dominance and submission.

Sexy Beast (2001) Drama ΨΨΨ
Ben Kingsley portrays a brutal antisocial personality who is anything but sexy.

Shadow of Fear (2004) Drama/Suspense Ψ
Disappointing film about a young businessman who is blackmailed after he accidentally kills a man with his car and tries to cover it up. James Spader's character displays strong antisocial characteristics.

Shape of Things, The (2003) Comedy ΨΨΨ
Disturbing comedy of a woman who helps transform an anxious, insecure man through physical alteration and love only to later reveal it was all a manipulative, self-serving project. Another film by director Neil LaBute who has been appropriately nicknamed by some film critics as Neil La-Brute because of his often brutal character portrayal of people and society.

Shattered Glass (2003) Drama ΨΨΨ
Based on a true story of a young journalist for the popular New Republic magazine, Stephen Glass (well acted by Hayden Christensen), who in 1998 made up several of his published stories. He was fraudulent with people, places, and events, making up fake business cards, notes, websites, numbers, and voice mails. Great depiction of "the antisocial in trouble," where the person becomes neurotic and remorseful. The "real" Glass, a self-proclaimed "pathological liar" in reference to the events in the film, admits that 27 of his 41 published magazine stories were partially or completely made up.

"I wanted every story to be a home run."

The real Stephen Glass in a *60 Minutes* interview, speaking of being out of control and doing anything to please his readers

---

Silence of the Lambs, The (1991) Drama/Suspense ΨΨΨΨ
Anthony Hopkins plays one of film history's greatest antisocial personalities, psychiatrist and cannibal Hannibal Lector. Jodi Foster is the FBI agent.

"A census taker once tried to test me. I ate his liver with some fava beans and a nice Chianti."

The Silence of the Lambs (1991)

Sleeping with the Enemy (1991) Suspense ΨΨ
Julia Roberts plays the battered wife of a possessive and sadistic husband played by Patrick Bergin. Roberts fakes her death and assumes a new identity in a desperate attempt to escape.

Small Time Crooks (2000) Comedy Ψ
Woody Allen plays a "foolish antisocial" who devises a plan to rob a bank with his not-so-bright pals. Hugh Grant plays a manipulative, charming, self-serving narcissist.

Sneakers (1992) Drama/Comedy ΨΨ
This film has a star cast that includes Dan Akroyd, who plays an ex-convict with paranoid traits who sees conspiracy in almost every situation.

Solitary Man (2009) Drama ΨΨΨ
Michael Douglas plays the role of Ben Kalmen, a man with a narcissistic personality disorder who has failed as a salesman, father, grandfather, husband, lover, and friend.

Speed (1994) Drama ΨΨ
Dennis Hopper plays a deranged sociopath who programs a bomb to explode if a city bus slows to less than 50 miles per hour.

Stagecoach (1939) Western ΨΨΨ
Classic John Ford movie, with Thomas Mitchell playing a drunken physician. Mitchell won an Academy Award for Best Supporting Actor for his role.

Strangers on a Train (1951) Thriller ΨΨΨΨ
Classic Hitchcock film in which Farley Granger is unable to extricate himself from his involvement with sociopath Robert Walker.

Streetcar Named Desire, A (1951) Drama ΨΨΨΨ
Elia Kazan film starring Marlon Brando and Vivian Leigh. Blanche DuBois offers a striking example of a histrionic personality. Brando is unforgettable in the role of Stanley Kowalski. (Compare this film with Woody Allen's *Blue Jasmine*.)

"They're dead, they're finished! There was a time in this business when they had the eyes of the whole wide world. But that wasn't good enough for them. Oh, no. They had to have the ears of the world, too. So they opened their big mouths, and out came talk. Talk! Talk!"

Sunset Blvd. (1950)

Sunset Blvd. (1950) Drama ΨΨΨΨ
Billy Wilder film in which a narcissistic, histrionic, and delusional Gloria Swanson clings to the memories of her former greatness as a silent screen star. William Holden plays a young man who exchanges attention and sexual favors for security.

Suspect Zero (2004) Thriller/Crime ΨΨ
Ben Kingsley plays a serial killer who tries to catch a serial killer by attempting to tune into the killer's thoughts, intentions, and feelings.

Swimfan (2002) Drama/Suspense Ψ
Girl's one-night-stand with a fellow classmate shifts from infatuation to the conviction "If I can't have you, no one will."

Swimming Pool (2002) Drama/Mystery ΨΨΨΨ
Mystery writer leaves London to find peace, quiet, and inspiration at her publisher's secluded home in a French village. She overcomes her writer's block by writing about the adventures of a seductive, provocative young woman, the publisher's daughter, who has spontaneously moved in.

Swimming With Sharks (1994) Comedy ΨΨ
Dark comedy with Kevin Spacey as a nasty, heartless, business executive who is held hostage and tortured by an employee he has verbally abused over the years.

"I always thought it would be better to be a fake somebody than a real nobody."

Tom Ripley describing his secretive double life in *The Talented Mr. Ripley* (1999)

Talented Mr. Ripley, The (1999) Drama ΨΨΨΨΨ
Matt Damon is the deceitful, charming, clever impersonator, Tom Ripley, who manipulates anyone in his path until he can no longer get away with his deceit. Breakthrough film for supporting actor Jude Law.

Tao of Steve, The (2000) Comedy Ψ
Self-serving, amateur philosopher uses some ideas from Buddhist philosophy to pursue and sleep with women.

Tape (2001) Drama ΨΨΨΨ
Creative, engaging, and honest story of how people manipulate one another to meet their own desires and how they react when their secrets are exposed. It also shows what can happen when someone has unresolved psychological issues. The entire film takes place in one motel room with only three characters – all young veterans – Ethan Hawke, Robert Sean Leonard, and Uma Thurman.

"You talkin' to me? [slower] You talking to me? You talking to me? Well, then, who the hell else are you talking – you talking to me? Well, I'm the only one here."

Travis Bickle rehearsing in *Taxi Driver* (1976)

Taxi Driver (1976) Drama ΨΨΨΨΨ
The premorbid personality of Travis Bickle illustrates delusional paranoid thinking. Bickle would probably meet the criteria for a diagnosis of schizotypal personality disorder.

There Will Be Blood (2007) Drama/Thriller ΨΨΨΨ
Daniel Day-Lewis portrays Daniel Plainview, a charismatic, ruthless oil prospector in this story of greed, religion, and family. Plainview is a good illustration of an antisocial personality disorder.

Thin Blue Line, The (1988) Documentary ΨΨΨ
Gripping documentary examining the unjust incarceration of a man accused of the murder of a Texas policeman.

To Die For (1995) Drama ΨΨ
Nicole Kidman plays the role of a newswoman who will do anything to advance her career, including having her husband killed.

Toto le Heros (1991) Drama/Comedy ΨΨΨΨ
An old man in a nursing home reviews his life and his lifelong hatred for his next-door neighbor, who appeared to have every advantage. Wonderful example of a paranoid personality disorder.

Town, The (2010) Drama ΨΨΨ
A bank robber seduces the teller her and his partners had earlier taken hostage; he falls in love with her, but finds it hard to leave his criminal past behind him. Ben Affleck's character meets many of the criteria for antisocial personality disorder.

Trucker (2008) Drama ΨΨ
A self-reliant woman finds her isolated life is turned upside down when her long abandoned 11-year-old son turns up. It is useful for students to speculate about whether Michelle Monaghan's character meets *DSM-5* criteria for a personality disorder.

Tsotsi (2005, UK, South Africa) Crime/Drama ΨΨΨΨ
An African gangster accidentally kidnaps an infant and in learning to care for the child makes some changes in himself.

Unfaithful (2002) Drama/Suspense ΨΨ
A married man (Richard Gere) finds out his wife (Diane Lane) is having an affair and he seeks revenge.

Very Bad Things (1999) Comedy Ψ
Dark comedy about a bachelor party gone horribly wrong. As the five men try to cover up an accidental murder, more problems arise.

Vicky Cristina Barcelona (2008) Drama ΨΨΨ
High quality, Woody Allen film about two young women touring Barcelona for the summer who encounter a handsome man and his erratic, labile ex-wife (Penelope Cruz).

Violette Noziere (1978) Biography/Crime ΨΨ
Claude Chabrol film based on the true story about a teenage girl who poisoned her parents, eventually killing her father, whom she claimed had raped and abused her.

Wall Street (1987) Drama ΨΨΨΨ
Michael Douglas is memorable as Gordon Gekko, a man who clearly meets criteria for a diagnosis of antisocial personality disorder.

> "The richest one percent of this country owns half our country's wealth, five trillion dollars. One third of that comes from hard work, two thirds comes from inheritance, interest on interest accumulating to widows and idiot sons and what I do, stock and real estate speculation. It's bullshit. You got ninety percent of the American public out there with little or no net worth. I create nothing. I own. We make the rules, pal."
>
> Gordon Gekko explains capitalism to Bud Fox in *Wall Street* (1987)

Wall Street: Money Never Sleeps (2010) Drama ΨΨΨ
Gordon Gekko returns to Wall Street after serving an 8-year sentence for securities fraud.

Wannsee Conference, The (1984) Historical/War ΨΨΨ
Recreation of the Berlin meeting in which Nazi officers first outlined the "final solution" for dealing with the "Jewish problem."

Whisperers, The (1966) Drama Ψ
Dame Edith Evans stars as a lonely old woman, divorced from her husband and estranged from her son, who devotes her days to worry and paranoid ramblings.

White Oleander (2002) Drama ΨΨΨΨ
Young girl is tossed around from home to home when her mother is incarcerated. The mother figures include characters played by Michelle Pfeiffer (antisocial), Renée Zellweger (dependent), and Robin Wright-Penn (histrionic). Fascinating dynamics of a young girl's resilience with each personality disordered mother-figure.

> "Loneliness is the human condition. Love humiliates you. Hatred cradles you."
>
> A mother teaching her philosophy to her teenage daughter in *White Oleander* (2002)

Who Loves the Sun (2006) Drama ΨΨ
Will discovers that his wife is having an affair with Daniel, the best man from their wedding, and he copes by dropping out of sight for 5 years. Daniel's character illustrates narcissistic personality disorder.

Wild at Heart (1990) Comedy/Drama/Romance ΨΨΨ
David Lynch film with ex-con Nicolas Cage and his lover, Laura Dern, as two antisocial personalities (despite their apparent commitment to each other). Won the Palme d'Or at Cannes, but not all critics were impressed. Too violent for some tastes.

Willard (2003) Drama Ψ
Crispin Glover plays a schizoid man whose only contact is his critical mother and numerous rats living in his basement. He uses the rats for revenge until they turn on him.

Wise Blood (1979) Drama ΨΨΨ
John Huston's adaptation of Flannery O'Connor's gothic Southern novel about an obsessed preacher.

Zoolander (2001) Comedy Ψ
Absurd, over-the-top depiction of a narcissistic model who is brainwashed to become an assassin. Ben Stiller directed, co-wrote, and starred in this film.

Paraphilic Disorders

8MM (1999) Mystery/Thriller ΨΨ
Joel Schumacher film about the underground world of "snuff" films. Depicts the worst kind of sadism.

Adjuster, The (1991) Drama ΨΨΨ
This interesting Canadian film explores voyeurism and exhibitionism.

Aleksandr's Price (2013) Drama ΨΨ
A Russian immigrant loses his mother, becomes involved with drugs, and then is drawn into the gay underworld as a male prostitute.

Angels and Insects (1995) Drama ΨΨΨ
Complex drama about social class, passion, incest, and hidden sexual secrets in a wealthy Victorian household.

Another Time, Another Place (1983) Drama ΨΨΨ
Sensitive film in which a Scottish woman in an unhappy marriage has a brief affair with an Italian prisoner of war working as a laborer on the farm. The man is accused of a rape he did not commit; his lover can save him, but only at the cost of revealing her adultery.

Antichrist (2009) Drama/Horror ΨΨΨ
A controversial Lars von Trier film about a grieving couple that lost their infant son when the child fell from a window while the man and his wife were making love. They retreat to a country cabin where the woman quickly decompensates and becomes psychotic and the couple engage in sadomasochistic behavior. The film has four chapters, titled Grief, Pain (Chaos Reigns), Despair (Gynocide) and The Three Beggars. The film, dedicated to the Russian director Andrei Tarkovsky, stars Willem Dafoe as the therapist husband and Charlotte Gainsbourg as the grieving wife.

Bad Timing: A Sensual Obsession (1980) Drama ΨΨ
Art Garfunkel (playing a psychology professor), Harvey Keitel, and Theresa Russell star in a provocative and explicit film about a psychiatrist who becomes sexually obsessed with a young woman after she makes a suicide attempt.

Beginner's Luck (1983) Comedy ΨΨ
Lightweight comedy about a law student who becomes involved in a ménage à trois.

Blame It on Rio (1984) Comedy ΨΨ
Two men take their teenage daughters to Rio's topless beaches, and one of the men, 43 years old, has an affair with the 15-year-old daughter of the other. The film has a vaguely incestuous theme and is modeled after the French film *One Wild Moment*.

Bliss (1997) Drama Ψ
Very fragile woman with a borderline personality disorder goes to a charming sex therapist who sleeps with his patients. The husband finds out; when he confronts the therapist, the husband converts and becomes his disciple. The film illustrates numerous ethical violations, and it demeans sacred Hindu tantric practices.

Blue Angel, The (1930) Drama ΨΨΨΨΨ
Classic film about a phlegmatic professor who loses everything because of his obsession with a cabaret singer.

Blue Car (2002) Drama ΨΨΨ
Independent film about an adolescent girl who is seduced by her teacher. Good depiction of the disturbing, subtle aspects of seduction and sexual exploitation.

Blue Velvet (1986) Mystery ΨΨΨΨ
A powerful and engrossing David Lynch film about drugs, sexual violence, and sadomasochism. Dennis Hopper portrays Frank Booth, one of the most sociopathic and sadistic villains in film history.

Bound (1996) Suspense/Drama ΨΨ
A tough female ex-con and her new female lover concoct a scheme to steal mob money. This film noir is the Wachowski brothers' directorial debut.

Breaking the Waves (1996, Denmark) Drama ΨΨΨ
A Danish film in which a devout Catholic wife submits to sexual degradation to satisfy the voyeuristic demands of her paralyzed husband.

"Are you sleeping with other men just to feed his sick fantasies?"

A question put to Bess in
Breaking the Waves (1996)

Cabaret (1972) Musical/Drama/Dance ΨΨΨΨ
Liza Minnelli in a film about sadomasochism, bisexuality, and the relationship between sex and power. *Cabaret* won Oscars for Best Actor, Best Actress, and Best Director. One scene in the film is as unforgettable as the classic confession of incest in *Chinatown*.

Caesar and Rosalie (1972) Comedy/Romance ΨΨ
Lighthearted and amusing examination of a ménage à trois.

Capturing the Friedmans (2003) Documentary ΨΨΨΨ
Extraordinarily disturbing and emotional documentary about a father and son accused of pedophilia. Important film to see regarding sex addiction, pedophilia, and the importance of not casting judgment too quickly.

"Don't worry, you've got everything under control."

A therapist's comments to a pedophile who was worried he might molest his own children; he later molests numerous children in a class he teaches out of his home in
Capturing the Friedmans (2003)

Chinatown (1974) Mystery ΨΨΨΨ
A film about power, incest, and the complexity of human relationships. Actors includes Jack Nicholson, Faye Dunaway and John Huston.

"You see, Mr. Gettes, most people never have to face the fact that, at the right time and in the right place, they are capable of anything."

Chinatown (1974)

Claire's Knee (1971, France) Drama ΨΨΨ
An intelligent film in which a middle-aged man becomes obsessed with a young girl's knee.

Close My Eyes (1991) Drama ΨΨ
A British film about brother-sister incest.

Collector, The (1965) Drama ΨΨΨ
Terence Stamp stars as a young man who collects butterflies. He becomes obsessed with Samantha Eggar, kidnaps her, and winds up inadvertently killing her.

Crash (1996) Drama ΨΨΨ
A David Cronenberg film about people who become sexually aroused by automobile accidents. The film presents a plausible hypothesis: people have developed fetishes

for stranger things, and there are erotic overtones to both cars and speed.

"You couldn't wait for me? You did the Jane Mansfield crash without me!"

One of many strange interactions in David Cronenberg's Crash (1996)

Cruising (1980) Crime Ψ
Controversial William Friedkin film starring Al Pacino as an undercover police officer who infiltrates gay bars and bathhouses. Gay activists condemned the film because it perpetuates stigma and stereotypes.

Dahmer (2002) Biography/Drama ΨΨ
A docudrama about the life of serial killer and cannibal Jeffrey Dahmer who served two years of a life sentence before being killed by another inmate on November 28, 1994. Dahmer was 34 years old when he died.

Day in the Country, A (1936) Romance ΨΨΨΨ
Jean Renoir's adaptation of a short story by Guy de Maupassant that describes the seductions of a man's wife and daughter.

Dark Tourist (2013) Drama ΨΨ
Michael is a "dark tourist" – he travels to places where atrocities have been committed such as mass murders. While visiting an arson site in California, Michael becomes involved with a waitress played by Melanie Griffith.

Desert Flower (2009) Biography ΨΨΨ
This autobiographical film details the life of a Somalian nomad who was subjected to female genital mutilation (FGM) as a child to ensure she would not be able to experience sexual pleasure as an adult. She was forced to marry a much older man when she was 13, but escaped and moved to London where she eventually became a celebrated model – and an outspoken opponent of FGM.

Disconnect (2013) Drama ΨΨΨ
This film presents 3 stories, all of which relate to social media and online communications. One story involves a teenage male prostitute who engages in online chat room sex; one involves identity theft of a couple, both of who are involved with illicit online activities; and one story is about two high school boys who impersonate a girl and persuade a shy boy to send them a nude photo of himself. The photo is sent to everyone in his high school class, and he attempts suicide, ending up in a coma.

Door in the Floor, The (2003) Drama ΨΨ
A couple separates after the death of their twin sons. The catalyst for the breakup is Eddie, a 16 year old who takes

a job as Jeff Bridges' assistant. Eddie is infatuated by Kim Bassinger's character and masturbates using her photos and undergarments to become aroused. Bassinger eventually seduces Eddie, who reminds her of her dead sons. Based on a novel by John Irving.

Dreamers, The (2003) Drama ΨΨΨ
Fraternal twins take in a roommate in this Bernardo Bertolucci exploration of politics, cinema, and sexuality. The dynamics become complicated when the new roommate falls in love with the female twin, taking her virginity and challenging her enmeshment with her brother.

"A filmmaker is like a peeping Tom, a voyeur. It's as if the camera is the key to your parent's bedroom and you spy on them and you're disgusted and you feel guilty but you can't ... you can't look away."

The Dreamers (2003

Eros (2004) Drama ΨΨΨ
Three noted directors (Michelangelo Antonioni, Steven Soderbergh and Wong Kar Wai) each contribute a short film dealing with some aspect of sexuality (e.g., a ménage à trois, voyeurism, and prostitution).

Everything You Always Wanted to Know About Sex * But Were Afraid to Ask (1972) Comedy ΨΨΨ
Woody Allen classic includes vignettes on crossing dressing, bestiality, sex in public, and the inner workings of the brain during sexual excitement.

Evil Alien Conquerors (2002) Comedy Ψ
Painfully bad film in which former Saturday Night Live star, Chris Parnell, has a foot fetish.

Eyes Wide Shut (1999) Drama ΨΨΨΨΨ
The final Stanley Kubrick film about a man (Tom Cruise) who discovers a sexual underworld after his wife (Nicole Kidman) tells him of her fantasies and previous sexual encounters. Depiction of ephebophilia (sexual attraction of adults to adolescents), orgies, sexual rituals, exhibitionism, prostitution, infidelity, sexual fantasy, seduction, and betrayal. Mythological and Jungian psychology themes are omnipresent.

Fellini Satyricon (1970) Historical ΨΨΨΨ
Controversial Fellini film about the decadence of ancient Rome. The film is visually stunning and explores human vices ranging from pedophilia to cannibalism. The film can be a springboard for a discussion of hedonism.

Female Perversions (1996) Drama ΨΨΨ
Confused and often confusing examination of the relationship between women, power, sexuality, and psycho-

pathology. Based on a scholarly book with the same title by psychoanalyst Louise J. Kaplan.

Fetishes (1996) Documentary ΨΨΨ
True examination of the clients of Pandora's Box, an elite club catering to the sexual fetishes of New York City.

Fist in His Pocket (1966) Drama ΨΨΨ
Italian film about a dysfunctional family with multiple examples of psychopathology including epilepsy, murder, and incest.

Girl 6 (1996) Drama/Comedy Ψ
Spike Lee film about a woman who takes a job as a phone sex operator for the money.

God's Little Acre (1958) Drama Ψ
Buddy Hackett and Michael Landon star in this adaptation of Erskine Caldwell's tale of depravity and Georgia farm life.

Good Mother, The (1988) Drama ΨΨΨ
A provocative film in which Diane Keaton plays the divorced mother of a six-year-old daughter. Keaton falls in love with an iconoclastic artist, who allows the daughter to touch his penis when she sees him in the bath and expresses normal childhood curiosity. Keaton is eventually forced to denounce her new lover in order to maintain a relationship with her daughter.

Happiness (1998) Comedy/Drama ΨΨΨ
Disturbing dark comedy portraying a variety of quirky characters. The most striking are the pedophiliac psychiatrist who drugs and rapes his son's best friend and Philip Seymour Hoffman as a man who is obsessed with telephone scatologia. Director Todd Solondz has a cameo as a doorman.

Joe: "What do you think would happen if I got him a professional ... you know ..."
Bill: "A professional?"
Joe: "Hooker. You know, the kind that can teach things ... first-timers, you know ... break him in."
Bill: "But Joe, he's 11."
Joe: "You're right, you're right. It's too late."

Cultures clash in *Happiness* (1998)

Hard Candy (2005) Drama ΨΨ
A pedophile arranges to meet a 14-year-old girl who turns things around and winds up being the aggressor.

Henry & June (1990) Drama ΨΨ
Adaptation of Anais Nin diary detailing her ménage à trois with novelist Henry Miller and his wife June.

Holy Smoke (1999) Drama ΨΨΨ
Jane Campion film about a family who believes their daughter (Kate Winslet) is under the power of a cult leader. They hire a renowned "cult exiter" (Harvey Keitel) whose role is to isolate the subject, provoke them, and then reintegrate them into the family. After an interesting role reversal, he finds himself developing a sexual obsession.

Hunt, The (2013, Denmark) Drama ΨΨΨ
A schoolteacher loses his job and is going through a divorce; however, his life seems to be improving until he is unfairly accused of pedophilia.

Human Nature (2001) Comedy ΨΨ
Fascinating study on instinct and desire about a man raised in the wild and the scientists he encounters.

In the Realm of the Senses (1977, Japan) Drama ΨΨΨ
A sadomasochistic relationship intensifies into highly graphic and unforgettable scenes of autoerotic asphyxiation and the severing of a penis.

Intimacy (2000) Drama ΨΨ
Depressed man and woman meet for anonymous sex in a dilapidated apartment once a week. The man becomes curious about the woman and follows her to learn more about her. Slow, dark film that depicts the double life of the addict.

Ju Dou (1990, China) Drama/Historical/Romance ΨΨΨΨ
Wonderful, visually stunning film examining the complex links that bind a husband, his wife, her lover, and the son of the illicit union. Good illustrations of sexual passion and sexual torment.

Jules and Jim (1962, France) Drama ΨΨΨΨΨ
Beautiful and engaging Truffaut film about a complex ménage à trois and an ultimate suicide. The film deals with far more than sexuality; it explores fundamental dimensions of human relationships and the boundaries of friendship and love.

"Love is the answer, isn't it? But, sex raises a lot of very interesting questions."

Kinsey (2004)

Kinsey (2004) Drama/Biography ΨΨΨΨ
Examination of the life of Alfred Kinsey, a sex researcher who revolutionized the way Americans viewed sexuality. The film depicts Kinsey's obsessive-compulsive personality, his inability to connect in a deep way, and the fail-

ure to set boundaries for his own (and his research team's) sexual practices.

Kissed (1996) Drama ΨΨΨ
A controversial but sensitive film dealing seriously with necrophilia. Molly Parker is the protagonist, a young woman obsessed from childhood with death. She gets a job in a mortuary and has ritualistic sex ("crossing over") with the bodies she embalms. Her boyfriend commits suicide in an attempt to compete for her affection and attention.

Last Exit to Brooklyn (1989) Drama ΨΨ
A film based on a controversial book about life in a sordid Brooklyn neighborhood. The film deals with rape, prostitution, homosexuality, and transvestism, but mostly with the sad and bleak reality of the lives of its characters.

Leap Year (2011, Mexico) Drama ΨΨΨΨ
Laura, a 25-year-old journalist, has numerous one-night stands until she meets Arturo who introduces her to the world of sadomasochistic sex. She embraces and expands this new sexual role as her lover beats her, urinates on her, chokes her, burns her, and rolls a knife over her naked body.

Little Children (2007) Drama ΨΨΨΨ
This film portrays a number of sexually troubled characters, but is especially memorable for the roles of Jackie Earle Haley playing a pedophile and Kate Winslet playing the role of a parent who overcomes her repugnance to befriend him.

"What drives me insane is the twofold nature of this nymphet ... this mixture in my Lolita of tender, dreamy childishness and a kind of eerie vulgarity."

Humbert Humbert in *Lolita* (1962)

Lolita (1962) Drama ΨΨΨΨ
James Mason and Sue Lyons star in a loose adaptation of Vladimir Nabokov's novel about pedophilia and murder. Laurence Olivier turned down the role of Humbert Humbert. Directed by Stanley Kubrick; watch for Peter Sellers as Dr. Zempf, the Beardsley High School psychologist.

Lust, Caution (2007) Drama ΨΨΨ
An Ang Lee film about a young Chinese woman who seduces a sadistic Japanese leader

Luna (1979) Drama ΨΨ
A Bertolucci film that explores mother-son incest and addiction. The film is not Bertolucci's best effort.

M (1931, Germany) Crime/Drama/Thriller ΨΨΨΨ
A Fritz Lang film about a psychopathic Berlin pedophile who is murdering small children.

Manhattan (1979) Comedy/Romance ΨΨΨΨ
Classic Woody Allen film in which his former wife, played by Meryl Streep, has taken a lover, found happiness, and written a book to tell the world about Allen's kinky habits. Allen's character (in an example of art imitating life) is consumed with guilt over the fact that he is living with a teenage girl.

Mark, The (1961) Drama ΨΨΨΨ
A British film about a pedophile who serves his sentence and is released, supposedly cured. However, a journalist who reveals the man's past hampers his rehabilitation. Interesting film in light of recent court decisions about sex offenders.

Matador (1986) Comedy/Drama ΨΨ
Almodóvar film about a bullfighter who acts in snuff films.

Menage (1986, France) Comedy ΨΨ
A French film that examines sex roles, sexual stereotypes, and the need for novelty and excitement in sexual relationships.

Midsummer Night's Sex Comedy, A (1982) ΨΨ
Excellent Woody Allen film about friends and acquaintances who gather at a country house in the woods at the turn of the century. Sexual boundaries blur in this homage to Shakespeare, Renoir, and others.

Mona Lisa (1986) Crime ΨΨΨ
Interesting Neil Jordan film about prostitution, exploitation, drug addiction, and love. Filmed in Soho, the film gives some insight into the two different worlds of prostitution: that of the call girl and that of the streetwalker.

Murmur of the Heart (1971) Comedy ΨΨ
A sensitive, intelligent, and funny French film about an incestuous relationship between a young mother and her adolescent son.

My Favorite Season (1993, France) Drama ΨΨΨ
A French film dealing with adolescent sexuality, family dynamics, and love between a brother and sister.

My Life to Live (1962, France) ΨΨΨ
Jean-Luc Godard's 12-part examination of the life of a prostitute, starring Anna Karina.

My Own Private Idaho (1991) Drama ΨΨ
River Phoenix, who subsequently died of a drug overdose, plays a homosexual prostitute.

Nine ½ Weeks (1986) Drama/Suspense ΨΨ
Excellent character portrayals by Mickey Rourke and Kim Bassinger who meet at a grocery store and later engage in sensual sexual exploration and mild sadomasochism.

Of Human Bondage (1934) Drama ΨΨ
Bette Davis stars in this film about the sexual obsession of a club-footed physician for a cruel, vulgar, and manipulative waitress. Based on a novel by Somerset Maugham. This film is far superior to the two adaptations that followed it.

"You dirty swine! I never cared for you ... It made me sick when you kissed me. I only did it because you drove me crazy. And after you kissed me I always used to wipe my mouth – wipe my mouth!"

Of Human Bondage (1934)

Oldboy (2003) Drama ΨΨΨ
This is an unforgettable Korean film directed by Chan-Wook Park about a man kidnapped and imprisoned for 15 years who becomes involved in an unwitting incestuous relationship with the daughter he had not seen for 15 years.

On_Line (2002) Drama ΨΨΨ
A film about internet addiction. Emphasis on the lack of connection and relational intimacy of the addict. Depicts an obsession with fantasy that becomes confused as reality.

Oscar Wilde (1960) Biography Ψ
Robert Morley plays Oscar Wilde, the playwright who was convicted of sodomy.

Peeping Tom (1960) Thriller ΨΨΨ
Controversial film about a sexual psychopath who photographs his victims as they are dying. Look for the full-length version of the film, which was released in 1979.

"It's being aware of what it means to lose oneself before being completely abandoned."

The Piano Teacher (2001)

Piano Teacher, The (2001) Drama ΨΨΨ
This is a powerful French film about a prominent, masochistic piano teacher who becomes sexually involved with one of her pupils. The film makes sexual obsession understandable and plausible.

Pillow Book (1997) Drama ΨΨΨ
Complex Peter Greenaway film about a woman who becomes sexually obsessed with calligraphy. This film is a meditation on love, art and imagination, eroticism, order, and decay.

Pretty Baby (1978) Drama ΨΨ
This Louis Malle film about pedophilia introduces Brooke Shields as a 12-year-old New Orleans prostitute.

Pretty When You Cry (2001) Drama/Suspense Ψ
Mostly flashbacks as detectives follow up a murder investigation with a young man who tells the story of his infatuation and love for a beautiful woman who was in an abusive relationship. The masochistic-sadistic relationship is portrayed, as well as physical, verbal, and emotional abuse.

Priest (1994) Drama ΨΨ
A priest struggles to deal with the sanctity of confession after a young girl tells him she is being molested by her father.

Private Lessons (1981) Drama Ψ
A French maid seduces a 15-year-old boy and betrays his trust.

Private Parts (1997) Comedy Ψ
Inside look at radio personality Howard Stern and his obsession with sex and outlandish comedy.

Psychopathia Sexualis (2006) Drama Ψ
Based directly on the classic Krafft-Ebing text, the film depicts a variety of fetishes and other paraphilias.

"Look, maybe your method of massage differs from mine, but touchin' his lady's feet, and stickin' your tongue in her holiest of holies, ain't the same ballpark, ain't the same league, ain't even the same fuckin' sport. Foot massages don't mean shit."

A discussion of foot massage in *Pulp Fiction* (1994)

Pulp Fiction (1994) Drama ΨΨΨΨ
Quentin Tarantino film depicts an underworld sadomasochistic den of iniquity run by two sexual sadists in the basement of an Army surplus store. A masochistic slave dressed totally in leather lives in a box in the back of the room.

Quills (2000) Drama ΨΨΨ
Depiction of the last years of the Marquis de Sade (well played by Geoffrey Rush) who was sent to the Charenton

Insane Asylum as punishment for his erotic writings. Interesting portrayal of various paraphilias.

Reader, The (2008) Drama ΨΨΨΨ
Kate Winslet plays Hanna Schmitz, a Nazi concentration camp guard who seduces a young boy who later grows up and becomes a prominent attorney.

Rita, Sue and Bob Too (1986) Comedy ΨΨΨ
British film about a married man who winds up in a sexual relationship with the two working-class teenage girls who babysit for his children. Interesting examination of the appropriate age for consent and issues of sexual exploitation.

Rocky Horror Picture Show, The (1975) Comedy/Horror/Musical/Dance Ψ
A fun film about a Transylvanian transsexual. From a psychological perspective, the film is not nearly as interesting as those fans who have turned it into a cult classic.

Salò, or the 120 Days of Sodom (1975, Italy) Drama Ψ
Based on the writings of the Marquis de Sade, and arguably an allegory film denouncing the excesses of fascism. Some reviewers consider this controversial last film of Italian director Pier Paolo Pasolini a classic. We are less impressed and believe the coprophagia and extreme sexual violence are largely gratuitous.

Sergeant, The (1968) Drama ΨΨ
Rod Steiger plays an Army sergeant sexually obsessed with a young private in his outfit. Filmed in France.

> "In one way or another I've always suffered. I didn't know why exactly. But I do know that I'm not so scared of suffering now. I feel more than I've ever felt and I've found someone to feel with. To play with. To love in a way that feels right for me."
>
> Reflections on masochism in *Secretary* (2002

Secretary (2002) Drama ΨΨΨ
A self-injurious, depressed woman is hired as a secretary after leaving a mental hospital; she takes a new job and begins to enjoy the criticism and punishment of her boss. They develop a sadomasochistic relationship in the work setting and eventually fall in love and marry.

Sex and Zen (1993) Comedy Ψ
Second rate film about a Buddhist who leaves his master and new wife to seek out a life of debauchery and erotic pleasures.

Sex is Zero (2002) Comedy Ψ
A Korean *Animal House*, but not as clever. The film involves lots of teens sexually acting out in a variety of ways.

Sex, Lies and Videotape (1989) Drama ΨΨΨ
The film revolves around an impotent young man who can achieve orgasm only when masturbating while watching videotapes of women whom he has persuaded to share the most intimate details of their sexual lives. This film won the top award at the Cannes Film Festival.

Short Cuts (1993) Drama ΨΨ
Most memorable for a scene in which a bored woman talks dirty on the phone to earn a few dollars while she changes her baby's diapers. Her husband wonders why she never talks to *him* like that.

Short Eyes (1977) Prison ΨΨΨΨ
A powerful film about life in "The Tombs," New York City's Men's House of Detention. Short Eyes is prison slang for a child molester.

Short Film About Love, A (1988, Poland) Drama ΨΨΨ
This Krzysztof Kieslowski film deals with themes of voyeurism, exhibitionism, humiliation and suicide.

Skin I Live In (2011, Spain) Thriller ΨΨΨΨ
Pedro Almodóvar film staring Antonio Banderas as Dr. Robert Ledgard, a gifted but troubled plastic surgeon. This film is too good to spoil with a plot summary, but it is highly recommended.

Sliver (1993) Drama Ψ
William Baldwin plays a voyeur who is the landlord of an apartment complex with high tech cameras set up in the tenants' rooms.

Something About Amelia (1984) Drama ΨΨ
Popular made-for-TV movie about father-daughter incest.

Strange One, The (1957) Drama ΨΨ
Ben Gazzara stars in this film about homosexuality and sadism in a Southern military academy.

This World, Then the Fireworks (1997) Drama ΨΨ
This film traces the development of incestuous twins who eventually become con artists.

Three (2010, Germany) Drama ΨΨ
In this Tom Tykwer film, a long time couple wind up independently having an affair with the same man, a stem cell scientist and a sex addict.

Tie Me Up! Tie Me Down! (1990, Spain) Comedy/Romance ΨΨΨ
A Pedro Almodóvar film about a former mental patient, kidnapping, masochism, and sex roles. Some critics have maintained that the film trivializes the problem of sexual violence and denigrates women.

Torch Song Trilogy (1988) Drama ΨΨΨ
Anne Bancroft and Matthew Broderick in a film adaptation of Harvey Fierstein's play about a homosexual drag queen and his lovers, enemies, and mother.

Towelhead (2007) Drama ΨΨΨ
A naïve, 13-year-old, Arab-American girl moves from Syracuse to Houston and encounters a number of challenges associated with her emerging sexuality, including being the victim of ephebophilia.

Venus (2006) Drama ΨΨΨ
Peter O'Toole plays an aging actor with prostate cancer who falls in love with a teenage girl.

Viridiana (1961, Spain) Drama ΨΨΨΨ
This complex Luis Buñuel film tells the story of a young woman who returns home to visit her uncle just before taking vows as a nun. She resembles her dead aunt, and her uncle drugs her while she is wearing her aunt's wedding dress. He plans to rape her but is unable to commit the act. He commits suicide; she inherits his estate and devotes her life to serving the poor.

Visiting Desire (1996) Documentary ΨΨ
Twelve strangers are brought together to act out their sexual fantasies.

"Stealing images from life is my life."

A voyeur describes himself in
Voyeur Confessions (2001)

Voyeur Confessions (2001) Drama ΨΨ
This film captures the pain associated with the life of the voyeur. The movie touches on the etiology of voyeurism, and helps serious students better understand the paraphilias.

Wild Orchid 2: Two Shades of Blue (1991) Drama Ψ
Disappointing film about the daughter of a heroin addict who becomes a prostitute to support her father's habit while maintaining a double identity.

Woodsman, The (2004) Drama ΨΨΨ
Kevin Bacon plays a pedophile recently released from prison struggling to establish a satisfying sexual relationship with a mature coworker.

Violence, Physical and Sexual Abuse

2LDK (2002) Drama/Action ΨΨΨ
A little known but striking independent film about two girls rooming together temporarily as they compete in an acting audition. A simple argument turns into a violent battle between the two roommates. The methods of violence are unique and extraordinary, despite being contained in one apartment.

3-Iron (2004, South Korea) ΨΨΨ
A man breaks into houses when people are away for vacation and engages in mundane activities while living there temporarily. He encounters a mute woman who is the victim of domestic violence and they continue his activities together.

5 x 2 (2004, France) Drama ΨΨΨ
Five stages of a couple's romance are portrayed backwards from their divorce; the film depicts conflict, rape, emotional stonewalling, poor decisions-making, and relationship neglect.

8 Mile (2002) Drama ΨΨ
Director Curtis Hanson depicts the struggles, racism, and abuse of rapper, Eminem. "8 mile" is a road in Detroit that represents several cinematic themes: it is the borderline and boundary between black and white, city and suburbia, and the authentic and non-authentic.

300 (2006) Action/History ΨΨΨ
Leonidas, the fearless leader of Sparta, leads 300 men against the vast Persian army of well over 100,000 in the infamous 480 B.C. Battle of Thermopylae.

Accused, The (1988) Drama ΨΨΨΨ
Jodi Foster won an Academy Award for Best Actress for her role as a woman who is gang raped in a bar. Her character chooses to prosecute for rape rather than aggravated assault; and the film examines the legal relevance of lifestyle (alcohol, drugs, and promiscuity) to the event and the complicity of bystanders. Based on a true story.

Aileen: Life and Death of a Serial Killer (2003) Documentary ΨΨΨ
Nick Broomfield directed this documentary about serial killer Aileen Carol Wuornos, a highway prostitute who was executed in Florida in 2002 for killing seven men. The film includes the filmmaker's testimony at Wuornos' trial. (See also *Monster*.)

Air I Breathe, The (2007) Crime/Drama ΨΨ
Violent, action-filled gangster movie that takes interesting themes – happiness, pleasure, sorrow, and love – yet falls short in delivering something meaningful.

Alphabet Killer, The (2008) Drama Ψ
A detective is determined to arrest the alphabet killer, a man who is both a serial rapist and murderer; however, her work is set back when she is diagnosed with paranoid schizophrenia.

American History X (1998) Drama/Suspense ΨΨΨ
Edward Norton plays a former skinhead who has decided to leave gang life but must also convince his younger brother.

American Psycho (1999) Drama/Suspense ΨΨΨ
Christian Bale is Patrick Bateman, a narcissistic Wall Street executive, who emphasizes excess and style over substance in everything from business cards and facial cleansers to restaurant selection and conversation. He is depicted as a serial killer who saves the victim's heads in his refrigerator. However, there is enough cinematic evidence to suggest that there were no murders at all, and everything in the film simply reflects the fantasies of an antisocial mind.

Amores Perros (2000) Action/Suspense ΨΨΨ
Mexican film with a non-linear plot with various hit men, murderers, and other perpetrators of highly graphic violence. Abuse and senseless killing of humans and animals are depicted.

Anatomy of a Murder (1959) Drama ΨΨΨΨ
Classic courtroom drama in which Jimmy Stewart plays a prosecuting attorney in a case involving rape and promiscuity. The film presents an interesting analysis of the "irresistible impulse" defense.

Antonia's Line (1995) Comedy ΨΨΨΨ
Remarkable film about the resiliency of the human spirit, the power of love, and the importance of families. It is included here because of its treatment of a rapist, but also because of its treatment of people with an intellectual disability, the suicide of a major character, the film's open acceptance of sexual differences, and its healthy attitudes about aging and death.

> "Every man has got a breaking point. You and I have. Walter Kurtz has reached his. And, very obviously, he has gone insane."
>
> An Army general tries to describe the aberrant behavior of Colonel Kurtz in *Apocalypse Now* (1979)

Apocalypse Now (1979) War ΨΨΨΨΨ
Francis Ford Coppola produced and directed this classic war film, which stars Marlon Brando, Robert Duvall, and Martin Sheen. The film is loosely based on Joseph Conrad's *Heart of Darkness* and was designed to drive home the madness of war, as well as its folly. Perhaps the best-known line in the film is "I love the smell of Napalm in the morning."

Apocalypto (2006) Thriller/Drama ΨΨ
Exceedingly violent Mel Gibson film depicting the collapse of the Mayan civilization.

Babel (2006) Drama ΨΨΨΨΨ
Stories from a variety of cultures (Morocco, Mexico, Japan) interweave around themes of communication and the tragic consequences of violence and miscommunication.

Bad Lieutenant (1992) Drama ΨΨΨ
Cocaine-addicted, alcoholic police officer who abuses his position and his family reexamines his life and values after investigating the case of a nun who refuses to identify the man who has raped her.

Badlands (1973) Crime/Drama ΨΨΨ
Film based on a true story about a sociopathic young man who takes up with a 15-year-old girl and goes on a killing spree. The film effectively portrays the lack of guilt and remorse that in part defines the antisocial personality.

Ballast (2008) Drama ΨΨ
A man's suicide profoundly affects three lonely people living in the Mississippi Delta.

Beyond Right And Wrong: Stories of Justice And Forgiveness (2012) Documentary ΨΨΨΨ
This sensitive film examines survivors of atrocities around the globe and emphasized the healing that can come through forgiveness.

Blood Diamond (2006) Action/Drama ΨΨΨΨ
Leonardo DiCaprio portrays a rough, mercenary, diamond smuggler who grapples with an American journalist (Jennifer Connelly) and must decide between money and assisting a fisherman (Djimon Hounsou) whose child has been kidnapped and turned into a terrorist. The film is a wake-up call on the topic of conflict diamonds.

> "He kidnapped them to control her, to make her do things. Then she wanted to commit suicide so he started cutting off ears as a warning to her to stay alive. I'm not kidding. Frank loved blue. Blue velvet."
>
> *Blue Velvet* (1986)

Blue Velvet (1986) Mystery ΨΨΨΨ
A powerful and engrossing film about drugs, sexual violence, and sadomasochism. Dennis Hopper plays Frank Booth, a sociopathic and sadistic drug addict who appears to be evil personified.

Bonnie and Clyde (1967) Crime ΨΨΨΨΨ
Perhaps the best of its genre, this landmark film examines the lives of five of the most fascinating characters in the history of crime.

"I ain't much of a lover boy. But that don't mean nothin' personal about you. I never saw no percentage in it. Ain't nothin' wrong with me. I don't like boys...."

Clyde Barrow to Bonnie Parker in
Bonnie and Clyde (1967)

Boston Strangler, The (1968) Crime ΨΨ
Tony Curtis, George Kennedy, and Henry Fonda in a film that attempts to portray the inner life of a serial killer.

Bridge on the River Kwai, The (1957) Drama ΨΨΨΨ
Alec Guinness plays an Academy Award–winning role as a British colonel who becomes so obsessed with building a bridge that he loses sight of his loyalty and allegiance to the allied forces.

"Do not speak to me of rules. This is war. This is not a game of cricket. He's mad, your Colonel. Quite mad."

The Bridge on the River Kwai (1957)

Boy A (2007, United Kingdom) Drama ΨΨΨ
Two young boys commit murder and are sent away; when Boy A (Jack) is eventually released, he attempts to establish a new life, but Jack's past catches up with him and makes renewal impossible. There is a sympathetic portrayal of a rehabilitation counselor in the film.

Cape Fear (1991) Thriller ΨΨΨΨ
Interesting Scorsese remake of a 1962 classic. This version includes Nick Nolte playing a sleazy attorney and Robert De Niro is a sociopathic ex-con out to get revenge by hurting Nolte and his family and seducing his teenage daughter.

Casualties of War (1989) Drama ΨΨΨ
Sean Penn leads a group of five soldiers who kidnap and rape a Vietnamese girl and subsequently kill her. Michael J. Fox subsequently shows the moral courage to confront the four rapists and murderers. Based on a true story.

Celebration, The (1998, Denmark/Sweden) Drama ΨΨΨ
A man confronts his sexually abusive father during a family gathering celebrating his father's 60th birthday. Film attempts to depict a realistic approach to abuse confrontation and its effect on a family.

City of God (2003, Brazil) Drama/Foreign ΨΨΨΨ
Painfully sobering and graphic look at violence associated with child and adolescent gang-life, drug trafficking, and poverty in a section of Rio de Janeiro, Brazil. Depiction of young children and adolescents walking around with no fear, guns, and only revenge on their minds.

Clockwork Orange, A (1971) Science Fiction ΨΨΨΨΨ
Stanley Kubrick's masterpiece about "ultra-violence," stereotypes, Beethoven, pathological youth, the future of society, the evils of aversion therapy, good versus evil, the rehabilitation of prisoners, and free will versus determinism. It is regarded by many film experts as one of the greatest films ever made.

"There was me, that is Alex, and my three droogs, that is Pete, Georgie, and Dim, and we sat in the Korova Milkbar trying to make up our rassoodocks what to do with the evening. The Korova milkbar sold milk-plus, milk plus vellocet or synthemesc or drencrom, which is what we were drinking. This would sharpen you up and make you ready for a bit of the old ultra-violence."

Opening lines in *A Clockwork Orange* (1971)

Cold Mountain (2003) Drama/Romance ΨΨ
Amidst a dramatic love story (between characters played by Jude Law and Nicole Kidman) is a lot of antisocial behavior, violence, immoral behavior, attempted rape, and senseless tortures and killings.

Compulsion (1959) Crime ΨΨΨ
Two homosexual law students kidnap and kill a young boy. Based on the Leopold-Loeb case, the film examines the morality of capital punishment and features Orson Wells in the role played by Clarence Darrow in the actual case.

Cook, the Thief, His Wife & Her Lover, The (1989) Drama ΨΨΨΨ
Peter Greenaway film far too complex to capture in a sentence or two. Full of psychopathology, the film deals with passion, deceit, gluttony, murder, cannibalism, and man's inhumanity to man.

Crash (2004) Drama ΨΨΨΨ
Director Paul Haggis blends several stories in this eclectic mix of races and ethnicities in Los Angeles that takes a meaningful look at racism, discrimination, corruption, and the possibility of redemption.

Das Experiment (2001) Drama/Suspense ΨΨΨ
Depiction of psychological research experiment in a prison setting where subjects are divided into prisoners who waive their civil rights and guards who are to maintain peace and order. While this film bears some initial structural similarity to the famous Zimbardo Prison Experiment, it in no way portrays it accurately as the film's violence goes well beyond actual events.

> "They got me on a greased rail to the Death House here."
>
> *Dead Man Walking* (1995)

Dead Man Walking (1995) Drama ΨΨΨΨ
Susan Sarandon and Sean Penn star in this dramatic examination of a nun's need to understand and help a man sentenced to die for the rape and murder of two teenagers. The film skillfully examines the death penalty, family dynamics, themes of redemption, and the mitigating role of drugs without ever providing easy answers. Sarandon won an Academy Award for her performance in this film.

Deliberate Stranger, The (1986) Drama Ψ
Made-for-TV movie about serial killer Ted Bundy.

> "Lewis, don't play games with these people."
>
> *Deliverance* (1972)

Deliverance (1972) Adventure ΨΨΨΨ
Jon Voight, Ned Beatty, and Burt Reynolds on a white water rafting trip in Appalachia. Beatty winds up being sodomized, and Reynolds kills the rapist, using a bow and arrow. Based on a James Dickey novel, the film raises interesting questions about personal responsibility and social justice.

Dentist, The (1996) Horror Ψ
A successful Beverly Hills dentist goes mad when he discovers his wife having oral sex with the boy who cleans their pool.

Disclosure (1994) Drama ΨΨ
A less-than-illuminating film about reverse sexual discrimination. Stars include Demi Moore and Michael Douglas; based on a novel by Michael Crichton.

Disco Pigs (2001, Ireland) Drama ΨΨ
A boy and a girl born moments apart become inseparable until the age of 17 when sexual tension complicates their lives.

Dog Day Afternoon (1975) Crime ΨΨΨ
Al Pacino holds up a bank to get enough money to fund a sex-change operation for his homosexual lover. Good illustration of a basically good person caught up in an stressful situation.

Domino (2005) Action Ψ
A tough, rebellious, female bounty hunter tries to fight fair.

Don't Tell (2005, Italy/UK/France/Spain) Drama ΨΨΨΨ
A young adult woman realizes she has repressed nearly all of her childhood, and following the death of her parents, begins to have nightmares of her father sexually abusing her as a young girl. She consults with her brother to put the pieces together.

Down and Dirty (1976) Drama ΨΨ
An interesting examination of the effects of poverty, squalor, and alcoholism on an Italian family.

Dressed to Kill (1980) Thriller Ψ
The film confuses transsexualism and schizophrenia but offers good suspense. Mimics Hitchcock.

Eastern Promises (2007) Thriller/Drama ΨΨΨ
David Cronenberg film about Russian gangsters. The film features an unforgettable, intense battle scene in steam room.

Elephant (2003) Drama ΨΨΨΨ
Well-crafted, foreboding, eerie Gus Van Sant film that attempts to explain a tragic school shooting. Powerful parallels with Columbine. Winner of the Palm award at Cannes for Best Picture and Director.

End of Violence, The (1997) Drama/Suspense ΨΨΨ
Bill Pullman plays an action/violence film director who is almost murdered so he hides out from society and starts a new life. While his character both promotes and greatly fears violence, a secret government worker (Gabriel Byrne) tries to prevent violence by watching over the city with thousands of cameras.

Executioner's Song, The (1982) Made for TV Drama ΨΨ
Tommy Lee Jones plays serial killer Gary Gilmore. Based on a story by Norman Mailer.

Extremities (1986) Drama Ψ
Farrah Fawcett plays a victimized woman who gets revenge on the man who rapes her.

Fight Club (1999) Drama/Suspense ΨΨΨΨ
A disillusioned, insomniac (Edward Norton) meets a dangerous, malcontent part of himself in the character of Brad Pitt. Norton then establishes "fight clubs" where men can violently release their aggressions by fighting one another.

"The first rule of Fight Club is: you do not talk about Fight Club. The second rule of Fight Club is: you DO NOT talk about Fight Club! Third rule of Fight Club: someone yells "stop!", goes limp, taps out, the fight is over. Fourth rule: only two guys to a fight. Fifth rule: one fight at a time, fellas. Sixth rule: No shirts, no shoes. Seventh rule: fights will go on as long as they have to. And the eighth and final rule: if this is your first time at Fight Club, you have to fight.

The rules of *Fight Club* (1999)

Freedomland (2006) Mystery/Drama Ψ
Julianne Moore portrays a neglectful mother; her character stands in marked contrast to Samuel L. Jackson's character who is attempting to redeem himself by caring for his adult son who is in prison.

Funny Games (1997, Austria; Remake 2007) Drama/Horror ΨΨΨ
Two sadistic, psychopathic killers ask to borrow eggs and then go on to capture, torture and kill a vacationing family.

Gangs of New York (2002) Crime/Drama ΨΨΨ
Martin Scorsese film about the revenge perpetrated upon a gang kingpin named Bill "the Butcher" Cutting (Daniel Day-Lewis).

Godfather, The (1972), **The Godfather, Part II** (1974), and **The Godfather, Part III** (1990) Drama ΨΨΨΨ
The three-part gangster trilogy, directed by Francis Ford Coppola, examines violence, corruption, and crime in America.

"We'll make him an offer he can't refuse."

The Godfather (1972)

Gone Baby Gone (2007) Crime/Drama ΨΨΨΨ
An interesting and complex film, and Ben Affleck's directorial debut. The film is about a young girl who has been neglected by her drug-dependent mother and has gone missing. The movie raises fascinating questions about how to raise children and the role of society.

Good Son, The (1993) Drama ΨΨ
A 12-year-old boy goes to stay with his uncle, aunt and cousin, only to discover that the cousin is a psychopath and a killer. The boy's aunt eventually discovers the truth about her son and has to make a difficult decision that pits the love of her son against her sense of right and justice.

Grindhouse: Death Proof (2007) and **Grindhouse: Planet Terror** (2007) Thrillers ΨΨΨ
Two feature lengths films often shown together that pay homage to gory exploitation films. Both feature significant violence – the first involves a gang of women who face off with a murderous racecar driver and the second features an army of flesh-eating zombies. Not surprisingly, the Tarantino-directed film (the first one) is more engaging and interesting than the second one (directed by Robert Rodriguez).

Halloween and its sequels (1978, 1981, 1982, 1988, 1998, 2002, 2006, 2007, 2009) Horror Ψ
Infamous mass murderer depicted as an escaped mental patient and a deranged toy maker. These films have contributed significantly to the negative stereotypes of mental illness.

Hand That Rocks the Cradle, The (1992) Thriller/Drama Ψ
Sociopathic woman seeks revenge for the suicide of her husband by moving in and taking over the family of the woman she holds responsible for her husband's death. Predictable performances, but still an engrossing film.

Heavenly Creatures (1994) Drama ΨΨΨΨ
A New Zealand film directed by Peter Jackson and based on the true story of two adolescent girls who grow up sharing a fantasy world. When the mother of one of the girls decides to separate the children, they murder her. One of the girls, Ann Perry, now lives in England and writes mystery novels.

Henry: Portrait of a Serial Killer (1990) Crime/Horror ΨΨΨΨ
A violent, controversial film about mass murderer and sociopath Henry Lee Lucas. A scene in which Lucas and his roommate videotape one of their murders is especially unnerving.

History of Violence, A (2005) Drama/Mystery ΨΨΨΨ
David Cronenberg film about a quiet, unassuming family man who springs to action when the workers and customers of his café are threatened by thugs. His fighting prowess causes his family to question his past and who he really is.

> "She'd make me watch it... She'd beat me when I wouldn't watch her... She'd make me wear a dress and they would laugh."
>
> Henry Lee Lucas describing abuse by his prostitute mother in *Henry: Portrait of a Serial Killer* (1990)

Honeymoon Killers, The (1970) Crime Ψ
A very realistic black-and-white film based on the true story of a couple who lured, exploited, and then killed lonely women. Both the man and the woman were executed at Sing-Sing Prison.

Hotel Rwanda (2004) Drama/Documentary ΨΨΨΨΨ
Depicts the genocide of the Hutus upon the Tutsis in Rwanda and the courageous efforts of Paul Rusesabagina, a hotel manager who saved over 1200 refugees. The film illustrates courage and persistence; it also shows how one ordinary man can be extraordinary and triumph over evil.

House of 1000 Corpses (2003) Horror Ψ
Musician Rob Zombie directed this film about a family of eerie serial killers that contains some comic relief.

Hunger Games, The (2012) Drama ΨΨΨ
Children between the ages of 12–18 are selected to compete to the death in televised games, the rules of which allow only one couple to survive.

Hunger Games, The: Catching Fire (2013) Drama ΨΨ
An engaging sequel in which the winners of the Hunger Games are required to compete once again.

I Spit on Your Grave (1980) Horror Ψ
A terrible film in which a woman systematically gets revenge on the four men who raped her.

> "They all felt physically inferior or sexually inadequate. Their childhood was violent.... They couldn't distinguish between fantasy and reality. They didn't hate their victims, they didn't even know them."
>
> A doctor describes serial killers in *In Cold Blood* (1967)

In Cold Blood (1967) Biography/Crime ΨΨΨ
This film is based on a Truman Capote biographical novel about two sociopaths who kill a Kansas family. The film explores the family dynamics that in part lead to the senseless murders.

Interrupters, The (2011) Documentary ΨΨΨ
Former gang members in Chicago work to curb street violence.

Kill Bill: Vol. 1 (2003) Action/Suspense ΨΨΨΨ
Dynamic Tarantino story of a samurai bride (Uma Thurman) betrayed by her ex-lover and boss. This first film sets up the mythology and the world of the characters. It has more extensive graphic violence than Vol. 2 and an "eastern" martial arts emphasis.

> "I've kept you alive for two reasons. First reason is information... But I am gonna ask you questions and every time you don't give me answers, I'm gonna cut something off. And I promise you they will be things you will miss!"
>
> The Bride in *Kill Bill: Vol. 1* (2003)

Kill Bill: Vol. 2 (2004) Action/Suspense ΨΨΨΨ
Tarantino's conclusion to the revenge story of The Bride. This part emphasizes the unfolding of the stories and further deepening of characters amongst a more "western" style.

> "I'm a killer. I'm a murdering bastard and there are consequences for breaking the heart of a murdering bastard."
>
> Bill in *Kill Bill: Vol. 2* (2004)

Killing Fields, The (1984) Drama ΨΨΨΨ
Gripping film about the horrors of war and the particularly gruesome and cruel practices of the Khmer Rouge in Cambodia following the evacuation of American soldiers from Vietnam in 1975.

Lilya 4-Ever (2002) Drama ΨΨΨ
A powerful depiction of the cruelty of violence. An adolescent girl experiences neglect, abandonment, rejection, physical and sexual abuse, gang rape, exploitation, and forced prostitution, all by the age of 16.

Looking for Mr. Goodbar (1977) Drama ΨΨ
Diane Keaton plays a special education teacher with a compulsive need to pick up men in bars and engage in sadomasochistic sex. There are numerous examples of family pathology in the film, and it is interesting to remember how casual sexuality was in a time before AIDS.

Lovely Bones, The (2009): Drama/Suspense ΨΨΨ
Peter Jackson film about a young teenage girl who is raped and murdered by a pedophile in her neighborhood.

The focus in the film is on the perpetrator's acts of violence, his subsequent cover-up behaviors, his craving, obsession, intent, and plan to kill again, and the impact of the death on the girl's family.

M (1931, Germany) Crime/Drama/Horror ΨΨΨΨ
A must-see Fritz Lang film (his first "talkie") starring Peter Lorre as a sexual psychopath who molests and murders little girls. When tried by a vigilante jury, he pleads irresistible impulse, but the jury is not impressed.

Magdalene Sisters, The (2002) Docudrama ΨΨΨ
Troubled adolescent girls are sent to a dehumanizing, boarding home where they are treated by nuns who run the home with abuse, neglect, and humiliation. The film follows four girls in particular as they experience and respond differently to the highly abusive situation.

Metallica: Some Kind of Monster (2004) Documentary ΨΨΨ
Inside look at the heavy metal band, Metallica, and their personal and interpersonal struggles. The handling of anger is a key theme in the film. The honest expression of emotions by these "stars" is likely to have a positive impact on many fans.

Midnight Express (1978) Biography ΨΨΨ
True story about an American college student who is busted for trying to smuggle two kilograms of hashish out of Turkey and is treated brutally in Turkish prisons before eventually escaping.

Monster (2003) Drama ΨΨΨΨ
A powerful film based on the life of Aileen Carol Wuornos, a highway prostitute who was executed for killing seven men in the state of Florida during the 1980s. (See also *Aileen: Life and Death of a Serial Killer.*)

Murder in the First (1995) Drama ΨΨ
A man imprisoned in Alcatraz for petty theft in the 1930s is put in solitary confinement for three years, becomes deranged, and then kills a guard. The film suggests the system is to blame for the crime. Based on a true story.

Mysterious Skin (2004) Drama ΨΨΨ
A coach sexually molests two boys and their lives go in completely different directions. Intense, realistic portrayal of the ways sexual abuse affects children when they become adolescents and adults.

Natural Born Killers (1994) Crime/Drama ΨΨΨΨΨ
A violent Oliver Stone film based on a story written by Quentin Tarantino and starring Woody Harrelson and Juliette Lewis. The film depicts a couple who celebrate their roles as mass murderers and find their new status as cult

figures a welcome reprieve from the dreariness of the life they left behind.

"Insane, no. Psychotic, yes. A menace to living creatures, yes. But to suggest that they're insane gives the impression that they don't know right from wrong. Mickey and Mallory know the difference between right and wrong. They just don't give a damn."

A psychiatric opinion in *Natural Born Killers* (1994)

Night Porter, The (1974) Drama/War ΨΨ
A former Nazi officer who sexually abused a 14-year-old girl in a concentration camp has the tables turned on him when she shows up at the hotel in which he works. This is one of several films linking Nazi practices with sado-masochistic sex.

No Man's Land (2001) Drama/Suspense ΨΨΨΨ
A Bosnian escapes a firing attack and finds himself in "No Man's Land" between enemy lines. A Serb goes to ensure there were no survivors and finds himself in a standoff with the Bosnian. Another Bosnian survivor, barely alive, awakes on top of a land mine that will explode if he rises. Heated debates, murder attempts, threats, desperation, and hopelessness characterize each of the three men.

North Country (2005) Drama ΨΨΨΨ
Charlize Theron transforms herself again (following up her role as a serial killer in *Monster*), this time to play a woman who goes to great lengths to support her children by working in a blue-collar mine where she experiences significant sexual harassment.

"It's the same old story. I've got to learn to keep my mouth shut."

Beth blaming herself for the beating she has received from her husband in *Once Were Warriors* (1994)

Once Were Warriors (1994) Drama ΨΨΨΨ
Important New Zealand film about substance abuse and domestic violence among urban Maori tribal people. The film will help you understand a different culture, as well as the ways in which alcoholism interacts with spousal and child abuse in almost every society.

Osama (2003, Afghanistan) Drama ΨΨΨΨ
Based on a true story of the heavy discrimination, abuse, and oppression of women under Taliban rule.

Passion of the Christ, The (2004) Drama/Biography **ΨΨΨΨΨ**
Mel Gibson film depicting the violent torture and suffering of the final hours of Jesus Christ. This highly controversial film is intensely graphic and visual in its portrayal of violence. It is interesting to note that it is Mel Gibson's hand that nails Jesus to the cross.

Personal Velocity (2002) Drama **ΨΨΨ**
Independent film about three strong women divided into three segments. One segment addresses issues of domestic violence.

"She imagined going back to him like she had done so many times before but this time her body wouldn't follow."

Narration on the escape from an abusive husband in *Personal Velocity* (2002)

Play Misty for Me (1971) Thriller **ΨΨΨ**
The first film directed by Clint Eastwood. A California disc jockey becomes involved with a listener who is clinging, dependent, fanatical, and ultimately homicidal. Interesting portrayal of sexual obsession.

Precious (2009) Drama **ΨΨΨΨ**
Gabourey Sidibe gives a riveting performance as Claireece "Precious" Jones, an illiterate, obese, black 16 year-old, who is pregnant for the second time by her father. Living in Harlem with her abusive mother, Precious struggles to cope with constant degradation and abuse through fantasies and dissociation. She gradually builds self-esteem through the help of a teacher at an alternative school.

Prick Up Your Ears (1987) Biography **ΨΨΨΨ**
A film showing the homosexual relationship and eventual murder/suicide of playwright Joe Orton and his lover.

Princess Aurora (2005, Korea) Drama **ΨΨ**
A saleswoman goes on a killing spree and leaves a cartoon sticker of Princess Aurora at the scene of each crime.

Prophet, A (2009) Drama **ΨΨΨΨ**
A 19-year-old boy is sent to prison for six years where he confronts racial tension and extreme violence.

Rampage (1992) Drama/Thriller **ΨΨΨ**
This movie, directed by William Friedkin, challenges many of the assumptions educated people are likely to hold about the insanity defense.

Rashomon (1950) Drama **ΨΨΨΨΨ**
Classic Akira Kurosawa film in which a rape-murder is described from four different perspectives by the four

people involved. The film makes the point that reality is subjective and that truth, like beauty, is truly in the eye of the beholder.

Rendition (2007) Drama/Thriller **ΨΨ**
An Egyptian man traveling in South Africa at a conference is detained without due process. The film addresses "extraordinary rendition" – detaining suspected terrorists and interrogating them on foreign soil without judicial process – and depicts torture (e.g., water-boarding), brain-washing/training of suicide bombers, and the various realities politicians face.

Reservoir Dogs (1992) Drama **ΨΨΨΨΨ**
Extremely violent but powerful Tarantino film with a graphic and realistic torture scene in which a sociopathic sadist derives great pleasure from using a razor to slowly torment a bound and gagged undercover police officer.

River's Edge (1986) Drama **ΨΨΨΨ**
A riveting film based on a true-life incident in which a young man kills his girlfriend and then shows the decomposing body to a series of friends. It takes days before one of his friends finally notifies authorities about the murder.

"Now I'm not gonna bullshit you. I don't really care about what you know or don't know. I'm gonna torture you for a while regardless. Not to get information, but because torturing a cop amuses me. There's nothing you can say, there's nothing you can do. Except pray for death."

The sadistic Mr. Blonde in *Reservoir Dogs* (1992)

Rope (1948) **ΨΨΨΨΨ**
Experimental Hitchcock film about two young homosexual men who kill a friend for sport and then hide the body in a room in which they are hosting a cocktail party. Based on the Leopold-Loeb case.

Santa Sangre (1989) Horror/Thriller **ΨΨΨΨ**
A controversial but unquestionably powerful Jodorowsky film about a boy growing up in bizarre circumstances. There are strong themes of violence and incest. Roger Ebert called this film "a collision between Freud and Fellini."

Saving Private Ryan (1998) War/Action **ΨΨΨΨ**
Steven Spielberg World War II film regarded by some as the most realistic and powerful war film ever made.

Se7en (1995) Drama **ΨΨΨ**
Morgan Freeman and Brad Pitt star in this engrossing film about a serial killer (Kevin Spacey) who is obsessed with

the seven deadly sins (pride, envy, gluttony, lust, anger, covetousness, and sloth) and who kills his victims accordingly (e.g., a man who is gluttonous is forced to eat until he dies from overeating).

Series 7: The Contenders (2001) Suspense/Comedy ΨΨΨ
Highly violent, tongue-in-cheek film about a reality television show where the contestants must seek out and kill one another.

Seven Beauties (1976) Comedy/Drama ΨΨΨ
Lina Wertmuller film in which the protagonist (the brother of the seven sisters alluded to in the title) must perform degrading sexual acts for the female commandant of a German prison camp to survive the war.

Shelter Island (2003) Drama/Suspense Ψ
A lesbian couple goes to get away at an island house to relax. A stranger (Stephen Baldwin) appears on their doorstep during a storm and things are not what they seem. Simplistic psychology that is not well-applied or developed.

Sin City (2005) Action/Noir ΨΨΨ
Stylized graphic violence tempered by computerized graphics, based on Frank Miller's comic books, with an all-star cast.

Single White Female (1992) Drama/Horror ΨΨ
A woman breaks up with her boyfriend and takes in a roommate who admires and emulates her – and later tries to kill her.

Sleepers (1996) Drama ΨΨΨ
Guards at a reform school physically and sexually abuse young boys. After the boys grow up, they avenge their abuse and attempt to manipulate the courts to avoid sentencing. Many stellar actors including Robert De Niro, Dustin Hoffman, Brad Pitt, and Kevin Bacon.

Slumdog Millionaire (2008) Drama ΨΨΨΨΨ
The Academy Award–winning rags to riches story about a young man's destiny that intersperses his performance on "Who Wants to Be a Millionaire" with flashbacks showing significant life experiences that include poverty, abuse, and torture. The film is a classic underdog story with poignant themes of persistence, integrity/honesty, and self-confidence.

South Central (1992) Action/Suspense ΨΨ
A man is released from prison and tries to lead a "clean," gang-free life.

Stone Boy, The (1984) Drama ΨΨ
Robert Duvall and Glenn Close star in this slow-moving but intelligent film about a young man who accidentally

shoots his brother and the effect the shooting has on the entire family.

Straw Dogs (1971) Crime ΨΨΨ
Provocative and violent Sam Peckinpah film, with Dustin Hoffman as a peace-loving mathematician who resorts to violence after his wife is raped.

Sweeney Todd: The Demon Barber of Fleet Street (2007) Musical/Thriller ΨΨΨ
Extensive violence tuned to music and dance in Tim Burton's story of revenge starring Johnny Depp and Helena Bonham Carter.

Take My Eyes (2003, Spain) Drama ΨΨΨΨ
One of the most compelling films we know dealing with domestic violence.

Tattoo (1981) Drama Ψ
Mentally ill tattoo artist kidnaps a model and uses her body as a canvas for his art. This is a movie that perpetuates stigma and prejudice about mental illness.

Terribly Happy (2008, Denmark) Drama ΨΨ
A policeman from Copenhagen is transferred to a small Danish town and discovers both secrets and violence.

Thelma & Louise (1991) Drama/Comedy ΨΨΨ
Two women friends on the road for a weekend lark wind up fleeing from the law and end their lives in a defiant suicidal act. Powerful feminist film.

Time to Kill, A (1996) Drama ΨΨΨ
Samuel Jackson plays an angry father who murders two white men who have raped his daughter. The film explores themes of racial and social injustice, temporary insanity, and justifiable homicide.

Treasure of the Sierra Madre, The (1948) Drama ΨΨΨΨ
Tremendous John Huston film starring Humphrey Bogart. The movie explores obsessive greed, the folly of avarice, and the ways in which love of money can come to be the dominant force in one's life. Bogart's character is an example of a paranoid personality disorder.

"Badges? We ain't got no badges! We don't need no badges. I don't have to show you any stinkin' badges!"

The Treasure of the Sierra Madre (1948)

Triumph of the Spirit (1989) Biography ΨΨΨ
Story of Auschwitz concentration camp during World War II. Good introduction to the horrors and stress of concentration camp life.

Twist of Faith (2004) Documentary ΨΨ
A firefighter faces the trauma of childhood sexual abuse by a priest, speaking to the shame, horror, anger, and dissociation that occurs. He discusses the significant impact of abuse on his life.

Two Women (1960, Italy) War/Drama ΨΨΨ
This Vittorio De Sica film starring Sophia Loren examines war, rape, coming of age, and mother-daughter relations. Loren won an Academy Award for Best Actress for this film.

Virgin Spring, The (1959) Drama ΨΨΨ
An Ingmar Bergman film examining the rape and murder of a young girl by three bandits.

Vulgar (2002) Drama ΨΨ
A man working as a clown for children decides he can make more money working as a clown at bachelor parties. He is tortured, gang raped, and blackmailed by a psychopath and his two sons. The film graphically depicts trauma and violence, but there are also comic moments.

Waitress (2007) Comedy/Drama ΨΨΨΨΨ
Inspirational story of a young, pregnant waitress (Keri Russell) who is not enthusiastic about her pregnancy because the child's father is her psychologically abusive and controlling husband (Jeremy Sisko). Sadly, the film's director, Adrienne Shelly, was murdered before the film was widely released to critical acclaim (Shelly's young daughter appears in the final scene).

War of the Roses, The (1989) Drama/Thriller ΨΨ
Marital conflict slowly progresses into an incredible, destructive battle between Oliver and Barbara Rose (Michael Douglas and Kathleen Turner).

Warrior, The (2001, UK/France/Germany) Drama/Adventure ΨΨΨ
A warrior, working for a cruel lord as an executioner in feudal India, takes up the practice of nonviolence. His new mission becomes particularly challenging when his son is kidnapped and killed in front of him.

We Need To Talk About Kevin (2011) Drama ΨΨΨΨ
A successful woman puts her career on hold to have two children, one of whom is distant, withdrawn and hostile. He eventually commits mass murder at his high school after killing his father and sister. He spares his mother, wanting to maximize the grief and suffering she will have to endure.

White Ribbon, The (2009, Germany) Drama ΨΨΨ
Strange things happen in a small German village in the months leading up to World War I. These include a wire being strung that almost kills the local doctor when he is thrown from his horse, cabbages beheaded in a field, the suicide of a farmer, an a handicapped child is bound to a tree and tortured.

Whore's Glory (2011) Documentary ΨΨΨ
A fascinating and nonjudgmental examination of prostitutes and the lives they lead in Thailand, Bangladesh and Mexico.

Zodiac (2007) Crime/Biography ΨΨ
Jake Gyllenhaal portrays an amateur detective in San Francisco who becomes obsessed with tracking down a serial killer in this David Fincher film.

Treatment

Antwone Fisher (2003) Drama/Biography ΨΨΨ
Troubled and angry sailor gets in fights and is referred to a psychiatrist (Denzel Washington). Their relationship develops and he becomes comfortable sharing his history of childhood abuse and trauma; he makes amends with his past and healing begins. Fair and balanced portrayal of a psychiatrist.

Article 99 (1992) Comedy Ψ
Unsuccessful M*A*S*H*-like attempt to ridicule the quality of care provided in Veterans Administration medical centers.

Bad Timing: A Sensual Obsession (1980) Drama ΨΨ
Interesting and provocative film in which a psychiatrist becomes sexually involved with a troubled and self-destructive woman.

> "Without treatment, John, the fantasies may take over entirely."
>
> Dr. Rosen attempting to educate John Nash on the importance of continuing his treatment regimen in *A Beautiful Mind* (2001)

Beautiful Mind, A (2001) Drama ΨΨΨΨΨ
Based on Sylvia Nasar's biography with the same name. Russell Crowe portrays John Forbes Nash, a mathematical genius and Nobel Prize laureate in Economics, who battles schizophrenia and is treated with antipsychotics and insulin-shock therapy.

Beautiful Dreamers (1992) Drama/Biography ΨΨΨ
True story about poet Walt Whitman's visit to an asylum in London, Ontario. Whitman is shocked by what he sees and persuades the hospital director to offer humane treatment. Eventually, the patients wind up playing the townspeople in a game of cricket.

Beyond Therapy (1987) Comedy Ψ
Disappointing Robert Altman film about New York yuppies and their psychiatrists.

Butcher's Wife, The (1991) Romance/Fantasy ΨΨ
Greenwich Village psychiatrist Jeff Daniels finds Demi Moore, the butcher's wife, is giving advice at least as good as his own.

Cabinet of Dr. Caligari, The (1920) Horror ΨΨΨΨΨ
German expressionistic film about hypnosis and the power of a hypnotist to induce others to do his bidding. One of the earliest stereotypic presentations of the madman who runs a psychiatric hospital.

Captain Newman, M. D. (1963) Comedy/Drama ΨΨΨ
Sympathetic story about an Army psychiatrist (Gregory Peck) taking on the military bureaucracy to provide effective treatment for Bobby Darin. Darin is clearly manic and ultimately commits suicide.

Carefree (1938) Musical/Dance ΨΨ
Fred Astaire is a psychiatrist who was talked out of being a dancer. Ginger Rogers is referred to him for treatment (hypnosis) so she can learn to love one of Astair's friends; he complies with her request, but predictably falls in love with her himself.

Caretakers, The (1963) Drama Ψ
Second-rate film that documents life in a West Coast psychiatric hospital and portrays some of the problems associated with introducing innovations in hospital settings.

Changeling (2008) Drama ΨΨΨ
Based on a true story, Angelina Jolie portrays a desperate but persistent mother whose son is kidnapped by a serial child murderer. She battles with a corrupt Los Angeles police force and a manipulative psychiatrist who twists her words, attempts to blackmail her, uses ECT to punish his patients, and holds innocent women captive in the hospital to protect the police department.

Chattahoochee (1990) Drama ΨΨΨ
Korean War veteran with a PTSD is hospitalized and treated. Dennis Hopper has a major role as a fellow patient.

Clockwork Orange, A (1971) Science Fiction ΨΨΨΨΨ
Fascinating interpretation of Anthony Burgess's novel. The portrayal of aversion therapy is somewhat heavy-handed but raises legitimate questions about the appropriate limits of behavior modification.

Color of Night (1994) Drama Ψ
Bruce Willis plays a disillusioned psychologist who gives up his practice after a patient commits suicide. Willis discovers he is no longer able to perceive the color red. Much of the plot revolves around a patient with multiple personalities who is simultaneously a group therapy patient (as a male) and, unknown to Willis, his lover (in a core personality named Rose).

"There was me, that is Alex, and my three droogs, that is Pete, Georgie, and Dim … and we sat in the Korova Milkbar trying to make up our rassoodocks what to do with the evening."

Alex in *A Clockwork Orange* (1971)

Couch Trip, The (1988) Comedy Ψ
Dan Aykroyd plays the role of a psychiatric patient who escapes from an institution and then passes himself off as a Beverly Hills psychiatrist. The film reinforces the notion that psychiatry is mainly pretentious language and social manipulation.

Dark Past, The (1948) Crime ΨΨΨ
A psychologist who is taken prisoner tries to use his training to help his captor. Remake of the film *Blind Alley*.

David and Lisa (1962) Drama ΨΨΨΨ
A dated but still sensitive portrayal of life in a psychiatric institution. Perpetuates the myth that love will conquer mental illness. Strong and balanced portrayal of a compassionate psychiatrist.

Dead Man Out (1989) Drama ΨΨ
Superior and timely made-for-TV movie about a psychiatrist treating a convict so the man will be sane enough to be executed. The film raises meaningful questions about ethical issues and the appropriate limits of professional practice.

Jack McDermott: "What about dinner? Who's gonna get us our dinner?"
Billy: "… aren't you the same guy who changed water into wine? Huh? J. C.? Ain't the son of God good for a burger in his town? You get us something!"

The Dream Team (1989)

Dream Team, The (1989) Comedy ΨΨ
Four psychiatric patients are being taken to a game in Yankee Stadium when their doctor/escort is knocked unconscious and hospitalized. The entire film appears to be based on the well-known (and better done) shipboard outing by Jack Nicholson and his friends in *One Flew Over the Cuckoo's Nest*.

Face to Face (1976, Sweden) Drama ΨΨΨΨ
Liv Ullmann plays a psychiatrist whose life is falling apart. She attempts suicide by taking an overdose and winds up in a coma. Interesting dream sequences with Bergman's usual presumption of childhood trauma as the trigger for adult unhappiness.

Fear Strikes Out (1957) Biography/Sports ΨΨΨ
Anthony Perkins as baseball player Jimmy Piersall, who suffers a mental breakdown as a result of his inability to please a domineering, demanding father. Piersall was successfully treated with psychotherapy and ECT and eventually staged a comeback.

Final Analysis (1992) Thriller/Drama ΨΨ
A complex film that pays homage to Hitchcock; interesting issues of childhood sexual abuse, repressed memories, professional responsibility, and the doctor–patient relationship.

> "Just repeat the last two words they say and phrase it like a question."
>
> A psychiatrist joking about his profession in *Final Analysis* (1992)

Fine Madness, A (1966) Drama ΨΨΨ
Sean Connery plays Samson Shillitoe, an eccentric and unconventional poet who is hospitalized and lobotomized because of his sexual peccadilloes and the fact that he can't conform to societal expectations. The film was ahead of its time in raising important issues about the rights of people with mental illness.

Flame Within, The (1935) Drama Ψ
Dated and insipid film about a psychiatrist who falls in love with a patient.

Frances (1982) Biography ΨΨΨΨΨ
A vivid portrayal of the life of actress Frances Farmer, including her institutionalization, lobotomy, and alcoholism.

Good Will Hunting (1997) Drama ΨΨΨΨ
Robin Williams won an Academy Award for Best Supporting Actor for his role as a counseling psychologist

teaching at a community college and treating a troubled young man who is extraordinarily gifted mathematically.

High Anxiety (1977) Comedy ΨΨ
Mel Brooks spoofs Hitchcock films and introduces The Psycho-Neurotic Institute for the Very, Very Nervous.

House of Fools (2002) Drama ΨΨΨΨ
Based on a true story: the chief psychiatrist and treatment staff of a mental institution flee due to conflicts in Chechnya, leaving the patients to fend for themselves. Soon soldiers occupy the hospital and the viewer is left with various questions of war, politics, mental health treatment and which is more crazy – the mentally ill or the politics of war. The film is loaded with examples of psychopathology.

I Heart Huckabees (2005) Comedy/Mystery ΨΨΨ
Dustin Hoffman and Lilly Tomlin play existential psychologists in this quirky, offbeat comedy. Although there is no formal therapy, there are plenty of therapeutic moments.

Inside/Out (1997) Drama ΨΨΨ
A Rob Tregenza film about life in a psychiatric hospital that was well received at the 1998 Sundance Film Festival. The film documents that both patients and staff find it hard to cope with the difficult demands of life.

Intimate Strangers (2004, France) Drama ΨΨΨΨ
A woman mistakenly receives psychotherapy from an accountant in this thoughtful film.

It's Kind of a Funny Story (2010) Comedy/Drama ΨΨΨ
A suicidal 16-year-old high school student checks himself into a psychiatric hospital where he is mentored by an older and more experienced patient (played by Zach Galifianakis).

King of Hearts (1966) Comedy/Drama/War ΨΨΨΨ
A Scotsman separated from his unit wanders into town, abandoned by all except the inmates of the local insane asylum. Must-see film for those interested in public attitudes about mental illness.

Ladybird, Ladybird (1993) Drama ΨΨΨΨ
Dramatic presentation of the clash between the rights of a parent and society's need to protect children.

Lilith (1964) Drama ΨΨ
Strong cast (Peter Fonda, Gene Hackman, Warren Beatty, and Kim Hunter) supports a weak script about a psychiatric inpatient who seduces a neophyte therapist.

Lost Angels (1989) Drama ΨΨ
Donald Sutherland plays a psychiatrist treating a Los Angeles adolescent who is angry and troubled but probably not mentally ill.

"When insurance paid for a year in a place like this, we said it took a year to help a kid. Now insurance pays for three months, and, presto, it takes three months to turn a kid around."

Dr. Charles Loftis complaining about the
system in *Lost Angels* (1989)

Ludwig (1973) Biography Ψ
Long and somewhat tedious film about the mad King Ludwig of Bavaria. Good costumes and scenery, but the film teaches us little about mental illness or Ludwig himself.

Macbeth (1971) Drama ΨΨΨ
Powerful Roman Polanski adaptation of Shakespeare's play. It is interesting to speculate about the obsessions of Lady Macbeth and to compare Polanski's version with the earlier Orson Welles' adaptation.

Man Facing Southeast (1986) Drama ΨΨΨΨ
Fascinating Argentine film about a man without identity who shows up at a psychiatric hospital claiming to be from another planet. It seems that this is not just another patient, and neither the hospital staff nor the film's audience ever figures out exactly what is happening.

Man Who Loved Women, The (1983) Comedy Ψ
A remake of the François Truffaut film of the same name. This film involves long sequences in which Burt Reynolds unburdens himself to his psychiatrist.

Manic (2001) Drama ΨΨΨ
A psychologist played by Don Cheadle tries to help an angry adolescent. Interesting group therapy sessions and inpatient hospital scenes with adolescents who have bipolar disorder, intermittent explosive disorder, major depression, self-injurious behavior, and night terrors.

Marat/Sade (1966) Drama ΨΨΨΨ
In the early 1800s, the inmates of a French asylum put on a play directed by the Marquis de Sade (a patient) based on the bathtub assassination of Jean Paul Marat. The play incites the patients to riot.

Mine Own Executioner (1947) Drama ΨΨ
Confused and troubled psychoanalyst tries to help out a schizophrenic veteran.

Mr. Deeds Goes to Town (1936) Comedy ΨΨΨ
Frank Capra film in which Gary Cooper inherits $20 million and is judged insane when he decides to give it all away to needy farmers.

Mr. Jones (1993) Drama/Comedy ΨΨΨ
Richard Gere portrays a bipolar patient treated by a psychiatrist who falls in love with him. This film raises interesting questions about the therapeutic relationship and boundary issues in psychotherapy.

Mumford (1999) Drama ΨΨΨ
A man named Mumford pretending to be a psychologist sets up shop in a small town named Mumford and begins to help the townspeople.

No Time for Sergeants (1958) Comedy Ψ
Andy Griffith stars; Don Knotts plays an Army psychiatrist.

No Way Out (1950) Drama ΨΨΨ
This was Sidney Poitier's first film. Poitier plays a black physician treating two racist hoodlums. When one dies, his brother (Richard Widmark) incites a race riot. The film was one of the earliest serious examinations of racism in postwar America.

Nobody's Child (1986) Biography ΨΨ
Marlo Thomas won an Emmy for her role as a woman who experiences tremendous personal and professional success when she is released after spending 20 years in a mental hospital.

"Oh Jerry, don't let's ask for the moon. We have the stars."

Charlotte Vale addressing her married lover
in *Now, Voyager* (1942)

Now, Voyager (1942) Drama ΨΨΨ
Her psychiatrist and inpatient treatment help sexually repressed Bette Davis find meaning and purpose in her life by serving as a surrogate mother for the daughter of a man she loves. The title comes from Walt Whitman's *Leaves of Grass* ("The untold want by life and land ne'er granted/ Now voyager sail thou forth to seek and find.")

Nuts (1987) Drama ΨΨΨ
Barbra Streisand plays a prostitute who has killed a patron. She is resisting an insanity defense, and through flashbacks we learn that she was sexually abused as a child. Interesting examination of civil liberties and forensic psychiatry.

Office Space (1999) Comedy Ψ
A hypnotherapist induces a trance in a patient but suffers a heart attack before the patient comes out of the trance.

Oil on Water (2007, South Africa) Drama Romance ΨΨΨ
An interesting examination of the ways in which a relationship is affected by schizophrenia.

One Flew Over the Cuckoo's Nest (1975) Drama ΨΨΨΨΨ
Classic film with Jack Nicholson as Randle P. McMurphy, who takes on Nurse Ratched and the psychiatric establishment. The film offers good insight into life on an inpatient ward, although the portrayal of ECT is stereotyped and inaccurate; in addition, the suicide of Billy seems to be simplistically linked to his domineering mother. This film took all five of the top Oscars in 1975: Best Picture, Best Actor, Best Actress, Best Director, and Best Screenplay.

> "They was giving me ten thousand watts a day, you know, and I'm hot to trot! The next woman takes me on is gonna light up like a pinball machine and pay off in silver dollars!"
>
> Randle P. McMurphy commenting on ECT in
> *One Flew Over the Cuckoo's Nest* (1975)

Passion of Joan of Arc, The (1928) Historical ΨΨΨ
Historically important silent film that portrays the burning of Joan of Arc as a heretic. The mental status of Joan of Arc remains a controversial subject for historians interested in psychopathology.

President's Analyst, The (1967) Spy/Comedy ΨΨ
James Coburn plays a psychoanalyst working for the President of the United States.

Pressure Point (1962) Drama ΨΨΨ
A black psychiatrist (Sidney Poitier) treats a racist patient (Bobby Darin). Based on a case from Linder's *The Fifty-Minute Hour*.

Prime (2005) Drama ΨΨ
A therapist discovers that her patient is having an affair with the therapist's son and fails to disclose this dual relationship.

Prince of Tides, The (1991) Drama/Romance ΨΨΨ
Barbra Streisand plays a psychiatrist who becomes sexually involved with the brother of one of her patients (Nick Nolte). The film raises interesting questions about the proper limits of the doctor–patient relationship.

Quills (2000) Drama ΨΨΨ
Geoffrey Rush stars in this Philip Kaufman film about the notorious French author who is responsible for the word sadism. The film depicts the abuses that occurred in the 18th century in the Charenton Insane Asylum, a mental hospital located in the suburbs of Paris. The Marquis de Sade died at Charenton in 1814.

> "I write of the great, eternal truths that bind together all mankind. The whole world over, we eat, we shit, we fuck, we kill and we die."
>
> The Marquis de Sade describes his views on
> literature in *Quills* (2000)

Rachel Getting Married (2008) Drama ΨΨΨ
Kym has been in a rehabilitation center for 9 months, but she gets a few days off to attend her sister's wedding. Predictable tensions result, most of which result from Kym's role in the death of her younger brother when Kym, who was drunk at the time, lost control of her car and drove off a bridge. Her brother was killed. The film highlights the links between substance abuse and depression and the ways in which family dramas serve as triggers for relapse in recovering alcoholics or drug addicts. Rachel also meets *DSM-5* criteria for narcissistic personality disorder.

Rampage (1992) Drama/Thriller ΨΨΨ
William Friedkin film about a sociopath who is arrested and tried for murder. The film raises important questions about capital punishment, the not guilty by reason of insanity (NGRI) plea, and the role of the expert witness in the courtroom.

Saving Grace B. Jones (2009) Drama Ψ
A disappointing story about how life is affected when a woman is discharged from a psychiatric hospital and comes to live with her brother and sister-in-law in a small Missouri town.

See You in the Morning (1989) Drama ΨΨ
A film about a Manhattan psychiatrist with multiple problems, including a failed first marriage. Interesting group therapy sequences and lots of speculation about motivation and purpose.

Shock Corridor (1963) Drama ΨΨ
Samuel Fuller film in which a journalist has himself admitted to an insane asylum in order to get an inside story on a murder but soon becomes psychotic himself. The film is better than it sounds.

Shrink (2009) Drama ΨΨ

Kevin Spacey plays a burned out therapist who writes popular self-help books and provides therapy for movie stars; however he is depressed after his wife's suicide and increasingly believes that his profession and his life are futile and pointless.

"Good night and sweet dreams ... which we'll analyze in the morning."

Spellbound (1945)

Spellbound (1945) Thriller ΨΨΨΨΨ

Ingrid Bergman plays a psychiatrist treating Gregory Peck's amnesia. Salvador Dali helped design the film's dream sequence. Producer David Selznick wanted the film to be based on his own experiences with psychotherapy and he used his own analyst as a technical advisor. Watch for the Hitchcock cameo.

Still of the Night (1982) Thriller Ψ

A psychiatrist becomes romantically involved with a woman who may have murdered one of his patients.

Teresa (1951) Drama Ψ

Notable only because it stars Rod Steiger in his first role. Steiger plays a psychiatrist in the film.

Through a Glass Darkly (1962) Drama ΨΨΨΨΨ

Classic Bergman film that follows the life of a mentally ill woman after she is treated with ECT and released from a mental hospital.

Tin Cup (1996) Comedy ΨΨ

A promiscuous Texas real estate sales person becomes a psychologist and trades off psychotherapy for golf lessons, eventually winding up in bed with the golf pro.

Touched (1983) Romance Ψ

Two patients on a psychiatric ward fall in love and try to set up a life together after they escape.

What About Bob? (1991) Comedy ΨΨ

Bill Murray plays Bob Wiley, a patient who becomes overly dependent on his therapist, Leo Marvin, played by Richard Dreyfuss. The film is very funny, and it raises interesting questions about transference and countertransference. Note the inane discussion of potential psychotropic medications.

"I'm not a shmuck Bob, and I'm not going to let you breeze into town and steal my family away just because you're crazy enough to be fun."

Dr. Leo Marvin to patient Bob Wiley in
What About Bob? (1991)

Whispers in the Dark (1992) Thriller/Drama ΨΨ

This murder mystery revolves around a psychiatrist who becomes overly involved in the lives of her patients. Mainly useful as a vehicle for discussion of professional issues and lessons on how *not* to behave in therapy.

References

Agel, J. (1970). *The making of Kubrick's 2001.* New York: New American Library.

Allen, J. G., & Smith, W. H. (1993). Diagnosing dissociative disorders. *Bulletin of the Menninger Clinic, 57,* 328–343.

Alper, G. (2004). *Like a movie: Contemporary relationships without the popcorn.* St. Paul, MN: Paragon House.

American Psychiatric Association. (1994). *Diagnostic and statistical manual of mental disorders* (4th ed.). Washington, DC: Author.

American Psychiatric Association. (2000). *Diagnostic and statistical manual of mental disorders* (4th ed., text revision). Washington, DC: Author.

American Psychiatric Association, DSM-5 Task Force. (2013). *Diagnostic and statistical manual of mental disorders: DSM-5* (5th ed.). Arlington, VA: American Psychiatric Publishing.

Arendt, H. (2003). *The portable Hannah Arendt.* New York: Penguin Classics.

Arendt, H. (1963). *Eichmann in Jerusalem: A report on the banality of evil.* New York: Penguin.

Arndt, W. B. Jr. (1991). *Gender disorders and the paraphilias.* Madison, CT: International Universities Press.

Banks, G. (1990). Kubrick's psychopaths: Society and human nature in the films of Stanely Kubrick. Retrieved from http://www.gordonbanks.com/gordon/pubs/kubricks.html

Barnard, G., Fuller, A., Robbins, L., & Shaw, T. (1989). *The child molester: An integrated approach to evaluation and treatment.* New York: Brunner/Mazel.

Baron-Cohen, S. (2011). *The science of evil: On empathy and the origins of cruelty.* New York: Basic Books.

Barrett, D. (2006). Hypnosis in film and television. *American Journal of Clinical Hypnosis, 49,* 13–30. doi: 10.1080/00029157.2006.10401549

Bartlett, S. J. (2005). *The first comprehensive psychology of human evil. The pathology of man: A study of human evil.* Springfield, IL: Charles C. Thomas.

Beck, A. (1976). *Cognitive therapy and the emotional disorders.* New York: Meridian.

Beck, A., & Emery, G. (1985). *Anxiety disorders and phobias: A cognitive perspective.* New York: Basic Books.

Beck, A., Steer, R., Beck, J., & Newman, C. (1993). Hopelessness, depression, suicidal ideation, and clinical diagnosis of depression. *Suicide and Life–Threatening Behavior, 23,* 139–145.

Bergsma, A., ten Have, M., Veenhoven, R., & de Graaf, R. (2011). Most people with mental disorders are happy: A 3-year follow-up in the Dutch general population. *The Journal of Positive Psychology, 6*(4), 253–259. doi: 10.1080/17439760.2011.577086

Bernstein, E. M., & Putnam, F. W. (1986). Development, reliability, and validity of a dissociation scale. *Journal of Nervous & Mental Disease, 174,* 727–735.

Blanchard, R., & Hucker, S. J. (1991). Age, transvestism, bondage, and concurrent paraphilic activities in 117 fatal cases of autoerotic asphyxia. *British Journal of Psychiatry, 159,* 371–377. doi: 10.1192/bjp.159.3.371

Bordwell, D., & Thompson, K. (1993). *Film art: An introduction.* New York: McGraw-Hill.

Briere, J. (1989). University males' sexual interest in children: Predicting potential indices of "pedophilia" in a nonforensic sample. *Child Abuse and Neglect, 13,* 65–75. doi: 10.1016/0145-2134(89)90030-6

Brown, G. R. (1994). Women in relationships with cross-dressing men: A descriptive study from a nonclinical setting. *Archives of Sexual Behavior, 23*(5), 515–530. doi: 10.1007/BF01541495

Burns, T. (2013). *Our necessary shadow: The nature and meaning of psychiatry.* London: Allen Lane/Penguin.

Butler, L. D., & Palesh, O. (2004). Spellbound: Dissociation in the movies. *Journal of Trauma & Dissociation, 5,* 61–87. doi: 10.1300/J229v05n02_04

Byrne, B. (2009). Why psychiatrists should watch films (or what has cinema ever done for psychiatry?). *Advances in psychiatric treatment, 15,* 286–296.

Canby, V. (1981, July 17). Review of *Arthur. The New York Times,* p. 10.

Cape, G. S. (2003). Addiction, stigma and movies. *Acta Psychiatrica Scandinavica, 107*(3), 163–169. doi: 10.1034/j.1600-0447.2003.00075.x

Cardena, E., & Spiegel, D. (1993). Dissociative reactions to the Bay Area earthquake. *American Journal of Psychiatry, 150,* 474–478.

Casson, I. R., Siegel, O., Sham, R., Campbell, E. A., Tarlau, M., & DiDomenico, A. (1984). Brain damage in modern boxers. *The Journal of the American Medical Association, 251,* 2663–2667. doi: 10.1001/jama.1984.03340440021020

Centerwall, B. S. (1992). Hiding in plain sight: Nabokov and pedophilia. *Texas Studies in Literature and Language, 32,* 468–484.

Chalkey, A. J., & Powell, G. E. (1983). The clinical description of forty-eight cases of sexual fetishism. *British Journal of Psychiatry, 142,* 292–295.

Classen, C., Koopman, C., & Spiegel, D. (1993). Trauma and dissociation. *Bulletin of the Menninger Clinic, 57,* 178–194.

Corrigan, P. W., Roe, D., & Tsang, H. W. H. (2011). *Challenging the stigma of mental illness: Lessons for therapists and advocates.* New York: Wiley-Blackwell. doi: 10.1002/9780470977507 de Leo, D., & Heller, T. (2008). Social modeling in the transmission of suicidality. *Crisis: The Journal of Crisis Intervention and Suicide Prevention, 29,* 11–19. doi: 10.1027/0227-5910.29.1.11

Denzin, N. K. (1991). *Hollywood shot by shot: Alcoholism in American cinema.* New York: Aldine De Gruyter.

Dick, B. F. (2004). *Anatomy of film* (5th ed.). Boston: Bedford/St. Martin's.

Dietz, P. E., & Evans, B. (1982). Pornographic imagery and prevalence of paraphilia. *American Journal of Psychiatry, 139,* 1493–1495.

Ellis, A., & Ellis, D. J. (Collaborator). (2010). *All out! An autobiography.* Amherst, NY: Prometheus.

Fleming, M., & Manvell, R. (1985). *Images of madness: The portrayal of insanity in the feature film.* Rutherford, NJ: Fairleigh Dickinson University Press.

Floriano, M. A. H. (2008). The cinema as therapy: Psychoanalysis in the work of Woody Allen. *Journal of Medicine and Movies, 4,* 17–26.

Frances, A. (2013). *Saving normal: An insider's revolt against out-of-control psychiatric diagnosis, DSM-5, Big Pharma, and the medicalization of ordinary life.* New York: William Morrow.

Frese, F. J. (2006). Another beautiful mind – with daughters [Review of the film *Proof*]. *PsycCRITIQUES, 51*(33). Retrieved from http://www.apa.org/psyccritiques/ doi: 10.1037/a0003503

Freund, K., & Watson, R. J. (1990). Assessment of the sensitivity and specificity of a phallometric test: An update of "Phallometric diagnosis of pedophilia." *Psychological Assessment, 3,* 254–260.

Fullerton, C. S., Ursano, R. J., & Wang, L. (2004). Acute stress disorder, posttraumatic stress disorder, and depression in disaster or rescue workers. *American Journal of Psychiatry, 161*(8), 1370–1376. doi: 10.1176/appi.ajp.161.8.1370

Gabbard, K., & Gabbard, G. (1992). *Psychiatry and the cinema.* Chicago: University of Chicago Press.

Gabbard, K., & Gabbard, G. (1999). *Psychiatry and the cinema* (2nd ed.). Washington, DC: American Psychiatric Press.

Geller, J., & Harris, M. (Eds.). (1994). *Women of the asylum: Voices from behind the walls, 1840–1945.* New York: Doubleday.

Gergen, K. (1991). *The saturated self: Dilemmas of identity in contemporary life.* New York: Basic Books.

Ghiselli, & Davis (2010). Stuttering: Fact or fiction [Review of the film *The King's Speech*]. *PsycCRITIQUES, 56*(13). doi: 10.1037/a0023604

Giannetti, L. (1993). *Understanding movies.* Englewood Cliffs, NJ: Prentice Hall.

Goffman, E. (1986). *Frame analysis: An essay on the organization of experience.* Boston: Northeastern University Press.

Goldstein, A. (1996). *Violence in America.* Palo Alto, CA: Davies-Black.

Greenberg, G. (2013). *The book of woe: The DSM and the unmaking of psychiatry.* New York: Blue Rider Press/Penguin.

Greenberg, H. R. (1993). *Screen memories: Hollywood cinema on the psychoanalytic couch.* New York: Columbia University Press.

Hacker, K., Collins, J., Gross-Young, L., Almeida, S., & Burke, N. (2008). Coping with youth suicide and overdose: One community's efforts to investigate, intervene, and prevent suicide contagion. *Crisis: The Journal of Crisis Intervention and Suicide Prevention, 29,* 86–95.

Hagglund, K. J. (2005, September 7). Million dollar baby: An Oscar's worth of grit [Review of the motion picture Million Dollar Baby]. *PsycCRITIQUES, 50*(36). Retrieved from http://www.apa.org/psyccritiques/

Hare, R. D. (2006). Psychopathy: A clinical and forensic overview. *Psychiatric Clinics of North America, 29,* 709–724.

Hesse, M., Schliewe, S., & Thomsen, R. R. (2005). Rating of personality disorder features in popular movie characters. *BMC Psychiatry, 5,* 45.

Hiller, W., & Fichter, M. M. (2004). High utilizers of medical care: A crucial subgroup among somatizing patients. *Journal of Psychosomatic Research, 56*(4), 437–443. doi: 10.1016/S0022-3999(03)00628-7

Huta, V., & Hawley, L. (2010). Psychological strengths and cognitive vulnerabilities: Are they two ends of the same continuum or do they have independent relationships with well-being and ill-being? *Journal of Happiness Studies, 11*(1), 71–93. doi: 10.1007/s10902-008-9123-4

Hyler, S. E. (1988). DSM–III at the cinema: Madness in the movies. *Comprehensive Psychiatry, 29,* 195–206. doi: 10.1016/0010-440X(88)90014-4

Hyler, S. E., & Bujold, A. E. (1994). Computers and psychiatric education: The "Taxi Driver" mental status examination. *Psychiatric Annals, 24,* 13–19.

Hyler, S. E., Gabbard, G. O., & Schneider, I. (1991). Homicidal maniacs and narcissistic parasites: Stigmatization of mentally ill persons in the movies. *Hospital and Community Psychiatry, 42,* 1044–1048.

Iaccino, J. F., & Dondero, J. E. (2013a). Technology can be deadly: A female serial killer for the new age. [Review of the film *Scream 4*]. *PsycCRITIQUES, 57*(50). doi: 10.1037/a0031286

Iaccino, J. F., & Dondero, J. E. (2013b). Edgar Allan Poe matches with with one of the first identified serial killers! [Review of the film *The Raven*]. *PsycCRITIQUES, 59*(2). doi: 10.1037/a0035401

Innala, S. M., & Ernulf, K. E. (1992). Understanding male homosexual attraction: An analysis of restroom graffiti. *Journal of Social Behavior and Personality, 7,* 503–510.

Institute of Medicine (2014). *New directions in child abuse and neglect research.* Washington, DC: The National Academies Press.

Jackson, E. (2006). A stutter's perspective: A stutter's challenge. *Journal of Stuttering, Advocacy & Research, 1*(3), 114–118.

Jamison, K. R. (1993). *Touched with fire: Manic-depressive illness and the artistic temperament.* New York: Free Press.

Kashdan, T. B. (2009). *Curious? Discover the missing ingredient to a fulfilling life.* New York: William Morrow.

Kieseppa, T., Partonen, T., Haukka, J., Kaprio, J., & Lonnqvist, J. (2004). High concordance of bipolar I disorder in a nationwide sample of twins. *American Journal of Psychiatry, 161*(10), 1814–1821. doi: 10.1176/appi.ajp.161.10.1814

Kinney, D. K., & Richards, R. L. (2011). Bipolar Mood Disorders. In M. A. Runco & R. Pritzker (Eds.), *Encyclopedia of Creativity* (2nd ed., pp. 140–148). San Diego: Academic Press.

Konigsberg, I. (1987). *The complete film dictionary.* New York: Meridian.

Kuo, W. H., Gallo, J. J., & Eaton, W. W. (2004). Hopelessness, depression, substance disorder, and suicidality: A 3-year community-based study. *Social Psychiatry Psychiatric Epidemiology, 39*(6), 497–501.

Lazarus, R. S. (1999). *Stress and emotion: A new synthesis.* New York: Springer.

Lazarus, R. S. (2000). Toward better research on stress and coping. *American Psychologist, 55*(6), 665–673. doi: 10.1037/0003-066X.55.6.665

Lazarus, R. S. (2001). Relational meaning and discrete emotions. In K. R. Schere, A. Schorr, & T. Johnstone (Eds.), *Appraisal processes in emotion: Theory, methods, research* (pp. 37–67). New York: Oxford University Press.

Leitner, L. M., & Imai, H. (2011). Many people labeled mentally ill have broken hearts [Review of the film *Crooked Beauty*]. *PsycCRITIQUES, 56*(10). doi: 10.1037/a0022905

Lilienfeld, S. O., & Berg, J. M. (2012). A psychological urban legend with disastrous consequences. *PsycCRITIQUES, 57*(20). doi: 10.1037/a0028043

Lothstein, L. (2012). Shame and sexual compulsivity: Enactments that fuel addiction. [Review of the film *Shame*, directed by S. McQueen]. *PsycCRITIQUES, 57*(20). doi: 10.1037/a0028224

Ludwig, A. M. (1998). Method and madness in the arts and sciences. *Creativity Research Journal, 11,* 93–101. doi: 10.1207/s15326934crj1102_1

Mann, C. E., & Himelein, M. J. (2004). *Psychiatric Services, 55*(2), 185–187.

Martin, F., & Farnum, J. (2002). Animal-assisted therapy for children with pervasive developmental disorders. *Western Journal of Nursing Research, 24,* 657–670. doi: 10.1177/019394502320555403

McCabe, P. (1992). *The butcher boy.* London: Picador.

McDonald, A., & Walter, G. (2001). The portrayal of ECT in American movies. *The Journal of ECT, 17,* 264–274. doi: 10.1097/00124509-200112000-00006

McEwen, B. S. (2005). Stessed or stressed out: What is the difference? *Journal of Psychiatry Neuroscience, 30,* 315–318.

Mehlum, L. (2000). The Internet, suicide, and suicide prevention. *Crisis: The Journal of Crisis Intervention and Suicide Prevention, 21,* 186–188. doi: 10.1027//0227-5910.21.4.186

Micali, N., Chakrabarti, S., & Fombonne, E. (2004). The broad autism phenotype: Findings from an epidemiological survey. *Autism, 8*(1), 21–37. doi: 10.1177/1362361304040636

Mikulincer, M., & Shaver, P. R. (Eds.). (2012). *The social psychology of morality: Exploring the causes of good and evil.* Washington, DC: American Psychological Association. doi: 10.1037/13091-000

Millon, T. (2013). Let's help psychiatry get back on the right track … Again! [Review of the books Diagnostic and Statistical Manual of Mental Disorders: DSM-5 (5th ed.), Desk Reference to the Diagnostic Criteria From DSM-5., & The Pocket Guide to the DSM-5 Diagnostic Exam. American Psychiatric Association, American Psychiatric Association, & A. M. Nussbaum]. *PsycCRITIQUES, 58*(45). doi: 10.1037/a0034713

Mueser, K. T., Salyers, M. P., Rosenberg, S. D., Goodman, L. A., Essock, S. M., Osher, F. C., & Swartz, M. S. (2004). Interpersonal trauma and posttraumatic stress disorder in patients with severe mental illness: Demographic, clinical, and health correlates. *Schizophrenia Bulletin, 30*(1), 45–57.

Nathan, D. (2011). *Sybil exposed: The extraordinary story behind the famous multiple personality case.* New York: Free Press.

Nathan, P. E. (2013). DSM–5: The perfect storm [Review of the books Saving normal: An insider's revolt against out-of-control psychiatric diagnosis, DSM–5, Big Pharma, and the medicalization of ordinary life; The Book of woe: The DSM and the unmaking of psychiatry; & Our necessary shadow: The nature and meaning of psychiatry. A. Frances, G. Greenberg, & T. Burns]. *PsycCRITIQUES, 58*(45). doi: 10.1037/a0034634

National Institute of Mental Health. (2003). In harm's way: Suicide in America (NIH Publication Number 03–4594). Retrieved from http://www.nimh.nih.gov/publicat/NIMHharmsway.pdf

National Institute on Alcohol Abuse and Alcoholism. (2000). Alcohol Alert. *Children of alcoholics: Are they different?* (NIH Publication Number 09–PH 288). Retrieved from http://www.niaaa.nih.gov/publications/aa09.htm

Neimeyer, G. J. (2013). On the origin of the specious: The evolution of the DSM–5 [Review of the books *Diag-*

nostic and Statistical Manual of Mental Disorders: DSM–5 (5th ed.), Desk Reference to the Diagnostic Criteria From DSM–5, & The Pocket Guide to the DSM–5 Diagnostic Exam. American Psychiatric Association, American Psychiatric Association, & A. M. Nussbaum]. PsycCRITIQUES, 58(45). doi: 10.1037/a0034699d

Niemiec, R. M., & Ferland, D. (2006). The layers of transformation [Review of the film Batman Begins]. PsycCRITIQUES, 51(2). doi: 10.1037/05206611

Niemiec, R. M., & Wedding, D. (2006). The role of the psychotherapist in movies. Advances in Medical Psychotherapy and Psychodiagnosis, 12, 73–83.

Niemiec, R. M., & Wedding, D. (2014). Positive psychology at the movies 2: Using films to build character strengths and well being. Cambridge, MA: Hogrefe.

Nimer, J., & Lundahl, B. (2007). Animal-assisted therapy: A meta-analysis. Anthrozoös, 20, 225–238. doi: 10.2752/089279307X224773

Norcross, J. C., & Norcross, J. (2005, October 2). A distant look at psychotherapeutic intimacy [Review of the film Intimate Strangers]. PsycCRITIQUES, 50(41). doi: 10.1037/05188711

Norcross, J. C., & Norcross, J. (2006, May 24). Psychotherapist conundrum: My son is sleeping with my patient [Review of the film Prime]. PsycCRITIQUES, 51(21). doi: 10.1037/a0002505

Norcross, J. C., & Norcross, J. (2007, July 11). The ubiquitous Number 23 [Review of the film The Number 23]. PsycCRITIQUES, 52(28). doi: 10.1037/a0008323

Norden, M. (1994). The cinema of isolation. New Brunswick, NJ: Rutgers University Press.

North, C., & Smith, E. (1992). Posttraumatic stress disorder among homeless men and women. Hospital and Community Psychiatry, 43, 1010–1016.

Orchowski, L. M., Spickard, B. A., & McNamara, J. R. (2006). Cinema and the valuing of psychotherapy: Implication for clinical practice. Professional Psychology: Research and Practice, 37, 506–514.

Oswald, D. (2011). Horses and autism [Review of the film The Horse Boy]. PsycCRITIQUES, 56(6). doi: 10.1037/a0022831.

Owen, P. (2007). Dispelling myths about schizophrenia using film. Journal of Applied Social Psychology, 37, 60–75. doi: 10.1111/j.0021-9029.2007.00147.x

Owen, P. R. (2012). Portrayals of schizophrenia by entertainment media: A content analysis contemporary movies. Psychiatric Services, 63(7), 655–659.

Park, N., & Peterson, C. (2009). Character strengths: Research and practice. Journal of College and Character, 10(4), np. doi: 10.2202/1940-1639.1042

Peake, T. H. (2004). Cinema and life development: Healing lives and training therapists. Westport, CT: Praeger.

Peterson, C., & Seligman, M. E. P. (2004). Character strengths and virtues: A handbook and classification.

Washington, DC: American Psychological Association.

Pinker, S. (2011). The better angels of our nature: Why violence has declined. New York: Viking.

Piper, A., & Merskey, H. (2004). The persistence of folly: A critical examination of dissociative identity disorder: Part I. The excesses of an improbable concept. Canadian Journal of Psychiatry, 49(9), 592–600.

Putnam, F. (1985). Multiple personality disorder. Medical Aspects of Human Sexuality, 19, 59–74.

Rastogi, M. (2011). Hurt people, hurt people. [Review of the film Greenberg]. PsycCRITIQUES, 56(35). doi: 10.1037/a0025055

Ressler, R. K., Burgess, A. W., Souglas, J. E., Hartman, C. R., & D'Agostino, R. B. (1986). Sexual killers and their victims: Identifying patterns through crime scene analysis. Journal of Interpersonal Violence, 1, 288–308.

Russell, D. E. H. (1983). The incidence and prevalence of intrafamilial and extrafamilial sexual abuse of female children. Child Abuse and Neglect, 7, 133–146.

Russell, D. E. H. (1984). Sexual exploitation: Rape, child sexual abuse, and workplace harassment. Beverly Hills, CA: Sage.

Saunders, E. B., & Awad, G. A. (1991). Male adolescent sexual offenders: Exhibitionism and obscene phone calls. Child Psychiatry and Human Development, 21(3), 169–178. doi: 10.1007/BF00705902

Scahill, L., Hamrin, V., Deering, C., & Pachlar, M. (2008). Psychiatric disorders diagnosed in childhood and adolescence. In M. Boyd (Ed.), Psychiatric nursing: Contemporary practice (pp. 633–672). Philadelphia: Lippincott, Williams, & Wilkins.

Seyle, H. (1956). The stress of life. New York: McGraw-Hill.

Seyle, H. (1974). Stress without distress. Philadelphia: J. B. Lippincott.

Shriver, T. (2008, August 11). What Tropic Thunder thinks is funny. The Washington Post.

Sieff, E. M. (2003). Media frames of mental illnesses: The potential impact of negative frames. Journal of Mental Health, 12, 259–269. doi: 10.1080/0963823031000118249

Simonton, D. K. (2009). Teaching creativity: Current findings, trends, and controversies in the psychology of creativity. Teaching of Psychology, 39(3), 217–222. doi: 10.1177/0098628312450444

Simonton, D. K. (in press). So you want to become a creative genius? You must be crazy! In D. Cropley, J. Kaufmann, A. Cropley, & M. Runco (Eds.), The dark side of creativity. New York: Cambridge University Press.

Solomon, O. (2010). What a dog can do: Children with autism and therapy dogs in social interaction. Ethos, 38, 143–166. doi: 10.1111/j.1548-1352.2010.01085.x

Steinberg, M. (1991). The spectrum of depersonalization: Assessment and treatment. In A. Tasman, & S. Goldfinger (Eds.), *Review of psychiatry* (Vol. 10; pp. 223–247). Washington, DC: American Psychiatric Press.

Stuart, H. (2003). Violence and mental illness: An overview. *World Psychiatry, 2*, 121–124.

Swenson, L. P., & Schwartz-Mette, R. A. (2011). Heists and heartbreak: Social pressures in the town. [Review of the film *The Town*]. *PsycCRITIQUES, 56*(28). doi: 10.1037/a0023723

Szasz, T. S. (1974). *The myth of mental Illness: Foundations of a theory of personal conduct* (Revised ed.). New York: Harper Row.

Szasz, T. S. (1977). *Psychiatric slavery: When confinement and coercion masquerade as cure.* New York: Free Press.

Szymanski, L. S., & Crocker, A. C. (1989). In B. J. Sadock (Ed.), *Comprehensive textbook of psychiatry* (5th ed.). Baltimore, MD: Williams & Wilkins.

Taylor, E. (2012). Did Jung really sleep with Sabina? [A review of the film *A Dangerous Method*]. *PsycCRITIQUES, 57*(16). doi: 10.1037/a0028020

Taylor, K. (2009). *Cruelty: Human evil and the human brain.* New York: Oxford University Press.

Taylor, T., & Hsu, M. (2003). *Digital cinema: The Hollywood insider's guide to the evolution of storytelling.* Studio City, CA: Michael Wiese Productions.

Trachtenberg, R. (1986). Destigmatizing mental illness. *The Psychiatric Hospital, 17*, 111–114.

Uhde, T., Tancer, M., Black, B., & Brown, T. (1991). Phenomenology and neurobiology of social phobia: Comparison with panic disorder. *Journal of Clinical Psychiatry, 52*, 31–40.

Uva, J. L. (1995). Autoerotic asphyxiation in the United States. *Journal of Forensic Sciences, 40*(4), 574–581.

Valentine, D. & Freeman, M. (2002). Film portrayals of social workers doing child welfare work. *Child and Adolescent Social Work Journal, 19*(6), 455–471.

Van Ameringen, M., Allgulander, C., Bandelow, B., Greist, J. H., Hollander, E., Montgomery, S. A., … Swinson, R. P. (2003). World Council Association recommendations for the long-term treatment of social phobia. *CNS Spectrums, 8*(8 Suppl. 1), 40–52.

VanDyke, M. M., & Anderson, V. H. (2013). Acquiring fear, learning safety, and modeling growth: The Croods flourish. [Review of the film *The Croods*]. *PsycCRITIQUES, 59*(6). doi: 10.1037/a0035402

Veitia, M. C., & McGahee, C. L. (2001). Nicotine and alcohol addiction. In D. Wedding (Ed.), *Behavior and medicine* (3rd ed.; pp. 247–261). Göttingen, Germany: Hogrefe & Huber.

Wahl, O. (1995). *Media madness: Public images of mental illness.* New Brunswick, NJ: Rutgers University Press.

Wahl, O., & Lefkowits, J. (1989). Impact of a television film on attitudes toward mental illness. *American Journal of Community Psychology, 17*(4), 521–528. doi: 10.1007/BF00931176

Walker, E. F., Grimes, K. E., Davis, D. M., & Smith, A. J. (1993). Childhood precursors of schizophrenia: Facial expressions of emotion. *The American Journal of Psychiatry, 150*(11), 1654–1660.

Walker, E. F., Savoie, T., & Davis, D. (1994). Neuromotor precursors of schizophrenia. *Schizophrenia Bulletin, 20*(3), 441–451. doi: 10.1093/schbul/20.3.441

Walter, G., McDonald, A., Rey, J., & Rosen, A. (2002). Medical student knowledge and attitudes regarding ECT prior to and after viewing ECT scenes from movies. *Journal of ECT, 18*(1), 43–46. doi: 10.1097/00124509-200203000-00012

Warburton, W. (2012). Growing up fast and furious in a media saturated world. In W. Warburton & D. Braunstein (Eds.), *Growing up fast and furious: Reviewing the impacts of violent and sexualised media on children* (pp. 1–33). Annandale, NSW, Australia: Federation Press.

Wedding, D. (2000). Cognitive distortions in the poetry of Anne Sexton. *Suicide & Life-Threatening Behavior, 30*, 150–154.

Wedding, D. (2001). The portrayal of alcohol and alcoholism in the western genre. *Journal of Alcohol & Drug Education, 46*, 3–11.

Wedding, D., & Niemiec, R. (2003). The clinical use of films in psychotherapy. *Journal of Clinical Psychology, 59*(2), 207–215. doi: 10.1002/jclp.10142

Wehmeyer, M. L., Buntinx, W. H. E., Lachapelle, Y., Luckasson, R. A., Schalock, R. L., Verdugo, M. A., … Yeager, M. H. (2008). The intellectual disability construct and its relation to human functioning. *Intellectual and Developmental Disabilities, 46*, 311–318.

White, J. W., Koss, M. P., & Kazdin, A. E. (Eds.). (2011). *Violence against women and children, Vol. 1. Mapping the terrain.* Washinton, DC: American Psychological Association. doi: 10.1037/12307-000

World Health Organization. (1992). *ICD-10 classifications of mental and behavioural disorder: Clinical descriptions and diagnostic guidelines.* Geneva, Switzerland: The author.

Zhang, L., Ravdin, L. D., Relkin, N., Zimmerman, R. D., Jordan, B., Lathan, W. E., & Ulug, A. M. (2003). Increased diffusion in the brain of professional boxers: A preclinical sign of traumatic brain injury. *American Journal of Neuroradiololgy, 24*(1), 52–57.

Zimbardo, P. (2007). *The Lucifer effect: Understanding how good people turn evil.* New York: Random House.

Zimmerman, J. N. (2003). *People like ourselves: Portrayals of mental illness in the movies.* Lanham, MD: Scarecrow Press.

Film Index

Steven Stack and Barbara Bowman

Suicide Movies
Social Patterns
1900–2009

HOGREFE

Steven Stack & Barbara Bowman

Suicide Movies

Social Patterns 1900-2009

2012, x + 298 pp. + numerous frame grabs
hardcover
ISBN 978-0-88937-390-7
US $59.00 / € 41.95 / £ 34.00

How is suicide portrayed in the cinema and what does it mean for suicide prevention? The first-ever comprehensive study of film suicide analyzes more than 1,500 film suicides

The portrayal of suicide in cinema can impact public understanding and effective prevention of suicide. This book presents the first-ever comprehensive analysis of how suicide has been portrayed in films over 110 years, based on a thorough evaluation of more than 1,500 film suicides – 1,377 in American films, 135 in British films.

One striking finding is that while the research literature generally attributes suicide to individual psychiatric or mental health issues, cinema and film solidly endorse more social causes.

In a compelling blend of social science and humanities approaches, the authors use quantitative methods, as well as the voices of scriptwriters, directors, actors, and actresses, dozens of illustrative framegrabs, and numerous case examples to answer core questions such as: Are we guilty of over-neglecting social factors in suicide prevention and research? Do cinematic portrayals distort or accurately reflect the nature of suicide in the real world? Has film presentation of suicide changed over 110 years? What are the literary roots of cinema portrayals?

This unique book makes fascinating reading for all concerned with suicide prevention, as well as areas such as sociology, film and media studies, and mass communication.

Table of Contents:

Hogrefe Publishing
30 Amberwood Parkway · Ashland, OH 44805 · USA
Tel: (800) 228-3749 · Fax: (419) 281-6883
E-Mail: customerservice@hogrefe.com

Hogrefe Publishing
Merkelstr. 3 · 37085 Göttingen · Germany
Tel: +49 551 999 500 · Fax: +49 551 999 50 111
E-Mail: customerservice@hogrefe.de

Hogrefe Publishing c/o Marston Book Services Ltd
160 Eastern Ave., Milton Park · Abingdon, OX14 4SB · UK
Tel: +44 1235 465577 · Fax +44 1235 465592
direct.orders@marston.co.uk

HOGREFE

Order online at **www.hogrefe.com**
or call toll-free **(800) 228-3749** (US only)

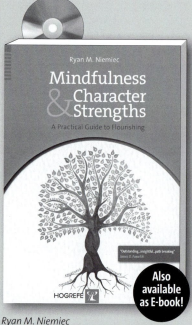